THE ROUGH GUIDE TO
KOREA

**ROUGH
GUIDES**

This fourth edition updated by
Norbert Paxton

Contents

Introduction to
Korea

Pine-clad mountains, Buddhist temples, emerald-green rice paddies... on the surface, Korea seems like a typical slice of Asia. But look beyond simple topography, and you'll discover something truly unique: seriously fiery cuisine, a complex alphabet and customs which – whether modern or ancient – have few equivalents beyond the peninsula. While North Korea continues to befuddle and trouble, South Korea has developed into a major regional power, an inspiration for much of Asia's youth. Koreans themselves long looked towards America for guidance, but a young, confident generation is bringing back some of the nuances their parents and grandparents had to relinquish while dragging the country out of poverty – change is now coming to the land that was once more accustomed to extremes.

The two Koreas, now separated by the spiky twin frontiers of the Demilitarized Zone, went their separate ways in 1953 after the catastrophic **Korean War** – essentially a civil war, but one largely brought about by external forces, it left millions dead and flattened almost the whole peninsula. **North Korea** has armed itself to the teeth since 1953, stagnated in its pursuit of a local brand of **Communism**, and become one of the least-accessible countries in the world. **South Korea**, on the other hand, has become an East Asian economic and cultural dynamo – the Western world may be able to pin down little bar *kimchi*, taekwondo, Samsung and *Gangnam Style*, but the soft-power effects of the Hallyu "New Wave" have been felt quite clearly across the region.

South Korea's **cities** are a pulsating feast of eye-searing neon, feverish activity and round-the-clock business. Here you can shop till you drop at markets that never close, feast on eye-wateringly spicy food, get giddy on a bottle or two of *soju*, then sweat out the day's exertions at a night-time sauna. However, set foot outside the urban centres and your mere presence will cause quite a stir – in the remote **rural areas** life continues much as it did before the "Economic Miracle" of the 1970s, and pockets of **islands** exist where few foreigners have ever set foot.

And for all its new-found prosperity, the South remains a land steeped in **tradition**. Before being abruptly choked off by the Japanese occupation in 1910, an unbroken line of more than one hundred kings existed for almost two thousand years – their grassy burial mounds have yielded thousands of golden relics – and even the capital, Seoul, has a number of **palaces** dating back to the fourteenth century. The wooden *hanok* housing of decades gone by may have largely given way to rows of apartment blocks, but these traditional dwellings can still be found in places, and you'll never be more than a walk away from an immaculately painted **Buddhist temple**. Meanwhile, Confucian-style formal ceremonies continue to play an important part in local life, and some mountains still even host shamanistic rituals.

As for the **Korean people** themselves, they are a real delight: fiercely proud, and with a character almost as spicy as their food, they're markedly eager to please foreigners who come to live or holiday in their country. Within hours of arriving, you may well find yourself with new friends in tow, racing up a mountainside, lunching over a delicious barbecued *galbi*, throwing back rice beer until dawn or singing the night away at a *noraebang*. Few travellers leave without tales of the kindness of Korean strangers – it's likely you'll be left wondering why the country isn't a more popular stop on the international travel circuit.

FACT FILE

- The Korean peninsula is split in two by the 4km-wide Demilitarized Zone (DMZ). **North Korea's** population of around 25 million live in an area half the size of the UK. Slightly smaller **South Korea** has a population of 51 million, meaning that if reunited, the peninsula would be the world's 20th most populous country.

- Ethnic Koreans dominate both countries, making them two of the most **ethnically homogenous** societies on Earth. Before splitting, both North and South Korea were traditionally Buddhist nations. Since then the North has followed Juche, a local brand of Communism, while Christianity has become the most popular religion in the South.

- There are over seven million ethnic Koreans living overseas; famous **"gyopo"** include golfer Michelle Wie, Yunjin Kim of TV show Lost, Joe Hahn of nu-metal band Linkin Park and Woody Allen's wife Soonyi Previn.

- The **economies** of South and North Korea were almost equal in size until the mid-1970s. The "Economic Miracle" that followed in the South has propelled it to the cusp of the world's top ten economies, while the North languishes just above 100th place.

- Psy's **Gangnam Style** went ultra-viral in 2012, becoming by far the most-watched video in YouTube history.

Where to go

Korea is still something of a mystery to most non-natives, and more than half of all its visitors get no further than **Seoul**. One of the largest and most technically advanced cities in the world, the capital confounds many expectations by proving itself steeped in history. Here, fourteenth-century palaces, imperial gardens, teeming markets and

secluded tearooms continue to charm amid a maze of skyscrapers and shopping malls. From Seoul, anywhere in the country is reachable within a day, but the best day-trip by far is to the **DMZ**, the strip of land that separates the two Koreas from coast to coast.

Gyeonggi, the province that surrounds Seoul, is a largely unappealing area dissected by the roads and railways that snake their way into the capital, but two of its cities certainly deserve a visit: **Suwon**, home to a wonderful UNESCO-listed fortress dating from the late eighteenth century; and cosmopolitan **Incheon**, gateway to the **islands** of the West Sea. By contrast, the neighbouring province of **Gangwon** is unspoiled and stuffed full of attractions: in addition to a number of national parks, of which craggy **Seoraksan** is the most visited, you can head to quirky **Sokcho** city, the giant caves near **Samcheok**, or peek inside a genuine American warship and North Korean submarine north of the sleepy fishing village of **Jeongdongjin**.

Stretching down from Gangwon to the South Sea lie the markedly traditional **Gyeongsang** provinces, home to some of the peninsula's most popular attractions. Foremost among these is gorgeous **Gyeongju**; capital of the Silla dynasty for almost a thousand years, and extremely laidback by Korean standards, it's dotted with the

---

THE CREATION OF HANGEUL

One thing that will strike you on a trip around Korea is **hangeul**, the peninsula's distinctive, almost Tetris-like alphabet. Amazingly, this was a royal creation, having been the brainchild of **King Sejong** in the 1440s. Most of this creative king's subjects were unable to read the Chinese script used across the land at the time, so he devised a system that would be easier for ordinary people to learn. Sejong was forced to do much of his work in secret, as the plan did not go down well with the *yangban* – Confucian scholars who were even more powerful than royalty at the time. As the only truly educated members of society, the *yangban* argued fiercely against the change in an effort to maintain their monopoly over knowledge.

Hangeul experienced periodic bursts of popularity, but was almost erased entirely by the Japanese during their occupation of the peninsula (1910–45). However, it's now the **official writing system** in both North and South Korea, as well as a small autonomous Korean pocket in the Chinese province of Jilin.

The alphabet, while it appears complex, is surprisingly **easy to learn**, and demonstrating that you can read even a handful of simple words will generate gasps of admiration across Korea. Just a few hours of hard study should suffice – to get started, turn to the table of characters in the Language section (see page 388).

grassy burial tombs of the many kings and queens who ruled here. There's enough in the surrounding area to fill at least a week of sightseeing – most notable are **Namsan**, a small mountain area peppered with trails, tombs and some intriguing Buddhas, and the sumptuously decorated **Bulguksa** temple, another sight on the UNESCO World Heritage list. Although less picturesque as a town, **Andong** is almost as relaxed as Gyeongju, and a superb base from which to access **Dosan Seowon**, a remote Confucian academy, and the charmingly dusty village of **Hahoe**, a functioning showcase of traditional Korean life. The region's rustic charm is actually best appreciated offshore on the windswept island of **Ulleungdo**, an extinct volcanic cone that rises precipitously from the East Sea, and where tiny fishing settlements cling barnacle-like to its coast. Thrills with a more urban flavour can be had in **Busan**, Korea's second city, which has an atmosphere markedly different from Seoul; as well as the most raucous nightlife outside the capital, it has the best fish market in the country, and a number of excellent beaches on its fringes.

GET YOUR MAK ON

Korea has plenty of local booze (see page 42), but the milky-coloured rice beer known as **makgeolli** is by far the most interesting. Drinking *makgeolli* is not really a case of "when in Rome…", since Koreans themselves are far more partial to beer and *soju* (a clear spirit). However, this dynastic-era drink has been making a sustained comeback in recent years: trendy "mak-bars" have been opening up in Seoul (see page 43), with the wave now slowly spreading across the land. Some serve the drink mixed with fruit juice, which may be too faddish for purists, but breweries have long mixed the main constituent rice with local ingredients such as black bean, ginseng and berry juice.

Even more characterful are the **Jeolla** provinces, which make up the southwest of the peninsula. Left to stagnate by the government while Korea's economy kicked into gear in the 1970s, they have long played the role of the renegade, though this energy is now being rechannelled. A violent massacre took place in regional capital **Gwangju** as recently as 1980, though the city has reinvented itself to become one of the artiest and most business-savvy in the land. **Jeonju** has a similar feel, plus a delightful district of traditional *hanok* housing, and is justly famed for its wonderful, flavoursome cuisine. Earthy **Mokpo** is the hub for ferry trips to a mind-boggling number of **West Sea islands**, dotted with fishing communities where life has changed little in decades, while inland there are a clutch of excellent national parks.

The **Chungcheong** provinces at the centre of the country are bypassed by many travellers, but this is a shame, as they contain some fine sights. The old Baekje capitals of **Gongju** and **Buyeo** provide glimpses of a dynasty long dead, **Daecheon beach** hosts a rumbustious annual mud festival that may well be Korea's most enjoyable event, and

TITLES AND TRANSLITERATION

The Korean peninsula is split into South Korea, officially known as the **Republic of Korea**; and North Korea, officially named the **Democratic People's Republic of Korea** (or DPRK for short). Most of this book is about the former, which is referred to throughout as "Korea"; this is how locals refer to their nation when talking to outsiders, though in Korean they use the term "*Hanguk*" (한국). North Korea has, where necessary, been referred to as such, or as "the DPRK"; North Koreans' own word for both country and peninsula is "*Choson*" (조선).

Also note that a uniform system of **transliteration** is used throughout this book, bar a few entities that are better known in another form (such as *kimchi*, and certain people's names). However, as older generations have been schooled with different methods (including one still used in North Korea) you may well spot a few varieties of the same word on your travels – see the Language section (see page 388) for more information.

there are temples galore: the gigantic golden Buddha at **Beopjusa** is surrounded by 1000m-high peaks, while the meandering trails and vivid colour schemes at **Guinsa** make it the most visually stimulating temple in the land.

Lying within a ferry ride of the mainland's southern shore is the island of **Jeju**, a popular honeymoon destination for Koreans. While it's undoubtedly touristy, it has its remote stretches and anyone who has climbed the volcanic cone of **Hallasan**, walked through the lava tubes of **Manjanggul** or watched the sun go down from **Yakcheonsa** temple will tell you the trip is more than worthwhile.

And finally, of course, there's **North Korea**. A visit to one of the world's most feared and most fascinating countries will instantly garner you some extra travel kudos – even experienced travellers routinely put the DPRK at the top of their "most interesting" list. Visits don't come cheap and can only be made as part of a guided tour, but the country's inaccessibility brings an epic quality to its few officially sanctioned sights.

When to go

Korea's year is split into **four distinct seasons**. **Spring** generally lasts from April to June, and is one of the best times to visit: flowers are in bloom, and a frothy spray of cherry blossom washes a brief wave of pinkish white from south to north. Locals head for the hills, making use of the country's many national parks, and the effects of the change in weather can also be seen in a number of interesting festivals.

Korea's **summer**, on the other hand, can be unbearably muggy, and you may find yourself leaping from one air-conditioned sanctuary to the next. It's best to avoid the **monsoon** season: more than half of the country's annual rain falls from early July to late August. In a neat reversal of history, Japan and China protect Korea from most of the area's typhoons, but one or two manage to get through the gap each year.

The very best time of the year to visit is **autumn** (Sept–Nov), when temperatures are mild, rainfall is generally low and festivals are easy to come across. Korea's mountains erupt in a magnificent array of reds, yellows and oranges, and locals flock to national parks to picnic under their fiery canopies. T-shirt weather can continue long into October, though you're likely to need some extra layers by then.

The Korean **winter** is long and cold, with the effects of the Siberian weather system more pronounced the further north

THE TAEGEUKKI

South Korea's national flag – the **Taegeukki** – is one of the most distinctive around, and is heavily imbued with philosophical meaning. The design itself has changed a little since its first unveiling in the 1880s, though its fundamental elements remain the same: a red-and-blue circle surrounded by four black trigams, all set on a white background. The puritanical connotations of the white are obvious, whereas the circle and trigams offer greater food for thought. The four trigams make up half of the eight used in the *I Ching*, an ancient Chinese book of divination. Each can represent a number of different concepts: moving clockwise from the top-left of the flag, these may be read as spring, winter, summer and autumn; heaven, moon, earth and sun; father, son, mother and daughter; as well as many more besides.

The circle is split into the "Yin-Yang" shape (again, of Chinese origin), its two halves representing opposites such as light and dark, male and female, day and night. Though coincidental, connections with the divided Korean peninsula are easy to find, with two opposing halves forming part of the same whole – the red half is even on top.

DOSAN SEOWON, GYEONGSANG

you go. However, travel at this time is far from impossible – public transport services continue undaunted, underfloor *ondol* heating systems are cranked up and the lack of rain creates photogenic contrasts between powdery snow, crisp blue skies, off-black pine trees and the earthy yellow of dead grass.

AVERAGE MONTHLY TEMPERATURES AND RAINFALL

	Jan	Feb	Mar	Apr	May	Jun	Jul	Aug	Sep	Oct	Nov	Dec
BUSAN												
Max/Min(°C)	6/-2	7/-1	12/3	17/8	21/13	24/17	27/22	29/23	26/18	21/12	15/6	9/1
Max/Min (°F)	43/28	45/30	54/38	63/47	70/55	75/63	81/72	84/73	79/64	70/54	59/43	48/34
Rainfall (mm)	43	36	69	140	132	201	295	130	173	74	41	31
JEJU CITY												
Max/Min (°C)	10/5	12/6	15/8	19/10	23/14	26/18	28/23	29/24	27/20	23/14	17/8	13/6
Max/Min (°F)	50/41	54/43	59/46	66/50	73/57	79/64	82/73	84/75	81/68	73/57	63/46	55/43
Rainfall (mm)	84	89	94	176	171	205	356	243	184	95	93	82
PYONGYANG												
Max/Min (°C)	-3/-13	1/-10	7/-4	16/3	22/9	26/15	29/20	29/20	24/14	18/6	9/-2	0/-10
Max/Min (°F)	27/7	34/14	45/25	61/37	72/48	79/59	84/68	84/68	75/57	64/43	48/28	32/14
Rainfall (mm)	15	11	25	46	67	76	237	228	112	45	41	21
SEOUL												
Max/Min (°C)	0/-9	3/-7	8/-2	17/5	22/11	27/16	29/21	31/22	26/15	19/7	11/0	3/-7
Max/Min (°F)	32/16	37/19	46/28	63/41	72/52	81/61	84/70	88/72	79/59	66/45	52/32	37/19
Rainfall (mm)	31	20	38	76	81	130	376	267	119	41	46	25

HONGDO, JEOLLA

Author picks

Our intrepid author has crisscrossed South Korea multiple times, and made several trips to reclusive North Korea, in a quest to better understand the workings of this fascinating peninsula. These are some of his favourite experiences.

Local booze Sample a fantastic selection of unique local tipples, some of which may actually improve your health – a cup of *makgeolli*, a sort of rice beer, contains more "friendly" bacteria than a pot of yoghurt; while whisky-coloured *baekseju* is made with ginseng, liquorice, cinnamon and ginger (see page 42).

Travel to Abai Island Sokcho (see page 151) is one of the most pleasant cities in the land, and for a few coins one can ride a truly bonkers little winch-ferry to Abai Island, famed for its stuffed squid.

Gyeongju by night Gyeongju (see page 186) is effectively an open-air museum, and one can spend an evening wandering through the grassy spaces surrounding its hundreds of regal burial mounds.

Ferry rides There are almost 500 inhabited islands dotted around the South Korean mainland, and catching a ferry to one of them will give you both a pleasant ride and a trip back in time – islands such as Hongdo (see page 246), Heuksando (see page 246) and Ulleungdo (see page 201) have changed little in decades.

The Farmers' Dance A dynastic tradition, with colourfully clad gents whirling super-long head-ribbons to a cacophony of clangs and drum beats – a real "this is Korea" sight. The Korean Folk Village (see page 132) puts on daily shows.

Munsu Water Park A fun embodiment of the strides recently taken by the North Korean economy (and largely ignored by the Western press), this is one of the only places in the country in which you'll be allowed to chill – and take selfies – with "regular" locals (see page 350).

Our author recommendations don't end here. We've flagged up our favourite places – a perfectly sited hotel, an atmospheric café, a special restaurant – throughout the Guide, highlighted with the ★ symbol.

THE FARMERS' DANCE

FERRY NEAR NAMI ISLAND, GANGWON

25

things not to miss

It's not possible to see everything that Korea has to offer in a short trip – and we don't suggest you try. What follows, in no particular order, is a selective taste of the peninsula's highlights: idyllic islands, spectacular temples and delicious food. All entries have a page reference to take you straight into the Guide, where you can find out more.

1 GWANGJANG MARKET
See page 78

One of Korea's most earthly atmospheric places to eat, Gwangjang is a Seoul institution, with sights and smells redolent of decades gone by.

2 PYONGYANG MARATHON
See page 351

Running 26 miles can be tough enough – now try it in one of the world's most mysterious nations.

3 MAKGEOLLI
See page 43

Get drunk the local way with *makgeolli*, a milk-coloured rice drink brewed across the land since the days of dynasty.

4 PAEKDUSAN
See page 356

The legendary birthplace of the Korean nation, this dormant volcano – the highest peak on the peninsula – rises up through the Chinese-North Korean border, its crater lake a preternatural blue when not frozen over.

5 SOKCHO
See page 151

The harbourfront of this pleasant city is a grand place to eat – sample some of its signature squid sausage on tiny Abai island, accessible on a ferry that you have to pull along yourself.

6 PYONGYANG
See page 343
The world's least-visited
capital – a rhapsody of
brutalist architecture,
and red *hangeul* slogans
extolling the virtues of the
government and its leaders.

7 GONGSANSEONG
See page 277
Overlooking the river in
sleepy Gongju, the walls of
this fortress follow an almost
caldera-like course; in the
middle you'll find dreamy
pavilions and walking paths.

8 JEONGDONGJIN
See page 166
Korea's most surreal village
has a train station on the
beach, a ship-hotel atop a cliff,
an American warship and a
North Korean spy submarine.

9 BEOPJUSA
See page 290
This delightful temple
boasts one of the world's
tallest bronze Buddhas – a
33m-high figure surrounded
by mountains that just beg
to be hiked across.

10 BORYEONG MUD FESTIVAL
See page 284
Korea's dirtiest, most
enjoyable festival takes place
each July on the west coast –
even if you forget your soap,
you can buy a bar made of
mud right here.

11 YAKCHEONSA
See page 320
This large, splendid temple on the southern coast of Jeju Island is almost unique among Korean temples in that it faces the sea – pop along for sundown and evening prayers.

12 WALKING THE JEJU OLLE TRAIL
See page 305
Get to know Korea's largest island by tackling part of this wonderful trail, which passes beaches, temples and mini-volcanoes on its circumnavigation of the island.

13 JIRISAN NATIONAL PARK
See page 225
The largest of Korea's many national parks, Jirisan offers some superlative multi-day hiking possibilities.

14 BIBIMBAP
See pages 37 and 263
A delectable dish derived from the five principal colours of local Buddhism: red for the paste, yellow for the egg, white for the rice, blue for the meat and green for the veggies.

15 INSADONG TEAROOMS
See page 109
Tea may have ceded ground to coffee across the nation, but Seoul's traditional Insadong district still has dozens of secluded places serving traditional brews.

11

12

16 CYCLING
See page 33
Excellent bike paths have been laid out across the country, and it's now possible to cycle from Seoul to Busan in under a week.

17 CHANGDEOKGUNG
See page 69
Saunter, as kings once did, though this dreamy, UNESCO-listed palace in central Seoul.

18 NORAEBANG
See page 88
A near-mandatory part of a Korean night out is a trip to a "singing room", the local take on Japan's karaoke bars.

19 BARBECUED MEAT
See page 38
A fire at the centre of your table and a plate of raw meat to fling onto it – could this be the world's most fun-to-eat dish?

20 THE DMZ
See pages 135 and 355
Take a step inside the 4km-wide Demilitarized Zone separating North and South Korea: the world's frostiest remnant of the Cold War.

21 GYEONGJU

See page 186

Dotted with the grassy burial mounds of Silla-dynasty royals, this ancient capital is the most traditional city in Korea, and should be on every visitor's itinerary.

22 WEST SEA ISLANDS

See pages 127, 246 and 286

Over three thousand islands are sprinkled like confetti around Korea's western coast – pick up a map in Mokpo, get on a ferry and lose track of time.

23 UDO

See page 313

This bucolic, beach-fringed island makes the ideal spot for a cycle ride – race past flower-filled fields whose borders are marked with walls of hand-stacked volcanic rock.

24 HONGDAE

See page 86

If you're itching to dive into Korean nightlife, this Seoul 'burb is the place to head – it's like walking through an extremely noisy kaleidoscope, full of sozzled students.

25 HAHOE FOLK VILLAGE

See page 179

Near the agreeable city of Andong, this rural hamlet provides a rare peek into what Korea was once like – think wooden buildings, views of rice fields and some actual truth to the phrase "Land of Morning Calm".

Itineraries

Despite Korea's relatively diminutive size, you'll need to do some planning if you're to make the most of the country. Seoul demands at least a couple of days, but with a little more time on your hands you could soon be racing up mountains, hopping between far-flung islands or tracking down the peninsula's best beaches and temples.

THE FULL MONTY

Korea's compact size and excellent public transportation makes it very simple to check off its main sights, and a couple of quirkier ones – even a week in the country is enough to give you a good idea of what Korea's all about. The number-one rule is to get out of Seoul – a great city it may be, but there's just so much else on offer across the land.

❶ Seoul Where to start with Korea's fascinating capital? Ancient palaces and shrines, a beguiling array of galleries, a national park on its doorstep and some of the best food and shopping in Asia – and that's just for starters. See page 58

❷ Sokcho This east-coast city offers day-trips into the mountains, as well as some simply fantastic restaurants – a great place to expand your waistline. See page 151

❸ Seoraksan National Park The undisputed number-one national park in a country full of mountains, Seoraksan delivers on lofty promises with a series of jagged, tremendously photogenic peaks. See page 156

❹ Jeongdongjin This small coastal village is perhaps Korea's best sunrise spot, and is also home to the country's most distinctive hotel – a ship-shaped establishment perched atop a cliff. See page 166

❺ Gyeongju If you've only got time for one place outside Seoul, make it quiet Gyeongju, dynastic capital for almost a millennium and still home to a mind-boggling assortment of treasures, as well as some superb temples and hiking routes. See page 186

❻ Busan Korea's second city is an easy place to love – if the beaches and seafood don't get you, the nightlife will. See page 205

❼ Jeju Island An extinct volcano jutting out of the sea, Jeju is far more natural in feel than the mainland: think beaches, farmland, lava tubes and volcanic craters. And now you can walk around the whole island on the Jeju Olle Trail. See page 300

RIDING THE JUNGANG LINE

Bypass the high-speed KTX services linking Seoul and Busan, and take the Jungang line instead – slower it may be, but it'll take you to some beautiful places, and give you a far better perspective of Korea's history and traditions.

❶ Seoul Start out with a few days in Korea's dynamic, open-all-hours capital, before catching the train south. See page 58

❷ Danyang First stop, Danyang – a delightful town set along a lakeside and surrounded by mountains. Drink in the superb views, then drink down some local *makgeolli*. See page 292

❸ **Guinsa** The most visually arresting temple in the land, shoehorned into a tight mountain valley a short bus ride from Danyang. See page 295

❹ **Andong** Further down the Jungang line is Andong, a relaxing, traditionally minded city famed for its *soju*. See page 177

❺ **Hahoe Folk Village** Step back in time at the quaint Hahoe Folk Village near Andong. Entirely made up of low-rise wooden buildings and surrounded by farmland, this charming village is a present-day sampler of Korea in dynastic times. See page 179

❻ **Gyeongju** There are more echoes of the past in Gyeongju, the capital of the Silla dynasty for almost one thousand years. Explore the city's regal burial mounds by bike. See page 186

❼ **Oksan Seowon** Established during the Goryeo dynasty, this shrine was once one of the most important Confucian academies in the land, and remains a fantastic draw on account of its beauty and idyllic location. See page 200

❽ **Busan** The Jungang line comes to an end in Busan, Korea's second city – head to Haeundae, Korea's most famous beach, to kick back with seafood and cocktails after a rail journey across the country. See page 205

WEST SIDE STORY

Korea's west side is relatively off the radar, but features some of the most beguiling places in the land: national parks aplenty, ancient capitals, dazzling temples and more islands than you could ever count.

❶ **Gongju** The one-time capital of the Baekje dynasty boasts a giant fortress, several regal burial mounds, a district of wooden *hanok* housing and a museum full of ancient riches. See page 276

❷ **Daecheon beach** Not as pristine as Haeundae beach, but far more Korean in feel – come here to splash around in the sea and wolf down a yummy shellfish barbecue. Daecheon is also home to the Boryeong Mud Festival, by far the most popular festival in the country with international visitors. See page 283

❸ **Jeonju** Most of Korea's traditional wooden housing has been flattened in the name of progress, but this earthy city boasts a whole swathe of it. It's also renowned for having the best food in the country. See page 257

❹ **Naejangsan National Park** Achingly beautiful in the autumn, this national park's circle of modest peaks makes for some great hiking at any time of year. See page 253

❺ **Mokpo** A pleasingly odd city surrounded by a spray of unspoiled islands, salty Mokpo is the best place to comprehend the provincial nuances of the Jeolla area. See page 242

❻ **Hongdo** Essentially as far west as Korea goes, this tiny, beautiful island juts dramatically from the sea – an emphatic full stop to your journey. See page 246

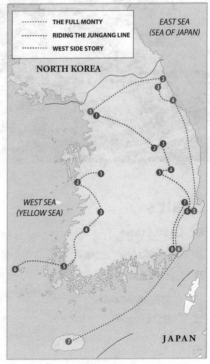

HAEMUL-JJIM

Basics

Getting there

With no way to travel to Korea by road or rail, the vast majority of travellers arrive at the gleaming Incheon International Airport; often referred to as "Seoul Incheon" on international departure boards, this offshore beast is touch-down territory for most of the world's major airlines, though some provincial airports also receive international flights. The only other way in is by sea – there are services from both China and Japan.

Korean Air (W koreanair.com) and Asiana (W flyasiana.com) are the two big Korean **airlines**, operating direct flights from a number of destinations around the world. Seoul increasingly features as a stopover on round-the-world trips, and the country is well served by dozens of international carriers. **Fares** increase for travel in the summer months and at Christmas time. A **departure tax** applies when leaving Korea, but will almost certainly be factored in to your ticket price.

Flights from the UK and Ireland

British Airways (W britishairways.com), Korean Air and Asiana have direct daily connections from **London Heathrow** to Incheon. The journey takes eleven hours, with return fares costing around £600; this can rise to over £800 during summer and at Christmas, when it's common for all flights to be fully booked weeks in advance. You can save money by taking an **indirect flight**, with prices often dipping to around £400 return during low season; good options include Finnair via Helsinki (W finnair.com), Qatar Airways via Doha (W qatarairways.com), Aeroflot via Moscow (W aeroflot.ru) and Emirates via Dubai (W emirates.com). It's also worth checking deals with KLM (W klm.com) and Air France (W airfrance.com), whose routes are as close to direct as possible.

There are no direct flights to Korea from **Ireland,** so you'll have to transfer in the UK or in mainland Europe.

Flights from the US and Canada

If you are coming from the **US** you have a number of options available to you: there are **direct** flights to Incheon from New York, Dallas, Las Vegas, Los Angeles, San Francisco, Detroit, Seattle, Chicago, Atlanta, Houston, Washington and Honolulu; carriers include Delta (W delta.com) and United (W united.com), as well as Asiana and Korean Air. Sample low-season return fares are $1400 from New York (a journey of around 14hr), $1200 from Chicago (14hr) and $1150 from Los Angeles (13hr). In all cases you may save hundreds of dollars by transferring – Beijing and Tokyo are popular hubs. Fares on many routes can almost double during summer and Christmas time.

Korean Air and Air Canada (W aircanada.com) have direct flights from Incheon from two **Canadian** cities, Vancouver (11hr) and Toronto (13hr), but these can be very expensive when demand is high (over Can$2500 return); low-season prices can drop under Can$1000. Again, you're likely to save money by taking an indirect flight.

Flights from Australia, New Zealand and South Africa

From **Australia**, the only cities with direct connections to Korea are Sydney (10hr) and Brisbane (9hr). There have, in the past, also been direct flights from Melbourne and Cairns – check to see whether these connections have reappeared. The number of Koreans going to Australia means that bargain direct flights are few and far between, so check around for indirect flights via a Southeast Asian hub; return prices via Kuala Lumpur, Singapore or Hong Kong can often drop below Aus$1000. For those travelling from **New Zealand**, there are direct flights from Auckland (11hr), though indirect flights are cheaper (sometimes under NZ$700 return). Going direct, keep your fingers crossed for a NZ$1400 fare, but assume you'll pay around NZ$1900. At the time of writing, there were no direct flights from **South Africa**.

Flights from other Asian countries

There are flights to Incheon from many cities across **Japan** (from $150 return) and **China** (starting at around $250 return from the major east-coast cities, but often cheaper from Qingdao). If Seoul isn't your final destination, it may be worth checking for a connection to another Korean international airport: in decreasing order of importance, these include

Unless otherwise stated, this Basics section is referring to South Korea, calling that country "Korea" as the locals do. For North Korea travel basics, see page 331.

A BETTER KIND OF TRAVEL

At Rough Guides we are passionately committed to travel. We feel that travelling is the best way to understand the world we live in and the people we share it with – plus tourism has brought a great deal of benefit to developing economies around the world over the last few decades. But the growth in tourism has also damaged some places irreparably, and climate change is exacerbated by most forms of transport, especially flying. All Rough Guides' trips are carbon-offset, and every year we donate money to a variety of charities devoted to combating the effects of climate change.

Busan's Gimhae Airport, Jeju, Daegu and Gwangju. There's also a handy, and extremely regular, connection between Seoul's Gimpo Airport and Tokyo Haneda, both of which are closer to the centre of their respective capitals than the larger hubs, Incheon and Narita.

China and Japan aside, Incheon is served by flights from an ever-increasing number of **other Asian countries**, and the good news is that many of these routes are run by budget airlines; local carriers Eastar Jet (W eastarjet.com), Jin Air (W jinair.com), Jeju Air (W en.jejuair.net) and T-way (W twayair.com) have services from Thailand, the Philippines, Hong Kong, Vietnam, Laos, Cambodia and more besides.

Ferries

Flights aside, access from abroad takes the form of **ferries** from Japan or China, possibly via a ride on the Trans-Siberian Railway (see W seat61.com for more information).

There are several ferry routes from **China**'s eastern coast (see page 28 for information on departure days and journey times), almost all of which head to Incheon's international termini (see page 120). All vessels have numerous classes of comfort, with one-way prices starting at around 850RMB. The most popular connections are Dalian and Qingdao, and Tianjin's port in Tanggu, which is the most convenient for those heading to or from Beijing.

Services from **Japan** run from Fukuoka, Osaka and Shimonoseki to Busan (see page 205), and arrive almost alongside Busan train station, so you can be heading to other Korean destinations in no time. **Fukuoka** is by far the best choice, since there are, in fact, three different services to and from Korea – the slowest is a regular ferry, departing Fukuoka every day except Sunday (6hr daytime from Japan, 11hr overnight back from Korea; ¥9000; W korea ferry.co.kr), the other a faster jetfoil with at least five services per day (3hr; ¥13,000; W jrbeetle.co.jp). The longer ferry from **Osaka** (19hr; from ¥14,000) runs three days a week – a beautiful ride through Japan's island-studded inland sea.

Overland

Despite the fact that South Korea is part of the Eurasian landmass, and technically connected to the rest of it by rail, the Demilitarized Zone (DMZ) and North Korean red tape means that the country is currently **inaccessible by land**. Two old lines across the DMZ have been renovated, and 2007 saw trains rumble across the border as part of a peace ceremony, but overnight trains from Beijing to Seoul station remain a distant prospect.

INTERNATIONAL AGENTS

ebookers W ebookers.com. Low fares on an extensive selection of scheduled flights and package deals.

FERRIES FROM CHINA

Chinese ports	Departure from China	Journey times
Dalian	Mon, Wed & Fri 6pm	17hr
Dandong	Tues, Thurs & Sun 6pm	16hr
Qingdao	Mon, Wed & Fri 5.30pm	17hr
Qinhuangdao	Wed & Sun 1pm	24hr
Shidao	Tues, Thurs & Sun 7pm	14hr
Tanggu (Tianjin)	Thurs & Sun 11am	24hr
Weihai	Tues, Thurs & Sun 6pm	14hr
Yantai	Mon, Wed & Fri 6.30pm	14hr
Yingkou	Mon & Thurs noon	24hr

North South Travel ⓦ northsouthtravel.co.uk. Friendly, competitive travel agency, offering discounted fares worldwide. Profits are used to support projects in the developing world, especially the promotion of sustainable tourism.

STA Travel ⓦ statravel.com. Worldwide specialists in independent travel; also student IDs, travel insurance, car rental, rail passes, and more. Good discounts for students and under-26s.

Trailfinders ⓦ trailfinders.com. One of the best-informed and most efficient agents for independent travellers.

LOCAL TOUR OPERATORS

Grace Travel ⓦ triptokorea.com. Outfit offering a wide range of good-value tours, including ski trips, Jeju excursions, hiking adventures and a "Royal Relics" journey.

HaB Korea ⓦ habkorea.com. In addition to the regular itineraries, this group also offers specialist tours dedicated to things such as K-pop (including the chance to meet a star or three) and photography. Can also set you up with tickets to musicals, shows and amusement parks.

HanaTour ⓦ hanatouritc.com. Korea's largest tour company by far offers a few interesting additions to the regular Seoul tours and DMZ trips, including nature, skiing and culinary tours.

O'ngo ⓦ ongofood.com. Interesting food tours, mostly focused on Seoul but sometimes heading to the hinterlands; you'll be able to wrap up the experience with a cooking class or two.

Visas and entry requirements

At the time of writing, citizens of almost any Western nation can enter Korea visa-free with an onward ticket, though the duration of the permit varies. Most West European nationals qualify for a visa exemption of three months or ninety days (there *is* a difference), as do citizens of the USA, New Zealand and Australia; Portuguese are allowed sixty days, South Africans just thirty, and Canadians a full six months. If you need more than this, apply before entering Korea. One exception is Jeju Island, which is visa-free for citizens of most nations, as long as they fly (or sail) directly in and out.

Overstaying your visa will result in a large fine (up to W500,000 per day), with exceptions only being made in emergencies such as illness or loss of passport. Getting a new passport is time-consuming and troublesome, though the process will be simplified if your passport has been registered with your embassy in Seoul, or if you can prove your existence with a birth certificate or copy of your old passport.

Work visas

Work visas, valid for one year and extendable for at least one more, can be applied for before or after entering Korea. Applications can take up to a month to be processed by Korean embassies, but once inside the country it can take as little as a week. Your **employer** will do all the hard work with the authorities, then provide you with a visa confirmation slip; the visa must be picked up outside Korea (the nearest consulate is in Fukuoka, Japan; visas here can be issued on the day of application). Visas with the same employer can be extended without leaving Korea. An **alien card** must be applied for at the local immigration office within ninety days of arrival – again, this is usually taken care of by the employer. Work visas are forfeited on leaving Korea, though re-entry visas can be applied for at your provincial immigration office. Citizens of seventeen countries – including Americans, Australians, British, Canadians and New Zealanders – can apply for a **working holiday** visa at their local South Korean embassy, as long as they're aged between 18 and 30.

SOUTH KOREAN EMBASSIES AND CONSULATES ABROAD

Australia 113 Empire Circuit, Yarralumla ☏ 02 6270 4100, ⓦ aus-act.mofa.go.kr.

Canada 150 Boteler St, Ottawa, Ontario ☏ 613 244 5010, ⓦ can-ottawa.mofa.go.kr.

China 20 Dongfang East Rd, Sanyunqiao, Beijing 100600 ☏ 10 8531 0700.

Ireland 20 Clyde Rd, Ballsbridge, Dublin ☏ 01 660 8800, ⓦ irl.mofa.go.kr.

Japan 1-2-5 Minami-Azabu, 1-chome, Minato, Tokyo ☏ 03 3452 7611, ⓦ jpn-tokyo.mofa.go.kr.

New Zealand 11th Floor, ASB Bank Tower, 2 Hunter St, Wellington ☏ 04 473 9073, ⓦ nzl-wellington.mofa.go.kr.

Singapore 47 Scotts Rd, Goldbell Towers, Singapore ☏ 6256 1188, ⓦ sgp.mofat.go.kr.

South Africa 265 Melk St, Nieuw Muckleneuk, Pretoria ☏ 012 460 2508, ⓦ zaf.mofat.go.kr.

UK 60 Buckingham Gate, London ☏ 020 7227 5500, ⓦ gbr.mofa.go.kr.

US 2450 Massachusetts Ave NW, Washington, DC ☏ 202 939 5600, ⓦ usa.mofa.go.kr.

Getting around

Travelling around the country is simple – even if the train won't take you where you want to go, there's almost always a bus that will; should you have a choice, it's usually

faster but more expensive to take the train. Travel prices are reasonable by international standards, even if you choose to hop on one of the surprisingly numerous domestic flights. Korea is surrounded by islands, and should you take a ferry to one of these, it may well be the most pleasurable part of your visit. All cities have comprehensive (if slightly incomprehensible) bus networks, and many now have subway lines. Taxis are remarkably good value, and can even be feasible modes of transport from city to city.

Wherever you are, it's wise to avoid **peak travel seasons** if possible. During the two biggest holidays (Seollal and Chuseok; see page 44) it can often feel as if the whole country is on the move, as people rush to their home towns and back again – there's gridlock on the roads, it's hard to find a seat on trains or buses, and many shops and businesses (including some hotels) close down. Weekend or rush-hour train tickets can also be hard to come by throughout the year. For **travel information**, it's best to ask at a tourist office, or call the English-speaking information line on ☎1330 (you'll need to add an area code if dialling from a mobile phone or abroad – see page 53).

By plane

For such a small country, Korea is surprisingly well served by **domestic flights**. The two **national carriers**, Korean Air (W koreanair.com) and Asiana (W flyasiana.com), have near-identical services – with near-identical fares – linking over a dozen airports across the nation, with the two main hubs being Gimpo in Seoul, and the holiday hotspot of Jeju Island. A glut of **budget carriers** head to Jeju from various Korean airports, including T'way (W twayair. com), Eastar Jet (W eastarjet.com), Jin (W jinair. com) and Jeju Air (W en.jejuair.net). All this said, the country is so small (and well covered by train and bus) that only a trip to Jeju would see the average traveller need to use a domestic flight. Prices are reasonable – almost always under W100,000 one way, and sometimes down to W20,000 – which is hardly surprising given that few trips take longer than an hour. Don't forget your **passport**, as you're likely to need it for identification purposes.

By ferry

With several thousand islands sprinkled around Korea's western and southern shores, no trip to the

MOVING ON FROM INCHEON AIRPORT

Connections to Seoul from **Incheon Airport** are excellent (see page 124 for more details), but if you're headed elsewhere there's no need to transit in the capital. Express buses dash from the airport to all of the country's major cities at pleasingly regular intervals. Wherever you're going, useful signs help point the way, or you can ask at the information desk to find the most suitable route.

country would be complete without a **ferry ride**. Several towns and cities have connections, though the main ports of entry to Korea's offshore kingdom are Incheon, Mokpo, Wando, Yeosu and Busan, all of which embrace sizeable island communities. The choice from **Mokpo**, in particular, is incredible – some travellers have inadvertently made trailblazers of themselves, finding their way onto islands that had never seen a foreign face. Popular **Jeju Island** is quite the opposite, and although the vast majority of Koreans travel here by plane, it has ferry connections to a number of south-coast mainland cities (see page 308 for details).

Fares, on the whole, are reasonable – short hops may cost as little as W5000, but for return fares to outlying islands such as Jeju, Hongdo or Ulleungdo you'll probably have to shell out at least ten times that. Only tickets to these destinations will be in much danger of selling out, and even then, only in high season; at these times, it's best to head to a Korean travel agency.

By train

A fleet of excellent **trains** ply the mainland provinces – sleek, affordable and punctual to a fault. There are two **main lines**, both starting in Seoul; these split in Daejeon, with one heading to Daegu and Busan to the southeast, and the other to Mokpo to the southwest.

The highest of three main classes of train is the **KTX** – these high-speed machines can reach speeds of over 300km per hour. The Gyeongbu line runs from Seoul to Busan and connects cities in around 2hr 40min (W59,800). The KTX has taken over from the previous lord of the tracks, the **Saemaeul**; though slower (Seoul to Busan takes over four hours), travelling on this class cuts KTX costs by around a third (W42,600 Seoul to Busan) and the greater legroom usually makes for a more comfortable journey. A third cheaper again is the network's third class of train, the **Mugunghwa**, on which the Seoul to Busan journey (W28,600) is a haul of over five hours.

The line from Seoul to Mokpo also carries all three types of train, though the final high-speed upgrade of the section from Gwangju to Mokpo was not complete at the time of writing. Late 2017 also saw the start of a new KTX line heading east to Gangneung, though this mountain-crosser is a bit slower than the others.

There are other lines away from the inverted "Y"-shape ploughed by the high-speed trains. The south-coast line has irregular services, but can come in handy, while the Jungang line takes a more rural route between Seoul and Busan, lassoing together some of Korea's most wonderful sights (see "Itineraries", page 24).

All trains have **toilets**, and salesfolk pushing trolleys of beer, peanuts, chocolate and *gimbap* for sale down the carriages with pleasing frequency. For fare and schedule information, check ⓦletskorail.com.

Tickets

Almost all stations have English-language signs where necessary, and schedules can also be checked online – it's also now possible to purchase tickets online, and use your smartphone instead of printing anything out. Aside from weekends (when you should buy in advance if you're heading out of Seoul on a Friday evening, or back into Seoul on Sundays), on the main routes it's usually easy to just show up at the station and be away in no time – simply state your destination and the class you require, and the cashier will swing a computer screen in your direction, showing the price and seat availability. If they're pointing at a zero and looking apologetic, you'll probably need another train. You'll be given a carriage and seat number, though there are also slightly cheaper "standing" tickets available.

Tickets for all classes go on sale a month ahead of travel, and can be bought at any station. A **return ticket** costs the same as two single ones, though prices for the KTX routes increase slightly on weekends.

Subway trains

Six Korean cities now have **underground** networks: Busan, Daegu, Daejeon and Gwangju have independent systems, while Incheon's lines are linked to the marauding Seoul network. Prices start at about W1300 for a short hop, and increase

---

KOREAN ADDRESSES

First, the good news – almost all Korean road signs are dual-language, spelling the Korean *hangeul* out in Roman characters. The bad news is that the whole concept of **street names** is fairly new in Korea, since addresses were, for a long time, based on **city sections** rather than roads. The numbers within these sections often ran non-sequentially, making things a nightmare for local postmen, and anyone asking – or giving – directions.

In 2010 the government, in an attempt to bring order to the system, gave all of the roads in the country names (often, confusingly, featuring numbers); consequently, every address in Korea now has **two addresses**: one old, one new. It'll be a while before the new ones find common usage – many Koreans still don't even know what road they live on. This guide has given the "new" addresses for each establishment, since those are the ones you'll see on road signs, and also the ones you're most likely to find on Internet search or mapping engines.

Alternative help is at hand. It's common for hotels and restaurants to include a small map on their **business cards**; wherever you're staying, pop one of their cards in your pocket, and it'll either help you find your way back, or enable locals to point you in the right direction. With a precise address, whether "new" or "old", taxi drivers will also be able to get you where you want to go – satnav systems have, understandably, become rather popular.

Despite the general confusion, addresses fit into a very rigid system. Unlike in the Western world, components are usually listed from largest to smallest when writing an address, the elements of which are discernable by their suffix. The country is split into nine **provinces** (도; –*do*), inside which you'll find **cities** (시; –*si*, pronounced "shee"), **towns** (읍; –*eup*) and **villages** (리; –*ri* or –*li*). The larger cities are split into a number of **districts** (구; –*gu*); the number will vary with the city's size (Seoul, for example, has 25 such sections), and these are further subdivided into **neighbourhoods** (동; *dong*). The new address system dispenses with the *dong* and replaces it with a **road name**; large roads end with 로 (–*no*, –*ro* or –*lo*), and smaller ones with –*gil* (길), and many of the latter are numbered side-roads off a larger (though not necessarily connecting) one. Finally, addresses end with the **number** of the house or establishment – under the new system, these run sequentially along the road. Happy hunting!

with distance in the bigger cities, though even the full run through Seoul from Soyosan to Cheonan – about one-third of the country, and one of the longest metro routes in the world at three hours plus – will only set you back just over W3000. Signs are dual-language, and station maps easy to read.

By bus

There are a staggering number of **long-distance buses** in Korea – during rush hour, some scheduled services can run as often as every two minutes, with all of them departing on time. They come in two types: **express** (고속; *gosok*), and **intercity** (시외; *si-oe*, pronounced "shee-way"). Although the express services are more expensive and tend to be used for longer journeys, they are likely to run in tandem with intercity buses on many routes. Allied to this, the two bus types use **separate stations** in most cities, and even the locals don't always know which one to go to, or which one they'll be arriving at – very frustrating, though some cities are starting to see sense and group both bus stations into one building. Some cities have even more than two bus stations, so all in all it pays to keep a loose schedule when using buses, even more so if the highways are full.

Longer journeys are broken at **service stations**, housing fast-food bars and snack shops. You typically get fifteen minutes to make your purchases and use the **toilets** (there aren't any on the buses), but many a traveller has come a cropper after exiting the building to be confronted by forty near-identical vehicles, of which half-a-dozen may be heading to the same destination – your bus won't wait for you, so make sure that you know where it's parked, and make a note of the registration number and colour of your bus.

Buses are so frequent that it's rare for them to sell out, though the last service of the day between major cities tends to be quite full. This can be surprisingly early: many services make their last trips at 7pm, though some have overnight connections. **Prices** are reasonable and usually lower than the trains, with intercity services slightly cheaper than express if the two coexist – Seoul to Busan is around W25,000 (5hr) on the former, W35,000 (4hr 30min) on the latter. Journeys take longer than the fastest trains, and are more prone to delays. Tickets are often checked at the start of the journey, but also at the end, so if possible try to avoid losing your ticket, lest the driver refuse to release you from his bus (which does happen).

City buses

With little English language on the signs or vehicles, Korea's **city bus** networks can be more than a little confusing for the first-time visitor. Once you are familiar with a route, city buses can be a good way of getting around – they're pleasingly frequent, and very affordable at around W1300 per ride.

Throw your money into the collection box next to the driver; change will be spat out just below – make sure that you've an ample supply of coins or W1000 notes with you, as higher-value bills are unlikely to be accepted (though foreigners in such situations may be waved on with a grin). The bigger cities have started to avoid these problems by introducing **pre-paid cards** (see page 32), and in some cities (notably Seoul) you're no longer able to pay in cash at all. Cards work out cheaper per journey than paying by cash, and some are also valid on subway networks or longer-distance buses. They last for as long as you have credit, and can be topped up in increments of W1000 at kiosks or ticket booths.

By taxi

Korean **taxis** are pleasingly cheap for a developed country. **Rates** start at W3000 in Seoul, and sometimes a little less in the provinces, meaning that over short distances, cab rides may work out cheaper than taking buses if you're in a group. All taxis are **metered,** and dishonesty is rarely an issue, though late at night in Seoul some drivers will (understandably) only want to head towards the commuter town they call home, and you may have to negotiate a fare. Taxis are pretty ubiquitous, and in any city you shouldn't have to wait long to spot one – look for cars with illuminated blocks on top, usually something resembling a plastic pyramid. Those whose blocks aren't illuminated are taken

---

PUBLIC TRANSPORT CARDS

If you're in Korea for anything more than a few days, and intending to use public transport to get around its cities, having a pre-paid **transport card** is a good idea. Different cities use different systems, but Seoul's T-money (see page 97) is a good one to pick up, since it can be used in most cities nationwide.

or on call; others can be **waved down** from the roadside, though to make sure of being understood you'll have to do it the Korean way – arm out, palm to the ground, fingers dangling underneath. As few drivers speak English, it's a good idea to have your destination **written down**, if possible – even the cheapest motels have business cards with their address on.

If you're wondering whether **Uber** exists in Korea, the answer is... maybe. The app was usable in Seoul and parts of Gangwon province, but in 2017 authorities buckled to pressure from the taxi-driver lobby, and you may not be able to use it. Koreans themselves tend to use local app **KakaoTaxi** (available in English); this uses regular, metered cabs, and you pay in cash, but in Seoul it has become so popular that simply standing by the roadside for a taxi often doesn't cut it any more.

By car

Korea's public transport network is so good that few foreigners end up renting a car here – in many cases it would simply lose you time, especially when getting around cities. Exceptions include Jeju Island and rural Gangwon province in the northeast, where the roads are relatively calm and traffic-free.

To **hire a car** you will need an international driving licence, and to be at least 21 years of age. Rental offices can be found at all airports and many train stations, as well as around the cities. **Prices** usually start at W50,000 per day, though as insurance is compulsory, you should budget on a little extra. Vehicles drive on the right-hand side of the road.

By motorbike

You'll be hard pushed to find two-wheeled vehicles above **125cc** in the country, as the vast majority of its superbikes are exported for use in Europe or America. Despite this, though, a sizeable number of expats still don leather during their Korean stint. One good place to hunt for information or cycle partners is **Yongsan Motorcycle Club**, whose website (Ⓦ roaddragons.com) features a calendar of forthcoming trips and events.

By bicycle

There are nowhere near as many **bikes** on the roads of Korea as there are in other Asian countries – cyclists are obliged to use pedestrian areas on major roads within most cities. There are, however, a few pleasant areas to cycle along rural roads; particular recommendations are the sparsely populated provinces of **Gangwon** and **Jeju Island**. Rides circumnavigating the latter take three or four days at a steady pace, and are becoming more and more commonplace. Those confined to a city will usually be able to go for a ride on a **riverbank**, with bikes available for hire at the most popular spots; at many such places foreigners are effectively barred from renting cycles, since a Korean ID card is required, though details have been included in this guide where appropriate.

In recent years, **long-distance bike routes** have been laid across the country; it's now possible to cycle much of the way from Seoul to Busan – a trip of up to one week – on dedicated cycle-and-walking paths. Other routes are set to follow – exciting times for Korean cyclists.

By hitchhiking

Foreigners who attempt to cover long distances by **hitching rides** in Korea generally have a hard time of things. Even with your destination on a handwritten sign, and even after having confirmed to the driver where it is that you want to go, you're likely to be dropped at the nearest bus or train station. After all, to Koreans, this is the only sensible way to travel if you don't have a vehicle of your own – hitching is almost unheard of as a money-saving or experiential device. **Short-distance** rides are a different proposition altogether; although the scope of Korea's public transport system means that you'd be very unfortunate to find yourself stuck without a bus or train, it can happen, and in such circumstances hitching a ride can be as easy as flagging down the first car that you see. Of course, accepting lifts with strangers isn't devoid of risk anywhere on Earth, but if you're ever determined to give it a try, there can be few easier and safer places to do it than the Korean countryside.

ONLINE TRAVEL RESOURCES

Google Maps Ⓦ maps.google.com. National security regulations mean that Google Maps isn't as useful as it is in most countries, but if you type in an A and a B, you'll often get accurate bus, train or subway times between them.

Incheon International Airport Ⓦ airport.or.kr. Information on flights into and out of Korea's main airport.

Korail Ⓦ letskorail.com. Information on train times and passes, including discounted combined train and ferry tickets to Japan.

Seoul Metropolitan Rapid Transport (SMRT) Ⓦ smrt.co.kr. Timetables, and a useful best-route subway map.

Visit Korea Ⓦ english.visitkorea.co.kr. Good for bus connections between major cities, with cursory information on trains and ferries.

Accommodation

Accommodation is likely to swallow up a large chunk of your travel budget, especially for those who favour Western-style luxuries, but for adventurous travellers there are ways to keep costs to a minimum. Finding a place is less likely to be a problem – Korea has an incredible number of places to stay, and one would be forgiven for thinking that there are actually more beds than there are people in the country. Do note, however, that the vast majority of these are on the cheaper side – only a few places around the country have top-drawer hotel facilities, though the number of boutique-style arrangements has certainly increased of late.

Luxury hotels can be found in all cities and major tourist areas, as well as a number of specially dedicated tourist hotels, though with space at such a premium, rooms are generally on the small side. At the lower end of the price scale, budget travellers can choose from thousands of motels and guesthouses – many of which have nicer rooms than the dedicated tourist hotels and at far lower prices – or even sleep in a *jjimjilbang* (a Korean sauna; see page 36). Reservations at these levels were once almost unheard of, but many motels – even in the provinces – are now on international booking engines. English is spoken to varying degrees in all top hotels, but elsewhere it pays to know a few keywords in Korean (or to have good miming skills).

Hotels

The big **hotel** (호텔) chains are present and correct in Korea, and there's at least one five-star option in every major city. You're most likely to pay full rack rates in July or August, though high season at national parks and ski resorts will be autumn and winter respectively. Standards are high, by and large, though even at the top end it's hard to find rooms of a decent size.

Korean hotels are split by **class**; from top to bottom, these are super-deluxe, deluxe, first-class, second-

class and third-class. Categories are marked by a plaque at the front showing a number of flowers – five for super-deluxe down to one for third-class. Many "**tourist hotels**" (관광호텔) were built as Korea was getting rich in the 1980s, and now offer questionable value; some of the more recently built motels offer better rooms, and at much lower prices. Most hotels have "Western" or "Korean" rooms; there are no beds in the latter (the sandwich of blankets on a heated *ondol* floor represents the traditional Korean way to sleep), and prices for both are about the same.

When booking, bear in mind that the 10 percent **tax** levied on hotel rooms is not always factored into the quoted prices; in higher-end establishments, you're also likely to be hit with an additional 10 percent service charge.

Motels

Bearing little resemblance to their American counterparts, **motels** (모텔) are absolutely all over the place – in any urban centre, you should never be more than a walk from the nearest one. Most offer fairly uniform en-suite doubles for W30,000–50,000, and standard facilities include shampoo and shower gel, hairdryers, televisions, a water fountain and free cans of coffee or "vitamin juice". Extortion of foreigners is extremely rare, and you shouldn't be afraid to haggle the price down if you're travelling alone, especially outside summer.

Korean motels won't appeal to everybody, as they're generally used as a much-needed source of privacy by young couples (or those who need to keep their relationship secret). A few would be more honestly described as "love hotels" – pink neon and Cinderella turrets are the most obvious giveaways, while the interior may feature heart-shaped beds, condom machines and more mirrors than you can shake a stick at. That said, the majority of establishments are quite tame, any seediness i[s] kept behind closed doors and they make accept[-]able places to stay even for lone women – indeed those who can put up with the decor will fin[d] them Korea's best-value accommodation optio[n]. The motels that have gone up since the turn o[f] the century, in particular, often have cleaner room[s] than the average tourist hotel, typically featurin[g] huge flatscreen TVs and internet-ready compute[r] terminals; most have wi-fi.

Guesthouses

Yeogwan (여관) are older, smaller, less polishe[d] versions of motels. Slightly cheaper, but often a litt[le]

ACCOMMODATION PRICES

The **prices** given for all establishments listed in this guide are for the cheapest double room, in high season, with all taxes and service charges included.

FIVE QUIRKY PLACES TO STAY

Sun Cruise, Jeongdongjin Ship-shape in a most literal sense, this hotel sits on top of a cliff overlooking the East Sea (see page 168).

Rakkojae, Hahoe Folk Village A delightful wooden guesthouse, brooding away in one of Korea's prettiest, quietest villages (see page 180).

Birosanjang, Songnisan One of the only accommodation options inside a Korean national park, here you can fall asleep to the sound of nothing but nature (see page 291).

Deungmeoeul, Biyangdo Basically the only inhabited building on this tiny islet, accessible from another tiny islet, which is accessible in turn by ferry from Jeju Island – a great place to get away from it all (see page 314).

Jjimjilbang Not a specific place, but a concept: found by the dozen in every city, these bathhouses have communal sleeping rooms in which you can get a night's rest for next to nothing (see page 36).

grubby, they once formed the backbone of Korea's budget travel accommodation, and can still be found in teams around bus and train stations. With whole streets full of them, it's easy to hunt around for the best deal – a double room usually costs W25,000–35,000, though prices are higher in Seoul, and tend to rise in high season. Single rooms do not exist, but almost all have en-suite bathrooms.

Minbak rooms (민박) are usually rented-out parts of a residential property, and are less likely to have private bathrooms. These are most commonly found on islands and by popular beaches or national parks, and though the prices are comparable to *yeogwan* rates for much of the year they can quadruple if there's enough demand – summer is peak season for the beaches and islands, spring and autumn for the national parks.

Even cheaper rooms can be found at a **yeoinsuk** (여인숙) – around W15,000 per night. Slowly disappearing, these are a noisier, more spartan variation of the *yeogwan*, invariably found in older areas of town, with rooms containing nothing more than a couple of blankets, a television and a heated linoleum *ondol* floor to sleep on. Such wipe-clean minimalism generally makes for clean rooms, though some have a cockroach problem, and the communal toilets and showers can be quite off-putting; in addition, some of them are used by prostitutes and their clients.

Hostels

Hostels (호스텔) in Korea come in two distinct varieties: official and independent. The official hostels are created for, and primarily used by, the nation's youth, with the resultant atmosphere more boarding school than bohemian – none have been listed in this guide. The **independent** hostels will be much more familiar to international backpackers, and have really taken off of late –

every major city now has one, and Seoul an almost countless number. However, they're not always great value: with W20,000 now normal for a dorm bed, you'd almost always be able to score a private motel room for a few dollars more, often in a far more convenient location. Many hostels also offer **private rooms**, though at W50,000–60,000, they're double the aforementioned motel prices. Still, if you're keen to socialize with other travellers, hostels remain a great way to go, and they're becoming ever more numerous.

Camping and mountain huts

Most national parks have at least one **campsite** to cater for the swarms of Korean hikers who spend their weekends in the mountains. Most are free, but those that charge (typically under W5000) have excellent toilet and shower facilities. Jirisan and Seoraksan, two of the largest parks, have well-signposted **shelters** or **huts** dotted around the hiking trails; these cost under W8000 per person, though they may only open from summer until autumn, and you're advised to book ahead – check the national park website (**W** english.knps.or.kr). At both campsites and shelters, drinking water should always be available, and though simple snacks may also be on offer, it's best to bring your own food.

Templestays, hanok guesthouses and alternative accommodation

If you're looking for a more traditional experience, you could try staying at a **temple**. Though temples with sufficient room are pretty much obliged to take in needy travellers for the night, many offer interesting, prearranged **templestay programmes** for around W50,000 per night, some with the

STAYING AT A JJIMJILBANG

For travellers willing to take the plunge and bare all in front of curious strangers, sauna establishments (known locally as **jjimjilbang**; 찜질방) are some of the cheapest and most uniquely Korean places in which to get a night's sleep. Almost entirely devoid of the seedy reputations that may dog similar facilities abroad, *jjimjilbang* are large, round-the-clock venues primarily used by families escaping their homes for the night, businessmen who've worked or partied beyond their last trains, or teenage groups having a safe night out together. They can be found in any Korean city, typically costing W5000–8000, and consist of a shower and pool area, a sauna or steam room, and a large playschool-style quiet room or two for communal napping; most also have snack bars and internet terminals. Upon entry, guests are given a locker key for their shoes, another for their clothing, and matching T-shirts and shorts to change into – outside clothes are not allowed to be worn inside the complex, though it's OK to wear underwear beneath your robe. All must be sacrificed on entry to the pools, which are segregated by gender. The common rooms are uniformly clean but vary in style; some have TVs and hi-tech recliner chairs, others invite you to roll out a mini-mattress, but all will have a floorful of snoring Koreans – not the quietest night's sleep you'll ever have, but a wonderfully local experience.

capacity for English-language translation (see Ⓦeng.templestay.com for more details). A stay generally involves meditation, grounds-sweeping, a tea ceremony and a meal or two, but be prepared for spartan sleeping arrangements and a pre-dawn wake-up call.

If you're after something traditional but without the routine, try hunting down a **hanok**. These are traditional Korean buildings, replete with wooden frames, sliding doors and a woodfired underfloor heating system. Few such buildings cater for travellers, though some can be found at the traditional villages scattered around the country (Hahoe near Andong is the best; see page 179), and there are dedicated districts in Seoul (see page 101) and Jeonju (see page 258). Many include tea ceremonies and other activities such as *kimchi*-making in the cost.

Lastly, **Airbnb** (Ⓦairbnb.co.uk) has made inroads into the Korean accommodation market, though it usually provides questionable value for money relative to motels and cheaper hotels, and locations can be less than convenient. However, some travellers (particularly vegetarians) will be delighted to have access to their own cooking facilities. Beware of the very cheapest places though, since many are actually *goshiwon* – usually used as student accommodation, these minuscule rooms are nominally private (though noise carries very easily), and their Airbnb rates can be three or four times the usual price.

ONLINE ACCOMMODATION RESOURCES

Ⓦ **booking.com** This major site has better sorting functions than most – enabling you to see the cheapest rooms without dorms, for example – and is regularly preferred to similar domestic sites by Koreans themselves.

Ⓦ **eng.templestay.com** Information on the various templestay programmes around the country.

Ⓦ **english.knps.or.kr** Korea National Park Service site detailing available shelters.

Ⓦ **hostelworld.com** Good listings of Seoul's budget accommodation, and a few more choices from around the country.

Ⓦ **khrc.com** Website for the Korea Hotel Reservation Centre, worth a look for occasional special deals.

Ⓦ **stay.visitseoul.net** City-sponsored site featuring a range of cheap accommodation in Seoul, all at places deemed suitable for foreigners; ironically, at the time of writing the "language" setting was only in Korean (it's at the top-right).

Ⓦ **trivago.com** User-friendly site that compares quotes from all the major hotel booking engines and directs you to the cheapest.

Food and drink

Korean cuisine deserves greater attention. A thrillingly spicy mishmash of simple but healthy ingredients, it's prepared with consummate attention, then doled out in hearty portions at more restaurants than you could possibly count – even if every person in the country suddenly decided to go out for dinner, there would probably still be some free tables. Most are open from early morning until late at night and a full 24 hours a day in many cases. You can usually find a restaurant to suit your budget, and there will always be an affordable option close by, a fact attested to by the great number of foreigners that live here quite happily for weeks, months or even years on end without doing a single bit of cooking for themselves.

The traditional Korean **restaurant** is filled with low tables; diners are required to remove their footwear and sit on floor cushions. There are a number of rules of restaurant **etiquette** (see page 49) but a substantial amount of custom also surrounds the food itself; while what often appears to be a culinary free-for-all can draw gasps from foreign observers (eat the meal; boil off the soup; throw in some rice to fry up with the scraps; add some noodles), Korea's great on conformity, and you may well provoke chuckles of derision by performing actions that you deem quite sensible – it's best just to follow the Korean lead.

Korean eating establishments are hard to pigeonhole. The lines between bar, restaurant, snack shop and even home are often blurry to say the least, and some places cover all bases: in provincial towns, you may well see the owner's children snoozing under empty tables.

Restaurant meals usually consist of communal servings of **meat** or **fish** around which are placed a bewildering assortment of **side dishes** (banchan; 반찬). Often, these are the best part of the meal – a range of fish, meat, vegetables and steamed egg broth, which come included in the price of the meal, and there may be as many as twenty of them on the table; when your favourite is finished, ask for a refill, and it'll be on the house. Amazing, really.

One common problem for visitors is the **spice** level of the food, an issue that has given Korea one of the world's highest rates of stomach cancer. It's not so much the spiciness of the individual dishes that causes problems (British travellers trained on curry, for example, rarely have any problems adjusting to Korean spice) but the fact that there's little respite from it – red pepper paste (gochujang; 고추장) is a component of almost every meal. Another common complaint by foreign visitors is the lack of attention paid to **vegetarians**, as such folk are extremely rare in Korea. Despite the high vegetable content of many meals, almost all have at least a little meat, and very few are cooked in meat-free environments. Most resort to asking for bibimbap without the meat, eating ramyeon (라면; instant noodles), or poking the bits of ham out of gimbap with a chopstick.

Many dishes are for **sharing**, a fantastic arrangement that fosters togetherness and increases mealtime variety, though this has adverse implications for single travellers – Koreans don't like to eat alone, and are likely to fret about those who do. One other point worth mentioning is the incredible number of foodstuffs that are claimed to be "good for **sexual stamina**"; at times it feels as if food is an augmenter of male potency first, and a necessary means of sustenance second. Raw fish and dog meat, in particular, are said to be good for this.

Rice dishes

Many meals involve **rice** in various forms: one that proves a hit with many foreigners is **bibimbap**, a mixture of shoots, leaves and vegetables on a bed of rice, flecked with meat, then topped with an egg and spicy gochujang pepper sauce. Bibimbap was originally a religious dish derived from the five principal colours of Korean Buddhism – red for the paste, yellow for the egg yolk, white for the rice, blue for the meat and green for the vegetables – and is one of the easiest dishes to find in Korea. It can cost as little as W4000, though there are sometimes a few varieties to choose from. Some restaurants serve it in a heated stone bowl (dolsot bibimbap; 돌솥 비빔밥); those in the countryside may make it using only vegetables sourced from

---

KIMCHI

No country on Earth is as closely entwined with its national dish as Korea is with its beloved **kimchi**: a spicy mix of fermented vegetables, which is served as a complimentary **side dish** at pretty much every restaurant in the land. Many traditionally minded families still ferment their own in distinctive earthenware jars, but home-made or not it's an important part of breakfast, lunch and dinner in most Korean homes. Lots of families even have a dedicated kimchi fridge, quartered off to separate the four main types. The two most common varieties are **baechu kimchi**, made with cabbage, and **ggakdugi kimchi**, which are cubes of radish in a red-pepper sauce, but there are others made with cucumber or other vegetables.

Salt, garlic and a hearty dollop of **red-pepper paste** are almost mandatory in a good kimchi, though additional ingredients vary from home to home and restaurant to restaurant. Many of the best recipes are shrouded in secrecy and handed down through the generations, but some of the most popular components include onion, brine, ginger and fish paste. The effect on the breath can be dramatic, to say the least, but there are few better ways to endear yourself to the locals than by chowing down on a bowlful of kimchi.

TOP 10 DINING SPOTS

Balwoo Buddhist temple food, Seoul (see page 104).

Korea House Royal banquets, Seoul (see page 105).

Bukcheong Sundae Noodle sausages and a ferry trip, Sokcho (see page 154).

Dosol Maeul Pancakes and rice beer in a traditional wooden abode, Gyeongju (see page 195).

Jagalchi fish market Busan (see page 216).

Hwangsolchon Some of Korea's best barbecued meat, Gwangju (see page 251).

Gomanaru Feasts of flowers and leaves, Gongju (see page 280).

Daecheon beach The best place in Korea for a shellfish barbecue (see page 285).

Haechon Eat cutlassfish *bibimbap* with a prime view of Sunrise Peak, Seongsan (see page 313).

North Korea Anywhere and anything, for sheer excitement value (see page 351).

the surrounding mountains (*sanchae bibimbap*; 산채 비빔밥); and certain establishments in Jeonju have elevated the dish to an art form, serving it with a whole witch's cauldron of fascinating ingredients including pine kernels, fern bracken and slices of jujube, and up to a dozen individual side dishes.

Other dishes to be served on a bed of rice include beef (*bulgogi deop-bap*; 불고기 덮밥), highly spicy squid (*ojingeo deop-bap*; 오징어 덮밥) or *donkasseu* (돈까스), a breaded pork cutlet dish imported from Japan (and particularly popular with those who want to avoid spice). Also fulfilling this need are rolls of **gimbap** (김밥): *gim* means laver seaweed, *bap* means rice, and the former is rolled around the latter, which itself surrounds strips of egg, ham and pickled radish; the resulting tube is then cut into circular segments with a sharp knife to make the dish chopstick-friendly. The regular ones are filling and only cost W1500–2000, but for a little more you'll usually have a variety of fillings to choose from, including tuna (*chamchi*; 참치), minced beef (*sogogi*; 소고기), processed cheese (*chi-jeu*; 치즈) and *kimchi*.

Noodle dishes

Noodles are used as a base in many dishes, and can be extremely cheap – a bowl of **ramyeon** (라면) can go for just W3000. This is a block of instant noodles boiled up in a spicy red-pepper soup, and usually mixed in with an egg and some onion. For a little more you can have dumplings (*mandu*; 만두), rice cake (*ddeok*; 떡) or processed cheese thrown in. Those travelling in the sticky Korean summer will find it hard to throw back a bowl of hot, spicy soup; a better choice may be **naengmyeon** (냉면), bowls of grey buckwheat noodles served with a boiled egg and vegetable slices in a spicy paste

or an ice-cold spicy soup; it'll set you back around W5000, though more like double that at the best establishments.

Soups and broths

The names of **soup** dishes usually end with *-tang* (탕) or *-guk* (국), though special mention must be made of the spicy **jjigae** broths (찌개). These are bargain meals that cost W4500 and up, and come with rice and a range of vegetable side dishes; the red-pepper broth contains chopped-up -vegetables, as well as a choice of tofu (*sundubu*; 순두부), tuna, soybean paste (*doenjang*; 된장) or *kimchi*.

Barbecued meat

Barbecued meat is one of Korea's signature foods, and a whole lot of fun – for carnivores, at least. Here, you get to play chef with a plate of raw meat commonly placed on a grill over charcoal, and a pair of scissors to slice it all up. As excess fat drips off the meat onto the briquettes it releases the occasional tongue of flame, which lends a genuine air of excitement to the meal. Two of the most popular meat dishes are *galbi* and *samgyeopsal*, which are almost always cooked by the diners themselves in the centre of the table. **Galbi** is rib-meat, most often beef (*so-galbi*; 소갈비) but sometimes pork (*dwaeji-galbi*; 돼지갈비). **Samgyeopsal** (삼겹살) consists of strips of rather fatty pork belly. Prices vary but figure on around W13,000 per portion for beef and a little less for pork; a minimum of two diners is usually required.

In dedicated *galbi* restaurants the dish is usually eaten sitting on the floor, but many cheaper places have outdoor tables. In all cases, you'll be served fresh (and replenishable) side dishes, which may include pulses, tofu, leek, potato and tiny fish. A boiling bowl of egg broth and a tray of leaves are also usually thrown in for the group to share – barbecued meat is not a meal to eat on your own – and each person is given a bowl of chopped-up greens and a pot of salted sesame oil.

In Confucian Korea, it's common for the "lowest" adult member of the party – usually the youngest female – to cook and dish out the meat. To eat it, first place a leaf or two from the tray onto your left hand, then with your chopsticks add a piece of meat, and a smudge of soybean paste; roll the leaf around to make a ball, and you're ready to go. Lastly, meat is traditionally washed down with a bottle or three of *soju* – Korea's answer to vodka (see page 42).

Snack food

Though the most common variety of Korean **snack food** is *gimbap* there are many more options available. One is a dish called **ddeokbokki** (떡볶이), a mix of rice cake and processed fish boiled up in a highly spicy red-pepper sauce; this typically costs around W3000 per portion, and is doled out in bowls by street vendors and small roadside booths. The same places usually serve **twigim** (튀김), which are flash-fried pieces of squid, potato, seaweed-covered noodle-roll or stuffed chilli pepper, to name but a few ingredients. The price varies but is usually around W3000 for six pieces – choose from the display, and they'll be refried in front of you. You can have the resulting dish smothered in *ddeokbokki* sauce for no extra charge – delicious.

FAST-FOOD CHAINS

Such is the pace at which Koreans live their lives that many find it impossible to spare time for a leisurely meal, so it should come as no surprise that their city streets are packed with **fast-food outlets**. Korean fast food is something of a misnomer: fast it may well be, but in general the local offerings are far healthier than their Western equivalents – you could eat them every day and never get fat. One slight problem for travellers is that few of these cheap places are used to dealing with foreigners, so don't expect English-language menus or service (you'll find a menu reader on page 393). Below is a selection of the outlets you're most likely to come across in cities across the nation.

Gimbap Cheonguk (김밥천국) In Korean street-space terms, this ubiquitous orange-fronted franchise is rivalled only by internet bars and the more prominent convenience store chains. The concept is pretty miraculous – almost all basic Korean meals are served here for around W5000 per dish, and despite the variety on offer you'll usually be eating within minutes of sitting down. They also sell *gimbap* from W1500, and these can be made to go: perfect if you're off on a hike.

Isaac Toast (이삭토스트) Toast, but not as you know it. The Korean variety is made on a huge hotplate – first your perfectly square bread will be fried and smeared with weird kiwi-like jam, then joined by perfect squares of spam and/or fried egg (or even a burger, for those to whom the word "cholesterol" means nothing), and the whole lot squirted with two sauces, one spicy and one brown. No, it's not healthy, but it makes a tasty breakfast; prices start at around W2000.

Jaws (죠스) This chain has been on the wane of late, though you'll still find them in every city, selling rounds of street-eats *twigim* (see page 39) and *ddeokbokki* (see page 39) for less than the street stands, and at a much higher level of quality. W2500 will be enough for a plate of crispy *twigim*; ask to have it smothered with spicy *ddeokbokki* sauce.

Kim Ga Ne (김家네) A slightly more upmarket version of *Gimbap Cheonguk* (see above), serving more or less the same things with a few snazzy "fusion" additions. Most branches have their menu on the walls in pictorial form, handy if you don't speak Korean. Dishes W4000–8000.

Paris Baguette (파리빠게뜨) & **Tous Les Jours** (뚜레쥬르) A pair of near-identical bakery chains, whose offerings may satisfy if you need a breakfast devoid of spice or rice; many branches are also able to whip up a passable coffee. Baked goods start at around W1500, but note that even the savoury-looking ones are usually extremely sugary. You'll find branches all over the place; harder to spot is *Paris Croissant*, a slightly more upmarket version.

Yu Ga Ne (유가네) This chain serves tasty barbecued meat, cooked at your table by an apron-wearing attendant. Unlike most barbecue joints, there are dishes for those dining alone, such as the delectable *dak-galbi beokkeumbap*, which is something like a chicken kebab fried up with rice. W8000 should be enough to get a bellyful.

ROYAL CUISINE

As it's such an important part of daily Korean life, it's inevitable that food should wend its way into traditional events. The hundredth day of a child's life is marked with a feast of colourful rice cake, while a simpler variety is served in a soup (*ddeokguk*) to celebrate Lunar New Year. More interesting by far, however, is **royal court cuisine**: a remnant of the Joseon dynasty, which ruled over the Korean peninsula from 1392 to 1910, this was once served to Korean rulers and associated nobility. The exact ingredients and styles vary and go by several different names, but usually rice, soup and a charcoal-fired casserole form the centre of the banquets, and are then surrounded by an array of perfectly prepared dishes; twelve was once the royal number of dishes and banned to the peasant class, but now anyone can indulge as long as they have the money. The aim of the combination is to harmonize culinary opposites such as spicy and mild, solid and liquid, rough and smooth; a balance of colour and texture is thereby achieved – the Yin–Yang principle in edible form.

Some of the best places to try this kind of food are *Korea House* (see page 105) and *Balwoo* in Seoul (see page 104).

Convenience stores are usually good places to grab some food, as all sell sandwiches, rolls and triangles of *gimbap*, and instant noodles; boiling water will always be available for the latter, as well as a bench or table to eat it from, an activity that will mark you as an honorary Korean. A less appealing practice, but one that will endear you to Koreans more than anything else can, is the eating of **beonddegi** (번데기) – boiled silkworm larvae.

Desserts

You'll find **ice cream** in any convenience store, where prices can be as low as W500; if you want to keep your selection as Korean as possible, go for green tea, melon, or red-bean-paste flavours. An even more distinctively local variety, available from specialist snack bars, is *patbingsu* (팥빙수), a strange concoction of fruit, cream, shaved ice and red-bean paste – most Korean meals are for sharing, so it's inevitable that a dessert made for sharing is super-popular around the land. Also keep an eye out in colder months for a **hoddeok** (호떡) stand – these press out little fried pancakes of rice-mix filled with brown sugar and cinnamon for just W1000 per piece, and are extremely popular with foreigners.

Seafood, markets and mountain food

Some Korean eating places exude an essence little changed for decades – fish stalls around the coast, city-centre marketplaces and mountain restaurants are your best options for that traditional feeling.

Korean **seafood** is a bit of a maze for most foreigners, and much more expensive than other meals, though it's worth persevering. Some is served raw, while other dishes are boiled up in a spicy soup. Jagalchi market in Busan deserves a special mention (see page 209), but in small coastal villages – particularly on the islands of the West and South seas – there's little other industry to speak of; battered fishing flotillas yo-yo in and out with the tide, and you may be able to buy fish straight off the boat. This may seem as fresh as seafood can possibly be, but baby octopus is often served live (*sannakji*; 산낙지). Be warned: several people die each year when their prey decides to make a last futile stab at survival with its suckers (usually those trying to eat the thing whole). A far simpler choice is *hoe deop-bap* (회덮밥), a widely available dish similar to *bibimbap*, but with sliced raw fish in place of egg and meat. A halfway house in excitement terms is *jogae-gui* (조개구이), a shellfish barbecue – the creatures are grilled in front of you, and W50,000 will buy enough of them to fill two people.

Korean **markets** offer similar opportunities for culinary exploration. Here you're also likely to spot seafood on sale, along with fruits, vegetables, grilled or boiled meats and an assortment of snacks. Many options have been detailed under "Snack food" (see page 39), but one favourite more unique to the market is *sundae* (순대), a kind of sausage made with intestinal lining and noodles (see page 104). Sokcho on the Gangwon coast is the best place to sample this, and has a few dedicated restaurants on Abai Island (see page 154).

Korea's wonderful **national parks** feature some splendid eating opportunities located around the main entrances. One of the most popular hiking dishes is *sanchae bibimbap* (산채 비빔밥), a variety of the Korean staple made with roots, shoots and vegetables from the surrounding country side – knowing that everything is sourced locally somehow makes the dish taste better. Most popular, though, are *pajeon* (파전); locals may refer to these as "Korean pizza", but they're more similar to a savoury pancake. They usually contain strips of spring onion and seafood (*haemul*; 해물) *pajeon*, though other varieties are available; it's usually washed down with a bowl or three of *dongdongju*, a milky rice wine.

International cuisine

While many visitors fall head over heels for Korean food, it's not to everybody's taste, and after a while the near-permanent spicy tang of red-pepper paste can wear down even the most tolerant taste buds. One problem concerns **breakfast**, which, to most Koreans, is simply another time window for the intake of *kimchi* and rice. This is too heavy for many Westerners, but though a fry-up will be hard to find outside the major hotels, you may find some solace in the buns, cakes and pastries of major bakery chains such as *Tous Les Jours* and *Paris Baguette* (see page 39), or the mayonnaise-heavy sandwiches of the convenience stores.

International food is getting easier to come by in Korea, and now most major cities have a fairly cosmopolitan range. **American-style fast food**, however, can be found pretty much everywhere – *McDonald's* and *Burger King* are joined by *Lotteria*, a local chain, and there are also a great number of fried-chicken joints scattered around. Traditional **Japanese food** has made serious inroads into the

Korean scene, and the obligatory red lanterns of *izakaya*-style bar-restaurants are especially easy to spot in student areas. **Italian food** has long been popular with Koreans, who have added their own twists to pizzas and pasta – almost every single meal will be served with a small tub of pickled gherkin, an addition that locals assume to be de rigueur in the restaurants of Napoli or Palermo. **Chinese restaurants** are equally numerous, though unfortunately they're no more authentic than their counterparts in Western countries, even in the many cases where the restaurateurs themselves are Chinese. One recommendation, however, is *beokkeumbap* – fried rice mixed with cubes of ham and vegetable, topped with a fried egg and black bean sauce, and served with deliciously spicy seafood broth; the whole thing will cost about W5000, and is, therefore, a great way to fill up on the cheap.

Drink

A sweet potato wine named **soju** (소주) is the national drink – a cheap, clear Korean version of vodka that you'll either love or hate (or love, then hate the next morning) – but there's a pleasing variety of grog to choose from. The country also has a wealth of excellent tea on offer, though coffee is increasingly winning the urban caffeine battles.

Bars and hofs

Though the imbibing of *soju* is de rigueur at restaurants of an evening, most people do their serious

---

DOG MEAT

Korea's consumption of **dog meat** (*gae-gogi*; 개고기) became global knowledge when the country hosted the 1988 Olympics, at which time the government kowtowed to Western tastes and attempted to sweep the issue under the carpet.

Today, eating dog meat amounts to a shameful national secret. Foreigners looking for it on the menu or in their hamburgers are likely to be relieved, as it's almost nowhere to be seen. Should the issue be raised, even with a Korean you know well, they'll probably laugh and tell you that they don't eat dog, and that the practice only takes place behind closed doors, if at all.

That said, and though it's true that few young people consume dog, the soup *yeongyangtang*, for one, is still popular with older Koreans due to its purported health-giving properties, and can be hunted down in specialist restaurants.

Any fears of Koreans chowing down on an Alsatian or Border Collie should be quelled; almost all dog meat comes from a scraggly mongrel breed colloquially known as the *ddong-gae* (똥개), or "shit-dog", an animal named for its tendency to eat whatever it finds on the floor. Even so, the poor conditions that the animals are often kept in, and the continuing – and occasionally verified – stories of dogs being clubbed to death to tenderize the meat, are good reasons to avoid this kind of meal. For those who wish to know, it's a slightly stringy meat somewhere between duck and beef in texture, and is generally agreed to taste better than it smells.

DRINK THE LOCAL WAY

Though Koreans largely favour beer and imported drinks, the country has more than a few superb **local hooches**, many of which go down very well indeed with the few foreigners lucky enough to learn about them.

Baekseju (백세주) A nutty, whisky-coloured concoction, about the same strength as wine. Its name means "one-hundred-year alcohol", on account of healthy ingredients including ginseng and medicinal herbs. Surely the tastiest path towards becoming a centenarian, *baekseju* is available at all convenience stores (W5500) and many barbecue houses (W8000 or so).

Bokbunjaju (복분자주) Made with black raspberries, this sweet, fruity drink is somewhat similar to sugary, low-grade port. It's available at all convenience stores (W7000), though those off on a mountain hike in late summer may be lucky enough to try some freshly made: it's sold by farmers at makeshift stalls.

Dongdongju (동동주) Very similar to *makgeolli* (see page 43), *dongdongju* is a little heavier taste-wise, and since it can only be served fresh you'll have to head to a specialist place for a try. The restaurants most likely to have *dongdongju* are those also serving savoury pancakes known as *pajeon*; these establishments are usually rustic affairs decked out with Korean bric-a-brac, and serving *dongdongju* in large bowls (W8000). A word of warning: many foreigners have "hit the wall" on their first dabble, suddenly finding themselves floored by this deceptively quaffable drink.

Maehwasu (매화수) Similar to *baekseju* in colour, strength and price, this is made with the blossom of the *maesil*, a type of Korean plum, and some bottles come with said fruit steeping inside.

Makgeolli (막걸리) Milky rice beer that's usually around 6 percent alcohol by volume (see page 43).

Soju (소주) The national drink, for better or worse. Locals are fond of referring to it as "Korean vodka", but it's only half the strength – a good thing too, as it's usually fired down in staccato shots, preferably over barbecued meat. It's traditionally made with sweet potato, but these days most companies use cheap chemical concoctions: the resultant taste puts many foreigners off, but some find themselves near-addicted within days of arrival. Expect to pay W1300 from a convenience store, W3000 at a restaurant.

drinking in bars and "*hofs*". **Hofs**, pronounced more like "hop" (호프) (호프; 맥주) by the bucketload. The main beers are Cass, OB and Hite; prices are more or less the same for each, starting at about W2500 for a 500cc glass. Quite fascinating are the three- or five-litre plastic jugs of draught beer (*saeng-maekju*; 생맥주), which often come billowing dry ice and illuminated with flashing lights. The downside of such places is that customers are pretty much obliged to eat as well as drink; you'll be given free snacks, but customers are expected to order something from the menu, with American-style fried chicken available at most such places (try the sweet-spicy *yangnyeom* topping).

The "typical" Korean bar is a dark, neon-strewn dens; unlike in *hofs*, customers are not usually expected to eat and tend to take roost in an extensive cocktail menu, and beer will still be available, in draught or bottled form. Recently, more **adventurous** bars have been taking their place, and there has been a nationwide proliferation of craft-beer establishments (see page 42). Each city has one or more main "going-out" district, with the most raucous to be found outside the rear entrances of the **universities** (which maintain a veneer of respectability by keeping their main entrances free of such revelry). Most cities have at least one resident **expat bar**; these are usually the best places for foreigners to meet fellow *waeguk-in* (foreigners) or English-speaking Koreans. Often surrounded with tables and chairs for customer use, convenience stores are equally great places to meet new mates, and cheap as hell for local drinks. They also sell bottles of foreign **wine** for W7000 and up, though special mention must be made of a local variety named Jinro House Wine: this curiously pink liquid, which may or may not be derived from grapes, costs about W2500 per bottle and can only be described as "comedy wine" as it tends to give people the giggles.

The local drinking scene has recently been shaken up by sudden increases in demand for two particular alcoholic drinks. First of all came the **makgeolli** craze: for decades young Koreans pooh-poohed this delicious rice beer (see page 43), but it has been given a new lease of life and is now sold at mini-markets and convenience stores across the country; Seoul even has a bunch of chic bar-restaurants dedicated to the stuff. More recently, the "regular" beer scene has been stirred by the arrival of **smaller-scale breweries**; the ripples having emanated across the nation from Seoul's Itaewon district, a whole generation of Koreans is now experiencing craft ale for the first time.

Tea and coffee

Tea is big business in Korea. Unfortunately, most of the drinking takes place at home or work, though Insadong in Seoul has dozens of interesting tearooms (see page 109), and there are some gems outside national parks and in Jeonju's *hanok* district (see page 262). Green tea is by far the most popular, though if you find your way to a specialist tearoom, do take the opportunity to try something more special (see the page 43 for suggestions).

Korea is now a bona fide coffee nation. **Café culture** has found its way into the lives of Korean youth, and even in smaller towns you shouldn't have to look too far to find somewhere to sate your

---

KOREAN TEA VARIETIES

Daechu-cha 대추차 Jujube tea
Gukhwa-cha 국화차 Chrysanthemum tea
Gyepi-cha 계피차 Cinnamon tea
Ggulsam cha 꿀삼차 Honey ginseng tea
Insam-cha 인삼차 Ginseng tea
Ma-cha 마차 Wild herb tea
Maesil-cha 매실차 Plum tea
Nok-cha 녹차 Green tea
Omija-cha 오미자차 Five Flavours tea
Saenggang-cha 생강차 Ginger tea
Yak-cha 약차 Medicinal herb tea
Yuja-cha 유자차 Citron tea
Yulmu-cha 율무차 "Job's Tears" tea

---

caffeine cravings. In addition to coffee, modern cafés usually serve delicious **green tea latte**, with some of the more adventurous throwing in ginseng or sweet potato varieties for good measure. Though certainly not for purists, worth mentioning are the cans and cartons of coffee on sale in convenience stores, and

---

MAKGEOLLI

The milky-coloured rice beer known as **makgeolli** (막걸리) has become increasingly hip in recent years. It's somewhat similar to real ale, in that the drink is still "living" when you drink it – the best will last no longer than a week, even while refrigerated. The following are just some of the varieties available around the country, with most clocking in at precisely 6% ABV:

Sobaeksan Geomeunkong (소백산 검은콩) Made in Danyang (see page 295), this creamy number is the best of Korea's many black-bean *makgeolli* brands.

Baedari (배다리) Pleasantly sour brew from Ilsan (a satellite city west of Seoul), and a one-time favourite of ex-dictator Park Chung-hee – it was once delivered in caseloads to the Blue House (see page 68).

Busan Geumjeongsanseong (부산 금정산) Too sour for some, invigoratingly so and slightly appley to others, this hails from Busan but is actually easier to hunt down in the *mak*-bars of Seoul (see page 109).

Jeju Makgeolli (제주 막걸리) Jeju Island (see page 300) has some cloyingly disgusting varieties, but this pink-labelled one, made with "friendly" bacteria, is a real winner.

Boeun Daechu (보은 대추) You'll have to be in the Songnisan mountains (see page 290) to have any chance of finding this delicious *makgeolli*, made with local jujube dates.

Gongju Albam (공주 알밤) Found all over Gongju (see page 276), and even Seoul these days, this chestnut *makgeolli* is a good one for beginners to sample.

Jangsu (장수) Purists scoff at this sweet, fizzy brand, which has cornered much of the Seoul market, but the truth is that it's still pretty tasty – not to mention very easy to find in the capital's convenience stores.

Hongsam Jujo (삼 주조) One of the most notable of Jeonju's many brands (see page 264), and made with red ginseng.

Jipyeong (지평) A fresh-tasting, easy-to-quaff brand, which has since 1925 been made in Jipyeong – a village east of Seoul – in a giant *hanok* (traditional wooden house). Clever marketing means that it's all over Seoul now, and it can often even be found in the provinces.

Dosan (도산) Smooth brew that's only really available in Tongyeong (see page 220) – grab a bottle and drink it outside, next to the town's cute little harbour.

the three-in-one instant mixes that pop up all over the place, including most motel rooms.

The media

Korean media has come a long way since bursting out of the dictatorial straitjacket of the 1970s and 1980s, but most of it is only accessible to those fluent in Korean.

Newspapers, magazines and the web

The two big English-language **newspapers** are the *Korea Times* (Ⓦ koreatimes.co.kr) and *Korea Herald* (Ⓦ koreaherald.com), near-identical dailies with near-identical addictions to news agency output and dull business statistics. That said, both have decent listings sections in their weekend editions, which detail events around the country, as well as the goings-on in Seoul's restaurant, film and club scenes. For Korean news translated into English, try the websites of *Yonhap News* (Ⓦ english.yonhapnews.co.kr), or *Dong-a Ilbo* (Ⓦ english.donga.com); the *Chosun Ilbo* (Ⓦ english.chosun.com) has a translated version too, but it's rather conservative in nature.

The *International Herald Tribune* is pretty easy to track down in top hotels, with copies containing the eight-page *Joongang Daily* (Ⓦ koreajoongangdaily.joins.com), an interesting local news supplement. You should also be able to hunt down the previous week's *Time* or *The Economist* in most Korean cities – try the larger bookstores, or the book section of a large department store. Lastly, Seoul has its own clutch of useful websites and magazines (see page 100), some of which also cover destinations elsewhere in Korea.

Television

Korean **television** is a gaudy feast of madcap game shows and soppy period dramas, and there are few more accessible windows into the true nature of local society. **Arirang** (Ⓦ arirang.co.kr) is a 24hr English-language television network based in Seoul, which promotes the country with occasionally interesting (but often propaganda-like) documentaries, and has regular news bulletins. Arirang TV is free-to-air throughout much of the world, and though not free in Korea itself, it comes as part of most cable packages. Such packages are what you'll get on most hotel televisions (try OCN for films, SBS Sports for Premier League or local baseball, CNN for comedy news, or Tooniverse for midnight runs of old Simpsons episodes), but as with Internet access, many motels have beaten them to the punch, and offer video on demand – though it can sometimes be tricky to navigate the menus if you're not able to read Korean.

Festivals

On even a short trip around the country you're more than likely to stumble across a special event of some sort. Many are religious in nature, with Buddhist celebrations supplemented by Confucian and even animist events. Most festivals are concentrated around spring and autumn, but there are many spread throughout the year. If you're heading to one, don't be shy – the locals love to see foreigners joining in with traditional Korean events, and those who dare to get stuck in may finish the day with a whole troupe of new friends.

USEFUL APPS

Happy Cow Not a Korea-only app, but this veggie restaurant locator can be very useful in a country with so few dedicated veggie restaurants.

KakaoTalk Almost everyone with a smartphone in Korea has this (ie, almost everyone under 85), and so should you, if you want any kind of social life.

KakaoTaxi Also from the KakaoTalk folk, this taxi-hailing app can come in very handy.

Korean Dictionary, Translator, Phrasebook No prizes for guessing what this app does – not perfect, but none of its competitors are, either.

Seoul Bus Seoul's bus network can be hard for newbies to use, but this makes it slightly easier.

Subway Korea When you're in a crowded subway carriage and can't see the maps, it pays to have one in your pocket – this has every subway system in the land covered, and the "last train" function can save you from getting stranded.

Yogiyo Named after the word you'd utter to get attention from restaurant staff, this food-ordering app can get a tasty meal right to your doorstep.

Though there are some crackers on the calendar, it must be said that a fair number of **Korean festivals** are brazenly commercial, making no bones about being held to "promote the salted seafood industry", for example. Other festivals can be rather odd, including those dedicated to agricultural utensils, clean peppers and the "Joy of Rolled Laver" – you'll easily be able to spot the duds. The most interesting events are highlighted here, though bear in mind that celebrations for two of the big national festivals – **Seollal**, the Lunar New Year, and a Korean version of Thanksgiving named **Chuseok** – are family affairs that generally take place behind closed doors. There are also festivals specific to Seoul (see page 113) and Busan (see page 213).

SPRING

Cherry blossom festivals Usually early April. Heralding the arrival of spring, soft blossom wafts through the air across the country, a cue for all Koreans to lay down blankets at parks or riverbanks, barbecue some meat and throw back the *soju*.

Jeonju International Film Festival Ⓦ jiff.or.kr. Last week of April. Smaller and more underground than the biggie in Busan, JIFF focuses on the arty, independent side of the movie industry (see page 257).

Buddha's Birthday Late May. A public holiday during which temples across the land are adorned with colourful paper lanterns; there's an even more vibrant night parade in Seoul.

International Mime Festival Ⓦ mimefestival.com. May. Held in the Gangwonese capital of Chuncheon, this foreigner-friendly event is a showcase of soundless talent (see page 147).

Dano Usually June. A shamanist festival held on the fifth day of the fifth lunar month, featuring circus acts, ssireum wrestling, mask dramas and a whole lot more. The city of Gangneung (see page 161) is host to the biggest displays.

SUMMER

Boryeong Mud Festival Ⓦ mudfestival.or.kr. Late July. This annual expat favourite pulls mud-happy hordes to Daecheon beach (see page 284) for all kinds of muck-related fun.

Firefly Festival Aug. Glow worms are the tiny stars of the show at this modest night-time event, which takes place over a weekend near Muju (see page 265). One unexpected treat is the chance to don a firefly costume.

AUTUMN

Gwangju Biennale Ⓦ gwangjubiennale.org. Sept–Nov. A wide-ranging, two-month-long festival of contemporary art, the biennale usually takes place on alternate autumns, though it has also been held in spring.

Andong Mask Dance Festival Ⓦ maskdance.com. Late Sept or early Oct. Legend has it that if a person fails to attend a mask festival in their lifetime, they cannot get into heaven, so if you're in Korea in the autumn you might as well have a crack at salvation by participating

in one of the country's most popular events – a week of anonymous dancing, performed by the best troupes in the land (see page 179).

Chuncheon Puppet Festival Oct. Puppets and their masters come from around the world to flaunt their skills in Chuncheon (see page 147), a city in Gangwon province.

Busan International Film Festival Ⓦ biff.org. Usually Oct. One of Asia's biggest such events, BIFF draws in big-shots and hangers-on for a week of cinematic fun (see page 213).

Baekje Festival Ⓦ baekje.org. Early Oct. This annual event commemorating the Baekje dynasty is held each year in the old Baekje capitals of Gongju (see page 277) and Buyeo (see page 281).

Kimchi Festival Late Oct. In Gwangju. You'll be able to see, smell and taste dozens of varieties of the spicy stuff, and there's even a *kimchi*-making contest for foreigners keen to show off.

Pepero Day Nov 11. A crass marketing ploy, but amusing nonetheless – like Pocky, their Japanese cousins, Pepero are thin sticks of chocolate-coated biscuit, and on the date when it looks as if four of them are standing together, millions of Koreans say "I love you" by giving a box to their sweethearts, friends, parents or pets.

WINTER

New Year Jan 1. Korea sees in the New Year in the regular manner – Seoul Plaza is the place to be if you want to feel like a sardine, while Ilchulbong on Jeju Island (see page 312) and Jeongdongjin on the east coast (see page 166) are also popular choices.

Sports and outdoor activities

The 1988 Seoul Olympics did much to thrust Korea into the international spotlight, a trick repeated with the even more successful 2002 FIFA World Cup, an event co-hosted with Japan. But sport here is less about watching than doing, a fact evident in the well-trodden trails of the national parks, and the svelte proportions of the average Korean.

Hiking

The most popular activity in Korea is **hiking**, which is the national pastime owing to the country's abundance of mountains and national parks. There are no fewer than seventeen **national parks** on the mainland – their names all end with the suffix "-san", which means mountain or mountains – and these are supplemented by an even greater number of lesser parks, mountains and hills. English-language **maps** (W1000) are available at all park offices, trails are well marked with dual-language signs, and each national park has a cluster of accommodation and

POPULAR HIKES

Day-trips from the city With so much of the country covered by mountains, it's possible to see any Korean city from the vantage point of its surrounding peaks. Even Seoul has a national park. Bukhansan (see page 83) is the world's most visited, though it occasionally offers surprising serenity.

Multi-day hikes Only a couple of parks have shelters where you can stay the night. Jirisan (see page 225) is the largest in the country, and features a three-day, 26km-long spine route. Seoraksan (see page 156) is not quite as expansive, but is considered the most beautiful in the country, with great clumps of rock peeking out from the pines like giant skulls.

Scaling peaks South Korea's highest peak is on Jeju Island. The 1950m-high extinct volcanic cone of Hallasan (see page 326) dominates the island, but is surprisingly easy to climb, as long as Jeju's fickle weather agrees. The highest mountain on the whole peninsula is Paekdusan (2744m) on the Chinese-North Korean border (see page 356); its sumptuously blue crater lake, ringed by jagged peaks, is a font of myth and legend.

Getting away from it all Hiking is so popular in Korea that some trails resemble supermarket queues, but there are a few splendid ways to get away from it all. Taebaeksan (see page 170) has long been a shamanist place of worship, while the small park of Wolchulsan (see page 245) sees few visitors dash across the vertigo-inducing bridge that connects two of its peaks. Though popular on account of its enormous bronze Buddha, Songnisan (see page 290) has a tiny, secluded guesthouse; when the sun goes down, you'll be alone with nature, a trickling stream and a bowl of creamy *dongdongju*.

restaurants outside its main entrance. Some are mini-towns bursting with neon signs and karaoke rooms, which dilutes the experience somewhat, but a Korean hike is not complete unless it's finished off with a good **meal**: *pajeon* is the most popular post-hike dish, a kind of savoury pancake made with mountain vegetables, while the creamy rice wine *dongdongju* (see page 42) is the drink of choice. Deceptively mild, it can pack a punch, especially the next morning.

Despite the wealth of choice available, many of Korea's trails contrive to be packed to the gills, especially during **holidays** and warm **weekends**, when the parks are full with locals enjoying a day out. Many families bring along sizeable picnics to enjoy on their way to the peaks, and lone travellers may be invited to join in – Koreans hate to see people on their own.

Spectator sports

The two most popular spectator sports in the country are **football** and **baseball**. Koreans tend to follow one or the other, though football has been in the ascendancy of late, particularly with females and the younger generations. Those looking for something authentically Korean should try to hunt down a *ssireum* wrestling tournament.

Football

Soccer, or *chuk-gu* (축구), became the most popular sport in the country following its co-hosting of the World Cup in 2002. The ten gleaming new *gyeong-gi-jang* built for the tournament were swiftly moved into by teams from the national K-League, but the high attendances that the tournament spawned dropped sharply as spectators realized that their local boys weren't really better than Argentina – rows of empty seats mean that you'll always be able to get a ticket at the door, with prices generally W10,000–20,000.

The K-League championship trophy usually sits in or around Seoul: Suwon, Seongnam and FC Seoul have achieved domestic and international success, though Pohang and Jeonbuk have also won titles recently. Suwon and Daejeon (the latter in the second division at the time of writing) are said to have the rowdiest fans. Other teams are listed below, though note most teams operate as American-style "franchises" that can move lock, stock and barrel to more profitable locations at the drop of a hat. A few locals have escaped the K-League for more lucrative pastures, and Koreans are immensely proud of their sporting diaspora.

K-LEAGUE 1 TEAMS

Daegu FC Daegu Stadium, Daegu
FC Seoul World Cup Stadium, Seoul
Gangwon FC Songam Stadium, Chuncheon
Gyeongnam FC Football Center, Changwon
Incheon United Incheon Football Stadium, Incheon
Jeju United FC World Cup Stadium, Seogwipo
Jeonbuk Motors World Cup Stadium, Jeonju

Jeonnam Dragons Gwangyang Stadium, Gwangyang

Pohang Steelers Steel Yard, Pohang

Sangju Sangmu Civic Stadium, Sangju

Suwon Bluewings World Cup Stadium, Suwon

Ulsan Munsu Cup Stadium, Ulsan

Baseball

Until 2002, **baseball** (*yagu*; 야구) was the spectator sport of choice. Though its popularity has waned, you'll see a lot of games on Korean television, or you can attend a professional game at one of the *yagu-jang* listed below; seasons run from April to October, with a break at the height of summer. Though the fielding, in particular, isn't quite up to the level that American fans will be used to (and neither is the ballpark atmosphere), several Korean players have made their way into the Major League, including pitchers Kim Byung-hyun and Park Chan-ho. Since the turn of the century, the Unicorns, Lions and Wyverns have ruled the roost, though the Giants also deserve a mention thanks to their noisy support. Bear in mind that the team names listed below are subject to regular change, thanks to the franchise system.

KOREAN BASEBALL TEAMS

Doosan Bears Jamsil Baseball Stadium, Seoul

Hanhwa Eagles Hanbat Baseball Stadium, Daejeon

Kia Tigers Champions Field, Gwangju

KT Wiz Suwon Baseball Stadium, Suwon

LG Twins Jamsil Baseball Stadium, Seoul

Lotte Giants Sajik Baseball Stadium, Busan

NC Dinos Masan Baseball Stadium, Changwon

Nexen Heroes Gocheok Sky Dome, Seoul

Samsung Lions Lions Park, Daegu

SK Wyverns Munhak Baseball Stadium, Incheon

Ssireum

Though inevitably compared to *sumo*, this Korean form of wrestling (씨름) bears more resemblance to Mongolian styles – the wrestlers are chunky, rather than gargantuan, and they rely on grabs and throws, rather than slaps and pushes. As with *sumo*, the object of the wrestlers is to force their opponents to the floor, but in **ssireum** the fights start with both fighters interlocked. The sport is markedly less popular than its Japanese counterpart; few Koreans will be able to point you in the right direction if you wish to see a tournament, and even if you hunt one down the atmosphere will usually be low-key. The best place to catch a fight will be as part of a traditional festival, notably the early summer Dano in Gangneung (see page 161).

Participatory sports

In addition to being a nation of compulsive hikers, all Koreans are taught at school to exercise as a matter of course. Martial arts are among the nation's most famed exports, but Western activities such as golf and skiing have caught on in recent decades.

Martial arts

Most Korean martial arts are variations of those that originated in China or Japan. **Taekwondo** (태권도) is the best known – developed in Tang-dynasty China, it was given a Korean twist during the Three Kingdoms period, going on to become one of the country's most famed exports, and an Olympic sport to boot. The predominantly kick-based style is taught at schools, and forms the backbone of compulsory military service for the nation's men; it's possible to take classes around the country, though easiest in Seoul (see page 115). There are several less common local styles to choose from. These include *hapkido* (합기도), better known in the West as *aikido*, its Japanese counterpart; and *geomdo* (검도), a form in which participants get to bonk each other with wooden poles and likewise known to the world as *kendo*.

Golf

The success of professional Korean golfers, mainly females such as LPGA champ Park Se-ri, has tempted many into taking up the game. Over a hundred **courses** dot the country, mainly surrounding Seoul or on Jeju Island; most are members-only clubs, however, and those that aren't are pretty pricey – the fact that Korean golfers often go to Japan to save money says it all. If you come in with clubs, don't forget to **declare** them on arrival at the airport. Tourist offices will have information about nearby courses, though the average traveller will have to stick to the **driving ranges** dotted around the cities – scan the urban horizon for tower blocks topped by a large green net.

Skiing

With sub-zero winters and mountainous terrain, it's hardly surprising that **skiing** is big business in Korea – and a sport on the rise since the country played host to the 2018 Winter Olympics (see page 165). Non-Olympians looking to ski or snowboard in Korea should have few problems – there are a number of resorts, mainly in the northern provinces of Gyeonggi and Gangwon (see pages 120 and 144); most of these have ample accommodation facilities, though prices soar in the ski season (usually Dec–Feb). Clothes and ski equipment are available for hire, and many resorts have English-speaking instructors; **prices** vary from place to place, but expect lift passes to cost around W65,000 per day, with ski or snowboard rental another W40,000 on top of that.

Culture and etiquette

You may have mastered the art of the polite bow, worked out how to use the tricky steel chopsticks, and learnt a few words of the Korean language, but beware, you may upset new friends by accepting gifts with your hand in the wrong place. While even seasoned expats receive heartfelt congratulations for getting the easy bits right (some locals are even surprised when foreigners are able to use Korean money), there are still innumerable ways to offend the locals, and unfortunately it's the things that are hardest to guess that are most likely to see you come a cropper.

Korea is often said to be the world's most **Confucian** nation, such values having been instilled for over a thousand years across several dynasties (see page 374). Elements of Confucianism still linger on today – it's still basically true that anyone older, richer or more important than you (or just male as opposed to female) is simply "better" and deserving of more respect, a fact that becomes sorely clear to many working in Korea. Perhaps most evident to foreigners will be what amounts to a national obsession with **age** – you're likely to be asked how old you are soon after your first meeting with any Korean, and any similarity of birth years is likely to be greeted with a genuine whoop of delight (note that Koreans count years differently from Westerners – children are already 1 when they're born, and gain another digit at New Year, meaning that those born on December 31 are already two years old the very next day). Women have traditionally been treated as inferior to men, and are expected to ditch their job as soon as they give birth to their first child; however, recent years have shown a marked shift towards gender equality, with males more forgiving in the home and females more assertive in the workplace.

Foreigners are largely exempt from the code of conduct that would be required of both parties following their knowledge of age, employment and background, and little is expected of them in such terms, but this does have its drawbacks – in such an ethnically homogenous society, those that aren't Korean will always remain "outsiders", even if they speak the language fluently or have actually spent their whole lives in the country. Meanwhile, foreigners with Korean blood will be expected to behave as a local would, even if they can't speak a word of the language.

Conduct

The East Asian concept of "face" is very important in Korea, and known here as **gibun** (기분); the main goal is to avoid the **embarrassment** of self or others. Great lengths are taken to smooth out awkward situations, and foreigners getting unnecessarily angry are unlikely to invoke much sympathy. The traditional Korean retort to an uncomfortable question or incident is an embarrassed smile; remember that they're not laughing at you, merely trying to show empathy or move the topic onto safer ground. Foreigners may also see Koreans as disrespectful: nobody's going to thank you for holding open a door, and you're unlikely to get an apology if I bumped into. **Dressing well** has long been important, but though pretty much anything goes for local girls these days, foreign women may be assumed to be brazen hussies if they wear revealing clothing.

Meeting and greeting

Foreigners will see Koreans **bowing** all the time, even during telephone conversations. Though doing likewise will do much to endear you to locals, don't go overboard – a full, right-angled bow would only be appropriate for meeting royalty (and the monarchy ended in 1910). Generally, a short bow with eyes closed and the head directed downwards will do just fine, but it's best to observe the Koreans themselves, and the action will become quite natural after a short time. **Attracting attention** is also done differently here – you beckon with fingers fluttering beneath a downward-facing palm.

Koreans are great lovers of **business cards**, which are exchanged in all meetings that have even a whiff of commerce about them. The humble rectangles garner far greater respect than they do in the West, and folding or stuffing one into a pocket or wallet is a huge faux pas – accept your card with profuse thanks, leave it on the table for the duration of the meeting and file it away with respect (a card-holder is an essential purchase for anyone here on business). Also note that it's seen as incredibly rude to write someone's name in red ink – this colour is reserved for names of those who have died, a practice that most Koreans seem to think goes on all around the world.

If you're lucky enough to be invited to a Korean home, try to bring a **gift** – fruit, chocolates and flowers go down well. The offering is likely to be refused at first, and probably on the second attempt too – persevere and it will eventually be accepted with thanks. The manner of receiving is also important – the receiving hand should be held from underneath by the non-receiving one, the distance up or down the arm dependent on exactly how polite you want to be. This will only come with experience and will not be expected of most foreigners, but you will be expected to take your **shoes off** once inside the house or apartment, so try to ensure that your socks are clean and hole-free.

Dining

There are innumerable **codes of conduct** when it comes to dining, although Koreans will usually guide foreigners through the various dos and don'ts. Koreans will tolerate anything viewed as a "mistake" on the part of the foreigner, and offer great encouragement to those who are at least attempting to get things right. This can sometimes go a little too far – you're likely to be praised for your chopstick-handling abilities however long you've been around, and it's almost impossible to avoid the Korean Catch-22: locals love to ask foreigners questions during a meal, but anyone stopping to answer will likely fail to keep pace with the fast-eating Koreans, who will then assume that your dish is not disappearing quickly because you don't like it.

Chopsticks

Many rules surround the use of **chopsticks** – don't use these to point or to pick your teeth, and try not to spear food with them unless your skills are really poor. It's also bad form, as natural as it may seem, to leave your chopsticks in the bowl: this is said to resemble incense sticks used after a death, but to most Koreans it just looks wrong. Just leave the sticks balanced on the rim of the bowl.

Table manners

Many Korean meals are group affairs, and this has given rise to a number of rules surrounding who **serves the food** from the communal trays to the individual ones – it's usually the youngest woman at the table. Foreign women finding themselves in this position will be able to mop up a great deal of

respect by performing the duty, though as there are particular ways to serve each kind of food, it's probably best to watch first. The **serving of drinks** is a little less formal, though again the minutiae of recommended conduct could fill a small book – basically, you should never refill your own cup or glass, and should endeavour to keep topped up those belonging to others. The position of the hands is important – watch to see how the Koreans are doing it (both the pourer and the recipient), and you'll be increasing your "face" value in no time.

One minor no-no is to **blow your nose** during the meal – preposterously unfair, given the spice level of pretty much every Korean dish. Should you need to do so, make your excuses and head to the toilets. It's also proper form to wait for the **head of the table** – the one who is paying, in other words – to sit down first, as well as to allow them to be the first to stand at the end of the meal. The latter can be quite tricky, as many Korean restaurants are sit-on-the-floor affairs that play havoc on the knees and backs of foreigners unaccustomed to the practice.

Paying the bill

Korea's Confucian legacy can often be a great boon to foreigners, as it has long been customary for hosts (usually "betters") to **pay** – as with the rest of the local workforce, many English teachers get taken out for regular slap-up meals by their bosses, and don't have to pay a penny. Koreans also tend to make a big show of trying to pay, with the bill passing rapidly from hand to hand until the right person coughs up. Nowadays things are changing slowly – "going Dutch" is increasingly common where it would once have been unthinkable.

Travel essentials

Costs

Some people come to Korea expecting it to be a budget destination on a par with the Southeast Asian countries, while others arrive with expectations of Japanese-style prices. The latter is closer to the truth – those staying at five-star hotels and eating at Western-style restaurants will spend almost as much as they would in other developed countries, though there are numerous ways for budget travellers to make their trip a cheap one. Your biggest outlay is likely to be **accommodation** – Seoul has some grand places to stay for W400,000 and up, though most cities have dedicated tourist hotels for around W100,000, and decent mid-range options for W70,000 or so. Though they're not to everyone's taste, motels usually make acceptable places to stay; they cost around W30,000 (but often double that in Seoul). The capital has a few backpacker hostels with dorms for around W20,000, while real scrimpers can stay at a *jjimjilbang* sauna (see page 36).

Because the country is small, **transport** is unlikely to make too much of a dent in your wallet – even a high-speed KTX train from Seoul in the northwest to Busan in the southeast won't set you back much more than W50,000, and you can cut that in half by taking a slower service. Inner-city transport is also good value, with most journeys costing just over W1000, and **admission charges** to temples, museums and the like are similarly unlikely to cause your wallet discomfort.

By staying in motels or guesthouses (staying in a pair, at the former, since prices are generally for the room) and eating at reasonably cheap restaurants, you should be able to survive easily on a daily budget of W40,000, or even half this if seriously pushed. After you've added in transport costs and a few entry tickets, a realistic daily figure may be W60,000.

Tipping plays almost no part in Korean transactions – try not to leave unwanted change in the hands of a cashier, lest they feel forced to abandon their duties and chase you down the street with it. Exceptions are tourist hotels, most of which tack a 10 percent service charge onto the room bill; these are also among the few places in the country to omit **tax** – levied at 10 percent – from their quoted prices.

Climate

Korea is a land of extremes in many senses, and its weather is no exception. Temperatures can rise to over 35ºC in the **summer** (broadly June–Sept), when it's also incredibly humid – more than half of Korea's annual rainfall comes down in the summer monsoons. **Winters** (Nov–March), on the other hand, can be surprisingly chilly for a country at the same latitude as Iraq, Cyprus and California, with the mercury occasionally plummeting to -20ºC. **Spring** and **autumn** are very pleasant times to visit, though some years, blink and you'll miss them.

Crime and personal safety

Korea is a country in which you're far more likely to see someone running towards you with a dropped wallet than away with a stolen one – tales abound about travellers who have left a valuable possession on a restaurant table or park bench and returned

hours later to find it in the same place. Though you'd be very unlucky to fall victim to a crime, it's prudent to take a few simple precautions. The country has a poor **road safety** record, the statistics heightened by the number of vehicles that use pavements as shortcuts or parking spaces. Caution should also be exercised around any **street fights** that you may have the misfortune to come across – since Korean men practise taekwondo to a fairly high level during their compulsory national service, Korea is not a great place to get caught in a scuffle. These days many local women avoid taking taxis alone in the evening; you'd be extremely unlucky to have something untoward happen, but it may be prudent to keep a phone in your hand as a deterrent.

Electricity

The electrical **current** runs at 220v, 60Hz throughout the country, and requires European-style plugs with two round pins, though some older buildings, including many *yeogwan* and *yeoinsuk*, may still take flat-pinned plugs at 110v.

LGBT+ travellers

Despite Goryeo-era evidence suggesting that undisguised homosexuality was common in Royal and Buddhist circles, at the turn of the century Korea's LGBT+ scene formed a small, alienated section of society. Thankfully, a spate of **high-profile comings-out**, including that of Hong Seok-cheon (see page 384), countered the prevailing local belief that Korean homosexuality simply did not exist, and these days almost nobody regards it as what was once a "foreign disease", with high-profile entertainers such as Harisu raising the visibility of trans people in Korea further still.

Although local law makes no explicit reference to the **legality** of sexual intercourse between adults of the same sex, this is less a tacit nod of consent than a refusal of officialdom to discuss such matters, and LGBT+ activities may be punishable as sexual harassment, or even, shockingly, "mutual rape" if it takes place in the military. In the early 1990s, the first few LGBT+ websites were cracked down on by a government that, during the course of the subsequent appeal, made it clear that human rights did not fully apply to homosexuals – all the more reason for the "different people" (*iban-in*), already fearful of losing their jobs, friends and family, to lock themselves firmly in the closet.

Korean society has, however, become much **more liberal** in such regards. With more and more high-profile people coming out, a critical mass has been reached, and younger generations are markedly less prejudiced on – and more willing to discuss – the issue. LGBT+ clubs, bars and saunas, while still generally low-key outside "Homo Hill" in Seoul's Itaewon district and Ikseondong near Insadong (see page 112), can be found in every major city, and lobbyists have been making inroads into the Korean parliament. The **Korean Queer Culture Festival** – still the only pride event in the country – takes place over a fortnight in early June at locations across Seoul (see page 113).

LGBT+ INFORMATION

Chingusai ⓦ chingusai.net. Loosely meaning "Among Friends", *Chingusai's* trailblazing magazine is available at many LGBT+ bars in the capital. Mainly in Korean, but with some English-language information.
Travel Gay Asia ⓦ travelgayasia.com. Pan-Asian site featuring listings of bars, clubs and saunas, in the case of Korea mainly focused on Seoul and Busan.
Utopia Asia ⓦ utopia-asia.com. Useful information about bars, clubs and saunas, including a fair few non-Seoul spots.

Health

South Korea is pretty high in the world rankings as far as **healthcare** goes, and there are no compulsory vaccinations or diseases worth getting too worried about. Hospitals are clean and well staffed, and most doctors can speak English, so the main health concerns for foreign travellers are likely to be financial – without adequate insurance cover, a large bill may rub salt into your healing wounds if you end up in hospital (see page 52).

Though no **vaccinations** are legally required, get medical advice ahead of your trip, particularly regarding hepatitis A and B, typhoid and Japanese B encephalitis (which are all rare in Korea but it's better to err on the side of caution), and make sure that you're up to date with the usual boosters. It's also wise to bring along any medicines that you might need, especially for drugs that need to be prescribed – bring a copy of your prescription, as well as the generic name of the drug in question, as brand names may vary from country to country.

Despite the swarms of mosquitoes that blanket the country in warmer months, **malaria** is not prevalent in Korea. However, infected mosquitoes breed in the DMZ, so those planning to hang around the rural north of the Gyeonggi or Gangwon provinces should take extra precautions to prevent getting bitten. All travellers should get up-to-date malarial advice from their GP before arriving in Korea, and since mosquitoes are profuse all over the country during the late-summer monsoon season, health considerations aside it's a good idea to slap on some repellent before going out.

Drinking Korean **tap water** is not the best idea, and with free drinking fountains in every restaurant, hotel, supermarket, police station and department store in the country, there really should be no need. Water is also sold at train and bus stations from around W500 for a small bottle. Restaurant food will almost always be prepared and cooked adequately, and all necessary precautions are (usually) taken with raw fish.

In an **emergency**, you should first try to ask a local to call for an ambulance. Should you need to do so yourself, the number is ☎119, though it's possible that no English-speaker will be available to take your call. Alternatively, try the tourist information line on ☎1330 (see page 55). If you're in a major city and the problem isn't life-threatening, the local tourist office should be able to point you towards the most suitable doctor or **hospital**. Once there, you may find it surprisingly hard to get information about what's wrong with you. As in much of East Asia, patients are expected to trust doctors to do their jobs properly, and any sign that this trust is not in place results in a loss of face for the practitioner.

For minor complaints or medical advice, there are **pharmacies** all over the place, usually distinguished by the Korean character "*yak*" (약) at the entrance, though English-speakers are few and far between. To see a doctor, ask at your accommodation about the nearest suitable place; even as a non-resident, fees are usually around W15,000 per visit. The same can be said for dental check-ups, and treatments are also usually very affordable. Travellers can also visit a practitioner of **oriental medicine**, who uses acupuncture and pressure-point massage, among other techniques, to combat the problems that Western medicine cannot reach; if you have Korean friends, ask around for a personal recommendation in order to find a reputable practitioner.

Insurance

The price of hospital treatment in Korea can be quite high, so it's advisable to take out a decent **travel insurance** policy before you go. Bear in mind that most policies exclude "dangerous activities"; this term may well cover activities as seemingly benign as hiking or skiing. Keep the emergency number of your insurance company handy in the event of an accident and, as in any country, if you have anything stolen make sure to obtain a copy of the police report, as you will need this to make a claim.

ROUGH GUIDES TRAVEL INSURANCE

Rough Guides has teamed up with **WorldNomads.com** to offer great travel insurance deals. Policies are available to residents of more than 150 countries, with cover for a wide range of adventure sports, 24hr emergency assistance, high levels of medical and evacuation cover and a stream of travel safety information. Roughguides.com users can take advantage of their policies online 24/7, from anywhere in the world – even if you're already travelling. And since plans often change when you're on the road, you can extend your policy and even claim online. Roughguides.com users who buy travel insurance with WorldNomads.com can also leave a positive footprint and donate to a community development project. For more information go to ⓦ roughguides.com/shop.

Internet

You should have no problem getting online in South Korea, possibly the most connected nation on the planet. **Wi-fi** access is becoming ever more common, with many cafés allowing customers to use their connection for free. *Tom N' Toms* and *Hollys* are generally the best chains for this (though the coffee at the former is pretty poor). You should also be able to get online at your accommodation.

If wi-fi fails, **PC rooms** (PC 방; pronounced "*pishibang*") are everywhere. Though declining in number with each passing year, there should always be one within walking distance – just look for the letters "PC" in Roman characters. These cafés charge around W1500 per hour, with a one-hour minimum charge. If you need something printed out, ask your accommodation if they can help – if not, head to a PC room, or one of the many branches of FedEx Kinko's.

Laundry

Almost all tourist hotels provide a **laundry** service, and some of the Seoul backpacker hostels will wash your smalls for free, but with public laundries so thin on the ground those staying elsewhere may have to resort to a spot of DIY cleaning. All motels have 24-hour hot water, as well as soap, body lotion and/or shampoo in the bathrooms, and in the winter clothes dry in no time on the heated *ondol* floors. Summer is a different story, with the humidity making it very hard to dry clothes in a hurry.

Mail

The Korean postal system is cheap and trustworthy, and there are **post offices** in even the smallest town. Most are open Monday to Friday from 9am to 6pm; all should be able to handle international mail, and the larger ones offer free internet access. There's a relative dearth of **postcards** for sale, though if you do track some down you'll find that postal rates are cheap, at around W400 per card. Letters will cost

a little more, though as with **parcels** the tariff will vary depending on their destination – the largest box you can send (20kg) will cost about W150,000 to mail to the UK or USA, though this price drops to about W50,000 if you post via **surface mail**, a process that can take up to three months. All post offices have the necessary boxes for sale, and will even do your packing for a small fee. Alternatively, international courier chains such as UPS and FedEx can also ship from Korea.

Maps

Free maps – many of which are available in English – can be picked up at any tourist office or higher-end hotel, as well as most travel terminals. The main drawback with them is that distances and exact street patterns are hard to gauge, though it's a complaint the powers-that-be are slowly taking on board. Excellent **national park** maps, drawn to scale, cost W1000 from the ticket booths.

Money

The **Korean currency** is the won (W), which comes in notes of W1000, W5000, W10,000 and W50,000, and coins of W10, W50, W100 and W500. At the time of writing the **exchange rate** was approximately W1500 to £1, W1300 to €1, and W1100 to US$1.

ATMs are everywhere in Korea, not only in banks (은행; *eunhaeng*) but 24-hour convenience stores such as *7-Eleven* or *GS25*. Most machines are capable of dealing with foreign cards, and those that do are usually able to switch to English-language mode; note that you may have to try a few machines. Smaller towns may not have such facilities – stock up on cash in larger cities.

Foreign **credit and debit cards** are being accepted in more and more hotels, restaurants and shops. It shouldn't be too hard to **exchange** foreign notes for Korean cash; banks are all over the place, and the only likely problem when dealing in dollars pounds or euros is time – some places simply won't have exchanged money before, forcing staff to consult the procedure manual.

Opening hours and public holidays

Korea is one of the world's truest 24-hour societies – **opening hours** are such that almost everything you need is likely to be available whenever you require it. Most shops and almost all restaurants are open daily, often until late, as are tourist information offices. A quite incredible number of establishments are open 24/7, including convenience stores, saunas, Internet cafés and some of the busier shops and restaurants. Post offices (Mon–Fri 9am–6pm, sometimes Saturday mornings too) and banks (Mon–Fri 9.30am–4pm) keep more sensible hours.

Until recently, the country was one of the few in the world to have a **six-day working week**; though this has been officially altered to five, the changes haven't filtered through to all workers, and Korea's place at the top of the world's "average hours worked per year" table has not been affected. The number of **national holidays** has fallen, however, in an attempt to make up the slack, and as most of the country's population are forced to take their holiday at the same times, there can be chaos on the roads and rails. Three of the biggest holidays – Lunar New Year, Buddha's birthday and *Chuseok* – are based on the lunar calendar, and have no fixed dates (see page 53, for further details on national holidays and festivals).

Phones

Getting hold of a **mobile phone** while you're in the country is easy – there are 24-hour **rental booths** at Incheon Airport. Using your own phone can be more problematic, but you'll be able to rent a data-only SIM at the same places (or many of the larger convenience stores, where you can also top up your credit), or simply switch on roaming. If you're going to be in Korea for a while, you may care to register with a major service provider – KT and SK Telecom are two of the biggest chains, and so ubiquitous that the nearest store is likely to be within walking distance; bring a Korean friend along if you're not legally employed in the country.

Despite the prevalence of mobile phones, you'll still see **payphones** on every major street; many of these ageing units only take coins, meaning that you'll have to pump in change at a furious pace to avoid the deafening squawks that signal the end of your call time. Pre-paid travel cards (see page 32) work with some machines.

Korea's **international dialling code** is ❶82. When dialling from abroad, omit the initial zero from the

---

KOREAN PUBLIC HOLIDAYS

Sinjeong (New Year's Day) Jan 1. Seoul celebrates New Year in much the same fashion as Western countries, with huge crowds gathering around City Hall.

Seollal (Lunar New Year) Usually early Feb. One of the most important holidays on the calendar, Lunar New Year sees Koreans flock to their home towns for a three-day holiday of relaxed celebration, and many businesses close up.

Independence Movement Day March 1.

Children's Day May 5. Koreans make an even bigger fuss over their kids than usual on this national holiday – expect parks, zoos and amusement parks to be jam-packed.

Buddha's Birthday Usually late May. Many temples become a photogenic sea of lanterns.

Memorial Day June 6. Little more than a day off for most Koreans, this day honours those who fell in battle.

Independence Day Aug 15. The country becomes a sea of Korean flags on this holiday celebrating the end of Japanese rule in 1945.

Chuseok Late Sept or early Oct. One of the biggest events in the Korean calendar is this three-day national holiday, similar to Thanksgiving; families head to their home towns to venerate their ancestors in low-key ceremonies, and eat a special crescent-shaped rice cake.

National Foundation Day Oct 3. Celebrates the 2333 BC birth of Dangun, the legendary founder of the Korean nation. Shamanist celebrations take place at shrines around Seoul, with the most important on Inwangsan mountain.

Hangeul Day Oct 9. Koreans celebrate their unique alphabet.

Christmas Day Dec 25. Every evening looks like Christmas in neon-drenched Seoul, but on this occasion Santa Haraboji (Grandpa Santa) finally arrives.

area codes. Korean area codes are given throughout the guide.

Photography

Photography is a national obsession in Korea. If you want a personal shot, few locals will mind being photographed, though of course it's polite to ask first. One serious no-no is to go snap-happy on a tour of the DMZ (see page 135) – this can, and has, landed tourists in trouble. You may also see temple-keepers and monks poised at the ready to admonish would-be photographers of sacrosanct areas.

Studying in Korea

Korea has long been a popular place for the study of **martial arts**, while the country's ever-stronger ties with global business are also prompting many to gain a competitive advantage by studying the Korean language.

Language

Courses at the institutes run by many of the larger **universities** vary in terms of price, study time, skill level and accommodation. Most of the year-long courses are in Seoul and start in March – apply in good time. There's a good list at ⓦ english.visitkorea.or.kr, while information on study visas and how to apply for them can be found on the Ministry of Education's website (ⓦ studyinkorea.go.kr). There are **private institutes** dotted around Seoul and other major cities – ⓦ english.seoul.go.kr has a list of safe recommendations in the capital, while other official city websites are the best places to look for institutes elsewhere.

If you're working in Korea, you may not have time for intensive study; if so, it's worth looking into the **government-funded courses** run by a few major cities, some of which are so cheap that their price is barely an issue. Many people opt for an even higher degree of informality and take language lessons from friends or colleagues, but with so few English speakers around, just living in Korea can be all the practice you need.

Martial arts classes

Finding classes for the most popular styles (including **taekwondo**, *hapkido* and *geomdo*) isn't hard, but very few classes cater for foreigners – it's best to go hunting on the expat circuit. Those looking for something more advanced should seek advice from their home country's own *taekwondo* federation.

Buddhist teachings

Many **temples** offer teaching and templestay programmes for around W50,000 per night – a wonderful opportunity to see the "Land of Morning Calm" at its most serene (as long as you can stand the early mornings). Some temples are able to provide English-language instruction, and some not – see ⓦ eng.templestay.com for more details.

Teaching English in Korea

Uncomplicated entry requirements, low tax and decent pay cheques make Korea one of the most popular stops on the **English-teaching** circuit. Demand for native speakers is high, though it has fallen since the public school system phased out international teachers; the cost of living, though rising, is still below that in most English-speaking countries; English-teaching qualifications are far from essential (though they certainly help), and all that is usually required is a degree certificate, and a copy of your passport – many people have been taken on by a Korean school without so much as a telephone interview.

To land a full-time job from outside Korea you'll have to go **online**, and it's still the best option if you're already in Korea. Popular sites include Dave's ESL Café (ⓦ eslcafe.com) and HiTeacher (ⓦ hiteacher. com), though a thorough web search will yield more.

Most language schools are reputable; you can typically expect them to organize **free accommodation**, and to do the legwork with your **visa** application. Some countries operate Working Holiday visa schemes with Korea, but others will need a full working visa to be legally employed; those unable to collect this in their home country are usually given a plane ticket and directions for a quick visa-run to Japan (the closest embassy is in Fukuoka).

Most new entrants start off by teaching kids at a **language school** (학원; *hagwon*). There are a whole bunch of pan-national chains, with YBM and Pagoda among the two biggest; like the smaller-fry operations, they pay around W2,500,000 per month in Seoul, and a little less outside the capital. After a year or two, many teachers make their way to a **university** teaching post; pay is usually lower and responsibilities higher than at a *hagwon* (and these days a Master's degree is an almost essential qualification), though the holiday allowances (as much as five months per year, as opposed to less than two weeks per year in a *hagwon*) are hard to resist. Most teachers give their bank balance a nudge in the right direction by offering **private lessons** on the side –

an illegal practice, but largely tolerated unless you start organizing them for others.

One of the most regular *hagwon*-related complaints is the **long hours** many teachers have to work – figure on up to thirty per week. This may include Saturdays, or be spread quite liberally across the day from 9am to 9pm – try to find jobs with "no split shift" if possible. Questionable **school policies** also come in for stick; for example, teachers are often expected to be present at the school for show, even if they have no lessons on.

With the number of teaching jobs on offer, it's quite possible to hand-pick a city or province of your choice. Seoul is an obvious target and the easiest place from which to escape into Western pleasures if necessary, though note that a hefty proportion of positions listed as being in the capital are actually in uninteresting satellite cities such as Bundang, Anyang or Ilsan, all a long journey from central Seoul – try to find the nearest subway station to your prospective position on a map if possible. Those who head to provincial cities such as Daejeon, Mokpo or Busan generally seem to have a better time of things, and emerge with a truer appreciation of the country, as well as better Korean language skills.

Time

The Korean peninsula shares a **time zone** with Japan: one hour ahead of China, nine hours ahead of Greenwich Mean Time, seven hours ahead of South Africa, fourteen hours ahead of Eastern Standard Time in the US or Montreal in Canada, and one hour behind Sydney. Daylight Saving hours are not observed, so though noon in London will be 9pm in Seoul for much of the year, the difference drops to eight hours during British Summer Time.

Tourist information

The Korean tourist authorities churn out a commend-able number of English-language maps, pamphlets and books, most of which are handed out at **information booths** – you'll be able to find one in every city, usually outside the train or bus stations. Not all of these are staffed with an English-speaker, but you'll be able to get 24-hour assistance and advice on the dedicated **tourist information line** – dial ☎1330 and you'll be put through to helpful call-centre staff who speak a number of languages and can advise on transport, sights, accommodation, theatre ticket prices and much more. If calling from a mobile phone or abroad, you'll also need to put in a regional prefix – to reach Seoul,

for example, dial ☎02 1330. The official **Korean tourist website** (ⓦenglish.visitkorea.or.kr) is quite useful, and most cities and provinces have sites of their own.

Travelling with children

Korea is a country with high standards of **health and hygiene**, low levels of crime and plenty to see and do – bringing children of any age should pose no special problems. **Changing facilities** are most common in Seoul – department stores are good places to head – though few restau-rants have highchairs, and baby food labelled in English is almost nonexistent. A few hotels provide a **baby-sitting service**, though those in need can ask their concierge for a newspaper with baby-sitter adverts. Every city has cinemas, theme parks and a zoo or two to keep children amused; Everland (see page 133) and Seoul Land (see page 94) are the two most popular escapes from Seoul, while there are a number of interesting museums in the capital itself. Note that some of the restaurants listed in this guide – especially those serving *galbi*, a self-barbecued meat – have hotplates or charcoal in the centre of the table, which poses an obvious danger to little hands, and in a country where it's perfectly normal for cars to drive on the pavements, you may want to exercise a little more caution than normal when walking around town.

Travellers with disabilities

Despite its First World status, Korea can be filed under "developing countries" as far as **disabled accessibility** is concerned, and with rushing traffic and crowded streets, it's never going to be the easiest destination to get around. Until recently, very little attention was paid to those with disabilities, but things are changing. Streets are being made more wheelchair-friendly, and many subway and train stations have been fitted with lifts. Almost all motels and tourist hotels have these, too, though occasionally you'll come across an entrance that hasn't been built with wheel-chairs in mind. Some museums and tourist attrac-tions will be able to provide a helper if necessary, but wherever you are, Koreans are likely to jump at the chance to help travellers in obvious need of assistance.

Seoul

CHEONGGYECHEON

1 | Seoul

An intoxicating cocktail of high-rise buildings and people-thronged streets, the Korean capital, Seoul (서울), is a veritable assault on the senses. Even small streets find themselves alive with frenzied activity by day and searing neon after sunset, while eardrums are set pounding by clamouring shop assistants and the night-time thump of a thousand karaoke rooms. Restaurants serving Korea's delectably spicy national dishes lure you in with their amazing aromas and tastes while doing minimal damage to your figure (or wallet), and for tactile bliss, the hot pools and ice rooms of the ubiquitous *jjimjilbang* bathhouses have no equal. The city's open-all-hours culture gives it an almost unmatched vitality, and the temptation to throw yourself in at the deep end is almost impossible to resist.

With over twenty million souls packed sardine-like into a metropolitan area smaller than Luxembourg, this is one of the most densely populated places on the planet, but for all its nonstop consumption, Seoul is also a place of considerable tradition and history. **Joseon-dynasty palaces**, displayed like medals in the centre of the city, proclaim its status as a seat of regal power from as far back as 1392; the tiled roofs of wooden *hanok* houses gently make their way, fish-scale-like towards the ash-coloured granite crags of **Bukhansan**, the world's most-visited national park; and the ancient songs and dances of farmhands and court performers are still clashed out in a whirligig of sound and colour along the street of Insadonggil. A city with a hyper-efficient transport system, a negligible crime rate, locals eager to please foreign guests and an almost astonishing wealth of locally produced modern art: it's little wonder that so many visitors come away impressed.

Top of most tourists' agendas are the half-a-dozen sumptuous **palaces** dating from the late fourteenth century that surround the city centre; these include **Gyeongbokgung** and **Changdeokgung**, together with the nearby ancestral shrine of **Jongmyo**. Situated in the middle is **Insadong**; by far the most popular part of the city with tourists, its warren of tight streets is littered with traditional restaurants, quaint tearooms, art galleries and trinket shops, and makes for a great wander. **Samcheongdong** and **Bukchon Hanok Village** are two areas offering similar delights, though with fewer tourists. The amount of art on display in all three areas can come as quite a surprise – contemporary Korean work receives a fraction of the international press devoted to art from Japan or China,

GYEONGBOKGUNG

Highlights

❶ Royal palaces Five beautiful palaces remain from Seoul's time as capital of the Joseon dynasty, each with its own merits; most visitors find Gyeongbokgung and Changdeokgung the most charming. See page 65

❷ Bukchon Hanok Village Despite its central location, this area remains markedly traditional and filled with wooden *hanok* housing. See page 69

❸ Insadonggil There's enough to fill a day on Seoul's most popular street – tearooms, galleries and traditional restaurants crammed into a network of alleys. See page 70

❹ Namsan at sunset Make sure you're at the top of Seoul's mini-mountain for sunset and the spectacular city's transition from grey to neon. See page 76

❺ Gwangjang market A delectable slice of Korea, this market is a highly atmospheric place in which to get a handle on some of the country's earthier drinks and dishes. See page 78

❻ Hanok guesthouses Stay a night in a *hanok*, a wooden building kept warm in the winter by underfloor fires – an authentically Korean experience. See page 101

❼ Nightlife Seoul's nightlife gets better and better, and is best soaked up in the throbbing university area of Hongdae. See page 109

HIGHLIGHTS ARE MARKED ON THE MAP ON PAGE 60

1

but is just as creative. Also offering a modern-day fusion of Korea old and new are the colossal **markets** of **Dongdaemun** and **Namdaemun**, in whose sprawling reaches you'll find anything from pig intestines to clip-on ties. The more modern facets of the city can be seen in the shoppers' paradise of **Myeongdong** or achingly fashionable **Apgujeong**, while the number of American soldiers hanging out in cosmopolitan **Itaewon** hint at Seoul's proximity to North Korea – it's even possible to take a day-trip to the border.

To get a sense of what makes Seoul so unique, however, you'll need to do more than tick off the sights. To truly appreciate the subtle facets of this distinctive

HIGHLIGHTS

1. Royal palaces
2. Bukchon Hanok Village
3. Insadonggil
4. Namsan at sunset
5. Gwangjang Market
6. Hanok guesthouses
7. Nightlife

society, take a leap of faith into the local cuisine, follow the Korean lead on a wild night (and early morning) out, and spend a decent amount of time simply walking the streets.

Brief history

Contrary to the expectations of many a visitor, Seoul possesses a long and interesting past; after first rising to prominence at the beginning of the **Three Kingdoms** period, it was then ruled over by almost every major power in Korean history. In 18 AD, then named Wiryeseong, it became the first capital of the **Baekje** kingdom (see page 278);

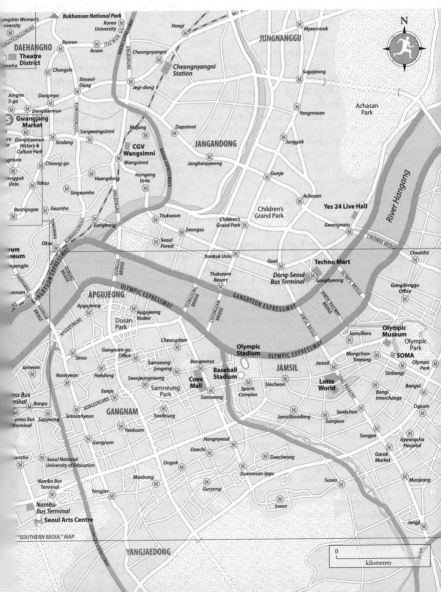

1

the exact location is believed to be a site just east of present-day Seoul, but this was to change several times. The kings and clans were forced far south to Gongju in 475, having been squeezed out by the rival **Goguryeo** kingdom; less than a century later, the city completed a Three Kingdoms clean-sweep when King Jinheung expanded the domain of his **Silla** kingdom (see page 188) far to the north, absorbing Seoul – then known as Hanseong – on the way. By 668, Silla forces held control of the whole peninsula, but having chosen Gyeongju as their capital, Seoul faded into the background. In the tenth century, Silla was usurped by the nascent **Goryeo** kingdom – they chose Kaesong, in modern-day North Korea, as the seat of their power, though Seoul was close enough to become an important trading hub, and soon earned yet another name, Namgyeong, meaning "Southern Capital".

The Joseon dynasty

It was not until the end of the Goryeo dynasty that Seoul really came into its own. In 1392, the "Hermit Kingdom" of **Joseon** kicked off over five centuries of power; after running the rule over a few prospective candidates, **King Taejo** – the inaugurator of the dynasty – chose Seoul as his new capital, impressed by its auspicious location. He immediately set about reorganizing the city with a series of major projects (see page 62). Exactly two hundred years after its birth, Joseon was invaded by **Japanese** forces from 1592 to 1598 under the control of warlord Hideyoshi; Seoul was pillaged in the course of the battles, and many of its most beautiful buildings lay in ruins. Though the country survived this particular struggle, mainly thanks to the heroic Admiral Yi (see page 237), the Japanese proved more obdurate on their return in the late nineteenth century.

Under Japanese occupation

After making tame inroads with a series of trade treaties, an escalating series of events – including the assassination of Queen Min in Gyeongbokgung (see page 66) – culminated in Japan's outright **annexation** of the peninsula in 1910, which lasted until the end of World War II, and closed the long chapters of Korean regal rule. During this time, Japan tried its best to erase any sense of Korean nationality; part of this was a drive to wipe out the Korean language, which earned Seoul yet another name – **Keijo**, which roughly translates as "Walled-off Capital". The city was to suffer greater indignity when its beloved palaces were modified in an attempt to make them "more Japanese"; a few of these alterations are still visible today.

To the present day

After the Japanese were defeated in World War II, peninsular infighting and global shifts in power and ideology resulted in the **Korean War** (1950–53). Seoul's position in the centre of the peninsula, as well as its obvious importance as the long-time Korean

---

BUILDING A CAPITAL

Rarely can a capital have been built so quickly. On the inauguration of his Joseon kingdom in 1392, the ambitious **King Taejo** immediately set his minions to work on a truly incredible number of gigantic projects. Even more astonishing is the fact that many of them can still be seen today, albeit in reproduction form, since few original structures survived the Japanese occupation and Korean War.

Gyeongbokgung Seoul's first palace, completed in 1394 (see page 66).
Changdeokgung Seoul's second palace, built in 1395 (see page 69).
Jongmyo The ancestral shrines, built in 1394 (see page 72).
Sungnyemun The city's south gate; construction started in 1395 (see page 75).
City walls Built in stages from 1396.
Dongdaemun The east gate, built in 1396 (see page 78).

SEOUL ORIENTATION

Seoul is colossal, its metropolitan area stretching far and wide in a confusion of concrete and cleaved in two by the **Hangang**, a wide river crossed by many bridges. But despite its size, a very definite city centre – just small enough to be traversed by foot – has been in place north of the Hangang River since the late fourteenth century.

GYEONGBOKGUNG AND AROUND

There are five grand palaces in "old" Seoul, of which **Gyeongbokgung** is the oldest and most famous; Changdeokgung is another great example, just to the east, and in between the two sit **Bukchon Hanok Village**, central Seoul's only area of traditional wooden housing, and artistic **Samcheongdong**.

INSADONG AND AROUND

Just to the south is **Insadong**, Seoul's tourist hub, full of traditional restaurants and tearooms, excellent souvenir shops, and more art galleries than you can count – with a beautiful temple and a small palace of its own, you could easily spend the whole day here. To the south is busy Jongno, Seoul's most important thoroughfare, and sketching a liquid parallel line south again is **Cheonggyecheon**, a gentrified stream lying beneath street level.

GWANGHWAMUN AND CITY HALL

Cheonggyecheon starts footsteps from **Gwanghwamun Plaza**, a city square surrounded by imposing buildings (including Gwanghwamun itself, the south gate of Gyeongbokgung). This area, and that surrounding **City Hall** to the south, constitute Korea's most important business district, and you'll see an awful lot of suits at mealtimes and rush hour.

MYEONGDONG AND DONGDAEMUN

The business area segues into **Myeongdong**, the busiest shopping area in the country, packed with clothes stores, restaurants and tourists from other Asian countries. It's flanked to the east and west by **Dongdaemun** and **Namdaemun**, two gargantuan market areas, and to the south by **Namsan**, Seoul's very own mountain, which affords fantastic views of the city centre and beyond.

NORTHERN SEOUL

Namsan once hemmed in Seoul to the south, while the imposing granite face of Bukhansan continues to do something similar to the north. **Northern Seoul** spreads around it to either side; head west and you'll get to cutesy **Buamdong**, or venture east instead and hit the student area of **Daehangno**.

WESTERN SEOUL

Western Seoul is all about students – there are tens of thousands at various massive establishments here. **Hongdae** is the most famous, but not purely due to its status as a vaunted school of artistic learning – it also possesses by far the most rocking nightlife in the country, a neon-drenched maze of hip-hop clubs, live music venues and trendy subterranean bars.

ITAEWON AND AROUND

South of Namsan is **Itaewon**, long the hub of foreign activity in the city; a curious mix of the sleazy and the cosmopolitan, it's home to some of Seoul's best restaurants, bars and clubs, and a happening LGBT+ area. Itaewon's scene has started to spread east and west, with much of Seoul's expat population choosing to hunker down in these newly fashionable areas.

SOUTHERN SEOUL

A number of important city districts lie south of the Han River. Most prominent is **Gangnam** (yes, from the song), a shop- and restaurant-filled south-bank alternative to Myeongdong, which merges with ultra-trendy **Apgujeong**, filled with boutiques and some of the best restaurants in the city. The **Coex Mall**, a gigantic underground shopping complex, is also in the south, as is the **Jamsil** area – home to **Lotte World**, one of the country's most popular theme parks – and **Olympic Park**, where Seoul's Summer Games were held in 1988.

1

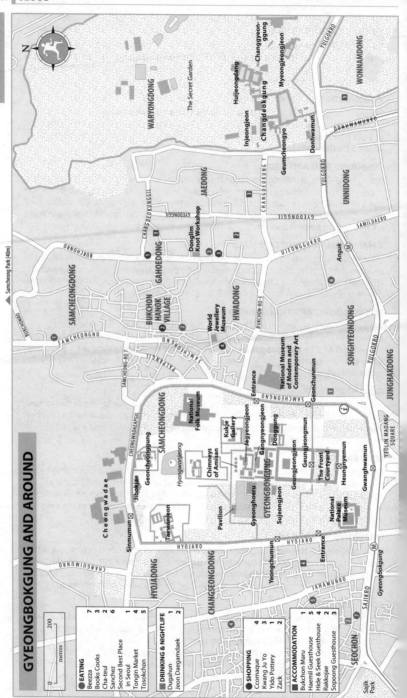

GYEONGBOKGUNG AND AROUND

0 metres 200

Samcheong Park (40m)

WARYONGDONG

The Secret Garden

Changgyeonggung

Myeongjeongjeon

Huijeongdang

Injeongjeon

Changdeokgung

Changdeokgyo

Geumcheongyo

Donhwamun

WONNAMDONG

DONHWAMUNRO

YULGOKRO

JAEDONG

Donglim Knot Workshop

SAMCHEONGDONG

GAHOEDONG

BUKCHON HANOK VILLAGE

HWADONG

World Jewellery Museum

UNNIDONG

GYEDONGGIL

SAMILDAERO

UIJEONGGUKRO

Anguk

SONGHYEONDONG

JUNGHAKDONG

YULGOKRO

National Museum of Modern and Contemporary Art

Geonchunmun

SAMCHEONGNO

National Folk Museum

Kukje Gallery

Jagyeongjeon

Gangnyeongjeon

Donggung

Geonjeongjeon

Geunjeongjeon

The Front Courtyard

Heunghyemun

Gwanghwamun

GYEONGBOKGUNG

Sujeongjeon

Gyeonghoeru

Pavilion

Chimneys of Amisan

Hyangwonjeong

Geoncheonggung

Jibokjae

Taewonjeon

Cheongwadae

Sinmumun

CHEONGMUDAEPGIL

CHANGUIMUNRO

HYOJADONG

HYOJARO

CHANGSEONGDONG

Yeongchumun

Entrance

National Palace Museum

YEOLIN MADANG SQUARE

JAHAMUNRO

SAJIKRO

SEOCHON

Gyeongbokgung

Sajik Park

capital, meant that it changed hands four times, coming under North Korean control twice before being wrested back. Seoul finally ended up under South Korean control, though most of the city lay in ruins. Despite – or perhaps, because of – all these setbacks, there has been no stopping it since then. The economic reforms inaugurated by president **Park Chung-hee** in the 1970s brought it global attention as a financial dynamo, and Seoul's population has ballooned to over ten million, more than double this if the whole metropolitan area is taken into account. The city has also played host to some of the world's largest events: the Summer Olympics in 1988, part of football's World Cup in 2002, and the G20 Summit in 2010.

Gyeongbokgung and around

Seoul is one of the world's largest urban agglomerations, racing out for mile after mile in every direction, and swallowing up whole cities well beyond its own official limits. As such, it's hard to imagine that the Korean capital was once a much smaller place, bounded by fortress walls erected shortly after the nascent Joseon dynasty chose it as their seat of power in 1392. The palace of **Gyeongbokgung** was erected during these fledgling years, and centuries down the line its environs are still the seat of national power – as well as the area of most interest to foreign visitors. To the east is **Changdeokgung**, a little more refined than Gyeongbokgung, and the only one of Seoul's five palaces to have been added to UNESCO's World Heritage list.

While the palaces are the main draw, there's much more to see in the area. Abutting Gyeongbokgung to the northeast is the neighbourhood of **Samcheongdong**, a trendy, laidback area filled with cafés, galleries, wine bars and clothing boutiques. Across a small ridge, hilly **Bukchon Hanok Village** provides the traditional counterpoint – you'll

---

WHICH PALACE?

Seoul has five **palaces** (and one "unofficial" palace) to choose from, and while they're all great, you may not have the time, energy or patience to traipse around all of them. The following is a short summary of their merits. Note that a **combination ticket** (W10,000) is available to the four palaces that charge admission – Gyeongbokgung, Changdeokgung (including the Secret Garden), Changgyeonggung and Deoksugung – as well as Jongmyo shrine (see page 72). Available at all venues, these tickets are valid for a month from first usage, though they're only really worth buying if you're visiting Changdeokgung and its garden; these days, you can also get into all palaces for free if you're wearing traditional *hanbok* clothing (see page 67). Note that certain venues are closed on Mondays or Tuesdays.

Gyeongbokgung (see page 66) The oldest and most historically important of the palaces, this attracts the greatest number of visitors and boasts a splendid mountain backdrop, as well as two great museums.

Changdeokgung (see page 69) Perhaps best viewed as the connoisseurs' choice, this has been listed as World Heritage on account of its superb architecture and charming garden.

Unhyeongung (see page 72) Never used as a regal residence and thus not an official palace, this is rarely busy and well worth tracking down if you're in the Insadong area.

Gyeonghuigung (see page 73) Viewed by Seoulites as the runt of the palace litter, this is the one to pick if you'd like to be away from the crowds – it's still a charming and beautiful place, and handily located next to the city's museum of history.

Deoksugung (see page 75) Used as a palace in the early twentieth century, when Korea was opening up to the wider world, Deoksugung's grounds contain some incongruous European-style structures, one of which now functions as one of the city's best art museums.

Changgyeonggung (see page 80) More natural in feel than the other palaces, Changgyeonggung has some delightful grassy areas – and a particularly intriguing history, involving Japanese desecration and a royal murder.

1

THE SECRET HISTORY OF SEOUL'S GRANDEST PALACE

Gyeongbokgung's construction was ordered by **King Taejo** in 1394, and the "Palace of Shining Happiness" held the regal throne for over two hundred years. At its peak, the palace housed over four hundred buildings within its vaguely rectangular perimeter walls, but most were burned down during the **Japanese invasions** in the 1590s. Though few Koreans will admit to it, the invaders were not directly to blame – the arsonists in one major incident were actually a group of local slaves, angered by their living and working conditions. The palace was only rebuilt following the coronation of child-king **Gojong** in 1863, but the Japanese were to invade again shortly afterwards, forcibly opening up Korea to foreign trade, and slowly ratcheting up their standing on the peninsula.

In 1895 **Empress Myeongseong**, one of Gojong's wives and an obstacle to the Japanese – who refer to her as "Queen Min" – was assassinated in the Gyeongbokgung grounds, a shady tale told in countless movies and soap operas, and a precursor to the full-scale **Japanese annexation** of Korea in 1910. During the occupation, which ended with World War II in 1945, the Japanese used Gyeongbokgung for police interrogation and torture, and made numerous changes to the building in an apparent effort to destroy Korean pride. The front gate, Gwanghwamun, was moved to the east of the complex, destroying the north–south geometric principles followed during the palace's creation, while a Japanese command post was built in the sacred first courtyard in a shape identical to the Japanese written character for "sun" (日). One interesting suggestion – and one certainly not beyond the scope of Japanese thinking at that time – is that Bukhansan mountain to the north resembled the character for "big" (大) and City Hall to the south that of "root" (本), thereby emblazoning Seoul's most prominent points with the three characters that made up the name of the Empire of the Rising Sun (大日本).

find plenty of tearooms and traditional culture among the splendidly tiled rooftops of its wooden buildings.

One popular **day-trip** itinerary is to start the morning at Gyeongbokgung and take in the on-site museums before heading to Samcheongdong for a meal and a cup of coffee; energy thus restored, you can head across hilly Bukchon towards the palace of Changdeokgung, then perhaps down into Insadong (see page 70) for dinner.

Gyeongbokgung

경복궁 • 161 Sajik-ro • Mon & Wed–Sun 9am–5pm; English-language tours 11am, 1.30pm & 3.30pm; changing of the guard 10am, 1pm & 3pm • W3000 or with combination ticket (see page 65); tours free • ⑩ royalpalace.go.kr • Gyeongbokgung subway (line 3)

The glorious palace of **Gyeongbokgung** is, with good reason, the most popular tourist sight in the city, and a focal point of the country as a whole. The place is absorbing, and the chance to stroll the dusty paths between its delicate tile-roofed buildings is one of the most enjoyable experiences Seoul has to offer. Gyeongbokgung was ground zero for Seoul's emergence as a place of power, having been built to house the royal family of the embryonic **Joseon dynasty**, shortly after they transferred their capital here in 1392. The complex has witnessed fires, repeated destruction and even a royal assassination (see pages 66 and 367), but careful reconstruction means that the regal atmosphere of old is still palpable, aided no end by the suitably majestic crags of Bugaksan to the north. A large historical complex with excellent on-site **museums**, it can easily eat up the best part of a day. Try to time your visit to coincide with the colourful **changing of the guard** ceremonies.

The palace

Most visitors will start their tour at **Gwanghwamun** (광화문), the palace's southern gate. Entering through the first courtyard you'll see **Geunjeongjeon** (근정전), the palace's former throne room, looming ahead. Despite being the largest wooden structure in the country, this two-level construction remains surprisingly graceful, the corners of its gently sloping roof home to lines of tiny guardian figurines. The central path leading up to the building was once used only by the king, but the best views of its interior are actually from the sides – from here you'll see the golden dragons on the hall ceiling, as well as the throne itself, backed by its traditional folding screen.

After Geunjeongjeon you can take one of a number of routes around the complex. To the east of the throne room are the buildings that once housed **crown princes**, deliberately placed here to give these regal pups the day's first light, while behind is **Gangnyeongjeon** (강녕전), the former living quarters of the king and queen, furnished with replica furniture. Also worth seeking out is **Jagyeongjeon** (자경전), a building backed by a beautiful stone wall, and chimneys decorated with animal figures.

West of the throne room is **Gyeonghoeru** (경회루), a colossal pavilion only visitable by pre-booking on the palace website (see page 66). It looks out over a tranquil **lotus pond** that was a favourite with artists in regal times, and remains so today. The pond was used both for leisure and as a ready source of water for the fires that regularly broke out around the palace (an unfortunate by-product of heating buildings with burning wood or charcoal under the floor), while the pavilion itself was once a place for banquets and civil service examinations.

North of the throne room, and right at the back of the complex, are a few buildings constructed in 1888 during the rule of King Gojong to house books and works of art. These structures were designed in the Chinese style that was the height of fashion at the time, and are markedly different from any other structures around the palace.

National Folk Museum

국립민속박물관 • Mon & Wed–Sun 9am–5pm • Entrance included in palace ticket • Ⓦ nfm.go.kr

On the east side of the palace complex is the **National Folk Museum**, a traditionally styled, multi-tier structure that fits in nicely with the palatial buildings. Despite its size, there's only one level, but this is stuffed with dioramas and explanations of Korean ways of life long since gone, from fishing and farming practices to examples of clothing worn during the Three Kingdoms era.

National Palace Museum

국립고궁박물관 • Mon–Fri 9am–6pm, Sat & Sun 9am–7pm; English-language tours 11am & 2.30pm • Free • Ⓦ gogung.go.kr

At the far southwest of the palace grounds is the **National Palace Museum**. The star of the show here is a **folding screen** which would have once been placed behind the imperial throne, and features the sun, moon and five peaks painted onto a dark blue background, symbolically positioning the seated kings at the nexus of heaven and earth. It's a glorious, deep piece of art that deserves to be better known. Other

---

HANBOK: THE RESURGENCE OF KOREAN COSTUME

Korea's traditional silken costume, known as **hanbok** (한복), has been around for centuries, though few would wear it outside family or educational events. However, since 2015 it has become impossible to walk for five minutes in the palace or Insadong areas without seeing outlets **renting out costumes** – and in that time, you'll probably see dozens of people (tourists and locals alike) swanning by in them. But why the sudden change? First you have to understand why they weren't worn much before: the original designs looked more than a little naff to the present generation, and there were few places to rent them cheaply. The solution was to tweak the designs to make them more visually appealing (though men may still feel a bit like Korean-style ice-hockey goalies), and rent them cheaply by the day or half-day – the demand is now simply staggering. You can get a costume for as little as W10,000 for an hour, or around W25,000 for a half-day – you won't have to walk far to find a rental spot. Remember that *hanbok*-wearers get into Seoul's palaces for free.

1

THE SAMCHEONGNO ART STRETCH

Perhaps Korea's most important road in artistic terms, **Samcheongno** sports a number of lauded **galleries**, all free to browse around, as well as the National Museum of Modern and Contemporary Art (see page 68).

Arario Seoul 84 Bukchon-ro 5-gil ⓦ ararioseoul.com; Anguk subway (line 3). This large venue lends itself to sculptures and large paintings, with artworks from renowned artists. With a sister gallery in Shanghai, the Arario is a great place to check out the latest offerings from the increasingly interesting Chinese art scene. Free entry. Tues–Sun 11am–7pm.

Gallery Hyundai 14 Samcheong-ro ⓦ galleryhyundai.com; Anguk subway (line 3). This large gallery possesses the most esteemed collection in the area; established in the 1960s, it's Korea's longest-running

commercial gallery. Its focus has long been on artists born before 1930, though there's an ever-increasing emphasis on newer trends. Free entry. Tues–Sun 10am–6pm.

Kukje Gallery 54 Samcheong-ro ⓦ kukjegallery.com; Anguk subway (line 3). The Kukje is one of the most important players in the area, actively promoting Korean artists abroad, and displaying a wide, well-selected range of exhibits in its own space. It's surrounded by excellent cafés, and there's an Italian restaurant in the same building. Free entry. Mon–Sat 10am–6pm, Sun 10am–5pm.

items in the fascinating display include a jade book belonging to King Taejo, paraphernalia relating to ancestral rites, and some of the wooden dragons taken from the temple eaves, whose size and detail can be better appreciated when seen up close. Equally meticulous is a map of the heavens engraved onto a stone slab in 1395.

Samcheongdong

삼청동

The youthful district of **Samcheongdong** is crammed with restaurants, cafés and galleries, most of which have a more contemporary appearance than their counterparts in Insadong. The area's charming main drag, Samcheongdonggil (삼청동길), heads off from Gyeongbokgung's northeastern corner – it's a mere five-minute walk from the palace's eastern exit. On the way between the two, be sure to pop into at least one of the excellent galleries on **Samcheongno**, a road running along the east flank of the palace (see above).

National Museum of Modern and Contemporary Art

국립미술관 • 30 Samcheong-ro • Tues, Thurs, Fri & Sun 10am–6pm, Wed & Sat 10am–9pm • W4000; free Wed & Sat after 6pm • ⓦ mmca.go.kr • Anguk subway (line 3)

Opened in late 2013, this wing of the **National Museum of Modern and Contemporary Art** (see pages 75 and 94 for the others) was erected to house the Japanese Defence Security Command during the occupation period. Despite this weighty history, the art on display is not just modern in nature, but on the very edge of contemporary. There's no permanent display, but each and every exhibition (there's usually a new one every two weeks) is highly creative, revolving around the open-air Madang Gallery, Seoul's own equivalent to the Turbine Hall in London's Tate Modern.

Cheongwadae

청와대 • 1 Sejong-ro • Guided tours Tues–Sat 10am, 11am, 2pm & 3pm • Free, but must be booked at ⓦ english.president.go.kr at least three weeks in advance; bring your passport and collect tickets at Gyeongbokgung • Gyeongbokgung or Anguk subway (both line 3)

What the White House is to Washington, **Cheongwadae** is to Seoul. Sitting directly behind Gyeongbokgung and surrounded by mountains, this official presidential residence is named the "Blue House" on account of the colour of its roof tiles. In

1

Joseon times, blue roofs were reserved for kings, but the office of the president is the nearest modern-day equivalent to regal rule. The road that borders the palace is open for public access, but don't venture too close to the entrance as it's understandably a high-security area. In 1968, a group of 31 North Korean soldiers were apprehended here during an attempt to assassinate then-President Park Chung-hee; while you're unlikely to be accused of doing the same, if you loiter or stray too close you may well be questioned.

Bukchon Hanok Village

북촌 한옥 마을

A few of Samcheongdong's cafés and galleries spill over into **Bukchon Hanok Village**, an area characterized by the prevalence of traditional wooden **hanok buildings**. These once covered the whole country, but most were torn down during Korea's economic revolution and replaced with row upon row of fifteen-storey blocks. The city council spared this area the wrecking ball, and as a result there's some delightful walking to be done among its quiet lanes, where tiny restaurants, tearooms and comic-book shops line the streets, and children play games on mini arcade machines, creating a pleasant air of indifference hard to find in the capital; a few of the buildings have even been converted into guesthouses (see page 101). Many Bukchon visitors make a beeline to **Bukchon Hanok Ilgil** (북촌 한옥 1길), a steep lane with a particularly good view of the *hanok* abodes.

Changdeokgung

창덕궁 • 99 Yulgok-ro • Tues–Sun: Feb–Oct 9am–6pm; Nov–Jan 9am–5.30pm; Secret Garden by tour only, usually on the hour 10am–4pm; English-language palace tours 10.30am, 11.30 & 2.30pm, plus 3.30pm Feb–Nov • Palace W3000; Secret Garden tour W5000; both also on combination ticket (see page 65) • ⓦ eng.cdg.go.kr • Anguk subway (line 3)

Sumptuous **Changdeokgung** is, for many, the pick of Seoul's palaces, with immaculate paintwork and carpentry augmenting a palpable sense of history; home to royalty as recently as 1910, this is the best-preserved palace in the city. Its construction was completed in 1412, under the reign of King Taejong. Like Gyeongbokgung, it suffered heavy damage during the **Japanese invasions** of the 1590s; Gyeongbokgung was left to fester, but Changdeokgung was rebuilt and in 1618 usurped its older brother as the seat of the **royal family**, an honour it held until 1872. In its later years, the palace became a symbol of Korea's opening up to the rest of the world: King Heonjong (who ruled 1834–49) added distinctively Chinese-style buildings to the complex, and his eventual successor King Sunjong (ruled 1907–10) was fond of driving Western cars around the grounds. Sunjong was, indeed, the last of Korea's long line of kings; Japanese annexation brought an end to his short rule, but he was allowed to live in Changdeokgung until his death in 1926.

SEOUL'S QUIRKY MUSEUMS

Samcheongdong and Bukchon are home to countless tiny museums, and it can be worth popping into one or two on your way around the area – especially if the weather is inclement.

Owl Art & Craft Museum 부엉이 박물관 143-10 Bukchon-ro; Anguk subway (line 3). The result of its founder's quirky (and slightly scary) obsession, this small museum is stuffed to the gills with anything and everything pertaining to owls. There's a small tearoom-cum-café in which you can purchase strigiform trinkets of your very own. W5000. Wed–Sat 10am–7pm.

World Jewellery Museum 세계 장신구 박물관 2 Bukchon-ro 5-gil, ⓦ wjmuseum.com; Anguk subway (line 3). With a name that's as coldly descriptive as they come, it may come as a surprise that this museum is the most rewarding in the area, with the pieces on display offering great subtlety and variety. W7000. Wed–Sun 11am–5pm.

1

The palace

The huge gate of **Donhwamun** is the first structure you'll come across – dating from 1609, this is the oldest extant palace gate in Seoul. Next is Changdeokgung's suitably impressive **throne room**, which is without doubt the most regal-looking of any Seoul palace – light from outside is filtered through paper doors and windows, bathing in a dim glow the elaborate wooden-beam structure, as well as the throne and its folding-screen backdrop. Beyond here, you'll pass a number of buildings pertaining to the various kings who occupied the palace, some of which still have the original furniture inside; one building even contains King Sunjong's old Daimler and Cadillac, which look more than a little incongruous in their palatial setting. Further on you'll come to **Nakseonjae**, built during the reign of King Heonjong; Qing-style latticed doors and arched pavilion reveal his taste for foreign cultures, and the colours of the bare wood are ignited with shades of gold and honey during sunset.

The Secret Garden

The palace's undoubted highlight is **Huwon** (후원), usually referred to in Seoul's tourist literature as the "Secret Garden". Approached via a suitably mysterious path, the garden is concealed by an arch of leaves. In the centre is a **lotus pond**, one of Seoul's most photographed sights, and alive with flowers in late June or early July. A small building overlooking the pond served as a library and study room in imperial times, and the gates blocking the entrance path were used as a checking mechanism by the king – needing to crouch to pass through, he'd be reminded of his duty to be humble.

Insadong and around

인사동

Insadong is the undisputed hub of Korea's tourist scene, and you could quite happily spend most of the day in this tight lattice of streets, full to the brim with art galleries, shops, tearooms and traditional restaurants. The appeal of the area lies in simply strolling around and taking it all in, but there are a fair few bona fide sights around, too, including the lesser-known palace of **Unhyeongung**; **Jongmyo**, a shrine where ancient ancestral ceremonies are still performed; and **Jogyesa**, Seoul's most-visited temple. Running along the southern edge of Insadong is **Cheonggyecheon**, a gentrified stream forming a below-street-level paradise for pedestrians and joggers.

Tapgol Park

탑골공원 · Daily 9am–6pm · Free · Jonggak subway (line 1)

Insadonggil finishes at small **Tapgol Park**, a small patch of land containing as much concrete as it does grass. It is, however, a place famed to Koreans as the venue for 1919's declaration of independence against Japanese rule (see page 367). It's also home to a huge, stunning Joseon-era **stone pagoda**, which sits resplendent at the park's northern end; grandly titled official "National Treasure Number Two", the pagoda has actually been the de facto number one since the burning down of Sungnyemun (see page 75), but sadly the beauty of its ancient design has been hugely diluted by the ugly glass box placed around it for protection.

Jogyesa

조계사 · 55 Ujeongguk-ro · Tues–Sun 9am–6pm · Free · Jonggak station (line 1)

Near the north end of Insadonggil, on the west side, is **Jogyesa**, the only major temple in the centre of Seoul. Created in 1910 and hemmed in by large buildings, it has neither history nor beauty to its credit (though the main hall is quite something), but

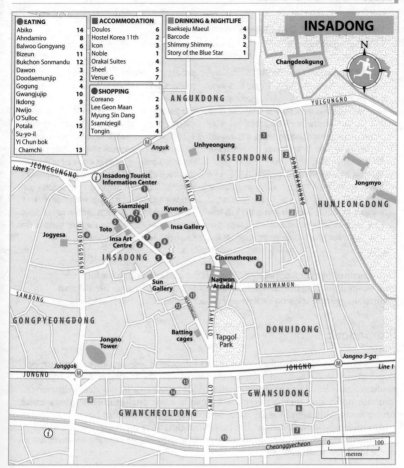

INSADONG

● EATING	
Abiko	14
Ahndamiro	8
Balwoo Gongyang	6
Bizeun	11
Bukchon Sonmandu	12
Dawon	3
Doodaemunjip	2
Gogung	4
Gwangjujip	10
Ikdong	9
Nwijo	1
O'Sulloc	5
Potala	15
Su-yo-il	7
Yi Chun bok Chamchi	13

■ ACCOMMODATION	
Doulos	6
Hostel Korea 11th	2
Icon	3
Noble	1
Orakai Suites	4
Sheel	5
Venue G	7

■ DRINKING & NIGHTLIFE	
Baekseju Maeul	4
Barcode	3
Shimmy Shimmy	2
Story of the Blue Star	1

● SHOPPING	
Coreano	2
Lee Geon Maan	5
Myung Sin Dang	3
Ssamiziegil	1
Tongin	4

for visitors with little time in the country it may represent the only chance to see a Korean temple of such size. The best times to visit are on Buddha's birthday (see page 45) and the Lotus Lantern festival.

Cheonggyecheon

청계천 • Daily 24hr • Free • Accessible from many stations, including Gwanghwamun (line 5) and Jonggak (line 1)

Until recently, **Cheonggyecheon** was a mucky stream running under an elevated highway, but in 2003 the Mayor of Seoul decided to ditch the road and beautify the creek – this controversial project saw heads rolling on corruption charges, grumbles from local businesses and protests from environmentalists, but since completion in 2005 it has been looked upon as a resounding success. Both the stream and the walkways that flank it are below street level, and on descending you'll notice that Seoul's ceaseless cacophony has been diluted and largely replaced by the sound of rushing water.

Cheonggyecheon starts just southeast of Gwanghwamun Plaza, at a point marked by a curious piece of **modern art**. Heading east, you'll pass a series of features, including fountains, sculpture and stepping stones; it's around 3km from the start to

1

INSADONG ART GALLERIES

All of these **galleries** are on or around **Insadonggil**, and are within easy walking distance of each other. Admission is free unless otherwise stated.

Insa Art Center 인사 아트 센터 41-1 Insadong-gil, ⓦinsaartcenter.com; Jonggak (line 1), Jongno 3-ga (lines 1, 3 & 5) or Anguk (line 3) subways. This interesting building's seven floors of exhibitions could keep you busy for some time – the acres of wall space display a wide range of modern styles, with exhibits changed every week to make room for new works. Daily 10am–7pm.

Kyungin Museum of Fine Art 경인 미술관 11-4 Insadong 10-gil, ⓦkyunginart.co.kr; Jonggak (line 1), Jongno 3-ga (lines 1, 3 & 5) or Anguk (line 3) subways. Exhibitions are rarely poor at this long-time local favourite, whose traditional-with-a-twist style fuses the conventional with the contemporary. Its four

pleasant and spacious rooms are centred around a leafy courtyard that's also home to *Dawon*, a decent tearoom (see page 109). Daily 10am–6pm.

Sun Gallery 선 갤러리 8 Insadong 5-gil, ⓦsun gallery.co.kr; Jonggak (line 1), Jongno 3-ga (lines 1, 3 & 5) or Anguk (line 3) subways. Spoken about in hushed tones by curators at other Insadong galleries, this houses probably the most renowned collection in the area. It mainly consists of early twentieth-century paintings, and shows that modern art in Korea goes back way before the country's growth into an economic power – look for pieces by Kim Sou, who had a Rubens-like obsession with flesh, or the floral works of Kim Chong Hak. Tues–Sun 10am–6pm.

Dongdaemun market (see page 78), though the paths continue on for a whopping 7km beyond, joining the Hangang near Oksu station – a stretch used almost exclusively by local joggers, cyclists and power-walkers.

Ikseondong
익선동

A neighbourhood largely made of small alleys known as *golmok*, **Ikseondong** surged in popularity in 2015, when Seoulites discovered that the alleyways and their many wooden *hanok* buildings made good selfie fodder – the area is now decidedly trendy. You may notice that there are very few women in many establishments – this area has been a favoured hangout for gay men for decades, though this fact has only become truly visible post-trendification. The bars hereabouts were once window-lite upper-floor places marked with subtle rainbow motifs, but many now sit proudly on street level – come by to see Seoul coming out.

Unhyeongung
운현궁 • 464 Samil-daero • Tues–Sun 9am–7pm • Free • Anguk subway (line 3)

Having never been an official royal residence, the tiny palace of **Unhyeongung** doesn't qualify as one of Seoul's "big five" palaces; accordingly, it's less showy than the others, but the relative paucity of tourists makes it a pleasant place to visit – the bare wood and paper doors would provide the perfect setting for a Japanese *anime*. Though he never lived here, King Gojong married the ill-fated Princess Myeongseong in Unhyeongung, and it was also the centre of neo-Confucian thought during the Joseon period, which sought to base civil progress on merit rather than lineage (see page 180 for information on Yi Toegye, one of the main instigators).

Jongmyo
종묘 • 157 Jongno • Sat 9am–6pm; English-language tours Wed–Fri & Sun 10am, noon, 2pm & 4pm • W1000 including tour, or on Palace combo ticket (see page 65) • Jongno 3-ga subway (lines 1, 3 & 5)

Along with the palace of Gyeongbokgung, the construction of **Jongmyo shrine** was on King Taejo's manifesto as he kicked off the Joseon dynasty in 1392. He decreed that dead kings and queens would be honoured here in true Confucian style, with a series of ancestral rites. These ceremonies were performed five times a year, once each season, with an extra one on the winter solstice, when the ruling king would pay his respects to those who died before him by bowing profusely, and explaining pertinent national issues to their **spirit tablets**. These wooden blocks, in which deceased royalty were believed to reside, are still stored in large wooden buildings that were said to be the biggest in Asia at the time of their construction. Jeongjeon was the first, but such was the length of the Joseon dynasty that another building – Yeongnyeongjeon – had to be added.

For most of the week the shrine is only accessible on **guided tours**, which remove the joy of simply wandering around the wooded complex – **go on Saturday** if at all possible, which is the one day on which you'll be given free rein. Whether on a tour or not, note that the buildings themselves remain locked, though the courtyards are open – take the opportunity to walk on the raised paths that were once reserved for kings. The one exception to this is on the first Sunday in May, which is the day of **Jongmyo Daeje** (see page 113), a long, solemn ceremony followed by traditional court dances – an absolute must-see.

Gwanghwamun and City Hall

Looking north from Gwanghwamun, the main gate of Gyeongbokgung palace, you can see little but cascading palace roofs, and the mountains beyond. Turn south instead, and the contrast is almost unbelievably stark – looming up behind **Gwanghwamun Plaza** are the ranked masses of high-rise blocks that announce Seoul's main **business district**, its walkways teeming with black-suited businessfolk and their civil servant brethren racing in and out of the grand new **City Hall**. However, there's more of tourist interest than you might expect in this *balli-balli* (Korean for "quickly, quickly!") area, including two palaces, a few major **museums** and **art galleries**, some fine examples of colonial architecture, and **Jeongdonggil**, one of Seoul's most charming roads, lined with ginkgo trees and popular with couples.

Gyeonghuigung

경희궁 • 45 Saemunan-ro • Tues–Sun 9am–6pm • Free • Gwanghwamun subway (line 5)

Humble **Gyeonghuigung** is the most anonymous and least visited of Seoul's Five Grand Palaces – even locals may struggle to point you towards it – but its simplicity tends to strike a chord with those who choose to track it down. Gyeonghuigung was built in 1616, and became a royal palace by default when Changdeokgung (see page 69) was burned down in 1624. Though a little forlorn, it's a pretty place nonetheless, and may be the palace for you if crowds, false-bearded guards in faux period clothing and the necessity of avoiding camera sightlines aren't to your liking. Unlike other palaces, you'll be able to enter the throne room – bare except for the throne, but worth a look – before scrambling up to the halls of the upper level, which have a visually pleasing backdrop of grass and rock.

Seoul Museum of History

서울 역사박물관 • 55 Saemunan-ro • Tues–Fri 9am–10pm, Sat & Sun 10am–7pm • Free; around W12,000 for big-name special exhibitions • ⓦ eng.museum.seoul.kr • Gwanghwamun subway (line 5)

Adjacent to Gyeonghuigung is the **Museum of History**, whose **permanent exhibition** on the third floor focuses on Joseon-era Seoul. Here you'll find lacquered boxes with mother-of-pearl inlay, porcelain bowls and vases thrown in gentle shapes, and silk gowns with embroidered leaves and dragons. Another room popular with visitors

1

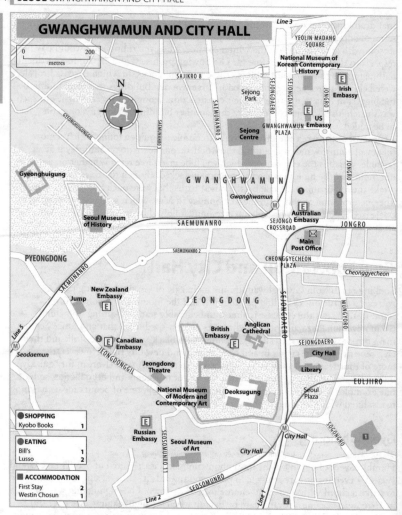

features a gigantic photographic image of Seoul covering its entire floor space. Certain halls play host to **rotating exhibitions**, which usually justify the extra charge.

Seoul Museum of Art

서울시립미술관 • 61 Deoksugung-gil • Tues–Fri 10am–9pm, Sat & Sun 10am–6pm • Admission price varies by exhibition; around W15,000 for major ones • ⓦ sema.seoul.go.kr • City Hall subway (lines 1 & 2)

The large, modern **Seoul Museum of Art**, otherwise known as SeMA, sits just off Jeongdonggil. More gallery than museum, it's well worth popping in for a look at what are invariably high-quality exhibitions of art from around the world – Picasso, Monet, Van Gogh and Renoir have all found temporary homes here. In addition, there are always free secondary exhibitions to peruse, most commonly the work of local (or at least Asian) artists. On exiting the museum look out for a strange piece of art across the road – a black metal statue of a man perpetually hammering, a mute reminder to folk from the nearby business district that life's not all about work.

Deoksugung

덕수궁 • 99 Sejong-daero • Tues–Sun 9am–9pm; free English-language tours 10.30am & 1.30pm; changing of the guard ceremonies 11am, 2pm & 3.30pm • W1000; also on combination ticket (see page 65) • Ⓦ deoksugung.go.kr • City Hall subway (lines 1 & 2)

Located in the very centre of Seoul's business district, the palace of **Deoksugung** receives plenty of visitors, a volume amplified by the compound's relatively small size. This was the last palace of Seoul's big five to be built, and it became the country's seat of power almost by default in 1592 when the Japanese destroyed Gyeongbokgung (see page 66); its reign was short, however, since only two kings lived here before the seat of power was transferred to a newly rebuilt Changdeokgung (see page 69). Deoksugung then became the de facto royal residence again in 1895; **King Gojong** fled here after the murder of his wife, and declared the short-lived **Empire of Korea** here before ceding control to Japan.

The **palace** is entered through **Daehanmun** (대한문), a gate on the eastern side of the complex – this goes against the tenets of *feng shui*, which usually result in south-facing palace entrances. Most visitors then make a beeline to the main hall, **Junghwajeon** (중화전), whose ceiling sports a pair of immaculate carved dragons. Be sure to check out **Jeonggwanheon** (정관헌), a pavilion used for **coffee-drinking** by King Gojong, who developed something of a taste for said beverage here.

National Museum of Modern and Contemporary Art

국립미술관 • Tues, Thurs, Fri & Sun 10am–7pm, Wed & Sat 10am–9pm • Admission price depends on the exhibition; usually W3000–10,000, plus the palace entrance fee (see page 75) • Ⓦ mmca.go.kr

Deoksugung contains a couple of **Western-style buildings**, dating back to when the "Hermit Kingdom" of the Joseon dynasty was being forcibly opened up to trade. At the end of a gorgeous rose garden is **Seokjojeon** (석조전), designed by an English architect and built by the Japanese in 1910; the first Western-style building in the country, it was actually used as the royal home for a short time. It now houses a wing of the **National Museum of Modern and Contemporary Art** (see pages 68 and 94 for the others), whose exhibits are usually quality works from local artists, more often than not blending elements of traditional Korean styles with those of the modern day.

Sungnyemun

숭례문 • 40 Sejong-daero • Tues–Sun 9am–6pm • Free • Hoehyeon subway (line 4)

Also known by its more literal name of Namdaemun ("Great South Gate"), **Sungnyemun** was built in 1398 by King Taejo as a means of glorifying and protecting

THE DEATH OF NATIONAL TREASURE NUMBER ONE

Also known as Namdaemun or "Great South Gate", **Sungnyemun** (see page 75) was feted as the country's official "**National Treasure Number One**" on account of its age, beauty and importance. It was the sole survivor from the Taejo era (see page 62), which made things all the more harrowing when after six centuries standing proud, it was destroyed in a matter of minutes by a lone **arsonist**, Chae Jong-gi. Chae had noticed that Namdaemun was guarded by nothing but a single set of motion sensors – not the best way to protect one of the oldest wooden structures in the land. Early in the morning on February 10, 2008, he mounted the gate armed with a few bottles of paint thinner – hours later, images of Seoul's smouldering city icon were being beamed around the world. However, Korea's incendiary history means that it has substantial experience of reconstructing its treasures, and **renovation** of Namdaemun was completed in 2013.

1

his embryonic capital. This was by no means the only major project to come out of Taejo's first years of rule (see page 62), but fires, Japanese invasions and civil war rubbed out the rest over the following centuries. This final survivor was destroyed by an arsonist in 2008, though reconstruction was completed in 2013, and the traffic-encircled gate makes for a very pleasant photo-op.

Myeongdong and Dongdaemun

To Koreans, and a whole generation of travellers from other Asian countries, the words **Myeongdong** and **Dongdaemun** mean one thing and one thing alone: **shopping**. Many visitors from China, Japan, Thailand and Taiwan pin their Korean travel plans on these two areas alone, and never venture beyond their wider perimeter – a pity, for sure, but testament to the zone's ever-increasing international reputation. Myeongdong's tightly packed web of streets features literally hundreds of shops selling clothing, cosmetics and street snacks, while Dongdaemun is the marketplace equivalent, and of more interest to those buying fabric or knock-off handbags. However, it's not all about consumption – **Myeongdong Cathedral** is up there with Korea's prettiest Christian places of worship, while just to the south rises **Namsan**, Seoul's own mini-mountain.

Myeongdong Cathedral

명동성당 • 74 Myeongdong-gil • Daily 9am–7pm; Korean-language mass daily 6.30am & 6pm; English-language mass Sun 9am • Free • Euljiro 1-ga subway (line 2)

The hub of Korea's large – and growing – **Catholic** community, **Myeongdong Cathedral** stands proudly over the shopping area. Designed in Gothic style by **French missionaries**, the elegant lines of its red-brick exterior are a breath of fresh air in the business district's maze of concrete cuboids. It was completed in 1898 at the bequest of King Gojong, who desired to make up for persecutions witnessed under his predecessors: the site on which the cathedral stands had previously been home to a Catholic faith community, many of whom were executed during the **purges** of 1866 (see page 376).

Namsangol Hanok Village

남산골 • 28 Toegyero 34-gil • Daily: April–Oct 9am–9pm; Nov–March 9am–8pm • Free • Chungmuro subway (lines 3 & 4)

On your way up to Namsan, you may care to stop by at **Namsangol**, a small recreated **folk village** of *hanok* housing. The area is pretty and quite photogenic; there are usually a few traditional games for kids (and the young at heart) to play, and occasional displays of dance and music. The buildings back onto a pleasing park, which makes as good an entry point as any for Namsan itself.

Namsan

남산 • Cable car daily 10am–11pm • W6000 one way, W8500 return • Buses (#2 from Chungmuro, #3 from Seoul station and Itaewon, #5 from Myeongdong and Chungmuro) run every 15–20min

South of Myeongdong station the roads rise up, eventually coming to a stop at the feet of **Namsan**, a 265m-high peak in the centre of Seoul. Though it may be hard to believe today, Namsan once marked the natural boundary of a city that has long since swelled over the edges and across the river – some restored sections of the old city wall can still be seen on the mountain, as can the remains of **fire beacons** that once formed part of an ingenious pan-national communication system. Most visitors reach the top by **cable car**, but don't be fooled into thinking you'll be whisked up without a bead of sweat,

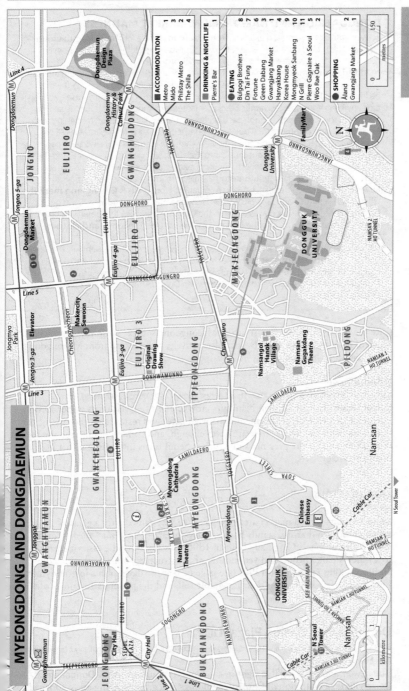

MYEONGDONG AND DONGDAEMUN

ACCOMMODATION
Metro	1
Mido	3
Philstay Metro	2
The Shilla	4

DRINKING & NIGHTLIFE
Pierre's Bar	1

EATING
Bulgogi Brothers	8
Din Tai Fung	7
Fortune	6
Green Dabang	3
Gwangjang Market	1
Hanyakbang	4
Korea House	9
Mongmyeok Sanbang	10
N Grill	11
Pierre Gagnaire à Seoul	5
Woo Rae Oak	2

SHOPPING
Åland	2
Gwangjang Market	1

1

DONGDAEMUN AND NAMDAEMUN: MARKET MADNESS

Between them, the colossal markets of **Dongdaemun** (동대문 시장) and **Namdaemun** (남대문 시장) could quite conceivably feed, and maybe even clothe, the world. Both are deservedly high on most visitors' list of sights to tick off in Seoul.

Dongdaemun market is the largest in the country, spread out, open-air and indoors, in various locations around the prettified Cheonggyecheon creek (see page 71). It would be impossible to list the whole range of things on sale here – you'll find yourself walking past anything from herbs to *hanbok* or paper lanterns to knock-off clothing, usually on sale for reasonable prices. Though each section of the market has its own opening and closing time, the complex as a whole simply never closes, so at least part of it will be open whenever you decide to come. Night-time is when the market is at its most atmospheric, with clothes stores pumping out music into the street at ear-splitting volume, and the air is filled with the smell of freshly made food sizzling at streetside stalls. Though some of the dishes on offer are utterly unrecognizable to many foreign visitors, it pays to be adventurous. One segment particularly popular with foreigners is **Gwangjang market** (광장 시장), a particularly salty offshoot of Dongdaemun to the northwest, and one of Seoul's most idiosyncratic places to eat in the evening – just look for something tasty and point. During the day, it's also the best place in Seoul to buy **secondhand clothes** (see page 116).

Smaller and more compact than Dongdaemun, where you'll find essentially the same goods, is **Namdaemun market**, which stretches out between City Hall and Seoul station. It's best accessed through Hoehyeon subway station (exits five or six), while Dongdaemun market's spine road runs between Dongdaemun and Dongdaemun Stadium stations.

---

since the base is an uphill slog south of Myeongdong subway station; you can chalk much of it off by taking a nearby lift. Alternatively, just walk up from Myeongdong, Seoul station or Itaewon.

N Seoul Tower

N서울타워 • Observatory Mon–Fri & Sun 10am–11pm, Sat 10am–midnight • W10,000 • ⓦ nseoultower.net

N Seoul Tower sits proudly on Namsan's crown. The five levels of its upper section are home to a **viewing platform**, and assorted **cafés and restaurants**. For many, the free views from the tower's base are good enough, and coming here to see the **sunset** is recommended – the grey mass of daytime Seoul turns in no time into a brilliant neon spectacle.

Dongdaemun

동대문

Dongdaemun's famed market area (see page 78) was named after a gigantic **ornamental gate** that still stands here – "*dong*" means "east", "*dae*" means "great" and "*mun*" means "gate". Originally built in 1396, this was once the eastern entrance to a much smaller Seoul, and yet another of the structures built by the incredibly ambitious **King Taejo** in the 1390s (see page 62), at the dawn of his Joseon dynasty; fires and warfare have taken their inevitable toll, and the present structure is of a mere 1869 vintage.

Dongdaemun Design Plaza (DDP)

동대문 디자인 플라자 • Daily 24hr • Most exhibitions around W8000 • ⓦ ddp.or.kr • Dongdaemun History & Culture Park subway (lines 2, 4 & 5)

The newest and most notable sight in the Dongdaemun area is the **Dongdaemun Design Plaza**, a collection of futuristic buildings and grassy walking areas. Opened in 2014 and colloquially referred to as the "DDP", this gargantuan city project was designed by Iraq-born architect **Zaha Hadid**, who won the tender with a design said to echo plumes of smoke – it was then altered slightly to its present shape, which, from above, is far more proximate to a high-heeled shoe. The reason for this change was the discovery of thousands of **dynastic relics** found in the earth; construction was delayed for over a year, and a small **museum** (daily 9am–6pm; free) added to display some of the bounty. Elsewhere, bar a café or two and a couple of gallery and **exhibition spaces**, the complex seems a little overlarge and underused.

Northern Seoul

North of Gyeongbokgung, Seoul appears to come to a rather abrupt end, with lofty mountains rearing up immediately behind the palace. The city did, indeed, once peter out here, but the "Economic Miracle" of the 1970s saw its population mushroom, and consequently Seoul's urban sprawl pushed around the mountainsides. Development was, however, not as rampant as in other parts of the city, and Seoul's **northern quarters** maintain a relatively secluded air. Northwest of Changdeokgung is the buzzing student district of **Daehangno**, a long-time favourite with visiting backpackers. Better for sightseeing is **Seongbukdong**, just north of Daehangno; here you'll find a secluded temple, plus the enchanting *Suyeon Sanbang* tearoom (see page 109), possibly the best in the city.

Seongbukdong lies on the eastern slopes of **Bugaksan**, a mountain whose trails provide some superb views of Seoul. On its western side is **Buamdong**, a quiet, hilly area becoming increasingly popular thanks to assorted clothing boutiques and swanky restaurants and a couple of superb galleries.

Finally, there are the peaks of **Bukhansan**, feted as the most-visited national park in the world, and possessing a range of historical sites and excellent hiking paths.

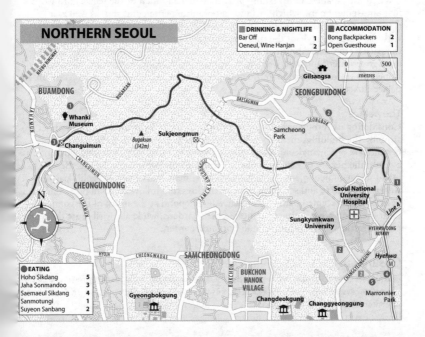

1

THE MURDER OF CROWN PRINCE SADO

In 1762, a sinister event occurred in the grounds of Changgyeonggung, one whose story is, for some reason, omitted from the information boards that dot the palace grounds – a **royal murder**. A young prince named **Sado** was heir to the throne of **King Yeongjo**, but occasionally abused his position of power, as evidenced by the apparently groundless murder of several servants. Fearing dire consequences if the nation's power were placed into his son's hands, Yeongjo escorted Sado to Seonninmun, a gate on the eastern side of the palace, and ordered him to climb into a rice casket; his son obeyed, was locked in, and starved to death. Sado's wife, Hyegyong, held the secret until after Yeongjo's death in 1776, at which point she spilled the beans in a book named *Hanjungnok* (published in English as *The Memoirs of Lady Hyegyong*). Sado's son **Jeongjo** became king on the death of Yeongjo, and built Hwaseong fortress in Suwon (see page 131) to house his father's remains. Jeongjo went on to become one of Korea's most respected rulers.

Changgyeonggung

창경궁 • 185 Changgyeonggung-ro • Mon & Wed–Sun 9am–5pm; tours 11.30am & 4pm (free) • W1000; also on combination ticket (see page 65) • 15min walk from Hyehwa subway (line 4), 30min walk from Insadong, or bus #150 or #171 from Anguk station

Separated from Changdeokgung (see page 69) by a perimeter wall, **Changgyeonggung** tends to split visitors into two camps – those who marvel at its history and the relatively natural beauty of grounds far greener than Seoul's other palaces, and those who feel that there's a little less to see. **King Sejong** built Changgyeonggung in 1418 as a resting place for his father, the recently abdicated King Taejong. In its heyday the palace had a far greater number of buildings than are visible today, but these were to suffer badly from fires and the damage inflicted during the Japanese invasions. Almost the whole of the complex burned down in the Japanese attacks of 1592, and then again during a devastating inferno in 1830, while in 1762 the palace witnessed the murder of a crown prince by his father (see page 80).

When the Japanese returned in 1907, they turned much of the palace into Korea's first **amusement park**, which included a botanical garden and zoo, as well as a museum; the red brick exterior and pointed steel roof were very much in keeping with the Japanese style of the time, and pictures of this era can still be seen around the palace entrance. Almost all of the Japanese-built features were tolerated by the local government for well over half a century, until almost everything was finally ripped down in 1983, though the **botanical garden** still remains today (access on palace ticket).

The palace

Considering its turbulent history, the **palace** is a markedly relaxed place to wander around. The buildings themselves are nowhere near as polished as those in the Gyeongbok or Changdeok palaces, though some feel that they look more authentic as a result; the history of each structure is chronicled on information boards. Be sure to look for **Myeongjeongjeon** (명정전), the oldest main hall of any of Seoul's palaces – it was built in 1616, and somehow escaped the fires that followed. From here, a number of lovely, herb-scented paths wind their way to a pond at the north of the complex. Near the pond are a couple of dedicated **herb gardens**, while also visible are the white-painted lattices of the Japanese-built **botanical garden**.

Gilsangsa

길상사 • 68 Seomjam-ro 5-gil • Daily 24hr • Free; templestay W50,000 – book in advance at ⓦ eng.templestay.com • ⓦ kilsangsa.info • Hansung University subway (line 4), then take the shuttle bus, or it's a 20min walk through a labyrinthine network of roads – the dearth of signage means that it's best to ask for directions

1

Way uphill in the Seongbukdong area is the wonderful Zen temple of **Gilsangsa**. This was once one of Seoul's most famous *gisaeng* (similar to the Japanese geisha) houses of entertainment, but was converted into a Seon (the Korean word for Zen) temple in 1997; it now makes one of the most convenient places for visitors to Seoul to experience a **templestay**, though it's only possible on one weekend each month. Gilsangsa's colouration is notably bland compared to most Korean temples, and as a result it looks its best under a thin blanket of winter snow; this is also the best time to take advantage of the little tearoom on the complex.

Buamdong

부암동 • Bus #7020 from Anguk subway (exit 1; head west to first bus stop), or #1020 from Gwanghwamun subway (just up the road from exit 2); 20min uphill walk from Gyeongbokgung subway – follow road flanking palace's western wall, and keep going straight

Hidden from central Seoul by the mountain of Bugaksan, **Buamdong** is one of the capital's quaintest and calmest corners. Recent years have seen its fame propelled by modern Korea's number-one cultural catalyst, the television drama: ever since the picturesque café *Sanmotungi* (see page 108) was used as a set in hit drama *The Coffee Prince*, young Seoulites have been heading to the area in ever greater numbers. Despite this, Buamdong retains a tranquillity that's almost impossible to find in other parts of Seoul, as well as a smattering of galleries and excellent places to eat and drink.

Whanki Museum

환기 미술관 • 63 Jahamun-ro 40-gil • Tues–Sun 10am–6pm • W8000 • ⓦ whankimuseum.org

The little-visited **Whanki Museum** is a shrine of sorts to Kim Whanki, one of Korea's first modern artists. In the 1940s, Kim proved a conduit between east and west, mopping up ideas from the Paris avant-garde movement while disseminating Asian techniques to a curious Europe. You may have to ask around to get to it – it's located down a small slope from the main road.

Bugaksan

북악산 • Hiking route daily 9am–5pm; last entry 3pm; bring passport or photo ID • Free • Western entrance at Changuimun gate in Buamdong; eastern entrance at Waryong Park, a taxi-ride or a 25min walk from Anguk station, and also accessible on local bus #8 from Hyehwa station

Rising up directly behind the palace of Gyeongbokgung (see page 66) is **Bugaksan**, one of the most significant mountains in Seoul. It provides some of the most glorious possible views of the capital, but for decades only soldiers were able to take them in, the mountain trails having been rendered off limits thanks to the rather important building nestling on its southern slopes – Cheongwadae, official home of the country's president (see page 68).

These protective measures were not without foundation: in 1968 Bugaksan was the scene of an **assassination attempt**, when a squad of North Korean commandos descended from the mountain with the intention of assassinating then-president **Park Chung-hee**. Near the mountain's eastern entrance, beside the gate of **Sukjeongmun**, a tree riddled with bullet holes is evidence of the shootout that occurred when the would-be assassins were sprung. You can now follow in their dubious footsteps, since the mountain was finally reopened to the public in 2006. Understandably, there's still a substantial military presence here, and those wishing to hike in the area must **register** with officials on arrival; photography is also not permitted at certain points.

The **hiking route** across Bugaksan is 3.8km long, and though it gets rather steep at times almost everyone will be able to get up and down in one piece. On the way you'll see remnants of Seoul's fortress wall, which once circled what was then a much smaller city.

Bukhansan National Park

북한산 국립공원

Few major cities can claim to have a national park right on their doorstep, but looming over central Seoul, and forming a natural northern boundary to the city, are the peaks of **Bukhansan National Park** – spears and spines of off-white granite that burst out of the undulating pine forests. While an undeniably beautiful place, its popularity means that trails are often very busy indeed – especially so on warm weekends – and some can be as crowded as shopping mall aisles, hikers literally having to queue up to reach the peaks.

The national park can be split into north and south areas. The southern section – **Bukhansan** proper – overlooks Seoul and is home to the fortress ruins, while 10km to the north is **Dobongsan**, a similar maze of stony peaks and hiking trails. Both offer

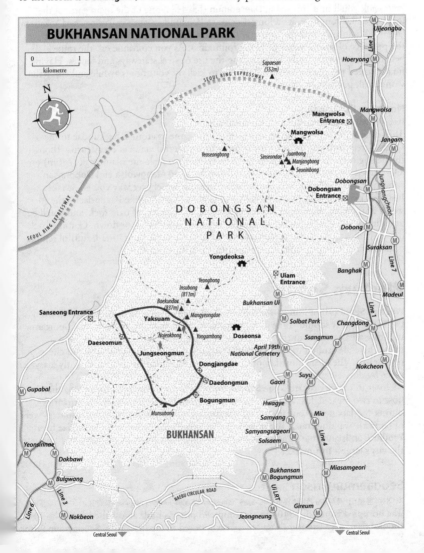

good day-trip routes which are easy enough to be tackled by most visitors, but still enough of a challenge to provide a good work-out. Maps are available at all entrances, and larger signboard versions can be seen at various points en route. Most local hikers choose to wear proper boots, but unless it's rainy a sturdy pair of trainers should suffice.

Southern Bukhansan
Gupabal station (line 3), then bus #704 to park entrance (10min)

The southern half of Bukhansan is best accessed through **Sanseong**, an entry point on the western side of the park. It's around two hours from the entrance to **Baekundae** (백운대; 837m), the highest peak in the park, though note that the masses tramping through Bukhansan have resulted in routes being closed off in rotation to allow them time to regenerate – bilingual signs will point the way. Around ten minutes into your walk you'll find yourself at **Daeseomun** (대서문), one of the main gates of the fortress wall. From here, it's a long slog up to Baekundae; once you've reached **Yaksuam** (약수암), a lofty hermitage, you're almost there (and will doubtless be grateful for the presence of spring-water drinking fountains). As you continue on, the route becomes more precipitous, necessitating the use of steel stairways and fences. Having finally scaled the peak itself, you'll be able to kick off your boots awhile and enjoy the wonderful, panoramic views.

Northern Bukhansan
Mangwolsa and Dobongsan subway (both line 1), then an uphill walk

The scenery in the **Dobongsan** area is much the same as around Baekundae to the south – trees, intriguing rock formations and wonderful views at every turn – though the hiking options are less numerous. Most choose to scale the main peak (740m) on a C-shaped route that curls uphill and down between **Mangwolsa** and **Dobongsan** subway stations. Most hikers start at the latter, but whichever way you go, it takes just over two hours up to the gathering of peaks at the top; like Baeundae to the south of the park, the upper reaches of the trail are patches of bare rock, and you'll be grateful for the steel ropes on which you can haul yourself up or down. Coming back down, you can take a rest at **Mangwolsa** (망월사), a small but rather beautiful temple originally built here in 639, before heading back into Seoul.

Western Seoul

Western Seoul is best known for the huge university area which spreads north from the Hangang. It should come as no surprise to learn that this is the most important nightlife area in the country, with the action going on all through the night – streets here are stuffed to the gills with bars, nightclubs, karaoke rooms and cheap restaurants. The area's most famous component, **Hongdae**, is also a pleasantly artsy place by day.

   Closer to the city centre is the **Seodaemun** district, an unprepossessing area that's host to two great sights: an eponymous **prison** that hosted innumerable atrocities during the Japanese occupation; and **Inwangsan**, a small mountain with a spider's web of fantastic walking trails. The **Hangang** river (see page 87) separates Hongdae from **Yeouido**, an island that's one of Korea's most important business districts, and home to the city's largest fish market.

Seodaemun Prison
서대문 형무소 역사관 · 251 Tongil-ro · Tues–Sun 9.30am–6pm · W3000 · Dongnimmun subway (line 3)

The occupied Korea of 1910–45 saw umpteen prisons built across the land to house thousands of activists and those otherwise opposed to Japanese rule. **Seodaemun Prison**

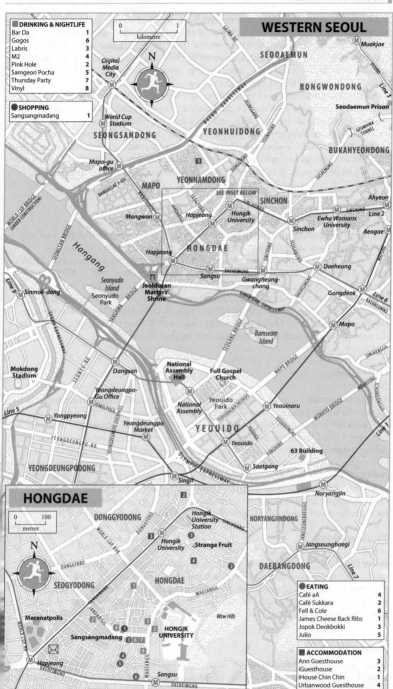

1

WESTERN SEOUL

DRINKING & NIGHTLIFE	
Bar Da	1
Gogos	6
Labris	3
M2	4
Pink Hole	2
Samgeori Pocha	5
Thursday Party	7
Vinyl	8

● SHOPPING	
Sangsangmadang	1

0 — 1
kilometre

N

Digital Media City

SEODAEMUN

Muakjae

BONGWONDONG

Line 3

Seodaemun Prison

GEUMHWA TUNNEL

World Cup Stadium

SEONGSANDONG

YEONHUIDONG

BUKAHYEONDONG

Mapo-gu office

MAPO

YEONNAMDONG

SEE INSET BELOW

SINCHON

Ahyeon

Mangwon

Hapjeong

Hongik University

Ewha Womans University

Line 2

Sinchon

Aeogae

Hapjeong

HONGDAE

DAEHEUNGNO

Daeheung

Hangang

Sangsu

Gwangheung-chang

Seoul

Seonyudo Island
Seonyudo Park

Jeoldusan Martyrs' Shrine

GANGBYEON EXPRESSWAY

Gongdeok

Line 6

BAEKBEOMNO

Sinmok-dong

Line 9

SEONGSAN BRIDGE (UNDER CONSTRUCTION)

WORLD CUP BRIDGE (UNDER CONSTRUCTION)

YANGHWA BRIDGE

SEOGANG BRIDGE

Mapo

SINCHANGGIL

Bamseom Island

Mokdong Stadium

Dangsan

National Assembly Hall

Full Gospel Church

MAPO BRIDGE

WONHYO BRIDGE

Line 1

Yeongdeungpo-Gu Office

JEMULPOGIL

National Assembly

Yeouido Park

Yeouinaru

Line 5

Yangpyeong

Yeongdeungpo Market

YEONGDEUNGPO-RO

YEOUIDO

Yeouido

63 Building

YEONGDEUNGPODONG

OLYMPIC EXPRESSWAY

Saetgang

Singil

Noryangjin

HONGDAE

0 — 100
metres

N

DONGGYODONG

Hongik University Station

NORYANGJINDONG

Jangseungbaegi

SEOGYODONG

Hongik University

Strange Fruit

Hongik University

HONGDAE

DAEBANGDONG

Line 7

Mecenatpolis

WAUSANGIL

Wow Hills

Sangsangmadang

HONGIK UNIVERSITY

Hapjeong

DAEHEUNGNO

Sangsu

DAEHEUNGNO

●EATING	
Café aA	4
Café Sukkara	2
Fell & Cole	6
James Cheese Back Ribs	1
Jopok Deokbokki	3
Julio	5

■ ACCOMMODATION	
Ann Guesthouse	3
iGuesthouse	2
iHouse Chin Chin	1
Urbanwood Guesthouse	4

was by far the most notorious, and the red-brick wings of its main barracks have now been reopened as a "history hall". Photos of the prison during occupation fill the rooms and corridors, together with written material from the period, and some televised documentaries. Few of these exhibits are in English, but the eerie vibe of the buildings themselves needs no translation, from the tiny vertical booths used for "coffin" torture to the lonely outpost where executions were conducted.

One piece of information not conveyed on any signboards, in any language, is the fact that the prison was not only used by the Japanese. Though independent, South Korea only became democratic in the late 1980s, and until then the prison was used to hold political activists and other enemies of the state. It was finally closed in 1987, immediately after the first fully democratic elections. Also absent is any information on the role played by local collaborators during resistance, or on how independence was actually achieved: it was simply part of the package in Japan's surrender to the United States (see page 368).

Inwangsan

인왕산 • Daily 24hr • Free • Dongnimmun subway (line 3), then a 15min walk uphill to Guksadang

Just north of Seodaemun Prison rise the craggy peaks of **Inwangsan**, which you may have noticed flanking the western side of Gyeongbokgung palace (see page 66). Here you'll find a number of **temples**, one of the longest sections of Seoul's old **fortress wall** and some **shamanist shrines**. One of these shrines, **Guksadang** (국사당), forms the main sight here; a boulder-surrounded prayer hall, it hosts at least three shamanist ceremonies known as *gut* (굿) each day, giving visitors a convenient opportunity to take in this surprisingly unheralded facet of Korea's religious make-up. The **peak** of Inwangsan itself (338m) lies a further 1km hike uphill from the shrine, and from here the massif's spider's web of routes continues further north.

Hongdae

홍대

Studenty **Hongdae** is one of the edgiest districts in the whole country, teeming with young and trendy people at almost every hour. The area only truly comes into its own after dark, its hundreds of bars and clubs buzzing with activity every night of the week (see page 110). During the daytime, it's fun to explore the streets lined with small shops selling stylish and secondhand clothing, and there are quirky cafés on every corner.

Hongdae's university itself specializes in the **arts**, a fact that'll be most evident in **Nolita Park** (놀이터 공원) – actually a triangular wedge of ground with almost no greenery – which plays host to anything and everything from punk-rock bands to choreographed street dance. On weekends there's an interesting **flea market** at which local students sell handmade jewellery and other trinkets.

Yeonnamdong

연남동

Seoul has its fair share of new "hipster" areas, but one of the best – and most relevant to overseas visitors – is trendy **Yeonnamdong**, effectively a suburb of Hongdae without the crowds and mass-market chaff. Centered on **Dongjin Market**, which comes to life on weekend markets and specializes in jewellery, its various alleyways are pleasant places for aimless wandering.

Yeouido

South of Hondae is **Yeouido** island, which is important to locals on account of it being Korea's centre of politics – it's home to the National Assembly – and one of Seoul's main business hubs.

1

HANGING ALONG THE HANGANG

The banks of the **Hangang** are a hive of activity, and proof of Seoul's open-all-hours nature: at any time of day or night, you'll see locals riding their **bikes**, puffing and panting on **exercise equipment** or going for a run. However, the river and its banks also offer up a whole raft of other possibilities, the best of which are detailed below.

COFFEE AND COCKTAILS

Six bridges now have stylish cafés at their northern and southern ends, providing great views of the river and the teeming bridge traffic. They're a little tricky to get to, and unless you're on a river walk they're best approached by taxi; all are open daily from 10am–2am, making them equally good spots for an evening cocktail. The Dongjak bridge cafés are particularly recommended, since they provide great views of the sunset, and the Banpo bridge fountain shows (see below).

CYCLING

The Hangang is the most popular spot for cycling in Seoul, and a scoot along the grassy riverbanks constitutes one of the city's most pleasurable and picturesque activities. The main route runs for a whopping 21km between World Cup Stadium to the west (see page 114), and Olympic Park in the east (see page 94). Bikes can be rented from various points along the river, including several in Yeouido Park, for around W3000 an hour.

FOUNTAIN SHOWS

Banpo bridge, located between the Seobinggo and Express Bus Terminal subway stations, plays host to some eye-catching fountain shows from April–Oct. Jets of water burst from the bridge for ten minutes at noon, 2pm, 4pm, 8pm and 9pm (more shows at weekends); the night-time shows are particularly recommended, since the fountains are illuminated in eye-catching colours.

PICNICKING

On balmy summer evenings in Seoul, the Hangang's banks are packed with locals barbecuing meat, throwing back beer and supping *soju* on mats known as *dotjari* (돗자리). These mats, and disposable barbecue sets, are sold for a pittance at most convenience stores close to the river – or just amble along the river looking curious, and you may well get an invite to a *dotjari* party.

SWIMMING

There are seven open-air swimming pools along the Hangang, with those on Yeouido easiest to reach for foreign visitors (see map, p.000). All are open 9am–8pm from June–Aug, and entry costs W5000; note that they may be closed during bad weather.

63 Building

63 빌딩 • 50 63-ro • **63 Art observation deck** daily 10am–10pm • W13,000 • **Aqua Planet** daily 10am–10pm • W21,000 • Ⓦ 63.co.kr • Shuttle buses (every 20–30min; free) from Yeouinaru (line 5) or Yeouido subway (lines 5 & 9)

A short walk south of Wonhyo bridge, the **63 Building** is one of the largest and most notable of Seoul's innumerable towers. A distinctive golden monolith 249m in height, it was the tallest structure in Asia when completed in 1985, though had already lost the title by the time the Olympics rolled into town three years later – today, it's not even in the national top ten. Right at the top of the building, the stylish sixtieth-floor **observation deck**-cum-gallery provides predictably good views of Seoul, while lower levels house the **Aqua Planet** aquarium, home to over twenty thousand sea creatures.

The Full Gospel Church

순복음 교회 • 15 Gukhwa-daero 76-gil • Services most days; check website for details • Ⓦ english.fgtv.com • National Assembly subway (line 9)

Yeouido is also home to the almost sinfully ugly **Full Gospel Church**, by some measures the largest church on earth – it has a membership exceeding one

1

A BANGING GOOD TIME

University areas are a good place to get a grip on the **"bang"** culture that pervades modern Korean life. The term is a suffix meaning "room", and is attached to all sorts of places where locals – and occasional foreigners – like to have fun. Below are a few of the most popular:

DVD-bang Imagine a small room with wipe-clean sofas, tissue paper on hand and a large television for movies – if it sounds a little sleazy, you'd be absolutely right. Though people do occasionally come to appreciate plot, cinematography or Oscar-winning performances, these places are more often used by couples looking for a cheap bit of privacy – going in by yourself, or with a person of the same sex, would draw some baffled looks. Figure on around W11,000 per movie.

Jjimjilbang Popular with families, teenagers and the occasional budget-minded traveller, these steam rooms have sauna rooms, a range of hot and cold pools, and often services from massage treatments to internet booths. Though they might sound dodgy, the reality is somewhat tamer; most are open all night, making them an incredibly cheap way to get a night's sleep – prices tend to be around W6000 (see page 36 for more information).

Noraebang These "singing rooms", found all over the country, are wildly popular with people of all ages; if you have Korean friends, they're bound to invite you, as *noraebang* are usually *sam-cha* in a Korean night out – the "third step" after a meal and drinks. You don't sing in front of a crowd, but in a small room with your friends, where you'll find sofas, a TV, books full of songs to choose from and a couple of maracas or tambourines to play. Foreigners are usually intimidated at first, but after a few drinks it can be tough to get the microphone out of people's hands. Figure on around W20,000 per hour between the group.

million. Obviously, not all of them pop along for prayers at the same time, but to meet the needs of Seoul's huge Protestant population there are no fewer than seven separate Sunday services, translated into sixteen languages. On occasion half of the congregation ends up in tears, as Korean pastors have a habit of ratcheting up the rhetoric.

Noryangjin fish market

노량진 시장 • Daily 24hr; auctions 4–6am • Noryangjin subway (lines 1 & 9)

Dongdaemun (see page 78) and Namdaemun (see page 78) may be the city's best-known markets, but for **seafood** there's only one winner: **Noryangjin**, which remains well off the radar for most foreign visitors. During the evening the place is particularly picturesque – under strings of bright lights, you can wander around whole soggy acres of shells, seaworms, spider crabs and other salty fare. Prime time is early morning, when noisy **fish auctions** are held.

Seonyudo

선유도 • Daily 24hr • Free • Seonyudo subway (line 9), or walkable from Hongdae and Hapjeong over Yanghwa bridge

A tiny island just west of Yeouido, **Seonyudo** was once the site of a gargantuan water treatment plant; gentrified in 2009, it has begun a new lease of life as a strolling and picnicking place. It has since become extremely popular, especially on weekends, when you'll see Seoulites arriving in their hundreds for a spot of cycling rollerblading, or a family meal; stay until evening time to see **Seonyugyo** – a bridge that links Seonyudo to the north and south banks of the Hangang – lit up in pretty colours.

Itaewon and around

이태원

Itaewon has gone through something of a metamorphosis of late. Following the Korean War, it became known for its association with the American military, thanks to the nearby Dragon Hill garrison – after the inevitable red-light district sprang up, it became one of the only places in the country in which "Western" items such as leather jackets, deodorant, tampons or Hershey's Kisses could be found. While the military have now been phased out of the area, the English teachers and other expats stationed here remain, and the bars and restaurants initially aimed at them

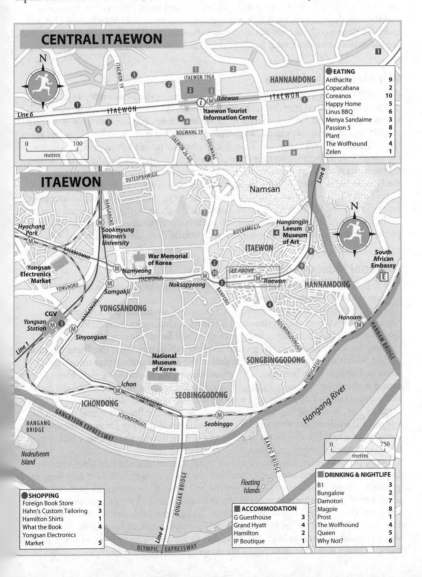

CENTRAL ITAEWON

HANNAMDONG

Itaewon Tourist Information Center

EATING	
Anthacite	9
Copacabana	2
Coreanos	10
Happy Home	5
Linus BBQ	6
Menya Sandaime	3
Passion 5	8
Plant	7
The Wolfhound	4
Zelen	1

ITAEWON

Namsan

Hyochang Park

Sookmyung Women's University

War Memorial of Korea

Hangangjin Leeum Museum of Art

ITAEWON

South African Embassy

Yongsan Electronics Market

Namyeong

Noksapyeong

SEE ABOVE

Itaewon

HANNAMDONG

Samgakji

YONGSANDONG

Hannam

CGV
Yongsan Station

Sinyongsan

National Museum of Korea

SONGBINGGODONG

Hangang River

Ichon

SEOBINGGODONG

SEOBINGGODONG

Seobinggo

HANGANG BRIDGE

ICHONDONG

Nodeulseom Island

Floating Islands

SHOPPING	
Foreign Book Store	2
Hahn's Custom Tailoring	3
Hamilton Shirts	1
What the Book	4
Yongsan Electronics Market	5

ACCOMMODATION	
G Guesthouse	3
Grand Hyatt	4
Hamilton	2
IP Boutique	1

DRINKING & NIGHTLIFE	
B1	3
Bungalow	2
Damotori	7
Magpie	8
Prost	1
The Wolfhound	4
Queen	5
Why Not?	6

1

have increasingly found favour with Koreans themselves. As such, Itaewon is not the "foreign ghetto" it once was, more a sort of north-of-the-river Gangnam, with cosmopolitan eateries, high prices – and little to actually see. Still, it's worth popping by, especially for a night out.

Leeum Museum of Art

리움미술관 • 60-16 Itaewon-ro 55-gil • Tues–Sun 10.30am–6pm • W10,000, plus W7000 for special exhibitions • ⓦ leeum. samsungfoundation.org • Hangangjin or Itaewon (both line 6)

The excellent **Leeum Museum of Art** is not so much a museum as one of the most esteemed galleries in the country. It's split into several halls, each with a distinctive and original design; one, built in black concrete, was designed by acclaimed Dutch architect Rem Koolhaas. The museum hosts the occasional special exhibition of world-famous artists, including such luminaries as Mark Rothko and Damien Hirst.

War Memorial of Korea

전쟁기념관 • 29 Itaewon-ro • Tues– Sun 9.30am–5.30pm • Free • ⓦ warmemo.or.kr • Samgakji subway (lines 4 & 6)

To the west of central Itaewon is the **War Memorial Museum**, a huge venue that charts the history of Korean warfare from ancient stones and arrows to more modern machinery. The museum's park-like periphery is riddled with B-52 bombers and other flying machines; with some, you'll be able to clamber up ladders to cockpit windows for a look inside. Before entering the main building itself, look for the names written on the outer wall: these are the names of every known member of Allied forces who died in the **Korean War**, and the list seems to go on forever. This is particularly heart-wrenching when you consider the fact that a far greater number of people, unmarked here, died on the Chinese and North Korean side – in total, the war claimed over two million souls. After all this, the main hall itself is a little disappointing, but you'll find plenty of exhibits and video displays relaying information about the Korean War.

National Museum of Korea

국립 중앙 박물관 • 137 Seobinggo-ro • Mon, Tues, Thurs & Fri 10am–6pm, Wed & Sat 10am–9pm, Sun 10am–7pm • Free • ⓦ museum.go.kr • Ichon subway (line 4 & Jungang line)

The huge **National Museum of Korea** is a Seoul must-see for anyone interested in history. It houses over eleven thousand artefacts, including an incredible 94 official National Treasures, but only a fraction of these will be on show at any one time. Among the many rooms on the ground level are exhibitions from the **Three Kingdoms** period, which showcase the incredible skill of the artisans during that time – gold, silver and bronze have been cast into ornate shapes, the highlight being a fifth-century crown and belt set that once belonged to a Silla king. Move up a floor and the focus shifts to paintings, calligraphy and wooden art, and there's usually a colossal **Buddhist scroll** or two, over 10m high; some were hung behind the Buddha statue in temples' main halls, while others were used for such purposes as praying for rain. The museum owns quite a few, but due to the fragility of the material, they're put on a rota system and displays are changed regularly.

The uppermost floor contains countless metal sculptures and a beautiful assortment of pots – some of these are over a thousand years old, though look as if they were made yesterday. From this floor you'll also get the best view of the museum's pride and joy, a ten-storey stone **pagoda** that sits in the main museum hall on the ground level and stretches almost all the way to the top floor. It's in remarkable condition for something that was taken apart by the Japanese in 1907, hauled overseas then all the way back some years later; from on high, you'll be able to appreciate more fully its true size, and the difficulties this must have posed for the people who built it.

Southern Seoul

Meaning "South of the River", **Gangnam** (강남) is the name for a huge swathe of land south of the Hangang, and an all-encompassing term for several distinct city districts. Before Seoul outgrew its boundaries and spread over most of the northwest of the country, the city's southern perimeter ran through Namsan, north of the river – and, accordingly, the capital's historical sights become sparser on the south side of the Han river. Still, to appreciate just how life ticks along in this fine city you'd do well to spend some time here.

Bongeunsa is the most enchanting temple in Southern Seoul, while just down the road, are the **royal tombs** in **Samneung Park**, the grassy resting place of a few dynastic kings and queens. In terms of modern-day attractions, there's **Coex**, a large underground shopping mall, and **Lotte World**, a colossal theme park. However, southern Seoul is perhaps best viewed as a window into modern Korean society – the teeming streets surrounding Gangnam station are pulsating with neon and noise, and loomed over by innumerable tower blocks rising into the heavens. In addition, the restaurants, cafés and **boutique shops** of the classy **Apgujeong** district are without doubt the costliest and most exclusive in the land.

Samsung D'light

삼성 딜라이트 • 11 Seochodae-ro 74-gil • Mon–Sat 10am–7pm • Free • Gangnam subway (line 2)

The Gangnam station area has precious little in the way of sights. The single exception is **Samsung D'light**, a showroom of sorts for electronic goodies produced by Samsung, Korea's largest company. It's the place to come if you want a sneak preview of the gadgets that will be racing around the world in the near future.

Samneung Park

삼릉공원 • 1 Seolleung-ro 100-gil • Tues–Sun 6am–9pm • W1000 • Seolleung subway (line 2)

During the Three Kingdoms period and beyond, deceased Korean royalty were buried in highly distinctive **grass mounds**. While these are more numerous elsewhere in Korea – notably the former Silla capital Gyeongju way down in the southeast of the country (see page 186), or the Baekje capitals of Gongju (see page 276) and Buyeo (see page 281) – closer to the capital, Seoul has a few of its own. The easiest to reach are in **Samneung Park**, which is within walking distance of Gangnam station.

The park's name means "Three Mounds". One was for **King Seongjong** (ruled 1469–94), an esteemed leader who invited political opponents to have a say in national government. Two of his sons went on to rule: **Yeonsangun** (ruled 1494–1506) undid much of his father's hard work in a system of revenge-driven purges, and was overthrown to leave his half-brother **Jungjong** (ruled 1506–44) in control. Jungjong's mound can also be found in the park, as can one created to house one of Seongjong's wives. For all the history, it's the prettiness of the park itself that appeals to many visitors, a green refuge from grey Seoul crisscrossed by gorgeous tree-shaded **pathways**.

The Coex complex

코엑스 • 513 Yeongdong-daero • **Mall** Daily 10.30am–10pm • ⓦ coexmall.com • **Aquarium** Daily 10am–8pm • W28,000 • ⓦ coexaqua.com • Samseong subway (line 2)

The **Coex complex** houses a huge assortment of shops, restaurants, cafés, offices and a couple of five-star hotels. One of the few sizeable covered spaces in the whole city, its large underground **mall** attracts Seoulites in their droves when the weather is inclement, and special mention must be made of its large and incredibly well-designed bookstore (though it has no English-language books at all). The complex is also home

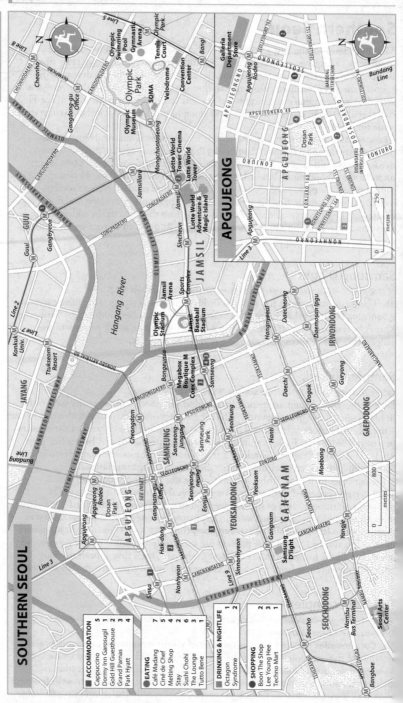

to the **Coex Aquarium** (코엑스 아쿠아리엄), which has been designed rather unusually – it must be the only aquarium in the world to use toilets as goldfish tanks, though mercifully there are normal facilities for public use. Sharks, manta rays and colourful shoals of smaller fish are on display.

Bongeunsa

봉은사 • 531 Bongeunsa-ro • Daily 24hr • Free • Bongeunsa subway (line 9)

Sitting directly across from the north face of COEX is **Bongeunsa**, the most appealing major Buddhist temple in Seoul. Despite an incongruous location amid a plethora of skyscrapers, this is a fairly decent rendition of a Korean temple; like Jogyesa, its uglier sibling to the north of the river (see page 70), it's affiliated to the **Jogye sect**, the largest Buddhist denomination in Korea. There has been a temple here since the late eighth century, but assorted fires and invasions mean that all of its buildings are of fairly recent vintage; still, it's worth peeking at its gorgeous main hall and clutch of small yet appealing outer buildings.

Apgujeong

압구정

Seoulites refer to **Apgujeong** as "Korea's Beverly Hills", and the comparison is both appropriate and ridiculous. If Louis Vuitton bags are your thing, look no further, though the tiny lanes hereabouts dash most thoughts of glamour, with expensive cars inching their way around in a manner unbecoming of luxury. Clothing boutiques, chic restaurants and European-style outdoor cafés line streets frequented by a disproportionate number of Seoul's young and beautiful, but note that their good looks may not be entirely natural – this is also Korea's plastic surgery capital, and clinics are ubiquitous. Though there are no real sights as such, Apgujeong is one of the most interesting places in Korea to sit down with a skinny latte and people-watch.

The best cafés and restaurants huddle in a pleasantly relaxed, leafy area outside the main entrance to **Dosan Park** (도산 공원). Heading further north, past the clothes shops and plastic surgeons, you'll eventually come out onto **Apgujeongno**, the area's main road, which features the most exclusive clothes shops and department stores in Korea (see page 115).

Garosugil

가로수길 • Sinsa station (line 3)

West of Dosan Park, though actually far closer to Sinsa station, is **Garosugil**, a particularly trendy street studded with hip cafés and sharp designer boutiques. Its name literally means "tree-lined street", bestowed on account of the roadside lines of gorgeous ginkgo trees, whose spectacular golden foliage makes this a superb place to stroll in Seoul's all-too-short autumn.

Lotte World

롯데월드 • Daily 9.30am–11pm • Lotte World Adventure W46,000, W26,000 after 4pm or W17,000 after 7pm; Lotte Water Park W35,000 or W30,000 after 2pm; Lotte World Tower W27,000 or W50,000 for fast track • ⓦ lotteworld.com • Jamsil subway (line 2 & 8)

This local version of Disneyland is incredibly popular – the **Lotte World** complex receives over five million visitors per year, and it's hard to find a Korean child, or even an adult, who hasn't been here at some point. While it may not be quite what some are looking for on their visit to "The Land of Morning Calm", Lotte World can be a lot of fun, particularly for those travelling with children. It comprises two theme parks: the indoor section is known as **Lotte World Adventure**, and this is connected by monorail to **Lotte Water Park**, an outdoor section located in the middle of a lake, and also home

1

to a spa. Also within the complex are a bowling alley, an overpriced ice rink and a large swimming pool.

The newest addition is **Lotte World Tower**, 555m tall and the fifth-highest building in the world at the time of writing; it's surprisingly elegant for its height, and visible from much of Seoul. They've gone a bit overkill with their observation levels – there's one on the 117th floor, a glass-floor sky deck on the 118th, a café on the 119th, a sky terrace on the 120th, and a shop, café and sky lounge spread between the 121st and 123rd floors – so you'll have plenty to keep you occupied.

Olympic Park

올림픽공원 • Daily 24hr • Free • Bikes W3000 per hour • Olympic Park Mongcheontoseong (line 8) or Olympic Park subway (line 5)

Built for the **1988 Summer Olympics**, this large **park** remains a popular picnicking place for Seoul families, and hosts a regular roster of small-scale municipal festivals; you're likely to see one if you turn up on a weekend. It's a very large place, around 2km square, and it's possible to **rent bikes** at the two main entrances. The **Olympic Stadium** itself is actually a few subway stops to the west (immediately north of Sports Complex station).

Seoul Grand Park and around

서울대공원 • 102 Daegongwongwangjang-ro • **Park** Daily 9.30am–9pm • Free • **Zoo** Daily 9am–6pm • W5000 • ⓦ grandpark.seoul.go.kr • Seoul Grand Park subway (line 4)

Seven subway stops south of the Hangang is **Seoul Grand Park**, one of the largest expanses of greenery in Seoul, and one of the best places to take children for a fun day out. There is a **zoo**, home to a diverse variety of animals from around the world, and, thankfully, several leagues above par for such venues in Asia. There are dolphin shows as well as other animal performances.

Elsewhere in the park is **Seoul Land** (서울랜드), a large amusement park with an abundance of roller coasters and spinning rides – around forty of them, at the last count. Like Lotte World, this is one of the most popular draws in the country for domestic tourists – they average almost three million visitors each year, and it's hard to find a Korean who hasn't been at least once.

National Museum of Contemporary Art

국립미술관 • March–Oct Mon–Fri 10am–6pm, Sat & Sun 10am–9pm; Nov–Feb Tues–Fri 10am–5pm, Sat & Sun 10am–8pm • Admission price varies by exhibition, usually W3000–10,000 • ⓦ mmca.go.kr • Seoul Grand Park subway (line 4), then a 15min walk or tram ride (W1000)

Nestled into the Seoul Grand Park area is the **National Museum of Contemporary Art**, an excellent collection of works by some of the biggest movers and shakers in the Korean modern art scene. It's affiliated to the facilities of the same name in central Seoul (see pages 68 and 75), though here the focus is on visual arts rather than paintings and sculpture – architecture, design and craft all get a look-in here.

ARRIVAL AND DEPARTURE   **SEOUL**

Korea has one of the best public transport systems in the whole world, and it should come as no surprise to learn that Seoul is extremely well connected to the rest of the country. However, given the choice, it's often best to leave or arrive **by train** – the stations are far more central than the bus terminals, which are rather confusing entities to boot, while trains themselves are more impervious to the traffic that occasionally snarls up the capital's access roads.

BY PLANE

INCHEON INTERNATIONAL AIRPORT

The vast majority of international planes to Korea touch down at Incheon International Airport (인천 공항), which sits in curvy, chrome-and-glass splendour on an

island about 50km west of central Seoul. The capital is the first and last Korean city that most foreign visitors see, and the main options linking it with the airport are buses, trains and taxis. Buses race all around the country from the airport – if you're headed elsewhere, there's usually no need to transit in Seoul.

Onward travel by bus There are umpteen services to destinations all over the capital (45min–1hr 30min; W10,000–15,000), and express buses to cities (even small ones) across the land – the airport's many information desks will let you know which one to catch.

Onward travel by train The AREX train (ⓦ www.arex. or.kr) heads to Seoul station several times an hour (1hr; around W4000), via Gimpo Airport and Hongdae; most services are subway-like in nature, though once an hour a more comfy train makes a direct run to Seoul station (43min; W9000). KTX high-speed train services now run direct from the airport – it's not worth taking these if you're only going to Seoul (it costs W12,500, and this stretch of line is no faster than the AREX), but they're worth considering if you're headed to Daejeon, Mokpo, Busan, Gangneung and the like.

Onward travel by taxi It's not all that expensive to travel to or from Seoul by taxi, especially if you're in a group; figure on W65,000–110,000 depending upon the time of day and your Seoul departure or arrival point, and don't be afraid to haggle. Black "deluxe" taxis are more expensive, and not worth the extra money.

GIMPO AIRPORT

Most domestic services run from Gimpo Airport (김포공항), which sits about halfway from the capital to Incheon Airport. Services have been scaled down since the expansion of the high-speed rail, bar the one to Jeju Island – the world's busiest air route (see page 308).

Destinations Busan (1–2 hourly; 1hr); Gwangju (2 daily; 50min); Jeju City (every 5–15min; 1hr 5min); Jinju (3 daily; 55min); Yeosu (4 daily; 55min).

Onward travel From Gimpo, plenty of bus services head into Seoul (around W7000; ask at information booths for the most appropriate one), while it's also a stop on the AREX train line to Seoul station (25min), via Hongdae. A taxi into town from Gimpo will be W30,000–50,000, depending on your destination and the time of day.

INFORMATION

Airport information The information line for both Incheon Airport (ⓦ airport.kr) and Gimpo Airport (ⓦ airport.co.kr) is ☎ 02 1577 2600, and there are excellent info-booths at both airports.

BY TRAIN

There are four main stations in Seoul, with trains generally heading south from the two biggest ones, Seoul station and Yongsan station. The line splits just north of Daejeon – trains heading to the southwest almost exclusively depart from Yongsan station, while those heading to the southeast do so from Seoul station. Smaller Cheongnyangni station generally deals with

trains heading to the east, and slower trains to the southeast. On most lines you'll have a choice of train classes, which vary in speed and price (see page 30 for more information). The durations between Seoul and the major cities listed below are for the fastest, most direct services; some KTX trains make more stops than others, and there are usually cheaper, slower options; see the Korail website (ⓦ letskorail.com) for schedules.

SEOUL STATION

Gleaming Seoul station (서울역), on subway lines 1 & 4, has startlingly regular services – most of them high-speed – towards Busan.

Destinations Busan (every 10–30min; 2hr 45min); Cheonan (every 10–40min; 50min); Daegu (every 10–30min; 1hr 50min); Daejeon (every 10–30min; 1hr); Gangneung (hourly; 2hr); Gyeongju (hourly; 2hr 5min); Suwon (every 20–40min; 30min).

YONGSAN STATION

Yongsan station (용산역) is just two stops from Seoul on subway line 1, and three on line 4; exit at Sinyongsan station for the latter. Services aren't quite as frequent as from Seoul station, but you'll rarely be waiting long.

Destinations Cheonan (every 15–40min; 1hr); Daecheon (hourly; 2hr 30min); Daejeon (Seodaejeon station; every 10–30min; 1hr); Gwangju (1–2 hourly; 1hr 45min); Jeonju (1–2 hourly; 1hr 40min); Mokpo (1–2 hourly; 2hr 30min); Suwon (every 20–40min; 30min).

CHEONGNYANGNI STATION

Seoul's third station is Cheongnyangni (청량리역), a short way to the east on subway line 1; this is the terminus of slow lines from Gangwon and Gyeongsang, and a stop on the new KTX line to Gangneung.

Destinations Andong (6 daily; 3hr 30min); Busan (Bujeon station; 1 daily; 7hr); Chuncheon (1–2 hourly; 1hr); Danyang (6 daily; 2hr 20min); Jeongdongjin (6 daily; 5hr 30min).

SUSEO STATION

Lastly, there's the new Suseo station on line 3 and the Bundang line; this hosts high-speed SRT services (ⓦ srail. co.kr; most info in Korean only), which are similar to KTX but independent of Korail, and are worth considering if you're headed to or from the Gangnam area, since they're often cheaper and faster.

Destinations Busan (1–2 hourly; 2hr 25min); Daegu (2–3 hourly; 1hr 40min); Daejeon (2–3 hourly; 55min); Gwangju (1–2 hourly; 1hr 40min); Mokpo (9 daily; 2hr 20min).

BY BUS

When travelling to or from other Korean cities by bus, you have a choice of Seoul terminals: most buses head to either the express bus terminal (고속 버스 터미널) on the south side of the river (subway lines 3, 7 & 9), or Dong-Seoul terminal (동서울 버스 터미널) to the east of town on line 2 (Gangbyeon station). There's also the smaller Nambu terminal (남부 버스 터미널), a few stations south of the express terminal on line 3. To find out which one is best for you, ask at a tourist information office, or call the foreigners' helpline on ☎ 1330 (with area code if calling from a mobile phone).

EXPRESS BUS TERMINAL

This mammoth venue – often referred to as "Gangnam" (강남) on departure boards around the land – has connections to most destinations around the country. It's made up of three different terminals: the Gyeongbu side serves areas to the southeast of Seoul, and the Honam building across the way serves the southwest, while the smaller Yeongdong terminal has buses to more local destinations in Gyeonggi province.

Destinations (Gyeongbu section) Busan (every 30min; 4hr 15min); Cheonan (every 10min; 1hr); Daegu (every 20min; 3hr 30min); Daejeon (every 15min; 2hr); Gongju (every 40min; 1hr 50min); Gyeongju (hourly; 3hr 45min); Pohang (every 20min; 4hr); Tongyeong (hourly; 4hr 10min).

Destinations (Honam section) Daecheon (hourly; 2hr 10min); Gwangju (every 10min; 3hr 30min); Jeonju (every 10min; 2hr 40min); Mokpo (every 45min; 4hr); Sokcho (every 30min; 2hr 30min); Wando (4 daily; 5hr); Yeosu (every 40min; 4hr 30min).

DONG-SEOUL TERMINAL

The equally huge Dong-Seoul terminal is the main launching point for intercity buses, but also hosts a bunch of express services.

Destinations (express section) Busan (11 daily; 4hr 20min); Daegu (every 30min; 3hr 40min); Daejeon (every 20min; 2hr); Gangneung (every 30min; 2hr 30min); Gwangju (every 20–30min; 4hr); Jeonju (every 30min; 2hr 50min); Jinju (5 daily; 3hr 50min); Samcheok (13 daily; 3hr).

Destinations (intercity section) include: Andong (every 20min; 2hr 50min); Busan (5 daily; 3hr 30min); Buyeo (8 daily; 2hr 30min); Cheonan (every 15min; 1hr 20min); Chuncheon (every 15min; 1hr 10min); Danyang (hourly; 2hr 30min); Gangneung (every 30min; 2hr 30min); Gongju (12 daily; 2hr 10min); Guinsa (12 daily; 3hr); Gyeongju (18 daily; 4hr); Haeundae (14 daily; 5hr 30min); Incheon (every 20min; 1hr 10min); Jeongdongjin (3 daily; 3hr 10min); Sokcho (every 20min; 2hr 20min); Songnisan (hourly; 3hr 30min); Taebaek (every 30min; 3hr 10min).

NAMBU TERMINAL

The smallest of Seoul's three main bus terminals is also the easiest to navigate, and hosts services to a seemingly random collection of destinations down south, including many of the same locations as the larger terminals.

Destinations Anmyeondo (12 daily; 3hr); Buyeo (every 30min; 2hr); Daecheon (3 daily; 2hr 50min); Gongju (every 50min; 1hr 30min); Jeonju (every 30min; 2hr 40min); Jinju (every 30min; 3hr 40min); Muju (5 daily; 2hr 30min); Songnisan (3 daily; 3hr 30min); Tongyeong (every 30min; 4hr 30min).

GETTING AROUND

Seoul is covered by a cheap, clean and highly comprehensive **public transport** system – the subway network is one of the best developed in the world, not least because of the sheer number of workers it has to speed from A to B. Buses dash around the city every which way, and even taxis are cheap enough to be viable for many routes. If you're staying in the city for more than a few days, invest in a **transport card** (see page 97), which saves you time waiting in ticket queues, and a little cash too.

BY SUBWAY

With nine underground lines, nine light-rail lines and over three hundred stations, Seoul's subway system is one of the most comprehensive on the planet – in the area bounded by the circular 2 line, you'll never be more than a short walk or taxi ride from the nearest station, while line 1 runs for a whole third of the country's length, stretching well over 100km from Soyosan in the north to Sinchang in the south.

Fares Ticket prices are reasonable, starting at W1350 for rides of less than 10km (W100 less if you use a travel card); this will get you almost everywhere you need to go in the centre, though even for further-flung locations it's very rare for the price to rise above W2000.

Buying tickets Unless you've invested in a transport card (highly recommended; see page 97), you'll have to buy a single-use card from a machine; though the operating system is a little curious, you should get there in the end. Each card

requires a deposit of W500, retrievable from machines outside the turnstiles when you've completed your journey.

Maps The subway system itself is very user-friendly: network maps are conveniently located around the stations, which are easily navigable with multilingual signs. You'll find maps of the surrounding area on walls near the station exits, though be warned that north only faces upwards a quarter of the time, since each map is oriented to the direction that it happens to be facing.

Operating hours The subway runs from around 5.30am to midnight, and trains are extremely frequent, though some lines are packed to bursting point at rush hour; services finish slightly earlier on weekends.

BY BUS

In comparison with the almost idiot-proof subway system, Seoul's bus network often proves too complicated

1

TRANSPORT CARDS AND PASSES

Transport cards such as T-Money or Cashbee are sold from W2500 at all subway stations, and some street-level kiosks. After loading them with credit (easiest at machines in the subway station), you'll save W50–100 on each subway or bus journey, and any remaining balance can be refunded at the end of your stay. These cards make it possible to switch at no extra cost from bus to subway – or vice versa – should you need to. In addition, you can use them to pay **taxi fares**, make **phone calls** from most streetside booths, and even pay your bill at **convenience stores**, plus they're useable for such purposes clean across the land (many cities have their own cards, but T-Money and Cashbee work nationwide). These cards often come in different forms, such as dongles one can attach to a smartphone.

Special **tourist cards** are also available (W15,000 for one day, up to W64,500 for one week), though they're a little ludicrous – you'd have to be doing an awful lot of travelling to make them value for money.

for foreign guests – English-language signage and announcements exist, but can be confusing all the same. Routes are given at almost every stop, though often in Korean only, or with only the main subway stations listed in English.

Bus types Buses are split into four coloured categories: blue buses travel long distances along major arterial roads; green buses are for shorter hops; red ones travel to the suburbs; and yellow (or sometimes small green) ones use tight loop routes.

Fares Tickets start at W1250 for blue and green buses, W2300 for red buses and W1100 for yellow buses, increasing on longer journeys; cash is no longer accepted on most buses, so travel cards are the way to go (see page 97), but always be sure to touch out at the end of your trip. Handily, a bus-plus-subway-plus-bus journey often counts as just one trip.

BY TAXI

As in every Korean city, Seoul's taxis are cheap and ubiquitous. You should never have to wait long for a cab, though when the subway starts to shut down at night, hawker cabs emerge, quoting far higher prices. Drivers do not expect tips, but it's also unlikely that they'll speak any English – having your destination written in *hangeul* is the easiest way to get the information across, though drivers are able to phone interpreters for no extra charge.

Fares A W3000 fare covers the first 2km, and goes up in W100 increments every 142m – given that bus and subway fares start at W1200 or so, it often works out almost as cheap for groups of three or four to travel short distances

by cab rather than public transport. Note that a twenty percent surcharge is added between midnight and 4am.

Mobeom cabs There are also deluxe *mobeom* cabs, which are black with yellow lights on top; these usually congregate around expensive hotels, charging W5000 for the first 3km and W200 for each additional 164m.

Smartphone apps Uber *has* existed in Seoul, but lobbying from taxi unions was severely complicating matters at the time of writing – it's worth checking to see whether the service is still in use. These days almost every Seoulite has the Kakao T taxi app, which alerts regular cabs to your presence, and brings them to your feet; in certain areas, at certain times of day, it'll be hard to hail a cab without it.

ON FOOT

Busy roads mean that walking through Seoul is rarely pleasurable, though getting around on foot is possible in some areas: Insadonggil is closed to traffic for most of the day; the shopping district of Myeongdong and club-heavy Hongdae are so swamped with people that vehicles tend to avoid these areas; and there are innumerable malls and underground shopping arcades. Special mention must be made of river banks, most pertinently the Hangang (see page 87) and the delightful Cheonggyecheon stream (see page 71), which often make grand walking territory.

BY BIKE

Riding a bike is only really advisable on specially designed routes along the river (see page 87 for further details).

INFORMATION

Seoul is dotted with **information booths**, all of which can dole out maps of the city, and help out with transportation enquiries, or information about attractions. Wherever you are in Korea, you can also make use of a supremely useful **dedicated foreigners' helpline** – just dial ☎ 1330 (with area code if calling from a mobile phone or abroad).

K-Style Hub 40 Cheonggyecheonno ☎ 02 729 9457. On the second-floor level of the Korea Tourist Organization's

HQ, this is the largest and most info-packed tourist office in town. They're able to help with anything from

SEOUL SUBWAY

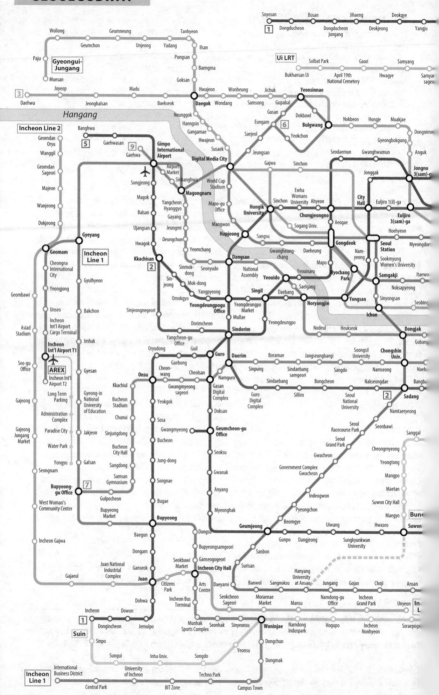

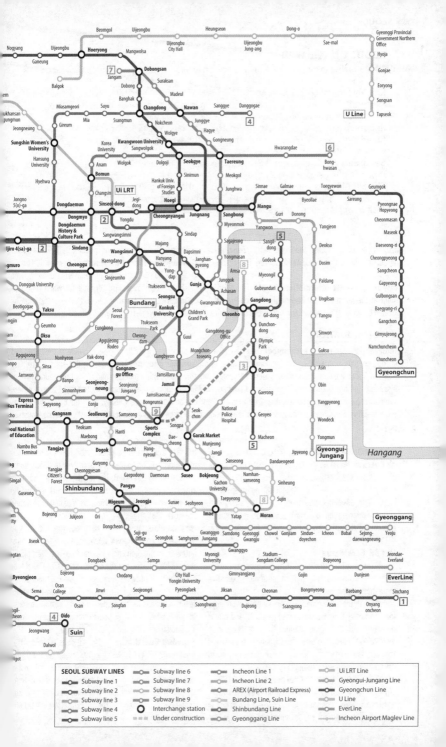

SEOUL ON THE WEB

10 Magazine ⓦ 10mag.com. A fun publication with good listings sections for Seoul and other Korean cities.

Kiss My Kimchi ⓦ kissmykimchi.com. Originally a food blog, with a pleasingly user-friendly interface, this has branched out in other directions of late, and includes good culture and shopping sections, as well as practical advice for those living in Seoul.

Roboseyo ⓦ roboseyo.blogspot.com. Expat blog that takes an often-offbeat view of Seoul society.

Seoul ⓦ magazine.seoulselection.com. City-sponsored magazine that's usually much more interesting than its name may suggest.

Seoul Eats ⓦ seouleats.com. Food blog with an admirable selection of restaurant reviews, though not updated as frequently as it once was.

The Seoul Times ⓦ theseoultimes.com. Though the news itself is stale to say the least, the site has good job listings and is a useful place to hunt for flatmates.

Visit Seoul ⓦ english.visitseoul.net. The official tourist site of Seoul's city government.

accommodation to tours, and have handy pamphlets detailing sights nationwide. English spoken. Daily 9am–8pm.

Insadong Tourist Information Center Yulgongno. Right at the north end of Insadonggil, and conveniently located for an array of surrounding sights, this small office can help with basic sightseeing queries. Daily 9am–6pm.

Myeongdong Tourist Information Center 66 Euljiro ☎ 02 778 0333. The largest of Seoul city's own array of tourist offices, though also very helpful when trying to glean advice for destinations around the country. English-speakers always on hand. Daily 9am–8pm.

ACCOMMODATION

Those seeking high-quality **accommodation** have a wealth of places to choose from in Seoul, while at the lower end of the price spectrum are the city's ballooning number of **backpacker guesthouses**. There are five-stars around City Hall and Gangnam, upper-class venues around Myeongdong, some good mid-rangers in and around the tourist hive of Insadong, and hostel clusters in Hongdae and Daehangno. **Motels** form a cheap alternative to official tourist hotels, sometimes having rooms of comparable size and quality, and can be found all over the city, while the Bukchon area has some traditional wooden guesthouses. **Airbnb** is an option, but beware places at the very cheapest end of the scale (see page 36).

GYEONGBOKGUNG AND AROUND

★ **Bukchon Maru** 북촌 마루 152 Changdeokgung-gil ☎ 02 744 8571, ⓦ bukchonmaru.com; Anguk subway; map p.64. Presided over by a delightful, English-speaking local couple, this *hanok* guesthouse is a homely affair, with granny whipping up breakfast (included), and guests encouraged to get to know each other. A lovely choice. W110,000

Haemil Guesthouse 해밀 게스트하우스 15-14 Yulgok-ro 10-gil ☎ 070 8950 1546, ⓦ haemilguesthouse.com; Anguk subway; map p.64. A touch more expensive than most *hanok* guesthouses in the area, though just about worth the extra expense on account of a wonderful location facing Jongmyo shrine (see page 72), and rooms decorated with even more attention to detail. Prices drop by W20,000 during the week, and a Korean breakfast is included (though they're more like Korean lunches – you can ask for a Western one instead). W120,000

★ **Hide & Seek Guesthouse** 하이덴식 게스트하우스 14 Jahamun-ro 6-gil ☎ 02 6925 5916, ⓦ hidenseek.co.kr; Anguk subway; map p.64. Set in a building dating from the Japanese occupation period, this is a truly charming place – the family who runs it makes every effort to please, especially with their yummy breakfasts (W7000 extra). The rooms are cosy, and there are sunloungers on the wide patio area, which is grand for an evening drink, too. Prices drop by W20,000 or so during the week. W80,000

★ **Rakkojae** 락고재 49-23 Gyedong-gil ☎ 02 742 3410, ⓦ rkj.co.kr; Anguk subway; map p.64. The most authentic of Bukchon's *hanoks*, character-wise. Not only is it an 1870s original, but the owners serve traditional food for dinner – a little like a Japanese *ryokan*. Studded with maple and pine trees, the courtyard is divine, with precious few concessions to the modern day; it's best appreciated at night, when soft light pours through the paper doors. Traditional breakfast included. W300,000

Sopoong Guesthouse 소풍 게스트하우스 10-Hyoja-ro 7-gil ☎ 010 6833 9159; Anguk subway; map p.64. A tiny place with only three rooms, this *hanok* guesthouse has proven a real winner with international guests. The owner will do everything possible to ensure that guests are happy – the breakfasts are particularly nice. W85,000

INSADONG AND AROUND

Doulos 돌로스 호텔 22 Supyo-ro 18-gil ☎ 02 2266 2244, ⓦ douloshotel.com; Jongno 3-ga subway; map p.71. Excellent value, comfy rooms, friendly staff and a convenient location... this mid-range hotel ticks all the boxes, even if it's a little tricky to find: take a few steps south of Jongno and you should be able to make out its sign. Usually gives discounts if booking online. W120,000

Hostel Korea 11th 호스텔 코리아 11th 85 Donhwamun-ro ☎ 070 4705 1900, ⓦ cdg.hostelkorea. com; Anguk subway; map p.71. High-rise hostel just down the road from the palace of Changdeokgung (see page 69). It's a trendy place with a café-like lobby area, and is often full on account of its popularity with tourists from other Asian countries. The rack rates for private rooms are ridiculous – they usually go for W45,000 on weekdays. Dorms W22,000, doubles W105,000

Icon 아이콘 호텔 20 Samil-daero 32-gil ☎ 02 766 3438; Anguk or Jongno 3-ga subway; map p.71. Many motels have restyled themselves as hotels in the Ikseondong area, some more successfully than most. This one is great value, especially since it's pretty much the only one to serve breakfast (included in rates, and not at all bad); it's also bookable on international accommodation engines. W40,000

Noble 노블 관광 호텔 13-3 Yulgok-ro 6-gil ☎ 02 742 4025, ⓦ noblehotel.co.kr; Anguk subway; map p.71. One of the least seedy options in this convenient, highly atmospheric area – unlike many of its neighbours, rooms here are not rentable by the hour. Some are rather small, but they're quiet, stylish and kept at the right temperature. W60,000

★ **Orakai Suites** 오라카이 스위츠 18 Insadong 4-gil ☎ 02 6262 8888, ⓦ orakaihotels.com; Jongno 3-ga subway; map p.71. Plush serviced residence, with rates starting at W6,500,000 per month for a single-bedroom suite. Also on site are a gym and swimming pool, as well as a rooftop driving range for golfers. The location, just off Insadonggil, is hard to beat. W300,000

Sheel 쉴 모텔 10 Supyo-ro 18-gil ☎ 02 2278 9993; Jongno 3-ga subway; map p.71. Something of a "high-end" love motel, filling its rooms with all sorts of interesting quirks. Lace curtains billow from the ceilings, projectors fill whole walls with computer or televisual output, and some bathrooms are decked out in the style of a sauna; there's free coffee and popcorn at reception (and condoms in the rooms). You can usually cut the price in half if checking in after 9pm. W100,000

Venue G 베뉴지 호텔 117 Cheonggyecheon-ro ☎ 02 2223 6500; Jongno 3-ga subway; map p.71. One of precious few hotels overlooking the Cheonggyecheon creek (see page 71), this has passed through several owners of late – and at least three different names. Only twin rooms face the stream, and these are the hotel's best in any case. Book online for discounts. W175,000

GWANGHWAMUN AND CITY HALL

First Stay 퍼스트 스테이 호텔 37 Namdaemun-ro 1-gil ☎ 02 756 1500; City Hall subway; map p. 74. Affordable option in the City Hall area, with rooms which are undeniably a little on the small side, but certainly cosy enough for a good night's sleep. Breakfast included. W70,000

★ **Westin Chosun** 웨스틴 조선 106 Sogong-ro ☎ 02 771 0500, ⓦ echosunhotel.com; City Hall subway; map p.74. Serious effort has been put into making this the most appealing hotel in central Seoul, with one of Korea's best swimming pools. An energetic group of knowledgeable staff preside over rooms that eschew the typical Korean concrete blockiness for plush carpets and curved sofas – even the bathrooms are graced with modern art, and a free mobile phone will be yours for the duration of your stay. Prices often fall to W250,000. W440,000

MYEONGDONG AND DONGDAEMUN

★ **Metro** 메트로 호텔 14 Myeongdong 2-gil ☎ 02 752 1112, ⓦ metrohotel.co.kr; Euljiro 1-ga subway; map p.77. A modern, squeaky-clean hotel away from the bustling Myeongdong main roads, where the staff are friendly and breakfast is included. Rooms are fresh and have free wi-fi, though views are generally poor – ask to see a few. W140,000

HANOK GUESTHOUSES

In **Bukchon Hanok Village**, a tranquil city sector north of Anguk subway station, lie some of Seoul's most interesting places to stay – here you can spend the night in traditional Korean housing known as **hanok** (혼옥). These are wooden buildings with tiled roofs, set around a dirt courtyard – a style that once blanketed the nation, but is rarely seen in today's high-rise Korea. The generally bed-less rooms – you'll be sleeping Korean-style in a sandwich of blankets – are kept deliberately rustic and heated in the winter with the underfloor *ondol* system; most, however, provide modern indoor toilets and free wi-fi.

There are a few "proper" *hanok* **guesthouses** dotted around (see "Gyeongbokgung and around" reviews, see page 100), as well as some charming **homestay** options bookable online (ⓦ hanokstay.org); the latter option will cost in the region of W50,000 per room.

1

Mido 호텔 미도 22 Toegye-ro 10-gil ☎02 7770088, ⓦhotelmido.com; Hoehyeon subway; map p.77. File this one under flashpacker – you can pay a lot more for a lot less in the Myeongdong area, and this is a decent mix of hotel and hostel. From the hostel side, neat little breakfasts (included) and informative staff. And from the hotel side, attractive rooms, many of which have computers. W80,000

Philstay Metro 필스테이 메트로 5F 19-3 Myeongdong 10-gil ☎02 771 8787; Myeongdong station; map p.77. There are silvery surfaces all over the place in this Myeongdong cheapie – maybe that's why it feels such good value. Other (more sensible) reasons include winning staff; a mix of cosy doubles, singles and triples; and a super location right in the thick of the shopping area. Breakfast included. W60,000

★**The Shilla** 더 신라 249 Dongho-ro ☎02 2233 3131, ⓦshilla.net; Dongguk University subway; map p.77. Tucked away in a quiet area on the eastern access road to Namsan, this hotel is characterized by the traditional style of its rooms and exterior. The lobby and restaurants are a luscious shade of brown, as if they've been dunked in tea, though the common areas can often be a little busy – this is one of Seoul's most popular conference venues. The rooms themselves are five-star quality, if a little overpriced, and feature genuine Joseon-era antiques. W480,000

NORTHERN SEOUL

Bong Backpackers 봉 배크패커스 3 Seonggyungwan-ro 5-gil ☎010 3388 8898; Hyehwa subway; map p.79. This building has been a hostel for donkey's years – formerly a rather loveable flophouse, it's now relatively swish, with the basement rooms given a new lease of life via the gift of epoxied walls and moody lighting. The owner speaks English very well, and breakfast is included in rates which are about as low as Seoul hostels go. Dorms W12,000, twins W40,000

Open Guesthouse 오픈 게스트하우스 8 Changgyeonggung-ro 35-gil ☎02 744 9000; Hansung University subway; map p.79. Hyehwa can be a bit busy for some, but just one subway station further out, the Hansung University area provides a calmer and more Korean experience. This is a great choice in this up-and-coming neighbourhood, with cheap private rooms – all en suite – and engaging staff. Also has single rooms (W25000), and rates include a simple breakfast. W30,000

WESTERN SEOUL

Ann Guesthouse 안 게스트하우스 157 Yanghwa-ro ☎010 9084 0837, ⓦannguesthouse.co.kr; Hongik University subway; map p.85. Terrific location, peering over Hongdae subway station. Despite being in the centre of Seoul's nightlife, it's a quiet and relaxed place, presided

over by a friendly couple. Free laundry service, and private rooms sleeping three to six for around W30,000 per person. Dorms W20,000

★**iGuesthouse** 아이 게스트하우스 10-14 Wausan-ro 23-gil ☎070 8779 6161, ⓦseouliguesthouse.com; Hongik University subway; map p.85. While Apple Corp probably wouldn't be too happy about the name, guests usually come away more than satisfied with this hostel, which is the best of a glut in this residential part of Hongdae. Dorms are more spacious and better-appointed than most of the competition, and staff keep abreast of the area's goings-on. Dorms W21,000

iHouse Chin Chin 아이 하우스 친친 24-11 Yeonnam-ro 7-gil ☎02 334 1476; Hongik University subway; map p.85. Something quite different, near trendy Yeonnamdong – with no signboard, and hidden behind foliage in an alley off a side-road, you'll need a decent command of maps to locate this secretive guesthouse. They've a range of artistically designed rooms, and an excellent breakfast is included in the rates. W75,000

★**Urbanwood Guesthouse** 어번우드 게스트하우스 5 Wausan-ro 29-gil ☎010 8320 0833, ⓦurbanwood.co.kr; Hongik University subway; map p.85. Run by an affable, English-speaking local who whips up a mean cup of coffee as part of breakfast (included), this is the most pleasant of the Hongdae station area's many boutique-style operations. Its few rooms are decorated along seasonal colour schemes (only the triple is en-suite), and it's usually booked out weeks in advance. W100,000

ITAEWON AND AROUND

★**G Guesthouse** G게스트하우스 14-38 Bogwang-ro 60-gil ☎02 795 0015; Itaewon subway; map p.89. Ticking off the backpacker and budget sections, this is an excellent addition to the area. The dorms (some female-only) are kept meticulously clean, and feature the same industrial-chic stylings as the rather pricey private rooms. The roof "garden" is a good place to mingle, and they throw the occasional barbecue; breakfast is also included in the rates. Dorms W19,000, twins W95,000

Grand Hyatt 그랜드 하야트 322 Sowol-ro ☎02 797 1234, ⓦseoul.grand.hyatt.com; Noksapyeong subway map p.89. A favourite of visiting dignitaries, this is one of Seoul's top hotels in more ways than one – perched on a hill overlooking Itaewon, almost every room has a fantastic view through floor-to-ceiling windows. There's a fitness centre, an ice rink and squash courts, as well as swimming pools, indoors and out. W410,000

Hamilton 해밀톤 호텔 179 Itaewon-ro ☎02 79 0171, ⓦhamilton.co.kr; Itaewon subway; map p.89 Long an Itaewon landmark, and a better place to stay since recent refurbishments, countless foreigners have made the their Seoul home. Staff are professional, and guests can make use of an outdoor pool in warmer months. **W135,000**

IP Boutique IP부티크 221 Itaewon-ro ☏02 3702 8000, ⓦ ipboutiquehotel.com; Itaewon subway; map p.89. A curious "boutique" (it's many floors high), whose rooms have all been individually decorated, with different colour schemes for each floor. They're mercifully a lot better than the nightmarish lobby, which looks something like the innards of a giant handbag. **W260,000**

SOUTHERN SEOUL

★**Cappuccino** 호텔 카푸치노 155 Bongeunsa-ro ☏02 518 5489, ⓦ hotelcappuccino.co.kr; Eonju subway; map p.92. Located on a crest just north of Gangman station and its surrounding mess of high-rises, this is a super mid-range choice. There's great coffee available in the lobby, though even more enticing is the rooftop bar, which provides simply superlative views over the wider Gangnam area, so you might want to be back home before sunset. Oh, and the rooms themselves – small, but absolutely fine. **W105,000**

★**Dormy Inn Garosugil** 도미인 가로수길 119 Dosan-daero ☏02 518 5489, ⓦ dormy.co.kr; Sinsa subway; map p.92. New mid-range option at the southern end of boutique-lined Garosugil (see page 93), with rooms which are really quite stylish for the price. Of even more note is the on-site spa-sauna, elements of which evoke the feeling of a Japanese *onsen*. It's worth paying a bit extra for breakfast. **W145,000**

Gold Hill Guesthouse 골드힐 게스트하우스 2F 60 Gangnam-daero 136-gil ☏070 4114 5887, ⓦ goldhillguesthouse.com; Nonhyeon subway; map p.92. Gangnam does have hostels and cheap places to stay, but they often consist of converted – or existing – student rooms. This is one of the better ones, with small dorms (some with just a single bunk-bed inside), twins resembling Korean bedrooms, clued-up staff, and a free brekkie. Dorm beds **W30,000**, twins **W65,000**

Grand Parnas 그랜드 파르나스 521 Teheran-ro ☏02 555 5656, ⓦ ihg.com; Samseong subway; map p.92. Designed with exceptional attention to detail, this Intercontinental hotel belies its age with regular overhauls. The rooms are fresh and tastefully decorated in pleasing tones, with modern furniture. Some great restaurants can be found on the lower floors (which are part of the Coex complex), and guests have access to a gym and indoor swimming pool. **W450,000**

★**Park Hyatt** 파크 하야트 606 Teheran-ro ☏02 2016 1234, ⓦ seoul.park.hyatt.com; Samseong subway; map p.92. First things first: this is Korea's best hotel. Its class will already be evident by the time you've entered the lobby, which is actually on the top floor, together with a gorgeous little pool. Rooms employ an almost Zen-like use of space, while staff are experts at making themselves available only when needed; in addition, those on a repeat visit will find their preferred room temperature, TV channels and light level all ready and waiting. Bliss. **W520,000**

EATING

Food in Seoul is cheap by international standards and invariably excellent, while the number of **restaurants** is nothing short of astonishing – there's almost one on every corner, and many more in between. Korean food has a well-deserved reputation as one of the spiciest around; those looking for something a little blander can stick to the ever-growing choice of restaurants serving global cuisine, or breakfast at one of the many **bakeries** strewn around the city. If you do get stuck, head for one of Seoul's seemingly infinite number of **convenience stores**. For something even more authentic, head to one of Seoul's many **markets**, those at Dongdaemun and Namdaemun being the most popular.

RESTAURANTS

Many parts of Seoul have their own particular culinary flavour. Most popular with tourists are the streets around Insadonggil, where restaurants serve traditional Korean food in a suitably fitting atmosphere. At the other end of the scale is Itaewon, where local restaurants are outnumbered by those serving Brazilian, Japanese and Bulgarian food, among others. Student areas such as Hongdae, Sinchon and Daehangno are filled with cheap restaurants, and the establishments of trendy Apgujeong cater to the fashionistas.

GYEONGBOKGUNG AND AROUND

Beezza 빛짜 113 Sajik-ro ☏02 737 8412; Gyeongbokgung subway; map p.64. The most appealing place to have a light meal on this trendy alley,

with a selection of small, wood-fired pizzas (W7500 and up), some of which have very interesting toppings. They also stock a range of locally produced craft beer. Mon–Fri 11.30am–midnight, Sat 1pm–midnight, Sun 1–11pm.

Sanchez 산체스 26 Yunboseon-gil ☏02 735 0723; Anguk subway; map p.64. This tiny basement place has a great range of fusion-esque Korean food – try the super-tasty "America-style" *gamjajeon* (미국감자전; W20,000), which sees the regular local potato pancake covered with bacon and egg. In addition, they have a superlative range of *makgeolli* sourced from breweries across the country. The only problem is that it's tiny and very popular, so you may well have to wait, or come back another day. Daily 6pm–2am.

Tongin Market 통인시장 Jahaun-ro 15-gil; Gyeongbokgung subway; map p.64. Hugely popular

1

CULINARY CURIOSITIES

While even "regular" Korean food may be utterly alien to most visitors, there are a few edibles that deserve special attention; you'll find some of the following at restaurants, but street stalls and markets are the best places to go hunting.

Beonddegi (번데기) In colder months, stalls selling this local delicacy – silkworm larvae – set up on pavements and riverbanks across the whole country. The smell of these mites boiled up in a broth is so disgusting that it may well breach international law. The treat is also served as a bar snack in many *hofs*, bursting in the mouth to release a grimy juice – perfect drinking-game material.

Dak-pal (닭발) So you've learnt the word for "chicken" in Korean (*dak*), spotted it on the menu and ordered a dish. Unfortunately, with this particular meal the suffix means "foot", and that's just what you get – dozens of sauced-up chicken feet on a plate, with not an ounce of meat in sight.

Gaegogi (개고기) This is dog meat, but let it be known that – contrary to the expectations of many a traveller – it rarely features on Korean menus: you're not going to get it on your plate unless you go to a dedicated restaurant. It's usually served in a soup: *yeongyangtang* and *bosintang* are its most common incarnations.

Sannakji (산낙지) Octopus tentacles served still wriggling on the plate – every year, people die of suffocation when their still-wriggling prey makes a last bid for freedom, but as long as you don't throw down your tiny octopod whole (as many Korean guys do, in an effort to impress) you should be okay.

Sundae (순대) Don't let the romanization fool you – this is nothing whatsoever to do with ice cream. In Korea, it's actually a sausage made with intestinal lining, and stuffed with clear noodles. Head to the nearest market to try some.

with local youngsters, this market has an intriguing payment system in place. First you pay W5000 for a batch of tokens shaped like ancient Korean coins, and then hand these over in exchange for food at the market's many stalls. Mon–Fri 9am–6pm, Sat 9am–1pm.

★ **Tosokchon** 토속촌 5 Jahamun-ro 5-gil ☎02 737 7444; Gyeongbokgung subway; map p.64. The grandest and most famous place in town for *samgyetang* (삼계탕), a delicious soup comprising chicken stuffed with ginseng, jujube and other healthy ingredients (W16,000). Fame and size aside, the food really does taste fantastic – be prepared to queue. Daily 11.30am–11.30pm.

INSANDONG AND AROUND

★ **Abiko** 아비코 20-1 Samil-daero 17-gil ☎02 730 3236; Jongno 3-ga subway; map p.71. Perhaps the spiciest food in Seoul, and it's not even Korean – *donkkaseu* (돈까스), from Japan, is a breaded pork cutlet, often served with curry, on rice. There are five levels of spice here – see if you can handle the hottest one. Various toppings and additions available; it'll work out at around W11,000 per head, all in. Daily 11am–9.30pm.

Ahndamiro 안다미로 6-3 Insadong 8-gil ☎02 730 5777; Anguk subway; map p.71. There's something rather romantic about this Italian restaurant, tucked into an Insadong side-alley. It's a great date spot, and if you're worried about paying for two then rock up before 3pm for the W10,000 pasta or pizza lunch specials – a bargain. Daily 10.30am–midnight.

★ **Balwoo Gongyang** 발우공양 Ujeonggungno 56 ☎02 2031 2081, ⓦbaru.or.kr; Anguk subway; map p.71. Overlooking Jogyesa temple (see page 70), this is one of the best places to eat in Seoul, particularly for vegetarians. The huge set meals are consummately prepared approximations of Buddhist temple food, and the balance of colour, texture, shape and taste is beyond reproach. Mung-bean pancakes, acorn jelly, sweet pumpkin tofu and sticky rice with ginkgo nuts are among the dozens of items that may appear on your table. Sets go from W30,000. Reservations recommended. Daily: lunch 11.40am–1.20pm & 1.30–3pm, dinner 6–9pm.

Bukchon Sonmandu 북촌 손만두 6 Insadong 3-gil ☎02 735 1238; Jonggak subway; map p.71. Cheap and tasty, this dumpling restaurant always has several different batches on the go, with portions selectable from a picture menu from W4000, or a selection platter for W8000. Good noodles, too. Daily 11.30am–11.30pm.

Doodaemunjip 두대문집 9 Insadong 12-gil ☎02 737 0538; Anguk subway; map p.71. Tucked into the Insadong alleys, this is perhaps the most attractive of the area's many traditional restaurants, with chandeliers lending elegance to the scene. Staple meals are super cheap (W7000–8000), with the broths particularly good choices, and they're served with tasty side-dishes. Daily 10.30am–10pm.

★ **Gwangjujip** 광주집 3 Donhwamun-ro 11-ga ☎02 764 3574; Jongno 3-ga subway; map p.71. You can get barbecued meat all across the city, but the litt three-way junction just north of Jongno 3-ga subway exit 6 is perhaps the most atmospheric in town – dozens and dozens of diners munch away outside every single night, eating from what look like overturned oil drums. This little venue usually has the best meat – W12,000 for a 200g portion of succulent beef. Daily 3pm–midnight.

Ikdong 익동 21-5 Supyo-ro 28-gil ☎02 765 8215; Jongno 3-ga subway; map p.71. Perhaps the classiest of Ikseondong's many fancy-looking *hanok*-style eateries (check out the mother-of-pearl furnishings), and no slouch on the food front either – this "butcher-bistro" whips up great steaks (around W30,000), as well as cheaper salads and pasta dishes. Daily noon–3pm & 5–10pm.

Nwijo 뉘조 Gyeongundong 84-13 ☎02 730 9301; Anguk subway; map p.71. Charmingly low-key restaurant where chefs create rounds of lovingly prepared traditional cuisine. Come before 4pm and you can take advantage of the great-value lunch meals (W18,000); dinner sets are W28,000 and up. Daily 10.30am–10pm.

★**Potala** 포탈라 99 Cheonggyecheon-ro ☎02 318 0094; Jongno 3-ga subway; map p.71. Run by a Nepali–Korean couple and centred on a functional Tibetan prayer wheel, this charmingly decorated basement restaurant serves Himalayan specialities (W15,000 for most curries, W10,000 for Tibetan *momo* dumplings). Highly recommended is the *samosa chat* – three large samosas served with chopped green onion, chickpeas, curry sauce and sour cream (W11,000). Daily noon–10pm.

Yi Chun Bok Chamchi 이춘복 참치 4 Jongno 14-gil ☎02 723 4558; Jonggak subway; map p.71. With its understatedly stylish design, beautiful lighting and immaculately attired chefs, this sushi joint wouldn't look out of place in Tokyo's swanky Ginza district. However, the fish served here (mostly tuna) runs along more Korean lines, making for a novel experience. Lunch prices are far lower (get here before 2pm); at this time you can try a sushi platter (W10,000), a full set (W12,000), or *hoedeopbap* (raw fish on rice; W7000). Daily 11am–2am.

MYEONGDONG AND DONGDAEMUN

★**Din Tai Fung** 딘타이펑 2F 13 Myeongdong 7-gil ☎02 3789 2778; Euljiro 1-ga subway; map p.77. This Taiwanese chain may be milking a decades-old magazine review, but it still makes darn good dumplings – perhaps even the best in Seoul. It's W9900 for ten of their famed *xiaolongbao*, or try the shrimp and wonton noodles (W10,000), or other Shanghainese fare. Daily 11am–10pm.

Fortune 포튠 154 Mareunnae-ro ☎02 2278 7770; Dongdaemun History & Culture Park subway; map p.77. The best restaurant in Dongdaemun's curious little Russiatown, with a mix of Russian and Central Asian dishes including meaty mains (W10,000), filling soups (W6000) and delicious salads (W5000). The Russian beer (W5000)

goes down nicely, and be sure to get some honey cake from the downstairs café before leaving. Daily noon–11pm.

Green Dabang 그린다방 3F Daerim Building, 157 Euiljiro ☎02 2273 7128; Euljiro 3-ga or Euljiro 4-ga subway; map p.77. Makercity Sewoon is the most unlikely hipster spot in the city, and this bistro-like affair was one of the first places to open up on the "wings" of this old-school market. Dinner can be a little pricey; better value is the super-thick pork cutlet (W8000), of which there are only 25 available each weekday lunchtime, so get here before noon. Mon–Fri 11.30am–2pm & 3pm–midnight, Sat 6pm–midnight.

Gogung 고궁 2F 27 Myeongdong 8-gil ☎02 776 3211; Myeongdong subway; map p.71. A good, well-located spot for simple Korean mains – best is the *Jeonju bibimbap* (W11,000), a tasty southwestern take on the Korean staple. Daily 11am–10pm.

★**Gwangjang Market** 광장시장 Off Jongno; Jongno 5-ga subway; map p.77. If you haven't had a meal at Gwangjang (see page 78), you haven't really been to Seoul. It's a beguiling place with all manner of indoor and outdoor places to eat; best is a *bindaeddeok* (mung-bean pancake; 빈대떡) in the central crossroads, though at lunchtime you should track down the alley selling *yukhoe* (raw beef tartare; 육회). Daily noon–2am.

Korea House 한국의집 10 Toegye-ro ☎02 2266 9101; ⓦkoreahouse.or.kr; Chungmuro subway; map p.77. Modelled on the court cuisine enjoyed by the kings of the Joseon dynasty, dinner sets here start at W68,000 (small lunch sets from W15,000), and are made up of at least thirteen separate components, usually including broiled eel, ginseng in honey, grilled sliced beef and a royal hotpot. Those eating dinner here will get discount from the performances of traditional song and dance (see page 113). Reservations recommended. Daily: lunch noon–2pm, dinner 5–6.30pm & 7–8.30pm.

★**Mongmyeok Sanbang** 목멱산방 Namsan ☎02 318 4790; Myeongdong subway; map p.77. On the Namsan walking track, a short walk uphill from the lower cable-car terminus, this traditionally styled venue is one of the most enchanting places to eat in Seoul – and also a great place for tea. They sell three types of *bibimbap*: normal (W8000), with *bulgogi* beef on top (W9000), or with raw beef (W11,000), and it's beautifully presented. Eat outside, under the maple trees. Daily 11.30am–9pm.

N Grill N그릴 7F N Seoul Tower ☎02 3455 9298, ⓦnseoultower.net; map p.77. Expensive French restaurant perched atop the N Seoul Tower (see page 78). You won't get much change from W100,000 per person, but the food is top-class, and there are few better views of Seoul. Mon–Fri 11am–2pm & 5–11pm, Sat & Sun 11am–11pm.

1

Pierre Gagnaire à Seoul 피에르가지에르 30 Euljiro ☏02 317 7181, ⓦpierregagnaire.co.kr; Euljiro 1-ga subway; map p.77. Molecular gastronomy hit Seoul when the unique creations of Michelin-starred French megachef Pierre Gagnaire started tickling tastebuds atop the *Lotte Hotel*. The menu has a discernible Korean twist, with ingredients such as ginger, sesame leaves and "five-flavoured" *omija* berries letting off little flavour bombs in certain dishes. Lunch menu W85,000, dinner from W170,000; reservations essential. Daily noon–3pm & 5–11pm.

★ **Woo Rae Oak** 우래옥 62-29 Changgyeonggung-ro ☏02 2265 0151; Euljiro 4-ga subway; map p.77. This meat-house and its elegant, hotel lobby-like atrium have been here since 1946 – just one year less than Korea itself. The customer base seems to have changed little in decades, and the sight of septuagenarians munching away in their Sunday best is rather charming. Most are here for the meat (W25,000 or so per head), though they also serve superb *naengmyeon*, cold buckwheat noodles similar to Japanese *soba* (W12,000). Daily 11am–10.30pm.

NORTHERN SEOUL

Hoho Sikdang 호호식당 35 Daehangno 9-gil ☏02 741 2384; Hyehwa subway; map p.79. This *hanok* venue is without doubt the most attractive restaurant in the Hyehwa area, and there are queues each mealtime to get in. It serves simple Japanese noodle and rice-bowl dishes – try *gyudon* (beef on rice; W9000), or *ebi*-fry (shrimp tempura on rice; W13,000). Daily 11am–3pm & 5–10pm.

★ **Jaha Sonmandoo** 자하 손만두 12 Baekseokdong-gil ☏02 379 2648; Gyeongbokgung subway; map p.79. Dumplings known as *mandu* are a cheap Korean staple, but unlike the regular processed fare, the handmade versions served here (from W6500) are delicious, filled with chunks of quality beef, radish, shiitake mushrooms and the like; you'll probably need two for a real meal. The setting is just as pleasant, a minimalist space with mountain views. Daily 11am–9.30pm.

Saemaeul Sikdang 새마을 식당 3 Daehangno 11-gil ☏02 3672 7004; Hyehwa subway; map p.79. So what if it's a chain restaurant – this pleasingly noisy venue still doles out the best-value barbecue meat in the wider Hyehwa area. Try the wafer-thin *yeoltan bulgogi* beef (열탄 불고기; W8000 per portion), washed down with some soybean broth (된장찌개; W6000). Daily 11.30am–midnight.

WESTERN SEOUL

Café Sukkara 카페 수까라 157 Wausan-ro ☏02 334 5919; Hongik University subway; map p.85. Not so much a café as a delightful light-food restaurant, in which vegan pumpkin pudding, chickpea salad, wholewheat spaghetti and the like are whipped up in the (very) open kitchen. Mains from W9000; wash them down with home-made ginger ale (W6000) or black shandy gaff (W7500). Tues–Sun 11am–3pm & 6–11pm.

James Cheese Back Ribs 제임스 등갈비 145-1 Eoulmadang-ro ☏02 324 3305; Hongik University subway; map p.85. Back in 2014, cheesy *deung-galbi* (barbecued pork ribs; 등갈비) was all the rage across Korea. Most places have since gone out of business, but there are two survivors almost next door to each other in Hongdae – this is the better one, and W16,000 will buy you a serving (single portions also allowed, which is rare), plus the plastic gloves you'll need to eat it. Wash it down with bottled craft beer from *The Booth*. Daily 11am–2am.

Jopok Deokbokki 조폭떡볶이 60 Eoulmadang-ro ☏02 337 9933; Sangsu subway; map p.85. A dish of rice-cakes in spicy sauce, *deokbokki* (떡볶이) is available at street-stands all across the city, though this small sit-down restaurant is by far the most famous venue, since its staff are rumoured to be connected to the local Mafia (*jopok*). Fact or fib, the food's pretty good, especially if you have a few *twigim* (refried treats; 튀김) thrown on top – just point at what you'd like. Most dishes W3000. Daily 11am–6am.

Julio 훌리오 40 Wausan-ro 13-gil ☏02 3141 5324; Sangsu subway; map p.85. Stylish restaurant selling Mexican staples such as tacos and burritos from W9000 – try one of their Korean fusion specials, such as the *carnitas kimchi* fries (W11,500). Daily noon–11pm.

ITAEWON AND AROUND

Copacabana 코파카바나 41 Itaewon-ro 27-gil ☏02 796 1660; Itaewon subway; map p.89. Anyone who's been to a Brazilian *churrascaria* will know exactly what to expect here – W29,000 buys as much grilled meat and salad as you can eat, or it's W15,000 for a single steak at weekday lunchtimes. Daily 11.30am–10pm.

★ **Coreanos** 코레아노스 46 Noksapyeong-daero 40-gil ☏02 795 4427; Noksapyeong subway; map p.89. Seoul expats almost unanimously vote this small Texan chain the best in the city for Mexican food, and there are great views from their Noksapyeong roost. Try some of their K-Mex options, such as galbi burritos (W12,000), or pork belly tacos (W7600). Daily noon–11pm.

Happy Home 해피홈 2-10 Itaewon-ro 20-gil ☏02 797 3185; Itaewon subway; map p.89. Itaewon has a sizeable Nigerian population, and a fair few restaurants catering to them. This is the best by far, a welcoming venue serving grilled plantains, black-eyed peas and beef-and-fish soups to eat with your *fufu* ("grinded" cassava). It's around W10,000 per dish. Daily noon–midnight.

★ **Linus' BBQ** 라이너스 바베큐 136-13 Itaewon-ro ☏02 790 2920; Noksapyeong subway; map p.89 A smash with both Seoul expats and Seoulites themselves, this atmospheric spot is the place to go for a taste of the

American south. Try a pulled pork sandwich (W7900), a mac and cheese (W4800), or mashed 'taters and gravy (W4800), and wash down with some craft beer. Daily 11am–10.30pm.

★ **Menya Sandaime** 멘야 산다이메 206 Itaewon-ro ☎02 790 4129; Itaewon subway; map p.89. Ramen joint serving noodles that are almost as good as you'd find across the pond in Japan. Bowls go from W8000, though in summertime consider the delicious *tsukemen* (W9000), in which you dip noodles into a spicy soup; the *gyoza* dumplings (W4000) always go down well, too. Daily 10am–10pm.

★ **Plant** 플렌트 2F 117 Bogwang-ro ☎02 749 1981; Itaewon subway; map p.89. So successful was the first branch of this vegan spot that they've opened this second – far better-located – one just south of Itaewon station. It's not easy to be vegan in Korea, but those dropping in here will be open-mouthed at a menu full of salads, wraps, soups, baked goods and more – you should eat well for under W15,000. Mon–Thu 11am–9pm, Fri & Sat 11am–10pm.

The Wolfhound 울프하운드 128-6 Bogwang-ro 59-gil ☎02 749 7971, ⊛wolfhoundpub.com; Itaewon subway; map p.89. Irish-style drinking hole notable for an authentic selection of pub grub, including burgers, fish & chips and shepherd's pie. Best, however, are the fried breakfasts, which cost from W7900, and go down quite nicely. Daily noon–11pm.

Zelen 젤렌 52 Itaewonno 27-gil ☎02 749 0600; Itaewon subway; map p.89. Bulgarian cuisine is one of the culinary world's best-kept secrets, taking hearty meat and veg dishes from the Slavic lands to the west, and fusing them with kebabs and breads from the Turkic east. Meals here (around W22,000) are well prepared, though best may be the gigantic "couple" *shashlik* kebab. Daily 11am–3pm & 6–11pm.

SOUTHERN SEOUL

Bulgogi Brothers 불고기 브라더스 Oakwood Premier Hotel, 46 Teheran-ro 87-gil ☎02 3466 8512; Samseong subway; map p.77. The barbecuing of raw meat at your table is one of the quintessential Korean experiences, but new arrivals can find it hard to jump straight in at the deep end. This elegant venue is a good place to learn the ropes, and the meat is always of exceptional quality. Around W30,000 per person, including side dishes and drinks. Mon–Fri 11am–3pm & 5–11pm, Sat & Sun 11am–11pm.

Ciné de Chef 씨네드쉐프 B5 848 Nonhyeon-ro ☎02 3446 0541; Apgujeong subway; map p.92. Immaculate Italian restaurant located in the bowels of the CGV cinema complex. The place is only really for couples, since sets (from W79,000 per head, and usually including soup, a steak or pasta dish and dessert) include tickets to

---

SEOUL'S TOP TEN PLACES TO EAT

Best naengmyeon noodles *Woo Rae Oak* (see page 106)

Best barbecued meat *Gwangjujip* (see page 104)

Best dumplings *Jaha Sonmandoo* (see page 106)

Best veggie food *Balwoo Gongyang* (see page 104)

Best bibimbap *Mongmyeok Sanbang* (see page 105)

Best soup *Tosokchon* (see page 104)

Best K-Mex *Coreanos* (see page 106)

Best views *Bill's* (see page 108)

Best desserts *Second Best Place in Seoul* (see page 108)

Best hidden café *Hanyakbang* (see page 108)

---

a private movie theatre, featuring just thirty comfy chairs laid out in couple formation; here you can watch the latest Hollywood blockbuster over a bottle of wine. Daily 10.30am–9pm.

Melting Shop 멜팅샵 55 Apgujeongno 46-gil ☎02 544 4256; Anguk subway; map p.92. Apgujeong probably has the full set of international comestibles now, after the addition of this dreamily pretty "retro ricotta bar". A ricotta caramel tart will set you back W16,500, while pasta dishes go for W24,000–33,000, and salads from W16,000. A place to impress, especially if you can score the seats overlooking Dosan Park. Daily 11.30am–3pm & 5pm–midnight.

Stay 스테이 81F Lotte World Tower ☎02 3213 1230; Jamsil subway; map p.92. Seoul's top restaurant – in a literal sense, at least, sitting as it does on the 81st floor of the new Lotte World Tower, with views every bit as good as you'd expect from such a height, and opulent decor to match. The food's pretty grand too – it's hard to pigeonhole the French-inspired creations of Michellin-starred chef Yannick Alléno, but if you can afford it, you'll enjoy it. Lunch sets start at W58,000, and dinner mains run from W35,000–75,000. Daily 11.30am–2.30am & 6–10pm.

★ **Sushi Chohi** 수시 초히 18-6 Dosan-daero 45-gil ☎02 545 8422; Apgujeong subway; map p.92. Sushi fans will be in their element at this pine-lined restaurant, overlooking Dosan Park. Absolutely no concessions are made regarding the fish or its preparation: the blades and chopping boards cost upwards of US$1000 each, while each fish is selected from the best possible place (and caught wild, rather than farm-raised), whether it be southwestern Korea or northern Japan. Grab a seat facing the chef, and watch the magic happen. Sets from W60,000. Daily 11am–10pm.

Tutto Bene 투또베네 5 Apgujeong-ro 77-gil ☎02 546 1489; Cheongdam subway; map p.92. The setting of this Italian restaurant is utterly gorgeous, its Orient Express-like wooden panelling offset by amber and honey-yellow lighting, and the scent of freshly cut flowers mingling with the creations of the chef. Pasta dishes are the most popular (from W25,000), but don't overlook the seafood menu – sourced from remote islands off Korea's west coast, the oysters are superb. Daily noon–midnight.

CAFÉS

Seoul's café society has come a long way since the turn of the millennium – good coffee is available on almost every corner, at almost any hour. There are a number of major chains knocking around, but far more interesting are the myriad privately run ventures; some effectively count as dessert cafés, focusing more on sweeties or baked goods than drinks.

GYEONGBOKGUNG AND AROUND

★ **Books Cooks** 북스쿡스 5 Bukchon-ro 8-gil ☎02 743 4003; Anguk subway; map p.64. *Hanok*-like venue strung with cool lighting, this place is famed for its scones – made to order and served with jam for just W4000. There are tea sets all over the walls, and you can have a brew yourself for W8000 or so. Daily 10am–9pm.

★ **Second Best Place in Seoul** 서울에서 두번째 로잘하는집 122-1 Samcheong-ro; Anguk subway; map p.64. A rarity on cosmopolitan and fast-changing Samcheongdonggil – not only has it been here for decades, but it also serves traditional fare. The menu is short and sweet, with an assortment of Korean teas and snacks. Best is the *patjuk* (W7000), something like a viscous red-bean fondue containing all manner of ingredients from cinnamon to chestnut chunks. Daily 10am–9pm.

INSADONG AND AROUND

Bizeun 비즌 16 Insadong-gil ☎02 738 1245; Jonggak subway; map p.71. Waffles and ice cream are the regular snacks in Korean cafés, but here you'll be able to chow down on something more traditional: sweet rice-cakes, known as *ddeok* (떡), which come in a wonderful kaleidoscope of colours, with flavours running the gamut from pumpkin to black sesame. Daily 8.30am–10pm.

★ **O'Sulloc** 오설록 45-1 Insadong-gil ☎02 732 6427; Anguk subway; map p.71. O'Sulloc is Korea's largest producer of green tea, but don't let that fool you into thinking that people come to their flagship tearoom to drink the stuff. Instead, this is a café and dessert bar *par excellence*, since the precious leaves have been blended into tiramisu, ice cream, lattes and chocolates (W5000–8000). Daily 9am–10pm.

GWANGHWAMUN AND CITY HALL

★ **Bill's** 빌즈 4F D Tower, 17 Jongno 3-gil ☎02 2251 8404; Gwanghwamun subway; map p.74. This Aussie import is one of the best cafes in the city, with great coffees, smoothies, teas and juices (W5000–9000) served in a swanky space boasting fantastic, massive-window views of the surrounding towers. A word of warning – don't look at their dessert selection (especially the disgustingly good Key lime pie), or you'll want one. Mon–Fri 9am–11pm, Sat & Sun 10am–10pm.

Lusso 루쏘 17 Jeongdong-gil ☎02 772 9935; City Hall subway; map p.74. Pretty Jeongdong-gil (see page 73) has a fair few cafés, but this one stands out for its second-floor views of the road's famed ginkgo trees – peer out into the leaves over an espresso and a croissant. Daily 9am–8pm.

MYEONGDONG AND DONGDAEMUN

★ **Hanyakbang** 한약방 16-6 Samil-daero 12-gil ☎070 4148 4242; Euljiro 3-ga subway; map p.77. If you can find this place, you're in for a real treat. Set in a side-alley off a side-alley off a side-road, there's next to no sign of its existence, which makes it all the more surprising that this is one of the most visually impressive cafés in the whole country – cups, furniture, wall art, the lot. The coffee itself is fantastic, and affordable at around W5000. Mon–Fri 8am–10pm, Sat 10.30am–10pm, Sun noon–10pm.

NORTHERN SEOUL

Sanmotungi 산모퉁이 153 Baekseokdong-gil ☎02 391 4737; map p.79. Made famous by its use as a set in Korean drama *The Coffee Prince*, this remote coffee house is worth a visit for the fresh air and mountain views on offer from its upper level – these help to explain the rather inflated prices (coffees from W8000). Daily 11am–10pm.

WESTERN SEOUL

Café aA 카페aA 19-18 Wausan-ro 17-gil ☎02 3143 7312; Sangsu subway; map p.85. Several things set this place apart from the regular Korean café: the huge, church-like front door; a ceiling at least three times higher than the national average; the bespectacled, artsy clientele; and a range of chairs imported from Europe. The upstairs floor functions as a sort of furniture museum, featuring examples from luminaries such as Jean Prouvé and Salvador Dalí. Art aside, the coffee here is excellent (around W5000), as are the various cakes. Daily noon–2am.

★ **Fell & Cole** 펠앤콜 7 Seopyongdaero 8-gil ☎010 8895 1434; Sangsu subway; map p.85. Divine ice cream in a tidy little hideyhole, secreted away in the alleys behind Sangsu station. Flavours change by the day, but expect things like carrot cake, fig mascarpone and caramel sweet potato. Daily noon–10pm.

ITAEWON AND AROUND
Anthracite 앤트러사이트 240 Itaewon-ro ☎ 02 797 7009; Hangangjin subway; map p.89. At this great café, prices are low by local standards (W4000–5500), the beans are roasted on site and from the upper level there are great views out towards the river. Daily 9am–10pm.

★ **Passion 5** 패션5 272 Itaewon-ro ☎ 02 2071 9505; Hangangjin subway; map p.89. Part bakery, part dessert café, part brunch spot, this stylish place is also the headquarters of the *Paris Baguette* chain. Their baked goods are delicious (from W2000), and the ice creams superb (W6000 for two scoops); there are several types of hand-dripped coffee to choose from, as well as the regular Italian options. Daily 7.30am–10pm.

SOUTHERN SEOUL
★ **Café Madang** 카페 마당 B1 7 Dosan-daero 45-gil ☎ 02 546 3643; Apgujeong subway; map p.92. The Hermès flagship store has a café discreetly tucked away on the basement level, and W10,000 will be enough to get you coffee. All cutlery, cups and glasses – plus the tables and chairs – are Hermès originals, and a fair proportion of the customers are local celebrities. There's no cheaper way to buy your way into high society. Daily 10am–9pm.

The Lounge 더 라운지 24F 606 Teheran-ro ☎ 02 2016 1205; Samseong subway; map p.92. Sitting atop the *Park Hyatt* (see page 103) alongside the infinity pool of the hotel's fitness centre, this is a superb place for a coffee or light snack. Better still is a range of amazingly good smoothies: well worth the W17,000 splurge. Daily 9am–midnight.

TEAROOMS
Insadonggil and its surrounding alleyways are studded with tearooms, typically decorated in a traditional style and therefore much in keeping with the area. The teas are high-quality products made with natural ingredients (see page 43 for some varieties), and often come with traditional Korean sweets.

GYEONGBOKGUNG AND AROUND
★ **Cha-teul** 차마시는뜰 26 Bukchon-ro 11-gil ☎ 02 722 7006; Anguk subway; map p.64. Utterly gorgeous *hanok* tearoom with a splendid range of fine brews, including unusual local varieties such as mistletoe and pine mushroom, and some imported from China. It's right next to a decaying brick smokestack – an easy landmark to spot. Teas go from W5500. Daily 10am–10pm.

INSADONG AND AROUND
★ **Dawon** 다원 11-4 Insadong 10-gil ☎ 02 730 6305; Anguk subway; map p.71. The most appealing tearoom in the area is located in the grounds of the Kyungin Museum of Fine Art (see page 72). In warm weather you can sit outside in the courtyard, while inside you'll find traditionally styled rooms where guests are encouraged to add their musings to the graffiti-filled walls. The menu lists teas (from W7000) alongside information about their purported health benefits. Daily 10am–11pm.

Su-yo-il 수요일 36 Insadong-gil ☎ 02 8723 0191; Anguk subway; map p.71. Fancy tearoom with a few tables overlooking Insadonggil – a fine place for people-watching. Teas cost W7500, and many are served with floating flowers; in addition to the Korean options, they also offer Earl Grey, Darjeeling and other more familiar teas, as well as some fine desserts. Daily 10am–10.30pm.

NORTHERN SEOUL
★ **Suyeon Sanbang** 수연산방 8 Seongbuk-ro 26-gil ☎ 02 764 1736; Hansung University subway; map p.79. Though a little out of the way and hard to find, this secluded *hanok* tearoom is highly recommended for those looking for a piece of old-world Seoul. Built in the 1930s, it exudes the charm of a bygone age, turning down the volume button of modern Seoul to leave only the sounds of bird chatter and running water. Teas around W10,000, desserts a little more. Daily 11.30am–10pm.

DRINKING AND NIGHTLIFE

Clubs pumping out techno, trance and hip-hop to wiggling masses; loungey subterranean lairs heavy with philosophical conversation; noisy joints serving up live jazz and rock; neon-tinged cocktail bars in the bowels of five-star hotels. After a lengthy gestation, Seoul's nightlife scene is finally wide open, and the drinkers themselves are becoming ever more liberal. Summer sees most of the city's convenience stores surround themselves with plastic tables and chairs; a cheap and popular way to start a night out (see page 42 for a rundown on local hooch).

GYEONGBOKGUNG AND AROUND
Dugahun 두가헌 14 Samcheong-ro ☎ 02 3210 2100; Anguk subway; map p.64. A charmingly characteristic venue to fall into for a glass of wine, set as it is in a revamped *hanok* building. Their selection runs the gamut from under W70,000 to well over W1,000,000 a bottle, augmented by fine European cuisine from the kitchens. Some of the views disappoint, so choose your table carefully. Mon–Sat noon–4pm & 6pm–midnight, Sun noon–4pm.

★ **Jeon Daegamdaek** 전대감댁 7-17 Jahamun-ro 1-gil ☎ 02 735 0723; Anguk subway; map p.64. An integral part of the newly trendy Seochon district, this bar-restaurant sells a great range of *makgeolli* for W4000–

1

A REAL KOREAN NIGHT OUT

The "proper" Korean night out has long followed the same format, one that entwines food, drink and entertainment. The venue for stage one (il-cha) is the **restaurant**, where a **meal** is chased down with copious shots of soju. This is followed by stage two (i-cha), a visit to a **bar**; here beers are followed with snacks (usually large dishes intended for groups). Those still able to walk then continue to stage three (sam-cha), the **entertainment** component of the night, which usually involves a trip to a noraebang room for a sing-along (see page 88), and yet more drinks. Stages four, five and beyond certainly exist, but few participants have ever remembered them clearly.

8000 – try the slightly sour Baedari brand (배다리), once beloved of ex-president Park Chung-hee. It's great for meals, too; most opt for the eponymous savoury jeon (전) pancakes. If there's room, head to the courtyard area at the back – an achingly beautiful place to drink, with occasional glimpses of the Seoul night sky. Daily 11pm–midnight.

INSADONG AND AROUND

Baekseju Maeul 백세주마을 10 Ujeongguk-ro 2-gil ☏02 0000; Jonggak subway; map p.71. Presentable bar-restaurant from the creators of baekseju (see page 42), serving local bar-food – entire meals, in other words – to go with it. It's also one of the few places in town where you'll find ihwaju (이화주; W29,000); something like evaporated makgeolli, it's pleasantly gloopy. Daily 5pm–2am.

Shimmy Shimmy 시미시미 39 Samil-daero 30-gil ☏010 9049 8393; Jongno 3-ga subway; map p.71. Good choice among the many new Ikseondong drinking holes, with a faintly Boho atmosphere, soju for W4000 (or try the tasty Hallasan variety from Jeju for W1000 more), beer for W5000, and good Korean bar snacks. Mon–Sat 6pm–1am.

Story of the Blue Star 푸른별주막 17-1 Insadong 16-gil ☏02 734 3095; Anguk subway; map p.71. Though technically a restaurant, this artily decorated hanok-style venue really comes alive in the evening. Though still highly atmospheric, it has gone downhill since a change of ownership, and their range of flavoured makgeolli has dwindled, but you can still choose from mulberry leaf or aronia berry (W12,000 for a large bowl). You'll need to order at least one dish. Daily 6–11pm.

MYEONGDONG AND DONGDAEMUN

Pierre's Bar 피에르스바 30 Euljiro ☏02 317 7183, ⓦpierregagnaire.co.kr; Euljiro 1-ga subway; map p.77. Adjoining the superb Pierre Gagnaire restaurant (see page 106) at the top of the Lotte Hotel, this stylish bar is a firm favourite with international businessmen. Despite the modern yet opulent surroundings, and the sky-high food prices next door, drinks aren't that dear – beer and spirits start at W13,000. Daily 6–11pm.

NORTHERN SEOUL

Bar Off 바오프 67-2 Changgyeonggung-ro 27-gil; Hyehwa subway; map p.79. Up near the university entrance, this is one of the few places in Seoul to have somehow contravened Korea's smoking laws – not even the owner seems to know how it has survived when most shisha bars have fallen by the wayside. Have a smoke (W10,000), and a cheap cocktail (most W4000). Daily 6pm–2am.

★ Oneul, Wine Hanjan 오늘, 와인한잔 240-7 Changgyeonggung-ro, ☏02 741 7786; Hyehwa subway; map p.79. Far more classy-looking than most student drinking holes, "Today, a Glass of Wine" sells house plonk for just W3900. The food's very cheap too. Daily noon–3am.

WESTERN SEOUL

Bar Da 바다 11 Hongik-ro 3-gil ☏02 334 5572; Sangsu subway; map p.85. Getting to this bar is an adventure in itself – finding the entrance, crawling up the steep steps, then back outdoors to navigate what probably used to be a fire escape for the final leg to the top. Once you're there, it's wonderful: a broodingly dim, candle-studded hideaway for a nice drink. Beers go from W4000, and they've plenty of single malts from W8000. Daily 7pm–3am.

Gogos 고고스 12 Wausan-ro 17-gil ☏02 337 8083; Sangsu subway; map p.85. Let's cut to the chase here – this is one of Hongdae's prime meat markets, with a good mix of Koreans and foreigners, cheap drinks, a fun vibe, and a W5000 entry fee on weekends. Tues–Thurs & Sun 8pm–2am, Fri & Sat 6pm–6am.

M2 클럽 엠투 20-5 Jandari-ro ☏02 3143 7573; Sangsu subway; map p.85. Focusing on electronica, this is the area's largest nightclub, which manages to rope in the occasional top international DJ. It's packed to the gills at weekends, when you may spend more than an hour waiting in line to get in. Entry W10,000–20,000. Tues–Thurs & Sun 9.30pm–5am, Fri & Sat 9.30pm–7am.

Samgeori Pocha 삼거리포차 70 Wausan-ro; Sangsu subway; map p.85. Technically a restaurant though an integral part of Hongdae's nightlife – after a dance or a drink, Koreans love to eat (and drink a little more), so you may well find yourself dragged along to thi rustic-looking place. Having a bit of *soju* for Dutch courage makes it easier to handle the house speciality, *sannakji* (W15,000) – chopped-up baby octopus that, while not exactly alive, is so fresh that it's still writhing on your plate when served. Daily 6pm–late.

Thursday Party 썰스데이파티 14 Wausan-ro 17-gil ☎02 322 0063; Sangsu subway; map p.85. This bar-chain originated way down south in Busan, but it has proven a hit in Seoul too – cheap drinks (cocktails from W3800), no entry fee, bar games (including beer pong), and plenty of opportunity to mingle. What more could you want? Daily 10am–4am.

★**Vinyl** 바이닐 61-1 Wausan-ro ☎02 322 4161; Sangsu subway; map p.85. Get takeaway cocktails from the window of this small bar, where pina coladas are served in what appear, at first glance, to be colostomy bags. Such ingenuity brings the price down – just W5000 for a cocktail. It's a great place to drink too, if you can find a seat free, or just swagger down the street with your booze-pouch. Mon–Thurs & Sun 4pm–midnight, Fri & Sat 4pm–2am.

ITAEWON AND AROUND

B1 클럽 비원 179 Itaewon-ro ☎02 749 6164; Itaewon subway; map p.89. Underground club with a decent sound system, and usually DJs who know how to make the most of it – a mix of house, techno, electronic and more. With lounge areas and snazzy decoration, it's far classier than most dance venues in the area – at the beginning of the night, at least. W10,000–20,000 entrance fee at weekends. Daily 7pm–4am.

Bungalow 번갈로 8 Itaewon-ro 27-gil ☎02 793 2344; Itaewon subway; map p.89. There are drinking options aplenty in this loungey, multilevel bar – sup sangria on the swing-seats, drink martinis (W10,000) in the sand pit, have a romantic glass of wine on a candle-lit table or kick back with a beer on the outdoor terrace. Daily 4.30pm–3am.

Damotori 다모토리 31 Sinheung-ro ☎070 8950 8362; Noksapyeong subway; map p.89. One of the best *makgeolli* bars in Seoul – the *mak*-menu is laid out geographically, showing you exactly which part of Korea your chosen hooch hails from. The best way to pick a bottle (W5000–11,000) is by using their ridiculously good-value sampler sets – W3000 for five cups of *makgeolli*, selected to range from light to heavy. Food's good, too. Daily 6pm–1am.

Flower Gin 플라워진 250 Noksapyeong-daero ☎02 412 1983; Noksapyeong subway. Part florist, part gin joint, this tiny place is up there with the most distinctive bars in Seoul. Come drain a Hendrick's with a slice of cucumber and a freshly cut flower. Mon, Wed & Thu 2pm–midnight, Fri–Sun noon–midnight.

★**Magpie** 맥파이 244-1 Noksapyeong-daero ☎02 749 2537; Noksapyeong subway; map p.89. Started by a beer-curious expat, this little brewery has seen so much demand that the chain just keeps on spreading; there are already branches in Hongdae, and on Jeju Island, and bars around the country are stocking their excellent beers. The pizzas are splendid, too. Daily 3pm–1am.

Prost 프로스트 26 Itaewon-ro 27-gil ☎02 796 6854; Itaewon subway; map p.89. This multi-floor drinking venue behind the *Hamilton Hotel* has been full to bursting almost every night since it first opened. Sassy staff, a global range of beers (including some of their own), and a bunch of people to rub shoulders with – whether you like it or not. Bring ID. Daily 11.30am–2am.

The Wolfhound 울프하운드 128-6 Bogwang-ro 59-gil ☎02 749 7971, ⊚wolfhoundpub.com; Itaewon subway; map p.89. If you're feeling homesick, this Irish-style pub isn't a bad choice – they sell a bunch of good beers, and it's also a fine place to eat (see page 107). Daily noon–2am.

KNOW YOUR NEIGHBOURHOOD: GOING OUT IN SEOUL

Koreans love going out, whether it's with family, colleagues, social acquaintances or old study friends, making Seoul a truly **24-hour city** – day and night, year-round, its streets are a thrilling merry-go-round of noise, which ramps up as evening approaches, and stays at a maximum until the early hours. Each area of Seoul has its own particular flavour, with **Hongdae** by far the busiest. Its streets are saturated with bars, clubs and restaurants, and full every day of the week from early evening on; towards midnight, clubbers disembark the last trains, party all night, then slink off home as dawn breaks. Almost as busy at the weekend is **Itaewon**, which has some of the best bars, clubs and restaurants in the capital. It has become trendified of late, and also functions as the most popular **LGBT+** area in the whole country, with some excellent bars catering to Seoul's ever-growing pink community (see page 112 for details). Also worth mentioning are studenty **Daehangno**, which is busy every evening (though most drift towards Hongdae as midnight approaches); and **Samcheongdong**, which has a few relaxing places to wine and dine in. South of the river, **Gangnam** has a couple of good clubs, and there are trendy bars aplenty in nearby **Apgujeong**.

1

SOUTHERN SEOUL

★**Octagon** 오크타곤 645 Nonhyeon-ro, ☎02 516 8847; Hakdong subway; map p.92. Seoul's most popular club at the time of writing, this EDM venue has state-of-the-art light and sound systems (and even a gourmet chef), and regularly hauls in superstar DJs from across the globe – Nic Fanciulli and Coyu have both played here. Entry is W30,000 on weekend evenings, and you'll have to be dressed up. Thurs–Sat 10pm–7am.

Syndrome 신드롬 205 Dosan-daero, ☎02 544 7227; Apgujeong subway; map p.92. A club with a swimming pool – no wonder this "new electronica" stomping ground was an immediate hit on opening in late 2013. Cover usually W10,000 before midnight, W30,000 after. Thurs–Sun 10pm–7am.

LGBT+ SEOUL

Seoul's burgeoning **LGBT+ nightlife** scene has come on in leaps and bounds since 2000, when star actor Hong Seok-cheon came out of the closet – the first Korean celebrity to do so. He has since opened up a whole raft of LGBT+-friendly bars and restaurants in **Itaewon**, which remains the best LGBT+ area for foreigners; the best are listed here. Seoul does have other LGBT+ zones; the area around Jongno 3-ga station has long been home to underground bars, but those in Ikseondong are now often out and proud. Additionally, the university district of **Sinchon** is popular with the local lesbian community, many of whom congregate in the evenings in "Triangle Park", a patch of concrete near exit 1 of Sinchon subway station (take the first right).

INSADONG AND AROUND

Barcode 바코드 2F 41 Donhwamun-ro ☎02 3672 0940; Jongno 3-ga subway; map p.71. Longstanding Jongno bar popular with gay men, a fun place with English-speaking staff, and a bearish, thirty-something clientele. Daily 7.30pm–3am.

ITAEWON AND AROUND

Queen 퀸 7 Usadan-ro 12-gil ☎010 9039 2583; Itaewon subway; map p.89. The two most popular LGBT+ bars on "Homo Hill" are Queen and Always Homme, but visitors often get fleeced at the latter; head instead to this attractive venue, with inviting staff and highly comfortable chairs. On warm weekend evenings, even these can't stop the crowd – usually quite a mixed bag in terms of race and persuasion – spilling out onto the street for a dance. Fri & Sat 10.30pm–5am.

★**Why Not?** 와이낫? 10 Usadan-ro 12-gil ☎02 795 8193; Itaewon subway; map p.89. Now, this is a trip.

Here you're likely to see dozens of young locals performing expertly choreographed K-pop dances – some of these guys are seriously talented. Other nights have drag shows, or more "regular" house music. Cover W10,000, includes a free drink. Daily 7.30pm–5am.

WESTERN SEOUL

Labris 라브리 8F 81 Wausan-ro ☎02 333 5276; Sangsu subway; map p.85. A long-established mainstay of the Seoul lesbian scene, this women-only (that includes FTM trans) bar and social space is one of the most welcoming places for foreigners. Entry W15,000. Fri & Sat 9pm–5am.

Pink Hole 핑크홀 24 Yanghwa-ro 12-gil; Hapjeong subway; map p.85. There are plenty of lesbian establishments in the wider Hongdae area, but this is one of the few options for those who feel like a dance – a pity, then, that they seem to put the same pop playlist on every night. Usually W10,000 entrance fee, with two free drinks. Daily 9pm–2am.

ENTERTAINMENT

There's no real excuse for being bored in Seoul. The city has a jaw-dropping amount going on almost every single day of the year, anything from **traditional dance** performances to **classical music** or **live jazz**; in addition, Hongdae functions as a breeding ground for local **rock** acts. The big bookstores (see page 115) have ticket booths, or you can get a Korean friend to help you book online at ⊕ ticketlink.co.kr.

CINEMA

Wherever you find yourself in Seoul, you won't be too far from the nearest cinema. CVG and Megabox are the two major cinema chains; foreign films are shown in their original language with Korean subtitles.

★**Cinematheque** 시네마테크 13 Donhwamun-ro ☎02 741 9782; Jongno 3-ga subway. Also going under the name of "Seoul Art Cinema", this sits on top of the characterful Nagwon Arcade, offering a rolling calendar of themed events, some of which are based around foreign films; pop by and pick up a pamphlet. Tickets around W8000.

★**CGV Wangsimni** 17 Gwangjang-ro ☎1544 1122; Wangsimni subway. The Wangsimni branch of Korea's biggest cinema chain has a "Gold Class" theatre, designed to resemble the first-class section on a plane, and seating just thirty. Tickets W35,000.

Megabox Boutique M 메가박스 부틱M B1 Coex 524 Bongeunsa-ro ☎1544 0070; Samseong subway. The chain's huge COEX branch has theatres resembling

SEOUL FESTIVALS

As long as you're not in Seoul during the long, cold winter, you'll almost certainly be able to catch a festival of some kind. In addition to national festivals (see page 44) and the traditional parades and street performances taking place on Insadonggil (usually every Thursday, Friday and Saturday), there are a whole host of events. A selection is detailed below.

Seoul Fashion Week March & Oct ⓦ seoulfashionweek.org. Since it started in 2000, this has become Asia's largest fashion event, functioning as a great showcase for Seoul's up-and-coming designers.

International Women's Film Festival Late April ⓦ siwff.or.kr. A week-long succession of films that "see the world through women's eyes" (even if some were created by men).

Jongmyo Daeje First Sun of May. Korean kings performed their ancestral rites at the Jongmyo shrine for hundreds of years, a tradition that's been carried forward to this day; the event is necessarily sober but very interesting, and is followed by traditional court dances.

Seoul International Cartoon & Animation Festival Late May ⓦ sicaf.org. Koreans young and old are major cartoon addicts, but while most of the national fix is sated by Japanese fare, there's still a lot of local talent: *The Simpsons*, *Family Guy* and *Spongebob Squarepants* are among the shows inked and lined here.

Korean Queer Culture Festival June ⓦ kqcf.org. Not exactly an event trumpeted by the local tourist authorities – in fact, not so long ago the police were still trying to ban it – this is a great way to see Korea crawling out of its Confucian shell. A fortnight-long programme includes a film festival, art exhibitions and the obligatory street parade.

Jisan Valley and Pentaport Rock Festivals July/Aug ⓦ valleyrockfestival.com & ⓦ pentaportrock.com. Two competing European-style music festivals (think tents, mud and portaloos) which manage to rope in major international acts, though admittedly ones usually on the wane in their homelands. Both events stretch across three alcohol-fuelled nights.

Seoul Performing Arts Festival Sept/Oct ⓦ spaf.or.kr. This increasingly acclaimed event has seen performances from as far afield as Latvia and Israel, though its main aim is to showcase Korean talent. It takes place in various locations around Seoul over a three-week period.

Seoul Drum Festival Early Oct. The crashes and bangs of all things percussive ring out at this annual event, which takes place in the Gwanghwamun area.

Jarasum Jazz Festival Oct ⓦ jarasumjazz.com. Very popular with expats, this takes place on Jara-seom, an islet east of Seoul, near Gapyeong.

Seoul Street Art Festival Oct ⓦ festivalseoul.or.kr. With everything from choreographed firework displays and tea ceremonies to men walking across the Han River by tightrope, this ten-day-long celebration is the best time to be in the city.

---

something from the not-too-distant future – the perfect place to watch a sci-fi flick. The experience is akin to being in a luxury hotel – "guests" are given slippers, a blanket and a bottle of Evian on check-in, and you can order a cocktail during the screening. Tickets from W12,000.

Sangsangmadang 상상마당 65 Eoulmadang-ro ⓣ02 330 6243; Sangsu subway. The basement of this arts complex has some arty English-language screenings, of which around half are from abroad. Interestingly, they try to show films whose themes match what's on show in the second-floor gallery. Tickets W8000.

THEATRE AND PERFORMANCE ARTS

Seoul's wide array of traditional performances and musicals are particularly popular with foreign travellers.

Jeongdong Theatre 정동극장 43 Jeongdong-gil ⓣ02 751 1500, ⓦ jeongdongtheater.com; City Hall subway. Seoul's most popular venue for traditional shows of song and dance. Previous performances have looked

at mask dances and love stories from dynastic times – whatever's on, it's bound to be well produced. Tickets usually from W30,000.

Jump 점프 3F 47 Mareunnae-ro ⓣ02 722 3995, ⓦ hijump.co.kr; Euljiro 3-ga subway. Ever wondered what a family entirely made up of martial arts experts would be like? Experience all the inevitable jumps and kicks in this entertaining musical. Tickets from W40,000. Performances Mon 8pm, Tues–Sat 5pm & 8pm, Sun 2pm & 6pm.

Korea House 한국의집 10 Toegye-ro ⓣ02 2266 9101, ⓦ koreahouse.or.kr; Chungmuro subway. Highly polished traditional performances from some of Korea's top artistes, combined with some of Seoul's best food (see page 105): this is one of the city's most popular nights out. The wonderful shows include fan dances, *pansori* opera and the long-ribboned hats of the "farmers' dance". Tickets W50,000; 50% off if you've had dinner here. Performances daily at 6.30pm & 8.30pm.

1

Namsan Gugakdang 남간 국악당 28 Toegyero 34-gil ☎ 02 2261 0500; Chungmuro subway. Those looking for a traditional Korean performance should make this their first port of call. Part of the Namsangol complex (see page 76), its shows revolve around *gugak*, an ancient style of Korean music, but the savvy curators bring a pleasant variety to the offerings with regular themed events of song, music, dance or a combination of the three. Ticket prices vary but are usually in the region of W30,000.

Nanta 난타 26 Myeongdong-gil ☎ 02 739 8288, ⓦ nanta.i-pmc.co.kr; City Hall subway. This madcap kitchen-based musical has gone down a storm since opening in 1997 (making it Korea's longest-running show), with songs, circus tricks and all sorts of utensil drumming mixed with a nice line in audience participation. Tickets from W40,000. Performances daily at 2pm, 5pm & 8pm.

Sejong Centre 세종 문화 회관 175 Sejong-daero ☎ 02 399 1114, ⓦ sejongpac.or.kr; Gwanghwamun subway. Gigantic venue offering a truly diverse array of music: everything from traditional Korean *gugak* to concerts from world-famous pianists. There's something going on every night of the week; check the website for details.

LIVE MUSIC

There's a decent little indie scene centred around Hongdae (check out ⓦ koreagigguide.com for listings). In addition, there are a few venues at which you can hear more highbrow offerings such as jazz or classical music.

All That Jazz 올댓재즈 12 Itaewon-ro 27-gil ☎ 02 795 5701, ⓦ allthatjazz.kr; Itaewon subway. An Itaewon institution, this place has been attracting jazz lovers for donkey's years. The atmosphere is fun, and audience interaction is commonplace – some spectators have ended up playing on stage with the band. Tickets usually W5000. Performances begin Mon 8.30pm, Tues–Thurs 6.30pm & 9.30pm, Fri & Sat 7pm & 10.30pm, Sun 6.30pm & 9.30pm.

FF 클럽FF 12 Wausan-ro 17-gil ☎ 010 9025 3407; Sangsu subway. Both Fs stand for "funky", though you're more likely to see some good ol' rock at this highly popular live music venue. A great many of the bands are foreign, bringing their pals and Korean hangers-on, then staying for the DJ sets afterwards. A great place to make new friends. Entry W10,000–15,000. Tues–Thurs & Sun 8–11pm, Fri & Sat 6pm–6am.

Once in a Blue Moon 원스인어블루문 824 Seolleung-ro ☎ 02 549 5490; Apgujeong subway. Perhaps the most renowned of Seoul's many jazz bars, and certainly the closest approximation to a Western venue. The music spans the full gamut of styles, played while customers dine on French or Mexican cuisine, accompanied by a choice from the lengthy wine and cocktail lists. Admission free. Performances begin 7.30pm.

★ Strange Fruit 스트레인지 프루트 64 Wausan-ro 29-gil ☎ 02 333 2919; Hongik University subway. Intimate live music venue with no stage – you'll be up close and personal with the band, and most probably with everyone else too. These walls have reverberated to almost every musical genre, and they offer cheap whisky and beer on tap. Entrance fee around W15,000. Daily 7pm–1am.

Yes 24 Live Hall 예스24라이브홀 20 Gucheonmyeon-ro ☎ 02 457 5114; Gwangnaru subway. Formerly the *Ax*, this venue has room for 2000 spectators, and is where many international bands play during their time in Seoul. Ticket prices vary.

SPORTS AND ACTIVITIES

Seoul has a small but pleasing range of ways to keep **sport** nuts entertained, as well as simple **exercise equipment** on almost every mountainside, as well as in parks, and dotting the banks of the Hangang and other waterways. The local **spectator sport** scene is also worth diving into.

BASEBALL

Pro baseball Seoul has three main professional teams. The two biggest are the LG Twins and the Doosan Bears, long-time rivals who both play in Jamsil Baseball Stadium (Sports Complex subway); the Nexen Heroes are a newer team playing west of Yeouido in Mokdong (Omokgyo subway). Games take place most days from April to October, and tickets can cost as little as W5000.

Batting cages Avid players can get some practice at a number of batting nets dotted around the city, particularly in student areas; these cost just W1000 for a minute's worth of balls. One is marked on the Insadong map (see map p.71).

FOOTBALL

K-League Those wanting to watch some professional K-League action can catch FC Seoul at the World Cup Stadium (ⓦ fcseoul.com; tickets from W10,000), with games taking place on weekends from March to October. Seongnam and Suwon, two of the most dominant Korean teams of recent times, also play near Seoul; the atmosphere at all grounds is fun but they can be on the empty side, unless you're lucky enough to be around for a major international game (ⓦ fifa.com).

ICE-SKATING

Outdoor rinks Those visiting in winter will be able to skate outdoors at various points in the city: Seoul Plaza and Gwanghwamun Plaza (see page 73) often turn into gigantic ice rinks for the season (usually Dec–Feb; daily 10am–10pm; W1000), though skaters are turfed off every 15min or so for surfacing.

Indoor rinks There's a year-round rink in Lotte World (see page 93), which charges W15,000 for entry and skate rental (daily 10am–9.30pm); far cheaper is the Olympic-size rink at Korea National University (daily 2–6pm; W5000), which is within walking distance of Korea University subway station.

SWIMMING

Outdoor pools In summer months (generally June–Aug), a number of outdoor pools open up around the Hangang; most convenient for visitors are those on the western side of Yeouido park (daily 9am–6pm; W5000). The *Hamilton Hotel* (see page 102) also opens its rooftop pool during the summer months (daily 9am–6pm; W22,000).

TAEKWONDO

Performances and practical sessions There are a number of places where foreign visitors can watch, or have a go at, this Korean martial art. The best place is Namsangol Hanok Village (see page 76), which puts on free performances every day bar Tuesday, and in summer often runs hands-on programmes for people to try themselves; alternatively, there are free practice sessions by Sungnyemun gate (see page 75) every Sat at 4pm (Jun, Sept & Oct only). Tourist information offices (see page 97) can advise on these as well as organizing longer programmes: figure on around W50,000 per day. In addition, there are occasional performances and tournaments at Kukkiwon (Mon–Fri 9am–5pm; free), a hall near Gangnam station and the home of Korea's national sport.

SHOPPING

Shopaholics will be quite at home in Seoul: the city has everything from trendy to traditional, markets to malls. High on the itinerary of many tourists are the colossal markets of **Dongdaemun** and **Namdaemun** (see page 78). There are **department stores** all over the city; the bustling streets of **Myeongdong** host department stores from the biggest nationwide chains – Migliore, Shinsaegae, Lotte and Galleria – and there are also luxury examples in Apgujeong. Perhaps more interesting are the city's **boutiques**; these are most numerous (and expensive) around Apgujeong, though there are cheaper versions of the same in Hongdae and Samcheongdong. Itaewon is also worth a mention for its excellent **tailored suits**. The best place to head for anything vaguely arty is **Insadonggil** and its side streets, which have numerous **craft** shops selling paints, brushes, calligraphy ink and handmade paper. There are also a few shops selling **antiques** here, and more of the same in Itaewon.

ARTS, CRAFTS AND ANTIQUES

★ **Kwang Ju Yo** 광주요 42-2 Bukchon-ro ☎ 02 741 4801, ⓦ kwangjuyo.com; Anguk subway; map p.64. Korea has been at the forefront of world pottery for centuries, and this store is one of the best places to buy it. Celadon bowls and porcelain vases are among the items on offer, while they also sell Andong *soju* (a particularly potent form of the national drink, at 41 percent ABV) in elaborate jars: perfect souvenirs. Daily 10am–9pm.

Myung Sin Dang 명신당 34 Insadong-gil ☎ 02 722 4846; Anguk subway; map p.71. The most renowned of Insadong's many art supplies shops (Queen Elizabeth II once popped by), focusing solely on the humble paintbrush – there are hundreds of styles on offer here, including some made with baby hair. Daily 10am–6pm.

Sangsangmadang 상상마당 65 Eoulmadang-ro ☎ 02 330 6243; Sangsu subway; map p.85. Although Hongdae is better known today for its bars than its art, the university that the area is named after is still artistically focused. This arty complex features a gallery, café and cinema, while the ground floor sells small lifestyle goods designed by local students. Daily 9am–9pm.

★ **Ssamiziegil** 쌈지길 44 Insadong-gil; Anguk subway; map p.71. A wonderfully designed building whose spiral walkway plays host to countless small shops selling traditional clothing, handmade paper, jewellery and the like. There's also a rooftop market at weekends,

selling all manner of quirky arts and crafts. Daily 10.30am–9pm.

Tongin 통인 가게 32 Insadong-gil ☎ 02 733 4867, ⓦ tonginstore.com; Anguk subway; map p.71. Colonial structure with whole floors full of antique cases, cupboards, medicine racks and other furniture, much of it in a distinctively oriental style; at least one of the proprietors speaks English, and the store can arrange shipping. Daily 10am–8pm.

★ **Yido Pottery** 이도 본점 191 Changdeokgung-gil ☎ 02 722 0756, ⓦ yido.kr; Anguk subway; map p.64. Just up the road from Kwang Ju Yo (see above), this pottery store is perhaps even more interesting. Here you'll find tea sets, plates and other great offerings from some of the country's top talents, many of whom learned their craft at Hongdae. Daily 10am–7pm.

Zack 잭 26 Samcheon-ro 4-gil ☎ 010 4183 0499; Anguk subway; map p.64. It may be exaggerating to call Kim Hyunkwan's tiny stall a shop, but what a find this is – he sells prints of his gorgeous etchings of the area's *hanok* buildings, and they're very affordable (from W5000 for a little one). The views from here are suitably impressive too. Daily 11am–5pm.

BOOKS

Foreign Book Store 포린북스토어 208 Noksapyeong-daero ☎ 02 793 8249; Noksapyeong

1

subway; map p.89. A rambling affair, and pleasingly messy, selling a selection of mostly secondhand books. Stick around a while and you're bound to find a gem or two, remnants of decades' worth of Itaewon expats. Daily 10am–9pm.

Kyobo Books 교보 문고 Kyobo Building B1, 1 Jongno ☎1544 1900; Gwanghwamun subway; map p.74. Filling the basement level of the huge Kyobo building, this is the country's largest bookshop, and fantastic for foreign-language books. There's also a branch in Gangnam, just south of Sinnonhyeon station. Daily 9.30am–10pm.

★ **What the Book** 윗더북 2F 86 Bogwang-ro ☎02 797 2342, ⓦwhatthebook.com; Itaewon subway; map p.89. Dedicated foreign-language bookshop that's extremely popular with expats; everyone seems to end up here at some point. They've an extensive secondhand selection too. Daily 10am–9pm.

CLOTHING

★ **Åland** 에이렌드 30 Myeongdong 6-gil ☎02 3210 5890; Myeongdong subway; map p.77. There are several branches of this popular around the city, but the Myeongdong one is usually best – the lower levels are full of clothing from some of Korea's edgier designers, while the top floor has a surprisingly well-stocked vintage section. Daily 11am–10pm.

Boon The Shop 스페이스 뮤 분더샵 21 Apgujeong-ro 60-gil ☎02 2056 1234; Apgujeong Rodeo subway; map p.92. This Apgujeong multishop (a Konglish term for a store selling various brands) sells clothing from upmarket international brands, but even if you can't afford to spend US$100 on a T-shirt it's worth popping into for the gorgeous interior alone. Daily 11am–8pm.

Ccomaque 꼬마 25 Bukchon-ro 5-gil ☎02 722 1547, ⓦccomaque.com; Anguk subway; map p.64. This chain has spread all around the city of late, selling skirts and dresses featuring cutesey, cartoonish designs based around purportedly Korean motifs, including animals such as deer, turtles and cranes, and natural elements such as clouds and pine trees. Daily 10am–8pm.

Coreano 코레아노 39 Insadong-gil ☎02 720 0301; Anguk subway; map p.71. If you've rented some *hanbok* for a walk around the palaces, but feel like bringing your own home (though don't dare use one as a Hallowe'en costume, or the ghosts of dynastic kings will haunt you forever), this is a great choice, with contemporary styles in gentle colours; skirts go for W75,000 or so, dresses for double that. Daily 10.30am–9pm.

DIRECTORY

Banks and exchange Banks will exchange foreign currency, but it can be cumbersome, and you'll get better rates in the

Gwangjang Market 광장시장; Jongno 5-ga subway; map p.77. Though best known for its culinary offerings (see page 105), this sprawling market has an excellent secondhand section, selling all manner of zany shirts, coats and jackets imported from abroad. It's a little hard to find: hunt down the staircase on the western side of the market, and head for the second floor. Mon–Sat 9am–6pm.

★ **Hahn's Custom Tailoring** 한스 양복 134 Itaewon-ro ☎02 793 0830, ⓔhanstailor@hotmail. com; Itaewon subway; map p.89. Get a perfectly tailored suit for around US$500. Affable owner Hahn speaks excellent English, and will be pleased to discuss the particular style you're after; his tailors also make good shirts. Daily 10am–9pm.

Hamilton Shirts 해밀튼 셔츠 153 Itaewon-ro ☎02 798 5693, ⓦhs76.com; Itaewon subway; map p.89. Tailored shirts at prices less than you'd pay for factory-made fare on your local high street: most shirts go for around W45,000. The quality is amazingly high for the price. Daily 10am–9.30pm.

★ **Lee Geon Maan** 이건만 29 Insadong-gil ☎02 733 8265, ⓦleegeonmaan.com; Anguk subway; map p.71. Well-located store selling ties for men and handbags for women. Their unique selling point is an innovative use of *hangeul*, the Korean text conspicuous by its absence on Korean clothing. Daily 10.30am–8pm.

★ **Lee Young Hee** 이영희 3 Seolleung-ro 155-gil ☎02 544 0630, ⓦleeyounghee.co.kr; Apgujeong subway; map p.92. The popularity of Korea's traditional clothing, *hanbok* (한복), has gone through the roof of late, and much of the credit is due to designers like Lee Young Hee, who altered traditional shapes and fabrics to cater for more contemporary tastes. Hillary Clinton has been a customer at their New York branch. Daily 11am–6.30pm.

ELECTRONIC EQUIPMENT

Techno Mart 테크노 마트 85 Gwangnaru-ro 56-gil; Gangbyeon subway; map p.92. Out near the Dongseoul bus terminal in eastern Seoul, this is a gigantic place stocking all manner of electronic goods. Daily 10am–7pm.

Yongsan Electronics Market 용산 전자 상가 125 Cheongpa-ro; Yongsan subway; map p.89. This multi-level giant rises up alongside the Yongsan train station. Many staff speak a little English, and it's a great place just to look around, even if you're not buying. It's a bit more expensive than Techno Mart for some goods. Daily 10am–7.30pm.

booths dotted around Myeongdong. Many ATMs can be used with international cards (see page 52 for advice).

Embassies Australia ☎ 02 2003 0100; Canada ☎ 02 3783 6000; China ☎ 02 738 1038; Ireland ☎ 02 721 7200; New Zealand ☎ 02 3701 7700; Russia ☎ 02 318 2116; South Africa ☎ 02 2077 5900; UK ☎ 02 3210 5500; US ☎ 02 397 4114.

Hospitals and clinics To find an English-speaking doctor, or a clinic suited to your needs, call the Seoul Help Center's medical line on ☎ 02 2075 4180.

Immigration There are immigration offices (ⓦ immigration. go.kr) at both Incheon and Gimpo airports, but the main one is way out west near Mokdong station (line 5), 151 Mokdongdong-ro (☎ 02 2650 6211).

Left luggage Most subway, train and bus stations have storage lockers costing from W2000 for a few hours, though these are too small to accommodate suitcases or large backpacks. Some hotels offer left luggage facilities, and a couple of guesthouses are willing to put your bags somewhere safe while you travel around the country.

Lost property There's a national lost property hotline (☎ 02 2299 1282), but since staff are unlikely to speak English it may be best to go through the tourist information line (☎ 1330). There are also lost property offices in City Hall and Chungmuro subway stations, as well as the main train stations.

Post offices There's a post office in every neighbourhood, all of which can handle international mail – just ask for the nearest *ucheguk* (usually Mon–Fri 9am–5pm). The main office on Jongno is open until 8pm on weekdays, 6pm on weekends (☎ 02 3703 9011).

Gyeonggi

KOREAN FOLK VILLAGE

Gyeonggi

If you meet a Korean who claims to live in Seoul, there's a fifty-fifty chance that they actually mean Gyeonggi (경기), a province encircling the capital and bristling with high-rise hives for many of its worker bees. Gyeonggi and Seoul have a combined urban mass of over 25 million people – around half of the country's population, meaning it's one of the world's most densely populated areas. Seoul functions as the province's beating heart, and while most of its satellite cities are commuter-filled nonentities, there's still plenty to see for those willing to put in the miles: a giant fortress from the days of dynasty; the country's biggest Chinatown; more islands than you could possibly count; and – most excitingly of all – the chance to tiptoe across the border to the forbidden North.

Of the province's cities, **Incheon** to the west of the capital and **Suwon** to the south merit a visit. Suwon's main draw is its UNESCO-listed fortress, while Incheon was the first city in the country to be opened up to international trade, and remains Korea's most important link with the outside world thanks to its international airport and ferry terminals.

A residue of traditional Korean life can be found off the mainland in the **islands** of the West Sea – better known internationally as the Yellow Sea – from whose shores fishermen roll in and out with the tide as they have for generations. Two of the more notable isles are **Deokjeokdo**, a laidback and refreshingly unspoiled retreat from Seoul; and **Gyodongdo**, an island with great views over to North Korea.

Those who want to catch a glimpse of the neighbours should head to **Panmunjeom**, a village inside the **Demilitarized Zone** that separates North and South Korea. With security so tight, access is understandably subject to the conditions of the time, but most should be lucky enough to take a step across the world's most fortified border to what is technically **North Korean territory**. Alternatively, you can make do with a view of the empty "Propaganda Village" on the opposite side of the DMZ, or a scramble through tunnels built by the North in readiness for an assault on Seoul.

Incheon

인천

Almost every international visitor to Korea gets to see some of **INCHEON**. Korea's third most populous city, it's home to the main airport and receives almost all ferries from China, though most new arrivals head straight to Seoul as soon as they set foot on Korean territory. However, in view of its colourful recent history, it's worth at least a day-trip from the capital – this was where Korea's "Hermit Kingdom" finally crawled out of self-imposed isolation in the late nineteenth century and opened itself

---

General MacArthur and the Incheon
    landings p.125
Incheon airport sleeping options
    p.126
Chinese food, Korean-style p.126

The Yellow Sea p.127
Mr Toilet p.132
The Axe Murder Incident p.137
"Freedom Village" and "Propaganda
    Village" p.139

HWASEONG FORTRESS

Highlights

❶ **Incheon** Climb Jayu Park to gaze out over the Lego-like jumble of container ships surrounding the city, before trotting down the hill into Korea's largest Chinatown. See page 120

❷ **West Sea islands** Clean air, homely villages and a thriving fishing industry are what make a visit to the islands worthwhile; all this and only a day-trip from Seoul. See page 127

❸ **Suwon** Scramble up a UNESCO-listed fortress wall, visit a nearby folk village, or hunt down a house shaped like a toilet. See page 131

❹ **Yangsu-ri** Seoul's best sunsets can be found way out east of the centre, on this charming island surrounded by mountains. See page 135

❺ **The DMZ** Walk through a tunnel under the world's most heavily fortified border, or take a couple of steps into official North Korean territory in the eerie Joint Security Area. See page 135

❻ **Paju** With its fun Book City and arts complex, Paju is more than just the average Seoul satellite suburb. See page 140

HIGHLIGHTS ARE MARKED ON THE MAP ON PAGE 122

up to international trade, spurred on by the Japanese following similar events in their own country (the Meiji Restoration). Incheon was also the landing site for **Douglas MacArthur** and his troops in a manoeuvre that turned the tide of the Korean War (see page 125). However, despite its obvious importance to Korea past and present, there's a palpable absence of civic pride, possibly due to the fact that Incheon is inextricably connected to the huge Seoul metropolis – the buildings simply don't stop on their long march from the capital.

Incheon's various sights can easily be visited on a day-trip from Seoul, though getting here can be tedious – it's around an hour on the capital's often-rammed subway line 1. The most interesting area is **Jung-gu**, where you can wander around the country's largest Chinatown, a small but appealing area where you can rub shoulders with the Russian sailors and Filipino merchants who – after the Chinese – make up most of Incheon's sizeable foreign contingent. Jung-gu sits below **Jayu Park**, where a statue of MacArthur gazes out over the sea. The only other area of note is **Songdo New Town**, an area being built on land reclaimed from the sea. Lastly, Incheon is also a jumping-off point for ferries to a number of islands in the **West Sea** (see page 127).

Jung-gu

중구 • Incheon subway (line 1)

Though it means "Central District", **Jung-gu** actually lies way out on the western fringe of Incheon – it does, however, form the centre of the city's tourist appeal. On exiting the gate at Incheon station, you'll immediately be confronted by the city's gentrified

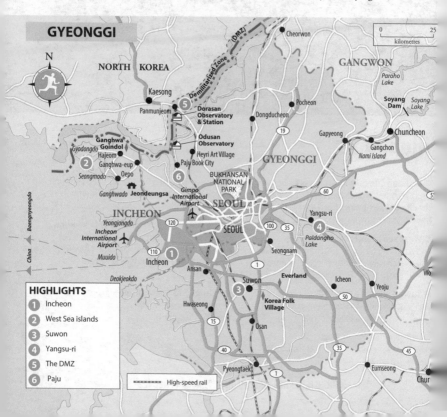

GYEONGGI

0   25
kilometres

NORTH KOREA

GANGWON

Kaesong

Demilitarized Zone (DMZ)

Cheorwon

Paroho Lake

Panmunjeom

Dorasan Observatory & Station

Pocheon

Soyang Dam   Soyang Lake

Dongducheon

19

Odusan Observatory

Gapyeong   Chuncheon

Gangchon   Nami Island

Ganghwa Goindol
Gyodongdo   Hajeom

Heyri Art Village

GYEONGGI

Paju Book City

Seongmodo   Ganghwa-eup   Oepo
Ganghwado   Jeondeungsa

BUKHANSAN NATIONAL PARK

60

Gimpo International Airport

SEOUL

5

Baengnyeongdo

INCHEON

Yeongjongdo

120

SEOUL

Yangsu-ri

China

Incheon International Airport

100   35

Paldangho Lake

110

Muuido

Seongnam

Incheon

Ansan

Deokjeokdo

Suwon   Everland

Icheon   Yeoju

HIGHLIGHTS

1   Incheon
2   West Sea islands
3   Suwon
4   Yangsu-ri
5   The DMZ
6   Paju

Korea Folk Village

50

Hwaseong

Osan

15

40

Eumseong

Pyeongtaek

1

Chur

35   45

High-speed rail

Chinatown; sitting across the main road and demarcated by the requisite oriental gate, it's a pleasant and surprisingly quiet area to walk around with a belly full of Chinese food. Uphill roads lead northeast to **Jayu Park**, which topples down to the south into a quiet but cosmopolitan part of town, where many Japanese lived during the colonial era.

Jayu Park

자유 공원 • Daily 24hr • Free

Within easy walking distance of the subway station, **Jayu Park** is most notable for its statue of **General Douglas MacArthur**, staring proudly out over the seas that he conquered during the Korean War (see page 125). Also in the park is the Korean–American **Centennial Monument**, made up of eight black triangular shards that stretch up towards each other but never quite touch – feel free to make your own comparisons with the relationship between the two countries. Views from certain parts of the park expose Incheon's port, a colourful maze of cranes and container ships that provide a vivid reminder of the city's trade links with its neighbours across the seas.

The Street of Culture and History

역사문화의 거리 • Daily 24hr • Free

South of Jayu Park, Incheon has tried to evoke its colonial past on the slightly bizarre **Street of Culture and History**; the new wooden fronts added to the buildings are the only discernable things that constitute such a grand title, though they look decidedly pretty. Most of the businesses that received a face-lift were simple shops such as confectioners, laundries and electrical stores; many are still going, though they're now being augmented by bars, arty cafés and such like.

The former Japanese banks

Sinpo-ro 23-gil • Both daily 9am–5.30pm • W500 each

One block south of the odd Street of Culture and History is a road more genuinely cultural and historic. Here you'll find a few distinctive **Japanese colonial buildings** which are surprisingly Western in appearance (that being the Japanese architectural fashion of the time). Three of the buildings were originally banks, of which two have now been turned into small **museums**. The former **58th Bank of Japan** offers interesting photo and video displays of life in colonial times, while the former **1st Bank** down the road has a less interesting display of documents, flags and the like. Sitting in a small outdoor display area between the two, there are some fascinating pictures taken here in the 1890s, on what was then a quiet, dusty road almost entirely devoid of traffic, peopled with white-robed gents in horsehair hats – images of a Korea long gone.

Incheon Art Platform

인천 아트 프래트폼 • ⓦ inartplatform.kr

It's usually worth popping by to see what's going on in and around **Incheon Art Platform**, a rambling culture and arts centre sprawled across several buildings just south of the former Japanese banks. There's nothing like a permanent exhibition here, since it's more a hub for artistic creativity than a place for displays, but there'll always be at least an outdoor installation to get your teeth into.

Wolmido

월미도 • Ferry cruises daily at noon, 2pm, 4pm & 6pm (1hr 20min; W15,000) • #2 (every 7min; W1300) is the best of several bus routes from Incheon station, or you can take a taxi (less than W5000)

Famed across the land as the place where the tides turned the tide of the Korean War, the island of **Wolmido** – 1km from Jung-gu and connected to the mainland by road – is now renowned for some pretty sorry-looking funfair rides and a musical fountain. It's possible to embark on a **ferry cruise** here, though, and there are umpteen restaurants

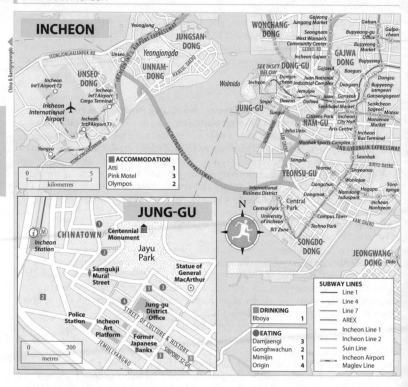

in which to wolf down a round of super-fresh seafood. You may also notice a monorail heading here from Incheon station – stalled for years at the time of writing, and quite possibly never to return.

Songdo New Town

송도 • Central Park station (Incheon subway line 1), or a W12,000 taxi ride from Incheon subway

Built on a man-made island just south of central Incheon, **Songdo New Town** is essentially a gigantic, $40bn experiment in modern-day urban development. Centred on the **Northeast Asia Trade Tower** (305m), which was for a time the tallest building in South Korea, this symphony of chrome and glass was created with an ambitiously green, eco-friendly manifesto – "City of the Future", "High-Tech Utopia" and "The World's Smartest City" were phrases bandied about by government bureaucrats. The vast majority of its buildings were in place at the time of writing, making use of fancy underground waste-disposal systems, super-fast Internet connections and other unexcitingly incremental improvements on modern life. It's all a bit dull, and more than a little creepy in feel, but the difference with "regular" Korean cities is quite striking, and it can be quite pleasurable strolling through or along one of the many parks and canals.

ARRIVAL AND INFORMATION   INCHEON

By plane Importantly, there's no need to hit central Incheon itself to get to and from the international airport, which is actually on an island west of the city proper and connected to the mainland by bridge: there are dedicated airport bus connections from Seoul and all over the country. Several limousine bus routes connect the airport with central Incheon, or take city bus #306 (W1300) to Incheon subway station.

GENERAL MACARTHUR AND THE INCHEON LANDINGS

"We drew up a list of every natural and geographic handicap... Incheon had 'em all."
Commander Arlie G. Capps

On the morning of September 15, 1950, the most daring move of the **Korean War** was made, an event that was to alter the course of the conflict entirely, and is now seen as one of the greatest military manoeuvres in history. At this point the Allied forces had been pushed by the North Korean People's Army into a small corner of the peninsula around Busan, but **General Douglas MacArthur** was convinced that a single decisive movement behind enemy lines could be enough to turn the tide.

MacArthur wanted to attempt an amphibious landing on the Incheon coast, but his plan was greeted with scepticism by many of his colleagues – both the South Korean and American armies were severely under-equipped (the latter only just recovering from the tolls of World War II), Incheon was heavily fortified, and its natural island-peppered defences and fast tides made it an even more dangerous choice.

The People's Army had simply not anticipated an attack on this scale in this area, reasoning that if one were to happen, it would take place at a more sensible location further down the coast. However, the plan went ahead and the Allied forces performed **successful landings** at Wolmido island and two other Incheon beaches, during which time North Korean forces were shelled heavily to quell any counterattacks. The city was taken with relative ease. MacArthur had correctly deduced that a poor movement of supplies was his enemy's Achilles heel – landing behind enemy lines gave Allied forces a chance to cut the supply line to KPA forces further south, and Seoul was duly retaken on September 25.

Despite the Incheon victory and its consequences, MacArthur is not viewed by Koreans – or, indeed, the world in general – in an entirely positive light, feelings exacerbated by the continued American military presence in the country. While many in Korea venerate the General as a hero, repeated demonstrations have called for the **tearing down** of his statue in Jayu Park, denouncing him as a "war criminal who massacred civilians during the Korean War", and whose statue "greatly injures the dignity of the Korean people". Documents obtained after his eventual dismissal from the Army suggest that he would even have been willing to bring nuclear weapons into play – on December 24, 1950, he requested the shipment of 38 atomic bombs to Korea, intending to string them "across the neck of Manchuria". Douglas MacArthur remains a controversial character, even in death.

By subway Despite the city's size, there's no train station: it's best to take subway line 1 from Seoul (1hr), though be sure that your train is bound for Incheon, as the line splits when leaving the capital. Some slightly faster services starting at Yongsan skip a few stations en route, and you might even be able to get a seat if you start your journey there.

By ferry Ferries from China dock at one of two terminals (see page 28 for details on these services). Terminal 2 is the closer to the city centre, and is best accessed by taxi (W4000 from Incheon or Dong-Incheon subway stations). Terminal 1 is further out; a taxi will be less than W10,000, or buses #28 and #24 head the same way from Incheon and Dong-Incheon stations respectively. Right next to Terminal 1 is the Yeonan terminal, which caters for domestic ferries

to almost all of the accessible islands in the West Sea (see details in the relevant island accounts).

By bus Incheon bus terminal is located next to a subway station of the same name on Incheon line 1, six stops south of Bupyeong, where it meets Seoul's own line 1.

Destinations Chuncheon (1–2 hourly; 2hr); Daegu (1–2 hourly; 3hr 45min); Daejeon (every 30min; 2hr); Gangneung (hourly; 3hr 30min); Gwangju (1–2 hourly; 3hr 30min); Jeonju (1–2 hourly; 2hr 50min); Seoul (Dong-Seoul terminal; every 30min; 1hr 10min).

Tourist information The helpful booth outside Incheon subway station (daily 9am–6pm; ☎ 032 773 2225) usually has an English-speaker; further offices can be found in the ferry terminals.

ACCOMMODATION

Incheon's proximity to Seoul means that most people choose to visit on a **day-trip**, but it's quite possible to spend a night here. There are a number of **motels** in and around Incheon and Dong-Incheon subway stations, as well as in Chinatown itself.

2

INCHEON AIRPORT SLEEPING OPTIONS

Travellers with untimely arrivals or departures often find themselves sleeping at or near Incheon International Airport (see page 124), which is almost an hour from Seoul at the best of times. The good news is that there's a range of accommodation options around the airport, with many bookable on the usual search engines – those that are a little more distant usually throw in free transfers. There's also a 24hr capsule hotel within the airport itself (☎032 743 5000), which is great if you just need a few hours' rest; rates start at W7700 per hour. Alternatively, there's a spa facility with a basic common sleeping area (W20,000), and there are free shower facilities if you just want a wash.

Atti 아띠 호텔 88 Sinpo-ro 35-gil ☎032 772 5233; map p.124. This little gem is tucked away in a quiet area behind the Jung-gu district office, near *Damjaengi* restaurant (see page 126). Recent renovations have seen it become a little too trendy – the big bugbears here are the glass partitions that make the bathrooms a little too visible. However, the surrounding area is highly pleasant, making it easy to put big-city bustle out of mind. **W65,000**

Pink Motel 핑크 모텔 4F 49 Sinpo-ro 23-gil ☎032 773 9984; map p.124. If you can find it (it's tucked away on the fourth floor of a large building), this is the cheapest motel in the area – rooms have carpets, which is a real rarity at this price level, and they're clean enough. **W25,000**

Olympos 올림포스 호텔 257 Jemullyangno ☎032 762 5181, ⓦolymposhotel.co.kr; map p.124. Formerly the *Paradise*, this is the best hotel in Jung-gu, though the crane-filled views may not appeal to some. Despite being just a stone's throw from Incheon subway station, the hotel entrance is uphill and hard to reach, so you may prefer to take a taxi. Rates can drop to as little as W65,000 midweek. **W250,000**

EATING

Rarely for a Korean city, and perhaps uniquely for a Korean port, Incheon isn't renowned for its food, though the presence of a large and thriving **Chinatown** is a boon to visitors. Don't expect the food to be terribly authentic, since Koreans have their own take on Chinese cuisine (see below).

★**Damjaengi** 담쟁이 12 Jayugongwonnam-ro ☎032 772 0153; map p.124. Pleasantly old-fashioned venue under Jayu Park, selling various forms of *bibimbap* (most W11,000), plus Korean bar-food meant for sharing (most plates W10,000–30,000). There's a garden out back, also featuring a tiny museum of sorts. Daily 11.30am–9pm.

Gonghwachun 공화춘 43 Chinatown-ro ☎032 765 0571; map p.124. This is where Korea's *jjajangmyeon* fad started – it has been served here since the 1890s. W5000 will buy you a bowl, or you could try the spicy tofu on rice (W8000) or something more exotic, like the sautéed shredded beef with green pepper (W20,000), and finish off your meal with fried, honey-dipped rice balls. Not the most attractive venue, but the views from the top level are lovely. Daily 11am–11pm.

Mimijin 미미진 27 Chinatown-ro ☎032 762 8988; map p.124. Something a little different to the area's norm, with food from the "other" side of China – namely the one associated with dim sum and dumplings (most W6000 a tray, though you'll need a few to fill up). Also home to an admirable quantity of carved wood. Daily 10.30am–10pm.

Origin 오리진 96 Sinpo-ro 27-gil ☎032 777 5527; map p.124. Many cafés on Culture Street have gone for "old-school" decor, but this one has been most faithful to the area's Japanese past – their single tatami-based table is the obvious target, plus there's a sculpted garden area out back. Mon & Wed–Sun 11am–10pm.

CHINESE FOOD, KOREAN-STYLE

Korea's biggest **Chinatown** can be found in Incheon, and there are some decent restaurants hereabouts (see above=). However, even at these, the food is not exactly what you'd expect to find across the West Sea – even though the majority of the restaurateurs are Chinese, Korean visitors usually order precisely the same dishes as they would at any Chinese restaurant across the land. When with the Romans, do as the Romans do: the **top choices** here, and available at every single restaurant, are sweet-and-sour pork (탕수육; *tangsuyuk*), fried rice topped with a fried egg and black-bean paste (볶음밥; *beokkeumbap*), spicy seafood broth (짬뽕; *jjambbong*), and the undisputed number one, *jjajangmyeon* (자장면), noodles topped with black-bean paste.

DRINKING

Bboya 뽀야 Jungangdong 3-ga 1-8 ☎ 032 762 8800; map p.124. Many bars in Korea decorate themselves with beer bottle tops, but here the concept is taken to its logical extreme – both interior and exterior alike are smothered with them. Despite the busy decor, it's a relaxing place to drink. Daily 7pm–1am.

The West Sea islands

Gyeonggi's perforated western coast topples into the **West Sea** in an expanse of mud flats – the **tidal range** here is said to be the second biggest in the world after the Bay of Fundy in eastern Canada, though this is challenged by Britain's Bristol Channel. Whichever is the silver medallist, the retreat of the tides is fantastic news for hunters of clams and other sea fare; it does, however, mean that beaches are in short supply. Fear not, Korean land rises again across the waves in the form of dozens of **islands**, almost all of which have remained pleasantly green and unspoiled; some also have excellent **beaches**. Life here is predominantly fishing-based and dawdles by at a snail's pace – a world away from Seoul and its environs, despite a few being close enough to be visited on a day-trip. Quite a number of these islands have next to no traffic, making them ideal places for a ride if you can find a bike to bring along.

Up the Gyeonggi coast from Incheon is **Ganghwado**, an island whose **dolmens** betray its ancient history. Just to the west is delightfully pastoral **Gyodongdo**, which sits just 5km from North Korea. Ganghwado is connected to the mainland by bus, but there are other islands that can take hours to reach by ferry; two of these are **Deokjeokdo** and **Baengnyeongdo**, both beautiful and sufficiently far away from "regular" Korea to provide perfect escapes for those in need of a break. Swarms of less-visited islands are also there for the taking, if you're in an adventurous mood. The suffix **-do** (도) means "island" in Korean; accordingly, you may see signs for "Deokjeok Island" and so on.

Ganghwado

강화도 • Bus #3000 (every 15–20min; 1hr 40min) from Sinchon subway in Seoul (line 2); walk directly up from exit 1

Unlike most West Sea islands, **Ganghwado** is close enough to the mainland to be connected by road – buses run regularly from Seoul to **Ganghwa-eup** (강화읍), the ugly main settlement; from here local buses dash to destinations across the island, though the place is so small that journeys rarely take more than thirty minutes. While this accessibility means that Ganghwado lacks the beauty of some of its more distant cousins, there's plenty to see. One look at a map should make clear the strategic importance of the island, which not only sits at the mouth of Seoul's main river, the Han, but whose northern flank is within a Frisbee's throw of the **North Korean border**. Would-be adventurers should note that this area is chock-full of military installations, and closed to the public.

Before the latest conflict, this unfortunate isle saw **battles** with Mongol, Manchu, French, American and Japanese forces, among others (see page 365). However, Ganghwado's foremost sights date from further back than even the earliest of these

> ### THE YELLOW SEA
>
> The West Sea is far better known abroad as the "**Yellow Sea**", a reference to the vast quantity of silt deposited into it by the Yellow River, which flows from the Chinese desert. Be warned that few Koreans will take kindly to this term, even though it's the accepted international name; there's nowhere near the intensity of debate that the East Sea/Sea of Japan on the other side of the country has inspired (see page 166), but those who want to stay on the better side of their Korean friends should refer to the body of water off the Gyeonggi coast as the "**West Sea**", or even better, the Korean name, **Seohae** (서해).

2

confrontations – a clutch of **dolmen** scattered around the northern part of the island date from the first century BC and are now on UNESCO's World Heritage list.

Ganghwa Goindol

강화 고인돌 • Daily 24hr • Free • From Ganghwa-eup, take one of the buses bound for Changhu-ri or Gyodongdo (every hour or so), and make sure that the driver knows where you want to go

Misty remnants from bygone millennia, Ganghwa's **dolmens** are overground burial chambers consisting of flat capstones supported by three or more vertical megaliths. The Korean peninsula contains more than 30,000 of these ancient tombs – almost half of the world's total – and Ganghwado has one of the highest concentrations in the country. Most can only be reached by car or bike, though one, **Ganghwa Goindol**, is situated near a main road and accessible by bus. The granite tomb sits unobtrusively in a field, as it has for centuries: a stone skeleton long divested of its original earth covering, with a large capstone.

Hajeom and around

하점

The countryside surrounding Goindol is extremely beautiful, and you can combine a visit to the dolmen with a delightful walk. One of the best places to head to is the village of **HAJEOM**, not far to the west, where the roofs of some houses have been traditionally decorated with distinctive patterns. From the hills above Hajeom it's possible to view the North Korean bank of the Hangang, though the propaganda that the North used to boom across the border from giant speakers can no longer be heard. Visual propaganda still remains, however, in the form of giant slogans best seen from the small mountain of **Bongcheonsan** (봉천산), a forty-minute walk north of Hajeom – the message visible across the border translates as "Yankees go home", a request that would doubtless be more effective were it not written in Korean.

Jeondeungsa

전등사 • Daily 8am–6pm • W3000, or free out of hours • From Ganghwa-eup, take one of the half-hourly buses bound for Onsu-ri; the #3100 also runs here from Sinchon in Seoul

In the south of the island is **Jeondeungsa**, a pretty temple dating from the fourth century – when Buddhism was just taking root on the peninsula – making it one of the oldest temples in the country. It was also the venue for the creation of the famed **Tripitaka Koreana**, eighty-thousand-plus blocks of carved Buddhist doctrine which now reside in Haeinsa temple near Daegu (see page 181). These days, due in part to its proximity to Seoul, it's a highly popular place to **templestay** (see page 35).

Gyodongdo and Seongmodo

교동도 • Buses from Ganghwa-eup (11 daily; 1hr; W1300); those driving may have to register with local military • Bicycles available for hire from the visitor centre, by main road in Gyodong-myeon

West of Ganghwado lie two smaller, even less densely populated islands. The southernmost of the duo, **Seongmodo**, was once a popular getaway for stressed-out Seoulites, though its remote appeal has diminished significantly since the building of a new bridge to Ganghwa, and the grounding of the cute ferries which once provided the island's only real link to the outside world. **Gyodongdo** to the north is now tethered to Ganghwa by bridge in a similar fashion, but has better retained its bucolic air – most of the place is pancake flat, and perfect for touring by bicycle, with views across to North Korea (just 5km away) under normal weather conditions. In fact, before crossing the bridge to the island, soldiers may board the bus and ask for your reason to visit – just say "tourist" instead of "spy", and you're almost certain to be waved across.

2

Unlike Seongmodo, there's next to no accommodation on Gyodongdo, though locals are extra friendly to the few international visitors who make it this far. The main "town", **Gyodong-myeon** (교동면), is nothing more than a country village, and boasts the island's only convenience store and bank, as well as a bizarre number of *dabang* (다방), Korea's original take on the whole café experience, though now in rapid decline across the nation. Poke around and you'll also see some quirky wall art. Abutting a small mountain south of Gyodong-myeon are the island's two main sights – **Gyodong Hyanggo** (교동향교), a simple Confucian academy which is one of the oldest in Korea, and **Hwagaesa** (화개사), a charming temple just to the west.

Deokjeokdo

덕적도 • Ferries from Incheon's Yeonan pier (1–3 daily; 1hr 30min; W21,900 one way)

Possibly the prettiest and most tranquil of the West Sea isles, **Deokjeokdo** feels a world away from Seoul, though it's quite possible to visit from the capital on a day-trip. There's little in the way of sightseeing, and not much to do, but that's just the point – the island has a couple of stunning beaches and some gorgeous mountain trails, and makes a refreshing break from the hustle and bustle of the mainland. Around the ferry berth are a few shops, restaurants and *minbak*, while a bus meets the ferries and makes its way round to grassy **Seopori beach** (서포리 해수욕장) on the other, quieter side of the island – also home to a few *minbak*. Most who stay here for a day or two spend their time chatting to locals, lazing or throwing back beers on the beach, going fishing or taking the easy climb up to the island's main peak.

Some adventurous souls make their way to **Soyado** (소야도), an island facing the ferry berth, and only a few minutes away if you can flag down a fishing boat. There's even less to do here than on Seongmodo, though there are a couple of motels and *minbak* if you look hard enough, and you can rest assured you'll be one of very few foreigners to have overnighted on the island.

Baengnyeongdo

백령도 • Ferries (2–5 weekly; 4hr 30min; W66,500 one way) run from Incheon's Yeonan pier, departing at 7.50am or 8.30am; ferries return to Incheon fairly quickly after arrival

A tortuous ferry-ride from Incheon is **Baengnyeongdo**, almost tickling the North Korean coastline and as such home to many military installations. In 2010 the **Cheonan**, a South Korean naval vessel, sank just off the island in suspicious circumstances, seriously damaging relations between the two Koreas (see page 372). Baengnyeongdo literally means "White Wing Island", due to its apparent resemblance to an ibis taking flight, and although the reality is somewhat different you will find yourself gawping at Baengnyeongdo's spectacular **rock formations**, best seen from one of the tour boats that regularly depart the port. Some of the most popular are off Dumujin, to the west of the island, while at Sagot beach the stone cliffs plunge diagonally into the sea.

The tranquil nature of these islands is sometimes diluted by swarms of summer visitors – it's best to visit on weekdays, or outside the warmest months. Given the island's distance from Incheon, and the occasional military problems, you should organize accommodation at a tourist information office before heading out.

ACCOMMODATION AND EATING   THE WEST SEA ISLAND

GYODONGDO

★**Pundarika** 푼다리카   184 Gyondongnam-ro 64-gil ☎010 9872 3221. By far the best place to stay on Gyodongdo, this place's comfy, pine-lined rooms are presided over by an English-speaking lady who does her best to g visitors acquainted with the island. As well as private roor and a dorm, they also have a tent, sleeping up to four, a bicycles for free use. Dorms W25,000, doubles W55,000

Yeonan Jeongyuk Sikdang 연안 정육 식당
508-2 Daeryong-ni ☎010 2204 7632. This barbecue
house is often Gyodongdo's only place with any evening
atmosphere. The proprietor is a butcher, as were his father
and grandfather, and the cuts of pork *moksal* (neck-meat;
W13,000 per portion, minimum two) are rather sublime.
Plenty of booze available too. Daily noon–9pm.

DEOKJEOKDO
Sonamu Pension 소나무 팬션 612 Deokjeoknam-
ro ☎010 9737 0007. The best choice by Seopori,

Deokjeokdo's best beach, its generously sized rooms also
featuring cooking facilities – and if you're too lazy to make
your own food, the building also sports a convenience store
at ground level. W60,000

BAENGNYEONGDO
Baengnyeong Motel 백령 모텔 700-6 Jinchon-
ri ☎032 836 0633. One of the island's few reliable
accommodation options, with decent – if inevitably rather
dated – rooms, and a helpful owner (Korean-speaking
only). W40,000

Suwon and around

수원

All but swallowed up by Seoul, **SUWON** is a city with an identity crisis. Despite a
million-strong population, and an impressive history – best embodied by the **UNESCO-
listed fortress** at its centre – it has had to resort to unconventional means to distance
itself culturally from the capital, the best example being the dozens of individually
commissioned **public toilets** that pepper the city (see page 132). Suwon, in fact,
came close to usurping Seoul as Korea's seat of power following the construction of its
fortress in the final years of the eighteenth century, but though the move was doomed
to failure, Suwon grew in importance in a way that remains visible to this day – from
the higher parts of the fortress wall, it's evident that this once-small settlement burst
through its stone confines, eventually creating the noisy hotchpotch of buildings that
now forms one of Korea's largest cities.

An hour away from central Seoul, Suwon is certainly an easy **day-trip** from the capital,
though those who choose to stay will benefit from cheaper accommodation, and a
wholesomely provincial experience. East of the centre lie **Everland** and the **Korean Folk
Village**, two sites ideal for anyone
travelling with children, though just as
easily accessible from Seoul.

Hwaseong fortress
화성 • Daily 9am–6pm • W1000 • ⓦ english.swcf.or.kr •
Buses #2-2, #11 and any beginning with #13, #16 or #50
from train station; #36 from bus terminal

Central Suwon has but one notable
sight – **Hwaseong fortress**, whose
gigantic walls wend their way around
the city centre. Completed in 1796, the
complex was built on the orders of **King
Jeongjo**, one of the Joseon dynasty's
most famous rulers, in order to house
the remains of his father, **Prince Sado**.
Sado never became king, and met an
early end in Seoul's Changgyeonggung
palace at the hands of his own father,
King Yeongjo (see page 80); it may
have been the gravity of the situation
that spurred Jeongjo's attempts to move
the capital away from Seoul.

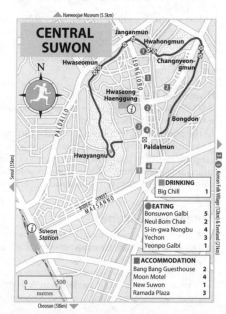

CENTRAL SUWON

Haewoojae Museum (5.5km)

Janganmun
Hwahongmun
Hwaseomun
Changnyeon-gmun
Hwaseong Haenggung
Bongdon
Paldalmun
Hwayangnu

Seoul (35km)
ROBERO STREET MAESANNO
Suwon Station

Cheonan (58km)

Korean Folk Village (13km) & Everland (21km)

DRINKING
Big Chill 1

EATING
Bonsuwon Galbi 5
Neul Bom Chae 2
Si-in-gwa Nongbu 4
Yechon 3
Yeonpo Galbi 1

ACCOMMODATION
Bang Bang Guesthouse . 2
Moon Motel 4
New Suwon 1
Ramada Plaza 3

0 ___ 500
metres

2

MR TOILET

Bar its fortress, central Suwon carries precious little sightseeing potential, though one interesting facet is what may be the world's greatest concentration of public toilets – they all have names, and some are even marked on tourist maps. This concept was the brainchild of **Sim Jae-deok**, a man referred to, especially by himself, as "**Mr Toilet**". Apparently afflicted by something of a cloacal obsession, Sim claimed to have been born in a public restroom, but transcended these humble beginnings to become mayor of Suwon and a member of the national assembly. He then went on to create, and declare himself head of, the *other* WTO – the **World Toilet Organization**. Undoubtedly spurred on by his team's debatable findings that the average human being spends three years of their life on the toilet, Sim desired to improve his home city's facilities for the World Cup in 2002, commissioning dozens of individually designed public toilets. Armed with the relevant pamphlet from the tourist office, it's even possible to fashion some kind of **toilet tour**. Features may include skylights, mountain views or piped classical music, though such refinement is sadly sullied, as it is all over Korea, by the baskets of used toilet paper discarded throne-side. Sim himself died in 2009, and his old home – custom-built to resemble a giant loo – was subsequently opened to the public as the **Haewoojae Museum** (해우재); if you fancy tracking it down, it's about 7km northwest of central Suwon.

The fortress

Towering almost 10m high for the bulk of its course, the **fortress wall** rises and falls in a 5.7km-long stretch, most of which is walkable, the various peaks and troughs marked by sentry posts and ornate entrance gates. From the higher vantage points you'll be able to soak up **superb views** of the city, but while there's also plenty to see from the wall itself, the interior is disappointing: other fortresses around the country – notably those at Gongju (see page 276) and Buyeo (see page 281) – have green, tranquil grounds with little inside save for trees, squirrels, pagodas and meandering paths, but Hwaseong's has had concrete poured into it, and is now a cityscape filled with restaurants, honking traffic and ropey motels. Even on the wall itself, it's hard to escape the noise, which is often punctuated by screaming aircraft from the nearby military base.

  Most visitors start their wall walk at **Paldalmun** (팔달문), a gate at the lower end of the fortress, exuding a well-preserved magnificence now diluted by its position in the middle of a traffic-filled roundabout. From here a steep path leads uphill to Seonammun, the western gate. At various points you may be able to practice your **archery** skills.

Hwaseong Haenggung

화성 행궁 • March–Oct daily 9am–6pm; Nov–Feb 9am–5pm; martial arts displays Tues–Sun 11am; traditional dance and music performances April–Nov Sat & Sun 2pm • W1500

In the centre of the area bounded by the fortress walls is **Hwaseong Haenggung**, once a government office, then a palace, and now a fine place to amble around; its pink walls are punctuated by the green lattice frames of windows and doors, which overlook dirt courtyards from where you can admire the fortress wall that looms above. There's a daily **martial arts display**, and occasional performances of traditional **dance and music**.

Korean Folk Village

한국 민속촌 • Daily 9.30am–6pm (though hours can vary); farmers' dance 11am & 2pm; tightrope walk 11.30am & 2.30pm; wedding ceremony 12pm & 4pm • W18,000 • ⓦ koreanfolk.co.kr • Shuttle buses (30min; free) from Suwon station at 10.30am, 12.30pm & 2.30pm (returning at 1.50pm & 4pm), or take regular city bus #10-5 or #37 (50min; W1300). From Seoul take bus #5001-1 or #1560 from Gangnam station (1hr; W2500), or #5500 from Jonggak station (1hr 20min; W2500)

This recreation of a traditional **Korean Folk Village** has become one of the most popular day-trips for foreign visitors to Seoul, its thatch-roofed houses and dirt paths evoking the sights, sounds and some of the more pleasant smells of a bygone time, when farming was the mainstay of the country. Its proximity to the capital makes this village by far the most visited of the many such facilities dotted around the country, which tends to diminish the authenticity of the experience. Nevertheless, the riverbank setting and its old-fashioned buildings are impressive, though the emphasis is squarely on performance – **shows** of tightrope walking and horseriding take place regularly throughout the day. **Traditional wedding ceremonies** provide a glimpse into Confucian society, with painstaking attention to detail including gifts of live chickens wrapped up in cloth like Egyptian mummies. Don't miss the **farmers' dance**, in which costumed performers prance around in highly distinctive ribbon-topped hats amid a cacophony of drums and crashes – quintessential Korea.

Everland

에버랜드 • Daily 10am–9pm (though hours can vary) • W54,000, W45,000 after 5pm • ⓦ everland.com • Buses from Suwon train station (depart on the half-hour; around 1hr); from Seoul, bus #5700 from the Dong-Seoul bus terminal via Jamsil subway station (1hr 10min; W2500), or #5002 from Gangnam subway station, via Yangjae (45min; W2500); more expensive daily shuttles (50min; W12,000 return) run at 9am from Hongdae and Yongsan via City Hall, Jongno 3-ga, Gangnam and more (see website for details); or take the Everline, a spur running from the Bundang line (around 2hr in total)

Everland is a colossal theme park that ranks as one of the most popular domestic tourist attractions in the country – male or female, young or old, it's hard to find a *hangukin* (Korean person) who hasn't taken this modern-day rite of passage, and more than seven million visitors pass through the turnstiles each year. Most are here for the fairground rides, and the park has all that a roller-coaster connoisseur could possibly wish for. Other attractions include a **zoo** (which features a safari zone that can be toured by bus, jeep or even at night), a speedway track and a golf course.

Caribbean Bay

케리비안 베이 • Daily, usually 9.30am–6pm; outdoor section June–Aug only • W42,000, W36,000 after 2.30pm; discount and combination tickets often available on website • ⓦ everland.com

The most popular part of the theme park is **Caribbean Bay**, with a year-round indoor zone containing several pools, a sauna and a short river that you can float down on a tube, as well as massage machines and relaxation capsules. The **outdoor section**, with its man-made beach, is what really draws the summer crowds – it's not just the beach that's artificial, since this has become one of the most popular places for Korea's silicon crowd to show off their new curves. Off the beach, facilities include a water bobsleigh, which drops you the height of a ten-floor building in just ten seconds, and an artificial surfing facility.

ARRIVAL AND INFORMATION   SUWON AND AROUND

By train and subway Suwon's main train station is a convenient place to arrive, and just about within walking distance of the fortress. It handles both national rail and Seoul subway trains (line 1; though note that this splits south of Seoul). If you're coming from the capital it's faster and far more comfortable to go by train (30min; from W2700) rather than subway (1hr; W1950), though this doesn't save much time, once transfers at Seoul or Yongsan stations have been factored in.

Destinations Busan (1–2 hourly; 2hr 45min); Daejeon (every 15–30min; 1hr 10min); Daegu (every 10–30min; 2hr 50min); Gwangju (16 daily; 3hr 30min); Jeonju (10 daily; 2hr 30min); Seoul (every 5–15 min; 30min).

By bus Buses run from several parts of Suwon to several parts of Seoul (usually W2500) – ask at your accommodation if you think that this may benefit you. Otherwise, Suwon's main bus terminal handles services to destinations all across the country.

Destinations Busan (7 daily; 5hr); Daegu (14 daily; 3hr 30min); Daejeon (8 daily; 1hr 30min); Gwangju (every 30min; 3hr 30min); Jeonju (12 daily; 2hr 40min); Mokpo (7 daily; 4hr 30min); Sokcho (8 daily; 4hr 30min).

Tourist information The main information office is just to the left of the main station exit (daily 9am–8pm; ☏ 031 228 4672), and there's a small office visible from Hwaseong Haenggung.

2

ACCOMMODATION

Most travellers visit on **day-trips** from the capital; there are troops of motels in the area bounded by the fortress wall, but you'd do well to disregard all images that staying inside a UNESCO-listed sight may bring to mind, as it's one of the seedier parts of the city. True budget-seekers can make use of an excellent *jjimjilbang* just off Rodeo Street (W7000).

★**Bang Bang Guesthouse** 방방 게스트하우스 16 Changnyong-daero 41-gil ☎010 3792 3525; map p.131. The best of Suwon's several hostel-like affairs, and just a short walk from the fortress walls (if a little distant from the train station). Beds are surprisingly large for a hostel, the common areas encourage mingling and the owners are friendly English-speakers. Breakfast included. Dorms W25,000, doubles W60,000

Moon Motel 문 모텔 3 Jeongjo-ro 742-gil ☎031 246 2285; map p.131. The best of the love motels in the Paldalmun area – the galloping horses on top are just about visible from the gate itself. Rooms are large, comfortable, clean and quiet, and that's all you really need in this type of place. W30,000

New Suwon 뉴 수원 호텔 33 Hwaseomun-ro 72-gil ☎031 245 2405; map p.131. A good mid-budget option, close to the fortress. Rooms feature all mod cons from slippers to hairdryers, but since some are a little on the small side, ask to see before checking in; it's often worth shelling out the extra W10,000 or so for a deluxe berth. W55,000

Ramada Plaza 라마다프라자 150 Jungbu-daero ☎031 230 0001, ⊛ramadaplazasuwon.com; map p.131. Suwon's best hotel, though in an uninteresting corner of the city, attracts well-heeled visitors – primarily Europeans on business – and offers all the comfort you'd expect of the chain. Some of the suites are truly stunning, and even standard rooms have been designed with care; oddly, rates often drop on weekends. W220,000

EATING

Suwon is famous for a local variety of *galbi*, whereby the regular meat dish is given a salty seasoning. There's a pleasingly styled food court in the basement level of the train station complex – good for Korean staples – and a couple of chain cafés offering good views of Paldalmun.

RESTAURANTS

Bonsuwon Galbi 본수원 갈비 41 Jungbu-daero 223-gil ☎031 211 8434; map p.131. A few kilometres east of the fortress, this may well be the best *galbi* restaurant in the city. The succulent meat doesn't come cheap (at least W25,000 per portion), but is worth it for the chance to try Suwon's local take on Korea's most pyromaniacal eating experience. Daily 11.30am–10pm.

Neul Bom Chae 늘봄채 3F 820 Jeongjo-ro ☎031 247 4565; map p.131. If you feel like meat but not like Suwon's famed barbecued version, give this attractive spot a try – delectable Korean-style *shabu-shabu*, plus all the relevant goodies to throw into the broth and a go at the veggie buffet, for just W10,000 per person. Daily 11am–3pm & 5pm–10pm.

Yechon 예촌 49-4 Haenggung-ro ☎031 254 9190; map p.131. It's retro to the max at this little hidey-hole near Paldalmun, a folk-styled establishment serving savoury pancakes known as *jeon* (전) in many different styles (from W10,000), as well as superb *makgeolli* from

Jeonju, a city in the southwest of the country. Tues–Sun 3.30pm–midnight.

★**Yeonpo Galbi** 연포 갈비 56-1 Jeongjo-ro 906-gil ☎031 255 1337; map p.131. In a quiet area just inside the fortress wall lies the best restaurant in the area. The meat is fair value (W14,000 a portion, minimum two) but cheaper noodle dishes are available, and those who arrive before 3pm can get a huge *jeongsik* (set meal) for W20,000, which includes several small fish and vegetable dishes. Daily 9am–9pm.

TEAROOMS

Si-in-gwa Nongbu 시인과 농부 8 Jeongjo-ro 796-gil ☎031 245 0049; map p.131. Great little tearoom just north of Paldalmun, "The Poet and the Farmer" has charming decor and the usual range of Korean teas (most around W5500; see page 43 for a hit-list); alternatively think about trying something more left-field, such as the sujeonggwa (cinnamon punch; W4500). Mon & Wed–Sun 10am–10pm.

DRINKING

You will more than likely find something appealing on **Rodeo Street**; the city's youth flocks here in the evenings to take advantage of the copious cheap restaurants, and eating segues into **drinking** as time goes on.

Big Chill 빅칠 3F 751-11 Jeongjo-ro ☎010 7600 2574; map p.131. The most popular bar in the central area, with a cast of expat regulars throwing down cheap beer

(W3000) and cocktails (from W5000), often over a game of pool or darts. Mon, Tues & Fri–Sun 8pm–5am, Wed & Thurs 8pm–2am.

Yangsu-ri

양수리

Taking the subway east of Seoul, it seems like an eternity before the capital's mess of high-rises comes to an end. The train then plunges through a long tunnel and shoots over a wide river, emerging in **YANGSU-RI**, a tranquil village surrounded by mountains and water – it sits at the confluence of the Namhangang and Bukhangang, two rivers that combine to create the Hangang, which pours through Seoul. The village has long been famed as a spot for extramarital affairs – a fact made evident by the number of seedy motels. However, in recent years its natural charm has also started to draw in an ever-increasing number of genuine couples, families, students and curious foreign visitors.

The focus of the area is a small **island**, one that's an easy walk from Yangsu station. Farmland takes up much of the interior, while a pleasant walking track skirts much of its perimeter – the stretch from the western railway bridge to the southern tip is particularly pleasant, and the latter also makes a spectacular place to watch the sunset, if the weather agrees.

ARRIVAL AND GETTING AROUND   YANGSU-RI

By subway Yangsu-ri is a stop on the Gyeongui-Jungang line – the journey takes around an hour from Yongsan. It's a 15min walk to the island from Yangsu station, though it's also possible to take a bus. It's also possible (and more pleasurable) to access the island from Ungilsan, the station immediately west of Yangsu – from here, simply find the bridge, and walk across.

By bike Though it may be more than 35km from central Seoul, Yangsu-ri is becoming more and more popular as a bike trip from the capital: it's certainly within day-trip distance for regular riders. You can also rent bikes at Yangsu-ri itself: there's a booth immediately outside Yangsu station, and another within visible distance of Ungilsan station. Cycling the island's perimeter is very pleasant, and the track even continues all the way down to Busan (see page 205).

ACCOMMODATION AND EATING

E-Motel 타모텔 35 Bukhangang-ro ☎ 031 771 8676. Sitting just north of the village hub, this motel is more modern than many others on the island, and some of the higher rooms have views of the river and mountains – thankfully the windows are slightly larger than the letterboxes more typical of Korean motels. W40,000

★ **Gelateria Panna** 빤나 4 Yangsu-ro 155-gil ☎ 031 75 4904. It's quite odd to think that wider Seoul's best ice cream could be found way out in Yangsu-ri, but it's true – the couple that run this tiny place lived in Milan for a decade, and during that time learned how to make some kick-ass gelato (from W3500 for a scoop). Their ice-cream roster changes daily (the ginger and vanilla are particularly

tasty), and they also make a mean espresso (W2500). It's in the village, just south of the main road. Wed–Sun 11am–8pm.

Jeongmune Jangeojip 정무네 장어집 27-1 Yangsu-ro 152-gil ☎ 031 577 8697. Yangsu-ri has found fame as a place for grilled river eel, and this pleasing clutch of wooden buildings – set near the river on the western side of the village, just north of the bridge – is as good a place as any to wolf some down (W24,000 per portion, min two). They also have cheap *jeon* pancakes, including a kimchi variety (W7000), and super-cheap *janchi-guksu* (noodles in an anchovy broth; W4000). Mon, Tues & Thurs–Sun 11am–8pm.

The Demilitarized Zone

"The visit to the Joint Security Area at Panmunjeom will entail entry into a hostile area, and possible injury or death as a direct result of enemy action." Disclaimer from form issued to visitors by United Nations Command

As the tour bus crawls out of Seoul and heads slowly north through the traffic, the seemingly endless urban jungle slowly diminishes in size before disappearing altogether. You're now well on the way to a place where the mists of the Cold War still linger on, and one that could still be ground zero for World War III – the **Demilitarized Zone**. More commonly referred to as "the DMZ", this no-man's-land is a 4km-wide buffer zone that came into being at the end of the Korean War in 1953. It sketches an unbroken spiky line across the peninsula from coast to coast, separating the two Koreas and their diametrically opposed ideologies. Although it sounds forbidding, it's actually possible to enter this zone, and take a few tentative steps into North Korean territory – thousands of civilians do so every month, though only as part of a **tightly controlled tour**. It's even home to two small communities, **Freedom Village** and **Propaganda Village** (see page 139). Elsewhere are a few platforms from which the curious can stare across the border, and a **tunnel** built by the North, which you can enter.

While most visitors content themselves with a packaged DMZ tour, there are more adventurous options available. The city of **Paju**, just southwest of Panmunjeom, has a few sights not at all related to North Korea – a small **arts village**, and a **publishing town** whose buildings are among the most adventurously designed in the land.

Brief history

For the first year of the **Korean War** (1950–53), the tide of control yo-yoed back and forth across the peninsula (see page 368 for more details). Then in June 1951, General Ridgeway of the United Nations Command got word that the Korean People's Army (KPA) would "not be averse to" armistice talks. These talks took place in the city of Kaesong, now a major North Korean city (see page 353), but were soon shifted south to **Panmunjeom**, a tiny farming village that suddenly found itself the subject of international attention.

Ceasefire talks went ahead for two long years and often degenerated into venomous verbal battles littered with expletives. One of the most contentious issues was the repatriation of prisoners of war, and a breakthrough came in April 1953, when terms were agreed; exchanges took place on a bridge over the River Sachon, now referred to as the **Bridge of No Return**. "Operation Little Switch" came first, seeing the transfer of sick and injured prisoners (notably, six thousand returned to the North, while only a tenth of that number walked the other way); "Operation Big Switch" took place shortly afterwards, when the soldiers on both sides were asked to make a final choice over their preferred destination.

Though no **peace treaty** was ever signed, representatives of the KPA, the United Nations Command (UNC) and the Chinese Peoples' Liberation Army put their names to an **armistice** on July 27, 1953; South Korean delegates refused to do so. The room where the signing took place was built specially for the occasion, and cobbled together at lightning speed by KPA personnel; it now forms part of most tours to North Korea (see page 331).

After the armistice

An uneasy truce has prevailed since the end of the war – the longest military deadlock in history – and the DMZ is now something of a natural haven filled with flora and fauna that's been left to regenerate and breed in relative isolation. However, there have been regular spats along the way. In the early 1960s a small number of disaffected American soldiers **defected** to the North, after somehow managing to make it across the DMZ alive (see page 380), while in 1968 the crew of the captured USS *Pueblo* (see page 138) walked south over the Bridge of No Return after protracted negotiations. The most serious confrontation took place in 1976, when two American soldiers were killed in the **Axe Murder Incident** (see page 137), and in 1984, a young tour leader from the Soviet Union fled North Korea across the border, triggering a short gun battle that left three soldiers dead. Even now, most years still see at least a couple of incidents – in late 2017, for example, a North Korean soldier defected across the DMZ, with CCTV footage of his brave flight going viral.

Panmunjeom

판문점

There's nowhere in the world quite like the **Joint Security Area** ("the JSA"), a settlement squatting in the middle of Earth's most heavily fortified frontier, and the only place

THE AXE MURDER INCIDENT

Relations between the two Koreas took a sharp nose dive in 1976, when two American soldiers were killed by a group of **axe-wielding North Koreans**. The cause of the trouble was a **poplar tree** which stood next to the Bridge of No Return: a UNC outpost stood next to the bridge, but its direct line of sight to the next Allied checkpoint was blocked by the leaves of the tree, so on August 18 a five-man American detail was dispatched to perform some trimming. Although the mission had apparently been agreed in advance with the North, sixteen soldiers from the KPA turned up and demanded that the trimming stop. Met with refusal, they launched a swift attack on the UNC troops using the axes the team had been using to prune the tree. The attack lasted less than a minute, but claimed the life of First Lieutenant Mark Barrett, as well as Captain Bonifas (who was apparently killed instantly with a single karate chop to the neck). North Korea denied responsibility for the incident, claiming that the initial attack had come from the Americans.

Three days later, the US launched **Operation Paul Bunyan**, a show of force that must go down as the largest tree-trimming exercise in history. A convoy of 24 UNC vehicles streamed towards the tree, carrying more than 800 men, some trained in taekwondo, and all armed to the teeth. These were backed up by attack helicopters, fighter planes and B-52 bombers, while an aircraft carrier had also been stationed just off the Korean shore. This carefully managed operation drew no response from the KPA, and the tree was successfully cut down.

2

in DMZ territory where visitors are permitted. Visits here will create a curious dichotomy of feelings: on one hand, you'll be in what was once memorably described by Bill Clinton as "the scariest place on Earth", but as well as soldiers, barbed wire and brutalist buildings you'll see trees, hear birdsong and smell fresh air. The village of **PANMUNJEOM** itself is actually in North Korean territory, and has dwindled to almost nothing since it became the venue for armistice talks in 1951. But such is the force of the name that you'll see it on promotional material for most **DMZ tours** that run to the area; these tours are, in fact, the only way to get in.

The Joint Security Area

Situated just over an hour from Seoul is **Camp Bonifas**, an American army base just outside the DMZ. Here you'll meet your guides – usually young infantry recruits whose sense of humour makes it easy to overlook the seriousness of the situation –

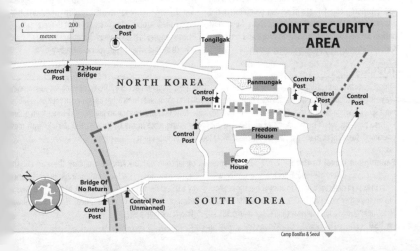

and be given a briefing session reminding you of the various dos and don'ts. Back on the bus look out for the white-marked stones pushed into the wire fence – these are detection devices that will fall out should anyone try to climb over. On both sides of the road you'll see hilltop points from where UNC forces keep a constant lookout across the border for any military build-up that would precede a large-scale attack.

Once inside the **JSA** itself, keep your fingers crossed that you'll be allowed to enter one of the three **meeting rooms** at the very centre of the complex, which offer some serious travel kudos – the chance to step into North Korea. The official Line of Control runs through the very centre of these cabins, the corners of which are guarded by South Korean soldiers, who are sometimes joined by their Northern counterparts, the enemy soldiers almost eyeball to eyeball. Note the microphones on the table inside the room – anything you say can be picked up by North Korean personnel. The rooms are closed to visitors when meetings are scheduled, which is just as well since some of them have descended into farce. One such fiasco occurred when members of one side – it's not clear which – brought a bigger flag than usual to a meeting. The others followed suit with an even larger banner, and the childish process continued until the flags were simply too large to take into the room; at this point, both sides agreed on a standard flag size.

From an outdoor **lookout point** near the cabins you can soak up views of the North, including the huge flag and shell-like buildings of "**Propaganda Village**" (see page 139). You may also be able to make out the jamming towers North Korea uses to keep out unwanted imperialist signals – check the reception on your phone. Closer to the lookout point, and actually within JSA territory, is the **Bridge of No Return**, the venue for POW exchange at the end of the Korean War (and also for James Bond in *Die Another Day* – though for obvious reasons it was filmed elsewhere).

On arriving back at Camp Bonifas you'll usually have time to pop into a gift shop, stocked with "I did the DMZ" T-shirts and, if you're in luck, North Korean blueberry wine. Also in the area is a golf course once named by *Sports Illustrated* as the most dangerous on Earth, but there's only one hole (a par three, for the record) and you won't be allowed to use it.

INFORMATION   THE JOINT SECURITY AREA

Note that each tour comes with a number of **restrictions**, most imposed by the United Nations Command. Be warned that schedules can change in an instant, and remember that you'll be entering an extremely dangerous area – this is no place for fooling around or wandering off by yourself.

Paperwork For all tours to the DMZ you'll need to bring your passport along. Citizens of certain countries are not allowed into DMZ territory, including those from most nations in the Middle East, some in Africa and territories such as Vietnam, Hong Kong and mainland China.

Dress code An official dress code applies (no flip-flops, ripped jeans, "clothing deemed faddish" or "shorts that expose the buttocks"), but in reality most things are OK.

Photography In certain areas photography is not allowed – you'll be told when to put your camera away.

TOURS

Almost all **tours** to the DMZ start and finish in Seoul, and there are a great number of outfits competing for your money. We've listed a couple of recommended operators here, but you'll find pamphlets from other operators in your hotel lobby; most speak enough English to accept reservations by telephone. Note that some operators are much cheaper than others – these probably won't be heading to **the JSA**, the most interesting place in the DMZ (W70,000–80,000 with most operators), so do check to see if it's on the schedule. Most tours also include lunch.

Panmunjom Travel Center ☎ 02 771 5593, ⊛ korea dmztour.com. Offers the regular tour, plus a session with a North Korean defector willing to answer questions about life on the other side (W85,000). Runs from the *Koreana Hotel*, near Myeongdong subway (line 4; see map p.98).

★ **USO** ☎ 02 6383 2570, ⊛ koridoor.co.kr. Run in conjunction with the American military, these are still the best tours to go for ($92), and include a 20min presentation by a US soldier in Camp Bonifas. Book at least four days in advance. Runs from Camp Kim, near Namyeong subway (line 1; see map p.98).

"FREEDOM VILLAGE" AND "PROPAGANDA VILLAGE"

The DMZ is actually home to two small settlements, one on each side of the Line of Control. With the southern village rich and tidy and its northern counterpart empty and sinister, both can be viewed as a microcosm of the countries they belong to.

The southern village – referred to as **"Freedom Village"** by the US military, but actually called **Daeseongdong** – is a small farming community, but one out of limits to all but those living or working here. These are among the richest farmers in Korea: they pay no rent or tax, and DMZ produce fetches big bucks at markets around the country. Technically, residents have to spend 240 days of the year at home, but most commute here from their condos in Seoul to "punch in", and get hired hands to do the dirty work; if they're staying, they must be back in town by nightfall, and have their doors and windows locked and bolted by midnight. Women are allowed to marry into this tight society, but men are not; those who choose to raise their children here also benefit from a school that at the last count had eleven teachers and only eight students.

North of the Line of Control lies an odd collection of empty buildings referred to by American soldiers as **"Propaganda Village"**. The purpose of its creation appears to have been to show citizens in the South the communist paradise that they're missing – a few dozen "villagers" arrive every morning by bus, spend the day taking part in wholesome activities and letting their children play games, then leave again in the evening. With the aid of binoculars, you'll be able to see that none of the buildings actually have any windows; lights turned on in the evening also seem to suggest that they're devoid of floors. Above the village flies a huge **North Korean flag**, one so large that it required a fifty-man detail to hoist, until the recent installation of a motor. It sits atop a 160m-high pole, the eventual victor in a bizarre game played out over a number of years by the two Koreas, each hell-bent on having the loftier flag. See page 138 for details of yet another flag-centred battle.

The Third Tunnel of Aggression

제3땅굴

In 1974, a South Korean army patrol unit discovered a tunnel that had been burrowed under the DMZ in apparent preparation for a military attack from the North; tip-offs from North Korean defectors and some strategic drilling soon led to the discovery of another two, and a fourth was found in 1990. North Korea has denied responsibility, claiming them to be coal mines (though they are strangely devoid of coal), but to be on the safe side the border area is now monitored from coast to coast by soldiers equipped with drills and sensors.

The third tunnel, now bombastically referred to as the **Third Tunnel of Aggression**, is the closest to Seoul, a city that would have been just a day's march away if the North's plan had succeeded. The tunnel is only accessible as part of a **tour** – either those covering the wider DMZ (see page 138), or shorter trips from Imjingang. Many visitors emerge from the depths underwhelmed – it is, after all, only a tunnel, even if you get to walk under **DMZ territory** up to the Line of Control that marks the actual border. On busy days it can become uncomfortably crowded – not a place for the claustrophobic.

Dorasan observatory and station

도라전망대 • Observatory Tues–Sun 10am–3pm • Free • Best accessed on the "DMZ Train" from Yongsan or Seoul station (Tues–Sun, departs Yongsan 10.08am and Seoul station 10.13am, returns from Dorasan 4pm; W9200 one-way)

South of the Third Tunnel is **Dorasan Observatory**, from which visitors are able to stare at the North through binoculars – W500 is a cheap price to satisfy a bit of curiosity. The observatory forms part of many DMZ **tour** schedules (see page 138); unlike the Joint Security Area you can also visit independently, but getting there takes forever unless you're on the **"DMZ Train"** services, pleasingly cheesy affairs with game-playing staff, gaudily decorated carriages and barbed wire souvenirs for sale.

Dorasan station lies at the end of the Gyeonghui light-rail line. This line continues to China, via Pyongyang: as one sign says, "it's not the last station from the South, but the first station towards the North". A gleaming, modern station was built at Dorasan in early 2007, and in May of that year the first train in decades rumbled up the track to Kaesong in North Korea (another going in the opposite direction on the east-coast line), while regular freight services got going that December. Such connections were soon cut, but there remains hope that this track will one day handle KTX services from Seoul to Pyongyang; in the meantime, there's a wall map showing which parts of the world Seoul will be connected to should the line ever see regular service, as well as a much-photographed sign pointing the way to Pyongyang.

Paju and around

파주

South of Imjingang is the Seoul satellite city of **PAJU**, which contains some of the most interesting sights in the border area; for once, some of these do not revolve solely around North Korea. There's **Paju Book City**, a publisher-heavy area actually more notable for its architecture than anything literary; **Heyri Art Valley**, a twee little artistic commune; and finally something pertaining to the North at **Odusan observatory**.

Paju Book City

파주 출판도시 문화재단 • ⓦ pajubookcity.org • Bus #200 (every 30min; 1hr) from Hapjeong subway (lines 2 & 6)

Quirky **Paju Book City** is ostensibly a publishing district. Many publishers were encouraged to move here from central Seoul (though a whole glut of small-fry printing houses remain in the fascinating alleyways around Euljiro) and most of the major companies based here have **bookstores** on their ground levels. However, the main attraction for visitors is the area's excellent **modern architecture** – quite a rarity in this land of sterile high-rises. There's no focus as such, but strolling the quiet streets is rather pleasurable, and there are a bunch of great little book cafés dotted around – none truly stand out but you can't really lose, so just walk into the first one you see.

Heyri Art Valley

헤이리 문화예술마을 • ⓦ heyri.net • Bus #2200 (every 30min; 1hr; W2700) from Hapjeong subway (lines 2 & 6)

Seven kilometres to the north of Paju Book City, similar architectural delights are on offer at **Heyri Art Valley**. This artists' village is home to dozens of small **galleries**, and its countryside air is making it an increasingly popular day-trip for young, arty Seoulites here to shop for paintings or quirky souvenirs, or drain a latte in one of several cafés. However, such mass-market appeal means that the complex in general is more twee than edgy.

Odusan observatory

오두산 통일전망대 • Daily 9am–5pm • W3000 • Bus #2200 (every 30min; 1hr; W2700) from Hapjeong subway (lines 2 & 6), or walking distance from Heyri Art Valley

Sitting atop a hill just 1km west of Heyri is **Odusan observatory**, where you'll be able to peer across the border through binoculars – the difference between the lush, busy South and the barren North is quite striking. When inter-Korean relations are good, the observatory sells alcoholic drinks from North Korea – but don't hold your breath.

ACCOMMODATION

★**Jijihyang** 지지향 145 Hoedong-gil ☏031 955 0090. A great boutique hotel sitting near the streamside in Paju Book City – both the complex in general and the rooms themselves are quite exquisite, and they don't co a fortune. W132,000

SHOPPING

Forest of Wisdom 지혜의숲 145 Hoedong-gil 524-3 ☎ 031 955 0077. More tempting than Paju Book City's many major bookstores is this one, selling discounted books of the used variety. It's attached to *Jijihyang* hotel (see page 140), and usually has hundreds of English-language books in store, as well as thousands of Korean ones. Daily 10am–7pm.

2

Gangwon

TEMPLE IN SEORAKSAN NATIONAL PARK

Gangwon

For Koreans, Gangwon (강원) exerts a magnetic pull. Enclosed by Gyeonggi to the west, Gyeongsang to the south, North Korea and the East Sea, it's a lush, green land blessed with beaches, lakes and muscular peaks. A lofty range of mountains scores its eastern flank, mopping up national and provincial parks along the way, and ensuring that Gangwon remains the most natural and least populated part of the country: despite being Korea's second-largest province, it has a smaller population than many of its cities. This isn't to say that Gangwon is an undiscovered paradise – those in the know will direct you here, rather than to the more obvious tourist draw of Jeju Island. In summer, the east-coast beaches and national parks are teeming with visitors, while skiers work their way around several resorts in the winter. Regardless of where you head, however, you're never likely to be far from a rushing blue river, a mountainside village, or lofty trees and peaks that recede into the distance – regular Korea can feel a world away.

Chuncheon is Gangwon's capital and major city, but though it's an agreeable enough place, and unhurried enough to allow for some pleasant bike riding, most people aren't visiting the province to sate urban pleasures. There are four **national parks** in Gangwon, each differing in topography and popularity; the acknowledged champion of them is **Seoraksan**, which contains some of the country's highest peaks. It sits alongside the city of **Sokcho**, a simple but highly enjoyable place with some of the best places to eat in the land. Gangwon's eastern shore sketches a fairly straight line from the North Korean border to the Gyeongsang provinces, so you're never far away from a perfect sunrise. Head down the coast and you'll come to **Gangneung**, home to a wonderful Confucian shrine; **Jeongdongjin** beach, the nation's favourite sunrise spot and home to a fascinating clifftop hotel; **Samcheok**, a dull city whose periphery includes Penis Park and one of the world's largest caves; and **Odaesan National Park**, similar to Seoraksan but much less touristed.

Brief history

Despite its natural attractions, Gangwon hasn't always been a paragon of serenity. Its historical boundaries actually extend far into North Korea, but since the end of the Korean War the province has been divided by the twin perimeters of the **Demilitarized Zone**. During the war, the mountainous terrain that for so long preserved Gangwon's tranquillity became a curse, with ferocious battles fought for strategically important peaks. Even today, the tension is palpable – much of the region's coast is fenced off to protect against attacks from the North, and even some of the most popular beaches

SUN CRUISE HOTEL, JEONGDONGJIN

Highlights

❶ Abai Island, Sokcho Getting to this tiny island is half the fun – pull yourself across the water from Sokcho on a specially customized winch-ferry, before tucking into the tasty blood sausage the island's famed for. See page 151

❷ Seoraksan National Park With its tall pines and naked rock, this is the most beautiful national park in the country according to the majority of Koreans. See page 156

❸ Gyeongpo beach The number one beach in the province, and perhaps the most popular nationwide after Busan's Haeundae. See page 161

❹ Jeongdongjin An American warship and a North Korean submarine lie side by side near this small village, just begging to be clambered around. See page 166

❺ Penis Park Overlooking the coast south of Samcheok, this may well be the weirdest park in Korea. See page 169

❻ Hwanseongul Explore 1.6km of subterranean passageways in one of the world's largest caves, hidden in the countryside west of Samcheok. See page 170

HIGHLIGHTS ARE MARKED ON THE MAP ON PAGE 146

are fringed with barbed wire and military installations – from the end of the Korean War until the signing of the armistice in 1953, all land above the 38th Parallel (which hits the coast at a point roughly halfway between Sokcho and Gangneung) came under **North Korean control**, and was eventually exchanged for an area almost equal in size north of Seoul. Tunnels under the DMZ were found in the 1970s, and a spy-filled North Korean submarine crashed on the Gangwon coast in 1996 (see page 167); the latter can still be seen, next to an old American warship, near the small village of **Jeongdongjin** (see page 166).

Chuncheon and around

춘천

Despite its status as Gangwon's capital city, **CHUNCHEON** remains small and relatively relaxed; in fact, it's the country's smallest provincial capital. Mountain-fringed and surrounded by rivers and artificial **lakes**, its fresh air comes as a welcome change for anyone who's been cooped up in a larger city. Its most popular sight, the island of **Jungdo** (중도), is now off limits as it transforms into the world's latest **Legoland** – initially due for completion in 2017, the project has been beset with problems, and its future was still unclear at the time of writing. Otherwise, Chuncheon's periphery is perhaps more popular than the city itself, with hordes of youngsters flocking to nearby **Gangchon** and **Nami Island** for some rural fun. Back in town there are a few good

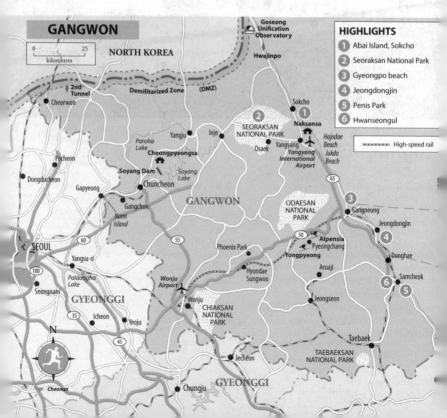

ENJOYING THE RIVERBANKS, CHUNCHEON-STYLE

Chuncheon is flanked to its west by the **Bukhangang** (북한강), a river that eventually forms part of the Hangang in Seoul. Much of the riverbank has been given a cycle-friendly revamp, and pedalling along these paths constitutes the best thing to do in a city of few actual sights. The best place to **rent a bike** (W3000 per hour or W10,000 per day) is on the west side of town, next to the Ethiopian Veterans' Memorial Hall (에티오피아 참전 기념관), a building that looks somewhat like a half-submerged Russian church; there are alternate rental points near both train stations. From the Memorial Hall, a **cycleway** runs along the lake-like river. Head **north** and you'll soon be upon a small war memorial; the path joins a road but does continue past the Skywalk (see page 147), and much further beyond. Heading **south**, you'll race through a park then hug a hillside on a purpose-built wooden path, before arriving at the former Jongdo ferry docks; again, the path goes much further – even as far as Seoul.

These days, motorized **stand-up scooters** are all the rage across Korea, and you can rent these from various points (W10,000 per hour), including just outside Chuncheon station. Near the Memorial Hall, you'll be able to rent duck-shaped **pedalloes** (W10,000 for 30min, seats up to four) – the ones sporting little crowns are particularly snazzy. There are also various **motorboat** courses on offer, starting from a pier just east of the Skywalk (W30,000–150,000 for up to four).

Lastly, it's possible to pedal **rail-bikes** on disused railway tracks, along a stretch between Chuncheon and the nearby "Membership Training" hamlet of Gangchon (see page 150).

bicycle tracks, though for many the city's main draw is the chance to sample *dak-galbi*, a famed local chicken dish (see page 148).

Each October, performers from Korea and abroad take part in a delightful **puppet festival**; most events take place at the Puppet Theatre, to the north of the city centre. Other popular annual events include a **mime festival** (Ⓦmimefestival.com), which takes place in May at venues across town.

Soyanggang Skywalk

소양강 스카이워크 • W2000 • Daily: March–Oct 10am–9pm; Nov–Feb 10am–6pm

A relatively new addition to Chuncheon's riverside sights is the **Soyanggang Skywalk**, a see-through pier jutting out over the waters. In good weather, it's certainly worth the effort of getting here, since the water- and mountain-filled views are rather impressive. Before stepping onto the walkway, you'll have to don some odd shoe covers which will make your feet look like Chewbacca's – they also make it easy to have a good slide around.

ARRIVAL AND GETTING AROUND   CHUNCHEON

By subway and train Chuncheon is the terminus of the Gyeongchun line from Seoul; as well as regular subway services (2hr 15min; W3250), comfier ITX trains also make the journey (every 30min; 1hr 15min from Yongsan; W7300), costing more but taking almost half the time. Seoul travel cards are valid for the subway services, but for the ITX ones you'll need a ticket. There are two stations in town – Namchuncheon, the south station, is actually a little closer to the centre than Chuncheon main station, though the latter is nearer the river.

By bus Chuncheon's intercity bus terminal is a bit old

school, with shops selling military surplus – and soldiers on their way to or from postings. Buses run here from the capital's Dongseoul and Gangnam terminals, and cities across Korea.

Destinations Busan (hourly; 5hr); Daegu (5 daily; 3hr 30min); Gangneung (1–2 hourly; 2hr 10min); Samcheok (hourly; 3hr 40min); Seoul (every 5–10min; 1hr 10min–1hr 30min); Sokcho (10 daily; 2hr 15min); Taebaek (1 daily; 4hr).

City transport To get anywhere in town it's advisable to take a taxi (almost always less than W5000), as bus routes are too confusing and irregular for most travellers.

ACCOMMODATION

There's a line of reasonable, fairly new **motels** across the main road and downhill from the bus station; older places are dotted around the city's shopping district, while on the lakes out of town the eagle-eyed may spot something rather unique – guesthouses made up of "floating" huts, usually used by fishermen looking to get away from it all.

CITY CENTRE

Egghouse 에그하우스 12-12 Chunghon-gil ☎ 070 8771 6311. Chuncheon finally has a hostel option – admittedly it's a converted apartment, but this only adds to the homely atmosphere. The hosts are kindly sorts, it's very close to the bus terminal and Namchuncheon station, and a simple breakfast is included in the rates. Dorms **W20,000**

Gyerim Motel 계림 모텔 342-1 Sportstown-gil ☎ 033 254 7392. Not the newest motel option in Chuncheon, and certainly not the most central, but there are some serious plus-points – this is one of the cheapest motels in town, and thanks to a location on the periphery of town winning river views are on offer from some rooms. **W30,000**

★ **Sangsangmadang** 상상마당 25 Sportstown 399-gil ☎ 033 818 4200, ⓦ sangsangmadang.com. Affiliated to the eponymous arts complex in Seoul (see page 115), this cheery hotel's three floors of bedrooms are every bit as quirkily designed as you might expect. The affiliated café, *Dancing Caffeine* (see page 148), is pretty good too, and decent breakfasts are available for an extra fee; use of laundry facilities is free, however. **W115,000**

OUTSIDE THE CENTRE

Jagalseom Nakksiteo 자갈섬 낚시터 Sports Town 223-gil 73 ☎ 033 253 9221. The "floating guesthouses" that featured in Kim Ki-duk chiller *The Isle* (see page 379) were no mere movie sets – there are a bunch of such places in Gangwon province, mostly catering to fishermen who want a bit of peace and quiet. This one is the most accessible of the lot, on the lakefront a short taxi ride from central Chuncheon, and facing the mountains; rooms have futon bedding only and are extremely basic, though they do have outhouse-like toilet facilities. You'll be taken to your lake-hut by boat, and then you're stuck for the night – all quite romantic, really. **W70,000**

EATING

Galbi is the word in Chuncheon; *dak-galbi*, to be precise (see below), and the shopping area in the city centre has a whole street of restaurants (Dakgalbi Golmok, 닭갈비골목) where you can sample this speciality. Another local favourite is the bargain *makguksu* (막국수) – cold buckwheat noodles with soup and hot-pepper paste.

Byeoldang Makguksu 별당 막국수 Chuncheon-ro 81-gil ☎ 033 254 9603. This vaguely *hanok*-styled restaurant may be a little out of the way, but it's worth it for the chance to sample their famed *makguksu* (W6000). However, do also consider giving the *memil jeonbyeong* (메밀 전병; W6000) a try; it's a sort of buckwheat pancake roll, wrapped around a mix of meat, *kimchi* and more. Daily 10am–8.30pm.

Dancing Caffeine 댄싱카핀 25 Sportstown 399-gil ☎ 033 243 4757. The nicest café in the city is actually outside the centre, on the bike route south along the Bukhangang (see page 147), and part of the *Sangsangmadang* guesthouse/arts complex (see page 148). There are great river and mountain vistas from the outdoor tables, and a sophisticated vibe inside. Coffees cost from W5500, or go for a gelato (W7500). Daily 10am–11pm.

Youme Dakgalbi 유미 닭갈비 12 Dakgalbi Golmok ☎ 033 244 4455. Of the restaurants on Dakgalbi Street, this place stands out simply because it's the most willing to serve single portions of the good stuff (W11,000); when you near the end of your meal, ask for some rice (볶음밥; *bokkeumbap*) to throw in for a crispy second course. Daily 9am–4am.

DRINKING

There's only really one place to head for a **drink**, and that's the area around **Gangwon University** (강원대); expats and locals alike often plan their night over a beer in front of the GS25 convenience store. Walk around here and you'll find a clutch of establishments with four-figure numbers in their name (most commonly 3900), corresponding to the amount of won you'll have to hand over for the cheapest beer, *soju* and/or light meal.

DAK-GALBI

You may have sampled regular *galbi*, whereby you cook (or to be more precise, set fire to) meat at your own table. **Dak-galbi** (닭갈비) is a little different – it's made with chicken meat, rather than beef or pork, and is grilled in a wide pan so there's no visible flame action for regular *galbi* arsonists to enjoy. You'll find this dish pretty much anywhere in Korea, but for some reason Chuncheon gets the glory. Imagine throwing a **raw chicken kebab** into a hot metal tray to boil up with a load of veggies and sesame leaves – you get to do this at your table for around W8000 per portion. You usually need at least two people for a meal, and once you're nearly finished it's common to throw some **rice or noodles** into the pan for a stomach-expanding second course. These days it's even more obligatory to chuck some **cheese** in too – a trend that has swept over Korea in recent years. And beware: once you go cheesy, you never go back.

Sheriff 셰리프 3F 245 Seobudaeseong-ro ☎033 256 9909. This bar has been a mainstay of the Gangwon University scene for years – head up the appropriately creaky stairs for some cheap booze (cocktails W6000–9000) and a game of darts. Daily 7pm–4am.

Gangchon

강천 • Three stops before Chuncheon (20min) on the Gyeongchun line from Seoul (every 30min; 55min)

Chuncheon's surrounding area is alluringly green and undulating, and well worth delving into. One of the most accessible places is the small town of **GANGCHON**, a pretty and (usually) tranquil place just west of Chuncheon. Although it has a national reputation as a student "MT" centre par excellence – **Membership Training** is a somewhat non-studious exercise that usually involves lots of drinking, singing and buzzing about on quad bikes – such revelry tends to confine itself to student holidays, and at other times it's a far more relaxing place to stay than Chuncheon for those who want a taste of inland Gangwon.

Gugok Waterfall

구곡폭포 • Daily 8am–7pm • W1600 • Bus #50 from Gangchon station

The major sight in Gangchon is **Gugok-pokpo**, a tumbling waterfall surrounded by hills and trails that make for a rewarding few hours of exploration. It's 5km away from Gangchon down a highly picturesque valley studded with tiny houses.

Gangchon Rail-bike

강천 레일바익 • Daily 9am–5pm (every 1hr) from Gimyujeong station (the stop between Gangchon and Namchuncheon; 10min from either) • W30,000 for two people

The opening of the new double-track railway from Seoul made the old Mugunghwa stretch obsolete, but part of it is enjoying a new lease of life – it's now known as the **Gangchon Rail-bike**, and you can pedal along the rails in little carriages. Groups leave in convoy on the hour from Gimyujeong station; the local proclivity to take as many selfies as humanly possible means that there'll most likely be a fair bit of idling, but it usually takes about fifty minutes to the end of the stretch. After this, you've a choice of a free shuttle bus back to Gimyujeong station, or (far more preferable) a twenty-minute ride on the "Romance Train" to Gangchon.

ACCOMMODATION AND EATING   GANGCHON

The village has enough **motels** and **restaurants** to cater for the students during their holidays, and an excess for the rest of the year. Cheaper and more rural *minbak* accommodation can be found in the valley linking the town with Gugok-pokpo.

Olive B&B 올리브 비엔비 418-10 Bangok-ri ☎010 5454 3554. This B&B is at least something a little different in the maze of motels and pensions surrounding Gangchon station. They've really gone for it with the decor in the rooms – maybe ask to see a couple before finalizing your check-in – and the friendly owners will most likely come to meet you at the station. W50,000

Nami Island

남이섬 • W10,000 • ⓦ namisum.com • Train to Gapyeong from Seoul (every 30min; 40min) or Chuncheon (every 30min; 20min), then a taxi (W5000); also visitable on tours from Seoul (W15,000 return; see website for details); ferries to the island (included in ticket price) every 10–30min, daily 7.30am–9.30pm; can also enter island by zip-wire (W38,000 including entry ticket), daily 9am–7pm

Further downstream from Gangchon is tiny **Nami Island**, which achieved international fame for being the scene of the main characters' first date and kiss on the hugely successful *Winter Sonata* soap opera (see page 151). For years, it was common to see crowds of middle-aged Japanese women patrolling the island in homage to their hero, but even though the soap hysteria has died down, Nami remains a common rite of pilgrimage for many visitors to Korea. The place is more than a little twee, but the "Naminara

> **WINTER SONATA**
>
> **Korean drama** has, of late, enjoyed sustained popularity across Asia and beyond, yet for all this recent success, **Winter Sonata** (2002) remains one of the most notable success stories. Though the storyline ran along familiar lines (a love-story between two diametrically opposed characters), male lead **Bae Yong-jun** got hearts racing all across Asia, and in the process became a continental superstar. Nowhere was he more successful than in Japan, where he remains revered as *Yon-sama*, a title roughly equivalent to an English knighthood. Junsang also helped the stereotypically strong-but-sensitive Korean male replace the martial arts hero as Asia's default male role model.

Republic", as authorities are now choosing to style it, has plenty of paths lined with ginkgo and chestnut trees, maples and white birches that make for a beautiful walk.

Cheongpyeongsa

청평사 • Daily 24hr • W2000 • Bus #11 or #12 (40min; W1200) to Soyang Dam from Chuncheon train station, then ferry (15min; W5000) from along the road; the temple is a 30min walk from the dock

The gorgeous, man-made **Soyang Lake** (소양호) lies just east of Chuncheon, hemmed in at its western end by the huge **Soyang dam** (소양댐). Ferries leave from the dam for **Cheongpyeongsa**, a majestic temple that, until fairly recently, was only accessible by boat; ferries remain the easiest way of getting here. The temple's appeal lies not in superb architecture or historical importance (though it's over a thousand years old, it was razed to the ground and rebuilt several times), but in the watery approach. Unfortunately, the secret is out, and the temple is now fronted by restaurants, snack stalls and *minbak* of a small tourist village.

Sokcho and around

속초

Most foreign visitors to **SOKCHO**, South Korea's northernmost city, wind up here by default – **Seoraksan**, the country's most popular national park, raises its granite fingers within visible range to the west (see page 156). However, this ugly yet appealing place certainly has merit of its own, lent a briny vibrancy by the local fishing industry. Fishing boats dock in Cheongcho Lake, around which Sokcho curls in a C-shape – loosely tied together in a very literal sense by the steel cables along which tiny ferry-platforms winch their way to **Abai Island**. This is the place to head for the city's culinary speciality – *sundae*, a sort of noodle-filled blood sausage. The harbourfront makes for a lovely walk at night – near the middle of the "C" you'll find a pier with some free-to-use binoculars at the end.

Bar Abai Island and the local **beach**, sights in Sokcho are thin on the ground, but there are some good day-trips on offer around the city: on the way north towards the barbed wire of the DMZ is **Hwajinpo lagoon**, while heading south will bring you to **Naksan beach** and its resident temple. All in all, it's one of Korea's most pleasant cities, and well worth a few days of your time.

Abai Island

아바이 마을 • Daily 24hr • Free • Ferries run 24hr (W200 one-way)

Connected to the mainland by road and winch-ferry, tiny **Abai Island** is the most brackish part of this salty city. Seemingly transported here from a bygone era, Abai's warren of tight lanes is well worth a wander; it's also famed for the peculiar local speciality food, *sundae* (see page 154). The island is connected on its southern side to the express bus terminal road by an unnecessarily large bridge, and to the City Hall area by an incredibly cute **ferry service**. Little more than a platform attached to steel cables, it runs day and night along a winch line, the two operators using what look like giant tuning forks to haul the ferry across. These days the pilots are in the habit of encouraging tourists to do the fork-hauling themselves, a truly unique experience that may well be the cheapest thrill you can get in Korea.

Yeongnangho

영랑호 • Bus #1 or #1-1 from Sokcho's main road

A twenty-minute walk north of the intercity bus terminal will bring you to **Yeongnangho**, a tranquil lake set away from Sokcho's brine and bustle. From its eastern shore, you can see Ulsanbawi – Seoraksan's distinctive spiny rock ridge – reflected in the water. It's a great area for a **bike ride** – the nearest rental outlets are in the city centre (see page 153).

Sokcho beach

속초 해수욕장

South of the city centre, and within walking distance of the express bus terminal, is **Sokcho beach**; this small stretch of sand can get extremely busy in the summer,

Hwajinpo (35km)

SOKCHO

0   500
metres

Yeongnangho
Lake

YEONGRANGDONG

BEONYEONG-RO
BESROAE-RO
JUNGANG-RO
JUNGANG-RO

Golf Course

DONGHAE-DAERO

MISURYEONG-RO

BEONYEONG-RO

1 Intercity
Bus Terminal
2

Old Ferry
Terminal

City
Hall
JUNGADGONG

1 **3**

2
3

EAST SEA

JUNGANG-RO

CHEONGCHOHOBAN-RO

4 Abai Ferry

SEORAKGEUMGANGDAE-GYO

SUPIEK-RO

JUYANG-RO

DONGHAE-DAERO

CHEONGDAE-RO

LEPEC-RO

Cheongcho
Lake

CHEONGRO-RO

ACCOMMODATION
Casa Seorak   7
Donggyeong Motel   1
The House Hostel   2
Ramada Gangwon   6
Rocustel Motel   4
Sokcho & Guesthouse   3
With U   5

DRINKING
Doghouse Beer   1

EATING
Bukcheong Sundae   3
Bulyaseong   5
Narutbae Sikdang   2
Tourist and Fishery Market 1
Twosome Place   4
Yeongrangjeong Garden   6

1
1

JOYANG-RO

Expo Park

EXPO-RO

E-Mart

DONGHAE-DAERO

6

JOYANGDONG

JOYANG-RO

CHEONGDAE-RO

Jangsu
Minimarket

Express
Bus Terminal
4

5

5
CHEONGHODONG

Sokcho
Beach

NAEGUHANG-RO

N

when you can rent out rubber rings or take a banana boat ride. At all times of year, you'll be able to dine on great seafood in the slew of **fish restaurants** (see page 154).

ARRIVAL AND DEPARTURE
SOKCHO AND AROUND

By plane The local airport is at Yangyang, down the coast. Though mostly used by charter flights, it fields scheduled flights to Busan (1 daily; 1hr 10min) and Jeju (1 daily; 2hr).

By bus To the north of the city is the intercity bus terminal, from which plenty of local buses trundle through the city centre to the express bus terminal in the south; the

latter now only serves Seoul (2–4 hourly; 2hr 10min) and Incheon airport (9 daily; 2hr 40min).

Destinations from intercity terminal Busan (5 daily; 9hr); Chuncheon (1–2 hourly; 2hr); Daegu (7 daily; 6hr 30min); Gangneung (1–4 hourly; 1hr 20min); Samcheok (9 daily; 2hr 45min).

GETTING AROUND

By bus Sokcho's C-shaped main road is ploughed by umpteen local bus routes – you can board almost any number to get between the two main bus terminals.

By bike Bikes can be rented next to the waterfront Expo Park for W6000 per hour.

INFORMATION

Tourist information Info booths are located outside both bus terminals. Both can give you maps, but for assistance it may be better to call tourist enquiries (☎033 1330).

Hiking equipment Those planning to hit one of the neighbouring national parks should track down one of numerous hiking stores on the main road of the city centre,

including North Face, Korean clone Red Face, and clone-of-a-clone Black Face. Alternatively, try Treksta, opposite City Hall.

Post office The main branch (Mon–Fri 9am–6pm) is located near the intercity bus terminal, just a short walk from City Hall.

ACCOMMODATION

Many places to stay in Sokcho were built in the 1970s, during the first big burst of domestic tourism, and today they're looking rather drab. **Motels** can be found around both bus terminals; pickings are best down south, around the express terminal, which has the bonus of a beach down the road. Seoraksan National Park (see page 156) and Naksan beach (see page 156) are alternate options.

CITY CENTRE

Donggyeong Motel 동경 모텔 4 Jungang-ro 2-gil ☎033 631 6444; map p.152. Right next to the intercity bus terminal, this is where the tourist office usually points budget travellers – rooms are great for the price, and the owners amiable. **W30,000**

★The House Hostel 더하우스 호스텔 5 Jungang-ro 205-gil ☎033 633 3477, ⓦthehouse-hostel.com; map p.152. This extremely amiable hostel has comfy rooms, and a homely atmosphere that makes meeting new friends almost inevitable; the free bike rental is a nice touch, and the free breakfasts are welcome. It's a short walk from the intercity terminal – look for the street signs. Dorms W23,000, doubles W45,000

Rocustel Motel 로커스텔 모텔 17 Cheongho-ro 1-gil ☎033 633 4959; map p.152. You'd once have found it impossible to miss this building behind the express bus terminal, but they recently replaced its shocking pink paint scheme with an off-white. The rooms remain too brash for some, but unlike most motels they have a few twins on offer; all in all, it's the best option in this price range. **W40,000**

Sokcho & Guesthouse 속초 & 게스트하우스 87 Jungangbudu-gil ☎070 8288 2016; map p.152. Although its name tends to lead to very confused Google searches, that's just about the only negative point of this excellent guesthouse, located close to the Abai winch-ferries. The simply decorated dorms and private rooms alike are kept spotless, and the hosts are helpful sorts. Breakfast included. Dorms W35,000, doubles W60,000

With U 위드유 호텔 3993 Donghae-daero ☎033 631 3620; map p.152. If you're after something a little classier than a hostel or motel, but cheaper than a tourist hotel, this is your best bet – decorated with a mix of pine and light greys, its rooms are soothing escapes from the noise of the express bus terminal area, and the beach is just a few minutes' walk away. **W70,000**

DAEPO PORT AND AROUND

★Casa Seorak 카사 설악 42 Hadomun-gil ☎033 636 0367; map p.152. South of Daepo Port, and close to the Seoraksan access road, this B&B is perhaps best described as "adventurous", splashing colour and quirky details across something resembling traditional Korean design. Some double rooms have spa baths – try to nab one of these if you can, especially when rates dip under W90,000, as they often do on weekdays. Excellent breakfast included. W120,000

Ramada Gangwon 라마다 강원 106 Daepohanghuiman-gil ☎033 630 6800, ⓦwyndham

hotels.com; map p.152. A new higher-end option in the Daepo port area, a few kilometres south of the city centre. Rooms have great views and are large, attractive and well equipped, though there's no breakfast or tourist assistance; rates often dive under W100,000 outside the tourist peak periods. W240,000

EATING

Like the accommodation, **restaurants** in Sokcho have a general air of decay about them; nonetheless, there are some very decent places to eat.

★**Bukcheong Sundae** 북청 식당 27–33 Abaimaeul-gil ☎033 632 7243; map p.152. If you really fancy getting into the local groove and chowing down on *Abai sundae* (W15,000), this friendly Abai Island restaurant is the best place to head. Go for the *modeum sundae* set (W25,000; feeds two) and you'll get the blood sausage, another version stuffed inside a squid, a small *bibimbap*, a broth, soy-marinated shrimp, salad, and more. For the full works, wash it down with some local corn *makgeolli*. Some of Gangwon's best-value food. Daily 8.30am–9pm.

Bulyaseong 불야성 Jeonjeokbi-ap ☎033 636 1346; map p.152. Off the north end of Sokcho beach, this tent-like venue is a great place for shellfish barbecue (조개구이; W50,000, feeds two) under a permanent Christmas of twinkly lights. Daily 1–10pm.

★**Narutbae Sikdang** 나룻배 식당 14 Abaimaeul-gil ☎033 636 1346; map p.152. *Saengseon-gui* (생선수이; grilled fish) dishes in Korea usually revolve around just the one grilled fish. In this unassuming Abai Island restaurant, there are no fewer than seven different fishes served at once – a veritable feast for W12,000 per person (minimum two, in theory, though they sometimes

serve solo diners). Daily 8am–10pm.

Tourist and Fishery Market 관광 수선 시장 Jungangdong; map p.152. The food arcade of this atmospheric market (formerly known as "Jungang Market") is a good place to track down some *dakgangjeong* (see page 154). Other items worth sniffing out are shrimp tempura and red-bean pancakes. Most stalls daily 8am–10pm.

Twosome Place 투썸 플레이스 324 Cheongchohoban-ro; map p.152. Yes, it's a chain café, but it's one of the better ones, plus the upper levels are ideal vantage point for taking in the insane majesty of the Abai winch-ferries. Coffees from W4000. Daily 8am–10pm.

Yeongrangjeong Garden 영랑정 가든 4083 Donghae-daero ☎033 636 4149; map p.152. Food in this mushroom-like building near Expo Park is up there with the best in town. The English-language menu has a list of succulent beef to barbecue from W15,000–40,000 per portion, or there are cheaper meals such as soybean broth (W7000) or cold *naengmyeon* noodles (W8000). Daily 10am–10pm.

SOKCHO SPECIALITY FOOD

Sokcho is famed for its **sundae** (순대), but be warned that this has nothing to do with ice cream. It's actually a kind of sausage with various odds and ends stuffed in; it's like haggis, and most people find the dish somehow tastes better than the sum of its parts. The Abai variety is so famous that its name appears on restaurant signs all across Korea; however, many prefer to opt for the stuffed squid option (오징어 순대; *ojingeo sundae*) while they're on the island itself. Nevertheless, Abai island is the best and most atmospheric place in Korea to eat either variety of the dish.

A few kilometres south of central Sokcho, Daepo Port (대포항) has burgeoned in popularity of late, with fish restaurants running in concentric circles around the harbour, which looks particularly pretty at night. The menus can be impenetrable for some foreigners, though a spot of pointing and finger-counting can land you some giant snow crab (대게; *daege*), or (활어; *hwal-eo*), a local flatfish. Perhaps easier for foreigners to enjoy are tempura-like *twigim* (튀김) available at various shacks (and even in one dedicated stand-alone section); W3000 will get you two plump shrimp.

Not all of the town's culinary specialities are hauled from the sea: all over town, you'll see domestic tourists toting around birthday cake-sized boxes of fried, spiced chicken known as *dakgangjeong* (닭강정). It's sold cold from W3000 for a small pack at the market (see page below) and makes great hiking fodder for those heading to Seoraksan.

DRINKING

Given Sokcho's importance as a tourist spot, it's surprisingly hard to find a decent place to **drink**. The beach occasionally gets pumping on weekends, when people often congregate outside – and buy cheap booze from – the Jangsu minimarket (장수 편의점; see map p.000).

Doghouse Beer 개집 비어 21 Meokgeori 6-gil ☎ 033 637 9774; map p.152. Sokcho does have a nightlife area for locals – but it's usually pretty lame. This is by far the best bar here; cocktails go from just W3000, local craft beer for double that, and unlike most such places there's no need to order food. Daily 6pm–5am.

Hwajinpo Lagoon

화진포 • Bus #1 or #1-1 from Sokcho (W5200); get off at Chodo (초도) stop, from which the lagoon is a short walk

As you travel north of Sokcho by road, tensions emanating from the area's proximity to North Korea become more and more apparent. Huge chunks of concrete sit suspended at the roadsides, ready to be dropped to block the path of any North Korean military vehicles that might one day come thundering along. Those with their own vehicle will be able to go all the way along to **Goseong unification observatory** at the border, but perhaps even more interesting is **Hwajinpo**, a stupendously beautiful **lagoon** en route. This was once used as a holiday escape by the Korean great and good – **summer villas** belonging to former Korean leaders can be visited on the same ticket. It's possible to walk between both villas mentioned here, but neither is particularly interesting; the beauty of the lagoon, however, makes a visit worthwhile, as does its sandy beach – white sands cordoned off by barbed wire and traps for North Korean frogmen (don't go swimming too far, if you're allowed in the water at all).

Summer Villa of Kim Il Sung

김일성 별장 • Daily 9am–5pm • Combined ticket with Syngman Rhee villa W3000

Kim Il Sung (North Korea's creator, "Great Leader" and still the country's president despite his death in 1994; see page 340) had a holiday home of sorts just south of Hwajinpo beach before the area was given to the South after the Korean War. This building was destroyed, but a replica has been built in its place, and now contains a mildly interesting collection of photographs; two particular displays are titled "Ceaseless provocations and atrocities by North Korea" and "Nothing has changed at all" – hardly in the spirit of reconciliation. Head up onto the rooftop for a grand view of the beach.

Summer Villa of Syngman Rhee

이승만 별장 • Daily 9am–5pm • Combined ticket with Kim Il-sung villa W3000

Syngman Rhee, president of South Korea from 1948 to 1960, also had a villa at Hwajinpo. Protests forced Rhee to flee to Hawaii in 1960, at which point his deputy, **Lee Ki-boong** (who also had a villa in this area) killed himself, shortly after shooting his parents. Visually this villa is less arresting than that of Kim Il Sung, though there are still some old costumes and photos to enjoy.

Hwajinpo Aquarium

화진포해양박물관 • Daily 9am–6pm • W5000

Korea often tries to soften up areas connected to the forbidden North with something more jovial – anything to take people's minds off the reality of what's going on over the border. In the case of Hwajinpo it's an **aquarium**, located to the north of the lagoon. It's not bad, and focuses more on local marine life than other Korean aquariums do.

Naksansa

낙산사 • Daily 24hr • Free • Bus #9 or #9-1 from Sokcho

Twelve kilometres south of Sokcho is **Naksansa**, a highly photogenic temple situated facing the sea – surprisingly rare in Korea. The complex was ravaged by fire in 2005, though rebuilding was swift and bold, with traditionalists perturbed by added accoutrements such as the white Goddess of Mercy statue now standing at the top of the hill. The hilltop does, however, afford great views of the sea to the east and Seoraksan National Park to the west. The temple is breezy and open, with plenty of nooks and crannies to explore, particularly around the rocky shore area; however, the number of domestic tourist arrivals has ballooned of late, and the place can feel horribly crowded on weekends.

Just south of the temple is **Naksan beach** (낙산 해수욕장), by far the longest on this stretch of coast. Almost unbearably popular in the summer, it is, accordingly, surrounded by hundreds of **motels** and seafood restaurants. If you fancy staying on, note that rates in the area go up and down with the temperature, but motels get newer and cheaper as you move away from the beach and main access road.

Seoraksan National Park

설악산 국립 공원 • Daily 24hr • W3500 fee levied at some park entrances • ⓦ english.knps.or.kr

Koreans gush about **SEORAKSAN NATIONAL PARK**, and with good reason. The nation's northernmost park, it contains some of the tallest peaks in the country, with mist-fringed bluffs of exposed crag that could have come straight from a Chinese painting. The name gains ambiguity in translation, but roughly translates as "Snow-cragged Mountains"; these bony peaks are pretty enough on a cloudy day, but in good weather they're set alight by the sun, bathed in spectacular hues during its rising and setting. Seoraksan is one of the highest parks in the country and, as a result, usually the first to display the reds, yellows and oranges of autumn.

The park stretches around 40km from east to west and about the same from north to south, with the wide area crisscrossed with myriad **hiking trails**: the routes mentioned here are by no means exhaustive. Also bear in mind that some are closed off from time to time in rotation in order to protect the land: in peak season there can be literally queues of hikers stomping along the more popular routes, and this pressure takes its toll. The park offers several two-day hikes heading around **Daecheonbong**, its highest peak, but the focal point is undoubtedly **Ulsanbawi**, a beautiful spine of jagged rock to the north which resembles a stegosaur spine, the fossilized jaw of a giant crocodile, or a thousand other things depending on your angle, the time of day, and the weather.

Seoraksan can be roughly split into three main areas: **Outer Seorak**, the most accessible part of the park from Sokcho, is where most of the action takes place; **South Seorak** looms above the small spa town of Osaek; while to the west are the less crowded peaks of **Inner Seorak**.

Outer Seorak

외설악 • Bus #7 or #7-1 from Sokcho main road (frequent; 30min) • Cable car W10,000 return

It's a very short trip from Sokcho to **Seorakdong** (설악동), the main **Outer Seorak** (*oe-seorak*) entrance – the transition from the beaches and seafood restaurants of the coast to the peaks and pine lodges of the mountains can be surprisingly swift, but on warm weekends and holidays the access road can be blanketed by one huge traffic jam. Just beyond the Seorakdong entrance is the entry terminal of a **cable car**, which whisks you up to the top of a nearby peak for some great views. Three easy and rewarding two-hour **round-trip hikes** head off the base of the cable car lead; everything is signposted in Korean and English, though it's prudent to nab a **map** from the park entrance.

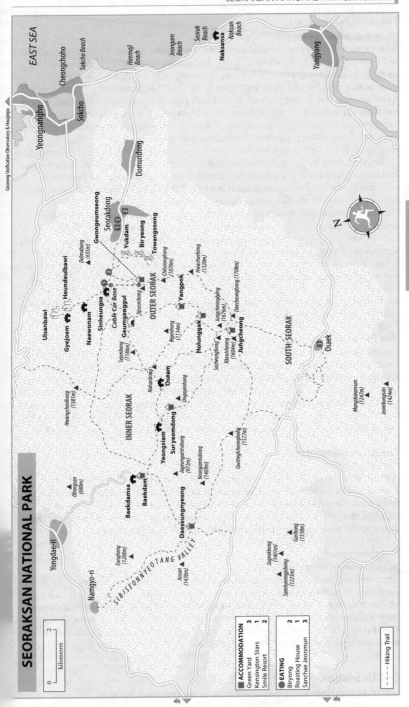

SEORAKSAN NATIONAL PARK

0 — 2 kilometres

ACCOMMODATION
Green Yard 3
Kensington Stars 1
Smile Resort 2

EATING
Biryong 2
Roasting House 1
Sanchae Jeonmun ... 3

- - - - Hiking Trail

The Heundeulbawi trail

3.8km to Ulsanbawi from Seorakdong (2hr)

Seoraksan's most popular (ie easy) trail heads north from the Seorakdong entrance to Heundeulbawi. On the way you'll pass **Sinheungsa**, a modest temple-with-a-view founded in the seventh century but rebuilt several times since; this is home to a large bronze Buddha and some wonderfully detailed "Heavenly Kings", four painted guardians that watch over the temple. The trail then continues up to Gyejoam, a **cave hermitage** chiselled from the rock – this has for centuries been a place of meditation, but given the popularity of the trail you'll have to arrive very early to get any sense of serenity – from where it's a short distance to **Heundeulbawi** (흔들바위; literally "the rocking rock"), a sixteen-ton boulder, which, despite its size, can be (and is, frequently) rocked to and fro by groups of people. Many visitors choose to stop here for a picnic, and there's also a small snack bar – it's hard to resist the sweet-smelling waffles on sale, though tea made from local fruits is a healthier option for those wishing to head beyond the rock, where the path becomes much steeper.

An hour up this trail, which consists of metal stairways, vertigo-inducing bridge passes and more than eight hundred steps, is the summit of **Ulsanbawi** (울산바위), a highly distinctive 873m-high granite crag thrusting out of the surrounding pine trees. Legend has it that the large rock formation was once a living being that came from Ulsan, a city in southeast Korea. It heard one day that a new mountain range was being put together – the Geumgang mountains in present-day North Korea – which were to be the most beautiful on the whole peninsula. Finding on arrival that there was no more room for gargantuan masses of rock, Ulsanbawi headed back home, but fell asleep in the Seorak mountains and never woke up.

The Towangseong trail

2.8km from cable car base to Towangseong (1hr 20min)

From the cable car base, a second popular hike heads southeast through a tight ravine, taking in a few **waterfalls** on the way – Yukdam, Biryeong and Towangseong. **Yukdam** is less a waterfall than a collection of tumbling cascades; hence its name, which means "Six Pools". The **Biryeong** fall further on is far taller, toppling almost forty metres down a cliff face. Almost an hour into the ravine, most hikers turn back, but though it looks like the end of the line the last waterfall, **Towangseong**, is a further twenty-minute hike away.

The Geumganggul trail

3.4km from Sinheungsa (2hr)

A third walk – arguably the most pleasant in the whole park – heads west from Sinheungsa to the lofty cave of **Geumganggul** (금강굴). Just over half an hour's walk from the cable car, this grotto sits almost halfway up one of the many spires of rock that line the valley; it was created as a place of meditation, though the height of the cave and the commanding views it provides make it hard to truly relax.

Daecheongbong

16km from Seorakdong (10hr); 5km from Osaek (4hr)

The park's highest peak, **Daecheongbong** (대청봉; 1708m), is an otherworldly confusion of rock that constitutes the third-highest point in the country. It's a tough all-day hike from Geumganggul cave, or there's a well-signed route from the top of the cable car that cuts out some of the upward climb. Either way, you'll probably need to spend the night at one of several **shelters** (see page 159 for details), unless you make the climb from Osaek to the south (see below).

South Seorak

남설악 • Bus #9 or #9-1 from Sokcho to Yangyang (every 10min; 1hr), then bus to Osaek (10 daily; 40min)

The **South Seorak** section sits pretty at the southern border of the national park, and boasts superlative views of the mountains beyond. The focus here is **OSAEK** (오색), a small village famed for the **hot spring waters** that course beneath its rolling hills. From here, it's possible to make an attempt on Daechongbong, which is just within day-hike territory – four hours up, three down. Osaek itself actually means "five colours", though this was a reference to the flowers fed by the nutritious springs, rather than the waters themselves. The subterranean bounty can be imbibed at several points in the village – the taste something close to an infusion made from flat lemonade and copper – or bathed in at the communal washrooms of numerous *yeogwan*, many of whose facilities are open to non-guests.

Inner Seorak

내설악 • Buses from Sokcho intercity terminal to Yongdae-ri (6 daily; 1hr); Baekdamsa is a 90min walk, or 15min on a shuttle bus

If you want a quiet hike, **Inner Seorak** (*nae-seorak*), is the place for you. Further away from Sokcho than the Outer Seorak range, there is less to see here, and it receives a fraction of the visitors. Inner Seorak is still accessible from Sokcho; a good target is **Baekdamsa** (pancake 백담사), a temple with a curious history in the northwestern side of the park. Baekdamsa started life much further west in the seventh century, but a series of unexplained fires led to several changes of location, until the monks finally settled in Seoraksan surrounded by water – Baekdamsa actually means "The Temple of a Hundred Pools".

From Baekdamsa, there are a number of **hiking** options – one day-long trail heads to Seorakdong in the east of the park, while others converge on Daecheongbong. One of the most pleasant trails is a ridge route that runs from **Daeseungnyeong**, a peak lying around four hours' hike south of Baekdamsa – unless you're starting extremely early, you may have to stay the night at a park shelter.

ACCOMMODATION   SEORAKSAN NATIONAL PARK

The bulk of Seoraksan's accommodation is situated a downhill walk from the **Seorakdong** entrance on the east of the park; there are a few classy hotels near the park gates, a clutch of much cheaper motels around twenty minutes' walk back down the access road, and a traditional hamlet of largely wooden accommodation further down still. It's also possible to stay at **Osaek**, the spa village at the southern end of the park; most of the *yeogwan* here pump hot spring water into the bedrooms, and some have communal hot spring baths that can be used by non-guests (W5000–10,000). Note that all around the park, **prices** from June to October tend to be far higher than at other times of year, especially on weekends.

SEORAKDONG

★**Kensington Stars** 켄싱튼 스타스 호텔 ☎033 635 4001, ⓦwww.kensington.co.kr; map p.157.

A favourite of visiting dignitaries, the *Kensington* has a genuinely English feel to it, with London buses parked up outside, suits of armour in the faux library and mahogany

---

MOUNTAIN SHELTERS AND CAMPING IN SEORAKSAN

If your hiking schedule necessitates an overnight stay in the mountains, you'll need to hunt down one of several basic **shelters**. These make for an atmospheric stay, and cost W8000 per night (an extra W1000 for blankets). While you're unlikely to be kicked out on a wet evening, to guarantee a place you'll have to book ahead on Korea's national park website (ⓦknps.or.kr) or reserve through the Seoraksan park office (☎033 636 7700). Unfortunately, you'll have to select the specific shelter in advance, which is a pain for those whose hike takes them longer than expected; most popular are the **Yangpok** and **Jungcheong** shelters, which generally allow for the most leeway. Sleeping at the peaks themselves is not allowed, though some intrepid hikers do so in their sleeping bags, waking sodden with dew in the midst of empty trails and wonderful views – just make sure you're well hidden. Rudimentary **camping facilities** are also available from W1000 per tent at Seorakdong and Jangsudae. Book ahead in summer or on weekends in the autumn, when the leaves are turning and the trails are at their busiest.

3

SURFING GANGWON

The coast between Sokcho and Gangneung has become popular with Korea's small – but growing – **surf** set; experienced boarders might not be all that impressed with the typically small **beach breaks**, but such conditions are ideal for beginners. You'll spot surfers on the beaches between Sokcho and Naksansa (see page 156), though there's more of a scene on **Jukdo beach** (죽도해변), south of Yangyang on the way to Gangneung, and accessible on buses shuttling between the two; as with surf-spots around the world, everything from cafés to cocktails comes prefixed with the S-word. **Joasurf** (☎033 673 6711, ⓦjoasurf.com) is one of the bigger players in the area, and can organize equipment rental or lessons. A little further north is **Hajodae** beach (하조대해변), a 1.5km-long stretch where **Surfyy** (☎033 672 0695, ⓦsurfyy.com) occupies a dedicated surf zone.

---

everywhere. Built in 1971, it's managed to keep itself on form, with excellent rooms; hefty discounts can be enjoyed off season (sometimes down to W70,000), plus slightly smaller ones if you give breakfast a miss. **W210,000**

Smile Resort 스마일 리조트 ☎033 636 7117; map p.157. Not so much a resort as a comfy, cosy guesthouse, located in a leafy setting just off the main road in Seorakdong's main motel area. Rooms have pine furnishings and exposed brickwork – quite pleasant for the

price, really. **W60,000**

OSAEK

★ **Green Yard** 그린야드 호텔 ☎033 670 1000, ⓦgreenyardhotel.com; map p.157. This huge, leisure-centre-like hotel just leaps out of nowhere in the calm, green Osaek area. Rooms are a bit old fashioned, but staying here can be rather pleasant – the presence of an on-site spa certainly helps. **W180,000**

EATING

The **Seorakdong** entrance has plenty of small restaurants, snack-stands and cafés, though few places are genuinely special. The places mentioned here are both on the hike towards Heundeulbawi. Like every other national park in the land, the done thing is to scoff down a *pajeon* (pancake) post-hike; the places within the park look nice from the outside but are not appealing to actually eat at, while there's a more old-school bunch serving better food a fifteen-minute walk down the hill from the Seorakdong entrance.

Biryong 비룡; map p.157. Inside the Seorakdong entrance, this is an acceptable place for mountain *bibimbap* (W9000) or *haemul pajeon* (W10,000); they also have a range of local *makgeolli*. Daily 9am–7pm.

Roasting House 커피볶는 하녹 ☎033 633 0079; map p.157. Just before you hit Sinheungsa (see page 158), you'll walk past this traditionally styled café, which roasts its own beans amid the trees, and serves quality hand-drip coffee from W8000 (cheaper Italian styles are available too). They're proud of their handmade cookies,

though they only rustle up a single batch in the morning – get them on your way up, since they'll be gone by the time you get back down. Sometimes closed in winter. Daily 8.30am–6pm.

Sanchae Jeonmun 산채 전문 ☎033 636 7477; map p.157. The best of the older venues downhill from the Seorakdong park entrance; their *bibimbap* (W8000) comes with a prodigious array of side-dishes, or you can splash out on a set meal centred on grilled bellflower root (더덕 정식; *deodeok jeongsik*; W28,000 for two). Daily 8am–8pm.

Gangneung and around

강릉

The biggest city on the northeastern coast, **GANGNEUNG** has blossomed since being selected as the de facto host city of the **2018 Winter Olympics**. Investment duly poured in, and the city was finally connected to Seoul by high-speed rail in late 2017; though some of the other Olympics-related projects will inevitably join the long, long chain of post-Games white elephants, the general feel of the place has changed – Gangneung now has substantial charm, though much of the nicer areas are on the periphery of the city, whose centre remains a little shoddy. Many of the best sights are located in a watery, semi-rural stretch between **Ojukheon**, a complex so important and tranquil that you'll see it on the W5000 note, and **Gyeongpo**, one of the most popula beaches in Korea. The lake of **Gyeongpoho** (경포호) effectively links the two; with innumerable paths, pavilions, lotus ponds and other selfie-friendly spots, it makes fantastic walking territory, and you'll also be able to rent a bike from various points (see page 162).

Gangneung has long been a jumping-off point for the superb **skiing** facilities at nearby **Pyeongchang** (see page 164), the official base of the Winter Olympics. Also in the area are **Odaesan National Park** (see page 163), a favourite with hikers and temple-hunters, and the charming coastal village of **Jeongdongjin** (see page 166).

Ojukheon

오죽헌 • Daily 8am–6pm • W3000 • Bus #202 from train station or bus terminals (tell the driver where you want to go, as it can be a little hard to know when to get off), or a W4500 taxi ride

Gangneung's main sight is **Ojukheon**, a network of floral paths and traditional buildings, and the birthplace of **Lee Yulgok**, also known as Yi-Yi, a member of the *yangban* – Korea's Confucian elite – and one of its most famous scholars (see box above). The complex is quite large, and much of it is paved, but there's a pleasant green picnic area surrounded by tall pines, as well as a patch of rare black bamboo to stroll through. Ojukheon is especially popular in the autumn, when its trees burst into a riot of flame. Rice fields surround the complex, which is a little set back from the main road and now near-surrounded by artsy cafés, and a couple of uninteresting galleries.

Chamsori Edison Gramophone Museum

참소리 축음기 에디슨 박물관 • Daily 9am–5.30pm • W7000 • Bus #202 from train station or bus terminals, or a W7000 taxi ride from the centre

East of Ojukheon is the slightly bizarre **Chamsori Edison Gramophone Museum**, which claims to be the largest gramophone museum in the world. There are around 4500 of the things here, as well as other items of Edisonnic provenance, and – rather tangentially – some invented by other contemporary geniuses.

Gyeongpo beach

경포 해수욕장 • Jetskis W50,000 for 10min; banana boat rides W10,000; speedboat trips from W40,000 for groups of up to five • Bus #202 from train station or bus terminals, or a W6000 taxi ride from the centre

The lake of Gyeongpoho almost tickles a near-eponymous beach – **Gyeongpo**, a long stretch of white sand that's one of the most popular beaches in the province; there is all kinds of water-based fun to be had in the summer, when it can be heaving with people. Well-informed locals prefer **Anmok beach** (안목 해수욕장), a more relaxed stretch of sand further south, which rarely fills up; you can walk between the two beaches, though those venturing too close to the military installations will get barked at by soldiers.

THE DANO FESTIVAL

The best time to be in Gangneung is around the fifth day of the fifth lunar moon, usually in June, when the riverside **Dano festival** is held. Events take place all over the country on this auspicious date, but Gangneung sees by far the biggest celebration – the five-day event has commemorated the "Double Fifth" with dancing and shamanist rituals for over four hundred years. Even hard-working Koreans, including students, sometimes get a day or two off for this. The festival provides your best opportunity to see **ssireum**, a Korean version of wrestling often compared to sumo, but far more similar to Mongolian forms.

3

YI-YI: STAR OF THE W5000 NOTE

Lee Yulgok (1536–84), more commonly known by his pen name **Yi-Yi**, is one of the most prominent Confucian scholars in Korea's history, and once lived in the **Ojukheon** complex in Gangneung. A member of the country's *yangban* elite, he was apparently able to write with Chinese characters at the age of three, and was composing poetry by the time he was seven years old, much of it on pavilions surrounding the glassy lake at Gyeongpoho just down the road. At nineteen he was taken to the hills to be educated in Buddhist doctrine, but abandoned this study to excel in **political circles**, rising through the ranks to hold several important posts, including Minister of Personnel and War. At one point, he advised the King to prepare an army of 100,000 to repel a potential **Japanese invasion** – the advice was ignored, and a huge attack came in 1592, just after Yi-Yi's death. His face is on one side of the **W5000 note**, while on the other is the famed "Insects and Plants" painting by his mother, **Sin Saimdang** (1504–51), who was a well-known poet and artist; you'll find her on the **W50,000 note**. Her selection, interestingly, managed to ruffle feathers with traditionalists and liberals alike – Confucian-thinking men were aghast that a woman should be on the front of Korea's most valuable note, while feminists were similarly distraught that this role model of "inferior" Confucian-era femininity should be chosen ahead of more progressive women.

ARRIVAL AND DEPARTURE   GANGNEUNG

By train Gangneung is now connected to Seoul by high-speed rail (hourly; 2hr), which has reduced travel times between the two significantly – it used to take triple the time.

By bus The express and intercity terminals are joined at the hip in the west of the city. Bus #202-1 will take you to the train station, though this only leaves every half-hour – it's far easier to take a taxi (W3000).

Destinations Busan (16 daily; from 5hr); Chuncheon (1–2 hourly; 2hr 10min); Samcheok (hourly; 1hr); Seoul (1–2 hourly; 2hr 30min); Sokcho (every 20–30min; 1hr 10min); Taebaek (hourly; 2hr 20min).

GETTING AROUND AND INFORMATION

By bus and taxi The city is well served by bus (W1300 per ride), with the #202 lassoing together the sights listed here; however, most foreigners find it far easier to simply hop in a cab, with rates rarely going above W8000 or so.

By bike Various places around the beaches and lake rent bikes for W5000/hr, or it's most like W20,000/hr for pedal buggies seating two.

Tourist information There's a helpful office between the bus terminals (daily 9am–6pm; ☎033 640 5129).

ACCOMMODATION

Half a dozen **motels** line the area behind the bus terminal, though it's better to base yourself elsewhere – try the glut of motels and boutique hotels near **Gyeongpo beach**. Alternatively, little Jeongdongjin (see page 166) just down the coast is a more pleasant place to stay.

Aark House 아크 하우스 4-5 Yongji-ro 96-gil ☎010 8977 4576. Excellent hostel option near the train station; it's homely on account of actually being a house, its dorm beds have comfy mattresses and curtains for privacy, and rates include breakfast, which makes the whole deal a bargain. Dorms W18,000

Herren Haus 헤렌 하우스 호텔 16 Changhae-ro 14-gil ☎033 651 4000. One of a bunch of hotels overlooking Anmok beach, this one stands out for its artistically decorated rooms, some with grand sea views. Rack rates almost halve on weekdays. W130,000

Hong C 홍시 호텔 2-6 Okcheon-ro 65-gil ☎033 641 8100, ⌨hongchotel.kr. The most comfortable place to stay in the centre, with rooms that are small but rather attractive – forget about the rack rates, which you can usually cut in two. Breakfast is cooked up by the hotel chef and comes as quite a treat. W180,000

★**Ojuk Hanok Village** 오죽 하녹 마을 11 Jukheon-gil ☎033 655 1117, ⌨ojuk.or.kr. What a fantastic addition to this city this has been. Created by the team responsible for a similar facility in Gongju (see page 276), it's effectively a mini-village of traditional wooden *hanok* housing. Such things can verge on the twee, but here the traditional feel wins out, and the bucolic surroundings should make for a very good night's sleep on floor-mattresses, of course. W60,000

EATING

There really isn't much of culinary interest in the city centre, but the **beach areas** have plenty of great seafood restaurants. The area around Anmok beach is absolutely riddled with cafés – youngsters come from far afield to drain a coffee here. None of them stand out, though several have good sea views from their balconies – take your pick.

Busan Hoetjip 부산 횟집 419 Changhae-ro ☎033 644 2240. Gangneung is famed for its *sundubu* (tofu), said to be particularly soft here on account of the local sea water used (don't ask how this works). The city has an area dedicated to the stuff near the Edison museum, but it's better to have precisely the same meal here, overlooking the sea. This Gyeongpo beach restaurant is a good choice; it's lined with pine and has a second-floor veranda. *Sundubu jjigae* (broth) will cost you W7000. Daily 9.30am–10pm.

Golondrina 골론드리나 4-11 Hassla-ro 206-gil ☎033 641 9138. Mexican restaurant nestled into Gangneung's most pleasant food-and-drink zone. It's run by a Peruvian-Korean couple, though sadly the most Peruvian things on the menu are the pisco cocktails; food options include good tacos (W3500), quesadillas (W8000) and burritos (W11,000), and the place has become extremely popular with local expats on account of an excellent range of Korean craft beer. Mon–Fri 6–11pm, Sat & Sun 6pm–midnight.

★ **L Coffee** L커피 933-16 Gyeongpo-dong ☎033 655 0075. Just around the corner from the Ojukheon entrance, this is the most pleasing café in the city by far – its garden setting is particularly appealing when the flowers are in bloom, and even the interior is filled with pot plants. Plenty of coffees and teas on offer for around W5000, and they have local ceramics on sale too. Daily 8am–10pm.

Odaesan National Park

오대산 국립 공원 • Daily 24hr; hiking prohibited from sunset until 2hr before sunrise • Free • ⓦ english.knps.or.kr

A short ride to the west of Gangneung is **Odaesan National Park**, which is markedly smooth and gentle compared with its jagged Gangwonese neighbours. A maze of tumbling waterfalls, bare peaks and thickly forested slopes, full of colour in the autumn, it's nevertheless relatively empty for a Korean national park as hikers tend to be sucked into the Seoraksan range a short way to the north.

Odaesan has **two main entrance points**: one in the pretty **Sogeumgang** area (소금강; "Little Geumgang"), named after the spectacular range just over the border in North Korea to the north of the park; and a south gate reached via the small town of **Jinbu** (진부). The south of the park contains more of historical interest, since it contains two sumptuous **temples** – Woljeongsa and Sangwonsa, both of which have little tearooms in which to rest. Throughout the park there are innumerable shrines, some of which are quite remote and receive next to no visitors – just the treat for adventurous hikers.

Woljeongsa

월정사 • Daily 24hr • W3000

Woljeongsa dates from 645, and contains an impressive octagonal nine-storey pagoda from the early Goryeo dynasty, adorned with wind chimes and striking a perfect balance with the thick fir trees surrounding the complex. It faces an ornate, and rare, kneeling Buddha. The complex as a whole addresses function rather than beauty, though in the main hall are two elaborate Buddhist paintings – most interesting is the one on the left, which features some hellish scenes of torture.

HIKING ODAESAN

A **hiking** trail leads from the temple of Sangwonsa to **Birobong**, the highest peak in the park at 1563m. Although the ascent can be made in less than two hours, plan for three – it's steep and not an easy walk. Those who get to the top can continue along a ridge trail to **Sangwangbong**, or even attempt a U-shaped day-hike to **Dongdaesan** via Durobong – this walk is particularly tough on the legs. A waterfall-strewn day-hike heads up through Sogeumgang via Noinbong to Odaesan's **spine road**; unfortunately, this twisty thoroughfare sees no public transport, limiting onward movement from the park to hitchhiking or a lengthy walk.

Sangwonsa

상원사 • Daily 24hr • Free

Ten kilometres through the pine trees from Woljeongsa is **Sangwonsa**, a complex containing what is believed to be Korea's oldest bronze bell, which dates from 725. Sangwonsa's appeal is its magical setting, facing a mountain ridge swathed with a largely deciduous wall of trees; in a country where pine green reigns supreme, the blaze of colour that these create in the autumn is rather welcome.

ARRIVAL AND DEPARTURE   ODAESAN NATIONAL PARK

By bus The Sogeumgang entrance is easiest to get to, with regular direct buses heading from Gangneung bus terminal (40min). To the south gate, you'll have to change in Jinbu (진부; 1–2 hourly; 45min from Gangneung), from where onward connections to the park are infrequent – there's one every hour or so, and some only go as far as Woljeongsa.

ACCOMMODATION

There's a pleasantly low-key **minbak** area downhill from both park entrances, with rooms in traditional houses going from W30,000. There's also a **campsite** between Woljeongsa and Sangwonsa; it costs up to W8000 per tent in July and August and is free for the rest of the year (though showering facilities will be unavailable).

Kensington Flora 켄싱튼 플로라 ☎033 330 5000, ⊕www.kensingtonflorahotel.co.kr. Downhill from the south entrance, this bank of high-rises constitutes the most luxuriant accommodation in or around the park. There's an outdoor swimming pool on site, as well as a pub and restaurant. W120,000

Pyeongchang

평창

PYEONGCHANG county – the hub of which is around 30km southwest of Gangneung – was thrust into the global limelight as the host of the **2018 Winter Olympics** (see page 165). It was awarded the Games in 2011, after narrow failures in the two previous rounds of voting – it lost out to Vancouver for the 2010 Games, and the Russian resort of Sochi for 2014. Third time lucky, then, and a full set of major sporting festivals for Korea after its hosting of the football World Cup in 2002 and Summer Games in 1988 – only France, Germany, Italy, Japan and the USA can make a similar boast. The main ski resorts in Pyeongchang are **Yongpyeong** and **Alpensia**; if you're looking for smaller, less crowded ski resorts, head to **Phoenix Park** and **Hyundae Sungwoo**, further down the Yeongdong highway, in the direction of Wonju.

Yongpyeong Ski Resort

용평 • Half-day passes around W60,000; ski/board rental for around W25,000; see website for full details • ⊕ yongpyong.co.kr

Also known as Dragon Valley, **Yongpyeong** is Korea's largest ski resort, though it was largely ignored for Olympic activities – it only hosted the alpine skiing. The resort has all kinds of activities from snowboarding to sledding available in the winter, and a mammoth **28 slopes** to choose from, accessed on fifteen ski lifts and gondolas.

Alpensia Ski Resort

알펜시아 • Range of passes available for W40,000–80,000; ski/board rental for W25,000–40,000; see website for full details • ⊕ alpensiaresort.co.kr

Newer and slightly smaller than Yongpyeong, the **Alpensia** resort hosted the opening ceremony of the 2018 Games, and much of its sporting activity. It's an excellent ski resort, with six slopes and counting, as well as a dedicated run for snowboarders; the hotels here are also a cut above anything else in the Gangwon mountains.

THE 2018 WINTER OLYMPICS

February 2018 saw the eyes of the sporting world trained on Korea's eastern seaboard, as the **Winter Olympics** came to town. The town in question, however, was open to debate – many of the events were held in the city of Gangneung (see page 160), but the official venue of the games was PyeongChang, a rural county, given a temporary extra capital letter in order to distinguish it from a certain capital city to the north.

North Korea was, in fact, the focus of initial proceedings – just over a month before the start of the games, **Kim Jong Un** suddenly proposed sending a delegation across the border, and diplomatic overtures went into overdrive. The two countries entered the opening ceremony together under a joint flag, and competed as a unified team in women's ice hockey (with such hasty preparations they lost all of their games, and finished last).

With Kim Jong Un's sister Kim Yo Jong in attendance, the games were opened by South Korean president **Moon Jae-in**, with the torch lit by Kim Yuna, a figure skater who retired with a clutch of medals in 2014, having made the podium in every single event that she competed in – she is arguably Korea's biggest sporting star of all time. Despite many locals seeking to usurp Kim Yuna, the breakout star in the games was actually a Korean-American – Chloe Kim, who stormed to snowboard halfpipe gold at the tender age of seventeen.

3

ARRIVAL AND DEPARTURE

PYEONGCHANG

By train Pyeongchang station is on the new KTX line, though Jinbu station (진부역) is far closer to the action, receiving trains from Seoul (5 daily; 1hr 40min) and Gangneung (12 daily; 19min).

By bus There are direct shuttle buses to the main ski resorts from far afield – even Seoul (daily departures from several stops; 2hr 30min) and Incheon Airport (5

daily; 3hr). Otherwise, Hoenggye (횐계) is the nearest town, receiving buses from Seoul (1–2 hourly; 2hr 30min) and Gangneung (every 30min; 30min), as well as some other Gangwon destinations. From Hoenggye there are free shuttle buses during the ski season; at other times you can take a local bus (4 daily; 25min; W1450), or taxi (W10,000).

ACCOMMODATION AND EATING

There are deluxe **accommodation** options at both resorts, though Yongpyeong also has several *yeogwan* and a youth hostel. During ski season this will all be booked out – at such times you may have to stay down the road in **Hoenggye**, where there are motels aplenty, though rates can be very poor value in peak season (W200,000 is not unheard of). For food, there are small clutches of **cafés**, **bars** and simple **restaurants** in both Alpensia and Dragon Valley.

YONGPYEONG

Dragon Valley 드래곤 밸리 호텔 Yongpyeong ☎033 330 7111, ⓦyongpyong.co.kr. The area's top dog for many years is now being upstaged somewhat by the Alpensia options, but still makes a great place to stay. Rooms are warm and cosy, which is just what you need in such a place, and if you don't fancy shelling out for meals at its restaurants, there are cheaper options just a walk away. Ask about discounts. W300,000

Yongpyeong Youth Hostel 용평 유스 호스텔 Yongpyeong ☎033 330 7512, ⓦyongpyong.co.kr. Immediately opposite the *Dragon Valley* hotel (who can handle bookings) is this spartan youth hostel, which is by far the cheapest place to stay in the vicinity of the slopes. As with all official Korean hostels, it's an otherwise dull place usually filled with families, teens and tweens. Open Nov–March & July–Aug. Dorms W18,000

ALPENSIA

Holiday Inn 홀리데이 인 Alpensia ☎033 335

5757, ⓦihg.com. The chain has a few buildings in the Alpensia resort area – both make great places to stay, and have fancy rooms boasting plush carpets and huge beds – perfect to wind down in after a hard day. W180,000

★**Intercontinental Alpensia** 인인터컨티넨탈 알펜시아 Alpensia ☎033 339 1225, ⓦihg.com. By far the best place to stay in the whole area, with immaculate rooms, an array of swanky places to eat and drink, and an atmosphere which somehow feels classy yet alpine-homely. Rates drop considerably outside ski season, though they rise again whenever major conferences are being held. W450,000

HOENGGYE

Daegwanryoung 대관령 호텔 90 Daegwallyeongno ☎033 336 3301. Good option near the bus terminal in Hoenggye, featuring six floors' worth of cheap, clean rooms, plus an unintentionally retro sky lounge for coffee or evening drinks, and a sauna on the first floor. W50,000

Jeongdongjin

정동진

For those bored with temples, war museums and national parks, the area around **JEONGDONGJIN** has some rather more unusual attractions to float your boat. Near this small, windswept coastal village lie two retired nautical vessels: an **American warship** from the Korean War, and an equally authentic **North Korean submarine**. From Gangneung, trains make the short trip down the coast, much of which is cordoned off with barbed wire, before stopping at what is apparently the world's closest train station to the sea. A short stretch of sand separates the track from the water, and it's here that Korean couples flock to hold hands and watch the sunrise – the area was featured in *Sandglass*, a romantic Korean soap opera.

Sun Cruise Hotel

썬크루즈 호텔 • Daily 24hr • W5000, free to guests; W2500 of entry price taken off bill in hotel bar or café • ⓦ english.esuncruise.com

There's not too much to see in the town itself, but the **Sun Cruise Hotel** is as much a tourist attraction as a place to stay (see page 168). It's designed to look like a boat, and you really can't miss it – just look for the ship hanging precariously from a cliff. Although its souvenir shop is only on the ninth floor, the combined height of hotel and cliff means that you're a whopping 165m above sea level, and as you walk out of the shop onto the **viewing platform**, it's tempting to let your mind soar and imagine that you're up on the deck of an impossibly large ship. One floor up is a revolving bar-cum-café, which makes a great place to while away some time (see page 168).

Sandglass Park

모래시계 공원 • Museum daily 9am–6pm • W6000 • Rail-bikes on the hour: Mon–Fri 9am–5pm, Sat & Sun noon–5pm • W20,000 for two-seater, W30,000 for four-seater

Look out for the **giant egg-timer** near the beach – couples gather to watch it being turned over each New Year. The egg-timer forms the centrepiece of **Sandglass Park**, a small expanse also featuring the **Time Museum**, an uninteresting look at the concept of time spread over seven disused train carriages. From here you can hop onto a customized **rail-bike** and zip along to the train station on a 5.2km course, which takes around an hour to complete (or just forty minutes if you set the machine to automatic, which rather takes the fun out of the whole thing).

Haslla Art World

하슬라 아트월드 • Daily 9am–6pm • Museum W7000; sculpture park W6000; combined ticket W10,000 • ⓦ haslla.kr • Bus #111, #112 or #113 from Gangneung or Jeongdongjin (every 30min or so), or around W4000 by taxi from Jeongdongjin

Around 2km north of Jeongdongjin is **Haslla Art World**, a superbly designed **contemporary art** complex ranged up a verdant hillside off the coast. There are a few

---

VICTIMS OF NAUTICAL NOMENCLATURE

The **victim mentality** drilled into Korean students during their history lessons is such that any perceived slant against the nation, no matter how slight, can turn into a serious issue that has the whole country boiling with rage. Anger is further magnified should the insult come from Korea's one-time colonial masters, the **Japanese** – witness the case of the waters east of the Korean mainland, generally known across the world as the "**Sea of Japan**". Koreans insist that this name is a symbol of Japan's imperial past, and youth hostel wall maps around the world have had the name crossed out by Korean travellers and replaced with "**East Sea**". Korean diplomats raised enough of a stink to take the issue to the United Nations, which tentatively sided with the Japanese, but left the topic open for further discussion. Although both terms have been used for centuries, neither is strictly correct – Korea controls a large portion of the waters, yet the sea lies plainly to Japan's west – so this storm in a teacup is set to rage on for a while yet.

ESPIONAGE IN THE EAST SEA

Those who deem the Cold War long finished should cast their minds back to September 1996. On the fourteenth, a submarine containing 26 **North Korean spies** arrived at Amin, on South Korea's Gangwon coast. Three disembarked, and made it back to the submarine after completing their surveillance mission on the Air Force base near Gangneung, but the waves were particularly strong that day and the sub came a cropper on the rocks. Eleven non-military crew members were killed by the soldiers, lest they leaked classified information to the South, and important documents were incinerated inside the vessel – the ceiling of the cabin in question is still charred with burnt North Korean spy material. The remaining fifteen soldiers attempted to return to the North overland, with their Southern counterparts understandably keen to stop them; the mission continued for 49 days, during which seventeen South Korean soldiers and civilians lost their lives. Thirteen of the spies were killed, one was captured, and the whereabouts of the last remains a mystery.

indoor halls, one of which features what may well be the world's only **Cow Dung Art Gallery** – note that only a few of the sculpted dollops are real. However, the bulk of the installations lie outdoors in the **sculpture park**: witness the metal spiders clambering up the hillside, or the much-photographed pair of adjoining chairs (again, Jeongdongjin is highly popular with couples) peering over the sea. The on-site "Sea Café" is an equally great place from which to watch the sunset, but perhaps best of all is the chance to stay in the wonderful **hotel** (see page 168).

Tongil Park

통일 공원 • Daily: March–Oct 9am–6pm; Nov–Feb 9am–5pm • W3000 • Bus #111, #112 or #113 from Gangneung or Jeongdongjin (every 30min or so), or W7000 by taxi from Jeongdongjin

Jeongdongjin's resident warship and sub are permanently moored next to each other at **Tongil Park**, 4km north of the village on the coast. The ship saw action, having served in the Korean War, but the **submarine** has an even more interesting tale to tell, having made a dramatic final voyage (see page 167). It's hard to imagine that this small metal tube could hold a crew of thirty, as even with nobody else on board it's tough enough to navigate without bumping your head; faced with just one dark, cramped corridor, you're unlikely to be inside for long. By comparison, the US-made **warship** is 120m long, and it can take an hour or so to hunt down every nook and cranny; in the bridge you can play with the chunky steering equipment, twiddle knobs, check dials and shoot imaginary torpedoes at your enemies. Though the ship is on dry land, nearby military installations and the waves crashing below can make it easy to let your imagination go wild, and if your karma is in credit there'll be fighter jets from the local Air Force base roaring overhead.

ARRIVAL AND DEPARTURE | JEONGDONGJIN

By train Jeongdongjin is best reached by train, and its station is right next to the beach – the closest station in the world to the sea, according to local authorities. The journey from Seoul (Cheongnyangni station; 6 daily; 5hr 30min) does take forever, though; in addition, Gangwon's coastal line operates a frustratingly infrequent service and the section to Gangneung was out of action at the time of writing), so it pays to find out times in advance. The relatively new introduction is the "Sea Train", a special service connecting Jeongdongjin and Samcheok (2–3 daily; 1hr 20min; W15,000); taking its lead from similar trains in Japan, its zanily decorated interior features swivel seats aimed at large, sea-facing windows. Tickets are available from the website (⊛ seatrain.co.kr), though it's in Korean only, so try to book at a train station ticket window.

By bus From Gangneung, bus #109 (40min) runs from the bus terminal direct to the *Sun Cruise* hotel, and #111, #112 and #113 from various stops around the city to central Jeongdongjin, passing Tongil Park and Hassla Art World on the way (30min).

3

ACCOMMODATION

Jeongdongjin trades on the romance dollar, with amorous couples arriving to hold hands and watch the sunset year round, so there are plenty of rooms to choose from – New Year and summer weekends are the only times you should have to book ahead.

Full House Motel 풀하우스 모텔 26 Jeongdongyeok-gil ☎033 644 5880. The pick of the roadside motels near the train station, with en-suite facilities and pleasantly decorated rooms; make sure to get one with a sea view. There's also a little veranda up on the roof. W45,000

★Haslla Museum 하슬라 호텔 1441 Yulgok-ro ☎033 644 9411, ⓦhaslla.kr. Forming part of the Haslla Art World complex just to the north of town (see page 166), this is without doubt the most distinctive hotel on the east coast. Each room has been individually, artistically designed; floor-to-ceiling windows provide wonderful sea views, and some rooms have their beds tucked away in gigantic wooden bowls – more comfortable than it may sound. Rack rates are high, though you can usually knock a fair chunk from this, and almost half on weekdays. W300,000

Hyanggi 향기 호텔 982-6 Heonhwa-ro ☎033 642 7512. Sitting in a prime location at the south end of the beach, this is a decent place to stay if you can nab a sea-facing berth, but rooms are a little stuffy and rather overpriced. W80,000

Suerte 수에르테 985 Heonhwa-ro ☎010 7766 9110. The best hostel option in the area, sat atop a nice café – the rooms are okay (dorms run from four to ten beds), but service can be next to nonexistent, since the staff are usually busy making coffee downstairs. Dorms W30,000

★Sun Cruise 썬크루즈 호텔 950-39 Heonhwa-ro ☎033 610 7000, ⓦenglish.esuncruise.com. You can't miss this place, perched as it is atop a cliff south of the station, and basically a tourist attraction in its own right (see page 166). It can be surprisingly cheap off season (down to W70,000 for a double), and, mercifully, the nautical theme isn't carried through into its plain rooms. A good place to go wild with a bunch of friends. W130,000

EATING AND DRINKING

Jeongdongjin has no shortage of **restaurants**, and it should come as no surprise that most (but by no means all) places focus on fish. Perhaps most fun for foreign visitors will be the chance to enjoy a **shellfish barbecue** (조개구이; *jogae gui*), which should cost from W50,000 for two people.

Café Sun 카페 썬 6 Jeongdongyeok-gil ☎033 644 5466. Pleasant café overlooking the sea, selling a range of coffees from around the world (W6000 and up), and cocktails in the evening. It opens up at crazy o'clock in order to sate the needs of couples itching to see the sunrise, but in need of caffeine and some warmth. Daily 4am–8pm.

★Jeonmangdae Hoetjip 전망대 횟집 982-2 Heonhwa-ro ☎033 644 5406. Just back from the *Hyanggi* hotel, this is the most friendly and reliable place for a shellfish barbecue (W50,000 for two), which comes with various tasty side dishes. Alternatively, go for *hoedeopbap* (sashimi on rice; W15,000), or *haemul kalguksu* (spicy seafood and noodle soup; W8000). Daily 10am–11pm.

Sseon Hansik 썬한식 1167 Yulgok-ro ☎033 644 5460. This European-style white cottage, sitting off the main road near the train station, deserves a mention for its *chodan sundubu* (초단 순두부), a Gangneung speciality made from super-soft tofu (W7000); they have plenty of other dishes besides, including hot-stone *bibimbap* (W9000). Opens early to nab sunrise-seekers. Daily 3.30am–9pm.

Sun Cruise 썬크루즈 호텔 950-39 Heonhwa-ro ☎033 610 7000. Come to the revolving café-bar atop the famous hotel (see page 168) for a coffee (around W10,000) or something stronger (cocktails W11,000). Prices are high, but you'll get W2500 off with your entrance ticket. Daily 24hr.

Samcheok and around

삼척

A typically ugly Gangwon coastal city, **SAMCHEOK** is nevertheless a good base for a range of interesting sights, including **Penis Park**, several secluded **beaches** and the gigantic cave of **Hwanseongul**. All of these are some way away, and there's little to see in the city itself, though the **port area** to the east is worth a stroll. Here, it's common to see acres of squid hung out like laundry to dry in the sun, and there are more fish restaurants than you can count. The **city centre** itself is bound by a rough quadrilateral

---

BEACHES SOUTH OF SAMCHEOK

The Gangwon coast continues on south of Samcheok, squeezing numerous **beaches** into a fairly short stretch along the way, although continued development of the coastal roads and the resulting increase in traffic means that in addition to the one in Samcheok only two beaches are actually worth visiting – **Maengbang** and **Yonghwa**. The former is one of the largest in the area and its calm waters make it good for swimming. Surrounded by pine trees, it's usually quite peaceful as it's a twenty-minute walk from the nearest bus stop and *minbak* village. The beach at Yonghwa is smaller – only 200m in length – and much closer to the road, but equally attractive.

---

of roads which are home to plenty of chain restaurants and high-street clothing stores; much of the area in between is taken up by an appealingly grimy market.

Samcheok beach

A few kilometres north of the centre is **Samcheok beach**, which attracts a young crowd in the summer; like many other beaches in the province, much of it is cordoned off with **barbed wire**. This makes it a rather interesting place to sunbathe; the wire is in place to prevent amphibious North Korean landings such as the one that occurred up the coast in Jeongdongjin in 1996 (see page 167); also look out at night for the large spotlights used to keep an eye on the seas.

ARRIVAL AND INFORMATION   SAMCHEOK

By bus Samcheok is best approached by bus, as the train station is some distance from the centre and in any case carries a sparse service, though the tourist train from Jeongdongjin is an option (see page 166). The city's two bus terminals – express and intercity – lie almost side-by-side on

the southern flank of town.
Destinations Busan (10 daily; 5hr); Chuncheon (10 daily; 4hr); Gangneung (hourly; 1hr); Gyeongju (hourly; 5hr); Seoul (8 daily; 4hr 30min); Sokcho (9 daily; 3hr); Taebaek (hourly; 1hr 10min).

ACCOMMODATION AND EATING

There are plenty of cheap sleeps in town, but for a more old-time coastal Gangwon atmosphere, adventurous travellers could do worse than head to the cheap guesthouses sprinkled around the **port area** east of town, an area whose restaurants and shops are almost entirely dedicated to fish, and which has something of an end-of-the-world vibe. **Samcheok beach** is also a pleasant place to stay, though prices at its various motels rise in summer.

★ **Moon Motel** 문 모텔 Jeongsangdong 432-63
☎ 033 572 4436. Set in a quiet part of town between

the bus terminal and the river, this motel has clean, comfy rooms that are remarkably stylish. W40,000

Penis Park

해신당 공원 • Daily 9am–6pm • W3000 • Bus #24 from Samcheok bus terminal (hourly; 40min)

South of Samcheok near Yonghwa beach is the rather curious **Penis Park**, whose paths are covered with **penis sculptures** of metal, stone and wood – one is lined with nails, several are carved into people-like shapes and one metal ithyphallus is mounted on cannon wheels. While it may seem bizarre, the park owes its existence to one of the area's most intriguing **folk tales**, the story of a young bride-to-be who died by the shore in a violent storm. After this, her angry spirit is said to have chased the fish from the seas, depriving locals of their major source of income and sustenance. The only way round this, apparently, was to placate the newly dead's soul with carved wooden phalluses, which were driven into the beach – spirit thus satisfied, the fish returned in record numbers.

The main building's **folk exhibition** can be safely ignored, and is interesting only for a small display showing how local squid are lured to their deaths, and an almost comically bad simulation of a boat ride. It gets better in the **sculpture zone**, which has replicas of ancient pornographic statuary from Asia and beyond – don't leave until you've checked out the Greek god's horny pose. Various **trails** make for a pleasant walk around the park – though one often made brisk by the seaside winds – with views of the sea crashing on to the crags below. You can go all the way down to the pebbly shore, which is certainly not safe for swimming thanks to the often fierce East Sea waves. A few *minbak* and stalls selling grilled fish from as little as W2000 can be found around the park's southern end.

Hwanseongul

환선굴 • Daily: March–Oct 8am–5.30pm; Nov–Feb 8am–4.30pm • W4500; monorail W4000 one-way, W7000 return • Bus from Samcheok bus terminal (6 daily, last useful bus 2.20pm; 45min); last bus back 7.30pm

Though Korea contains a fair number of navigable caves, **Hwanseongul**, hiding away under a sumptuous range of hills west of Samcheok, is the one that can most justly be described as "cavernous" – it's one of the **largest caves in Asia**, over 6km long and featuring umpteen rooms and some subterranean water features. Hwanseongul's largest chamber measures 100m by 30m, its dimensions, shading and vaguely creepy atmosphere bringing to mind a Gothic cathedral. Only 1.6km of the cave is open to the public, most of which is traversed by platforms and staircases; be sure to bring suitable shoes and an extra layer of clothing, as it's damp and not very warm down there – it'll take at least an hour to navigate the passageways if you want to see everything. Also bear in mind that the cave entrance is a rather steep half-hour trek from the ticket office, next to which are some examples of *gulpi*, the area's traditional wooden mountain housing; you can chalk some of this off on a short but steep **monorail** track, though the walk is beautiful, particularly in the autumn.

EATING AND DRINKING   HWANSEONGUL

Daemiri Golpijip 대미리 골페집 ☎033 541 7288. Heading up from the entrance to the cave, you'll spot three little restaurants. The first sells *gamja-jeon* (potato pancake) for W5000, the second for W4000, and the third for W3000 – a bargain, since it can be more like W15,000 in Seoul. The middle restaurant is best; it's set in a mocked-up version of a *gulpi*, and heated with a wooden stove in colder months – it looks like a good kick would bring the whole place crashing down. They're also proud of their acorn-jelly salad here (W5000). Daily 9am–5pm.

Taebaeksan National Park

태백산 국립 공원 • Daily 24hr • Free • Bus from Taebaek bus or train stations (every 30–45min; 30min), or around W20,000 by taxi

A thoroughly enjoyable maze of hiking trails, and especially beautiful in the winter months, **Taebaeksan National Park** lies around 40km southwest of Samcheok. Trails in the park are well signposted, but for peace of mind you can buy a map at the entrance. This is already 870m above sea level, and from here a pair of easy two-hour routes run to the twin peaks of **Munsubong** (1517m) and **Cheonjedan** (1561m), two of the highest in Korea. These are of particular importance to **shamanists**, as Taebaeksan is viewed as Korea's "motherly mountain" – ancient Korean kings were said to perform rituals here, and at the summits it's still common to see offerings left behind by hikers in honour of **Dangun**, the legendary founder of Korea (see page 361). Cheonjedan plays host to a shamanist ceremony every year on October 3 – "National Foundation Day" in Korea, and a public holiday – as does the Dangun hall near the entrance.

A rather less spiritual **coal museum** (daily 9am–6pm; W2000) sprawls out just below the park entrance; the Taebaeksan area was once the heart of Korea's coal industry, and this museum charts its gradual decline. The top floor shows some interesting pictures in a coal of village life, and there are a couple of surprise simulations in store too.

The park's main entrance lies a half-hour bus (or taxi) ride from the small, sedate city of **TAEBAEK** (태백) one of the most typical of the Gangwonese interior. Surrounded by mountains and with little large-scale commerce to speak of, its elevation means the air is clean and fresh, and the climate is usually a little colder here than on the coast. It's mainly used as a transit point for the national park.

ARRIVAL AND INFORMATION

By train Trains run from Jeongdongjin (6 daily; 1hr 40min) and Seoul's Cheongnyangni station (6 daily; 4hr) to Taebaek train station. From here you'll need to take an onward bus or taxi to the park.

By bus Taebaek's bus terminal is by the train station at the northern end of town.

Destinations Andong (5 daily; 3hr); Busan (5 daily; 4hr

TAEBAEKSAN NATIONAL PARK

30min); Gangneung (hourly; 2hr 30min); Samcheok (hourly; 1hr 10min); Seoul (hourly; 3hr 30min).

Tourist information There's an information booth (daily 9am–5pm; ☎033 550 2081) by the train and bus stations in Taebaek, and a smaller version of the same at the entrance to the park.

ACCOMMODATION AND EATING

There is a range of cheap sleeps near **Taebaek**'s train and bus stations; for decent food, though, you'll have to make your way into the city centre – walk down from the train station and turn right at the main road. The park itself makes a much prettier place to stay. A two-storey parade of buildings near the **park entrance** houses restaurants on the ground floor and *minbak* accommodation above. Nearby motels offer greater comfort. Further downhill is a bunch of newer, homelier *minbak*, all charging around W30,000 per room.

TAEBAEK

Aegis Motel 이지스 모텔 88 Seohwangji-ro ☎033 553 9980. You can't really miss this place, with its white frame towering over the train station. Rooms here are large and clean, though as the train line has some early morning services, it may not be ideal for light sleepers. W40,000

PARK ENTRANCE

Ujin Motel 우진 모텔 170-12 Cheonjedan-gil. Basic guesthouse across the stream from the park entrance. The attached restaurant allows you to eat in little private huts. W25,000

3

Gyeong-
sang

ULLEUNGDO

Gyeongsang

A land of mountains and majesty, folklore and heroes, the southeastern Gyeongsang provinces (경상) are home to some of the most wonderful sights that Korea has to offer. In terms of its history, Gyeongsang was the base of the Silla kingdom that ruled for nearly a thousand years; though this came to an end a similar timespan ago, a horde of jewellery, regal tombs and wonderful temples provide present-day evidence of past wonders. Next, tradition: in Gyeongsang's richly traditional hinterland you may see beasts ploughing the fields, villages of thatch-roofed houses or even ancestral rites being performed. Then there are more contemporary aces in the pack, with the south-coast city of Busan rivalling Seoul for Korea's best nightlife. Finally, there are natural attractions in abundance: a bunch of great beaches, a slew of scraggly islands and all the seafood you could wish for.

Though the Korean capital was transferred to Seoul following the collapse of the Silla dynasty, Gyeongsang has continued to exert influence on the running of the country. Since independence and the end of Japanese occupation, the majority of Korea's leaders have been Gyeongsang-born, with the resulting distribution of wealth and power making the area the country's most populated, and industrial, outside Greater Seoul.

Covering one-fifth of the country, the largely rural province of **Gyeongbuk** (경북; "North Gyeongsang") is South Korea's largest. Here, age-old tradition lingers on to a degree unmatched anywhere else in Korea, with sights strewn around the area providing a chronological view into more than two thousand years of history. Wonderful **Gyeongju** was capital of the **Silla empire** from 57 BC to 935 AD, and is now a repository to the resulting treasures. The main sights here are the **regal tombs**, small hillocks that held the city's kings, queens and nobles; **Bulguksa**, one of the country's most revered temples; and **Namsan**, a holy mountain crisscrossed with paths, and studded with relics of Silla times. Traces of the **Joseon dynasty**, which ruled the peninsula from 1392 until its annexation by the Japanese in 1910, are evident in a number of Confucian academies and traditional villages; both of these can also be found around **Andong**, a small, peaceful city that's becoming ever more popular with foreigners. The years immediately preceding Korea's mass industrialization in the 1980s can be savoured on the scenic island of **Ulleungdo**, where fishing and farming traditions exist unadulterated by factory smoke or sky-high apartment blocks. Meanwhile, the saccharine delights of present-day Korea can be savoured in **Daegu**, the largest city in the region, and a fun place to hole up for a couple of days.

HAHOE FOLK VILLAGE

Highlights

❶ **Folk villages** Savour a taste of Korean life long forgotten at Hahoe Folk Village near Andong, and at Yangdong, an equally gorgeous version near Gyeongju. See pages 179 and 200

❷ **Confucian academies** Two stunning Joseon-dynasty academies can be found in the Gyeongsang countryside – Dosan Seowon and Oksan Seowon. See pages 180 and 200

❸ **Cycling around Gyeongju** Once the Silla kingdom's capital and now Korea's most laidback city, Gyeongju has enough sights to fill at least a week – you can chalk many of them off on a bike-tour around Namsan, a mountain just to the south. See page 194

❹ **Ulleungdo** This island's isolation out in the East Sea makes it the perfect place to see traditional life first-hand, or you can kick back and relax for a few days. See page 201

❺ **Busan** This smaller, more characterful version of Seoul has many sights including Jagalchi Fish Market and Haeundae, the country's most popular beach. See page 205

❻ **Namhaedo** Swing by this laid-back island, quite literally at the end of the road, to get a taste of rural Korea. See page 224

❼ **Jirisan National Park** Korea's largest national park has umpteen lofty trails, including a three-day hike across the ridge. See page 225

HIGHLIGHTS ARE MARKED ON THE MAP ON PAGE 176

Korea's southeasternmost province, **Gyeongnam** (경남; "South Gyeongsang"), is as closely connected to the sea as its northern neighbour, Gyeongbuk, is to the land. The southern coast splinters off into an assortment of cliffs, peninsulas and **islands**, many of the latter preserved as the **Hallyeo Haesang National Park**. Here you can head by ferry to minute specks of land where life goes on as it has for decades, free of the smoke, noise and neon often hard to escape on the mainland. This greenery is not just confined to the province's shoreline – **Jirisan**, to the west, is the largest national park in the country. It's a real favourite among hikers, and not just for its size, or its beauty – a chain of **shelters** runs across the park's central spine, making multi-day hikes a possibility. Despite all this, Gyeongnam is no

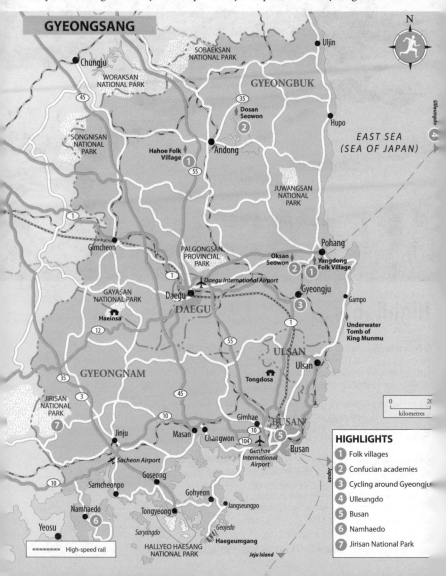

GYEONGSANG

N

Chungju

SOBAEKSAN
NATIONAL PARK

Uljin

WORAKSAN
NATIONAL PARK

GYEONGBUK

45

35

Dosan
Seowon ②

Hupo

EAST SEA
(SEA OF JAPAN)

Ulleungdo ④

SONGNISAN
NATIONAL
PARK

Hahoe Folk
Village ①

Andong

55

JUWANGSAN
NATIONAL
PARK

1

Gimcheon

PALGONGSAN
PROVINCIAL
PARK

1

Oksan
Seowon ②

Pohang

Yangdong ①
Folk Village

GAYASAN
NATIONAL PARK

Daegu International Airport

Daegu

Gyeongju

Gampo

Haeinsa

DAEGU

③

12

Underwater
Tomb of
King Munmu

55

1

35

GYEONGNAM

ULSAN

JIRISAN
NATIONAL
PARK

3

45

Tongdosa

Ulsan

⑦

10

Gimhae

Jinju

Masan

Changwon

10

BUSAN

⑤

Sacheon Airport

104

Gimhae
International
Airport

Busan

Goseong

10

Samcheonpo

Gohyeon

Jangseungpo

0   20
kilometres

Namhaedo

⑥

Tongyeong

Geojedo

Yeosu

Saryangdo

Haegeumgang

HALLYEO HAESANG
NATIONAL PARK

Jeju Island

┈┈┈┈ High-speed rail

HIGHLIGHTS
① Folk villages
② Confucian academies
③ Cycling around Gyeongju
④ Ulleungdo
⑤ Busan
⑥ Namhaedo
⑦ Jirisan National Park

natural paradise. Nearly eight million people live in the area, making it the most densely populated part of the country outside Greater Seoul. Here lies Korea's second city, **Busan**, a fantastic place with good beaches, excellent nightlife and a friendly, earthy nature.

Andong and around

안동

To walk around the unhurried streets of little **ANDONG**, you'd never guess that this is one of the most popular draws in the region for foreign travellers. It's true that there's little going on in the centre, but there are some truly magical sights in the highly picturesque countryside surrounding the city. **Dosan Seowon** to the north is a stunning Confucian academy dating from Joseon times, while to the west is **Hahoe Folk Village**, a rustic approximation of traditional Korean life that's a mainstay of present-day Korean tourist pamphlets. These sights are a little distant from town, but a similar folk village can be found nearer the centre, next to a rather absorbing **folklore museum**; access to this area has been improved of late, and it's possible to walk or cycle much of the stretch from central Andong.

Andong Folk Village

안동 민속 마을 • Daily 24hr • Free • Bus #3 from train station – get off immediately after crossing the river

Just outside the main body of the city lies **Andong Folk Village.** With its buildings mere models, rather than functioning abodes, this is basically a heavily diluted version of the terrific folk village at Hahoe (see page 179), but it's worth a quick nose around, especially if the bus schedules from Andong to Hahoe or Dosan Seowon have left you with an hour or two to spare. After seeing the village, it's possible to cross the river on a zigzagging pedestrian bridge, then catch the bus back to Andong from the other side of the road.

Folk museum

민속 박물관 • Daily 9am–6pm • W1000

Don't leave the folk village without seeing the **Folk museum** near the entrance to the complex, which is chock-full of interesting information about local culture and practices – including why Korean women traditionally give birth facing the south or east; it's altogether more explanatory and less obsessed with cold, hard facts than most Korean museums. Look out for dioramas portraying village games – some of which still go on in the countryside on occasion – and some fascinating collections of clothing and headwear; if you're in luck, you may even walk out with a free scroll of calligraphy from an on-site artist.

Andong Soju Museum

안동 소주 박물관 • Mon–Sat 9am–5pm • Free • Ⓦ andongsoju.net • A taxi from central Andong should cost less than W5000, or take bus #34 or #36 from the train station

Soju, of which Andong is home to a particularly strong variety, is the grog that oils Korea's wheels, and the town has a whole **museum** dedicated to the stuff, a couple of kilometres to the south of town. Unfortunately, it isn't too interesting, but you're welcome to buy a bottle of the local variety (see page 42).

ARRIVAL AND INFORMATION   **ANDONG**

By train Andong's train station is in the very thick of things, and within a 10min walk of all the accommodation and eating options listed here. However, at the time of writing, a new station was being constructed some way

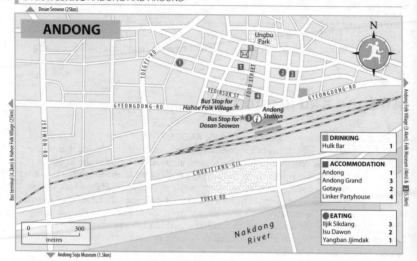

ANDONG

Dosan Seowon (25km)

Ungbu Park

YEDINSUK ST

Bus Stop for
Hahoe Folk Village ★

Bus Stop for
Dosan Seowon

Andong
Station

GYEONGDONG-RO

FOOD STREET

1OEGYE-RO

GYEONGDONG-RO

JEBIWON-RO

Bus terminal (4.2km) & Hahoe Folk Village (25km)

Andong Folk Village (13.4km); Folk Museum (4km) & (3.3km)

CHUKJEJANG-GIL

YUKSA-RO

Nakdong River

0   300
metres

Andong Soju Museum (1.5km)

■ **DRINKING**
Hulk Bar   1

■ **ACCOMMODATION**
Andong
Andong Grand   3
Gotaya   2
Linker Partyhouse   4

● **EATING**
Iljik Sikdang   3
Isu Dawon   2
Yangban Jjimdak   1

to the west, near the bus station – this will be far less convenient when it finally opens up for service, though journey times may decrease slightly.

Destinations Busan (Bujeon station; 3 daily; 3hr 45min); Daegu (Dongdaegu station; 2 daily; 1hr 50min); Danyang (7 daily; 1hr 15min); Gyeongju (3 daily; 2hr); Seoul (Cheongnyangni station; 7 daily; 3hr 20min).

By bus The new bus station is inconveniently located around 6km to the west of the town centre – bus #11 (20min; W1200) connects it to the train station. If you're heading to Hahoe Folk Village and not the town centre,

take bus #46 instead, and you'll save a lot of time.

Destinations Busan (1–2 hourly; 2hr 30min); Daegu (2–3 hourly; 1hr); Daejeon (14 daily; 2hr 10min); Gyeongju (7 daily; 2hr); Pohang (10 daily; 2hr); Seoul (2–3 hourly; 3hr); Sokcho (2 daily; 4hr).

Tourist information There's an excellent information office (daily 9am–6pm; ☎054 852 6800) outside the train station; staff are helpful and informative, especially with regard to finding a place to stay or eat, and there's usually an English-speaker on hand.

ACCOMMODATION

Andong's **accommodation** hasn't quite caught up with its increasing popularity as a tourist destination, but there are now some decent options at all levels. One intriguing option is staying out at Hahoe Folk Village (see page 179); the tourist office will ring ahead to book a room if required. Lastly, if you're on a bare-bones budget, there's a street filled with *yeoinsuk* (around W15,000) just north of the train station.

★**Andong** 안동 호텔 40-11 Munhwagwangjang-gil ☎054 858 1166; map p.178. The best-value motel in the area features flash rooms with great showers; some also have nice paintings. It may be worth paying extra for the more expensive deluxe rooms, which are huge. A café and noodle restaurant are attached to the base. **W50,000**

Andong Grand 안동 그랜드 호텔 346-84 Gwangwangdanji-ro ☎054 851 9000, ⒲andonggrand hotel.com; map p.178. Andong at last has a "luxury" option, set out of the centre in a park-like area near the folk village. They were still finding their feet at the time of writing, though these are by far the best rooms in town, and the breakfasts (included) are superb. **W175,000**

Gotaya 고타야 20 Dongheung 1-gil ☎010 4367 0226; map p.178. Good hostel option with informative

staff, spacious dorm rooms and a range of affordable private rooms. There's a nice common area up top near the dorms, which doubles as the place for breakfast (included in rates); however, note that alcohol is not allowed, and that there's a strictly enforced curfew – come back any later than 11pm and you won't be able to open the door. Dorms **W17,000**, doubles **W60,000**

Linker Partyhouse 링커 파티하우스 180-1 Daean-ro ☎010 4652 0070; map p.178. In stark contrast to the *Gotaya* (see above), at this hostel alcohol is not just allowed, but encouraged – guests are often found in a tight corral outside the front door, surrounded by soju bottles. Rooms are cosy enough, though few seem to remember going to bed. Dorms **W22,000**

EATING

A dedicated **food street** starts just opposite the train station – look for the gate with the mask – though the best restaurants are to be found away from this road. The tourist booth outside the train station is an excellent source of information; they even have a cursory **restaurant map** for visiting foreigners. The city is famed for its grilled, salted mackerel (*gangodeung-eo*; 간고등어), and steamed chicken in soy broth (*jjimdak*; 찜닭).

★ **Iljik Sikdang** 일직 식당 676 Gyeongdong-ro ☎054 859 6012; map p.178. Right next to the train station, here you can dine on grilled, salted mackerel, an Andong speciality. Ask for the *jeongsik* (정식) – a belly-filling set course featuring salted mackerel plus an array of side *dishes*, yours for just W9000. Daily 8am–9pm.

Isu Dawon 이수 다원 23 Dongheung 1-gil ☎054 859 9988; map p.178. Somehow Andong lends itself more to tea than coffee – try tracking down this small, quaint

tearoom, located just opposite the *Gotaya* guesthouse. Teas W5000–7000. Daily 11am–11.30pm.

Yangban Jjimdak 양반 찜닭 19 Beonyeong-gil ☎054 858 4455; map p.178. The best place in the market area to order a portion of *jjimdak* (see above); unlike most such places, they're also willing to serve half-sets, which will still get you a belly-full (W8500 per portion). Daily 9am–9pm.

DRINKING

Even more than its mackerel or chicken, Andong is known across the land for its *soju*. You'll see some local brands in the shops and convenience stores, alongside the generic, nationally available ones; note that some are far stronger than regular *soju*, topping out at about 45 percent alcohol.

Hulk Bar 홀크 바 170 Seodongmun-ro; map p.178. The most distinctive bar in the centre, with a picture of two snarling Hulks on the outside (saying "Have a good time, everybody", as Hulks often do), and inside a variety

of cheap beers (from W4000), available to take straight from the fridge. Usually one of the liveliest bars in town – though this is not exactly saying much, even on weekend evenings. Daily 6pm–1am.

Hahoe Folk Village

하회 마을 • Daily 9am–7pm, though open 24hr • W3000; W3000 for small-boat ride to Buyongdae • ⓦ hahoe.or.kr • Bus #46 from Andong (8 daily; 40min); bus stops 2km from the complex, and from the ticket office you can walk, or take one of the regular shuttle buses (included with ticket price)

Korea has made many efforts to keep alive its pastoral traditions in the face of rapid economic growth; one particularly interesting example is its preserved **folk villages**. While some – such as the one near central Andong (see page 177) – exist purely for show, others are functioning communities where life dawdles on at an intentionally slow pace, the residents surviving on a curious mix of home-grown vegetables, government subsidy and tourist-generated income. Now under World Heritage protection, **Hahoe Folk Village** is one of the best and most popular in the country, a charming mesh of over a hundred **traditional countryside houses** nestling in the gentle embrace of an idle river. This charming mix of mud walls, thatched roofs and dusty trails is no mere tourist construct, but a village with a history stretching back centuries, and you'll be able to eat up at least a couple of hours exploring the paths, inspecting the buildings and relaxing by the river. The village's past is told on information boards outside the most important structures – seek out the Yangjin residence, for example, the oldest in the village, and built in a blend of Goryeo- and Joseon-era styles. Also try to track down the little boats shuttling across to **Buyongdae**, a small peak across the river; the small effort expended on the gentle climb up will bring hugely rewarding views of the village and its surrounding countryside.

Hahoe can sometimes get a little busy with visitors, but it's easy to escape and find space. Even better, stay on to experience the village at night, when the vast majority of visitors have gone home – misty early morning walks can be rather wonderful, too. If you're around in October, you'll be able to catch Hahoe's absorbing **mask dance festival** (ⓦ maskdance.com).

4

ACCOMMODATION AND EATING   **HAHOE FOLK VILLAGE**

Temptingly, there are a number of *minbak* at which you can **stay the night** in Hahoe, costing about W50,000 for a spartan room, and heated in colder months with the underfloor *ondol* system. The tourist information office in Andong (see page 178) will be happy to book you into one of these guesthouses; all serve light meals, which is handy since there are **no restaurants** in the village; there are, however, a couple of simple **grocery stores**.

Daega 대가 Bus stop area ☎054 852 8361. The most appealing of the clutch of restaurants near the bus stop, with tables in an outdoor pavilion. Try the *jjimdak* (see page 179; W40,000, feeds two or three), or perhaps the savoury *pajeon* pancakes (W8000); the latter are best washed down with *dongdongju*, a creamy rice beer, sold here by the bowl (W6000). Daily 10am–8pm.

Rakkojae 락고재 695 Hahoe-ri ☎054 857 3410. The one upper-class option in Hahoe is this small yet extremely atmospheric complex, affiliated to a similar establishment of the same name in Seoul (see page 100), and equipped with its own *jjimjilbang*. You'll be able to eat breakfast just outside your room, overlooking the courtyard – quite a wonderful experience on misty mornings – and *samgyetang* (chicken soup) is available for W20,000 in the evenings if you book in advance. W180,000

Dosan Seowon

도산 서원 • Daily: March–Oct 9am–6pm; Nov–Feb 9am–5pm • W1500 • ⊕ dosanseowon.com • Bus #67 from Andong (5 daily; 50min)

Dosan Seowon is a Confucian academy, surrounded by some of the most gorgeous countryside that the area can offer – on the bus journey here from Andong, you'll find yourself winding your way past rice paddies and some pleasantly unspoiled countryside, before ducking down to the academy's entrance. From here it's a short walk to the complex itself; the wide **valley** to your right is simply stunning, the sound of rushing water from the stream occasionally augmented by the splutter of a faraway tractor.

The academy was established in 1574, in honour of Yi Hwang, a well-respected Confucian scholar also known as **Toegye** (see page 180). It no longer functions as a place of study, but a refurbishment in the 1970s helped re-establish the tranquillity of its original *raison d'être*: this was a highly important study place during the Joseon era, and the only one outside Seoul, for those who wished to pass the notoriously hard tests necessary for governmental officials.

Opposite the main entrance, you may notice a little man-made hill topped by a **traditional-style shelter**; the stele underneath once marked an important spot for the government exams, with the original location somewhere towards the bottom of the

---

TOEGYE, NEO-CONFUCIANIST

Poet, scholar, all-round good guy and bearded star of the thousand-won note, **Toegye** (퇴계; 1501–70) is one of Korea's most revered historical characters. Born Yi Hwang, but better known by his pen name (pronounced "Twegg-yeah"), he exerted a major influence on the politics and social structure of his time. The country was then ruled by the **Joseon dynasty**, one of the most staunchly **Confucian** societies the world has ever known – each person was born with a predefined limit as to what they could aspire to in life, forever restricted by their genetics. The aristocracy oversaw a caste-like system that dictated what clothes people could wear, who they could marry, and what position they could hold, among other things.

Toegye was lucky enough to be born into privileged society. He excelled in his studies from a young age, and eventually passed the notoriously difficult governmental exams necessary for advancement to the higher official posts. Once there, he refused to rest on his laurels – he hunted down those he thought to be corrupt, and as a reward for his integrity was **exiled**, several times, from the capital. However, his intelligence made him a force to be reckoned with, and he set about introducing **neo-Confucian thought**, much of it borrowed from the Song dynasty in China; he advocated, for example, advancement based on achievement rather than heredity. After his death, the Confucian academy **Dosan Seowon** was built in his honour; it retains the contemplative spirit of the time, and of Toegye himself.

DAEGU'S APPLE GIRLS

In a country obsessed with appearance, it's hard to talk to a Korean about Daegu without being told how beautiful its women are. The city is based in a geological bowl, which makes for very hot summers, very cold winters and very delicious **apples**, and the fruit from the surrounding countryside is said to keep the skin pimple-free. However, those who have spent some time in Seoul will notice that women in Daegu seem to dress at least a few years behind their counterparts from the capital – one of the most visible indications of the city's long-standing conservatism.

lake that you pass on the bus in. As you enter the complex, you'll see, beyond the flower gardens and up the steps, two libraries whose nameplates are said to have been carved by Toegye himself; the buildings were built on stilts to keep humidity to a minimum. Further on are structures that were used as living quarters, the main lecture hall, and a shrine to Toegye, though this last one is usually closed off. Passing back down under a cloak of maple – which flames roaring red in late autumn – you'll find an **exhibition hall** detailing the great man's life and times, as well as an astrolabe for measuring the movements of celestial bodies.

Daegu and around

대구

DAEGU is Korea's **fourth-largest city** by population, and a major centre of business. The core of town is effectively one large shopping mall, the department stores supplemented by a lattice of streets devoted to particular products. Herbal Medicine Street is the best known, as the city has for centuries been a centre of **herbal medicine**, but you could also head to Steamed Rib Meat Street or Rice Cake Street if you're hungry, Shoe Street or Sock Street if your feet need attending to, or Washing Machine Appliance Street if, well, your washing machine needs maintenance. Daegu is also one of the few places in Korea where you'll notice a substantial American military presence – the city's nightclubs are often prowled by grunts from the surrounding army bases.

It has to be said that Daegu as a city is not particularly attractive. There are few notable sights in the centre, but it's a pleasant place to shop, or to catch up on your **partying** if you've been trawling the Gyeongsang countryside. There are also a few surprisingly rustic restaurants and tearooms to hunt down in the city core; several alleyways in **Jingolmok**, which spreads out around the famed Herbal Medicine Market, have been given a gentle gentrification in recent years, and make for pleasant strolling. Head a little further afield **Palgongsan** and you'll find a wonderful park to the north of town, while **Haeinsa**, one of Korea's best-known temples, is just a short bus ride to the west.

Herbal Medicine Market

한약 시장 • Exhibition hall Mon–Sat 9am–5pm, Sun 10am–5pm • Free

Daegu's **Herbal Medicine Market** first got going in the 1650s. Today almost half of the country's buying and selling of medicinal herbage is undertaken on these streets – don't expect to see a physical market as such, more a prevalence of stores selling everything from fruits to roots, bark to bugs and lizard tails to deer antlers, with practitioners able to whip up combinations of weird and wonderful ingredients for a range of ailments. On the main street is the **Yangnyeongsi Exhibition Hall**, a mildly diverting display of medicinal ingredients and how they're used, though very little information is in English. Unfortunately, few places sell anything useful to the average foreign tourist – instead, try a herbal tea at nearby *Mido Dabang* (see page 184).

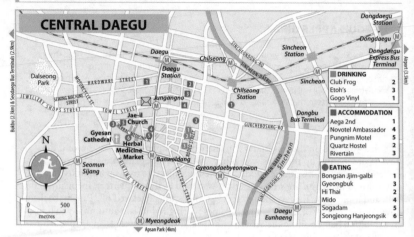

CENTRAL DAEGU

DRINKING	
Club Frog	2
Etoh's	3
Gogo Vinyl	1

ACCOMMODATION	
Aega 2nd	1
Novotel Ambassador	4
Pungnim Motel	5
Quartz Hostel	2
Rivertain	3

EATING	
Bongsan Jjim-galbi	1
Gyeongbuk	3
Hi Thai	2
Mido	4
Sogadam	5
Songjeong Hanjeongsik	6

The churches

Near the Herbal Medicine Market you'll be able to spot the spire of **Je-il Church** (제일 교회), a red-brick building that constitutes Daegu's first Christian place of worship, having been founded by Presbyterian missionaries in 1898 (the present building, though, only dates to 1933). Just around the corner is the more Gothic-style **Gyesan Cathedral** (계산 성당).

Apsan Park

앞산 공원 • Daily 24hr • Free; cable car W7500 one way, W9500 return • Bus #300, #410 or #750 from either train station

Daegu's most notable stretch of greenery is **Apsan Park**, around 6km to the south of the city centre. It's more of a mountain than a park, and there are some good trails to tackle; you'll find plenty of temples and pavilions, and a small exhibition on the Korean War. You can also walk or take a cable car to a ridge that provides wonderful views of Daegu's sprawl.

ARRIVAL AND INFORMATION

DAEGU

By plane The city's international airport is a short bus or taxi ride east of Dongdaegu train station, and has connections to Jeju (9 daily; 1hr) and Incheon (2 daily; 1hr), as well as flights to China, Japan, Taiwan, Thailand, Vietnam and even Guam.

By train Daegu station stares straight down at the main downtown area, and as such is the best place in which to arrive, but most services (including high-speed KTX trains) head to Dongdaegu station – this is three stops to the east by subway, but you can pretty much hop on any train heading between the two, since you're very unlikely to be asked for a ticket.

Destinations from Daegu station: Busan (1–2 hourly; 1hr 30min); Daejeon (1–3 hourly; 1hr 45min); Seoul (1–3 hourly; 3hr 45min).

Destinations from Dongdaegu station: Busan (every 10–20min; 50min); Daejeon (every 10–20min; 50min); Danyang (2 daily: 4hr 30min); Gyeongju (hourly; 1hr 10min); Pohang (hourly; 35min); Seoul (every 10–20min; 1hr 50min).

By bus Arriving by bus can be a little confusing since there are several terminals across the city, though only a few of these are likely to be used by tourists. The Bukbu terminal and Seodaegu express terminal are frustratingly far (9km) to the northwest of the centre, as is the Seobu terminal to the southwest. The Dongbu terminal is marginally more central, but best is the Dongdaegu express (고속; gosok) terminal, whose several buildings connect with trains and the subway system – to get here from other Korean cities you should head to their own gosok terminal.

Destinations from Express terminal Andong (2–3 hourly; 1hr 30min); Busan (every 50min; 1hr 40min); Daejeon (hourly; 2hr); Gwangju (every 40min; 3hr 20min); Gyeongju (every 40min; 50min); Jeonju (every 1hr 20min; 3hr 30min); Jinju (hourly; 2hr 10min); Seoul (hourly; 3hr 50min); Sokcho (3 daily; 4hr).

Destinations from Dongbu terminal Gangneung (15 daily; 5hr 30min); Gyeongju (every 10–15min; 1hr); Pohang (every 10–30min; 1hr 20min).

Destinations from Seobu terminal Busan (8 daily; 1hr 50min); Gyeongju (19 daily; 1hr 10min); Haeinsa (every 40min; 1hr 30min); Jinju (1–2 hourly; 1hr 40min) Tongyeong (1–2 hourly; 2hr 40min); Yeosu (7 daily; 4hr).

Destinations from Bukbu terminal Andong (2–3 hourly; 1hr 10min); Gangneung (9 daily; 4hr); Guinsa (1 daily; 4hr);

Muju (3 daily; 3hr 30min); Sokcho (5 daily; 5hr).

Tourist information Both train stations have information booths, with English-speakers most likely at Dongdaegu (daily 9am–7pm; ☎ 053 939 0080).

Travel card If you're staying in the city for more than a couple of days, you could use the Daegyong or Top Pass travel cards (W2000), which give slight discounts and avoid the need to rummage for change. Seoul's T-money cards also work in Daegu.

GETTING AROUND

By subway Daegu's two train stations are connected to the city's subway system, which consists of two lines and a monorail route; as with others across the land, it's cheap

(W1200 per ride) and efficient.

By bus Daegu's local bus network is comprehensive, though likely to bewilder foreign tourists. It's W1200 per ride.

ACCOMMODATION

There are a few good **hotels** around, **motels** aplenty can be found near both train stations and there are some cheaper **yeogwan** within staggering distance of the nightlife area around Jungangno subway station. For those on a real budget, or just in need of a good scrub, there's *Greenvill*, a decent **jjimjilbang** (W8000) outside Banwoldang subway station, and another right outside Daegu station.

Aega 2nd 애가 2호점 46-6 Seoseong-ro 16-gil ☎ 053 781 5215; map p.182. Surprisingly, there are a fair few old-fashioned *hanok*-style places to stay in and

around central Daegu. This second offering from an already successful guesthouse is the best of the bunch; as is par for the course with *hanok* accommodation, rooms are small

4

THE DAEGU SUBWAY FIRE

On February 18, 2003, a calamitous event took place under Daegu's downtown streets, one that was to have a heavy impact on the Korean psyche, and a terrible comedown after the spectacular success of the previous year's World Cup. The simple facts – around two hundred killed in a **subway fire** – do not even begin to tell the story, with failings before, during and after the event bringing about a national sense of shame, and a level of introspection previously unseen in a country accustomed to looking abroad for excuses.

A few months before the fire, a man named **Kim Dae-han** had suffered a stroke that left him partially paralysed. Ostracized by his family and friends, and losing his sanity, he decided to take his frustrations out on society. During a Tuesday morning rush hour, he wandered into a subway train armed with gasoline-filled containers, which caught fire as the train pulled into Jungangno station. The fire spread rapidly through the carriages, owing to the lack of any fire-extinguishing apparatus on board; both the seats and the flooring produced toxic smoke as they burned. Kim managed to escape, along with many passengers from his train, but the poor safety procedures on the line meant that the driver arriving in the opposite direction was not informed of the problem, and pulled in to a plume of thick, toxic smoke. At this point the fire detection system kicked in and shut off power on the line, leaving both trains stranded. The driver of the second train told passengers to remain seated while he attempted to contact the station manager, and when finally put through was told to leave the train immediately. He duly scurried upstairs, but in his haste had removed the train's key, shutting off power to the doors, and effectively sealing the remaining passengers inside – death on a large scale was inevitable. The total count has never been fully established, as some bodies were burnt beyond all recognition.

The families of the victims, and the country as a whole, needed someone to blame. The arsonist was sentenced to life in prison, avoiding the death penalty on the grounds of mental instability; he died in jail soon afterwards. The incident raised some serious questions, primarily about **safety** being compromised by a thirst for profit, and the treatment of the **disabled** in Korean society – a baptism of fire for incoming president Roh Moo-hyun. Safety on Daegu's subway has since been significantly improved, and facilities for the disabled have improved across Korea: at least some good came out of one of Korea's biggest modern-day disasters.

and you'll have to sleep on floor futons, but the charm of the courtyard and the hosts themselves mean that guests almost always enjoy the experience. Prices often drop to W40,000, at which times rooms are a steal. **W60,000**

Novotel Ambassador 노보텔 앰배서더 611 Gukchaebosang-ro ☎053 664 1101, ⓦnovotel.com; map p.182. The reception area may not exude class, but this is the best accommodation in the city centre, with stylish, carpetted rooms, a gym and sauna, and a few places to eat and drink within the complex. **W270,000**

Pungnim Motel 풍림 모텔 95-2 Jungang-daero 81-gil ☎053 254 9903; map p.182. Near Herbal Medicine Street, and therefore also within walking distance of downtown, this motel will suffice for anyone on a tight budget – while other motels in the area double their prices

at weekends, this one stays the same, and the rooms are fine. **W30,000**

Quartz Hostel 쿼츠 호스텔 16 Gyodong 4-gil ☎010 9072 0967; map p.182. The best of the city's many, many hostel options – the central location is obviously a plus (quite literally a stone's throw from Daegu station, if your arms are strong and you can find the right line), but throw in a sleek, spacious common area and affable staff. Dorms **W20,000**

Rivertain 리버틴 호텔 193 Gyeongsanggamyeong-gil ☎053 269 4000, ⓦrivertain.com; map p.182. Pronounced more like "Libertine", this place may be a little beyond flashpacker level price-wise, but it's worth a splurge – rooms this good usually go for double the price in Korea. The decor is adventurous from the lobby on up, and some rooms even have small balconies. **W120,000**

EATING

There's a good, cheap **restaurant** around every corner in Daegu, and the rising number of expats means that the choice is becoming ever more cosmopolitan; Indian restaurants are becoming particularly popular, but Spanish, Thai and Japanese options are all over the place too. **Coffee** and morning snacks are far easier to hunt down in the Jungangno downtown area, as are Western-style joints such as *TGI Friday's*.

RESTAURANTS

Bongsan Jjim-galbi 봉산 찜갈비 9-18 Dongdeok-ro 36-gil ☎053 425 4203; map p.182. Daegu has a number of dedicated shopping streets, so it should come as no surprise that there's one dedicated to the city speciality, steamed rib meat (*galbi-jjim*; 갈비찜). This is the oldest and most famous establishment hereabouts, having doled out the dish since the 1960s. You'll pay W18,000 per portion (minimum two). Daily 10am–10pm.

Hi Thai 하이 타이 70-3 Gongpyeongdong ☎053 255 0562; map p.182. A good reflection of Daegu's increasingly cosmopolitan nature, this tiny place serves curries, pad Thai and other basics for very fair prices (most mains around W10,000), with a choice of three Bangkok beers (plus Myanmar, which is even better) to wash them down with. Tues–Sun 11.30am–3.30pm & 5–9.30pm.

★**Sogadam** 소가담 38 Namseong-ro ☎053 255 6112; map p.182. Now, here's a good idea. This restaurant serves up some interesting takes on the humble pork cutlet (돈까스; *donkkaseu*) in a sleek, industrial-chic space. Try it chopped up in a salad, with balsamic vinegar and bread, or smothered with chilli – all variations cost W8900. Daily 10am–10pm.

Songjeong Hanjeongsik 송정 한정식 78 Jongno 2-ga ☎053 425 2221; map p.182. On the same cute road as *Mido* tearoom, this place offers earthy delights in a *hanok*-style setting – think sliding paper doors, yellow lino floors and a pleasantly leafy exterior. Their food's great,

too – plump for one of the W7000 *jeongsik* (정식) sets, which give you a choice of mackerel (고등어), *kimchi* broth (김치찌개) or soybean broth (된장찌개) as a centrepiece. Daily 10am–10pm.

TEAROOMS

Gyeongbuk 경북 32 Namseong-ro, no phone; map p.182. Not a tearoom as such, but a shop at the very western end of the herbal medicine street – it's one of the only places selling ginseng potions to passers by (W2000 for a pouch), and they're absolutely delicious. Daily 9am–9pm.

★**Mido** 미도 다방 75 Jongno 2-ga ☎053 252 9999; map p.182. Fancy a trip back in time? This tearoom seems to have been plucked straight from the Korean 1970s – with only its staff and customers showing any signs of ageing – old chaps are dressed in their Sunday best every day here, wearing a lot of trilbies, rhinestone-covered ties, chequered jackets and hiking trousers (often all at the same time). The sight of a foreigner walking in will likely cause quite a stir; a *hanbok*-clad lady will be guiding you to a silk cushion-covered couchette in no time, offering tea from W2000, and some ginger to dunk in sugar and munch. Since it's close to Herbal Medicine Street, the *ssanghwa-cha* (쌍화차; W4000) is perhaps most appropriate – a bitter concoction that one might expect a witch to make, it's made with medicinal herbs and full of jujube slices, pine nuts and much, much more. Daily 9am–10pm.

DRINKING

The downtown area has innumerable places to **drink**. The focus is Rodeo Street, which holds all of the city's most popular **clubs** and lures local expats (and plenty of American soldiers) at weekends to dance until dawn.

Club Frog 클럽 프로그 8-8 Samdeokdong 1-ga ☎010 8533 1828; map p.182. There isn't much to choose between the several clubs tightly jammed into this area, but this hip-hop venue has stood the test of time and remains enduringly popular despite verging on the cheesy. Daily 8pm–late.

Etoh's 12-3 Dongseong-ro 3-gil ☎053 211 9385; map p.182. Second-floor pizza-and-ale place, popular with expats and locals alike, swimming in an industrial-chic vibe that gets pretty rocking on weekend evenings. Drinks are

affordable (cocktails from W5000), as are the sandwiches, hot dogs and pizza, the latter also available by the slice. Mon & Wed–Sun 4pm–1am.

Gogo Vinyl 고고 비닐 58-19 Dongseong-ro ☎010 2333 6644; map p.182. A local institution ever since it became one of the first places in Korea to hit on the idea of selling cocktails in vinyl pouches (most W5000) – on weekends, the street outside is full of foreigners pre-gaming before heading to other bars and clubs, and it's quite the place to be at around 10pm. Daily 6pm–midnight.

Palgongsan Provincial Park

팔공산 도립 공원

Just 20km north of Daegu, the land rises and folds, creating a peak-lined ridge and a series of valleys now studded with temples, hermitages and the odd carved Buddha. This area, **Palgongsan Provincial Park**, is an ideal setting for a day of relaxed hiking.

Donghwasa

동화사 • Bus #401 from Dongdaegu station in Daegu (1hr)

Dating way back to 493, **Donghwasa** is the park's most famous temple, though a little over-hyped by the local authorities. Visitors are most likely to be impressed by a seated Buddha thought to date from the eighth century, and the gloriously intricate interior of the main hall. More modern is the mammoth **Tongil Buddha**, which stands next to some similarly outsized stone pagodas and lanterns. These uninspired creations were placed here in the hope that the two Koreas will one day become one – *tongil* means "reunification" – and though the religion-lite powers that be in Pyongyang are unlikely to approve of the Buddha, they're sure to be impressed by a liberal use of concrete rarely seen outside Communist societies.

Gatbawi

갓바위

Gatbawi, another carved Buddha, occupies a lofty and far more natural setting, providing a view that's not quite top-of-the-world, but at least high enough to present Daegu in all its apartment-block-filled glory. Situated up near the peak of Gwanbong (850m), it's around an hour's walk from the tourist village below Donghwasa, at the bottom of the trail. Many people make the journey on the 1st or 15th of the month to make a wish, as it is claimed that the Buddha will hear one from every visitor on these occasions.

Yeombulbong and Yeombulam

Cable car W5500 one-way, W9000 return

Beyond Gatbawi, a few hours should be enough to bring you to **Yeombulbong** (1121m), from where you can drop down the trail back to Donghwasa, stopping at **Yeombulam**, a hermitage on route. You could even take the **cable car** to or from an observation point near the hermitage – this runs from the tourist village beneath Donghwasa.

Haeinsa

해인사 • Daily 8.30am–6pm • W3000 • ⓦ haeinsa.or.kr • Bus from Daegu's Seobu terminal (every 40min; 1hr 30min; W6600)

A bus ride away from Daegu, the secluded temple of **Haeinsa** (해인사) is part of Korea's holy trinity of "Jewel Temples" – the other two are Tongdosa (see page 201) and Songgwangsa (see page 239), which represent the Buddha and Buddhist community respectively, while Haeinsa symbolizes the religion's teachings, or *dharma*. These doctrines have been carved onto more than eighty thousand wooden blocks, known as

THE TRIPITAKA KOREANA

One of the most famous sights in the land, the eighty-thousand-plus wooden blocks of Buddhist doctrine known as the **Tripitaka Koreana** were first carved out in the eleventh century, over a 76-year period, in an attempt to curry the favour of the Buddha in a time of perpetual war. Though the originals were destroyed by rampaging Mongol hordes in the thirteenth century, the present set were carved shortly after that, and once again every possible measure was taken to please the Buddha. The best wood in the area was tracked down then soaked for three years in sea water before being cut to shape and boiled. The slabs then spent another three years being sheltered from sun and rain but exposed to wind, until they were finally ready for carving. Incredibly, not a single mistake has yet been found in over **fifty million** Chinese characters, a fact that led other countries to base their own Tripitaka on the Korean version. The blocks represent a superb feat of craft, patience and devotion, and their outer spines blocks are still visible today at Haeinsa temple; and the set has been added to UNESCO's World Heritage list.

the **Tripitaka Koreana** (see page 186), and remain visible through the vertical wooden rungs of the buildings that house them. Still in use today, Haeinsa's various buildings are pleasant enough; its location, however, is nothing short of spectacular: the path leading up to the main entrance, lined on both sides with colossal trees, is worth the trip alone, while the complex backs onto **Gayasan National Park** (가야산 국립 공원). Fame and beauty conspire to make the complex uncomfortably crowded at times, but few venture off the beaten track to enjoy the surrounding area. This is a shame, as a few hermitages can be found on the opposite side of the stream, and innumerable paths snake their way through the trees to peaks, farmland and secluded villages.

ACCOMMODATION   HAEINSA

There are plenty of simple **places to stay** in the winding streets that surround the small bus terminal. Haeinsa itself is a grand place for at which to take a templestay programme (W40,000; ⓦeng.templestay.com) – you'll have to be up early, but dawn at the temple is simply magical.

Haeinsa Tourist Hotel 해인사 관광 호텔 Chi-in-ni 13-45 ☎ 053 933 2000. The best rooms in the area are on high at this tourist hotel, though it possesses the stained carpeting and slight chemical odour typical of official Korean tourist accommodation. The views, however, can be stunning, particularly on misty mornings. <u>W87,000</u>

Gyeongju

경주

Travellers seeking to delve headfirst into Korea's rich and storied history should make little **GYEONGJU** their primary target – here you can walk among kings from a dynasty long expired and view the treasures accumulated during a millennium of imperial rule. If this sounds a little like Kyoto, you'd be half right – unlike Japan's more illustrious ancient capital, Gyeongju remains decidedly semi-rural in nature, and a little rougher around the edges. Strangely, much of its present charm is all down to a bit of good, old-fashioned dictatorship: in the 1970s and 1980s, authoritarian **President Park Chung-hee** managed to ensure that Korea's most traditional city stayed that way at a time when rapid economic progress was turning the country upside down. He introduced height restrictions on structures built anywhere near historical remains, and passed a bill requiring many new constructions to sport a traditional Korean-style roof. The rules have, sadly, not always been followed, but the contrast with regular urban Korea remains quite striking; together with Seoul's palace district, it's one of the most popular (and appropriate) places in the country for the sporting of silken *hanbok* clothing, available to rent all over the place (see page 67).

Gyeongju's **city centre** is surprisingly mucky for a place of such dynastic repute. During harvest months, many of its streetsides are lined with old *chonnyeo* (a slang term for country ladies) hawking fruit, vegetables and all manner of roots and shoots – this gives a palpably bucolic twist to goings-on in one of Korea's foremost tourist centres. Recent demographic shifts have seen foreigners move into Gyeongju en masse, mostly factory workers from the stretch between here and Ulsan to the south; one intriguing sign of their presence is at local mobile phone shops, whose fronts often feature reams of text from South, Southeast and Central Asia.

Chief among Gyeongju's sights are the Silla-dynasty **royal tombs**, rounded grassy hills that you'll see all over the town's periphery (see page 189); in **Tumuli Park** it's even possible to enter one for a peek at the ornate way in which royalty were once buried. To the east of the centre there's **Anapji Pond**, a delightful place for an evening stroll under the stars, and the **National Museum**, which is filled with assorted trinkets and fascinating gold paraphernalia from Silla times.

South of the city centre, and accessible by bicycle (see page 194), is the small mountain of **Namsan**, centrepoint of a wonderful park filled with trails and carved Buddha images. Many more sights can be found in the countryside around Gyeongju; see the "Around Gyeongju" section (see page 196) for a few possibilities.

Brief history

The most interesting period of Gyeongju's lengthy history was during its near-millennium as capital of the Silla kingdom (see page 188). After so long as Korea's glamourpuss, Gyeongju faded into the background, and the degree to which it did is quite surprising – having relinquished its mantle of power, the city lived on for a while as a regional capital, but then fell into a **steep decline**. The Mongols rampaged through the city in the fourteenth century, the Japanese invasions a couple of hundred years later stripped away another few layers of beauty, and from a peak of over a million, Gyeongju's population fell to next to nothing.

4

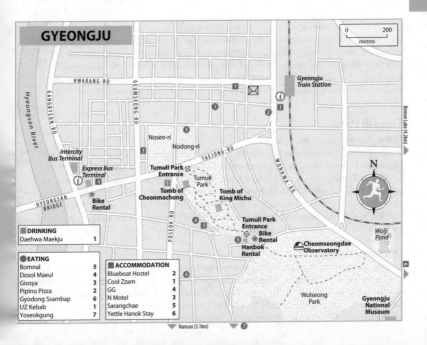

GYEONGJU

0 — 200 metres

Hyeongsan River

HWARANG-RO

GANGBYEON-RO

GEUMSEONG-RO

Gyeongju Train Station

Noseo-ri
Nodong-ri

TAEJONG-RO

WONHWA-RO

Intercity Bus Terminal

Express Bus Terminal

Tumuli Park Entrance
Tumuli Park

HYEONGSAN BRIDGE

Bike Rental

POSEOK-RO

Tomb of Cheonmachong

Tomb of King Michu

Tumuli Park Entrance
★ **Bike Rental**

Hanbok Rental

Cheomseongdae Observatory

N

Bomun Lake (4.2km)

Wolji Pond

Wolseong Park

Gyeongju National Museum

■ DRINKING	
Daehwa Maekju	1

● EATING	
Bomnal	5
Dosol Maeul	4
Gisoya	3
Pipino Pizza	2
Gyodong Ssambap	6
UZ Kebab	1
Yoseokgung	7

■ ACCOMMODATION	
Blueboat Hostel	2
Cool Zzam	1
GG	4
N Motel	3
Sarangchae	5
Yettle Hanok Stay	6

Namsan (3.1km)

THE SILLA DYNASTY

In 69 BC a young Herod was learning how to talk, Julius Caesar was busying himself in Gaul and Spartacus was leading slave revolts against Rome. Legend has it that at this time, a strange light shone down from the East Asian sky onto a **horse** of pure white. The beast was sheltering an egg, from which hatched **Hyeokgeose**, who went on to be appointed king by local chiefs at the tender age of 13. He inaugurated the **Silla dynasty** (sometimes spelt "Shilla", and pronounced that way), which was to go through no fewer than 56 monarchs before collapsing in 935, leaving behind a rich legacy still visible today in the form of jewellery, pottery and temples. Many of the regal burial mounds can still be seen in and around **Gyeongju**, the Silla seat of power.

Though it was initially no more than a powerful city-state, successive leaders gradually expanded the Silla boundaries, consuming the smaller **Gaya kingdom** to the south and becoming a fully fledged member of the **Three Kingdoms** that jostled for power on the Korean peninsula – Goguryeo in the north, Baekje to the west, and Silla in the east. Silla's **art and craft** flourished, Buddhism was adopted as the state religion, and as early as the sixth century a detailed social system was put into use – the *golpuljedo*, or "bone-rank system" – with lineage and status dictating what clothes people wore, who they could marry and where they could live, and placing strict limits on what they could achieve.

Perversely, given their geographical positions on the "wrong" sides of the peninsula, Baekje was allied to the Japanese and Silla to the Chinese Tang dynasty, and it was Chinese help that enabled Silla's **King Muyeol** to subjugate Baekje in 660 (see page 278). Muyeol died the year after, but his son, **King Munmu**, promptly went one better, defeating Goguryeo in 668 to bring about a first-ever unified rule of the Korean peninsula. The resulting increase in power drove the state forward, though abuse of this new wealth was inevitable; pressure from the people, and an increase in the power of the nobility, gradually started to undermine the power of the kings from the late eighth century. Gyeongju was sacked in 927, and eight years later **King Gyeongsun** – by that time little more than a figurehead – finally handed over the reigns of power to **King Taejo**, bringing almost a millennium of Silla rule to a close, and kicking off the Goryeo dynasty.

Ironically, centuries after carrying countless spoils of war across the sea after their successful invasion, it was the **Japanese** who reopened Gyeongju's treasure chest of history, during their occupation of the country in the early twentieth century. In went the diggers, and out came hundreds of thousands of relics, so that, even today, much visible evidence of the dynasty still remains around the city. Not all of this is above ground – excavations continue, and new discoveries are made every year.

Tumuli Park

대릉원 • Daily 9am–10pm • W2000

Gyeongju is often described by the Korean tourist board as an open-air museum, thanks to its large number of grassy regal, burial mounds. The tombs in question are known as **Tumuli**, which are prolific and impossible to miss. Right in the centre of town, the walled-off **Tumuli Park** contains over two dozen tombs. It's hard to imagine that this was until quite recently a functioning – though quiet – part of town, but in the 1970s the buildings were removed and the area beautified, creating a path- and tree-filled park that's wonderful for a stroll.

Cheonmachong

Entrances are located at the east and north of the complex, but its most famous hump sits to the far west. Here lies **Cheonmachong** (천마총), the only such tomb in Korea that you can actually enter. Its former inhabitant is not known for sure, but is believed to be a sixth- or seventh-century king whose many horse-related implements gave rise to the name – Cheonmachong means "Heavenly Horse Tomb". Excavated in 1973, it yielded over twelve thousand artefacts, which was the largest single haul in the country, and although many went to Gyeongju's National Museum, a few decorate the inner walls of the tomb. There's also a full-scale mock-up of how the inhabitant was buried.

Tomb of King Michu

Elsewhere in the complex is the large **tomb of King Michu**, who reigned from 262 to 284 and fought many battles to protect his empire from the neighbouring Baekje dynasty. According to legend, he even dispatched a ghost army from beyond the grave when his successor was losing one particular bout of fisticuffs; these phantoms disappeared during the resulting celebrations, leaving behind only the bamboo leaves that had infested the cavities of the enemy dead. For this reason, the tomb is often referred to as the "Tomb of the Bamboo Chief". One other tomb of note is the double-humped **Hwangnam Daechong**, which was almost certainly the resting place of a king and queen.

Noseo-ri and Nodong-ni

노서리 and 노동리 • Daily 24hr • Free

Across the main road from Tumuli Park, the tumuli continue, though less abundantly, into the city's main shopping district. Split by a road into two sections known as **Noseo-ri** and **Nodong-ni**, these areas are not walled off, and are free to enter at any time of the day or night. Here lie some colossal mounds, as big as those you'll find in Tumuli Park – one, known as Bonghwangdae, is 22m high, with a 250m circumference. Although you're not allowed to climb onto the tombs, faint paths heading up this largest hump indicate that some find the temptation too great to ignore, and you'll usually find a couple of people seated here after the sun has gone down. Opposite,

4

GYEONGJU'S SILLA TOMBS

Every culture has its own solutions for what to do with the deceased. Tibetan corpses are often left on a mountainside for vultures to carry away, certain Filipino societies place the departed in a coffin and pack it into a cliff, while the Yanomami of the Amazon rainforest choose to cremate their dead then eat the ashes with banana paste. Koreans have long preferred burial – a slightly more prosaic journey to the afterlife, for sure – and those who have travelled around the country a while will doubtless have seen the little green bumps that dot hills and mountains in the country's rural areas. Larger versions used to be a matter of course for Korean royalty.

Literally hundreds of **tombs** from the **Silla dynasty** can be found all over Gyeongju and its surrounding area. However, the identities of few of the tombs' occupants are known for sure – there were only 56 Silla kings, so it's clear that many were created for lesser royals, military leaders and other prominent members of society. Equally mysterious are the **interiors**, as the super-simple green parabolas give almost no hints as to their construction; however, a look inside **Cheonmacheong** in Tumuli Park should provide a few hints. Layers of gravel and stone make up the base of the tomb, with a wooden chamber placed in the centre to house the deceased – unlike a pharaoh, he or she would not have supervised the construction, but as in Egypt they would have been buried with some of their favourite belongings. The chamber was then covered with large, rounded stones (these would eventually crush the chamber, after sufficient putrefaction of the wood), which in turn was covered with clay and dirt, and sown with grass.

Given the riches inside, surprisingly few of the tombs were plundered for their treasures – while such an endeavour would be long and rather conspicuous, that didn't stop thievery elsewhere in the country. Over the past century, many tombs have been carefully excavated, yielding thousands of artefacts, many of which are now on display in Gyeongju's National Museum (see page 190).

in Noseo-ri, is a monument dedicated to **Prince Gustav Adolf VI** of Sweden, who participated in the excavations here in 1926 before inheriting his country's throne.

Wolseong Park

월성 공원 • Daily 24hr • Free • Grasshopper bus every 30min (W3000)

A short walk southeast of Tumuli Park will bring you to the pretty patch of greenery called **Wolseong Park**, in and around which are some of the city's most popular sights. The paths that run through the park are pedestrianized, but you can also take a short horse-and-carriage ride around the area – you'll see them lined up opposite the main entrance to Tumuli Park – or opt to travel around in a kid-friendly grasshopper bus.

Cheomseongdae observatory

첨성대 • Daily 9am–10pm • Free

There are plenty of tombs around, though most Koreans make an eastward beeline to have their picture taken next to **Cheomseongdae**, an astronomical observation tower dating from the seventh century. Looking a little like a rook from a giant chessboard, its simplicity conceals a surprising depth of design: the twelve stones that make up the base represent either the months of the year or the signs of the Chinese zodiac, while the 27 circular layers were a nod to Queen Seondeok, ruler during the tower's construction and the 27th ruler of the Silla dynasty. Added to the two square levels on top and the base, this equals thirty, which is the number of days in a lunar month, while the total number of blocks equals the number of days in a year. Even more amazingly, the various gaps and points on the structure are said to correspond to the movements of certain celestial bodies.

Wolji Pond

월지 • Daily 9am–10pm • W2000

Down the northern fringe and across the road from Cheomseongdae is **Wolji**, a pond and pleasure garden constructed in 674 by **King Munmu** (see page 188). Numerous battles in the preceding decade had led to a first-ever unification of the Korean peninsula, after which Munmu built what was – and still remains – a tranquil, tree-filled area around a **lotus pond** whose shape roughly mirrored that of his kingdom. In an interesting twist of fate, this was where the empire also came to an end, being the scene of King Gyeongsun's handover of power to King Taejo, founder of the Goryeo dynasty. In the following centuries, the area fell into disrepair until 1975, when it received its first modern makeover. When the pond was dredged it revealed a few relics from Silla times. That few then grew to hundreds, then thousands – much of the bounty, including a whole barge, now sits in the National Museum just down the road. The pond and gardens themselves are pleasantly illuminated at night – a great time to come for a walk among the bamboo.

Gyeongju National Museum

경주 국립 박물관 • Daily 10am–6pm • Free • ⓦ gyeongju.museum.go.kr

On the southern perimeter of Wolseong Park, **Gyeongju National Museum** is a repository of riches from the surrounding area, and with the exception of Seoul's National Museum (see page 90), it's quite possibly the best in the country. The rooms run in chronological order from locally sourced stone tools and ancient pottery to modern times, via the Bronze Age. But it's the **Silla** bling that most are here to see. Beautifully crafted earrings, pendants and other paraphernalia in gold, silver and bronze were cast into spectacular shapes, often adorned with tiny golden discs or leaves. You'll also find pottery, golden antlers and some uncomfortable-looking spiked bronze shoes, but the undisputed star of the show, hidden away in its own private room, is

---

THE EMILLE BELL

Outside Gyeongju National Museum lies the **Emille Bell**, a veritable beast dating from 771. Known to Koreans as the Bell of King Seongdeok – in whose memory it was created – this is the largest existing bell in the country, and one of the biggest in the world; though estimates of its weight vary, even the smallest – nineteen tons – makes it a whopper by any standard. Legend surrounding the bell says that when it was first cast it failed to ring, only doing so once its constituent metal was melted back down and mixed with the body of a young girl. Her death-cry "Emille" (which rhymes with "simile") was a word for mother in the Silla dialect, and can apparently still be heard in the ring of the bell.

---

a glorious golden sixth-century crown, intricately sculpted and boasting an array of dangling bean-shaped jades.

Bomun Lake

보문호 • Musical performances May & June Sat & Sun 8.30pm; July–Oct Mon, Tues & Thurs–Sun 8.30pm • Free • Bus #10 or #700 from Gyeongju (every 20min; W1700)

Travel a few kilometres east of Wolseong Park, and on the bus route towards Bulguksa temple (see page 197), and you'll come to **Bomun Lake**. Surrounded by five-star hotels, this tranquil expanse has become the Gyeongju venue of choice for the well-heeled; largely devoid of the historical sights found elsewhere in the city, it's still a good place to head for a bit of easy fun. You can hire swan-shaped pedalos – the doyens of Korea's artificial waterways – and bikes for the cycle-trails around the lake, or have fun in a cheesy **amusement park**. There are also regular cultural and **musical performances** at the Bomun Outdoor Performance Theater just down from the *Commodore Hotel*, and a number of **golf courses** can be found in the area, but for most visitors it's simply a great place to come for sundown.

Namsan

남산 • Buses #500 to #508 run down the western flank of Namsan (every 10min; W1300–1700); #10 and #11 can be used for some sights on the eastern side (every 30min; W1300–1700)

Central Gyeongju's ragtag assortment of buildings fades to the south, turning from urban to rural. Mercifully, development of this area is unlikely, as the city is hemmed in on its southern flank by **Namsan**, a small, park-like mountain area packed with trails and sights. New discoveries of ancient relics are made regularly, but even if you don't find yourself unearthing a piece of Silla jewellery, this is another of the city's must-sees. Roads run along the park's perimeter, giving access to a wealth of sights on both sides, while the interior is strewn with carved Buddhas and offers some fantastic hikes. Namsan is best tackled either by **bicycle** around its pleasantly traffic-free perimeter (see page 194), or with a pair of hiking boots through its interior.

Oreung

오릉 • Daily: March–Oct 9am–6pm; Nov–Feb 9am–5pm • W1000

The first sight that you'll come to on Namsan's western flank is **Oreung**, which means "five tombs". The grassy area just inside the perimeter wall is popular with picnicking families in the summer, but if you make your way through the pines along one of the park's lovely paths you'll soon come to the tomb of Hyeokgeose (ruled 57 BC to 4 AD), the **first king** of the Silla dynasty. Little else is known about him, but a history this long deserves to be acknowledged with a little perspective: Hyeokgeose was born in 69 BC, the same year as Cleopatra – Hyeokgeose's hump has been around for a seriously long time. Nearby mounds contain three of his immediate successors – Namhae, Yuri and Pasa were the second, third and fifth Silla monarchs respectively – as well as Hyeokgeose's wife, **Alyeong**, who was apparently born as a dragon in a nearby well, and therefore suitably auspicious. The well can still be seen; just follow the signs. Hyeokgeose himself trumped his future wife's spectacular birth by hatching from an egg laid by a phantom horse; his birthplace is outside the park, just down the road at **Najeong**, but the site is badly neglected in comparison.

Poseokjeong

포석정 • Daily 9am–6pm • W1000

Heading south and across the main road from Oreung you'll soon come across **Poseokjeong**, an uninteresting site, but one that's hugely popular with Korean tourists. Here once lay a villa in which Silla kings held regular banquets, but with the buildings long gone, you may wonder what all the fuss is about. The draw is actually a 6m-long water canal set within a loose perimeter of rocks – don't step inside – which was once used for royal **drinking games**: one member of the party would reel off a line of poetry, choose another guest to supply a suitable second line, and float a cup of wine down the watercourse. If the drink reached the challenger before he could think of a line, he had to drain the cup.

Just across the way, and signposted from the Poseokjeong car park, is the **Tomb of King Jima**, who was the sixth Silla king, but now finds himself isolated among the trees. The neighbouring village of **Poseok** remains charming, and is worth a nose around. It's also home to some good, cheap **restaurants**, which make a handy pit-stop for those touring the Namsan area.

Baeri Samjon-seokbul

배리 삼존 석불 • Daily 24hr • Free

Further south down either the road or the footpath from Posekjeong you'll find a couple of tiny temples housing a standing Buddha trio known as **Baeri Samjon-seokbul**, which are said to date back to the early seventh century. This is a pretty area, and the starting point for a number of paths into Namsan's interior.

Samneung

삼릉 • Daily 24hr • Free

Continuing south from Baeri Samjon-seokbul you come to **Samneung**, a small, pretty complex containing three tombs. Here lies Adalla, the eighth Silla king (ruled 154–184 AD), next to Sindeok and Gyeongmyeong, the 53rd and 54th leaders, who ruled for just a few years each in the early tenth century as the empire struggled to its close.

The eastern flank and the interior

A number of carved Buddhas were placed on Namsan's **eastern side** so that they may face the rising sun, though you'll need to trek a short way into the park to see them – the tourist office have detailed **maps** of the area, and some guesthouses create their own. One of the first you'll reach on your way from Gyeongju is also the most accessible – follow signs for **Woljeongsa** temple – but the one uphill behind **Borisa** (보리사), the largest functioning temple on Namsan, is more interesting; it dates from the eighth century and is backed by richly detailed stonework. A path from here leads all the way to a viewing platform on the top of the mountain, after which you'll have a choice between heading west to Poseokjeon (see page 192), or south to the ruin-surrounded peak of **Geumosan**.

West of the centre

The sights **west of Gyeongju** are quite scattered, making exploration a little tricky. For those not yet weary of dead Silla kings, a few **tomb complexes** lie a couple of kilometr beyond the River Hyeongsan, which tickles the western flank of the city. The closest two are accessible by bike (see page 194 for rental information).

Tomb of General Kim Yu-sin

김유신묘 • Daily 9am–6pm • W1000

A right turn after the Hyeongsan bridge near Gyeongju will take you in the direction of the **tomb of General Kim Yu-sin**. Records in the *Samguk Sagi* (see page 200) state that in between his birth in 595 and his death in 673, he led the battles that defeated the Baekje and Goguryeo kingdoms, paving the way for Silla rule over the whole peninsula. The road leading here is quieter than those heading elsewhere from the bridge, but unfortunately for walkers and cyclists there are no real side routes to make use of.

Tomb of King Muyeol

무열왕릉 • Daily 9am–6pm • W1000

The **tomb of King Muyeol** – who defeated the rival Baekje kingdom in 660, and essentially unified the Korean peninsula for the first time – lies just south of the Hyeongsan bridge, though as the road leading south of the bridge is both a little too narrow and a little too busy for comfortable walking or cycling, it's best to head through the fields. Turn left down the bumpy riverside track immediately after the bridge, then down the first decent road that falls off to the right, and under the railway bridge. The tomb itself is quite delightful, perhaps on account of the fact that you're likely to have it more or less to yourself.

Geumcheok

금척 • Daily 24hr • Free

Several kilometres down the main road leading west from the Hyeongsan bridge is the beguiling **Geumcheok** collection of tomb-mounds. Legend has it that Hyeokgeose, the first Silla king, once owned a golden stick (*geum-cheok*) that could restore the dead to life. However, the village got so overcrowded with Silla-dynasty undead that the townsfolk decided to bury the rod in a mound – forty decoy mounds were also raised in the area, and to this day nobody knows which one houses the stick.

ARRIVAL AND DEPARTURE
GYEONGJU

By train Gyeongju's small train station is on the east of the city centre, within easy walking distance of most accommodation and a number of central sights. The new Singyeongju high-speed station sits 10km to the west; from here, buses #50, #70 and #700 make their way to the bus terminal in town.

Destinations from Gyeongju station Andong (3 daily; 3hr); Busan (Bujeon station; 10 daily; 1hr 50min); Danyang (2 daily; 3hr); Daegu (Dongdaegu station; hourly; 1hr 10min); Pohang (6 daily; 35min).

Destinations from Singyeongju station Busan (1–2 hourly; 35min); Daejeon (hourly; 1hr); Seoul (1–2 hourly; 2hr).

By bus Gyeongju's main bus terminals – express (고속; *gosok*) and intercity (시외; *si-oe*) – sit side by side on the west of the city centre. It's an easy walk to most accommodation and the central attractions. Durations given here are the shortest possible, mostly from the express terminals.

Destinations Andong (8 daily; 3hr); Busan (every 10–20 min; 50min); Daegu (every 10–20 min; 50min); Daejeon (every 20–30min; 2hr 40min); Gangneung (9 daily; 6hr); Gwangju (3 daily; 3hr 20min); Jeonju (4 daily: 4hr); Jinju (6 daily; 2hr 20min); Pohang (every 10–20 min; 30min); Seoul (every 20–40min; 3hr 45min); Sokcho (2 daily; 8hr).

INFORMATION

Tourist information There are booths outside the train and bus stations (daily 9am–6pm; ☎054 772 3843), usually staffed by friendly English-speakers; they're eager to dole out pamphlets, and are adept at assisting with accommodation and travel queries.

Services Banks with ATMs and exchange facilities include the Korea First Bank opposite the train station, and there are plenty of ATMs at 24hr convenience stores such as GS25 or 7-Eleven. The main post office is opposite the train station (Mon–Fri 9am–5pm; ☎054 740 0114).

4

NAMSAN BY BICYCLE

The various sights strewn around the Namsan area are some of the most enjoyable Gyeongju has to offer; buses will get you from A to B, or at least close enough, but the mountain's periphery is far better explored by **bicycle**. The western flank is best for a bike trip, and with the right mix of luck and judgement, it's possible to do much of your riding on farming trails, rather than the over-busy main roads.

First, get yourself to **Oreung** (see page 191), just across the river from the city centre. Almost opposite the ticket booth, you'll see a small farming track heading south; this will only take you as far as the main road (turn left to cross safely at the crossroad traffic lights), but it continues far beyond, providing stunning views of rice fields and distant mountains. There are no signs on this track, but **Poseokjeong** (see page 192) lies behind the first sizeable clutch of buildings you'll see to the left. From here, skirt the mountain on a trail heading further south to the **Tomb of King Jima** (see page 192) and **Samneung** (see page 192); some of the course is a wooden path perfect for bicycles, though you may have to backtrack from time to time when you hit the woods. Worry not – the mountain will be to your east the whole time, and rarely is getting lost so pleasurable.

Hanbok rental You won't be able to walk for long around the centre before seeing booths and shops renting out *hanbok* costumes – prices are usually W10,000 for an hour, or W30,000 for the day. One obvious place to start looking is the main entrance to Tumuli Park, which has two such outlets immediately outside.

GETTING AROUND

On foot Central Gyeongju is small enough to walk around, while the number of landmarks dotted around town – and the fact that you can actually see them, without apartment blocks getting in the way – makes navigation easy in relation to other Korean cities.

By taxi Taxi rides between central locations shouldn't cost more than W5000, though many of the city's attractions are far-flung – ask at your accommodation about organizing a taxi for the day, which should work out somewhere in the region of W80,000–170,000, depending on precisely what you'd like to see.

By bicycle One excellent way of getting around – almost uniquely, for a Korean city – is by bike. Rental outlets can be found all over town, including outside the main entrance to Tumuli Park and opposite the bus terminal information booth. You'll need to hand over some form of ID for security (if unwilling to part with your passport, you may be able to use a library card or something similar), and a bike will be yours for around W10,000 per day, or W5000 for a few hours. Bikes are particularly good for touring Namsan (see page 194) or the wider Wolseong Park area (see page 190).

ACCOMMODATION

Cheaper **motels** can be found near the bus terminals, while there are a fair few backpacker-oriented hostels and **guesthouses**, which generally provide cooking facilities, and common rooms in which to hang out with fellow travellers. Of more note are a range of traditionally styled *hanok* guesthouses – along with Seoul's Bukchon area (see page 101) and the *hanok* village in Jeonju (see page 258), Gyeongju is one of Korea's best places to stay in such abodes. For anything more fancy, you'll need to head to the **five-stars** standing proud around Bomun Lake, a short way east of the centre (see page 191); rack rates can fall by up to half at quieter times of the year, but rooms are on the small side and lack character.

CITY CENTRE

★ **Blueboat Hostel** 블루보트 호스텔 2F 252-1 Wonhwa-ro ☏ 010 2188 9049, ⊛ blueboat-hostel.com; map p.187. Another great offering from Korea's foremost hostel empire. Their attention to detail is admirable (hair-straighteners in the ladies' bathrooms), curtains give the dorm beds some privacy and a decent breakfast is included in the rates. Quite simply, one of the best hostels in Korea. Dorms W24,000, doubles W60,000

Cool Zzam 꿀잠 9 Gyerim-ro 106-gil ☏ 054 8239 5006, ⊛ coolzaam.com; map p.187. Great little alpine cottage-like hostel, presided over by a friendly English-speaking lady. Two of the wood-ceilinged dorms have pleasant views out over a field, and there are some private bunk-bed rooms available. Often closed for a while during the winter – check ahead. Dorms W23,000, doubles W50,000

GG 지지 호텔 3 Taejong-ro 699-gil ☏ 054 701 009? ⊛ gghotel.co.kr; map p.187. The city centre's only official tourist hotel has had a couple of fancy makeovers of late, and the current iteration is quite pleasing, with generously sized and suitably plush rooms; in those sporting a massage chair, you can buzz travel cares away

Breakfast is optional at W19,000 per head, or you could nip to the *McDonald's* next door. **W98,000**

★ **N Motel** 엔모텔 260-6 Geumseong-ro ☎054 777 4364; map p.187. Forget the cluster of motels spreading out from the bus terminal – this is the best one in town. Evidence includes big TVs in big rooms, free Dutch coffee whenever you ask, snazzily illuminated corridors – oh, and a location right next to some of the regal tombs that Gyeongju is famed for. Lovely. **W50,000**

★ **Sarangchae** 사랑채 23 Poseok-ro 1068-gil ☎054 773 4868, ⓦkjstay.com; map p.187. Quite possibly the best guesthouse in the country, and housed in wooden *hanok* buildings, *Sarangchae* offers friendly, informative management, cooking facilities and some friendly dogs along with a gorgeously traditional courtyard setting. Book ahead though, as there are only a few rooms; also note that they're usually closed in Dec. **W45,000**

Yettle Hanok Stay 옛뜰 한옥 스테이 9 Balgeunmaeul-gil ☎010 4129 2494; map p.187. Stay outside the city, inside the city – this *hanok* guesthouse is a great option if the *Sarangchae* is full, but is also worth considering on its own terms, thanks to stellar service, and a location outside the town centre, surrounded by greenery. Rooms are traditional in nature, but the floor bedding is more like a mattress than a futon – some will find this far more comfortable. **W90,000**

BOMUN LAKE

Bomun World 보문 월드 Cheongundong 1444-2 ☎054 772 0062, ⓦbomunworld.com; map p.197. For a change from Bomun's five-star hotels try this collection of intriguingly designed villas south of the lake – a 20min walk, more if you choose to head the long way across the fields. Some of the rooms are duplex in nature, and they're predictably popular with young couples. **W70,000**

Commodore 코모도 호텔 422 Bomun-ro ☎054 745 7701, ⓦcommodorehotel.co.kr; map p.197. Rooms here are as tastefully designed as the lobby, with a choice of hill or lake views – the latter are best but marginally more expensive. There are a few good restaurants on site, as well as a lovely spa. **W230,000**

★ **Hilton** 힐튼 484-7 Bomun-ro ☎054 745 7788, ⓦhilton.com; map p.197. Possessing a slightly more international ambience than its neighbours, the *Hilton* has a swimming pool, gym, squash court and jogging track – and a Miró original in the lobby. Rooms are every bit as comfy as you'd expect for the price, with some nice touches and relatively large bathrooms, and service is very good; there are also Italian, Chinese, Korean and Japanese restaurants to choose from, as well as a bakery and cocktail lounge. **W320,000**

EATING

Gyeongju is not really known for its food, but there are a few places dotted here and there serving traditional food, often in a wooden *hanok* setting, or something similar. One interesting feature is the simply incredible number of small **bakeries** selling *gyeongju-bbang* (경주빵), small, sweet cakes that are eagerly snapped up by domestic and Japanese tourists; they're usually sold by the box, though ask around and you might get to sample one for W1500 or so.

RESTAURANTS

CITY CENTRE

★ **Dosol Maeul** 도솔 마을 8-13 Sonhyoja-gil ☎054 48 9232; map p.187. You can tuck into filling set meals (W9000, min two) or potato pancakes (W15,000) and quaff *dongdonju* – a milky Korean wine (W5000) – by the bucket-load at this simple, atmospheric place, in additional rooms set around an equally rustic courtyard. A great place to kick back after a day's sightseeing. Wed–Sun 11am–3pm & 5–9pm.

Kisoya 기소야 90 Wonhyo-ro ☎054 746 6020; map 187. Facing some of the city centre regal tombs, this simple Japanese restaurant which gets the basics right. Try the kimchi *katsudon* (W8500), or a tempura *soba* set (W11,000). Tues–Sun 10am–3pm & 5–10pm.

Pipino Pizza 피피노 피자 145-3 Wonhyo-ro ☎054 773 0987; map p.187. While there are Western pizza chains in Gyeongju, *Pipino* offers a slightly more Korean experience, for W10,500 and up. Toppings include vegetarian, sweet potato, *bulgogi* or "super special". If you speak Korean, or can find someone willing to translate, you can call for free delivery – perfect on a rainy day. Daily 10am–10pm.

★ **Gyodong Ssambap** 교동 쌈밥 77 Cheomseong-ro ☎054 773 3322; map p.187. Large eatery popular with tour groups – no matter, since the food is excellent. Their *ssambap* sets (W17,000, min two) see the table absolutely covered with delectable side-dishes; if you're dining alone, go for the utterly delicious *bibimbap* (W10,000), which also comes with generous number of side-dishes. Mon & Wed–Sun 9am–2pm & 4–9pm.

UZ Kebab 2F 114-1 Dongseong-ro; map p.187. This Uzbek restaurant is the best of the several which have popped up to cater for the city's recently ballooning number of foreign factory-workers. Try some pilaf (W8000), a *jizbiz* (lamb meat on chips; W10,000), or some Russian salads. Daily 10am–10pm.

Yoseokgung 요석궁 19-4 Gyochonan-gil ☎054 772 3347; maps p.187. A fabulous place for fabulous food, set around a traditional courtyard in a quiet area facing Namsan. There's no English menu, but good traditional food is guaranteed – set meals go from W33,000 to W132,000

4

GYEONGJU FESTIVALS

Throughout the year the city puts on many shows and events to please its guests. In warmer months, regular performances of traditional song and dance take place on **Bomun Lake** (see page 191) and around **Wolji Pond** (see page 190) at 8pm on Saturdays from April to October, but the biggest event by far is the three-day **Silla Cultural Festival**, in October, one of the best and most colourful in the land. On the menu are wrestling, archery, singing and dancing, and a parade in which a mock Silla king and queen are carried down the streets. Other events include the **Cherry Blossom Marathon**, held on the first Saturday of April, and a **Traditional Drink and Rice Cake Festival** in late March, while on December 31 the New Year's crowd heads to King Munmu's seaside tomb (see page 198) to ring in the change of digits and enjoy the first sunrise of the year.

---

per head, though there's a two-person minimum. Daily 11.30am–3.30pm & 5–9pm.

OUTSIDE THE CENTRE

Poseokjeong 포석정 633-5 Poseok-ro ☎054 777 3053; map p.197. Little bungalow-restaurant just off Namsan's western flank, and almost directly opposite the Tomb of King Jima (see page 192). Here you can get a filling meal such as *sundubu jjigae* (순두부 찌개; tofu broth) for just W8000 – perfect if you're touring the mountain by bike. Daily noon–8pm.

CAFÉS AND TEAROOMS

CITY CENTRE

Bomnal 봄날 62-4 Posok-ro 1092-gil ☎070 4795 4799; map p.187. The most attractive café in central Gyeongju; coffees are a wee bit pricey (from W5000), but there's a great view over to the tiled rooftops of an adjacent shrine. The vibe is suitably chilled, and one has to dig the 1970s-style green chairs here. Daily 8am–8pm.

OUTSIDE THE CENTRE

Aden 아덴 424-34 Bomun-ro ☎054 774 2016; map p.197. Industrial-chic café overlooking Bomun Lake, providing some of the best views around (especially at sunset time), and decent coffee (from W5000) and baked goods to boot. No under-sixteens allowed. Daily 10am–11pm.

★**Jeontong Chatjip** 전통 찻집 Samneung; map p.197. A wonderful find for those touring Namsan by bike, this is the sweetest-looking countryside tearoom imaginable, presided over by a cheery lady who'll ply you with fruit and sweet treats. The teas are great, too, and cost from W5000. Daily 10.30am–6pm.

DRINKING

There aren't many good places to drink in Gyeongju, though a few funky spots have opened up on Posok-ro, the road flanking the western fringe of Tumuli Park – little really stands out so far, though expect standards to improve once the wheat is sorted from the chaff.

Daehwa Maekju 대화맥주 1093 Posok-ro ☎054 771 3355; map p.187. The best place to pop up on this newly trendified street – very cosy, on account of having just five tables, with a modest selection of beers (W7000–8000), and very rustic bathrooms. Daily 11am–11pm.

Around Gyeongju

An almost overwhelming number of sights litter the countryside around Gyeongju – those listed here make up just a fraction of the possibilities, so be sure to scour local maps and pamphlets for things that might be of particular interest to you. East of the city centre is **Bulguksa**, one of Korea's most famous temples; splendidly decorated, it's on the UNESCO World Heritage list, as is **Seokguram**, a grotto hovering above it on a mountain ridge. Apart from that geared towards these two sights, **transport** in this area is not always regular – you may need to spend some time waiting for buses, so if possible, try to get the latest timetable from one of Gyeongju's tourist offices. While hitchhiking is never totally safe and can't be wholeheartedly recommended, you'll rarely get a better chance than on the run east to the **Underwater Tomb of King Munmu**, where traffic on the road is light and everyone is heading to or from Gyeongju. On the way see the king's watery grave, and easily combined as part of a day-trip, you'll pass a spur road leading to **Golgulsa**, an out-of-the-way temple famed for its martial arts. To the north of Gyeongju are **Oksan Seowon**, one of the country's best examples of a Joseon-era Confucian academy, and **Yangdong Folk Village**, a collection of traditional housing.

Bulguksa

불국사 • Daily 7am–6pm • W5000 • Bus #10, #11 or #700 from Gyeongju (every 20min; W1700)

Sitting comfortably under the tree-lined wings of the surrounding mountains is **Bulguksa**, which was built in 528 during the reign of King Beop-heung, under whose leadership Buddhism was adopted as the Silla state religion. It was almost destroyed by the Japanese invasions in 1593 and, though it's hard to believe now, was left to rot until the 1970s, when dictatorial president Park Chung-hee ordered its reconstruction. It has subsequently been added to the UNESCO World Heritage list. As one of the most-visited temples in the country, it can be thronged with people, many of whom combine their visit with a picnic on and around the path leading from the bus stop to the ticket office.

The temple

Once through the gates, you'll follow a pretty path past a pond and over a bridge, before being confronted by the temple. Here, **two staircases** lead to the upper level; these are officially "four bridges" rather than two flights of steps, leading followers from the worldly realm to that of the Buddha. Both are listed as national treasures, so you're not actually allowed to ascend them. Having entered the main courtyard, you'll be confronted by two three-level **stone pagodas** from the Unified Silla period – one plain and one ornately decorated, representing Yin and Yang.

From the courtyard, it's best to stroll aimlessly and appreciate the views. The whole complex has been elaborately painted, but the artistry is particularly impressive in **Daeungjeon**, the main hall behind the pagodas, whose eaves are decorated both inside and out with striking patterns. At the top of the complex, another hall – **Gwaneumjeon** – looks down over Bulguksa's pleasing array of roof tiles; the steep staircase down causes problems for Korean girls in high heels, but there are other ways back. Making

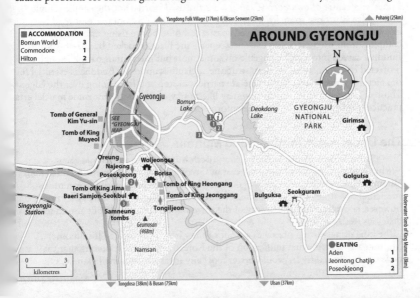

4

AROUND GYEONGJU

■ ACCOMMODATION	
Bomun World	3
Commodore	1
Hilton	2

●EATING	
Aden	1
Jeontong Chatjip	3
Poseokjeong	2

your way across the rear of the complex you'll come to **Nahanjeon**, a hall surrounded by bamboo and a cloak of maple leaves. Behind this lie small towers of stacked stones; you're welcome – expected – to add your own. The **tearoom** beneath the nearby trinket shop provides a useful rest stop.

Seokguram

석굴암 • Daily: March–Sept 6.30am–6pm; Oct–Feb 7am–5pm • W5000 • Bus #12 from Bulguksa (hourly; W1700; last bus back 6.20pm)

After Bulguksa, a visit to the Buddhist grotto of **Seokguram** may feel a little anti-climactic. However, the views from its lofty position alone justify the trip up, especially at sunrise. The East Sea is visible on a good day, and it is said that the statue was built to provide spiritual protection to the country from the Japanese across these waters. Until fairly recently, access was only possible via a 3km mountain path from Bulguksa, but today most choose to take the bus instead. It is still possible to hike the mountain path, if only to appreciate how hard it must have been for the grotto's builders to transport the necessary blocks of granite to such a height; you can judge for yourself how far it is by looking up at the horizon from the Bulguksa bus stop – that's the Seokguram ticket booth on top.

Once past the ticket booth, a winding but easy ten-minute walk through the trees leads to the grotto itself; inside its keyhole-shaped chamber sits an image of the Sakyamuni Buddha, surrounded by art of a similarly high calibre. However, the chamber has been sealed off in order to protect it from both the elements and visitors, and unfortunately, this could and should have been done better. A pane of glass separates you from the art and its beauty, and an ugly little protective hut now stands in the way of the grotto. As a result, it's almost impossible to appreciate the elegance and attention to detail that many experts consider to be the finest example of Buddhist art in the country.

Golgulsa

골굴사 • 24hr • Free • ⓦ golgulsa.com • Bus #100 or #150 from Gyeongju (every 30min; 45min; W1700); get off at the village of Andong-ni, from where it's just under 1km (10min) to the temple turn-off

Famed as a centre of *seonmudo* (선무도), a Zen-based martial art, the simple temple of **Golgulsa** sits above some lovely countryside. The walk up from the spur road is already quite inspiring; the track heads past a teahouse before rising into the small complex, from where it becomes even steeper – the place is backed by a sixth-century Buddha, carved into a cliff navigable on some short but precipitous paths. Though now protected by a monstrous modern structure, a clamber up to the Buddha is essential for the picture-perfect **view** alone; there are barriers to stop you from going over the edge. Those of an even steelier disposition may like to stay at the temple for some **martial arts practice** (visit their website for more information).

The Underwater Tomb of King Munmu

문무대왕 수중릉 • Daily 24hr • Free • Bus #150 from Gyeongju (hourly; W1700; 1hr); get off as soon as you hit the coast

Within wading distance of the coast east of Gyeongju is the **Underwater Tomb of King Munmu**. Though the name befits a good novel, and it's popular with Korean tourists, the actual signature of rocky crags may come as an anticlimax; it's worth the trip, however, not only to see the beauty of the surrounding countryside but also to feast on delicious fresh seafood.

The king's final resting place lies a stone's throw from the coast. In his lifetime, Munmu achieved the first unification of the Korean peninsula, reasoning that the power of his united forces would better repel any invasion from the Japanese. On

his deathbed, and still clearly concerned by the Nipponese threat, he asked to have his ashes scattered on the offshore rocks, believing that he would then become a **sea dragon**, offering eternal protection to the country's coast. Just 1km inland you'll be able to make out two giant stone pagodas, 13m high, which mark the former site of **Gameunsa** (감은사), a temple built on the orders of Munmu's son, Sinmun, in order to provide his sea-dragon father an inland retreat along the now-dry canal.

You may be lucky enough to witness one of the banana-heavy **shamanist ceremonies** that occasionally take place on the beach, honouring spirits of the local seas. Lining the beach are several **fish restaurants**, and it's possible to spend the night at one of several local **minbak**.

Oksan Seowon

옥산 서원 • Daily 9am–8pm • Free • Bus #203 from Gyeongju (10 daily; W1700; 1hr)

After enjoying the Silla-era delights in and around Gyeongju, you can leap forward in time to the **Joseon dynasty** by making a trip 30km north of town to **Oksan Seowon**, a Confucian school and shrine established in 1572 under the rule of King Seonjo. During this period Confucianism was the primary system of belief, particularly for the *yangban* aristocracy. However, most such places were closed in the 1870s at a time of social upheaval, and many were destroyed, making Oksan one of the oldest in the country, and quite possibly the most enjoyable to visit (though tiny Dosan Seowon near Andong gives it a run for its money, see page 180). It was dedicated to **Yi Eon-jeok** (1491–1533), a Confucian poet, **scholar** and all-round theological handyman who, while not as revered as his contemporaries Yi-Yi (see page 237) or Toegye (see page 180), certainly exerted an influence on neo-Confucian thought.

Now restored, following years of neglect and the occasional fire, the complex still manages to create a gentle atmosphere in keeping with its original function as a place of study and reflection, helped by the stream bubbling away below, as well as the gorgeousness of the surrounding countryside and the surprisingly low number of visitors. It's also home to a copy of the **Samguk Sagi**, the only concise records of the Three Kingdoms period (albeit one that seems to be biased towards the Silla dynasty).

Just a short walk beyond Oksan Seowon is Yi Eon-jeok's former abode at **Dongnakdang**. Some of his descendants still live in the cramped compound, which appears to be hiding under the skirt of a large tree, and is every bit as tranquil as the academy itself. Further ahead again are **Jonghyesa**, a temple famed for its curiously shaped pagoda, and **Dodeokam**, a tiny hermitage with a view balanced high up on the rocks. All are just about within walking distance of each other, though considering the rather poor bus connections from Gyeongju, it may be best to stay the night near Oksan Seowon – there's a motel and a few *minbak* around the academy, and a few places to eat.

Yangdong Folk Village

양동 민속 마을 • Daily 9am–6pm • W4000, free outside official visiting hours • Bus #203 from Gyeongju (10 daily; W1700; 1hr)

Korea has a number of "**folk villages**", a product of Park Chung-hee's desire to keep alive rural traditions at a time when large-scale economic growth was smothering the nation in concrete. Usually they consist of a rural group of houses and associate buildings; some openly exist for show alone, while others are living, breathing communities whose denizens work the local fields, rewarded for their enforced deprivation in terms of urban amenities with governmental subsidy. **Yangdong Folk Village**, tucked into a countryside fold near the village of Angang-ni, is one of the best in the country, and home to some real history – one reason behind its World Heritage status, received in 2010. Dating from the 1400s, this was once a thriving community of **yangban**, the aristocracy that ruled the country during the Joseon dynasty. Yi Eon-jeok, the great Confucian scholar to whom Oksan Seowon (see above) was dedicated, was born here in 1491; his life and the academy's history are relayed on information boards. As you walk around, try to suspend belief and imagine yourself back in nineteenth-century Korea (though it probably smells much more pleasant now). Some buildings are permanently open, and you may even be lucky enough to be invited into a private house.

Tongdosa

통도사 • Daily 8.30am–5.30pm • W3000 • ⓦ tongdosa.or.kr • Regular buses from Gyeongju (bus #12, #63 or #67; every 10min; 1hr 30min) and Busan (every 20min; 1hr)

Well worth a visit if you are zooming between Gyeongju and Busan, **Tongdosa** is one of Korea's three "Jewel Temples" (the others being Songgwansa and Haeinsa; see pages 239 and 185), and as such one of the most heralded in the land. It's a truly captivating place, especially around sunset, when its various buildings fall into a darkness amplified by their setting, shoehorned into a tight valley. From the entrance, it's a twenty-minute walk to the temple itself, along a gorgeous path that's illuminated after sunset with picturesque stone lanterns.

Part of the local **Jogye** sect, Tongdosa has been in existence since the mid-seventh century – long enough to pick up a few interesting quirks. Firstly, the candle is said to have stayed alight this whole time; easier to verify with your own eyes is the fact that there's no Buddha in the main hall. Rather, the main subject of veneration is a hall housing **sani**, a crystal-like substance said to be created inside the bodies of pure monks. Of course, it's not on public display. Lastly, take a look at the drum and bell tower: you'll see two of all four instruments (wooden fish, brass gong, drum and bell), rather than the more usual one. Despite its age, only the Daeungjeon hall withstood the Japanese attacks of the 1590s. However, most other buildings have been reconstructed with consummate care, and look rather beautiful.

The semi-rural location may tempt you to stay the night, and you'll have no problems finding a motel; their neon signs start right outside the temple entrance.

4

Ulleungdo

울릉도

With island groups dotted all around Korea's southern and western coasts, you may feel tempted to forgo the three-hour ferry ride to a small turret of land between Korea and Japan, and head instead to a closer isle. However, this would be a mistake – **Ulleungdo**, covered in a rich, green cloak of trees and fringed with juniper, is refreshingly unspoiled and simply stunning. It's essentially a volcano poking from the East Sea, and the flora splashed around on its nutritious soils mark it out as a mini Jeju; while it's increasingly popular with Korean travellers, Ulleungdo's isolation has kept it largely free from the ravages of mass tourism. Its armies of middle-aged Korean tourists are here mainly

---

HIKING ULLEUNGDO

Wherever you are on the island, you're likely to see the sea on one side, and a group of verdant peaks hovering over you on the other. These unspoiled, richly forested slopes offer some wonderful **hiking** opportunities, and fortunately the walk up to the main summit, **Seonginbong** (984m), and back can be done in one day. There are several paths into and around the interior, but the main access point is just north of Dodong-ni, near Daewonsa, a small temple. A spur-road just before the temple leads uphill to the right, marking the start of a clammy 4.1km walk to the top. From here, you can either turn back or make your way further north to the opposite trailhead at Naribunji, 4.5km from the summit (around 6hr in total). Trails are well signposted, though as there's almost nothing en route, be sure to bring water and snacks.

due to its proximity to **Dokdo**, an even smaller speck of land claimed by both Korea and Japan, and a focus of nationalistic demonstrations (see page 203). With no chain stores or five-star hotels, and just one bumpy main road tracing a vague parallel to the coast, the only time that the island's pulse seems to quicken is in the half-hour window surrounding ferry arrivals, when *ajummas* race around trying to draw tourists back to their *minbak* accommodation.

Few islands in Korea can provide as spectacular an arrival as Ulleungdo's main settlement, **Dodong-ni**, whose port makes a sudden appearance in a sumptuous pirate-like cove hidden and encircled by precipitous mountains, and squeezed in on both sides by the valley walls. Ulleungdo's second main settlement, **Jeodong-ni**, lies just up the coast, and is slightly smaller, but relatively open and rather different in character. These two villages, both an untidy but undeniably appealing mishmash of *minbak* and fish restaurants, give guests a taste of what Ulleungdo island is like. **Naribunji** is a farming area of tremendous beauty to the north of the island, whose flatness will come as a great surprise to those who've travelled the bumpy coastal road to get there. On the way, picturesque fishing settlements dot the coast, while there's some good **hiking** to be enjoyed around the rugged, volcanic peaks that rise up in the centre of the island, almost totally untouched by modern life.

Dodong-ni

도동리

Though still just a village in population terms, **DODONG-NI** is the largest settlement on Ulleungdo and its main port, and as a result houses most of the island's overnight guests. However, despite the visitor numbers, it has remained surprisingly true to its old ways. The atmospheric village sits in a tight valley up from the ferry terminal, its few roads all heading uphill past a looping parade of *minbak*, small shops and raw-fish

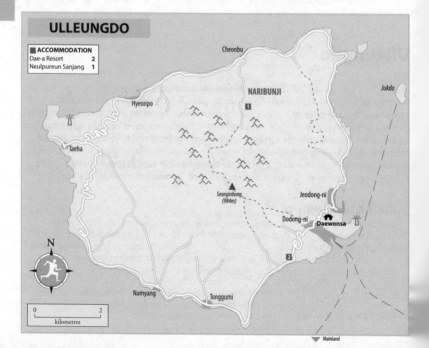

ULLEUNGDO

ACCOMMODATION
Dae-a Resort — 2
Neulpureun Sanjang — 1

Cheonbu

NARIBUNJI

Jukdo

Hyeonpo

Taeha

Seonginbong
(984m)

Jeodong-ni

Dodong-ni — Daewonsa

N

Namyang

Tonggumi

0 — 2
kilometres

Mainland

DOKDO

Ninety kilometres east of Ulleungdo lies a remote, straggly bunch of rocks, a small archipelago that seems to be good for little bar fishing, fighting and assertions of national identity. **Dokdo** (독도) to the Koreans, **Takeshima** (竹島) to the Japanese, it is claimed by both nations, and like the East Sea/Sea of Japan dispute (see page 166), the issue is unlikely to be resolved any time soon. The problem centres on political rivalry resulting from Korea's Japanese occupation, which lasted from 1910 until the end of World War II – Koreans tend to take even the slightest whiff of neo-imperialism quite seriously.

In the decades following the war, a number of **armed confrontations** took place in and around the islands, but after things eventually died down Korea took the upper hand, and built a wharf, a lighthouse and a helicopter-landing pad, around which are stationed a couple of permanent residents. In 2004, Korea issued a set of stamps featuring the islands; Japan took this as a claim of ownership, and a couple of years later sent two ships to Dokdo on an unauthorized survey mission. After protracted talks, Japan agreed to suspend the survey, but shortly afterwards Korea sent in ships to do exactly the same thing.

Today, **right-wing elements** in Korea use Dokdo in promotional materials, and the islands have become the focal point of a new nationalist wave. A few of the biggest mobile telecom operators in the country built communications towers on the island (totally for show, given the puny local population) and flag-waving ferry-loads of Korean tourists regularly make the journey across from Pohang on the mainland. It's quite possible for foreign travellers to do likewise, but few choose to take the **ferry tours** from Ulleungdo (March–Nov; 2–3 daily; W45,000 return).

The only form of access, if you're even allowed to disembark, is a spiral staircase with one step for each day of the year; after panting your way to the top you'll come out at the island's one lofty "town" (population: two civilians, to go with six lighthouse operators and around forty coastguards around the archipelago). A half-hour later, you're on the boat back out again – without the bombastic fervour, it's not exactly a thrilling trip.

restaurants. There are few sights as such, but many visitors find themselves heading to a **lighthouse** to the east of town, which can be reached on a number of routes; the most scenic is the half-hour walk around the jagged coast from the ferry terminal.

Following any one of Dodong-ni's upward trails from the ferry terminal will bring you, after what may seem like a never-ending climb, to the island's main "coastal" road. Turn left from the village exit, then immediately right, and you'll find **Daewonsa** (대원사), a tiny temple that marks the beginning of most hikes into the interior (see page 201).

Dokdo Museum

독도 박물관 • Museum daily 9am–6pm • Free • Cable car daily 5.30am–8pm • W7500 return

If you head uphill from the ferries and stick to the left, you'll eventually come across a sign pointing to the **Dokdo Museum**, which together with an adjacent historical museum forms part of a small park. The former is the most interesting, as it details the Korean claim on Dokdo, a tiny scrawl of rock east of Ulleungdo (see page 203). Also in the park is a "healthy water" spring, the metallic taste presumably proof of some kind of goodness. The walk up is quite a slog, and most who make the climb are heading to the base of a **cable car**, ready to be whisked up a nearby peak to take in some wonderful views: on clear days, you may be able to see Dokdo across the seas.

Jeodong-ni

저동리

A short taxi ride – or a half-hour walk – away from Dodong-ni is **JEODONG-NI**. Open-plan and spread out along a harbour, rather than wedged into a valley, it's something like a flattened version of its neighbour; here you'll see far fewer visitors, fewer *minbak*, and therefore an atmosphere more in keeping with the general nature of the island. It's the kind of place where you can idle away a fair few hours doing nothing at all.

The **harbour** is a great place for a walk, and is full of fishing boats dangling dozens of high-wattage bulbs, used to lure squid to their doom. The tall finger of stone that protrudes through the harbour's outer wall, called "**Candlestick Rock**", is the village's defining landmark.

Naribunji

나리분지 • Take the coastal road bus and get off at Cheonbu (천부), where a 4WD will be waiting to take passengers over the hill to Naribunji (W1000)

To the north of the island lies a geographic anomaly. **Naribunji** is literally the only flat space on Ulleungdo, a dreamy patchwork of fields entirely encircled by mountains; it's a fantastic place to base yourself and spend a day or two walking through fields, taking in the surrounding forest or doing absolutely nothing. It's also a good start or finish point for a **hiking trip** up and over the mountain; you may notice cable-car wires heading up into the hills, but unfortunately this service is for the use of local military only.

ARRIVAL AND DEPARTURE   ULLEUNGDO

Due to the absence of an airport on the island, there's only one way to arrive – by **ferry**. At the time of writing, all services were using the port at the main settlement of Dodong-ni, but plans have long been afoot to make a larger terminal elsewhere on the island. Ferry schedules were also in a constant state of flux – double-check with any tourist office before heading out.

From Pohang Most travellers get here from Pohang (포항), a large but uninteresting city near Gyeongju on the mainland's eastern coast. Services leave each morning at 9.50am (3hr; W64,500), returning at 3.30pm. The terminal at Pohang is a short taxi journey from the train station or either bus terminal; fortunately, the ferry bay is one of the quieter, more pleasant areas in a generally ugly city, and if you're unlikely to arrive in time for the ferry you can stay at one of several motels around the terminal. Alternatively, it's possible, with an early start, to wake up in Gyeongju and make it to Pohang in time to catch the ferry – be sure to arrive at the terminal before 9am. Note that the ferry has no windows on economy level, and will usually smell of *kimchi* – those likely to suffer sea-sickness should "splurge" the extra W6000 for first class.

From Gangneung A daily service (8am; 3hr; W54,000) leaves for Ulleungdo from Gangneung, a city in Gangwon province (see page 160). It's now connected to Seoul by high-speed trains, which are the quickest form of access from the capital – the earliest trains (followed by a taxi ride) will have you at the port in time.

GETTING AROUND

By bus Getting around the island is harder than you might expect – the coastal road runs in a "U" rather than a circle, ending in the northeast of the island, though eighteen daily buses (W1000–1500) now bump their way around, a recent increase.

By tour More convenient than public transport are the daily bus tours (4hr; W20,000) that leave from the ferry terminal; there'll be a scramble for the sea-side seats. It's also possible to take one of the round-island ferry tours (2hr; W25,000) which run six times a day in the summer, and twice a day at other times. Lastly, it's also possible to take a taxi tour for around W120,000 for the day.

INFORMATION

Tourist information There's a small office just uphill from the ferry terminal – where the water stops, look to your left. Though you'll be lucky to find an English-speaker here, staff will be able to hunt down accommodation across the island and arm you with the requisite maps and pamphlets. The island's website (ⓦ ulleung.go.kr) is also worth a look.

Money One very important thing to consider on Ulleungdo is money – those with non-Korean bank cards may not have much luck here, though the island's few banks may be able to exchange foreign cash.

ACCOMMODATION

Korea's developers must have a fear of long ferry rides – Ulleungdo is almost entirely devoid of modern **accommodation**, bar one tourist hotel and a few overpriced motels in the main settlements, Dodong-ni and Jeodong-ni. Every building in Dodong-ni seems to have **minbak** rooms, and these can also be found in Jeodong-ni and other settlements. You won't need to go hunting for offers, as elderly women will scream them at you on your walk up from the ferry. A fair price for a room sleeping two is usually around W30,000 in off season and W70,000 in peak summer months; don't be afraid to see a couple. Heading around the island, there are a few tiny settlements where it's possible to stay, but the best by far is **Naribunji** in the north: there's a campsite here, as well as a few **minbak**.

DODONG-NI

Seonginbong Motel 송인봉 모텔 26 Dodong-ni ☏054 791 2078. Just up from the ferries on the right-hand side of the road you'll find best motel in the village (recently renovated, too), though the quality and accessibility mean that it's often packed with tour groups, and the price is accordingly a little high. **W50,000**

Ulleung E Sa Bu 울릉 이사부 호텔 21-1 Dodong 1-gil ☏054 791 8253. This is the one official tourist hotel in the village, but not too overpriced, especially when the off-peak discounts kick in, and some of the more expensive rooms are colossal. **W90,000**

JEODONG-NI

★**Motel Jeil** 모텔 제일 38 Bongnae 2-gil ☏054 791 2637. Set back from the seafront, next to a small park visible from the waterfront, this is the best of Jeodong-ni's motley selection of accommodation. Rooms are surprisingly large and well appointed, and some have pretty sea or mountain views; there's also an attached sauna, in which you can take a scrub for a few thousand won. **W45,000**

ELSEWHERE

Dae-a Resort 대아 리조트 302-1 Sadong-ni ☏054 791 8800, ⓦdaearesort.com; map p.202. The most comfortable place to stay on the island by far, with stylish (if surprisingly small) rooms and good sea views, but little going on around it. **W150,000**

Neulpureun Sanjang 늘푸른 산장 Nari 49 ☏054 791 8181; map p.202. A standout among the several *minbak* of the Naribunji area, doubling as a good restaurant. At least one of the family members can speak English, though she may have to translate by phone if away from the island. **W40,000**

EATING

There are plenty of **restaurants** in Dodong-ni and Jeodong-ni, mostly centred around creatures culled from the sea, though less fishy things are available – the island's most famous edible product is, in fact, **pumpkin taffy**. Note that most places shut early (ie, before 9pm). A few **fish shacks** open in good weather and cling limpet-like to the cliffs near Dodong-ni's ferry terminal, and there's a more permanent upper-floor parade above the fish shack in Jeodong-ni; W30,000 per person should be enough for a belly full of fish. Those wanting something more Western can make use of small **bakeries** in both of the main villages.

99 Sikdang 99식당 89 Dodong-gil ☏054 791 2287. This friendly restaurant, in the very centre of Dodong-ni, has whipped up an army of fans following appearances on Korean TV. Prices have stayed low, and there's an English menu of sorts, including *bibimbap* (W12,000) and the house special – a spicy mix of pork and squid known as *ojingeo bulgogi* (오징어 불고기; W13,000). All meals come with seasonal side dishes. Daily 6am–9pm.

Eddiang 에띠앙 84 Dodong-gil ☏054 791 8484. Located under the *Ulleung Hotel*, this homely place offers reasonably priced spaghetti, steak and pizza for W15,000 or so – a respite, if necessary, from the ubiquitous fish restaurants. Daily 10.30am–11pm.

Busan

부산

Tell any Korean that you're about to visit **BUSAN**, and just watch their face light up – if one were to run a national census asking where everyone would most like to live, Korea's second city would likely wind up in first place. "Seoul by the sea", or so the saying goes, Busan is by turns brackish, glamorous, clumsy and charismatic, and prides itself on simply being different from the capital. It has beaches, for a start – **Haeundae** is by far the most popular in the land, and quite a sight with its attendant high-rise buildings and five-star hotels forming a modern-day amphitheatre of sorts. The connection to the sea is also evident at the city's other major draw – **Jagalchi**, the most renowned fish market in the country. Busan is also the world's fifth-largest container port – its salty fringes tumble away into a colourful, confetti-like jumble of corrugated containers. In the evenings, the setting sun throws these ships into cool silhouette on a sea of gold, and the youth come out to paint the town red.

BUSAN

Hopo

Nopo
Busan Central
Bus Terminal

Geumgeok

Beomeosa

Dongwon

Geumjeong
Sanseong

Beomeosa

Namsan

Dusil

Yulli

Guseo

GEUMJEONG-GU

Hwanmyeong

Dong-Busan
College

Jangjeon

Busan National
University

Youngsan
University

Pusan National
University

Banyeo
Agricultural
Market

Sujeong

Heosimcheong

Oncheonjang

Seokdae

Cable Car

Geumsa

Sukdeung
Mandeok

Myeongnyun

DONGNAE-GU

Seodong

Namsaan-
jeong

Deokcheon

Minam

Dongnae
Suam

Myeongjang

Sajik Baseball
Stadium

Sajik

Nakmin

Chungnyeolsa

Busan National University
of Education

Asiad Main
Stadium

Sport
Complex

Geoje

Yeonsan

City Hall

Mulmangol

Spa Land
Centum City

Busan Museum
of Art

Jung-dong

Jangsan

Yangjeong

Baesan

Centum City

Bujeon
Station

Busan
Global
Center

Mangmi

Suyeong

Haeundae
HAEUNDAE

SEOMYEON

Bujeon

Seomyeon

Millak

Dongbaek

SEE 'HAEUNDAE' MAP

Bunam

Jeonpo

Gwangan

Gaegeum

Dongeui
University

Gaya

SEE SEOMYEON'
MAP

Gwangalli
Beach

Naengjeong

Beomil

Munjeon

NAM-GU

Geumnyeonsan

DIAMOND BRIDGE

Jwacheon

Munhyeon

Namcheon

Beomnaegol

Jigegol

Motgol

Daeyeon

Kyungsung University

Busanjin

Choryang

Busan
Museum

UN Memorial
Cemetery

SEO-GU

International
Ferry Terminal

Busan
Station

Seodaesin

Dongdaesin

Busan Train
Station

Daeti

Toseong

Jungang

JUNG-GU

Jagalchi

Nampo

Gamcheon
Culture
Village

Pusan
National
University
Hospital

SEE 'CENTRAL
BUSAN' MAP

Songdo
Beach

Yeongdo

Cable Car

N

Taejongdae
Park

Pebble
Beach

Seobu Intercity Bus Terminal & Gimhae International Airport (15km)

Jeju Island   Japan

SUBWAY LINES

Line 1	
Line 2	
Line 3	
Line 4	

0   2
kilometres

DRINKING & NIGHTLIFE

Basement	1
Vinyl Underground	3
Yong Ggum	2

BUSAN ORIENTATION

With buildings sprawling across the whole horizon, filling the gaps between the city's mountains and swamping some of the smaller hills entirely, Busan can be quite confusing for the first-time visitor. The de facto centre of the city, known as **Jung-gu**, is the area heading south from the train station down to Jagalchi Fish Market; on the way, you'll pass the ferry terminals, Busan Tower and Nampodong's maze of shops, cinemas, markets and restaurants. A short way north of the train station is trendy **Seomyeon**, a brand-name shopper's paradise, but also home to some of the earthiest restaurants, and excellent nightlife. A way east of here you'll find **Haeundae**, a fascinating beach area that's home to rich Koreans and five-star hotels, but still manages to retain much of its fishing village character.

Indeed, it could be said that the locals alone make this city worth a visit: more characterful than those from the capital, Busanites talk almost as fast as their city moves, spouting provincial slang in a distinctive staccato that many foreigners initially mistake for Japanese. In fact, some locals aren't actually Korean at all – head across the road from the train station and you'll find a fascinatingly seedy district populated by **Russians**, **Chinese** and **Filipinos**.

Brief history

Even before it became the whirring economic dynamo that it is today, Busan played a pivotal role in the country's history. Though it was once part of the short-lived **Gaya kingdom** swallowed whole by the Silla dynasty (see page 188), it was at that time little more than a collection of fishing villages. In the fifteenth century it benefitted from its proximity to Japan, when a trade treaty opened it up as a port to international trade – up until that point, most goods had been leaving the area as loot on pirate ships. This competitive advantage promptly swung around and hit Busan squarely in the face when the city was attacked by the Japanese in 1592; under the astute leadership of **Admiral Yi Sun-shin** (see page 237) damage was limited, but still devastating.

Outside Busan's largest museum (see page 210) is a stone "stele of anti-compromise", whose Chinese characters read "All countrymen are hereby warned that anyone who does not fight against the Western barbarians is committing an act of treachery". Little did they know that Korea would eventually be consumed by its closest neighbour – the Japanese annexed the peninsula in 1910 – then fight a bloody civil war, only to be bailed out both times by said barbarians. Busan was at the forefront of the **Korean War**; indeed, for a time, the city and its surrounding area were the only places left under Allied control, the North Koreans having occupied the peninsula up to what was known as the **Pusan Perimeter** (Pusan being the correct romanization at the time). At this point, up to four million refugees from elsewhere on the peninsula crowded the city, before **General Douglas MacArthur** made a bold move at Incheon (see page 125) to reverse the tide of the war.

Jung-gu and around

The city's **downtown** spreads south from the train station to Jagalchi Fish Market. This area, referred to as **Jung-gu**, is dripping with character but rather run-down. Head across the main road from Busan train station and you'll come to **Shanghai Street**, a pedestrianized "Chinatown" road filled with restaurants, and marked with the oriental gates you'll find in all such areas. This joins **Texas Street**, which has lots of sleazy bars and some shops selling gold and/or clothing featuring eagles, wolves, tigers and other fierce animals. This area rivals Haeundae for the title of most cosmopolitan part of the city, though it has an

4

entirely different air: whereas Haeundae draws in beach bums and the convention crowd, here you may find yourself rubbing shoulders with Russian sailors, American soldiers, Filipino restaurateurs and lost tourists, and it makes a great place to people-watch.

Busan Modern History Museum

부산 근대 역사관 • Daily 9am–6pm • Free • Ⓦ modern.busan.go.kr • Jungang subway (line 1)

A relative newcomer to the city's roster of sights is the **Busan Modern History Museum**, set inside a building that dates back to the Japanese colonial period. Attractive on the outside, its innards are interesting too, charting the more recent episodes of Busan's history, including the opening of its port (with a recreated shopping street from the time), the havoc caused during wartime, and the effects of the economic boom.

Busan Tower

부산 타워 • Daily 10am–11pm • W8000 • Nampo subway (line 1)

Rising over Nampodong is **Busan Tower**, a long-standing city landmark affording **excellent views** of the city's boat-filled surroundings. The tower is the crowning glory of **Yongdusan Park** (용두산 공원), a popular area for walkers, though in all honesty the top of the park is already high enough for good views – take an early morning walk to

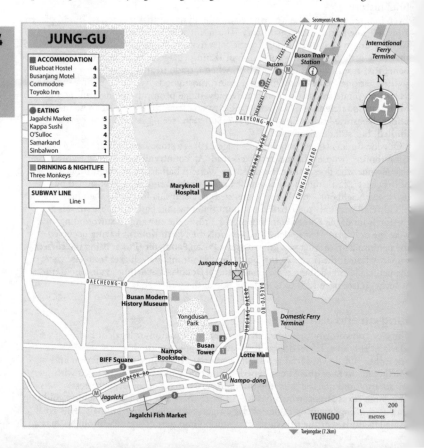

JUNG-GU

ACCOMMODATION
Blueboat Hostel	4
Busanjang Motel	3
Commodore	2
Toyoko Inn	1

EATING
Jagalchi Market	5
Kappa Sushi	3
O'Sulloc	4
Samarkand	2
Sinbalwon	1

DRINKING & NIGHTLIFE
| Three Monkeys | 1 |

SUBWAY LINE
——— Line 1

the top, buy some instant *ramyeon* from the convenience store or a coffee at the café, and watch the sun break through the mist.

Jagalchi Fish Market

자갈치 시장 • Daily 8am–10pm • Free • Jagalchi subway (line 1)

Every single person in Korea knows about **Jagalchi**, the largest and most popular **fish market** in the country. Wonderfully atmospheric, it's been used as a set in numerous movies and dramas. Mid-October is the best time to visit, when the **Jagalchi festival** offers a rare shot at hands-on fish preparation and a whole slew of freebies to munch. If you're just here on a regular day, you'll see that it's more a place in which to consume than simply somewhere to look around (see page 40 for some advice).

Gamcheon Culture Village

감천 문화마을 • Daily 24hr • Free • Toseong subway (line 1), then taxi (under W5000), walk (20min, mostly uphill) or local bus #1-1, #2 or #2-2

A residential area to the west of Jagalchi, **Gamcheon Culture Village** has recently become one of Busan's most popular visitor targets. It's often referred to as "**Korea's Santorini**", on account of the spectacular, colourful array of low-rise housing, cascading in tiers down an amphitheatre-shaped valley; if the weather's being cooperative, visit in the hours around sunset and sunrise, and you'll get some absolutely **magical views**. Plenty of little cafés and snack shacks have popped up along the horseshoe-shaped main road, but it's perhaps more pleasurable to poke around the various alleys above and below it, where you'll find plenty of galleries, wall murals, Instagram-famous dogs and the like.

4

Songdo beach

송도 해수욕장 • Jagalchi station (line 1), then bus #7, #26, #71 or #96, or taxi (around W5000) • Songdo Skywalk daily 6am–11pm • Free • Busan Air Cruise Mon–Thurs & Sun 9am–10pm, Fri & Sat 9am–11pm • W15,000 round-trip, or W20,000 for glass-bottomed "Crystal Cabins"

Little **Songdo beach** is a more intimate version of Haeundae, its big brother out east. This was actually Korea's first official tourist beach, having been designated as such way back in 1913, in the early years of Japanese occupation. The sands here are decent and the scenery picturesque; in addition, one can enjoy the **Songdo Skywalk**, a 365m-long path over the waves, or take a trip on the **Busan Air Cruise** cable car, which heads over the water to Annam Park, 1.6km to the south.

Yeongdo

영도 • Bus #88 from Seomyeon via the train station and ferry terminals, or #30 from Nampodong

Facing Jagalchi Fish Market in downtown Busan is **Yeongdo** – technically an island, though the double-bridge connection to downtown Busan makes it feel more like a peninsula. There's not much to see here, but a walk around **Taejongdae** (태종대), a pretty park at the far end of the island, is worthwhile; follow the crowds along the new paths leading to the lighthouse. From the main entrance, shuttle buses run to **Pebble beach**, a rocky outcrop at the very end of the island, but as roads are otherwise empty it makes an appealing walk, particularly in the evenings, when the sun sets over the mainland peninsula west of Yeongdo.

Nam-gu and around

남구

Nam-gu, a district splayed out between Busan station and Haeundae, holds a couple of sights relating to the city's fascinating history: the city's main **museum**, and a **cemetery** where many of the Allied forces who died in the Korean War were laid to rest. Also in the area are **Kyungsung University**, famed for its nightlife; and **Gwangalli beach**, a smaller, less interesting version of Haeundae.

Busan Museum

부산 박물관 • Daily 9am–8pm • Free • Daeyeon subway (line 2); bus #68 from Seomyeon, #139 from Haeundae or #134 from Busan station

A short walk south of Daeyeon subway station, **Busan Museum** charts the local area's history and its remains from the Neolithic era to the present day; exhibits include a **gilt-bronze crown** once worn by a Silla king, and a **standing Bodhisattva** of similar age and material. More recent history is generally presented in diorama form, with one of the more compelling displays showing Busan station in the 1920s; the building has, of course, changed somewhat. Unfortunately, the more modern part of the exhibit leaves a rather bad taste in the mouth, stemming from the sad inevitability of the museum's choice to focus on the Japanese occupation rather than the Korean War. There's just a single wall commemorating the tens of thousands of foreign troops who died here – a pattern repeated all over the country, in classrooms as well as museums, but particularly galling here since many of the fallen are lying just outside in the **UN Memorial Cemetery**.

The UN Memorial Cemetery

UN기념 공원 • Daily 9am–6pm • Free • Daeyeon subway (line 2); bus #68 from Seomyeon, #139 from Haeundae or #134 from Busan station

Adjacent to the museum grounds lies the **UN Memorial Cemetery**, where you'll find over two thousand dead soldiers from Britain, Turkey, Canada, Australia, the Netherlands, France, the USA, New Zealand, South Africa and Norway; many more, of course, were never found, and those from Belgium, Ethiopia, Colombia, Thailand, Greece, India and the Philippines, as well as the vast majority of Americans, were repatriated. A photographic exhibition on site provides a small, mute tribute, and the grounds are welcoming and pretty. At 2pm on every second Saturday, there are moving ceremonies featuring marching bands and rifle salutes.

Gwangalli beach

광안리 해수욕장 • Gwangan subway (line 2)

At 1.4km in length, **Gwangalli beach** is a shorter, marginally less popular version of Haeundae; locals still arrive here in droves, as do students from the nearby university. Its most famous feature is actually located off the coast – the Gwangan suspension bridge, usually referred to as the **Diamond Bridge**, which is certainly quite dazzling when the sun has gone down.

Haeundae and around

해운대

On the eastern side of Busan, and half an hour away from downtown by subway, is **Haeundae**, without a doubt the most popular **beach** in Korea. Whether it's the best or not is open to question – in the summer it draws in families, teens and bronzed beach bums by the bucketload, though at only 2km in length, space here is tighter than a pair of Speedos, while the sand gradually becomes a composite of cigarette butts, firework ash and other debris. Like it or not, it's an interesting place.

Haeundae is not just the name of the beach, but also the surrounding area, which attracts all sorts throughout the year. The **Busan Film Festival**, one of the biggest in Asia, rolls into town each October with a cast of directors, actors, wannabes and hangers-on; hungry Koreans come to chow down on **raw fish** and throw back a few bottles of *soju* from the comfort of a plastic chair; affluent expats, trendy locals and the international convention crowd populate the many luxury apartments and **five-star hotels**; and youngsters come from all over the country to spend a starry night on the beach. If you catch it at the right time, Haeundae can be quite magical.

The **beach** itself is good for swimming; tubes and boats are also available to rent, and the purchase of puny, multi-round fireworks is near compulsory. At the end of the beach, past a clutch of raw-fish stalls and behind the *Westin Chosun*, there's **Dongbaek**

Park, a pleasant place for a stroll, skate or bike ride. It's also possible to take pleasure-boat rides around the surrounding coast (see page 214).

Sea Life Busan Aquarium

시라이브 부산 아쿠아리움 • Mon–Thurs 10am–8pm, Fri–Sun 9am–10pm • W29,000 • ⓦ busanaquarium.com • Haeundae subway (line 2)

Sitting on the beach is the **Sea Life Busan Aquarium**, where three million litres of water host up to thirty thousand fish. Penguins and crocodiles are also on the complex, and there's a touch pool for the kids. There's an underwater tunnel for those who want to see fish from below, or you can pay an extra W5000 to ride a glass-bottomed boat and see them from above instead.

Busan Museum of Art

부산 시립 미술관 • Tues–Sun 10am–8pm • Free • ⓦ art.busan.go.kr • Museum of Art subway (line 2)

One subway stop away from Haeundae is the **Busan Museum of Art**, an excellent gallery that keeps its exhibitions fresh and interesting – no mean feat considering the fact that they're arrayed in umpteen halls across two main levels. Displays often seem to reference the sea, sometimes in a manner that feels a little forced.

Spa Land Centum City

스파랜드 센텀시티 • Daily 6am–midnight; no children under 12 allowed • Mon–Fri W15,000, Sat & Sun W18,000 • ⓦ shinsegae. com • Centum City subway (line 2)

Built on the site of Busan's former airport (many locals wish that the new one was half as convenient), **Centum City** is the city's latest urban mega-development, bankrolled

4

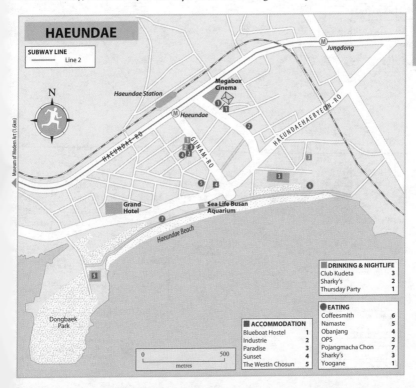

HAEUNDAE

SUBWAY LINE
Line 2

N

Jungdong

Megabox
Cinema

Haeundae Station

Ⓜ Haeundae

HAEUNDAE-RO

GUNAM-RO

HAEUNDAEHAEBYEON-RO

Museum of Modern Art (1.6km)

Grand
Hotel

Sea Life Busan
Aquarium

Haeundae Beach

Dongbaek
Park

0   500
metres

DRINKING & NIGHTLIFE
Club Kudeta	3
Sharky's	2
Thursday Party	1

EATING
Coffeesmith	6
Namaste	5
Obanjang	4
OPS	2
Pojangmacha Chon	7
Sharky's	3
Yoogane	1

ACCOMMODATION
Blueboat Hostel	1
Industrie	2
Paradise	3
Sunset	4
The Westin Chosun	5

by the good folks at Shinsegae Corporation. The mall areas are typically bland, but it's certainly worth swinging by the **Spa Land** section – the largest bathing facility in a country absolutely full of them. Size is not the only difference, since the whole place has been designed with a rare attention to detail – the outdoor footbaths are particularly lovely, though the themed steam rooms look a bit cheesy.

Haedong Yonggungsa

해동 용궁사 • Daily 5am–sunset • Free • Bus #181 (every 15min; W1300) from Haeundae subway (line 2)

Korea is absolutely full of delightful temples, but given the country's lengthy coastline, it's surprising how few of them are located next to the sea. One notable exception is **Haedong Yonggungsa**, located on the coast just east of Haeundae; first built in 1376, it was lovingly reconstructed in the 1970s, and the surrounding shore and the buildings themselves are undeniably photogenic.

Northern Busan

Most of the foreigners you'll see around Busan's **northern fringes** are international students, or teachers, from Pusan National University. However, there are a few tourist sights hereabouts – and, for once, they've nothing to do with water or the sea. Busan's foremost temple, **Beomeosa**, can be found here, as well as a splendid **fortress**.

BUSAN FESTIVALS

Busan hosts an incredible number of **festivals**, and many of them are a little bit comical in nature – you may care to visit one dedicated to anchovy-rubbing or egg-rolling, for example.

Busan International Film Festival ⓦ biff.kr. The most popular festival in town, BIFF takes place over a week or so each October. One of the biggest such events in Asia, it draws the cream of the continent's talent, and has recently expanded its scope to please non-mainstreamers too. Most of the action takes place around Nampodong and Haeundae, with the latter a great place to star-spot – you could even find yourself pitching ideas to a director over *soju*.

Busan Biennale (ⓦ busanbiennale.org). Interesting festival of contemporary art which takes place on even-numbered years, though in seemingly random months. It alternates with the less interesting Sea Art Festival, which is held in odd-numbered years.

Busan International Rock Festival (ⓦ bfo.or.kr). Busan's major music event takes place in early August on Dadaepo beach.

Polar Bear Swim Contest This competition sees participants splash through the cold Haeundae waters each January.

Mass-Media Cutting-Edge Marine Fireworks Festival. Worth mentioning for the name alone, this event sees things go bang over Gwangalli beach each November.

Beomeosa

범어사 • Daily 24hr • Free • ⓦ beomeo.kr • Beomeosa subway (line 1), then a 3km uphill walk or bus #90 (every 15min)

A half-hour subway ride to the north of central Busan is where you'll find one of the best sights in the city. The temple of **Beomeosa**, dating from 678, occupies a spectacular setting high above town and is a popular choice for travellers looking to **templestay** (see page 35). Despite the age of the complex, most of its buildings were built much later, the result of the occasional fire or destruction during the Japanese invasion. The first main gate, Iljumun, dates from 1781 and continues to carry its age well, the eaves radiating rich colour from its four pillars. Ascending past a patch of bamboo, you'll pass four bearded guardians to the main concourse, and Daeungjeon, the main hall and scene of fervent morning prayer. In the courtyard there's a three-storey stone pagoda dating from the ninth century.

However, the main appeal of the place lies not in its buildings, but in its **mountainous setting**. The forested slopes are impressive, and there's a surprising preponderance of deciduous trees for a Korean mountain area – a beautiful sight in the autumn. On the complex itself, smaller trees and shrubs lend their own spindly nuances to an enchanting scene.

Geumjeong Sanseong

금정산성 • Daily 9am–6pm • Oncheonjang subway (line 1), then bus #203 or cable car (starts within walking distance of station; ₩8000 return)

Looming above Beomeosa is **Geumjeong Sanseong**, a mountaintop fortress that's popular with hikers at weekends – sheer numbers mean that it's best to visit during the week. The fortress was built in the early eighteenth century, far too late to provide protection from the Japanese invasions of the 1590s, or the repeat attacks of the following century. Though it fell into disrepair, much of the wall still stands, as do the main gates. It's quite a walk up from Beomeosa, or a **cable car** can do most of the work for you.

ARRIVAL AND DEPARTURE   BUSAN

Busan's unwieldy size means that the best way to arrive largely depends on exactly where you want to go. In general, most prefer train to bus as the train station is right in the centre of the city, whereas the two main bus terminals are on the fringes.

By plane Gimhae International Airport lies in a flat estuary area around 15km west of the city centre. There's an extraordinary number of flights to Jeju (every 20min; 50min) and Seoul (every 30min; 55min), as well as services to Japan, Thailand, China, Vietnam, Taiwan, the Philippines and Cambodia. The airport sits on a light-rail spur-line on the subway system, but the limousine buses are generally faster, especially if you want to get across the city to Haeundae. In addition, there are direct buses to the airport from most of the main cities in the Gyeongsang region.

By train Busan station forms the terminus of the Gyeongbu railway line, which starts in Seoul and hurtles through Daejeon and Daegu en route. The fantastic slow line from also finishes in Busan (Bujeon station, just north of the main station), just after it hits Sin-Haeundae station out east – this latter stop is fairly close to Haeundae beach.

Destinations (Busan station) Daegu (Dongdaegu station; every 10–20min; 50min); Daejeon (every 10–20min; 1hr 40min); Gyeongju (Singyeongju station; 1–2 hourly; 35min); Seoul (every 10–20min; 2hr 40min).

Destinations (Bujeon station) Andong (5 daily; 3hr 45min); Danyang (2 daily; 5hr); Gyeongju (15 daily; 1hr 30min); Seoul (Cheongnyangni station; 2 daily; 7hr 30min).

By bus Arriving in Busan by bus is not really recommended, unless you're heading somewhere specific near either of the two main terminals. The so-called "central terminal" is way

to the north (Nopodong subway, line 1), and is actually made up of two separate stations – one express and one intercity, with the latter often referred to as the Dongbu terminal. The Seobu terminal is way out west (Sasang subway, line 2).

Destinations (Central bus terminal) Andong (1–2 hourly; 3hr); Chuncheon (14 daily; 6hr); Daegu (3–4 hourly; 1hr 20min); Daejeon (2–3 hourly; 3hr); Gangneung (10 daily; 5hr); Gwangju (2–3 hourly; 3hr 40min); Gyeongju (2–3 hourly; 50min); Incheon (11 daily; 4hr 30min); Jeonju (12 daily; 3hr 20min); Jinju (1–2 hourly; 2hr); Pohang (every 10min; 1hr 30min); Seoul (2–3 hourly; 4hr 30min); Sokcho (12 daily; 7hr); Yeosu (13 daily; 3hr 20min).

Destinations (Seobu bus terminal) Gwangju (2–3 hourly; 3hr 30min); Jinju (2 hourly; 1hr 30min); Mokpo (7 daily; 5hr 40min); Ssanggyesa (3 daily; 2hr); Tongyeong (1–2 hourly; 2hr); Wando (5 daily; 6hr 40min).

By ferry The most spectacular way to arrive into Busan is by sea, though, sadly, domestic connections have been curtailed of late. The city has two ferry terminals (one international, one domestic), both near Jungangdong subway station in the centre of town, just minutes from each other by foot. All international ferries head to Japan (see page 28), with the Fukuoka connection especially popular with *hagwon* teachers on visa runs; there are other ferries to Shimonoseki. The only domestic connections are to Jeju Island (Mon, Wed & Fri 7pm; 12hr; from W48,500).

GETTING AROUND

By subway Busan's subway system now boasts four lines, with a light-rail spur heading to Gimhae airport. The city is divided into two sections (vaguely inner and outer); tickets cost W1300 for one section, W1500 for two. Given Busan's topography, rides can feel like they take forever – it's 21 stations from Nopodong (where the "central" bus terminal is) to Busan train station, and a full 31 to Haeundae beach.

By bus As with every Korean city, the bus system is comprehensive and convenient, but often incomprehensible for foreign travellers; fares start at W1300. The Busan City Tour (ⓦ citytourbusan.com) buses are also worth a mention; buses run along each of the two routes every 30min, and day-tickets cost W15,000.

By taxi Taxis start at W3000, but given Busan's size fares can stack up quickly – rides totalling W30,000 are not uncommon.

By boat Boats leave on the hour from Haeundae's tiny port (daily 8am–10pm; W22,000) for tours of the surrounding coastline; daytime boats go to the nearby island of Oryukdo and back, while night trips aim instead for the sparkly Gwangalli bridge.

Pre-paid cards Busan's own pre-paid travel cards – the Hanaro Card and Digital Busan Card – are available at subway stations and kiosks around the city, but Seoul's T-Money cards are also useable here.

INFORMATION

Tourist information For a city of such size, and with so many foreign visitors, Busan has a surprisingly poor network of information offices. The most useful one is in Busan train station (ⓣ 051 441 6565): you're unlikely to find any English-speakers at the offices in Haeundae and Seomyeon. Five-star hotels can come in very handy, but if you need some English-language information in a hurry,

it's best to call ⓣ 1330 (add an area code if using a mobile phone – Busan's is ⓣ 051).

Expat services The Busan Global Center (ⓣ 051 66 7900, ⓦ bfia.or.kr) near Yangjeong subway (line 1) can come in handy for expats living in Busan – they run Korean classes, host lectures, help with banking, offer counselling and more.

ACCOMMODATION

Busan has plenty of choice at the top end of the accommodation range. Most of the five-stars are in **Haeundae**, the beach district to the east of the centre; it's by far the most interesting place to stay, but the motels here can get expensive weekends and during summer, and cheaper places are disappearing. Elsewhere, there are cheap motels all over the city; if you want to go out at night you're best basing yourself in **Seomyeon** or around the **university** drinking areas (see page 218), whereas sightseers should consider heading for the cheap areas around the **train station** or **ferry terminal**. There are now a few **hostels** kicking around, while those who want to save even more cash can get a night's sleep for less than W10,000 in a **jjimjilbang** (see page 36); two of the most convenient are *Vesta*, east of the main hotel district in Haeundae, and *Nokju* in central Seomyeon.

JUNG-GU

★**Blueboat Hostel** 블루보트 호스텔 4F 10-4 Donggwangdong 2-ga ☎010 8511 9049, ⓦblueboat-hostel.com; Nampo subway (line 1); map p.208. Surprisingly elegant hostel choice in the Nampodong neighbourhood – snazzy lighting in the huge common area and even, in what may be a world hostel first, a "powder room" for the ladies. The dorm rooms are fine, but the twins are poky for the price; all rates get cut a bit out of season. They've another venue out near Haeundae (see page 215). Dorms W29,000, twins W73,000

Busanjang Motel 부산장 여관 32-1 Daecheong-ro 126-gil ☎051 245 1371; Nampo subway (line 1); map p.208. The pick of a dirt-cheap bunch in the appealingly rustic area near the ferry terminal, with acceptable en-suite rooms, a rambling layout, and a free trip back in time. On some online booking engines, though usually with a W5000 surcharge. W30,000

Commodore 코모도 호텔 151 Junggu-ro ☎051 466 9101; Busan station subway (line 1); map p.208. Visible from the port, this distinctive fusion of skyscraper and temple has acceptable rooms, and lies a short taxi ride from the main train station. The sliding windows are a nice feature, even more so given the views – Busan's crane-filled port on one side, and what passes for a Korean version of Naples on the other. However, many guests find the place as a whole a little overblown. W180,000

★**Toyoko Inn** 토요코 인 12 Jungangdae-ro 196-gil ☎051 466 1045, ⓦtoyoko-inn.com; Busan station subway (line 1); map p.208. Japan's biggest business hotel chain has a few branches in Busan, including this one, conveniently just a few steps from the train station. If you've stayed at a *Toyoko* before you'll know what to expect – small but perfectly clean rooms, near-total silence, free bathrobe and slippers and a decent breakfast... like a little trip to the Land of the Rising Sun. W70,000

HAEUNDAE

Blueboat Hostel 블루보트 호스텔 2F 13-4 Jungdong-ro ☎010 2990 9049, ⓦblueboat-hostel. com; Haeundae subway (line 2); map p.211. Almost as fancy as its namesake in Nampodong (see page 215), this calm hostel has a female-only floor, and a charming common area which doubles as a kitchen, coffee and breakfast space (the latter is included in the rates). Management are switched on, and the place is a short walk from the beach. Dorms W29,000

★**Industrie** 인더스트리 호텔 16 Gunam-ro 24-gil ☎051 742 4777, ⓦindustriehotel.com; Haeundae subway (line 2); map p.211. Motel prices in Haeundae often go through the roof, but amazingly this place is often about the same rate – quite a surprise, given the sleek, minimalist design hinted at by its name. The rooms themselves are a little more functional, but overall this place is great value, and you'll surely feel a purr of pride when returning to somewhere this stylish. W90,000

Paradise 파라다이스 호텔 296 Haebin-ro ☎051 749 2111, ⓦbusanparadisehotel.co.kr; Haeundae subway (line 2); map p.211. With widescreen TVs in the rooms, stylish lighting in the corridors and W8,000,000 suites, this perennial favourite has been carefully designed in a refreshingly modern style. It's a busy place with all manner of bars and restaurants, and there's even a boutique mall; the pine-fringed outdoor pool stays open year-round and has views over the beach – an absolute must. Try to stay in the newer main building, and book online for the best deals. W400,000

Sunset 선셋 비지니스 호텔 46 Gunam-ro ☎051 730 9900, ⓦsunsethotel.co.kr; Haeundae subway (line 2); map p.211. Stylish, hotel-like rooms with good views from certain parts of the building; the only thing lacking is good service. Prices often drop below W100,000 during the week, especially in off-season, though the cheapest rooms are Korean-style floor-mattress affairs. W150,000

★**The Westin Chosun** 웨스틴 초선 호텔 61 Dongbaeng-ro ☎051 749 7428, ⓦwestin.com; Haeundae subway (line 2); map p.211. This Haeundae landmark provides great views of the beach, which comes to an abrupt end here. Though perfectly acceptable, rooms are surprisingly drab compared with the sleek lobby area, which includes an oh-so-trendy beach-facing bar, as well as an Irish "pub" that pulls a mean Guinness. Reserve through the website for the cheapest deals. W390,000

SEOMYEON

Lotte 롯데 호텔 772 Gayadae-ro ☎051 810 1000, ⓦlottehotelbusan.com; Seomyeon subway (lines 1 & 2); map p.212. Located in trendy Seomyeon, the small-but-stylish rooms and mall-like atmosphere found here are typical of the chain, which caters almost exclusively to shopaholics from Korea and other East Asian countries. The place is huge – as is the attached shopping mall. W545,000

★**Travelight Hostel** 트래블라이트 호스텔 7F 52 Seomyeon-ro 68-gil ☎010 9428 7281, ⓦtravelight.

co.kr; Seomyeon subway (lines 1 & 2); map p.212. The best of Seomyeon's many hostel choices, and certainly worth considering for those travelling as a pair, since the private rooms (all en suite) are very affordable. Dorms,

doubles and twins alike have been decorated with wooden flourishes, and a decent breakfast is included in the rates. Dorms W24,000, doubles W58,000

EATING

Busan's cosmopolitan nature is reflected in its culinary options. One of the most interesting eating areas is opposite the train station – no five-star paradise, but rather a motley crew of snack bars catering to sailors and assorted night-crawlers. Here, "**Shanghai Street**" provides a wealth of similar **Chinese** restaurants, before merging effortlessly into "**Texas Street**", home to a lower-key choice of outlets. The area running from the station to Jagalchi Fish Market is uninspired, though Korean staples are easy to track down, while the student areas (see "Nightlife", page 217) are predictably cheap – take your pick from innumerable **meat houses** or *izakaya*-style **Japanese** restaurant-bars. If you're looking for something a little classier, head to one of the five-star hotels around **Haeundae** beach.

RESTAURANTS

JUNG-GU

★**Jagalchi Market** 자갈치 시장 Nampodong; Jagalchi subway (line 1); map p.208. One of Busan's foremost attractions (see page 209), this huge market can be utterly confusing for the average non-Korean (see page 40 for some advice on local seafood). Many of the outlets in the large indoor market have picture menus, or you could simple point at what you fancy (figure on at least W35,000 per head for a mixed platter). Easier on brain, palate and wallet are the fried slabs of tuna (참치; *chamchi*) served at the outdoor stalls (W5000). Daily 8am–10pm.

Kappa Sushi 갓파 스시 20 BIFF Square-ro ☎051 343 4377; Nampo subway (line 1); map p.208. Jagalchi can be intimidating for first-timers, who may prefer the comforting familiarity of Japanese-style sushi. This revolving-sushi place is pretty good; although the quality isn't stellar (it never is at such places), prices are low (from W1800 a plate), with their lunch buffets (W18,800) particularly good value if you plan on eating a lot. Daily 11.30am–10pm.

Samarkand 사마르칸트 37 Shanghai Street ☎051 465 4734; Busan station subway (line 1); map p.208. Very luridly decorated, but the pick of the train station area's Russian restaurants, serving tasty dishes such as borshch (W6000) and *pilmeny* dumplings (W8000), as well as grilled meat meals (W10,000 and up), some of which are Uzbek in nature, just like the owners (and, of course, the restaurant's name). As with most Russian restaurants, order without adding a salad, and they'll think you're bonkers. Daily 9am–11pm.

★**Sinbalwon** 신발원 62 Shanghai Street ☎051 467 0177; Busan station subway (line 1); map p.208. Of the Chinese restaurants on "Shanghai Street", this is one of the smallest, but certainly the most distinctive. Long queues form for their *xiaolongbao* soup-dumplings (W5000 a portion), which are whipped up at lightning speed by a team of Chinese ladies, in a manner similar to *Din Tai Fung* – and they're not far behind the world-renowned Taiwanese chain in terms of quality, either. Also consider

the fried dough-sticks and hot soybean milk (W3000 for both); unlike in Beijing or Taipei, the sticks are chopped and served inside the milk, which is not exactly traditional but arguably tastes even better. Daily 11.30am–7.30pm.

HAEUNDAE

★**Namaste** 나마스테 7 Haeundaehaebyeon-ro 265-gil ☎051 746 1946; Haeundae subway (line 2); map p.211. Underground restaurant serving delectable Indian food. All of the main curry styles are on the menu (W15,000 or so); the tandoori dishes are particularly recommended, as is the rare chance to try ginseng lassi. Daily noon–midnight.

Obanjang 오반장 20 Gunam-ro 24-gil ☎051 747 8085; Haeundae subway (line 2); map p.211. The most popular meat-joint on the strip, at the time of writing – especially the fairy-light-studded outdoor section. Meat portions cost around W9500 but are a little small, so you may have to order more than one per head. Daily noon–1am.

Pojangmacha Chon 포장마차촌 Udong; Haeundae subway (line 2); map p.211. A quintessential Korean dining experience – raw fish and assorted seafood served up by an equally salty *ajumma*. Look for the tarpaulin-covered stands sheltering tanks of fish, and prepare your stomach – some of your prey may still be moving. Happily, all stalls now have English-language menus; most things cost W20,000 per portion. Daily 6pm–midnight.

Sharky's 샤키스 1305 Udong ☎010 6533 2959 ⊛sharkysbusan.com; Haeundae subway (line 2); map p.211. This place is primarily a bar (see page 217), but the great food on offer may drag you back the morning after – tempting hangover-busters include spic chimichangas (W14,000) and a range of burgers (from W14,000). Mon–Thurs 5–11pm, Fri & Sat noon–1am Sun noon–11pm.

Yoogane 유가네 11-1 Jungdong 1-ro ☎051 74 9912; Haeundae sunway (line 2); map p.211. Exceller chain restaurant serving rounds of succulent barbecue chicken (닭갈비; *dak-galbi*). Staff will do the necessa chopping and mixing on your table – meat and fried rice are yours from around W5500 per head, and unlike most places that serve such food, single diners are welcome. There are branches around the city, including ones in Seomyeon and Nampo-dong. Daily 11am–midnight.

SEOMYEON

Toh Lim 터림 43F Lotte Hotel, 772 Gayadae-ro ☎051 810 6340; Seomyeon subway (lines 1 & 2); map p.212. The top floor of the *Lotte* has the usual five-star-hotel medley of Japanese, Chinese and Korean restaurants, but best for decor and price is this Chinese one, where you can score basic rice and noodle dishes for around W20,000. Otherwise the sky's the limit on their vast menu, and the views are absolutely stunning. Daily noon–3pm & 6–10pm.

Ramen Truck 서면 라멘 트럭 80-17 Jungang-daero 680-gil ☎010 9922 9313; Seomyeon subway (lines 1 & 2); map p.212. First of all, good luck finding this small place (note: not actually a truck), squeezed into a small alley away from the Seomyeon main drags. It's worth persevering, though, for excellent ramen – just W7000 for a great bowl of the good stuff, or W8000 for a spicy one. Daily noon–3pm & 5–11pm.

CAFÉS, TEAROOMS AND DESSERTS

JUNG-GU

O'Sulloc 오설록 70 Gwangbongno ☎051 246 5285; Nampo subway (line 1); map p.208. Korea's green-tea phenomenon shows no sights of abating, and this Jeju Island tea company (see page 324) has a café-like tearoom in central Busan. Most people aren't here for the tea but for the green-tea lattes, tiramisu and *patbingsu* (a dessert made with red bean and shaved ice). Daily 8am–10pm.

HAEUNDAE

Coffeesmith 24 Haeundaehaebyeon-ro 298-gil ☎051 731 1066; Haeundae subway (line 2); map p.211. Yes, it's a coffee chain, but with sweeping – almost tropical – beach views from the second level, who cares? The coffee's better than at most chains, too (from W4000). Daily 7am–midnight.

OPS 31 Jungdong 1-ro ☎051 747 6886; Haeundae subway (line 2); map p.211. Heralded local bakery chain with branches across the city. The one in Haeundae is perhaps the most conveniently located – don't leave without trying the delectable *pains au chocolats* (W2500). Daily 8am–11pm.

SEOMYEON

Byeolnan-ssi Hoddeok 별난씨 호떡 29 Gaya-daero 784-gil ☎051 783 8008; Seomyeon subway (lines 1 & 2); map p.212. Fried, sugar-filled pancakes known as *hoddeok* are available across the land, but their finest iteration – in which a clutch of seeds are poured into the thing too – originated here in Seomyeon. This truck is as good a place as any to try one of Korea's best desserts, yours for just W1000. Daily 11.30am–8pm.

4

DRINKING AND NIGHTLIFE

Busan has an excellent and varied **nightlife scene** – a single evening can see you sipping *soju* over raw fish at sunset, rubbing shoulders with Russian sailors near the train station, throwing back beer with students in one of the university areas, then dancing all night at a beachside hip-hop club. However, to avoid expensive taxi trips, it's a good idea to pick one area and stick with it (see page 218 for some advice).

JUNG-GU

Three Monkeys 원숭이 세마리 Gwanbok-ro ☎051 245 2160; Nampo subway (line 1); map p.208. Microbrewery named after the range of ales it sells – there are now actually four monkeys on offer for W7000 each, namely red, white and black, plus a "green" pilsner. Free nachos and garlic chips. Daily 5pm–2am.

HAEUNDAE

Club Kudeta 클럽 쿠데타 25 Haeundaehaebyeon-ro ☎1899 5605; Haeundae subway (line 2); map p.211. The owners describe this as a "bistro and beach" club – they do indeed offer good dining, as well as a wide spectrum of music including electro, house, funk and R&B. Entry W20,000 for men, W10,000 for women. Often closed off season. Fri–Sun 11pm–7am.

Sharky's 샤키스 1305 Udong ☎010 4038 2907; Haeundae subway (line 2); map p.211. This bar is perhaps better for its food (see page 216), but it has a range of craft beer and makes a pleasant place to be most nights. Mon–Thurs 5–11pm, Fri & Sat noon–1am, Sun noon–11pm.

Thursday Party 썰스데이 파티 22 Gunam-ro ☎051 744 6621; Haeundae subway (line 2); map p.211. You'll find branches of this Busanese bar chain all over the city; cheap beer and cocktails (some under W4000) and clever choices of location mean that most of them are busy every night. The Haeundae branches are fun places to be on weekends, this one in particular. Daily 3pm–2am.

SEOMYEON

★**Guri Bar** 구리빠 Bujeonno 66-gil; Seomyeon subway (lines 1 & 2); map p.212. You'll find bar-restaurants known as *pojangmacha* all over Korea – tarp-

---

BUSAN NIGHTLIFE: WHICH NEIGHBOURHOOD?

Busan's nightlife scene is spread in uneven clumps across various parts of the city – to avoid spending a small fortune on taxi fares, it's best to simply pick an area and hunker down for the night. The two main student areas – **Busan National University** to the north, and **Kyungsung University** west of Haeundae – are among the most interesting places to go out, and certainly the cheapest. Weekdays can be tame, but on weekends the partying goes on until the wee hours. The same can be said for the two beach areas – **Haeundae** and **Gwangalli** – which cater to a more upmarket crowd, and throw a couple of clubs and cocktail bars into the mix; there's also the option of buying some cans at a convenience store and drinking on the beach. Central Busan is markedly less interesting: **Seomyeon** has a few clubs, though these never seem to stick around for long, while the bars around **Busan station** tend to be populated with Russian working girls and men in the market for them.

---

covered shacks selling seafood and cheap booze. This one's been pimped up, and now functions as a weird little outdoor bar – grab a cocktail (W7000) and get chatting to whoever's sitting next to you. Daily 7pm–late.

OTHER AREAS

★**Basement** 베이스멘트 62 Busandaehak-ro; Pusan National University subway (line 1); map p.206. This underground lair has, for many a year, been by far the most popular bar in the Busan National University area. Drinks are cheap, staff are super friendly, and there are regular theme and live music nights. Tues–Sun 7pm–2am.

Vinyl Underground 바이늘 언더그라운드 Suyeongno 322-gil ☎010 9239 9792; Kyungsung University subway (line 2); map p.206. Vibrant, stylish, student-friendly bar which hosts occasional movie nights, live music and other events – look out for the Warholesque banana out front. Sat & Sun 8pm–late.

Yong Ggum 용꿈 19 Beomgok-ro ☎051 642 3355; Beomil subway (line 1); map p.206. A cab ride from the main train station, this is Busan's oddest place to eat or drink – it's set in a cave used for munitions storage during the war era. Head to the back and the air will become awfully clammy – the cave goes further, but you can't. You'll have to buy food to go with your *soju* (W4000) or *makgeolli* (W3000); cheapest is a portion of spicy fish soup (대구탕; W9000). Hard to find, but it's still worth it, at least once, for the atmosphere. Daily noon–10pm.

DIRECTORY

Cinemas Four large multiscreens stand almost eyeball-to-eyeball on BIFF Square in Nampodong. When the film festival rolls into town in October (see page 213) there are also showings at the big cinemas in Haeundae.

Embassies and consulates China, 25 Haeundae-ro 294-gil ☎051 743 7990; Japan, 18 Gogwan-ro ☎051 465 5101; Russia, 10F Korea Exchange Bank BD, 94 Jungang-daero ☎051 441 9904.

Hospitals Pusan National University Hospital, 179 Gudeok-ro (☎051 240 7000), is most likely to offer English-language help, or try the more central Maryknoll Hospital, 121 Junggu-ro (☎051 465 8801).

Post The largest post office is just south of Jungangdong subway station on the main road (Mon–Fri 9am–8pm, Sat 9am–6pm), but there are smaller branches in every city suburb.

Sport Despite being the country's second-largest city, Busan's sporting teams usually fail to make waves in their national leagues. Busan I'Park is the city's football team, and plays in red-and-white-quartered shirts at the Asiad Main Stadium (see map, p.000). The Lotte Giants are one of the best-known baseball teams in Korea, and you can catch them – and their noisy supporters – at the Sajik Baseball Stadium (see map, p.000).

Geojedo

거제도

Connected to the mainland by giant bridges, **GEOJEDO** is Korea's second-largest island; measuring 40km by 25km, it's a craggy paradox of stone and steel. Here can be found large tracks of forest and some of the most impressive **coastal scenery** in the land, but while the island is famed for its natural vistas, parts of it have been shattered by industry – around a third of the world's container ships are built here in the two mammoth **shipyards** that now define the island, and provide much of its employment. The island's biggest town and main travel hub is **Gohyeon** (고현), tucked in to the north and sheltered from the South Sea. Other sights include **Haegeumgang**, where a simply gorgeous rock formation – quite possibly the most beautiful on the whole Korean coast – rises from the sea just offshore, and **Oedo**, a tiny, flower-covered island that's incredibly popular with Korean tourists.

Prisoner of War Camp Museum

포로수용소 유적공원 • Daily 9am–5pm • W7000 • Within walking distance of Gohyeon bus terminal, but poorly signed – a taxi won't cost more than a few thousand won

During the Korean War, Geojedo was the base of one of the Allied forces' main **prisoner of war camps**, which kept Chinese and North Korean captives almost as far as possible from the wavering line of control. The largest of several such bases was in Gohyeon, where the freshly spruced-up **Prisoner of War Camp Museum** recreates part of the original camp. Despite being diorama-heavy, the open-air display is surprisingly diverting for a Korean historical exhibition, right from the introductory escalator-based greeting from Mao, MacArthur, Kim and their cardboard comrades. Simulated gunfire, explosions and revolutionary music crackle around the squat buildings and dirt tracks, much of which are cordoned off by barbed wire. There's little information in English, but keep an eye out for the video footage of what life was like in the camp.

Haegeumgang

해금강 • Bus from Tongyeong (8 daily; 1hr; W5700), or Gohyeon (every 30min; 1hr 30min; W2500)

The Geumgang Mountains in North Korea are rightly revered as the most beautiful on the peninsula, a Chinese painting come to life, where tree-fringed scoops of sculpted rock rise through the mist. Similar sights – far smaller, but infinitely more accessible – are on offer at **Haegeumgang** off the south coast of Geojedo (*hae* means sea), where the precipitous crags lift through the waters rather than the North Korean hinterland. Topped with a sprinkling of camellia and highly photogenic, Haegeumgang can also be seen from dry land – a network of trails web out from the nearby village of Galgot-ri (갈곶리), heading to a viewing point that's perfect for a picnic, but becomes yet more majestic under the light of the moon.

Oedo Botania

외도 보타니아 • Daily: March–Oct 8am–7pm, Nov–Feb 8.30am–5pm • W11,000 • Ferries (10 daily; 3hr round-trip including 1hr 30min on island; W17,000 on weekdays, W19,000 on weekends) run from Jangsuengpo, accessible by bus or taxi from Gohyeon

The brainchild of a couple of botanists from Seoul, the islet of **Oedo** (pronounced "way-dough", and now rechristened "Oedo Botania"), has been almost entirely covered with flowers, and is now one of the most popular sights in the country for **Korean tourists**, pulling in a couple of million each year. Though the flowers are beautiful, it's one of those experiences that appeals to Koreans far more than it does to foreign visitors, and the island's tight paths can get uncomfortably crowded – don't dare to go against the current. Also note that you're only allowed on the island for a specified time – your ticket will say which vessel you have to return on.

ARRIVAL AND DEPARTURE   GEOJEDO

bus Thanks to the mammoth bridges linking the island to Tongyeong and Busan, Geojedo is easily accessible by bus from many mainland destinations. Gohyeon has by far the best connections, including Busan (every 30min; 1hr 30min), Jinju (every 30min; 2hr 30min), and Tongyeong (every 30min; 30min).

4

Tongyeong

통영

Straddling the neck of the Geosong peninsula, affable **TONGYEONG** occupies a special place in Korean hearts as the base from which **Admiral Yi Sun-shin** orchestrated some of his greatest victories against the invading Japanese (see page 237). The town is now a laidback place concentrating as much on its present as its past, with enough diversions to keep visitors occupied for a day, after which you may care to head off to the emerald confetti of islands that surround it (see page 221). Tongyeong's four-sided **harbour** – known as Ganguan – forms the focal point of the city, and is where you'll be able to see, and taste, the city's pride and joy – **Chungmu gimbap** (see below). The **promenade** lining its western flank can be a relaxing place to drink on warm evenings.

Tongyeong's popularity with domestic tourists has ballooned of late – half of the harbour is occasionally walled off with tour buses parked bumper to bumper. The increase in visitor numbers is, quite simply, down to an increase in sights – recent years have seen the opening of a **cable car** ride, and Korea's first **luge** experience. In addition, the small hill rising from the north bank of the harbour has been rechristened **Dongpirang Village**, its maze of houses and tiny lanes given a new lease of life via the gift of colourful wall murals – very popular with domestic tourists, though in reality almost every Korean city now boasts such an area.

Sebyeonggwan

세병관 • Daily 9am–6pm • W3000

A steep five-minute walk from the harbour brings you to **Sebyeonggwan**, a huge single-floor house built in 1605 as the headquarters of the Admiralty, and one of the oldest wooden structures in the country. Its lack of walls, windows or doors makes it almost unrecognizable as a house, but in the summer the giant roof, balanced on top of fifty carved wooden columns, provides welcome shade for *gimbap*-munching tourists.

Nammangsan

남망산 • Sculpture park daily 24hr • Free

East of the harbour, the hill-mountain of Nammangsan is home to an excellent international **modern sculpture park** and a statue of Lee Sun-shin. The bearded Admiral Yi stands with his back to the art, fixing a patriotic gaze at the island-peppered scene of his victories.

Mireukdo

미륵도 • Cable car daily 9.30am–6pm • W10,000 return • Luge ride daily: 10am–6pm, though varies by day and season • W11,000, including chairlift ride to top of track • Bus #141 from Tongyeong bus terminal, or around W10,000 by taxi

---

TONGYEONG TREATS

It would be a pity to leave Tongyeong without trying the city's famed **Chungmu gimbap** (충무 김밥). These are small rice rolls with radish *kimchi* and chillied squid, and though available in specialist *gimbap* restaurants across the land they taste infinitely better here – you'll find plenty of tiny outlets on the western side of the harbour. These days, far more visitors are here for "honey balls" (꿀빵; *gulbbang*); you'll find plenty of places selling them by the box on the northern side of the harbour. Lastly, try to hunt down a bottle of **Dosan** (도산), the delicious local *makgeolli* (rice wine), from any convenience store – best enjoyed by the harbour, on a picnic mat.

ISLANDS OF THE SOUTH SEA

An almost innumerable number of islands radiate out into the South Sea like emerald stepping stones. Much of this area is protected as the **Hallyeo Haesang National Park** (한려 해상 국립 공원) and, as do other island groups around the country, it offers a look into the heart of traditional Korean life. Here ports and villages have changed little for generations, and remain places inextricably connected to their surrounding waters, where the busy urban realities of modern Korea are little more than memory.

Mainland Tongyeong is the area's transport hub, and from here you can cross to dozens of islands by ferry. **Mireukdo** (미륵도) is immediately opposite the ferry terminal, but is built up and a little too industrial, and in any case connected to Tongyeong by bridge. Just 20km to the west of Tongyeong, the twin-peaked island of **Saryangdo** (사량도) is far more serene, and popular with young travellers in the summer on account of some good beaches; at these times, many choose to camp under the stars, but there are *minbak* available. **Hansando** (한산도) is even closer to Tongyeong, and was once home to Admiral Yi's main naval base; nowadays it's best known for **Jeseungdang**, a large shrine. Just off its northeastern flank is the relaxed island of **Bijindo** (비진도), whose long, east-facing beach is a wonderful place to watch the sunrise over a smattering of small islets. Further afield, **Yeonhwado** (연화도) is home to a remote temple, as well as the *Yongmeori* – needles of rock protruding from the eastern cape. These are just a few possibilities – allow yourself a few days, armed with a map of the area, and forget about the mainland for a while. Many of the islands have simple *minbak* accommodation, but as banking facilities are rare (you can try at some convenience store ATMs), it's wise to bring the necessary funds along from the mainland.

4

Just across the bridge from central Tongyeong, the island of **Mireukdo** is host to Korea's longest **cable car** ride, stretching almost 2km from its base to the peak of Mireuksan; from here there are utterly stupendous views of an island-splattered sea. In the same area you'll find Korea's first **luge** ride – essentially a downhill go-kart track, and nothing at all like the rather insane Winter Olympics event, it's pretty good fun.

ARRIVAL AND DEPARTURE

TONGYEONG

By ferry Tongyeong is a local ferry hub, with regular services heading to the surrounding islands in all seasons (see page 221). Most popular are trips to the twin peaks of Saryangdo (8 daily; 40min), and to Jeseungdang port on Hansangdo (hourly; 30min).

By bus The bus station, inconveniently hidden in the northern suburbs, offers regular services to most cities in Korea. Most city buses (30min; W1300) head into town from a stop immediately outside – ask if they're going to

Jungang Market (중앙시장; *jungang-shijang*), which is right on the harbour. Alternatively, it'll be just over W10,000 by taxi.

Destinations Busan (every 30min; 1hr 30min); Daegu (every 30min; 2hr 40min); Daejeon (hourly; 2hr 40min); Geojedo (every 30min; 30min); Gwangju (3 daily; 2hr 30min); Haegeumgang (2 daily; 1hr 30min); Jinju (every 30min; 1hr 15min); Seoul (1–2 hourly; 4hr 30min).

ACCOMMODATION AND EATING

There's **accommodation** all over the city, but by far the most pleasant place to stay is the harbour, where there's a clutch of cheap motels and *yeogwan*, as well as an acceptable *jjimjilbang*. For **food**, there are a few local specialities to get your teeth around (see page 220).

Ddungbo Halmae Gimbapjip 뚱보할매 김밥집 33 Tongyeonghaean-ro ☎ 055 645 2619. The town's best restaurant for *Chungmu gimbap* (see page 220), according to a straw poll of in-the-know locals. It'll cost you a mere W5000 for the town speciality. Daily 6am–10pm.

Friends of Loft 둥섬의 다락방 친구들 15-10 Hangnam 2-gil ☎ 010 5496 7977. Decent hostel option, located just a three-minute walk from the harbour. Rooms

are nothing special, but staff are cheery, and breakfast is included in the rates. Dorms **W20,000**

Napoli Motel 나폴리 모텔 355 Tongyeonghaean-ro ☎ 055 646 0202. Standing out like a sore thumb over the harbour, this motel is one of the tallest buildings around, and a little overpriced, but nice enough. It's attached to a café boasting good views out over the harbour – great for breakfast. **W60,000**

Jinju

진주

A small city typical of Korea's southern coast, **JINJU** is worth dropping into on account of its superb **fortress** alone. This was the scene of one of the most famous suicides in Korean history (see page 223), but such dark days are behind Jinju, and today you can walk for hours along pretty paths, gaze over the river from traditional pavilions and pop into the odd temple.

The beauty of Jinju is that all you need is within easy walking distance – the fortress is close to the intercity bus terminal, and surrounded by places to stay and eat. Unlike most towns in the region, the city is famed for its food, and a clutch of excellent **eel restaurants** can be found near the fortress. Jinju even has its own take on *bibimbap* – a popular dish across the nation, but prepared here with consummate attention. The city also makes a good base for nearby national park of **Jirisan** (see page 225), one of the most popular in the country.

Jinjuseong

진주성 • Daily 9am–10pm • W2000; free after 6pm

The focal point of the city, and its best sight by far, is the walled-off riverside fortress of **Jinjuseong**, which can easily eat up hours of your time. Constructed in 1379 to protect the city from Japanese invasions, it did its job in 1592 during the first attacks of what was to be a prolonged war (see page 223). Just in from the entrance you'll find **Chokseongnu**, a beautiful pavilion facing the river; if you're lucky, you may find it full of elderly men dressed in white, chatting and playing *baduk*. From here, a network of pretty, tree-lined trails forms a spider-web across the complex, with something to see at every turn. One of the most impressive sights is little **Hoguksa**, a temple at the opposite end – small and unheralded, but highly atmospheric. The compact central square is surrounded by an immaculately balanced amphitheatre of palms, bamboo and other foliage, with this leafy cocktail especially pleasing when augmented by the drones and wooden clacks of morning prayer. There's also a large **museum** on site, which has been built in an unnecessarily modern style, at odds with its surroundings. However, it is good on history, with an inevitable focus on the 1592 Japanese invasions, several battles from which are depicted on folding screens.

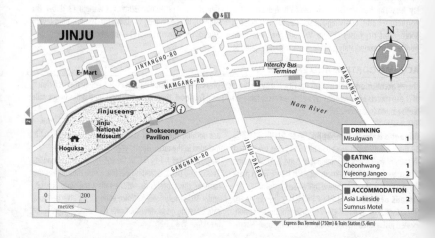

JINJU

Intercity Bus Terminal

E-Mart

JINYANGHO-RO

NAMGANG-RO

Nam River

NAMGANG-RO

Jinjuseong

Jinju National Museum

Chokseongnu Pavilion

Hoguksa

GANGNAM-RO

JINJU-DAERO

0   200
metres

DRINKING
Misulgwan   1

EATING
Cheonhwang   1
Yujeong Jangeo   2

ACCOMMODATION
Asia Lakeside   2
Sumnus Motel   1

Express Bus Terminal (750m) & Train Station (5.4km)

THE JAPANESE ATTACKS ON JINJU

Jinju's fortress received its first serious test in October of 1592, during the first attacks of what was to be a prolonged Japanese invasion. Like Admiral Yi along the coast in Yeosu (see page 235), **General Kim Si-min** held the fort despite being heavily outnumbered, with records claiming that 30,000 Japanese soldiers were seen off by just 3800 local troops. The following June, the Japanese returned in greater numbers, with up to 100,000 soldiers eager to obliterate the shame of their previous defeat, and it is estimated that 70,000 Koreans were killed during a week-long siege. Every tragedy needs a hero – or, in this case, a heroine – and this time a local girl named **Nongae**, one of several girls selected to "entertain" the Japanese top dogs after their victory, stepped into the breach. After using her charms to lure Japanese general Keyamura to what should have been a suspiciously lofty position on the riverside cliff, she jumped to her death, bringing the general down with her. A **festival** commemorating Nongae's patriotic valour takes place in the fortress each May, while General Kim's memory lives on in statue form at the centre of the fortress.

ARRIVAL AND DEPARTURE   JINJU

By plane Sacheon Airport is 20km away, and rather quiet at the best of times – the only flights are to Jeju (5 weekly; 45min) and Seoul (2 daily; 1hr).

By train The train line passing through Jinju sees precious few services – a pity, since the station's quite nice. One foreign travellers may be interested in is the long haul to Mokpo, which goes via Suncheon (for Jogyesan National Park), where you can also change for Yeosu. The scenic S-train (see page 240) links the city to Busan once a day. From the train station, it'll cost W7000 to the fortress area by taxi; a couple of bus routes head that way too.

Destinations Busan (1 daily; 1hr 50min); Mokpo (1 daily;

4hr 15min); Seoul (10 daily; 3hr 30min); Suncheon (5 daily; 55min).

By bus Most of Jinju's visitors arrive by bus. The express terminal is to the south of town, past the train station, but the intercity terminal is well located in the thick of things, just north of the river and within walking distance of the fortress. Destinations Busan (every 30min; 1hr 30min); Daegu (every 30min; 2hr); Daejeon (hourly; 2hr); Daewonsa (hourly; 1hr 10min); Gwangju (2 daily; 2hr 30min); Haeinsa (3 daily; 2hr 20min); Seoul (every 30min; 3hr 35min); Suncheon (15 daily; 1hr 30min); Tongyeong (every 30min; 1hr 30min); Yeosu (3 daily; 2hr 20min).

4

ACCOMMODATION

While there are **places to stay** all over the city, there's little point in basing yourself anywhere other than the strip running from the bus station to the fortress, which is dotted with a fair few motels and *yeogwan*.

Asia Lakeside 아시아 레이크사이드 호텔 133 Namgang-ro 1-gil ☎055 746 3734; map p.222. There are a few decent hotels in Jinju, but this is the only one with a decent location to match – it's set, as the name may suggest, by the lakeside west of the fortress. Rooms may not be carpeted, but they're large and decently appointed,

and breakfast is included in the rates. **W150,000**

Sumnus Motel 솜누스 모텔 53 Nongae-gil ☎055 748 7457; map p.222. Located facing the river, this is one of the nicest motels around. Rooms are all pretty colourful, and the best (sometimes available at no extra cost) feature computers, TVs and a tiny balcony. **W40,000**

EATING

The **Jeollanese** influence has clearly crept across the provincial border – meals are often served with a copious array of **side dishes**, and there's even a local version of that Jeonju favourite, the *bibimbap*, though surprisingly few Jinjuites will be able to point you to a restaurant serving this delectable dish. It's eel, instead, which is the local speciality – there was once a parade of near-identical restaurants serving it just downhill from the fortress entrance, but you'll have to walk a little further until the area's gentrification is complete.

Cheonhwang 천황 3 Chokseok-ro 207-gil ☎055 741 7646; map p.222. It takes a fair bit of hunting to find this super-cute shack-restaurant, one of the only places in town still serving Jinju *bibimbap* (W9000) – as it has done since 1927. With metal chair frames, blue cushioning and wooden tables, it's almost like eating lunch back at school.

Daily 9.30am–9pm.

Yujeong Jangeo 유정장어 2 Jinjuseong-ro ☎055 746 9235; map p.222. This spacious, attractive venue is the pick of the area's many eel restaurants. Choose between river (W27,000) or sea eel (W22,000), or just have a bowl of eel soup (W7000). Daily 11am–10pm.

JINJU FESTIVALS

The suicide of Nongae, who became a posthumous hero during the Japanese invasions (see page 223), is commemorated by an annual weekend festival at the end of May. The river comes alive during an annual **lantern festival** at the beginning of October; this usually coincides with one of Korea's only **bullfighting** events, where bulls fight each other until one of them flees.

DRINKING

Misulgwan 미술관 6 Jinjudae-ro 1079-gil ☎ 055 747 4449; map p.222. Quirky place for a drink, decorated like something out of a Miyazaki anime. They've plenty of varieties of cheap *soju* and *makgeolli*, though you'll need to buy food alongside – try one of their intriguing savoury pancakes, including a kimchi-pork one (W13,000), and something resembling a Swiss rosti (W12,500). Daily 7pm–3am.

Namhaedo

남해

An island dangling off Korea's southern coast, and tethered to the mainland by a couple of bridges, **Namhaedo** (or, more commonly, simply "Namhae") is, to Koreans, almost code for "the back of beyond". Tell city-dwelling locals that you're planning a weekend here, and they'll start to fret about your well-being – in reality, though, it's not too hard a place to visit, though getting around the island can be time-consuming if you're reliant on public transport.

Foreigners may not find Namhaedo the uninhabited paradise Koreans often claim it to be; however, it's a simple, down-to-earth kind of place, with a few good beaches, plenty of good seafood and an atmosphere that, though not quite the end of the world, is close enough to provide a good chill-out. You'll still see fields being ploughed by oxen here, and fishing villages clinging to the coast like barnacles, obdurately refusing to change.

The island's various sights are all over the place, but perhaps the best base is **Sangju beach**, way down to the southeast. This provides a point of attack for the island's stand-out sight, the temple-hermitage of **Boriam**.

Boriam

진주성 • Daily 24hr • Free • Take a Sangju-bound bus (W2300) or taxi (around W20,000) from Namhae-eup, then either walk up to the temple (1.5km, 45min), or take a shuttle bus (every 30min; W2000)

One of the most spectacularly located temples in all Korea, **Boriam** sits way, way up Geumsan mountain, surrounded by pinnacles of jagged rock. The view of the surrounding islands is absolutely wonderful, especially on a clear day when you've walked your way up. If the thought of that doesn't appeal, you can use one of the regular shuttle buses instead.

ARRIVAL AND GETTING AROUND   NAMHAEDO

By bus Most visitors to Namhaedo arrive by bus; these head to the bus terminal in the island's scruffy main town, Namhae-eup (남해읍). From here, various buses head around the island; most useful is the irregular service to Sangju beach (12 daily; 40min; W2500).
Destinations Busan (1–2 hourly; 2hr 30min); Jinju (1–2 hourly; 1hr 15min); Seoul (11 daily; 5hr 30min); Suncheon (4 daily; 1hr 30min).

ACCOMMODATION AND EATING

Accommodation can be expensive on Namhaedo, especially at weekends, when you should consider booking in advance.

Miga 미가 22 Sangju-ro ☎ 055 863 5679. Almost next door to the *Sangju Beach Motel*, this sit-on-the-floor joint is a terrific place to eat, with various fishy *bibimbap* option – try it with sea-squirt (*monggae*; W10,000), or just have

regular hoe-deop-bap (sashimi on rice; W12,000). Larger fish sets can be yours from W15,000, though with a two-person minimum. Daily 9am–9pm.
Sangju Beach Motel 상주 비치 모텔 24-3 Sangju-ro 1-gil ☎ 055 863 0807. Not the best place to stay in the area, but certainly the best value, especially if you get a room looking out over Sangju beach itself. All rooms have decent beds, and little tables on which to take a morning coffee (provided, but of the instant variety). <u>W40,000</u>

Jirisan National Park

지리산 국립공원 • Daily 24hr • Free, though small fees may be levied at or near certain entrances • ⓦ english.knps.or.kr

Korea's largest national park, **Jirisan**, pulls in hikers from all over the country, attracted by the dozen peaks measuring over 1000m in height, which include Cheonwangbong, the South Korean mainland's highest. It has also found fame for its **resident bear population**; a park camera spotted an Asiatic Black Bear wandering around in 2002, almost two decades after the last confirmed Korean sighting. The bear group was located and placed under protection, and continue to breed successfully. Although you're extremely unlikely to see them, it lends the park's various twists and turns an extra dash of excitement – nowhere else in Korea will you be fretting over the sound of a broken twig.

Jirisan is one of the only national parks in the country with an organized system of overnight **shelters** – there are few more atmospheric places to fall asleep in this corner of Korea. This makes **multi-day hikes** an exciting possibility; one popular route heads across the main spine of the park from east to west, and takes three days to walk (see page 225). It's impossible to detail all of the possible hikes and sights in the park, better instead to arm yourself with the **park map** (available at park entrances and nearby tourist offices for W1000) and find your own lofty piece of paradise.

The park actually sprawls across three provinces, with its most popular access point – the temple of **Hwa-eomsa** – on the west of the park, and actually located across the provincial border in Jeonnam. The eastern side of Jirisan, in Gyeongnam province, lacks such a focal point – there are dozens of entrances, but though none are particularly popular or easy to get to, this usually makes for a quieter visit

4

HIKING JIRISAN

Jirisan has literally hundreds of potential hiking iterations, which can make things a little confusing. Mercifully, a few are particularly popular. The biggest is the **26km-long trail** heading along the east–west main spine of the park. The hike connects **Nogodan** (1507m) in the west – best accessed from Hwa-eomsa (see page 227 for details) – and **Cheonwangbong** (1915m) in the east, the highest peak on the South Korean mainland and the second highest in the country. There are large peaks all the way along this central ridge, from which numerous picturesque valleys drop down to the fields and foothills below. The trail takes most people three days to walk, with a couple of overnight stays at the **shelters** sprinkled along the way; there are eight of these on the spine, costing from W5000 to W7000 per person, and all are marked on the map. The westernmost shelter, at **Nogodan**, is very often full due to its proximity to a bus stop, though you can't make reservations here; to guarantee a place at certain other shelters, reserve a berth in advance through Korea's national park website (ⓦ english.knps.or.kr). This can prove frustrating, as it's hard to tell where you will run out of daylight or energy on your hike, but reserving beds at Yeonhacheon and Seseok should give you enough leeway whether you're heading east or west.

Numerous valleys head up to the park's main spine, and most make for excellent day-hikes. One of the most popular runs from **Jungsan-ni** (중산리), a village connected to Jinju by bus, up to the principal peak of Cheonwangbong and back again, though many choose to continue north and emerge out of the park at Chuseong, down a valley lined with small waterfalls. Others start at the temples of Daewonsa and Ssanggyesa, which are a little far away from the spine for a day-trip, so you'd have to overnight at a shelter.

than you'd get at other national parks. One of the most popular trails is up from **Ssanggyesa** (쌍계사), a beautifully located temple at the south of the park. There's little of historical note here, bar a stone tablet apparently dating from 887, but the surroundings are delightful, particularly in the early morning before the sun has risen beyond Jirisan's muscular peaks; it may also be Korea's noisiest temple in terms of birdlife. **Daewonsa** (대원사) is another pretty temple, this one on the park's eastern fringe, and it also has trails leading up to the peaks.

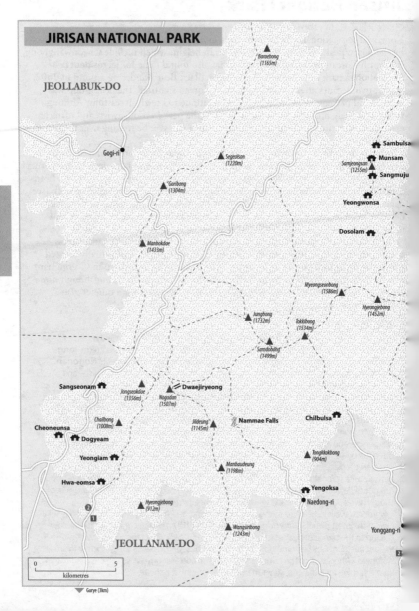

JIRISAN NATIONAL PARK

JEOLLABUK-DO

Baraebong (1165m)

Gogi-ri

Segeolsan (1220m)

Garibong (1304m)

Manbokdae (1433m)

Sambulsa
Munsam
Samjeongsan (1255m)
Sangmuju
Yeongwonsa

Dosolam

Myeongseonbong (1586m)
Hyeongjebong (1452m)

Jungbong (1732m)
Tokkibong (1534m)

Samdobong (1499m)

Sangseonam
Jongseokdae (1356m)
Nogodan (1507m)
Dwaejiryeong
Jildeung (1145m)
Nammae Falls
Chilbulsa

Chailbong (1008m)
Cheoneunsa
Dogyeam
Yeongiam
Manbaudeung (1198m)
Tongkkokbong (904m)

Hwa-eomsa
Yengoksa
Naedong-ri

Hyeongjebong (912m)

Yonggang-ri

Wangsiribong (1243m)

JEOLLANAM-DO

0   5
kilometres

Gurye (3km)

Hwa-eomsa

화엄사

Even if you're not up for a hike, the temple of **Hwa-eomsa**, locked in Jirisan's muscular embrace a short distance inside the park, is a highly worthy detour. An early morning visit is recommended, as you'll avoid any school groups and, hopefully, be able to see the sun rise over the peaks. A couple of hours' hike north of here is **Nogodan**, where you can begin the 26km-long multi-day hike across the park (see page 225).

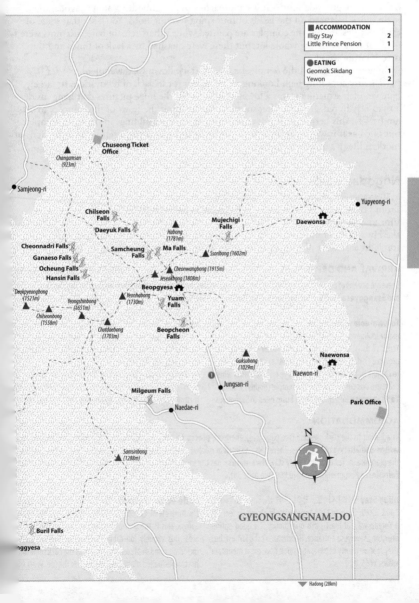

■ ACCOMMODATION	
Illigy Stay	2
Little Prince Pension	1

● EATING	
Geomok Sikdang	1
Yewon	2

Chuseong Ticket Office

Changamsan (923m)

Samjeong-ri

Yupyeong-ri

Chilseon Falls

Daeyuk Falls

Mujechigi Falls

Daewonsa

Habong (1781m)

Cheonnadri Falls

Samcheung Falls

Ma Falls

Ganaeso Falls

Ssaribong (1602m)

Ocheung Falls

Cheonwangbong (1915m)

Hansin Falls

Jeseokbong (1808m)

Beopgyesa

Deokpyeongbong (1521m)

Yeongshinbong (1651m)

Yeonhabong (1730m)

Yuam Falls

Chilseonbong (1558m)

Chotdaebong (1703m)

Beopcheon Falls

Guksubang (1029m)

Naewonsa

Naewon-ri

Milgeum Falls

Jungsan-ri

Naedae-ri

Park Office

N

Samsinbong (1288m)

GYEONGSANGNAM-DO

Buril Falls

...nggyesa

Hadong (28km)

4

The temple

Daily 7am–7.30pm • W3500, payable at park entrance • 1km walk from bus stop outside the park entrance

The **temple guardians** at the entrance to the temple of Hwa-eomsa are worth a look – the three regular bulgy-eyed fellows are joined by a serene, buck-toothed figure strumming an instrument with huge fingers. Inside the complex are two **pagodas**; the western one is the more interesting, carved in Silla times with Buddhist figures that remain visible to this day. Nearby is a **stone lantern** that is the largest such sculpture in Korea, an oversized beast emblazoned with cloud and lotus motifs, stretching over 6m from the ground. Subtler in its approach is the neighbouring stone pagoda, its main block balanced on the heads of four smug-looking lions. You'll see that some of the buildings around the complex are painted while others remain bare; attempts were made at repainting the whole lot, but these were quashed by a lack of funds and the deteriorating wood.

On your way around the temple, be sure to track down **Gakhwangjeon** (각황전), a particularly appealing hall. Looking all the better for its lack of renovation, its largely bare wooden structure forms a lovely contrast with the huge pictures that hang inside – a rhapsody in red. If you're after solitude, head behind the heart of the complex to **Gu-am** (구암); this hermitage is not as old or pretty as the buildings in the main complex, but filled as it is with vegetable plots, birdsong and mossy paths, and almost no signs of modern life, it's quite enchanting.

Nogodan peak

노고단 • Infrequent buses from Gurye (7 daily, 3.50am–5.40pm), via Hwa-eomsa

From Hwa-eomsa you can hike up to **Nogodan peak** (1507m; around 3hr), or save time and energy by taking a connecting bus most of the way up (you can catch it from the Hwa-eomsa mini-terminal). If you do take the bus, the remaining distance to the top is an easy walk of an hour or so – leave enough time if catching the last bus down.

ARRIVAL AND DEPARTURE   JIRISAN NATIONAL PARK

There are dozens of places to start an assault on the Jirisan peaks, but the temples of **Hwa-eomsa** (in the west of the park) and **Ssanggyesa** (in the south of the park) are usually the easiest to get to.

To Hwa-eomsa Direct buses run to Hwa-eomsa from the major Jeollanese cities of Gwangju (hourly; 1hr 40min) and Yeosu (7 daily; 2hr), as well as from Busan in Gyeongsang province (7 daily; 2hr 30min) From other cities, you'll have to change at the small town of Gurye (구례), from where there are bus connections to the temple (hourly; 15min).

To Ssangyesa Infrequent direct buses head to Ssanggyesa from Jinju, though these pass through Hadong (하동), a small town nearer the park that you may be able to get to directly from other cities. From Hadong there are buses to the temple (10 daily; 35min).

To Jungsan-ni Buses run to the village of Jungsan-ni from Jinju (hourly; 45min), but the park entrance is a frustratingly long (20min) uphill walk from the bus stop.

ACCOMMODATION

In addition to the park shelters (see page 225), there are **places to stay** outside both of the main park entrances, as well as a smattering of campsites. There's also a clutch of *minbak* at the **Jungsan** park entrance, though the isolation of the place makes for a rather lonely stay. **Hwa-eomsa** has the most extensive accommodation possibilities, and offers **templestay** programme for W40,000 (see page 35).

Illigy Stay 일리지 스테이 505 Hwagye-ro ☎010 7503 2270; map p.226. Appropriately alpine in feel (in a Korean way, at least), this guesthouse is a good option near the Ssangyesa entrance. Rooms aren't the largest, but they feature plenty of pine, and some have great mountain views. **W65,000**

Little Prince Pension 페티프랑스 펜션 521-Hwangjeon-ni ☎061 783 4700; map p.226. Near Hwa-eomsa, this is the best of a string of similar places in the area, this vaguely log-cabin-like pension has big rooms including some duplexes. The terrace at the back sometimes hosts *soju*-fuelled night-time feasts over the fire. **W60,00**

EATING

The **Ssanggyesa** entrance, bucolic and open-plan, has restaurants spread over a wide area. If you're on a multi-day hike you may be able to buy basic **provisions** in some park shelters, but while water is easier to find, it's advisable to bring your own food.

Geomok Sikdang 거목 식당 536 Jungsan-ni ☎055 972 1222; map p.226. If you're entering or exiting Jirisan via Jungsan-ni, track down this little place, which serves some pretty good *pajeon* pancakes (W10,000) – just the treat after a long hike. Daily 9am–8pm.

Yewon 예원 546 Hwangjeon-ni ☎061 782 9917; map p.226. The Hwa-eomsa area's best restaurant serves *sanchae jeongsik* (산채 정식), colossal, utterly delicious set meals of roots, shoots and mountain vegetables for just W13,000 (min two). Plenty of other hearty Korean meals on the menu, too, as well as cheap *dongdongju* rice beer (W3000). Daily 10am–8pm.

4

Jeolla

NAEJANGSAN NATIONAL PARK

5 Jeolla

If you're after top-notch food, craggy coastlines, vistas of undulating green fields and islands on which no foreigner has ever set foot, go no further. Jeju Island has its rock formations and palm trees, and Gangwon-do pulls in nature lovers by the truckload, but it's in the Jeolla provinces (전라) where you'll find the essence of Korea at its most potent – a somewhat ironic contention since the Jeollanese have long played the role of the renegade. Here, the national inferiority complex that many foreigners diagnose in the Korean psyche is compounded by a regional one: this is the most put-upon part of a much put-upon country. Although the differences between Jeolla and the rest of the country are being diluted year by year, they're still strong enough to help make it the most distinctive and absorbing part of the mainland.

The Korean coast dissolves into thousands of **islands**, the majority of which lie sprinkled like confetti in Jeollanese waters – many lie under the umbrella of the **Dadohae Haesang National Park**, not a single entity but a clutch of islands accessible from places like Yeosu (see page 238), Wando (see page 241) and Mokpo (see page 245). Some islands – such as Hongdo and Geomundo – are popular holiday resorts, while others lie in wave-smashed obscurity, their inhabitants hauling their living from the sea and preserving a lifestyle little changed in decades. The few foreign visitors who make it this far find that the best way to enjoy the area is to pick a ferry at random, and simply go with the flow.

Jeollanese cuisine is the envy of the nation – pride of place on the regional menu goes to *Jeonju bibimbap*, a local take on one of Korea's favourite dishes (see page 263). Jeolla's culinary reputation arises from its status as one of Korea's main food-producing areas, with shimmering emerald rice paddies vying for space in and around the national parks. The **Jeollanese people** themselves are also pretty special – fiercely proud of their homeland, with a devotion born of decades of social and economic repression. Speaking a dialect sometimes incomprehensible to other Koreans, they revel in their outsider status and make a credible claim to be the friendliest people in the country.

Most of the islands trace a protective arc around **Jeonnam** (전남), a province whose name translates as "South Jeolla". On the map, this region bears a strong resemblance to Greece, and the similarities don't end there; the region is littered with ports and a constellation of islands, their surrounding waters bursting with seafood. Low-rise buildings snake up from the shores to the hills, and some towns are seemingly populated entirely with salty old pensioners. **Yeosu** and **Mokpo** are relatively small, unhurried cities exuding a worn, brackish charm; it's worth breaking the journey between the two to see **Jogyesan**, a provincial park home to two gorgeous temples, and the tea plantation at **Boseong**. Further inland is

TAPSA

Highlights

1 Hyangiram A tiny hermitage hanging onto cliffs south of Yeosu, and the best place in the country in which to see in the New Year. See page 237

2 Mokpo This characterful seaside city is the best jumping-off point for excursions to the emerald isles of the West Sea. See page 242

3 Naejangsan National Park The circular mountain ridge within this national park looks stunning in autumn, and is the best place in the land to enjoy the season. See page 253

4 Byeonsanbando Look out across the sea from the peaks of this peninsular national park,

then descend to the coast at low tide to see some terrific cliff formations. See page 256

5 Jeonju Hanok Village There are all sorts of traditional sights and activities to pursue in this wonderful area of *hanok* housing. See page 258

6 Jeollanese food Jeollanese cuisine offers the best ingredients and more side dishes than you'll find elsewhere; it's best exemplified by Jeonju's take on *bibimbap*. See page 263

7 Tapsa This cute temple, nestling in between the "horse-ear" peaks of Maisan Provincial Park, is surrounded by gravity-defying towers of hand-stacked rock. See page 264

HIGHLIGHTS ARE MARKED ON THE MAP ON PAGE 234

5

the region's capital and largest city, **Gwangju**, a young, trendy metropolis with a reputation for art and political activism.

The same can be said for likeable **Jeonju**, capital of **Jeonbuk** (전북; "North Jeolla") province to the north and one of the most inviting cities in the land; its **hanok district** of traditional buildings is a particular highlight. Green and gorgeous, Jeonju is also home to four excellent **national parks**, where most of the province's visitors head. Just east of Jeonju, the arresting "horse-ear" mountains of **Maisan Provincial Park** accentuate the appeal of Tapsa, a glorious temple that sits in between its distinctive twin peaks.

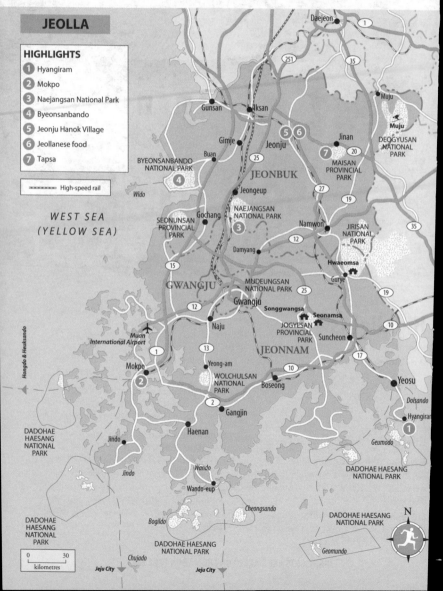

JEOLLA

HIGHLIGHTS

1. Hyangiram
2. Mokpo
3. Naejangsan National Park
4. Byeonsanbando
5. Jeonju Hanok Village
6. Jeollanese food
7. Tapsa

········ High-speed rail

WEST SEA (YELLOW SEA)

Brief history

Jeolla's gripe with the rest of the country is largely political. Despite its status as the **birthplace** of the Joseon dynasty that ruled Korea from 1392 until its annexation by the Japanese in 1910, most of the country's leaders since independence in 1945 have hailed from the northwest-to-southeast tangent of Seoul and the Gyeongsang provinces. Seeking to undermine their Jeollanese opposition, the central government deliberately withheld funding for the region, leaving its cities in relative decay while the country as a whole reaped the benefits of the "Economic Miracle". Political discord reached its nadir in 1980, when the city of Gwangju as the unfortunate location of a **massacre** that left hundreds of civilians dead (see page 249). National democratic reform was gradually fostered in the following years, culminating in the election of Jeolla native and eventual Nobel Peace Prize laureate **Kim Dae-jung**. Kim attempted to claw his home province's living standards up to scratch with a series of big-money projects, notably in the form of highway connections to the rest of the country, once so conspicuous by their absence. Despite these advances, with the exception of Gwangju and Jeonju, Jeolla's urban centres are still among the poorest places in Korea.

Yeosu and around

여수

Charming in an offbeat way, **YEOSU** is by far the most appealing city on Jeonnam's south coast, with more than enough here to eat up a whole day of sightseeing. It's beautifully set in a ring of emerald islands, so the wonderful views over the South Sea alone would justify a trip down the narrow peninsula Yeosu calls home. In 2012 the city hosted an international **Expo**, which brought in domestic tourists en masse, but the site has since morphed into the regular post-event white elephant.

Yeosu sprawls on for quite a distance, but for casual visitors the main area of interest is the "old" **downtown**, a surprisingly quiet area abutting the city's harbour. Here, many content themselves by wandering around the several **fish markets** and newly gentrified promenade – very popular with the city's youth (there's even a busking zone), it's a nice place to sample *samhap*, a local speciality meal (see page 238). However, there are a few interesting, unassuming sights within walking distance, including **Odongdo**, a bamboo-and-pine island popular with families, and a couple of replicas of Admiral Yi's famed **turtle ship**. Beyond the city limits are the black-sand beach of **Manseongni**, and **Hyangiram**, a magical hermitage at the end of the Yeosu peninsula.

Jinnamgwan

진남관 • Pavilion daily 9am–6pm • Free • Museum Tues–Sun 9am–6pm • Free

In the very centre of town, and just ten minutes' walk northeast of the ferry terminal, is **Jinnamgwan**, a pavilion once used as a guesthouse by the Korean navy. The site had previously been a command post of national hero Admiral Yi (see page 237), but a guesthouse was built here in 1599, a year after his death, and replaced by the current structure in 1718. At 54m long and 14m high it's the country's largest single-storey wooden structure. In front of the guesthouse is a **stone man** – initially one of a group of seven – that was used as a decoy in the 1592–98 Japanese invasions. Just below the pavilion is a small **museum** detailing the area's maritime fisticuffs, while crossing the footbridge over the main road will lead you to a quiet residential area with numerous specimens of **street art**.

5

Admiral Yi Square

이순신 광장 · Turtle ship daily 8am–8pm · Free

Just downhill from Jinnamgwan and abutting the port area is a statue of **Admiral Yi Sun Shin**, the town hero (and quite possibly the national one too – see page 237), who appears to be surfing one of the **turtle ships** for which he's famed; you'll be able to spot a larger replica just a few paces away. Such boats – small, rounded vessels with wooden dragon heads at the front – spearheaded the battles against the Japanese in the sixteenth century, and were so-called for their iron roofs covered with spiked metal, which made them tough to attack from the top. The interior of the ship can be prowled around, though it contains little bar a few dioramas and a modern-day regiment of mannequins.

Odongdo

오동도 · Daily 9am–6pm · Free; shuttle bus W800 · Cable car Daily 9am–9.30pm · W10,000/W13,000 one way/return · Pleasure cruises Approximately 1hr · W12,000 · Bus #333 from bus terminal or train station, or a short taxi ride from the city centre

Famed for its camellia trees, the small island of **Odongdo** is crisscrossed by a deliciously scented network of pine- and bamboo-lined paths, and has become a popular picnicking destination for local families. A 700m-long causeway connects it to the mainland, and if you don't feel like walking you can hop on the bus – resembling a train – for a small fee. The island's paths snake up to a lighthouse, the view from which gives clear rendition of Yeosu's contorted surroundings. In the summer, kids love to cool off in the fountain by the docks on the northern shore – the water show comes on every twenty minutes or so.

From the mainland side of the Odongdo bridge, you can take a lift up to the entrance of a new **cable car** system, the other side of which is over the waters on Dolsando island. In addition, a number of **boat tours** operate from Odongdo; most popular are the pleasure cruises across the harbour to Dolsan Bridge and back.

Expo Park

엑스포 공원 · Daily 10am–8pm, sometimes later in summer · Free · Sky Tower daily 10am–7pm · W2000 · Aqua Planet daily 10am–7pm · W25,000

You have to hand it to international Expos – they take years to prepare, are out-of-date by the time they come around and almost invariably become a waste of space

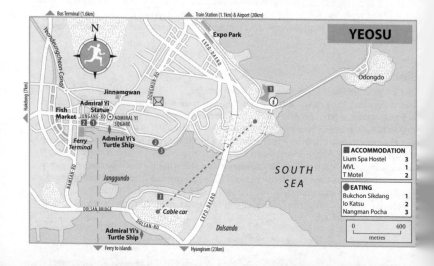

ADMIRAL YI, CONQUEROR OF THE SEAS

"…it seems, in truth, no exaggeration to assert that from first to last he never made a mistake, for his work was so complete under each variety of circumstances as to defy criticism."

Admiral George Alexander Ballard, The Influence of the Sea on the Political History of Japan

Were he not born during the Joseon dynasty, a period in which a nervous Korea largely shielded itself from the outside world, it is likely that **Admiral Yi Sun-shin** (이순신; 1545–98) would today be ranked alongside Napoleon and Horatio Nelson as one of the greatest generals of all time. A Korean national hero, you'll see his face on the W100 coin, and **statues** of the great man dot the country's shores. The two most pertinent are at Yeosu, where he was headquartered, and Tongyeong (then known as Chungmu; see page 220), the site of his most famous victory.

Yi Sun-shin was both a beneficiary and a victim of circumstance. A year after his first major posting as Naval Commander of Jeolla in 1591, there began a six-year wave of **Japanese invasions**. Although the Nipponese were setting their sights on an eventual assault on China, Korea had the misfortune to be in the way and loyal to the Chinese emperor, and 150,000 troops laid siege to the country. Admiral Yi achieved a string of well-orchestrated victories, spearheaded by his famed **turtle ships**, vessels topped with iron spikes that were adept at navigating the island-dotted waters with ease.

Despite his triumphs, the admiral fell victim to a Japanese spy and the workings of the Korean political system. A double agent persuaded a high-ranking Korean general that the Japanese would attack in a suspiciously treacherous area; seeing through the plan, Admiral Yi refused the general's orders, and as a result was stripped of his duties and sent to Seoul for torture. His successor, Won Gyeun, was far less successful, and within months had been killed by the Japanese after managing to lose the whole Korean fleet, bar twelve warships. Yi was hastily **reinstated**, and after hunting down the remaining ships managed to repel a Japanese armada ten times more numerous. Peppering the enemy's vessels with cannonballs and flaming arrows, Yi waited for the tide to change and rammed the tightly packed enemy ships into one another. Heroic to the last, Yi was killed by a stray bullet as the Japanese retreated from what was to be the final battle of the war, apparently using his final gasps to insist that his death be kept secret until victory had been assured.

once the circus leaves town. The zone created for **Expo 2012** is no exception, with few people generally present to watch the fountain shows put on through the day. The two redeeming features are the **Sky Tower**, from whose viewing deck you can gaze on Yeosu over a coffee; and **Aqua Planet**, a highly pleasing (once you've got over the ticket price) **aquarium** filled with all manner of marine life, including penguins, seals, otters, belugas and umpteen species of fish.

Hyangiram

향일암 • Daily pre-dawn to 8pm • W2000 • Bus #113 from central Yeosu, or #111 from central Yeosu, Yeosu station and Odongdo (all W1300; around 50min)

Clinging to the cliffs at the southeastern end of Dolsando is the magical hermitage of **Hyangiram**, an eastward-facing favourite of sunrise seekers and a popular place to ring in the New Year. Behind Hyangiram is a collection of angular boulders which – according to local monks – resembles an oriental folding screen, and is soaked with camellia blossom in the spring. The area outside the hermitage makes a lovely place to stay; there are plenty of motels and restaurants to choose from, though none really stand out.

ARRIVAL AND DEPARTURE

YEOSU AND AROUND

By plane The cute little airport lies around 20km to the north, and has flights to and from Seoul (4 daily; 55min) and Jeju Island (3 daily; 45min). Buses connect it with the city's main bus terminal.

5

ISLANDS AROUND YEOSU

South of Yeosu, the mainland soon melts into a host of **islands**, many of which lie under the protective umbrella of **Dadohae Haesang National Park** (다도해 해상 국립 공원). Many can be accessed from Yeosu's ferry terminal (see page 238), and as with Jeolla's other island archipelagos, these are best explored with no set plan; you'll find simple *minbak* accommodation on all islands. **Dolsando** (돌산도), connected to the mainland by road, is the most visited and most famed for **Hyangiram**, a hermitage dangling over the crashing seas (see page 237). Further south are **Geumodo** (금오도), a rural island fringed by rugged cliffs and rock faces, and **Geomundo** (거문도), far from Yeosu – and briefly occupied by Britain during the 1880s, during an ill-planned stab at colonizing Korea's southern coast – but now an increasingly popular holiday destination. From Geomundo you can take a tour boat around the assorted spires of rock that make up **Baekdo** (백도), a protected archipelago containing a number of impressive formations. There are daily **ferries** from Yeosu to both Geomundo (7.40am & 1pm; 2hr 30min; W36,600) and Geumodo (6.10am, 9.50am & 2.50pm; 1hr 25min; W18,900).

By train Trains arrive at Yeosu-Expo station, so named since it's adjacent to Expo Park. There are plenty of KTX services too, though note that they won't have been on high-speed tracks since the split at Iksan; additionally, if you want to get to or from Jinju or Gwangju by train, you'll have to change at Suncheon. It's possible to walk into the old town from the station, though taxis are cheap (around W5000).
Destinations Jeonju (1–2 hourly; 1hr 20min); Seoul (1–2 hourly; 3hr); Suncheon (1–2 hourly; 20min).
By bus The bus station is located frustratingly far to the north of town – just about walkable, though it's not fun,

so take one of the many bus routes (W1300), or hop into a cab (around W7000).
Destinations Busan (1–2 hourly; 3hr); Gwangju (1–2 hourly; 1hr 40min); Jeonju (9 daily; 3hr); Mokpo (1–3 hourly; 2hr 40min); Seoul (1–2 hourly; 4hr 20min).
By ferry Yeosu's ferry terminal has services to the islands making up Dadohae Haesang National Park (see page 238); the most popular trips are to Geomundo and Geumodo (see page 238). Ferries to Jeju (6 weekly; 5hr), have also restarted, after several years off the departure boards.

ACCOMMODATION

Yeosu's old **downtown** is the best place to stay, though **prices** are a cut above the national norm – motels here tend to charge W50,000 as a matter of course, though poke around and you'll find bare-bones places for W30,000.

Lium Spa Hostel 리움 스파 호스텔 72 Jinduhaean-gil 7 **☏**061 644 0306, **ⓦ**lium.co.kr; map p.236. Over on Dolsando island, this is something a bit different. Not a hostel at all, it's a pension of sorts (with kitchen facilities in all rooms); though aimed at small Korean groups, foreign couples may find the place to their liking – all rooms boast private spa tubs, set on balconies overlooking the city. **W85,000**
MVL 111 Odongdo-ro **☏**061 660 5800, **ⓦ**mvlhotel.com; map p.236. Built for the Expo, this is far and away

the fanciest place in central Yeosu – even the standard rooms are pretty plush. It's a big boy, so aim for as high a floor as possible – and, of course, for a sea view too. The fifth-floor sauna is quite gorgeous, though guests have to pay W18,000 for its use. **W190,000**
T Motel T모텔 5-13 Gyodongnam 1-gil 534 **☏**061 665 5757; map p.236. The best value of the downtown motels (though still a bit of a rip-off), this place has relatively swish rooms; a couple of bonus points, too, for the free can of beer waiting for you in the fridge. **W50,000**

EATING

Yeosu's **restaurants** are surprisingly poor by Jeolla standards. If you're feeling brave, try *samhap* (삼합), the local speciality food, a broiling mess of squid, scallops and pork belly served at various market-like areas around town; these are also the most atmospheric places to **drink** in the downtown area, which has basically no nightlife.

Bukchon Sikdang 북촌 식당 5-8 Gyodongnam 1-gil **☏**061 662 5260; map p.236. Sit-on-the-floor venue that's a real favourite with locals and domestic tourists, who come to gollop down raw tonguefish (서대회; W10,000), grilled cutlassfish (갈치구이; W10,000) or

spicy eel soup (장어탕; W9000). Daily 10am–10pm.
Io Katsu 이오 카츠 159 Yi Sun-shin Gwangjang-ro **☏**061 662 4201; map p.236. The best of the new places to have opened up by the waterfront, selling Japanese staples such as udon noodles and katsu (cutlet) curry-ric

for W8000. Daily 9am–10pm.
Nangman Pocha 낭만 포차 Yi Sun-shin Gwangjang-ro; map p.236. Not a restaurant, but a clutch of simple pojangmacha stands, most of them selling samhap

(W30,000 for a portion feeding two) and other fishy goodies. The one at #25 is especially recommended. Daily 4pm–midnight.

Jogyesan Provincial Park

조계산 국립 공원

Small but pretty, **Jogyesan Provincial Park** is flanked by two splendid temples, **Seonamsa** and **Songgwangsa**. If you get up early enough, it's possible to see both in a single day, taking either the four-hour hiking trail that runs between them, or one of the buses that heads the long way around the park. The park and its temples are accessible by bus from **Suncheon** (순천), an otherwise uninteresting city that's easy to get to by bus, and occasionally train, from elsewhere in the area.

Seonamsa

선암사 • Daily sunrise–sunset • W2000

Seonamsa, on the park's eastern side, is the closer temple of the two to Suncheon. On the way in from the ticket booth you'll pass **Seungsongyo**, an old rock bridge whose semicircular lower arch makes a full disc when reflected in the river below: slide down near the water to get the best view.

There has been a temple at Seonamsa since 861, but having fallen victim to fire several times, the present buildings are considerably more modern. Its **entrance gate** is ageing gracefully, though the dragon heads are a more recent addition – the originals can be found in the small museum inside. Notably, the temple eschews the usual four heavenly guardians at the entrance, relying instead on the surrounding mountains for protection – they look particularly imposing on a rainy day. The **main hall** in the central courtyard is also unconventional, with its blocked central entrance symbolically allowing only Buddhist knowledge through, and not even accessible to high-ranking monks – this is said to represent the egalitarian principles of the temple. The hall was apparently built without nails, and at the back contains a long coffin-like box which holds a large picture of the Buddha that was once unfurled during times of drought, to bring rain to the crops.

Songgwangsa

송광사 • Daily 9am–6pm • W3000 • ⊕ songgwangsa.org

To the west of the park is **Songgwangsa**, viewed by Koreans as one of the most important temples in the country, and one of the **"Three Jewels"** of Korean Buddhism – the others are Tongdosa (see page 201) and Haeinsa (see page 185). Large, well maintained and often full of devotees, it may disappoint those who've already appreciated the earthier delights of Seonamsa. The temple is accessed on a peculiar bridge-cum-pavilion, beyond which is **Seungbojeon**, a hall filled with 1250 individually sculpted figurines, the painstaking attention to detail echoed in the paintwork of the main hall; colourful and highly intricate patterns spread like a rash down the pillars, surrounding a trio of Buddha statues representing the past, present and future.

ARRIVAL AND DEPARTURE

JOGYESAN PROVINCIAL PARK

By train Suncheon is the closest train station; there are trains from here to Jeonju (1–2 hourly; 1hr 30min), Jinju (5 daily; 1hr 30min), and Yeosu (hourly; 35min).

By bus From central Suncheon, bus #1 runs to Seonamsa (hourly; 50min) and bus #111 to Songgwangsa (1–2

hourly; 1hr 20min); if travelling between the two, you'll save a lot of time by transferring at Seopyeong-maeul (서평마을), a small village where the bus routes split. Also note that there are occasional buses to Songgwangsa from Gwangju.

5

ACCOMMODATION AND EATING

There are low-key **accommodation** and **restaurant** facilities at both entrances to the park, with local *minbak* charging around W25,000 a night. It's more comfortable to overnight in Suncheon – head for the district of **Yeonhyangdong** (연향동), which has plenty of motels and restaurants.

Gilsang Sikdang 길상 식당 Seonamsa. This basic restaurant is a good pick; as in many Korean rural areas, *sanchae bibimbap* (산채 비빔밥; W8000) is a favoured dish, and is made with ingredients from the surrounding mountains. Daily 9am–8pm.

Boseong

보성

The town of **BOSEONG** is famed for the **tea plantations** that surround it; visitors flock here during warmer months to take pictures of the thousands of tea trees that line the slopes. They may not be as busy or as verdant as those in – for example – Sri Lanka or Laos, but they're still a magnificent sight, particularly when sepia-tinged on early summer evenings. **Green tea** (녹차; *nok-cha*) rode the crest of the "healthy living" wave that swept the country in the early 2000s, and by the Boseong fields you can imbibe the leaf in more ways than you could ever have imagined.

Daehan Dawon

대한 다원 • Daily: March–Oct 5am–8pm; Nov–Feb 8am–6pm • W4000 • Buses from outside Boseong train and bus stations (1–2 hourly; 15min), or W10,000 by taxi

Daehan Dawon is the area's main, and most scenic, tea plantation. Pluckers comb the well-manicured rows at all times of year, though spring (April–June) is the main harvest season, and if you're lucky you may be able to see the day's take being processed in the on-site factory. A couple of on-site **restaurants** and **cafés** serve up green tea-centric meals and drinks – if you've never tried a *nok-cha* latte, you'll never get a better opportunity (though, admittedly, it's on sale at pretty much every café up to the North Korean border).

ARRIVAL AND DEPARTURE

BOSEONG

By train Boseong's little station hosts arrivals from Gwangju (Songjeong station; 3 daily; 1hr 20min), Mokpo (1 daily; 2hr 20min) and Suncheon (4 daily; 1hr). There's also the scenic, gaudily decorated S-train, which comes from Busan in the morning (3hr 40min) via Suncheon, then heads back that way in the evening.

By bus Boseong's small bus terminal has surprisingly regular connections to nearby destinations, including Gwangju (1–2 hourly; 1hr 30min); Mokpo (1–2 hourly; 1hr 45min) and Yeosu (hourly; 2hr). Note that there are also direct buses from Gwangju to the Daehan Dawon tea fields (9 daily).

EATING

Hebeunddeul Sikdang 헤븐뜰 식당 Daehan Dawon ☎ 061 853 4900. Just before the ticket gate to the tea fields, this restaurant is better value than those inside the compound. More or less everything has green tea as a component ingredient, including *bibimbap* (W9000) and *samgyeopsal* (pork belly; W12,000, minimum two servings). Daily 7am–7pm.

Wando

완도

Dangling off Korea's southwestern tip is a motley bunch of more than a hundred islands. The hub of this group is **WANDO**, also the most popular owing to its connections to the mainland by bus and Jeju Island by sea. It's barely worth coming

ISLANDS AROUND WANDO

There are so many islands around Wando that you'll be quite spoiled for choice, with even the tiniest inhabited ones served by ferry from Wando-eup; many form part of **Dadohae Haesang National Park** (다도해 해상 국립 공원). **Maps** of the islands are available from the ferry terminal, where almost all services depart, with a few leaving from a small pier just to the north. At the time of writing, **Cheongsando** (청산도) was the island most visited by local tourists, mainly due to the fact that it was the location of *Spring Waltz*, a popular drama series. Naturally, spring is the busiest time of year here – and quite beautiful, with the island's fields bursting with flowers. More beautiful is pine-clad **Bogildo** (보길도), a well-kept secret accessible via a ferry terminal on the west of Wando – free hourly shuttle-buses make the pretty twenty-minute journey from Wando-eup's bus terminal. In the centre of tadpole-shaped Bogildo is a lake, while the island's craggy tail, stretching east, has a couple of popular beaches.

here if you're not planning to take a ferry elsewhere, but Wando does have a few diversions in its own right, and a journey away from **Wando-eup** (완도읍), the main town, will give you a glimpse of Jeolla's pleasing rural underbelly. Regular buses run from Wando-eup to **Gugyedeung** (구계등), a small, rocky beach in the coastal village of Jeongdo-ri, and to **Cheonghaejin** (청해진), a stone park looking over a tiny islet which, despite its unassuming pastoral mix of farms and mud walls, was once important enough to send trade ships to China.

ARRIVAL AND INFORMATION

WANDO

By bus Wando-eup's petite-size bus terminal has buses to plenty of Jeolla destinations, including Gwangju (1–2 hourly; 2hr 40min) and Mokpo (every 50min; 2hr); there are also buses to Seoul (4 daily; 6hr).

By ferry The ferry terminal is a 15min walk from the bus station, and very easy to find – hit the seafront and follow it along to the right. There are three daily services to Jeju, though the price and duration of these journeys varies substantially (1hr 40min–5hr). There are also services to

several islands around Wando (see page 241), including Cheongsando (1 daily; 50min); ferries to Bogildo (11 daily; 40min) actually leave from the Hwaheungpo port, which is around W10,000 away by taxi, or a 20min bus ride.

Banks There are a few Nonghyeop Bank branches around town, and ATMs in the bus station and most convenience stores, though there are regular reports of all failing to work with foreign cards – it's prudent to bring as much money as you'll need.

ACCOMMODATION AND EATING

Most of the action in Wando-eup is centred around the bus station, but the area around the main ferry terminal makes a quieter and more pleasant **place to stay**. There are plenty of **restaurants** serving both raw and cooked food in the town centre, as well as a fish market next to the ferry terminal.

Jeonsama 전사마 197 Jangbogo-daero ☎061 555 0838. A simple place on the main road between the bus and ferry terminals, this restaurant is the target of most Korean visitors to Wando, thanks to multiple appearances on TV – they're all here for the superb *Jeonbuk bulgogi* (전북 불고기; W15,000, minimum two portions), a beef-and-abalone dish which tastes even better when *kimchi* is added to the already odd-sounding mix. Daily 9am–9pm.

Naju Yeoinsuk 나주 여인숙 4-1 Jangbogodaero

333-gil ☎061 554 3884. Very close to the ferry terminal in a building painted a fetching aquamarine, this *yeoinsuk* has the cheapest rooms around – all mats-on-the-floor affairs, though most of them are, surprisingly, en suite. <u>W20,000</u>

Tower Motel 타워 모텔 302-1 Jangbogodae-ro ☎061 554 4747. Relatively new motel near to the ferry terminal, boasting loudly decorated rooms – try to nab one with a view of the sea and the fish market (the smell from the latter, mercifully, doesn't reach the motel). <u>W40,000</u>

5 Mokpo and around

목포

If you've been travelling around Korea for a while, you may well notice that **MOKPO** is, to put it bluntly, a little different. This charmingly ramshackle city is not just the end of the road, but the end of the rail line, too; indeed, Mokpo gives the impression that it would happily be an island if it could. For decades, it was the hotbed of **opposition** support to the entities ruling Korea; for much of the 1970s and 1980s, central funding was deliberately cut in an attempt to marginalize the city, which was once among the most populous and powerful in the land. Much of the city remains run-down, and Mokpo is probably the **poorest** urban centre in the country.

Though it'll be a while before Mokpo's salty charms are eroded, things are changing, and after being starved of funding for decades, the balance is now being redressed. However, much of the initial glut of money was poorly spent – for instance, the province paid through the nose to join the Formula One circuit in 2010, though mismanagement and a lack of public interest saw the Korean Grand Prix dropped just four years into its thirteen-year contract. Still, there have been better-thought-out changes of late – witness the huge new **museums** out east, or the new town of **Hadang**, built on land reclaimed from the sea a little further on. There's also a permanent Christmas of neon lights festooned around the **city centre**, though they impart a sort of dreary melancholy to this dying area. However, Mokpo's main travel draw remains the same as it ever was – this is the jumping-off point for literally hundreds of **islands**, which start ganging up in the seas just to the west (see page 245). Heading inland in the other direction is Korea's smallest national park, **Wolchulsan** (see page 245), an easy day-trip from the city.

Downtown

The city's **downtown** area, spreading from the train station down to the ferry terminals, is a curious mix of the old and the new – here you'll find a slew of generations-old restaurants and guesthouses, together with some newer (though rather empty) shopping streets. Many

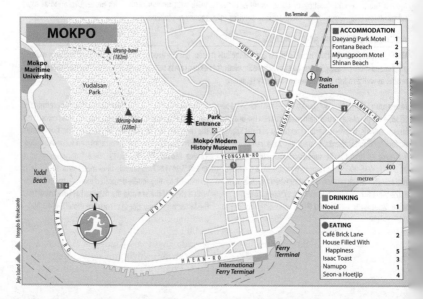

MOKPO

Ideung-bawi (182m)

Mokpo Maritime University

Yudalsan Park

Ideung-bawi (228m)

Park Entrance

Mokpo Modern History Museum

Yudal Beach

YUDAL-RO

YEONGSAN-RO

SUMUN-RO

Train Station

SAMHAK-RO

HAEAN-RO

Bus Terminal

Ferry Terminal

International Ferry Terminal

HAEAN-RO

Jeju Island ◀   Hongdo & Heuksando ◀

0   400
metres

ACCOMMODATION
Daeyang Park Motel	1
Fontana Beach	2
Myungpoom Motel	3
Shinan Beach	4

DRINKING
| Noeul | 1 |

EATING
Café Brick Lane	2
House Filled With Happiness	5
Isaac Toast	3
Namupo	1
Seon-a Hoetjip	4

of the latter have been pimped with decorative lighting, which looks pretty neat at night, if a little forlorn. Press on past the ferry terminals – or head clean across the mini-mountain of **Yudalsan** – and you'll get to **Yudal beach**, which isn't great for swimming or sand-lounging, but makes a pleasant place to sit and look at the surrounding ocean.

Yudalsan
유달산 • Daily 8am–6pm • Free

Many of the mind-boggling number of islands surrounding Mokpo are visible from the peaks of **Yudalsan**, a small hill-park within walking distance of the city centre and train station. It's a popular place, with troupes of hikers stomping their way up a maze of trails, past manicured gardens and a sculpture park, towards **Ildeung-bawi**, the park's main peak. After the slog to the top – a twenty-minute climb of 228m – you'll be rewarded with a **spectacular view**: a sea filled to the horizon with a swarm of emerald islands. Similar views can be had from Yudalsan's second-highest peak, **Ideung-bawi**, just along the ridge past a large, precariously balanced boulder.

Mokpo Modern History Museum
목포 자연사 박물관 • Tues–Sun 9am–6pm • W2000

Backing onto Yudalsan's foothills is the **Mokpo Modern History Museum**, housed in the former Japanese consulate. The building dates back to 1900 – made of red brick and with its wooden window frames painted baby-blue, it's probably the most beautiful in the city. The exhibits aren't as interesting as the architecture, but there are some fantastic photos of Mokpo in colonial times.

Hadang and around
하당

The city's "new" downtown is **Hadang**, an area around 6km east of the train station. There's little to see here, though there are a few decent hotels, and what passes for nightlife in Mokpo. One exception is the **Dancing Fountain** on the waterfront, which puts on a few twenty-minute-long shows each evening; the jets spurt up to 70m from a "floating" platform on the ocean, and the overall effect is pretty spectacular. A little west, and accessible from Hadang on a pleasing wooden walkway, are a cluster of museums.

Maritime Museum
해양 유물 전시관 • Tues–Fri 9am–6pm, Sat & Sun 9am–7pm • Free • Bus #15 from bus terminal or train station (W1350), but better approached by taxi (W5000 from the train station)

The most popular of Mokpo's cluster of modern museums is the **Maritime Museum**, around 3km east of the train station. Its prime exhibits are the remains of a ship sunk near Wando in the eleventh century – the oldest such find in the country. Preserved from looting by its sunken location, celadon bowls and other relics scavenged from the vessel are on display, alongside a mock-up of how the ship may have once looked. In an adjacent hall, there are two smaller wrecks from the Goryeo dynasty.

Natural History Museum
자연사 박물관 • Tues–Fri 9am–6pm, Sat & Sun 9am–7pm • W3000 • Bus #15 from bus terminal or train station (W1350), but better approached by taxi (W5000 from the train station)

Along the road from the Maritime Museum – and marginally more compelling – is the **Natural History Museum**, home to an artily arranged butterfly exhibit, as well as a collection of dinosaur skeletons that is sure to perk up any sleepy youngster. Accessible on the same ticket, the building next door contains rather more highbrow sights, including calligraphy and paintings from **Sochi**, a famed artist from the local area, and a nineteenth-century protégé of Chusa, one of the country's most revered calligraphers (see page 322).

5

Mokpo is not the easiest Korean city in which to get your bearings. The most logical way to arrive is by train, as the main station is in the centre of town, surrounded by shops, cafés and restaurants.

By plane The closest airport to Mokpo is Muan, 20km to the north; there are a few flights to Shanghai and the Philippines, though the only domestic services are to Jeju (1 daily; 50min).

By train The train station is the terminus of the Honam line, and receives plenty of services, including high-speed KTX ones – these still run on adapted lines from Gwangju, though some travel times given here will drop when the dedicated line is completed in 2018.
Destinations Boseong (1 daily; 2hr 20min); Daejeon (9 daily; 2hr 10min); Gwangju (Seongjeong station); 2–3 hourly; 40min); Jinju (1 daily; 4hr 15min); Seoul (Yongsan station; 1–2 hourly; 3hr 30min).

By bus Buses terminate some way to the north: taxis cost just W5000 to the centre, or there are several city bus routes (15min; W1350). The most useful of these is #1, which passes both the bus and the train stations on its way to the ferry terminal.
Destinations Boseong (1–2 hourly; 1hr 45min); Busan (9 daily; 4hr 20min); Gwangju (2–3 hourly; 1hr 20min); Jeonju (1–2 hourly; 2hr 30min); Jindo (every 30min; 1hr 10min); Seoul (1–2 hourly; 4hr 30min); Wando (5 daily; 2hr); Yeosu (1–2 hourly; 3hr).

By ferry Mokpo's huge terminal sits on the city's southern shore, a lavishly funded structure standing incongruously in an area of apparent decay, and as such one of the most telling symbols of modern Mokpo. There are services to and from many islands in the West Sea, including Heuksando (4 daily; 1hr 45min) and Hongdo (2 daily; 2hr 15min). Those to and from Jeju Island (2 daily; 3hr 10min–4hr 30min) use the inappropriately named "International" terminal a short way around the coast.

ACCOMMODATION

Despite the city's size and new-found wealth, there are few options at the **top end** of the accommodation range, though a few places have sprung up in Hadang, the "new" downtown out east. Further down the price scale, there are dozens of fairly decent **motels** by the train station, as well as some cheap – and seedy – *yeogwan*.

★**Daeyang Park Motel** 대양 파크 모텔 17 Samhak-ro 18-gil ☎061 243 4540; map p.242. One of the better options in the station area, this motel boasts stairwells and some corridors lit up with ultraviolet lights, stars and planets. After this NASA-friendly introduction the rooms are almost disappointingly plain – clean, with big TVs, internet-ready computers and free toiletries. W40,000

Fontana Beach 폰타나 비치 호텔 69 Pyeonghwa-ro ☎061 281 1963, ⓦfontanahotel.co.kr; map p.242. Large hotel by the water in Hadang district, a taxi-ride east of central Mokpo. Rooms are large and well kitted out (if occasionally a little old-fashioned in feel), and it's by far Mokpo's only decent option in this price range. Get a room at the front, and you'll have a great place from which to watch the fountain show (see page 243). W140,000

Myungpoom Motel 명품 모텔 14 Nambu-ro 51-gil ☎061 261 7701; map p.242. Of the many, many love motels out in Hadang, this is by far the most notable – rooms here feature the logos of Prada, Gucci and the like (without permission, of course), and have been designed in a suitably gaudy faux-label style. W70,000

Shinan Beach 신안 비치 호텔 2 Haean-ro ☎061 243 3399, ⓦshinanbeachhotel.com; map p.242. Cut off from the city centre by the mountains and with views of the sea, this was for decades Mokpo's only tourist hotel. Nowadays its stylings feel more than a little dated, but the price is fair. W88,000

EATING

You can't walk for five minutes in downtown Mokpo without passing a dozen **restaurants** serving cheap, delicious food – the area west of the train station is packed with all kinds of options, including cheap-as-chips snack bars, pizzerias and stacks of cafés.

Café Brick Lane 카페 브리크 레인 Jukdong 14-5 ☎061 244 2556; map p.242. Quite an oddity in grimy central Mokpo, this café wouldn't look out of place in Seoul. As well as good coffee (W3500 and up), they serve ciabatta filled with squid ink, tomato and mozzarella, or honey and camembert (both W9500). Daily 10am–midnight.

House Filled With Happiness 49 Beonhwa-ro ☎061 245 5887; map p.242. Housed in one of Mokpo's few extant colonial buildings (and just down the road from another one, the Modern History Museum), this café is a delightful spot on a sunny day – classical music will be playing over your coffee (from W5500) or Korean tea (W9000). There are several charmingly furnished rooms to choose from, though the garden is best if the weather agrees. Daily 11am–10pm.

Isaac Toast 이삭 토스트 91 Yeongsan-ro ☎061 273 5566; map p.242. Shack-restaurant across from the train station, selling Korean-style toast for W2000–3000, and tasty fruit shakes too. Mon–Sat 8am–9pm.

★ **Namupo** 나무포 19-1 Sumun-ro ☎ 061 243 8592; map p.242. Head here for the juiciest *galbi* in town (from W13,000). If you're not in a meat-burning mood, try other items from the picture menu, including excellent sashimi *bibimbap* (W10,000), and *naengmyeon* (W8000); these both come with umpteen delectable side dishes. Daily 8am–10pm.

Seon-a Hoetjip 선아 횟집 59 Haeandaehak-ro ☎ 061 281 9777; map p.242. The main road opposite the ferry terminal is alive with raw fish outlets, but this restaurant, out west and overlooking the sea, serves better food, for the same price, in a nicer location – try various fishy types of *bibimbap* including baby octopus (*nakji*; 낙지) or sea squirt (*meongge*; 멍게) for just W10,000, or splash out on a seafood platter (W50,000, feeds two or three). Daily 10am–10.30pm.

DRINKING

Hadang, out east, is the best place to head for a night out, though few bars are particularly interesting, and even weekend evenings can feel a little dead.

Noeul 노을 2-1 Haean-ro ☎ 061 242 1301; map p.242. West of the centre, this is a nice little place for a drink – coffee (from W4000) and yoghurt smoothies by day, and beer (from W3000) and cocktails (W7000) at

night. Blur the two by coming for sunset; after the sun has gone down, you'll be left with the twinkling bridge for company, and the fairy lights dotting a nearby island. Daily 10am–midnight.

Wolchulsan National Park

월출산 국립 공원 • Free • ⓦ english.knps.or.kr • Bus to Yeong-am from Mokpo (every 20min; 35min), then taxi to park

A short bus-ride east of Mokpo, **Wolchulsan National Park** is the smallest of Korea's national parks and one of its least visited – the lack of historic temples and its difficult access are a blessing in disguise. Set within the gorgeous Jeollanese countryside, Wolchulsan's jumble of maze-like rocks rises to more than 800m above sea level, casting jagged shadows over the rice paddies.

From the main entrance at **Cheonhwangsaji**, a short but steep hiking trail heads up for an hour or so to **Cheonhwangbong** (809m), the park's main peak. Along the way, you'll have to traverse the "Cloud Bridge", a steel structure slung between two peaks – not for sufferers of vertigo. Views from here, or the peak itself, are magnificent, and with an early enough start it's possible to make the tough hike to **Dogapsa** (도갑사), an

---

ISLANDS AROUND MOKPO

There are dozens of **islands** surrounding Mokpo in the West Sea, though few are truly noteworthy – no matter, since the key to enjoying them is to pick up a map, select an island at random, and make your way there; if you stop somewhere nice along the way, stay there instead. The **islanders** are among the friendliest people in Korea – some travellers have found themselves stuck on an island with no restaurants or accommodation, only to be taken in by a local family. These islands are not cut out for tourism and possess very few facilities, particularly in terms of banking – so be sure to take along enough **money** for your stay. It's also a good idea to bring a **bike** and/or **hiking boots**, as the natural surroundings mean that you're bound to be spending a lot of time outdoors.

All of the islands hereabouts are accessible from the ferry terminal in central Mokpo (see page 244); service at the **tourist information** office here is hit-and-miss, but at the very least you'll be able to pick up a **map** (in Korean only) of the islands and an up-to-date **ferry schedule**. One of the most pleasing ferry circuits connects some of Mokpo's closest island neighbours – a round trip will take around two hours, and there are several ferries per day. On this circuit, the only island that sees any tourists whatsoever is **Oedaldo** (외달도; 5 ferries daily; 50min), which has a decent range of accommodation and restaurants. Only a few kilometres from the mainland, though hidden by other islands, little **Dallido** (달리도; 5 ferries daily; 25min) offers some of the best walking opportunities. Beyond these lie a pack of much **larger islands**, accessible on several ferry routes from Mokpo. Most of these have swimming-friendly beaches, and hills to climb.

5

uninteresting temple on the other side of the park, while heeding the "no shamanism" warning signs along the way. There's no public transport to or from the temple, but a forty-minute walk south – all downhill – will bring you to **Gurim** (구림), a small village outside the park, on the main road between Mokpo and Yeong-am, where you can pick up a taxi.

West Sea islands

The Korean peninsula has thousands of **islands** on its fringes, but the seas around Mokpo have by far the greatest concentration. Though many of these are merely bluffs of barnacled rock that yo-yo in and out of the West Sea with the tide, plenty are large enough to support fishing communities; they're all accessible by **ferry** from Mokpo. The quantity of islands here is, in fact, so vast that it's easier to trailblaze here than in some less-developed Asian countries – many of the islands' inhabitants have never seen a foreigner, and it's hard to find a more quintessentially Korean experience.

Much of the area is under the umbrella of **Dadohae Haesang National Park**, which stretches offshore from Mokpo to Yeosu. The most popular islands are actually the furthest away – **Hongdo**, which rises steeply from the West Sea, and neighbouring **Heuksando**, a miniature archipelago of more than a hundred islets of rock.

Heuksando

흑산도 • Ferry from Mokpo (4 daily; 1hr 45min; W34,300) or Hongdo (2 daily; 40min; W11,000)

More than 100km west of the mainland, **Heuksando** is not one island but a jagged collection of forested bumps; the main ones offer good hiking opportunities. On the main island (also called Heuksando), the westerly trails are highly recommended at sunset, when Hongdo is thrown into silhouette on the West Sea; most people head to the 227m-high peak of Sangnabong. Ferries usually dock at **Yeri** (예리), a delightful little village on the main island, from where **boat tours** of the dramatic coast are available; three are available (all W22,000), though the best is number one, which loops around several rocky islets to the north.

Hongdo

홍도 • Ferry from Mokpo (2 daily; 2hr 15min; W42,000) or Heuksando (2 daily; 40min; W11,000) • Boat tours W15,000 (2hr 30min)

Another 25km further out from Heuksando is **Hongdo**, whose slightly peculiar rock colouration gave rise to its name, which means "Red Island". Those who make it this far are less likely to be interested in its pigment than its spectacular shape. Spanning around 6km from north to south, the island rises sheer from the waters of the West Sea to almost 380m above sea level. It may seem like a hikers' paradise, but much of the island is protected, and there's only one real **trail** – even on this, much of the ascent is on wooden steps. Indeed, the best views of the rock formations will be from a **tour boat**; these run from the tiny village where the ferry docks; most trips go around the rocky spires of **Goyerido** (고예리도), a beautiful formation poking out of the sea just north of Hongdo. The village itself, one of only two on an island whose population barely exceeds five hundred, sprawls saddle-like from one pinched side of the island to the other; it makes a marvellous place to stay, with the bunched-together buildings engendering a palpable sense of community.

ACCOMMODATION AND EATING

WEST SEA ISLAND

HEUKSANDO

There are several settlements around the Heuksando archipelago. Many visitors are whisked to distant, group-booked pensions on arrival, though it's actually best to stay in Yeri, the village surrounding the main ferry terminal – highly pleasant place to sleep and eat. Yeri also boasts karaoke salon, a billiards hall and a curious bar inside an o bus – great places in which to capture that frontier feelin

5

THE SINKING OF THE SEWOL

Until recently, the island of **Jindo** was the up there with the most popular in the wider Mokpo area – famed for a curly-tailed local dog, a highly loyal breed now exported across the world, the island was also a huge draw each March, when local tides would withdraw to reveal a 3km-long land bridge, a phenomenon referred to locally as "Moses' Miracle". However, no Koreans now desire to walk in the waters hereabouts – this is where the **Sewol ferry** sank on 16th April 2014, with truly catastrophic loss of life. Of the 476 people on board when the Jeju-bound ferry departed Incheon, only 172 survived – the vast majority of those who died were students from a high school in Ansan, just south of Seoul.

Following the event, and even during the brief window when hundreds were trapped alive beneath the waves, fingers were pointed in just about every direction. Questions were asked of the conduct and competence of the captain and crew, who escaped to safety after issuing a message telling passengers to remain in their bunks, despite the vessel listing heavily; it was actually one of the student victims who made the first emergency call to the coastguard, transcripts of whose communication with the crew paint a picture of confusion and incompetence. It later transpired that the ferry had made far too fast a turn, and was also travelling with double the cargo and half the ballast required by law, partially as a result of its being illegally reconfigured to carry more goods and passengers.

The event also had substantial **political ramifications**, with the opposition exploiting the situation in order to heap pressure on new president Park Geun-hye. Protests took place in Seoul for many months afterwards, during which time Park was lambasted by the general public for her failure to deal with the issue. The sad fact of the matter is that poor regulatory enforcement, poor stewardship and poor communications came together in a perfect storm – another national tragedy to add to Korea's ever-increasing list.

Daejungsusan Sikdang 대중수산 식당 42 Yeri 2-gil ☎061 275 9367. The local delicacy is fermented skate (홍어) – a truly revolting dish that even makes most Koreans retch – but this place is one of the very few restaurants serving the non-fermented (and therefore non-stinky) variety; ask for *shing-shing hong-eo* (싱싱 홍어). The powdery dipping mix they give you is also very tasty. It'll set you back W50,000 for a skate which, together with free side dishes, will feed three. Daily 8am–9pm.

Hwanggeum Motel 황금 모텔 12-5 Yeri 1-gil ☎061 246 5372. A short walk along the harbour from the ferry terminal in Yeri, this motel is, amazingly, the only place in town with beds. Rooms are nothing special, but many have

harbour views, and they do the job. W30,000

HONGDO

The main village on Hongdo is full of motels, *yeogwan* and *minbak*, though if you're coming during the summer holidays, you are advised to book your accommodation prior to arrival through the tourist offices in Mokpo or Gwangju.

1004 Hotel 1004 호텔 65-1 Hongdo 1-gil ☎061 246 3758. One of the few "hotels" (it's a guesthouse) offering sea views on the ferry terminal side of the island, with decent-enough rooms, a few of which have beds. The restaurant is pretty good (*hoe-deopbap* W15,000), and has a few outdoor tables on which to soak up the sunshine. W50,000

Gwangju and around

광주

The gleaming, busy face of "new Jeolla", **GWANGJU** is the region's most populous city by far. Once a centre of political activism, and arguably remaining so today, it's still associated, for most Koreans, with the brutal **massacre** that took place here in 1980 (see page 249). The event devastated the city but highlighted the faults of the then-government, thereby ushering in a more democratic era. Other than a **cemetery** for those who perished in the struggle, on the city outskirts, there's little of note to see in Gwangju itself, except perhaps the shop-and-dine area in its centre. Largely pedestrianized, this is one of the busiest and best such zones in the country – not only the best place in which to sample Jeollanese cuisine but also a great spot to observe why Gwangjuites are deemed to be among the most fashionable folk on the peninsula. Also in this area is "**Art Street**", a warren of studios and the hub of Gwangju's dynamic **art scene** (see page 250).

5

Apart from its art spaces, central Gwangju's only genuine tourist sights are the **museums** lying on the northern fringe of the city, around the Honam Expressway. Further afield, **Mudeungsan National Park** forms a natural eastern border to the city. Most tourists base themselves around **Geumnamno** (금남로), the major downtown artery, near the May 18th Democratic Plaza in Gwangju's main shopping district.

Asia Culture Center

아시아 문화 전당 • Most halls daily 10am–6pm • Complex entry free, though fee (typically W7000) charged for some exhibitions • ⓦ acc.go.kr • Direct access from Culture Complex subway station

Opened in 2015, Gwangju's **Asia Culture Center** is the pride of the city, though somewhat bravely set in a place of national shame – the central buildings here were used by the military during the 1980 massacre (see page 249). Rather than airbrush these out of modern Gwangju, the authorities chose to leave them standing in memoriam to those who perished, though most of the complex – much of which is below ground level – is daringly modern, and makes good strolling territory. Exhibitions usually focus on prominent Asian artists, and there are occasional performances.

Gwangju National Museum

광주 국립 박물관 • Mon–Fri 10am–6pm, Sat & Sun 10am–7pm • Free • ⓦ gwangju.museum.go.kr • Bus #48 from train station or #95 from city centre

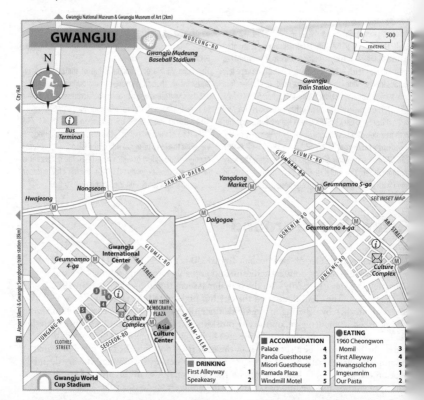

5

THE GWANGJU MASSACRE

"At 10.30 in the morning about a thousand Special Forces troops were brought in. They repeated the same actions as the day before, beating, stabbing and mutilating unarmed civilians, including children, young girls and aged grandmothers... Several sources tell of soldiers stabbing or cutting off the breasts of naked girls; one murdered student was found disembowelled, another with an X carved in his back... And so it continues, horror piled upon horror."
                                                                            Simon Winchester, Korea

Away from the bustle of Gwangju, in what may at first appear to be a field of contorted tea trees, lie those who took part in a 1980 **uprising** against the government, an event which resulted in a brutal **massacre** of civilians. The number that died is still not known for sure, and was exaggerated by both parties involved at the time; the official line says just over two hundred, but some estimates put it at over two thousand. Comparisons are inevitable with the **Tiananmen** massacre in China, an event better known to the Western world despite what some historians argue may have been a similar death toll. While Beijing keeps a tight lid on its nasty secret, Koreans flock to Gwangju each May to pay tribute to those who died.

In an intricate web of corruption, apparent Communist plots and a presidential assassination, trouble had been brewing for some time before **General Chun Doo-hwan** staged a **military coup** in December 1979. Chun had been part of a team given the responsibility of investigating the assassination of President Kim Jae-kyu, but used the event as a springboard towards his own leadership of the country. On May 17, 1980, he declared martial law in order to quash **student protests** against his rule. Similar revolts had seen the back of a few previous Korean leaders (notably Syngman Rhee, the country's first president); fearing the same fate, Chun authorized a ruthless show of force that left many dead. Reprisal demonstrations started up across the city – the MBC television station was burned down, with protestors aggrieved at being portrayed as Communist hooligans by the state-run operator. Hundreds of thousands of civilians grouped together, mimicking the tactics of previous protests on Jeju Island by attacking and seizing weapons from police stations. With transport connections to the city blocked, the government was able to retreat and pool its resources for the inevitable crackdown. This came on May 27, when troops attacked by land and air, retaking the city in less than two hours. After having the protest leaders executed, General Chun resigned from the Army in August, stepping shortly afterwards into presidential office. His leadership, though further tainted by continued erosions of civil rights, oversaw an economic boom; an export-hungry world remained relatively quiet on the matter.

Also sentenced to death, though eventually spared, was **Kim Dae-jung**. An opposition leader and fierce critic of the goings-on, he was charged with inciting the revolt, and spent much of the decade under house arrest. Chun, after seeing out his term in 1987, passed the country's leadership to his partner-in-crime during the massacre, **Roh Tae-woo**. Demonstrations soon flared up once more, though in an unexpectedly conciliatory response, Roh chose to release many political prisoners, including Kim Dae-jung. The murky world of Korean politics gradually became more transparent, culminating in charges of corruption and treason being levelled at Chun and Roh. Both were pardoned in 1997 by Kim Dae-jung, about to be elected president himself, in what was generally regarded as a gesture intended to draw a line under the troubles.

The **Gwangju National Museum** is set in a typically oversized, quasi-traditional building, a grubby place despite its relative youth. The most interesting rooms are those devoted to **Yuan-dynasty ceramics** scavenged from a Chinese trading boat, which was sunk off the Jeolla coast in the fourteenth century on its way to Japan, and lay undiscovered until 1975. Yuan-dynasty artisans were renowned across East Asia for their celadon pottery, and many of the pieces on display can be traced to **Jingdezhen**, China's most famous centre of ceramic production. Despite their centuries underwater, most pieces are in pretty good condition, a testament to the procedures of the time. Another section is devoted to items scavenged from a Korean wreck found nearby in 1983, though these pieces lack the gentle balance of their Middle Kingdom counterparts.

5

ON THE ART TRAIL IN GWANGJU

Outside Seoul, Gwangju is by far Korea's most artistically inclined city. Much of this can be ascribed to the fact that it's the largest city in Jeolla, which during the 1970s and 1980s was a hotbed of political activism (see page 235). Regional tensions have long since subsided, meaning that present-day Jeollanese have a little less to say, but it's still worth taking a stroll through some of the city's many galleries.

The best place to go hunting is a narrow road in the city centre, affectionately known as **Art Street**. This is a funky collection of shops and studios selling art materials and works by local artists. There are similar streets in other Korean cities, but this one is larger and much more accessible, and forms an active part of the city's life. Traditional art styles remain dominant, but are complemented by a more contemporary set. Also nearby is the site of the huge **Asia Culture Center** (see page 248), while further afield in Mudeungsan National Park, a small exhibition shows the work of a calligrapher named **Uijae** (see page 253).

Those visiting Gwangju in the autumn of even-numbered years will be able to attend the **Gwangju Biennale** (ⓦgwangjubiennale.org), the biggest and most important art festival in the land. Most of the action takes place at a huge dedicated hall north of the train station, and there's so much to see that even a full day is unlikely to be enough.

Gwangju Museum of Art

광주 시립 미술관 • Tues–Sun 9am–6pm • Free • Bus #48 from train station or #95 from city centre

From the National Museum, a tunnel under the expressway leads to the more interesting **Gwangju Museum of Art**, a relatively recent creation, and perhaps Korea's most important provincial art museum – they have wings in Seoul, and even Beijing. There are usually a few concurrent exhibitions in the main building, while the Ha Jungwoong hall features art from overseas (most pertinently from ethnic Koreans in Japan, just like the man it's named after), and there's also a hall focusing on photography. Very worth an hour or two of your time.

ARRIVAL AND DEPARTURE

GWANGJU

By plane Gwangju's little airport is just over 6km west of the centre, and you can actually walk there from some parts of town. The airport subway station sits 300m away from the terminal (a slightly confusing walk), while various bus routes run past the entrance; alternatively, a taxi to or from the centre should cost less than W15,000.

Destinations Jeju (11 daily; 50min); Seoul (2 daily; 50min).

By train The main station is very close to the city centre – you could walk, or a taxi will cost around W5000. High-speed trains use Gwangju-Songjeong, a larger station just past the airport to the west, and on the city subway network.

Destinations (Gwangju station) Daejeon (9 daily; 2hr); Mokpo (1 daily; 1hr 15min); Seoul (Yongsan station; 8 daily; 4hr).

Destinations (Gwangju-Songjeong station) Daejeon

(2 daily; 1hr 30min); Mokpo (1–3 hourly; 40min); Seoul (Yongsan station; 1–3 hourly; 1hr 50min).

By bus The city's express and intercity terminals sit side by side in a newish construction to the west of the centre; unfortunately the nearest subway stations are quite far, though there are plenty of onward buses and taxis.

Destinations Busan (every 30min; 3hr 40min); Daegu (every 40min; 3hr 40min); Daejeon (every 20min; 2hr 30min); Gurye (every 30min; 1hr 30min); Gyeongju (2 daily; 3hr 30min); Jeonju (every 30min; 1hr 20min); Jindo (every 40min; 3hr); Jinju (3 daily; 2hr); Mokpo (every 30min; 1hr); Naejangsan (5 daily; 1hr 30min); Seonunsan (8 daily; 1hr 40min); Seoul (every 5–10min; 4hr); Sokcho (4 daily; 7hr); Wando (every 40min; 2hr 40min); Yeosu (every 30min; 2hr)

GETTING AROUND

By subway A subway line (W1400 per ride, or W1250 with a pre-paid card) runs through the centre from east to west, but for some reason doesn't connect with the train station or bus terminal (both of which are fairly central). Line #2 is

in planning, but political infighting means that nobody ye knows where it will run.

By bus Bus journeys in the city cost W1300.

INFORMATION

Tourist information There are decent tourist information booths outside both train stations, and another on

Geumnamno (daily 9am–6pm; ☏062 226 105(The Gwangju International Center on Geumnamno ▪

Jungang-ro 196-gil, ☎ 062 226 2733, ⊚ eng.gic.or.kr) is an excellent source of local information, and has a selection of secondhand English-language books and films. The centre puts on Korean-language classes for expats, and also stocks the excellent monthly *Gwangju News* – one of the best expat magazines in the country, with listings sections (also online at ⊚ gwangjunewsgic.com) that are very useful for visitors.

ACCOMMODATION

There are a couple of decent **accommodation** options at the higher end of the price range, and motels can be found in groups around the train and bus stations, though those in the nightlife area around Geumnamno are far more appealing – poke around and you should find one for under W50,000.

Palace 호텔 팰리스 13 Jungang-ro 160-gil ☎ 062 222 2525; map p.248. Smallish, immaculate rooms in the centre of the city, and much better value than the more expensive hotels in the area. The entrance is on the fourth floor, but the place is slightly hard to find in the middle of a bank of bars and restaurants, and staff aren't always clued up. W65,000

Panda Guesthouse 팬더 게스트하우스 102 Jebong-ro ☎ 010 4669 2086, ⊚ pandaguesthouse. com; map p.248. Gwangju has witnessed something of a hostel boom of late, but most places are in dull areas – not this one, handily located just across from the Asia Culture Complex. Rooms are plain and the mattresses a little thin, but the welcoming owners help guests forget those flaws quickly. Rates include a simple breakfast. Dorms W18,000, doubles W48,000

Misori Guesthouse 미소리 게스트하우스 14-1 Dongmyeong-ro 67-gil ☎ 062 222 3753, ⊚ misori guesthouse.com; map p.248. There are a few hanok (traditional wooden house) accommodation options near the city centre, and this is the best pick, with immaculate rooms – you'll be taking plenty of photos – and a genteel air quite at odds with the nearby city bustle. Do note that bedding is on-the-floor style, which isn't for everyone. Rates include breakfast. W60,000

Ramada Plaza 라마다 프라자 149 Sangmujayu-ro ☎ 062 717 7000, ⊚ ramadagwangju.com; map p.248. Gwangju's top hotel, located in the Hadang "new town" area, and walkable from Sangmu subway station. The whole complex is superbly designed – if the swish lobby doesn't blow you away, then check out the stunning suites (particularly the "Spa Corner"). In addition, prices are very fair – the cheapest rooms often dip below W180,000. W285,000

Windmill Motel 윈드밀 모텔 150-8 Jungang-ro ☎ 062 223 5333; map p.248. Standing out from the local motel crowd by having a whacking great windmill sticking from the side (yes, hence the name), the rooms here are actually pretty decent, and they're a popular target for those who've been drinking nearby. W40,000

EATING

The Jeollanese pride themselves on their **food**, and Gwangju cuisine is excellent – whisper this quietly, but the "average" dish may actually be better than the more vaunted food from Jeonju, up the road. One place to pay attention to is the newly fashionable area just northeast of Art Street.

CITY CENTRE

1960 Cheongwon Momil 청원 모밀 174-1 Jungang-ro ☎ 062 222 2210; map p.248. This little restaurant has been serving cheap noodles since 1960, making it almost Jurassic in Korean terms. The spicy buckwheat noodles (*bibim momil*; W6000) are fantastic, or you can go for the more *soba*-like *mareun momil* (W5000), served cold and soupless. Daily 10.30am–8.30pm.

First Alleyway 퍼스트 앨리웨이 5-4 Chungjang-ro Angil ☎ 070 4127 8066; map p.248. If you're in the mood for something different, this Canadian-run restaurant is the place to come. They have yummy poutine (fries topped with gravy and cheese curds; from W5000), pizzas (W12,000), fish and chips (W10,000), sandwiches (W12,000) and much more. It's also a good place for drinks (see page 252). Wed–Thurs 5–10pm, Fri noon–1am, Sat noon–midnight, Sun 11am–9.30pm.

★ **Hwangsolchon** 황솔촌 Honamdong 73-2 ☎ 062 222 4815; map p.248. This opulent-looking meat restaurant serves absolutely delicious pork *galbi* (W11,000) in a pleasant atmosphere – if you're lucky, they'll crack eggs into the run-off tray to make a tasty omelette. There are also some cheapies available on the menu, including *galbitang* (a beef broth; W6500), *naengmyeon* (W6000) and *bibimbap* served in a sizzling bowl (W7500). Daily 11.30am–midnight.

Our Pasta 아우어 파스타 3 Dongmyeong-ro 26-gil ☎ 062 229 5056; map p.248. The most notable of the several eateries to have popped up near Art Street in recent years, selling pasta dishes (W11,500 and up) made by young chefs aspiring to work in the kitchens of top restaurants. Daily noon–3pm & 5–10pm.

DAMYANG

★ **Imgeumnim** 임금님 78-9 Jichim 6-gil ☎ 061 381 3050; map p.248. There are no fewer than five branches

5

DDEOK-GALBI: THE KOREAN BURGER

Koreans love to simplify their food in order to help poor foreigners get their heads around it. You've got *mandu* (translated as "Korean dumplings"), *pajeon* ("Korean pizza", though it's actually nothing like pizza), *soju* ("Korean vodka", though again it's very different in taste) and much more, though for some reason *ddeok-galbi* (떡갈비) is never referred to as a **Korean burger** – even though this is precisely what it is. Served bun-less on a hotplate with rounds of side dishes, *ddeok-galbi* is available around the country, though Gwangju has achieved national renown for this delicious dish – despite the fact that there's absolutely nowhere to eat it in the centre of the city. The place to head to is a parade of near-identical restaurants near **Gwangju-Songjeong** train station; the dish costs around W12,000 per portion at all of them.

---

of Imgeumnim in and around Gwangju; their Damyang branch is the most distant of the lot, but by far the best choice if you're visiting the nearby bamboo park (see page 253). The food is, in short, utterly divine – a modern take on the *hanjeongsik* (traditional banquet) experience, their *ddeok-galbi* (Korean burgers; see above) meals come with so many side-dishes that staff just plonk them all on a separate table, then wheel it over to the one you're sat by. Some of the best food in Korea, for just W14,000 a head – what a bargain. Daily 11am–8pm.

DRINKING

Gwangju's busiest central drinking zone is a knot of alleys just east of **Seoseongno**, centred on a curling, metal piece of street architecture – young local chaps lie in wait under this, and try to chat up any girl that walks past.

First Alleyway 퍼스트 앨리웨이 5-4 Chungjang-ro Angil ☏070 4127 8066; map p.248. This super restaurant (see page 251) has a range of Craftworks and Magpie beer on tap (from W7000), plus great bar snacks. Wed–Thurs 5–10pm, Fri noon–1am, Sat noon–midnight, Sun 11am–9.30pm.

Speakeasy 스피크이지 31-31 Jungang-ro 160-gil, wfacebook.com/speakeasygwangju; map p.248. A mainstay on the Gwangju bar scene, this is an expat teacher hive if ever there was one – everyone seems to know everyone, and Koreans are greatly outnumbered. It's fun, cheap (draught beer from W4000, strong cocktails for a little more) and good for meeting people – hence its meat-market reputation. Thurs–Sun 7pm–late.

DIRECTORY

Cinema Blockbusters are shown at the Lotte Cinema and Megabox, while the Gwangju International Center (see page 250) also puts on films from time to time.
Hospital Chonnam University Hospital lies just south of the Asia Culture Complex (☏062 220 5114).
Post office There's a post office in every district (usually Mon–Fri 9am–5pm). Those in the bus terminal and just west of the May 18th Democratic Plaza are most convenient

for visitors.
Spectator sports Gwangju FC are the city's football team; they play at the World Cup Stadium, to the south of the city, though rarely achieve much. The local baseball team is a different matter entirely – Kia Tigers have been one of the most successful outfits in Korea, and play at three different venues around the city.

May 18th National Cemetery

국립 5.18 묘지 • Daily 9am–6pm • Free • Bus #518 from train station (40min; W1400)

One of Gwangju's most important sights, the **May 18th National Cemetery**, lies in rolling countryside around forty minutes north of the city centre by bus. This is the resting place of those killed in the **1980 massacre** (see page 249); the thousands of participants who survived also have the right to be buried here. Though Gwangju has many sights related to this event, some even forming part of a rather macabre tour detailed in the official tourist literature, this is the least morbid and most factual.

An overlarge oval of walkways and sculpture, the **visitor centre** is more of a testament to concrete than to the lives of the demonstrators, though it's worth a visit for the **photograph exhibition hall** – there are some astonishing pictures on display, and the tension of the time is painfully palpable. Be warned that many images are rather

5

graphic, though the worst have mercifully been cordoned off into a section of their own. The cemetery itself is a badly signed five-minute walk away.

Damyang

담양 • Juknokwon daily 9am–6pm • W3000 • Bus #311 goes from Gwangju train station (1hr; exit through north gate; W2800) and bus terminal (1hr 15min; W3000) straight to Juknokwon

Perhaps the most popular sight in Gwangju is actually outside the city – famed for its profuse amounts of bamboo, **DAMYANG** is a sleepy town 25km to the north. Most visitors make a bee-line for **Juknokwon** (죽녹원), a park full of bamboo; paths lead up towards a small peak, on the northern side of which there's a small hanok village. It's all a little cutesy-poo, but a very pleasant place to spend an afternoon – just try to avoid weekends unless you love avoiding photo sight-lines. One of Gwangju's best restaurants, *Imgeumnim* (see page 251), can be found in Danyang too, and there are a couple of neat cafes in Juknokwon itself.

Mudeungsan National Park

무등산 국립 공원 • Daily 8am–5pm • Free • Bus #49 from train station or #9 from bus terminal to Jeungsimsa entrance; bus #59 from train station to Wonhyosa entrance

Small but pleasant, **Mudeungsan National Park** borders Gwangju on its eastern side, and is easily accessible by bus from the city centre. The park is named after its principal peak, a three-headed massif rising 1186m above sea level. The slopes here are gradual, and paths are well signed. One runs between two temples – Jeungsimsa (증심사) to the west, and Wonhyosa (원효사) to the north; it'll take around four hours to hike between them via Mudeungsan peak.

Uijae Gallery

의재 미술관 • By the entrance of Mudeungsan • Tues–Sun 9.30am–5pm • W2000

Near the entrance of Mudeungsan, the **Uijae Gallery** showcases the work of Ho Baeknyon (1891–1977), better known by his pen name **Uijae**. Uijae was an important painter-poet-calligrapher, and in uniting those fine arts was probably one of the main catalysts behind Gwangju's dynamic art scene. His old house and tea plantation, as well as a **gallery** dedicated to his work, stand in close proximity. The most interesting piece on show in the museum is a ten-picture **folding screen**, whose images are said to represent the world's rainbow of personal characteristics: are you bamboo-, blossom- or orchid-like in temperament?

Naejangsan National Park

내장산 국립 공원 • W3000 payable at some entrances • ⓦ english.knps.or.kr

Naejangsan National Park is one of Korea's most popular parks, its circle of peaks flaring up like a gas ring in the autumn. Maple trees are the stars of the show in this annual incandescence, with squads of elm, ash and hornbeam adding their hues to the mix. The many trails and peaks across the park keep hikers happy year-round, though most visitors head to the amphitheatre-shaped mountain circle in the northeast, where the nearby tourist village has plenty of accommodation and places to eat. The area's topography allows for two **hiking routes**: a short temple loop around the interior, and a far more punishing circuit around the almost circular ridge.

5

The temple route

The **temple route** takes less than two hours to complete. A pleasant, maple-lined path takes you from the park entrance to **Naejangsa**, an unremarkable but pretty temple whose complex is dotted with informative English-language signs. Head further up the valley and you'll come to isolated **Wonjeogam**, a tiny hermitage home to a couple of monks and an abnormally large golden statue, before the trail swings back along the mountain face towards **Baengnyeonam**, another hermitage that marks the final sight on this route. Built in 632, the structure has been destroyed and rebuilt several times since then, and enjoys the most arresting setting of the three – bamboo stalks in a grove behind the main building point up towards the sheer rock crags of Naejangsan's main ridge, while in the other direction is the awesome view of a distant pavilion nestling beneath the peaks.

The ridge route

Cable car daily 9am–6pm • W4000 one-way, W7000 return

There are eight main peaks on the **ridge route**, and it's possible to scale them all on a calf-burning 13.8km day-hike, but most visitors content themselves with a shorter trip up and down – wherever you are on this circular route, you won't be far from a path heading back towards Naejangsa in the centre. From a point on the approach from the park entrance to Naejangsa (around 40min from the entrance) it's even possible to take a **cable car** up to a restaurant that's within a short hike of the southern ridge and some great views.

ARRIVAL AND DEPARTURE

By bus The park lies almost midway between Gwangju and Jeonju, and there are occasional direct buses from both cities (around 1hr 30min for either). Otherwise you'll have to transfer in Jeongeup (정읍), a small town well serviced by buses and trains, and connected to Naejangsan

NAEJANGSAN NATIONAL PARK

by bus (1–2 hourly; 25min; W1400) or taxi (W12,000). Naejangsan's bus stop is outside a convenience store; it's a half-hour walk from here to the park entrance, and cheap shuttle buses also run through the day.

ACCOMMODATION AND EATING

Simple places to **sleep** and **eat** are clustered around Naejangsan bus stop. If you're looking for something more rustic, note that slightly uphill from the stop (in the opposite direction to the park entrance) is a small, friendly village of family homes, many of which lease out *minbak* rooms from W25,000 or so.

Hanok Hoegwan 하녹 회관 ☎ 063 538 9448. Located at the end of the long parade of restaurants heading from the bus stop towards the park entrance, this attractive venue serves good local dishes such as *sanchae bibimbap* (W9000), or filling set menus centred on mountain

mushrooms (버섯 벡반; W12,000). Daily 8am–9pm.
Sarangbang Motel 사랑방 모텔 ☎ 063 538 8186. Standing out simply because it stands apart, this motel lies across the stream on the way to the park entrance. Rooms are simple, but it'll do. **W40,000**

Seonunsan Provincial Park

선운산 도립 공원 • Daily sunrise–sunset • Free • Bus from Jeonju (3 daily; 1hr 30min) or Gwangju (4 daily; 1hr 30min), though access to the park is usually via Gochang (고창), the closest town to Seonunsan and connected to it by regular bus (every 30min; 30min)

Seonunsan Provincial Park has more than a few aces hidden up its leafy sleeves. It offers some of the country's best **rock-climbing** and a few enjoyable hikes; these may not be as well signed as others in Korea, but some may find this liberating. A streamside path, lined with stalls selling delicious mountain berry juice in the summer and autumn, heads straight from the main entrance to **Seonunsa** (선운사), a dusty collection of buildings, stupas and the like that appear to have been thrown together with little care.

5

It's quite possibly the least satisfying temple complex in the province, and the small hermitages strewn around the park are of more interest.

Once past Seonunsa, you'll have a diverse range of **hiking trails** to choose from. Keen hikers should head for the hills; the peaks are puny by Korean standards, rarely reaching above 400m, but this makes for some easy day-hikes, and you may be rewarded with occasional views of the West Sea. For more hard-core thrills, continue further on the temple path, across the river; hidden a ten-minute hike behind a small restaurant is a spectacular **rock-climbing** course. This is a tough route and should not be attempted alone or without equipment (see ⊛koreaontherocks.com for climb details, and to contact the few Koreans and expats au fait with holds, conglomerates and overhangs). Back towards the park entrance, an underused side path heads along the temple wall and up a gorgeous valley lined with rows of tea trees and a few rustic dwellings.

A motley collection of hotels and motels lies outside the park entrance – you're better off **staying** elsewhere.

Byeonsanbando National Park

변산반도 국립 공원 • Daily 24hr • Free • ⊛ english.knps.or.kr

In addition to the usual mix of peaks and temples found in Korea's parks, **Byeonsanbando National Park** throws in some wonderful sea views. It's spread around a small, rural **peninsula** on the west coast from which it takes its name – *bando* literally means "half-island". However, it's in the process of being hauled towards the mainland on its northern side with the aid of a 33km causeway, a development that will yield thousands of hectares of new farmland, but has caused one hell of a stink with Korean environmental groups.

Naesosa

내소사 • Daily 24hr • W3000

5

Off the charming southern side of the peninsula is the temple complex of **Naesosa**; this is more notable for its rural, mountain-backed setting than for any of its buildings, and is the most accessible place from which to start a hike. From the **entrance** – surrounded by persimmon trees, which shed their leaves at the slightest sniff of autumn, leaving behind baubles of bright-orange fruit – it's a short walk to the temple and its adjacent *minbak* village. The main temple building's exterior is almost entirely devoid of paint, while inside four dragons ascend to heaven, two headless, one gnawing a fish. From here, **hiking** routes head up to **Gwaneumbong** (425m).

Chaeseokgang

채석강 • Daily 9am–6pm • Free

The unusual rock formations of **Chaeseokgang** sit at the western tip of the peninsula. You have to time it right to get the most out of the place – for much of the day it's just a bunch of pretty cliffs, but the surrender of the tide reveals page-like leaves of rock piled up like rusty banknotes, and teeming with crabs and other oceanic fauna.

ARRIVAL AND DEPARTURE
BYEONSANBANDO NATIONAL PARK

By bus The park is accessible on a single daily bus from Jeonju; note that these head to the north of the peninsula first, then pass by Chaeseokgang (2hr) before wrapping around to Naesosa (2hr 40min). For Naesosa you'll save time transferring in the town of Buan (부안), accessible on regular buses from Jeonju (1hr) and Seoul (3hr); from Buan, hourly buses to the park (55min) depart from a stop diagonally across from the bus terminal, or it's W25,000 by taxi.

ACCOMMODATION AND EATING

There are simple places to stay around both Chaeseokgang and the Naesosa entrance, though nothing truly stands out bar the **templestay** programmes (W40,000) run by the temple. Rooms are surprisingly comfy, and there's free wi-fi – useful if you can't drop off at the early hour you'll be put to bed. There are also plenty of fish **restaurants** around Chaeseokgang.

Neuti Namu 느티나무 ☎063 581 7773; map p.256. Right next to the Naesosa ticket booth, this restaurant's outdoor tables have the nicest views of any in the area, looking over persimmon trees and into the park. The food's excellent, and best washed down with a splendid choice of local *makgeolli*; their "mountain food" set (산채 정식; W18,000; minimum two) comes with a dozen side dishes. Sometimes open later. Daily 8am–6pm.

Jeonju

전주

The small city of **JEONJU** is a place of considerable appeal; though it now attracts domestic tourists in the numbers it richly deserves, it remains largely off the radar of international visitors. This is ironic, since it's possibly the best place in the land in which to get a handle on **Korean customs**. Most visitors make a beeline for the city's splendid **hanok village** of traditional wooden housing, which contains more than enough for a full day of sightseeing, as well as being a good introduction to Korea's indigenous **arts and crafts**. In addition, spring sees Jeonju hosting JIFF (ⓦeng.jiff. r.kr), by far the most eclectic major **film festival** in the country.

However, it's **food** that Koreans most readily associate with Jeonju. Many of the differences are too subtle to be noticed by foreigners – and in the cheapest places, nonexistent – but you're likely to find a greater and more lovingly prepared number of *banchan* (반찬; side dishes) here, and a slightly greater emphasis on herbal seasoning than on the somewhat less cultivated tastebud-tinglers of salt and red-pepper paste. Particularly notable is the city's take on the tasty Korean staple, **bibimbap** (see page 53). The only downside is that Korean food just won't taste as good when you've moved on elsewhere.

5

Jeonju's ginkgo-lined streets help to create an ambience notably relaxed for a Korean city, but this disguises a hidden historical pedigree – this unassuming place marked the beginning of one of the longest lines of kings that the world has seen. It was here in the fourteenth century that the first kings of the **Joseon kingdom** were born, and the dynasty went on to rule Korea for over five centuries. Overlooked as the dynastic capital in favour of Seoul, today's Jeonju is not brimming with historical riches, but it has its charms, and is well worth a visit.

The hanok village
한옥마을

Jeonju's main attraction is undoubtedly its splendid **hanok village**, a city-centre thatch of largely **traditional housing**. Highlights here include a cathedral, an ancient shrine and a former Confucian academy, as well as museums for calligraphy, paper and wine; musical *pansori* performances are also frequent (see page 260), and you may even be able to participate in traditional activities such as weaving or lantern-making. Almost all sights are free, and there's enough to keep you busy for a full day. The best way to enjoy it is simply to turn up and wander around – whether it be a museum, a traditional restaurant or a photogenic house, there's something to see around every corner.

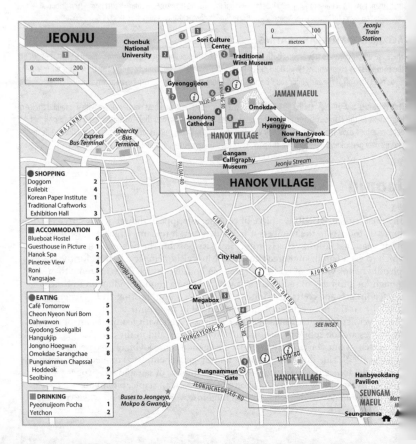

There are no opening times or entry fees to the area, and it remains a functioning part of the city, but recent years have seen the village pander massively to the needs of domestic tourists. The glut of traditional tearooms, which once made Jeonju rare among Korean cities, have been replaced by vendors selling cream-filled churros and slushies. However, the village retains a certain magic, especially at night, when some streets are illuminated with fairy lighting.

The best place to get your bearings is **Taejoro**, a road that bisects the *hanok* village from west to east; it has two information offices (see page 261) that can provide you with maps of the area. Rising south of Taejoro's eastern end is **Omokdae**, a small bluff that makes a great sunset-viewing spot.

Pungnammun
풍남문 • 24hr • Free

Just outside the village, across the main road that marks its western boundary, lies **Pungnammun**, an ornate city gate; the present structure dates from 1768, but it was originally built in the late fourteenth century as part of Jeonju's city wall. Now surrounded by a circle of rather ugly buildings, Pungnammun holds a gruesome secret – this is where the heads of martyred Christians were displayed after purges in 1801 (see page 376).

Gyeonggijeon
경기전 • Daily: Mar–Oct 9am–7pm; Nov–Feb 9am–6pm • W3000

Taking up much of the *hanok* village's northern half, **Gyeonggijeon** is a park-like shrine area full of ornate buildings and beautiful trees – quite a sight in the autumn. It was built in 1410 to preserve a portrait of **King Taejo**, first leader of the famed Joseon dynasty and native of Jeonju, who had died two years previously after arguably the most productive reign in Korea's long regal history (see page 62). The portrait shows Taejo resplendent in an embroidered robe, against a pale-yellow background, and sits proudly in a hall to the rear of the complex. It's surrounded by potraits of other members of his family, who were only officially made royals after Taejo's death, a move that gave posthumous legality to his bringing down of the Goryeo dynasty (see page 365).

Jeondong Cathedral
전동성당 • Services Mon 5.30am, Tues & Thurs 5.30am & 7am, Wed & Fri 5.30am & 10am, Sat 5.30am, 4pm & 6pm, Sun 5.30am, 9am, 10.30am, 5pm & 8pm • Free

Almost directly opposite Gyeonggijeon, on the southern side of Taejoro, sits **Jeondong Cathedral**, looking almost European, with its brown brick walls and soaring spire. It was one of the first cathedrals to be built in Korea, and remains an active place of worship. The entrance is often open to view outside service times.

TRADITIONAL ARTS AND CRAFTS IN THE HANOK VILLAGE

You'll find an abundance of places to sample traditional arts and crafts in the *hanok* village, with the greatest concentration in the alleys north of Taejoro, a road bisecting the village. One popular target is the **Traditional Wine Museum** (Tues–Sun 9am–6pm; free); the exhibits here aren't terribly interesting, but the beauty of the *hanok* building, and the fact that you can try three traditional tipples for just W5000, make it worth a quick peek. Of more interest is the **Korean Paper Institute** (Tues–Sun 9am–6pm; free), where beautiful examples of products made with handmade paper (한지; *hanji*) are on display, many available to buy (see page 264); if you ask nicely, you may even be able to try your hand at making a kite or lantern. Near the eastern end of Taejoro, you'll find the **Traditional Craftworks Exhibition Hall**, a traditionally styled wooden structure; this long held crafts created by Jeonju artisans, and though temporarily shut down at the time of writing, it's expected to reappear in more or less its previous form, though perhaps with a different name. Lastly, artistic beauty of a different kind can be found at a couple of cultural centres that put on occasional *pansori* shows (see page 260).

5

Gangam Calligraphy Museum

강암 서예관 • Daily 9am–6pm • Free

South of Taejoro, and overlooking the stream that marks the *hanok* village's southern boundary, is the **Gangam Calligraphy Museum**. Stored inside are wonderful examples of writing from some of Korea's best-known calligraphers – much of the work is that of Song Seongyong, a reputed maker of temple name-boards in dynastic times, though there are also pieces here from several former Korean presidents.

Jeonju Hyanggyo

전주 향교 • Daily: Mar–Oct 9am–7pm, Nov–Feb 9am–6pm • Free

Near the southeastern corner of the *hanok* village is **Jeonju Hyanggyo**, a former Confucian academy. Present here since 1603, and still housing a few of the original buildings, it sees surprisingly few visitors – a very good thing, as you'll appreciate more its contemplative *raison d'être*. Most notable are a number of large ginkgo trees, a couple of which – incredibly – actually predate the complex; with a majesty all of their own, these alone make a trip to this *hyanggyo* worthwhile.

Southeast of the hanok village

There are a few minor attractions just southeast of the *hanok* village's official boundary, including two small non-*hanok* villages and **Martyrs Hill**, which has quite a grim history. The best place to start is **Hanbyeokdang** (한벽당), a pavilion dangling off a rock face across the road from the *hanok* village's southeast corner; it was long a place for poets and contemplation, and one can only speculate on how beautiful the view must have been when this was built in 1404, before the main road arrived.

Jaman Maeul

자만 마을 • Daily 24hr • Free

Across the footbridge from Omokdae, the village of **JAMAN MAEUL** has recently become very popular with young, selfie-seeking out-of-towners. In keeping with what has become a national norm, the narrow lanes have been pimped out with colourful murals (including the world's worst depiction of John Lennon), and a few cafés have popped up here and there. Cheesy, but pleasant, and worth a wander.

Seungam Maeul

승암 마을 • Daily 24hr • Free

Head down the river from Jaman Maeul, and you'll soon be rewarded with **SEUNGAM MAEUL**, a more authentic village whose paths snake between walls of rock and up the

---

PANSORI

Usually marketed to foreigners as "Korean opera", **pansori** (판소리) performances are a modern-day derivative of the country's shamanist past. Songs and incantations chanted to fend off evil spirits or ensure a good harvest slowly mutated over the years into ritualized presentations; the themes evolved, too, with tales of love and despair replacing requests to spirits unseen.

A good *pansori* may go on for hours, but each segment will be performed by a cast of just two – a female singer (소리꾼; *sorikkun*) and a male percussionist (고수; *gosu*). The *sorikkun* holds aloft a paper fan, which she folds, unfolds and waves about to emphasize lyrics or a change of scene. While the *gosu* drums out his minimalist finger taps on the *janggo*, he gives his singer words – or, more commonly, grunts – of encouragement known as *chuimsae*, to which the audience are expected to add their own. The most common are "*chalhanda!*" and "*olshi-gu!*", which are roughly equivalent to "you're doing good!" and "hm!", a grunt acknowledging appreciation, usually delivered with a refined nod. Just follow the Korean lead, and enjoy the show (see page 263 for details of places to see them).

hill to the pine forest behind. The atmosphere here is something special, especially considering its proximity to the city centre; all the more surprising, then, that this little hamlet may have been the true **birthplace** of Joseon-era Korea – local rumours suggest that this was the source of the dynasty's first royals. Nowadays it's home to **Seungamsa** (승암사), a simple, deserted but intricately painted temple.

Martyrs Hill

It's possible to access **Martyrs Hill** via a path starting a little further down the river from Seungam Maeul. The martyrs in question include Yi Hang-geom, killed in 1801 along with six of his family for his religious beliefs; his head was displayed on Pungnammun (see page 259) in the city centre in order to show the populace what happened to Catholics. A thirty-minute slog will take you to his tomb, from where you can follow a number of paths back to the city, many of which are studded with yet more delightfully secluded temples and hermitages.

ARRIVAL AND INFORMATION   JEONJU

By train Jeonju's train station, which is shaped something like a giant temple building, hosts a number of KTX services, though the spur-line running here from Iksan is not a high-speed one. Several bus routes head from the station towards the *hanok* village, but it's far easier to take a cab (W7000).
Destinations Daejeon (hourly; 1hr 10min); Seoul (Yongsan station; 1–2 hourly; 3hr 35min); Suncheon (1–2 hourly; 1hr); Yeosu (1–2 hourly; 1hr 20min).

By bus Bus passengers are disgorged at one of two terminals – one express, one intercity – in a messy area to the north of the city centre. Plenty of buses run into town from the main road a short walk to the east. However, it's far easier to go by taxi, which is unlikely to cost more than W5000.

Destinations Buan (every 30min; 1hr); Busan (11 daily; 3hr 35min); Daegu (hourly; 3hr 30min); Daejeon (every 20min; 1hr 30min); Gurye (7 daily; 2hr); Gwangju (every 30min; 1hr 40min); Jeongeup (every 15min; 1hr); Jinan (every 20min; 50min); Jinju (hourly; 3hr 30min); Mokpo (1–2 hourly; 3hr); Muju (hourly; 2hr); Seoul (every 10min; 3hr); Suncheon (11 daily; 2hr 20min); Yeosu (11 daily; 3hr).

Tourist information There are two information booths inside the *hanok* village; the most useful is the one nearer the east end (daily 9am–6pm; ☎063 288 0105). Whichever you head to, pick up one of the excellent free maps of the *hanok* village; these should also be available at the train station and bus terminals.

ACCOMMODATION

For a place with such tourist potential, Jeonju has a surprising dearth of quality accommodation. However, the city does provide a rare opportunity to stay at specially adapted **hanok** buildings – an opportunity not to be missed (see page 262 for more). There's precious little point in basing yourself outside the *hanok* area, though there's a seedy motel cluster in the "downtown" area just west of the *hanok* village.

★**Blueboat Hostel** 블루보트 호스텔 75 Chunggyeong-ro ☎010 6545 9049, ⓦblueboat-hostel. com; map p.258. Yet another winner from the ever-expanding Blueboat Hostel empire, located on a rather over-busy road just north of the *hanok* village. That's about the only real negative. Dorm berths have charging sockets and privacy curtains, and the place looks surprisingly classy for the price. Modest breakfast included. Dorms W24,000, twins W60,000
Guesthouse in Picture 그림 속 여유 57-7 Dongmun-gil ☎010 2770 5042; map p.258. If you want to do the whole *hanok* thing but stick around the motel price level, this is a good bet. Rooms have been given a little artistic love (and, unlike many such places, they're all en suite), and the floor mattresses allow for a good night's sleep. W55,000
Hanok Spa 한옥 스파 40 Jeondongseongdang-gil ☎063 232 0015; map p.258. This *jjimjilbang*, north of

Gyeonggijeon, is the city's super-budget choice. It doesn't quite live up to the "*hanok*" component of its name, though there are a variety of pools to enjoy, with the waters hauled from 170m beneath the surface. W8000
★**Pinetree View** 황토 민박 42 Omokdae-gil ☎010 5685 0804; map p.258. This *hanok* guesthouse is larger and less homestay-like than most options in the village, though somehow contrives to be more charming – its setting in the less-developed southern half certainly helps. There's a rooftop viewing area, and a few secluded niches for night-time drinks around the complex. W65,000
Roni 로니 관광 호텔 74-50 Jeonjugaeksa 4-gil ☎063 281 1000; map p.258. There are still no proper high-end places in Jeonju – this is as swanky as the city gets, accommodation-wise, located in the bustling downtown area, just a short walk from the *hanok* village. Rooms are sharper than you might expect when seeing

5

SLEEPING THE TRADITIONAL WAY IN JEONJU

Somewhat ironically, one of Jeonju's main draws for domestic tourists is the opportunity to sleep in traditional Korean houses. Known as **hanok** (한옥), these have long been dwindling in number across the country, and few urban areas feature them in any significant quantity – Seoul's Bukchon neighbourhood being an honourable exception (see page 69). For foreign tourists, the chance to stay in such a place is perhaps even more enticing; both demand and supply have been rising of late, with an ever-increasing number of houses in Jeonju's *hanok* village allowing guests to stay. These are traditional dwellings, so don't expect large rooms or too much comfort. The experience is unique, nonetheless, especially in winter when your feet are toasted by the *ondol* floors, many of which are heated from beneath by burning wood.

One minor drawback is that very few *hanok* owners hereabouts will speak any English – this certainly complicates things when trying to make a booking. The city's tourist information offices (see page 261) will help find you a suitable room on arrival, and they have options listed on their website (🖥 tour-eng.jeonju.go.kr). Count on paying around W60,000 for a room.

the place for the first time, and a decent little breakfast is included in the rates. **W125,000**

Yangsajae 양사재 40 Omokdae-gil ☎ 063 282 4959; map p.258. Formerly home to a famed local poet, this is another of the *hanok* district's wooden dwellings, with *ondol*-heated rooms as pleasingly traditional as they are tiny. They're going for the "culture" experience, with a variety of teas to sample during your stay. **W60,000**

EATING

Jeonju has a national reputation as a city of culinary excellence and visitors should not leave without trying the city's wonderful **bibimbap** (see page 263). There exist a number of excellent **traditional restaurants** in the *hanok* village, together with some rustic **tearooms** and an ever-growing number of **cafés**. The *hanok* district isn't exactly a nightlife hotspot, though in good weather it would be a shame not to take advantage of the unique opportunities the *hanok* district provides for alfresco drinking (see page 264). Further afield, there are countless places to **drink** or dance the night away in the **student zones** around Jeonju's various universities; the area outside Chonbuk National University is generally regarded as the best.

RESTAURANTS

★**Cheon Nyeon Nuri Bom** 천년누리봄 Gyeongwondong 2-ga 53-1 ☎ 063 288 8813; map p.258. Just north of Gyeonggijeon, this is a thoroughly noble restaurant – the volunteer staff here are all female retirees. The food they whip up is great, too; try their super-cheap staple meals (from W7000), or drop by in the evening for the filling *makgeolli* sets (W25,000). Daily 11am–9pm.

★**Gyodong Seokgalbi** 교동 석갈비 26-1 Taejoro ☎ 063 288 2282; map p.258. Attractive restaurant in which succulent pieces of beef *galbi* are brought to you on a sizzling hotplate (W12,000 per portion, or W2000 more for a spicy one), and served with a selection of lovingly prepared side dishes. Gluttons can add rice or noodles to the mix. Daily 10.30am–9pm.

Hangukjip 한국집 119 Eojin-gil ☎ 063 284 2224; map p.258. Behind temple-like walls, decent Jeonju *bibimbap* (W11,000) is served plain or in a sizzling-hot bowl, with a charming garden view. For an extra W2000 you can have raw beef (something like a tartare) thrown into the mix – highly recommended, especially since the side dishes usually lack a little oomph. Daily 10am–9pm.

★**Jongno Hoegwan** 종로 회관 98 Jeondongseongdang-gil ☎ 063 283 4578; map p.258. This Jeonju *bibimbap* place may look fancy and new,

but don't let the recent renovation fool you – it has, for decades now, been one of the most venerated places in which to sample one of the country's most famous meals, and boasts Gyeonggijeon views to boot. For W10,000 (or W13,500 for the raw beef option) you get the meal and a mouthwatering array of side dishes – the mushrooms, in particular, are nothing short of heavenly. If you're not in a *bibimbap* mood, they also do good *naengmyeon* (W5000). Daily 9am–9.30pm.

Omokdae Sarangchae 오목대 사랑채 69 Eunhaeng-ro ☎ 063 232 8533; map p.258. Traditional food is on offer at this extremely beautiful restaurant – sitting in the rear, near the fish pond, is particularly recommended in the evening, when the interior is bathed in a soft glow. It's almost easy to forget about the food in such surrounds, but their speciality is *galbi tang* – beef bone served in a clear soup (W10,000). Daily 8am–10pm.

CAFÉS AND TEAROOMS

Café Tomorrow 카페 투모로 71-1 Girin-daero ☎ 063 288 6455; map p.258. Up there with the best views in town – nab a seat on the balcony or rooftop, and gaze down over the *hanok* district. Decent coffee, and cups of traditional tea, go from W4000. Daily 10am–10pm.

★**Dahwawon** 다화원 13 Choemyeonghui-g

☎ 063 284 6472; map p.258. The *hanok* district has been getting ever more gentrified of late, and the tearooms that have lasted the course have been those kowtowing to youthful trends such as waffles or cream-filled churros. Hurrah, then, for the one which has kept it real – nothing but tasty, traditional tea (W5000), a couple of traditional snacks, and an utterly beguiling interior boasting views of tiled rooftops and maple leaves. Wonderful. Daily 8am–10pm.

Pungmmunun Chapssal Hoddeok 풍남문 찹쌀 씨엇호떡 22 Pungnammun 2-gil ☎ 063 232 6993; map p.258. The name of this little booth is as much of a mouthful as the gloopy sugar-and-rice pancakes on sale for just W1000 each – *hoddeok* (호떡; pronounced a little like "hot dog") are extremely popular winter snacks, and on a cold evening are hard to beat. Here they're also filled with seeds – a fad that knocks socks off the original. Daily 9am–9pm.

Seolbing 설빙 33 Eunhaeng-ro ☎ 070 7799 8883; map p.258. Part of a dessert café chain which has swept the nation of late, this one stands out for the 500-year-old ginkgo tree standing outside – there are a couple of tables under its penta-centenarian branches. Try a *bingsu* – a Korean dessert made with shaved ice and red beans (from W7000). Daily 10am–10pm.

DRINKING

Pyeonuijeom Pocha 편의점 포차 17 Myeongnyun 4-gil ☎ 070 8210 0581; map p.258. There are a bunch of cheap, studenty drinking holes in the university area, but this is the cheapest (and, therefore, the most studenty) of the lot – it's basically a shop with a bar attached, and just W1900 will buy you a bottle of soju or beer. To round it out, have it with student snacks such as ice cream, instant noodles or a bag of crisps. Daily 6pm–6am.

Yetchon 옛촌 144-4 Paldal-ro ☎ 063 232 9991; map p.258. This local chain finally has a branch in the Hanok Village – hoorah! *Makgeolli* costs W8000 a kettle, and moju (see page 264) about the same. The atmosphere can be raucous, but you'll have to order food, but there are some insanely cheap things on the menu – try *kimchi* pancake (W4000) and stick fried eggs on top for good measure (W2000). Tues–Sun 3pm–midnight.

ENTERTAINMENT

There are a couple of places in which to catch traditional *pansori* shows (see page 260), though unfortunately these don't take place every day – all the more reason to stay in Jeonju longer. In addition, there are a few cinemas in the downtown area just northwest of the *hanok* village. CGV and Megabox are the largest, and both host screenings when the Jeonju Film Festival comes to town (see page 45).

Hanbyeok Culture Center 한벽 문화관 20 Jeonjucheon-dongro ☎ 063 280 7000. This large cultural centre, facing the stream at the south end of the *hanok* village, puts on occasional *pansori* shows. The performers are usually of an extremely high standard, and the shows are not over-long, making this an absolute must-see if you're in town at the right time. Free. Tues–Thurs 11am.

Sori Culture Center 소리 문화관 33-1 Pungnamdong 3-ga ☎ 063 231 0771. Smaller and more intimate than the Hanbyeok, the *pansori* shows put on here are perhaps more traditional in feel, though sadly they only take place once a week. W10,000. Sat 5pm.

JEONJU BIBIMBAP

Jeonju's most famous dish is, without doubt, its **bibimbap** (전주 비빔밥). Regular *bibimbap* – a mixture of vegetables served on a bed of rice, with a fried egg and meat on top – is available across the country, but in Jeonju they've picked up the formula and run with it. Recipes vary from place to place, but the ingredients are always well chosen and may include anything from pine kernels to bluebell roots or fern bracken in addition to the usual leaves and bean sprouts. In addition, your meal will invariably be surrounded by up to twenty free **side dishes**, made with just as much care, and an even greater variety of ingredients. Beware, however, of restaurants that claim to serve authentic Jeonju *bibimbap* – many places, particularly around the train station and bus terminals, will simply give you a regular version of the dish (though genuinely made in Jeonju, and thereby circumnavigating Korea's already weak product description laws). One way to sort Jeonju wheat from Jeonju chaff is the price – for the real deal, you shouldn't be paying less than W8000, but even at double this price it's likely to be money well spent.

5

DRINKING ALFRESCO

Korea is a great country for those who like drinking outdoors – cheap alcohol is available round the clock from ubiquitous convenience stores, and as long as you're not making a nuisance or on private property, **alfresco drinking** is completely legal. Jeonju is perhaps the best Korean city in which to take advantage of these possibilities – in addition to the romance bequeathed by streets lined with wooden housing and studded with fairy lights, it's the best place in the land for the milky rice beer known as **makgeolli**. About six percent ABV, this is available for as little as W1000 from any convenience store or mini-mart, and there are dozens of local varieties to enjoy – notable brands include *Myeongga* (명가) and *Namwonssal* (남원쌀), though you could also try hunting down red ginseng-infused *Hongsam Jujo* (홍삼주조). Jeonju actually seems most proud of a drink named **moju** (모주): flavoured with ginseng, jujube, ginger, cinnamon and liquorice, and browner than your average *makgeolli*, this tasty beverage is only three percent in strength, and usually W3000 for a tiny bottle. As for where to drink, a few recommendations include the grassy area behind the middle school east of Gyeonggijeon; a blue-and-green-lit footbath on the western side of Eunhaengno; and the hilltop behind the Traditional Craftworks Exhibition Hall.

SHOPPING

Doggom 도꼼 14-3 Taejo-ro ☎063 221 1222; map p.258. Many shops in the *hanok* district sell earthenware products, but those on offer here are clearly a class above. You can even try your hand at making a cup if you'll be in town long enough for it to get fired – one night should do. Daily 9am–7pm.

Eollebit 얼레빗 74 Eunhaeng-ro ☎063 286 3848; map p.258. Tiny store selling gorgeous wooden combs – for decorative as well as practical use – made from the wood of the *daechu* (jujube) tree. Daily 9.30am–7pm.

Korean Paper Institute 한지원 53-26 Pungnamdong 3-ga ☎010 8959 7757; map p.258.

Shop making and selling traditional hanji paper, as well as lanterns, brooches and other goodies made from it. Daily 10am–7pm.

Traditional Craftworks Exhibition Hall 전주 공예 풍전시관 15 Taejoro ☎063 285 0002; map p.258. Set in a large complex across several buildings, this is a grand place to hunt for souvenirs. Examples include silk goods such as pillowcases and shawls, a range of traditionally styled ties, masks, ceramics and fans made with *hanji* (handmade) paper. Closed at the time of writing, but likely to reappear more or less as was – check ahead. Daily 10am–7pm.

Maisan Provincial Park

마이산 도립 공원 • Daily 24hr • W3000 • For the northern entrance, take a bus (2–4 hourly from Jeonju; 1hr) to the small town of Jinan (진안), and then either another bus (hourly) or a taxi (W12,000) to the park; for the Tapsa entrance, take a bus from Jinan (3 daily), or Jeonju (3 direct buses daily) – Tapsa itself is a gentle 30min walk from the stop

Korea's pine-clad mountain ranges tend to look rather similar to each other. One exception is tiny **Maisan Provincial Park**, or "horse-ear mountains", so named after two of its peaks. From the **northern entrance** – where you'll find restaurants and a couple of places to stay – steep flights of energy-sapping stairs take you between the horses' ears and over the scalp, where you'll probably need a rest. Unfortunately it's not possible to climb the peaks, which remained closed for regeneration at the time of writing.

If you continue between the peaks, around a half-hour from the entrance you'll hit **Unsusa**, a dainty temple surrounded by flowers in warmer months. Another quick burst down the mountain is the highly popular temple of **Tapsa** (탑사), Maisan's real gem, which sits in a surreal clasp of stacked rock. Mildly Gaudíesque in appearance, the near-hundred-strong towers were the work of one monk, Yi Kap-myong (1860–1957), who apparently used no adhesive in their construction, even though some are over 10m high. Rather than head over the ridge again, you can pick up a bus from a stop another half-hour walk downhill from Tapsa, a pleasing stretch lined with little restaurants and snack-stands.

Deogyusan National Park

5

덕유산 국립 공원 • Daily 24hr • Free • ⓦ english.knps.or.kr

Locked into the northeast of Jeonbuk province is **Deogyusan National Park**, whose lofty yet gentle terrain rises up south of **Muju ski resort**, then spills down in an undulating series of valleys. Though it's most popular in the wintertime, the **warmer months** are actually a great time of year to visit, since accommodation prices plunge, and there's great hiking on hills that would otherwise be covered with snow and skiers.

Muju ski resort

무주 • ⓦ mujuresort.com

Despite being one of the warmest and most southerly ski resorts in Korea, **MUJU** is one of the peninsula's most popular, and attracts hordes of skiers throughout the winter, a season artificially elongated with the aid of some hefty snow machines. Less bulky ski equipment is available for hire, and whether you're a ski veteran or an absolute beginner, you'll have more than twenty slopes to choose from. It's also possible to sled or go cross-country skiing, or take part in non-snow related activities from golf and paintball to bungee-jumping and bike rides.

Muji–Gucheondong hike

A popular hike – one that almost every summertime visitor to Deogyusan follows – links Muju ski resort with the main park entrance at Gucheondong. Though it's not especially taxing, much of the upward slog can be chalked off by **cable car** from the resort, which whisks passengers up the 1520m peak of Seolcheon-bong. From here it's a 6.2km hike back down to the ski area, or a longer, more beautiful one along a trail riddled with rocks, small waterfalls and pools to the Gucheondong park entrance.

ARRIVAL AND DEPARTURE   DEOGYUSAN NATIONAL PARK

By bus The national park and ski resort can both be reached on regular buses via Muju town itself. The 19km drive in is astonishingly beautiful, taking you through a typically relaxed slice of rural Jeolla. Buses continue past the resort on to Gucheondong, the main entrance to the

national park; there are also free hourly shuttle buses linking this entrance with the ski resort.

Destinations (Muju): Daejeon (every 30min; 1hr 30min); Gwangju (every 30min; 3hr 40min); Jeonju (frequent; 2hr); Seoul (5 daily; 2hr 40min).

ACCOMMODATION AND EATING

It'll cost a pretty penny to stay in or next to the **ski resort** itself, where prices go through the roof during ski season. Things are much less expensive in the motel district down the hill; few establishments are worthy of special mention, and it will always pay to shop around. The area also has restaurants aplenty, but most notable during wintertime is **Carnival Street**, a quasi-Austrian collection of **restaurants** and cafés below the *Tirol* – a refreshing change if you've been in Korea for a while.

Muju In Guesthouse 무주 인 게스트하우스
Gucheondong ☎ 063 320 7000. Though not in the resort itself, there are ski slopes right by to this hostel-cum-guesthouse, which may be simple, but provides good value for money in the pricey winter season – it's just a pity that the beds in the private rooms offer no more comfort than the dorm beds. Breakfast included. Dorms W30,000, twins W85,000

Tirol 호텔 티롤 Muju resort ☎ 063 320 7200. Right next to the ski runs and resembling an Austrian cabin, this hotel is absurdly expensive during the peak winter season, and far from cheap at other times. It's a nice place, though, with well-appointed rooms that are piping hot, even in the depths of winter – the suites also come with four-poster beds, and breakfast is included in the price. W380,000

Chung-cheong

BEOPJUSA TEMPLE

Chungcheong

Of South Korea's principal regions, Chungcheong (충청) is the least visited by foreign travellers, most of whom choose to rush through it on buses and trains to Gyeongju or Busan in the southeast, or over it on planes to Jeju-do. But to do so is to bypass the heart of the country, a thrillingly rural mishmash of rice paddies, ginseng fields, national parks and unhurried islands. One less obvious Chungcheong attraction is the local populace – the Chungcheongese are noted throughout Korea for their relaxed nature. Here, you'll get less pressure at the markets, or perhaps even notice a delay of a second or two when the traffic lights change before being deafened by a cacophony of car horns. The region's main cities are noticeably laidback by Korean standards, and the Chungcheongese themselves, particularly those living in the countryside, speak at a markedly slower pace than other Koreans.

Today split into two provinces, Chungcheong was named in the fourteenth century by fusing the names of Chungju and Cheongju, then its two major cities – they're still around today, but of little interest to travellers (Cheongju did, however, produce the world's first book; see page 292). Administratively separate from the two Chungcheong provinces, and lying in between them, is **Daejeon**, the area's largest city and a fun place to sample some urban delights.

The westernmost of the two provinces is **Chungnam** (충남), whose name somewhat confusingly translates as "South Chungcheong". Its western edge is washed by the West Sea, and has a few good beaches – the strip of white sand in **Daecheon** is one of the busiest in the country, with the summer revelry hitting its zenith each July at an immensely popular **mud festival**. Off this coast are a number of accessible **islands** – tiny squads of rock stretch far beyond the horizon into the West Sea, and sustain fishing communities that provide a glimpse into pre-karaoke Korean life. Head inland instead and the pleasures take a turn for the traditional: the small cities of **Buyeo** and **Gongju** functioned as capitals of the **Baekje dynasty** (18 BC–660 AD; see page 278) just as the Roman Empire was collapsing, yet each still boasts a superb wealth of dynastic sights. Both are home to fortresses, regal tombs and museums filled with gleaming jewellery of the period, which went on to have a profound influence on Japanese craft. North of Gongju, and actually part of Seoul's sprawling subway network, is **Cheonan**, which is home to the country's largest, and possibly most revealing, museum.

To the east, the land becomes ever more mountainous as you enter the province of **Chungbuk** (충북; "North Chungcheong"). As Korea's only landlocked province, this could be said to represent the heart of the country, a predominantly rural patchwork of fields and peaks, with a handful of national parks within its borders. **Songnisan** is deservedly the most popular, and has a number of good day-hikes emanating from

GUINSA

Highlights

❶ Gongju and Buyeo Head to the former capitals of the Baekje dynasty to feast your eyes on their regal riches. See pages 276 and 281

❷ Boryeong mud festival Get dirty on the beach at the most enjoyable festival on the Korean calendar. See page 284

❸ West Sea islands Chungcheong boasts a number of tiny, beach-pocked isles, home to fishing communities and a relaxed way of life that's hard to find on the mainland. See page 286

❹ Independence Hall of Korea The nationalistic side of the Korean psyche is laid bare at this huge testament to the country's survival of Japanese occupation. See page 288

❺ Beopjusa temple This striking temple features an enormous bronze Buddha, and is surrounded by the hiker-friendly peaks of Songnisan National Park. See page 290

❻ Danyang Take a midnight stroll, *makgeolli* in hand, along this tiny town's lakeside promenade. See page 292

❼ Guinsa Clamber around the snake-like alleyways of what may well be Korea's most distinctive temple. See page 295

HIGHLIGHTS ARE MARKED ON THE MAP ON PAGE 270

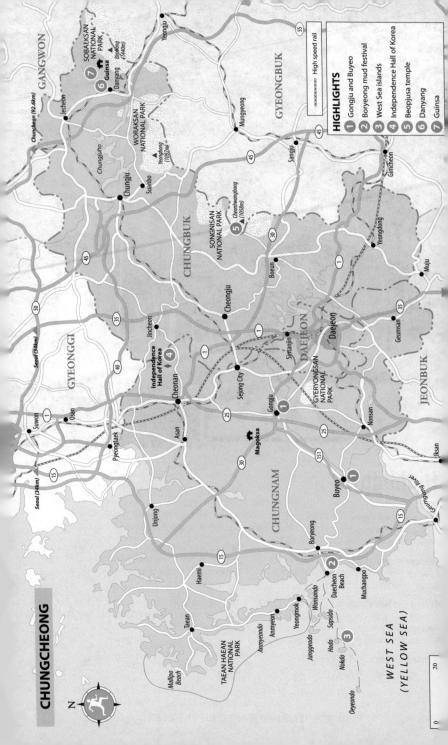

> **SLOW TALK**
>
> When passing through rural Chungcheong, those who've been travelling around Korea for a while may notice something special about the way locals talk. The **pace of conversation** here is slower than in the rest of the land (particularly the staccato patois of Gyeongsang province), with some locals speaking in a drawl that can even have non-native students of the language rolling their eyes and looking at their watches in frustration. One folk tale, retold across the nation, describes a Chungcheongese town that was destroyed by a falling boulder: apparently it was spotted early enough, but locals were unable to elucidate their warnings in a speedy enough manner.

6

Beopjusa, a highly picturesque temple near the park's main entrance. **Sobaeksan** is less visited but just as appealing to hikers; it surrounds the lakeside resort town of **Danyang**, which makes a comfortable base for exploring the caves, fortresses and sprawling temple of **Guinsa** on the province's eastern flank.

Daejeon

대전

Every country has a city like **DAEJEON** – somewhere pleasant to go about daily life, but with little to offer the casual visitor. These, however, arrive in surprisingly high numbers, many using the city as a default stopover on the high-speed rail line from Seoul to Busan. There are far better places in which to break this journey, including on the lesser-used slow line through Danyang, Andong and Gyeongju (see "Itineraries", see page 24), but if you do choose to hole up in Daejeon you'll find decent nightlife and a few mildly diverting attractions. The most vaunted of the latter is **Yuseong**, a therapeutic hot-spring resort sitting near the **Gapcheon River** on the western flank of the city. On the opposite side of the river lies the pleasant **Hanbat Arboretum**, while the peak of **Gyejoksan**, on the city fringes, makes for a rewarding climb. Lastly, and perhaps most importantly, Daejeon is also a good jumping-off point for **Gyeryongsan**, a small but pretty national park to the west (see page 274).

Yuseong Spa

유성온천 • Most springs open daily 9am–6pm • Entry to Yousung Hotel pools W9000 • Yuseong Spa subway

The **Yuseong** hot-spring district is revered across the land for its purportedly curative waters, which bubble up into the communal steam rooms of a series of middling hotels (the Yousung is recommended; see page 274); non-guests can usually use them for a small fee. Unfortunately, this is a heavily built-up – and, to be frank, rather ugly – slice of urban Korea. One recent attempt at partial prettification saw a small channel of spring water routed along the area's main stretch, which makes for a rather lovely footbath.

The Gapcheon

갑천 • Hanbat Arboretum Jan–March & Oct–Dec daily 9am–6pm, April–Sept daily 9am–9pm • Free • Daejeon Art Gallery Tues–Sun 10am–6pm • W500

Wide as it may appear, the **Gapcheon** is too short to qualify as a river, and is thus, according to Korean officialdom, officially a stream. Its banks come alive in the summer with picnickers, and the park-like area immediately south of the pedestrianized Expo Bridge is a popular weekend hangout for local families. You can rent bikes from a booth just south of the bridge (W5000 per hour). In the park-like expanse to the south, you'll also find the peaceful **Hanbat Arboretum**, and the excellent **Daejeon Museum of Art**, which tends to focus on modern art.

6

Gyejoksan

계족산 • On a number of bus routes, including the #720 and #102 (every 10–15min)

One of the best ways in which to enjoy Daejeon is to look down on it from one of the several mountains encircling the city. Budding hikers are advised to make their way to **Gyejoksan**, a 429m-high peak rising cone-like from a plateau on the city's northeastern fringe. After a simple, invigorating climb of under two hours, you'll have fantastic views of Daejeon on one side, and a man-made lake to the other; signs point the way to secluded temples and hermitages, and you can also see a couple of sections of fortress wall from the Baekje era. A more recent addition is the "eco-walking" **Red Clay Trail**, which stretches for 14km and apparently constitutes the nation's first barefoot mountain path – you don't have to do the whole lot.

ARRIVAL AND DEPARTURE   DAEJEON

By train The city has two train stations: Daejeon station is right in the centre and sits on the Seoul–Busan line, while Seodaejeon station is a W4500 taxi ride away to the west (or a 15min walk from Oryong subway station), sitting on a line that splits off north of Daejeon for Gwangju and Mokpo. Both handle high-speed KTX services, though slower, cheaper trains are available too.

Destinations (Daejeon station) Busan (3–6 hourly; 1hr 40min); Cheonan (1–3 hourly; 30min); Daegu (Dongdaegu station; 3–6 hourly; 45min); Seoul (3–6 hourly; 1hr).

Destinations (Seodaejeon station) Cheonan (6 daily; 25min); Gwangju (Songjeong station; 9 daily; 1hr 30min); Jeonju (14 daily; 1hr 15min); Seoul (Yongsan station; 1–3 hourly; 1hr).

By bus Daejeon has excellent bus connections to every major city in the country, though arrivals are often hampered by the city's incessant traffic – and the fact that there are several terminals to choose from. The main one is the mammoth Terminal Complex (복합 터미널) to the northeast of the city (sadly nowhere near the subway line);

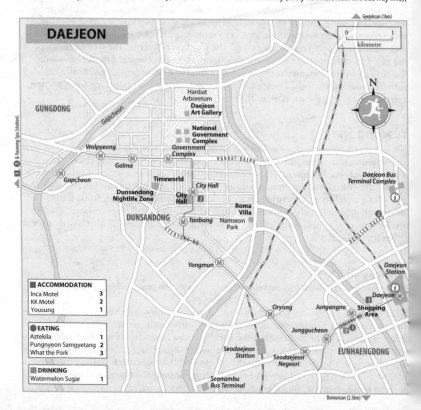

DAEJEON

Gyejoksan (1km)

0   1
kilometre

N

GUNGDONG

Hanbat Arboretum
Daejeon Art Gallery

Gapcheon

National Government Complex

Wolpyeong

Government Complex

HANBAT-DAERO

Galma

Gapcheon

Timeworld

Dunsandong Nightlife Zone

City Hall

City Hall

Roma Villa

Daejeon Bus Terminal Complex

DUNSANDONG

Tanbang

Namseon Park

DONGSEO-DAERO

GYERYONG-RO

Yongmun

Daejeon Station

Daejeon

ACCOMMODATION
Inca Motel	3
KK Motel	2
Yousung	1

EATING
Aztekila	1
Pungnyeon Samgyetang	2
What the Pork	3

DRINKING
Watermelon Sugar	1

Oryong

Jungangno

Shopping Area

Junggucheon

JUNGANG-RO

Seodaejeon Station

Seodaejeon Negeori

EUNHAENGDONG

Seonambu Bus Terminal

Bomunsan (2.5km)

& Yuseong Spa (station)

THE CURE-ALL ROOT

For centuries, perhaps even millennia, the **ginseng root** has been used in Asia for its medicinal qualities, particularly its ability to retain or restore the body's **Yin–Yang** balance; for a time, it was valued more highly by weight than gold. Even today, Korean ginseng is much sought after on the global market, due to the country's ideal climatic conditions; known locally as **insam** (인삼), much of it is grown in the Chungcheong provinces under slanted nets of black plastic. The roots take anything up to six years to mature, and suck up so much nutrition from the soil that, once harvested, no more ginseng can be planted in the same field for over a decade.

The **health benefits** of ginseng have been much debated, and most of the evidence in favour of the root is anecdotal rather than scientific. There are, nonetheless, hordes of admirers, and it's possible to get your fix in pills, capsules, jellies, chewing gum or boiled sweets, as well as the more traditional tea. As the purported benefits depend on the dosage and type of ginseng used (red or white), it's best to consult a practitioner of oriental medicines, but one safe – and delicious – dish is **samgyetang** (삼계탕), a tasty and extremely healthy soup made with a ginseng-stuffed chicken, available for W8000–15,000 across the land. Or for a slightly quirky drink, try mixing a sachet of ginseng granules and a spoon of brown sugar into hot milk – your very own **ginseng latte**.

6

its express and intercity wings are connected by walkway. Buses from most Chungcheong destinations arrive at the Seonambu (서남부) terminal to the south of the city, though you'll get to some faster from the tiny Yuseong (유성) terminal, in the eponymous hot-spring area to Daejeon's west, and nearer to the city subway than any other Daejeon bus terminal.

Destinations (Terminal Complex intercity) Andong (1–3 hourly; 2hr 10min); Gongju (1–3 hourly; 1hr); Muju (1–2 hourly; 50min); Songnisan (11 daily; 1hr 40min); Seoul (every 20–30min; 2hr).

Destinations (Terminal Complex express) Busan (6 daily; 3hr); Cheonan (every 40min; 1hr); Daegu (1–2 hourly; 1hr 40min); Gwangju (every 40min; 2hr 30min); Gyeongju (2 daily; 2hr 40min); Jeonju (every 30min; 1hr 20min); Seoul (every 15min; 2hr).

Destinations (Seonambu terminal) Buyeo (1–2 hourly; 1hr 45min); Daecheon (10 daily; 2hr); Gongju (1–3 hourly; 1hr).

Destinations (Yuseong terminal) Buyeo (1–2 hourly; 1hr 40min); Daecheon (1–2 hourly; 2hr).

GETTING AROUND

By bus The city's size and levels of traffic can make getting around frustrating. The city bus network is comprehensive but complicated, with hundreds of routes (tickets W1400) – two of the most useful are #841, which connects Daejeon station to all three bus terminals, and #107, which runs from the express terminal via Yuseong to Gyeryongsan National Park (see page 274).

By subway Given the traffic, it's usually better to make

use of the single subway line bisecting the city whenever possible; the network is not exactly all-encompassing, but it's good for heading from Daejeon station to Yuseong, or the bars of Dunsandong. Tickets cost W1400 a pop.

By taxi This is Korea – taxis are absolutely everywhere (the ones with their roof lights on are available), and a ride across town is unlikely to set you back more than W10,000.

ACCOMMODATION

Finding a **place to stay** shouldn't be too much trouble, though don't expect much in the centre. The higher-end lodgings are all out west in **Yuseong** (see page 271), and many squat over **hot springs**, the mineral-heavy waters coursing up into bathrooms and communal steam rooms. The city centre's main **motel** areas are notoriously sleazy, particularly the one surrounding the main bus terminal. Pickings are even slimmer in Eunhaengdong, the area west of the main train station.

Inca Motel 인카 모텔 570 Daejeoncheondong-ro ☎ 042 226 3000; map p.272. An easy walk from the main train station, this snazzy love motel also makes a suitable mid-range-ish place to stay. Rooms are large and gaudily decorated, though this being Korea, even those facing the adjacent river have no real view. **W60,000**

KK Motel 케이케이 모텔 27 Dunsanjung-ro 40-gil

☎ 042 487 3009; map p.272. Though some of its neighbours are bookable on international accommodation sites, this place is the most amenable to bargaining of all the motels in the wider Dunsandong party area – and has the largest rooms to boot. Your cash will buy a neat room with a comfy bed and far too many mirrors, plus all the motel regulars such as free toothpaste and power showers. **W40,000**

6

A CAPITAL IDEA

Thrusting up from the very centre of Daejeon are the buildings of the **National Government Complex** – four large, sinister cuboids whose red lights blink in eerie non-unison at night. While there's nothing for the Ordinary Joe to see inside, these buildings represent the most visible examples of Korea's attempts to shift a bunch of government agencies from Seoul. As well as the generic decentralization-driven rationale propping up such plans around the globe, the North Korea issue was a prime factor in the decision to relocate – Seoul lies just 50km from the border of a country with which it remains at war. The initial plans were to move the capital entirely from Seoul, though these were watered down following the discovery that doing so would violate the national constitution. Busan will now get fisheries and maritime agencies; Chuncheon gets tourism; Ulsan will house those pertaining to labour and energy, and so on. The main focus, however, is now **Sejong City**, a new development currently taking shape just north of Daejeon; though many government bureaucrats have been somewhat miffed about being sent "to live in the countryside", the city is growing at pace, and expected to be home to over half a million by 2030.

Yousung 유성 9 Oncheonno ☎042 820 0100, ⓦyousunghotel.com; map p.272. Yuseong's grand old dame (its name, appropriately, using now-retired Romanization) is ticking over nicely. Its partly outdoor on-site spa is the big draw, if functional rather than attractive,

and it's open to non-guests for W9000. The hotel rooms themselves are spacious and furnished with all mod cons; though the views aren't great, it still pays to plump for as high a floor as possible. <u>W235,000</u>

EATING

Daejeon's culinary scene is decidedly unremarkable, but this being Korea, you should still eat well. Of particular note are international places serving the many local expat teachers.

Aztekila 아즈테낄라 2F 27 Oncheonbuk-ro ☎010 8733 8033; map p.272. Mexican-run joint in the Yuseong Spa neighbourhood, serving decent quesadillas, tacos and burritos for W9000–13,000. Wash them down with a tequila slammer (W7000). Mon–Fri & Sun 11.30am–10pm.

Pungnyeon Samgyetang 풍년 삼계탕 407 Gyejok-ro ☎042 632 5757; map p.272. This is the best place in town to hunt down the healthy local favourite, *samgyetang* (삼계탕), a ginseng-infused chicken soup (W11,000); the roots used here come from nearby Geumsan, one of the world's most vaunted locations for the growing of ginseng

(see page 273). A ten-minute walk southwest of the bus terminals, though several places closer to the buses serve the same dish. Daily 10am–10pm.

What the Pork 왓더포크 24 Jungang-ro 130-gil ☎010 4080 9364; map p.272. You have to admire such a name, yet this place has become super-popular with Daejeon's English-teacher set on account of its succulent ribs – we're talking American-style, rather than Korean galbi, but good meat is good meat, and you should eat well for around W20,000 per head. Mon–Fri 5pm–midnight, Sat & Sun noon–2am.

DRINKING

Eunhaengdong, the zone west of the train station, constitutes the old nightlife area, but much of the action has shifted to **Dunsandong**, near City Hall; there's also a nice little student scene in **Gungdong**, around Chungnam University.

Watermelon Sugar 수박설탕 2F 29 Bomun-ro 262-gil ☎042 221 0474; map p.272. This tiny club has been going since the turn of the century – they often seem to be

using the same playlist from 2002, but young Daejeonites, and a few expats, come to "booby booby" (a local term for bump and grind) weekend nights away. Daily 7pm–3am.

Gyeryongsan National Park

계룡산 국립 공원 • Daily from 2hr before sunrise to sunset • Free • ⓦenglish.knps.or.kr

Despite its comparatively puny size relative to its Korean brethren, **Gyeryongsan National Park** (see map, p.276) is a true delight, with herons flitting along the trickling streams, wild boar rifling through the woods and bizarre long-net stinkhorn mushrooms – like regular mushrooms, but with a yellow honeycombed veil – found on the forest floors. It is said to have the most *gi* (기; life-force) of any national park in Korea, one of several factors that haul in 1.4 million people per year, making it the most visited national park in the Chungcheong region. The main reasons for this are accessibility and manageability: it lies equidistant from Gongju to the west and Daejeon to the east, and easy day-hikes run up and over the central peaks, connecting **Gapsa** and **Donghaksa**, two temples flanking the park, and each more than a millennium old.

6

Gapsa

갑사 • Daily 5.30am–8pm • W3000

On the western side of the park, **Gapsa** is the larger and more enchanting of Gyeryongsan's pair of temples, its beauty enhanced further when surrounded by the fiery colours of autumn – maple and ginkgo trees make a near-complete ring around the complex, and if you're here at the right time you'll be treated to a joyous snowfall of yellow and red. It was established in 420, during the dawn of Korean Buddhism, though needless to say no extant structures are of anything approaching this vintage.

Donghaksa

동학사 • Daily 5.30am–8pm • W3000

On the other side of the park entirely, and connected to Gapsa with umpteen hiking trails (see page 275), **Donghaksa** is best accessed from Daejeon and is said to look at its most beautiful in the spring. It has served as a college for Buddhist nuns since 724, and its various buildings exude an air of restraint; some have, sadly, been renovated without much care, though be sure to check out the fantastic carvings on the doors to its main hall.

ARRIVAL AND DEPARTURE
GYERYONGSAN NATIONAL PARK

To Gapsa Bus #320 heads to the Gapsa entrance on the park's west side from Gongju's local bus terminal (1–2 hourly; 30min); it's also accessible from Yuseong terminal in Daejeon (7 daily; 50min). To get there from Gongju's main bus terminal, it's fastest to grab the next bus heading to or through Gyeryong-myeon, then wait to pick up the aforementioned local service. Lastly, a taxi from Gongju shouldn't set you back more than W30,000.

To Donghaksa Bus #107 (every 15min) runs from Daejeon train station to the Donghaksa entrance on the park's east side, though it can take over an hour; you're best advised to head to the Yuseong terminal by subway, from where the same bus takes as little as 25min. You can also take bus #350 from Gongju's local bus terminal (3 daily; 1hr 20min).

HIKING GYERYONGSAN

Although Gyeryongsan's temples are pretty, most visitors to the park are actually here for the **hike** between them – two main routes scale the ridge and both should have you up and down within four hours, including rests. Given the terrain, it's slightly easier to hike east to west if you have a choice; heading in this direction, most people choose to take the path that runs up the east side of Donghaksa, which takes in a couple of ornate stone pagodas on its way to Gapsa. Others take a faster but more challenging route leading west from the temple, which heads up the 816m-high peak of **Gwaneumbong**; these two routes are connected by a beautiful **ridge path** boasting particularly sumptuous views. Whichever way you go, routes are well signposted, though the tracks can get uncomfortably busy at weekends; a less crowded (and much tougher) day-hike runs from **Byeongsagol** ticket booth – on the road north of the main eastern entrance to the park – to Gwaneumbong, taking in at least seven peaks before finally dropping down to Gapsa.

6

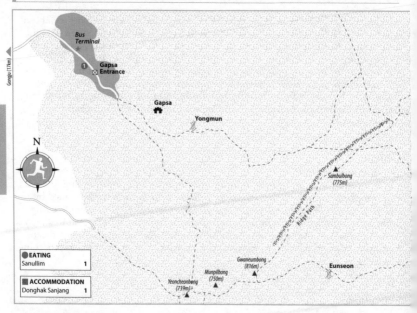

EATING
Sanullim   1

ACCOMMODATION
Donghak Sanjang   1

Map labels: Bus Terminal · Gongju (17km) · Gapsa Entrance · Gapsa · Yongmun · Sambulbong (775m) · N · Ridge Path · Gwaneumbong (816m) · Munpilbong (750m) · Eunseon · Yeoncheonbong (739m)

ACCOMMODATION

Most visitors to the park stay in nearby Gongju or Daejeon, but with time on your side a night in the park can come as a pleasant change of pace. The bulk of Gyeryongsan's **rooms** are around the bus terminal below Donghaksa, but not all are of high quality; there's also a campsite here (from W5000 per head). The Gapsa end is prettier and more relaxed; below the temple are some very rural *minbak*, while on the other side of the car park is a sweet village of **traditional houses** with simple rooms for rent (W20,000 or so) – at night the cramped, yellow-lit alleyways create a scene redolent of a bygone era, and make for a truly atmospheric stay. Finally, note that both temples offer **templestay** programmes for W40,000 per head (see page 35 for more).

Donghak Sanjang 동학산장 735-2 Hakbong-ri ☏ 042 825 4301, ⓦ dhsanjang.co.kr; map above. What a difference a renovation can make: once a run-of-the-mill flophouse, this is now a spick-and-span pension with a stylish lobby and conference facilities. It's angled at families and groups, though there are a few rooms sleeping two – a bit plain, but with comfy beds and sleek bathrooms. Prices drop on weekdays. **W100,000**

EATING

Sanullim 산울림 Jungjang-ri 28-10 ☏ 041 857 5206; map above. On both sides of the park, local *ajummas* will go out of their way to lure you into their restaurants. The first one you come to on the approach to Gapsa is recommended, and has been so since the 1970s – look for the big water wheel outside. Dishes here include acorn jelly pancakes (도토리전; W8000), while the mountain-vegetable sets (된장벽반; W8000) are excellent value. As with any national park restaurant worth its salt, there's plenty of *makgeolli* (rice beer) here too. Daily 8am–9pm.

Gongju and around

공주

Is this Korea's most underrated travel destination? Presided over by the large fortress of Gongsanseong, small, sleepy **GONGJU** is one of the most charming cities in the land, and deserving of a little more fame. It's also the best place in which to see relics from the **Baekje dynasty** that it ruled, as capital, in the fifth and sixth centuries (see page 278). **King Muryeong**, the city's most famous inhabitant, lay here undisturbed

for over 1400 years, after which his tomb yielded thousands of pieces of jewellery that provided a hitherto unattainable insight into the splendid craft of the Baekje people. It's tempting to think that the city has changed little in the meantime – notably, it remains off the national rail network, the result of traditionalist lobbying in the 1970s. Largely devoid of bustle, clutter and chain stores, and with a number of wonderful sights, Gongju is worthy of at least a day of your time – and perhaps more if you want to explore **Magoksa** temple or other sights in the wider area, and take full advantage of some surprisingly good restaurants.

The **Baekje Cultural Festival** (⑩baekje.org) takes place each September and/or early October, with colourful parades and traditional performances in and around Gongju.

Gongsanseong

공산성 • Daily 9am–6pm • Changing of the guard April–June, Sept & Oct daily 2pm • W1200

For centuries, Gongju's focal point has been the hilltop fortress of **Gongsanseong**, whose 2.6km-long **perimeter wall** was built from local mud in Baekje times, before receiving a stone upgrade in the seventeenth century. It's possible to walk the entire circumference of the wall, a flag-pocked, up-and-down course that occasionally affords splendid views of Gongju and its surrounding area. The grounds inside are worth a look too, inhabited by stripey squirrels and riddled with paths leading to a number of carefully painted **pavilions**. Of these, **Ssangsujeong** has the most interesting history: where the pavilion now stands, a Joseon-dynasty king named Injo (ruled 1623–49) once hid under a couple of trees during a peasant-led rebellion against his rule; when this was quashed, the trees were made government officials, though sadly they're no longer around to lend their leafy views to civil proceedings. Airy, green **Imnyugak**, painted with meticulous care, is the most beautiful pavilion; press on further west down a small path for great views of eastern Gongju.

Down by the river there's a small temple, a refuge to monks who fought the Japanese in 1592, and on summer weekends visitors have the opportunity to dress up as a Baekje

6

THE BAEKJE DYNASTY

The **Baekje dynasty** was one of Korea's famed **Three Kingdoms** – Goguryeo and Silla being the other two – and controlled much of southwestern Korea for almost seven hundred years. The *Samguk Sagi*, Korea's only real historical account of the peninsula in these times, claims that Baekje was a product of sibling rivalry – it was founded in 18 BC by **Onjo**, whose father had kick-started the Goguryeo dynasty less than twenty years beforehand, in present-day North Korea; seeing the reins of power passed on to his elder brother Yuri, Onjo promptly moved south and set up his own kingdom.

Strangely, given its position facing China on the western side of the Korean peninsula, Baekje was more closely allied with the kingdom of Wa in Japan – at least one Baekje king was born across the East Sea – and it became a conduit for art, religion and customs from the Asian mainland. This fact is perhaps best embodied by the **Baekje artefacts** displayed in the museums in Buyeo (see page 282) and Gongju (see page 279), which contain lacquer boxes, pottery and folding screens not dissimilar to the craftwork that Japan is now famed for. Unabashedly excessive, yet at the same time achieving an ornate simplicity, Baekje jewellery also attained an international reputation, and went on to exert an influence on the Japanese craft of jewellery-making.

Though the exact location of the first Baekje capitals is unclear, it's certain that Gongju and Buyeo were its last two seats of power. **Gongju**, then known as Ungjin, was **capital** from 475 to 538; during this period the aforementioned Three Kingdoms were jostling for power, and while Baekje leaders formed an uneasy alliance with their Silla counterparts the large fortress of Gongsanseong (see page 277) was built to protect the city from Goguryeo attacks. The capital was transferred to **Sabi** – present-day **Buyeo** – which also received a fortress-shaped upgrade (see page 281). However, it was here that the Baekje kingdom finally ground to a halt in 660, succumbing to the Silla forces that, following their crushing of Goguryeo shortly afterwards, went on to rule the whole peninsula.

Though local rebellions briefly brought Baekje back to power in the years leading up to the disintegration of Unified Silla, it was finally stamped out by the nascent Goryeo dynasty in 935. Despite the many centuries that have elapsed since, much evidence of Baekje times can still be seen today in the form of the regal **burial mounds** found in Gongju and Buyeo.

warrior and shoot off a few arrows. Lastly, note that *Gomanaru*, one of Gongju's – nay, Korea's – best **restaurants**, is a stone's throw from the fortress entrance (see page 280).

The tomb of King Muryeong

무령왕릉 • Daily 9am–6pm • W1500

Heading west over the creek from Gongsanseong, you'll eventually come to the **Tomb of King Muryeong**, one of many regal burial groups dotted around the country from the Three Kingdoms period, but the only Baekje mound whose occupant is known for sure. Muryeong, who ruled for the first quarter of the sixth century, was credited with strengthening his kingdom by improving relations with those in China and Japan; some accounts suggest that the design of Japanese jewellery was influenced by gifts that he sent across. His gentle green **burial mound** was discovered by accident in 1971 during a civic construction project – after one and a half millennia, Muryeong's tomb was the only one that hadn't been looted. Everything has now been sealed off for preservation – the fact that you can't peek inside is disappointing, but the sound of summer cicadas whirring in the trees, and the views of the rolling tomb mounds themselves, make for a pleasant stroll. A small **exhibition hall** contains replicas of Muryeong's tomb and the artefacts found within (the originals are in the Gongju National Museum – see below).

Gongju Hanok Village

공주 한옥 마을 • Daily 24hr • Free

A short walk from the regal tombs is **Gongju Hanok Village**, a fairly decent recreation of a Baekje-era village – though one complete with café, restaurants and a convenience store. Unlike its counterparts in Seoul (see page 69) and Jeonju (see page 258), this is a tourist construct rather than a functional part of the city; nevertheless, it makes good camera fodder, and you may find yourself tempted to sleep (see page 280) or eat in these unusual environs.

Gongju National Museum

공주 국립 박물관 • Tues–Sun 9am–6pm • Free • ⓦ gongju.museum.go.kr • Get bus #108 from the bus terminal (W1400), or take a taxi (around W4000)

To see the actual riches retrieved from Muryeong's tomb, head west to **Gongju National Museum**, set in a quiet wooded area by the turn of the river. Much of the museum is devoted to jewellery, and an impressive collection of Baekje bling reveals the dynasty's penchant for gold, silver and bronze. Artefacts such as elaborate golden earrings show an impressive attention to detail, but manage to be dignified and restrained in their use of shape and texture. The highlight is the king's flame-like **golden headwear**, once worn like rabbit ears on the royal scalp, and now one of the most important symbols not just of Gongju, but of the Baekje dynasty itself. Elsewhere in the museum exhibits of wood and clay show the dynasty's history of trade with Japan and China.

ARRIVAL AND INFORMATION GONGJU

By bus There are direct buses to Gongju's intercity bus terminal from cities and towns across the Chungcheong provinces, as well as Seoul and other major Korean cities. From the terminal, it's a beautiful 15min walk to Gongsanseong, along the river and over the bridge. There's another small local bus terminal near the fortress,

serving destinations around Gongju's periphery, including Magoksa and Gyeryongsan National Park.

Destinations Buyeo (1–3 hourly; 1hr); Cheonan (1–2 hourly; 1hr 10min); Daecheon (1–2 hourly; 1hr 40min); Daejeon (every 5–15min; 50min); Seoul (1–2 hourly; 1hr 20min).

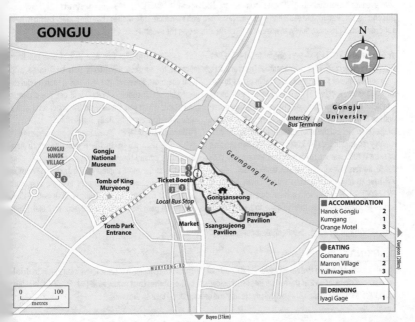

■ ACCOMMODATION	
Hanok Gongju	2
Kumgang	1
Orange Motel	3

● EATING	
Gomanaru	1
Marron Village	2
Yulhwagwan	3

■ DRINKING	
Iyagi Gage	1

By train In the 1980s, Gongju locals successfully protested against plans to run a train line here – as such, in 2015 it became perhaps the first city on earth whose first-ever trains were of the high-speed variety. However, the station is annoyingly far (25km south; bus #200 connects it to the city for W1400, and a cab will be around W20,000), and as such it's only worth considering if you're looking to KTX it to or from Gwangju, Jeonju or Mokpo.

Destinations Gwangju (7 daily; 50min); Jeonju (8 daily; 35min); Mokpo (5 daily; 1hr 30min); Seoul (Yongsan station; 14 daily; 1hr).

Tourist information The main tourist information centre (daily 9am–6pm; ☎041 856 7700) is under Gongsanseong.

ACCOMMODATION

Gongju's poor range of **accommodation** is no doubt the main reason why the city still fails to attract international tourists in any decent numbers. **Motels** are centred in two areas: a bunch of new establishments to the west of the bus terminal (including a couple of cheesy replica "castles" north of the river), and a group of older cheapies south of the river across the road from Gongsanseong. The latter is a quainter and more atmospheric area, and slightly closer to the sights, but the newer places are far more comfortable.

★ **Hanok Gongju** 한옥 공주 12 Gwangwangdanji-gil ☎041 840 8900; map p.279. A splendidly pretty little faux hamlet of traditional wooden *hanok* housing, sitting in calm isolation between the tombs and museum. Though recently constructed, the buildings certainly feel real enough, and are heated from beneath by burning wood; they're spartan, for sure, but the location is relaxing and the experience somewhat unique. Prices come down to W50,000 on weekdays. W70,000

★ **Kumgang** 호텔 금강 Singwandong 595-8 ☎041 852 1071; map p.279. The only official "hotel" in town, though in reality it's basically a smarter-than-average motel with a few twins and triples. However, it has friendly staff, spacious bathrooms and on-demand TV in all rooms, and should suffice for all but the fussiest travellers. Prices come down a little on weekdays. W60,000

Orange Motel 오렌지 모텔 22 Neutinamu-gil ☎041 856 5033; map p.279. This creekside *yeogwan* is the best option south of the river, and has decent-enough rooms; some have minor views of the adjacent stream area. W35,000

EATING

Food in Gongju is almost uniformly excellent, yet this wonderfully enjoyable facet of the city remains surprisingly off the radar, even for Korean tourists. The local specialities are **duck meat** (오리고기; *ori-gogi*), **chestnuts** (밤; *bam*) and **ginseng** (인삼; *insam*), and you'll find your table festooned with even more **side dishes** than the national norm (which is already a lot). Criminally, however, no restaurants have a view over the river.

★ **Gomanaru** 고마나루 5-9 Bengmigoeul-gil ☎041 857 9999; map p.279. This unassuming restaurant is, quite simply, one of Korea's most enjoyable places to eat. Their huge *ssam-bap* (쌈밥) sets feature a – quite literal – tableful of largely veggie side dishes, and over a dozen kinds of leaves to eat them with. There are a few choices for the centrepiece of the meal, though the barbecued duck is highly recommended (W13,000, minimum two people); an extra W7000 will see the whole shebang covered with edible flowers, which is absolute heaven. Solo diners will have to content themselves with a flower *bibimbap* (W12,000) – this comes with a mere dozen side-dishes, and vegetarians will think they've gone to heaven early. Daily 11am–9pm.

Marron Village 밤마을 5-9 Bengmigoeul-gil ☎041 853 3489; map p.279. One of a pair of pine buildings opposite the fortress, this bakery sells buns made with local chestnuts. However, you may find it more useful for incredibly cheap coffee – W2000 will get you a decent Americano, which you can have on the upper level with a view of the fortress walls. Daily 9am–10pm.

Yulhwagwan 율화관 12 Gwangwangdanji-gil ☎041 840 8900; map p.279. Of the restaurants which have popped up around the *Hanok Gongju* complex (see page 280), this is the most appropriate to travellers; most of their dishes feature local chestnuts in some way, such as the cold noodles (*naengmyeon*; W7000) and seafood buckwheat pancake (*memil haemul jeon*; W12,000). Daily 10am–8pm.

DRINKING

The area around **Gongju University** (공주대), north of the main bus terminal, has some interesting places to drink. Convenience stores, as well as the restaurants listed below, sell bottles of **chestnut makgeolli** (밤 막걸리; W1800 in a shop, W5000 in a restaurant), a particularly creamy and delicious local take on the drink.

★ **Iyagi Gage** 이야기 가게_3F Gongjudaehak-ro ☎ 010 5507 7457; map p.279. A little away from the most vibrant bit of the student zone, this is by far the most attractive drinking hole in the area, and commonly frequented by expat teachers. Those who drop by regularly refer to it as the "Art Bar", since there's all sorts of arty paraphernalia dangling from the ceilings and strewn across the tables, and there's a modest range of beers and cocktails to enjoy. Daily 6pm–4am.

Magoksa

마곡사 • Daily sunrise–sunset • W3000 • Bus #600 or #601 from Gongju bus terminal, or #770 from Gongju local bus terminal (all 45min; W1400)

A beautiful bus ride through the countryside west of Gongju is **Magoksa**. The exact year of this temple's creation remains as mysterious as its remote, forested environs, but it's believed to date from the early 640s. It is now a principal temple of the **Jogye** order, the largest sect in Korean Buddhism. Although the most important buildings huddle together in a tight pack, rustic farmyard dwellings and auxiliary hermitages extend into nearby fields and forest, and can easily fill up a half-day of pleasant meandering. The hushed vibe of the complex is the main attraction, though a few of the buildings are worthy of attention. **Yeongsanjeon** (영산전) is a hall of a thousand individually crafted figurines, and has a nameplate said to have been written by King Sejo (ruled 1455–68), a Joseon-dynasty monarch perhaps best famed for putting his brother to the sword. At the top of the complex, **Daeungbojeon** (대웅보전) is a high point in more than one sense; the three golden statues in this main hall are backed by a large, highly detailed Buddhist painting, and look down on a sea of fish-scaled black roof tiles.

EATING   MAGOKSA

Gareung Binga 가릉빈가 33 Magoksangga-gil. Just down the hill from the main clutch of accommodation, this is a restaurant-cum-teahouse that serenades diners with traditional piped music. Most teas go for around W6000; this being Chungcheong, the ginseng tea (인삼차) is recommended. Daily 8am–6pm.

Buyeo

부여

Smaller and sleepier than Gongju, its Baekje buddy to the east, **BUYEO** is almost equally worthy of a visit. The Baekje seat of power was transferred here from Gongju in 538, and saw six kings come and go before the abrupt termination of the dynasty in 660, when General Gyebaek led his five thousand men into one last battle against a Silla-Chinese coalition ten times that size. Knowing that his resistance would prove futile, the general killed his wife and children before heading into combat, preferring to see them dead than condemn them to slavery. Legend has it that thousands of the town's women threw themselves off a riverside cliff when the battle had been lost, drowning both themselves and the Baekje dynasty. Today, this cliff and the large, verdant **fortress** surrounding it are the town's biggest draw, along with an excellent **museum**.

Buyeo's main street runs between two roundabouts – Boganso Rotary to the north, and Guncheon Rotary 1km to the south. You can orient yourself with the **statue of General Gyebaek**, which stands at the latter.

Busosan

부소산 • Daily: March–Oct 9am–6pm; Nov–Feb 9am–5pm • W2000; ferry rides W4000

Buyeo's centre is dominated by its large fortress. **Busosan** lacks the perimeter wall of Gongju's Gongsanseong, but with its position perched high over the Baengman river, plus a greater variety of trees and a thoroughly enjoyable network of trails, many

6

BUYEO'S ELIXIR OF YOUTH

Tucked behind Goransa temple, which sits on the river side of the Busosan fortress complex, is a small **water spring** which once provided water to the Baekje kings on account of its purported health benefits – servants had to prove that they'd climbed all the way here by serving the water with a distinctive leaf that only grew on a nearby plant. The spring water is said to make you three years younger for every glass you drink – throw down enough and, presumably, you'll be prenatal in no time.

---

visitors find this one even more beautiful. It also has history on its side, as this is where the great Baekje dynasty came to an end after almost seven centuries of rule.

On entering the fortress, you'll soon happen upon **Yeonggillu** pavilion; one of many such structures dotting the grounds, this is where kings often brought local nobility for sunrise meetings, presided over by a pair of snake-like wooden dragons that remain today. Paths wind up to Sajaru, the highest point in the fortress and originally built as a moon-viewing platform. The path continues on to the **clifftop of Nakhwa-am**; from here, it is said, three thousand wives and daughters jumped to their deaths after General Gyebaek's defeat by the Silla-Chinese coalition, choosing suicide over probable rape and servitude. This tragic act gave Nakhwa-am its name – **Falling Flowers Rock** – and has been the subject of countless TV epics.

Down by the river is **Goransa**, a small temple backed by a spring with a bit of a history (see page 282). The best way to finish a trip to the fortress is to take a **ferry ride** from a launch downhill from the spring. These sail a short way down the river to a **sculpture park**, though you'll have to wait for the vessel to fill up before departure, which can be annoyingly infrequent in winter.

Jeongnimsaji

정림사지 • Daily: March–Oct 7am–7pm; Nov–Feb 8am–5pm • W1000

Heading south of Busosan's main entrance, you might want to swing by **Jeongnimsaji**, a small but pretty site once home to a large temple. Several buildings here have been recreated, and you'll also find a five-storey stone pagoda – one of only three survivors from Baekje times – and a seated stone Buddha dating back to the Goryeo era.

Buyeo National Museum

부여 국립 박물관 • Tues–Fri 9am–6pm, Sat & Sun 9am–7pm • Free • ⓦ buyeo.museum.go.kr

As with other "national" museums in Korea, the **Buyeo National Museum** focuses exclusively on artefacts found in its local area; here there's an understandable emphasis on Baekje riches. Some rooms examine Buyeo's gradual shift from the Stone to the Bronze Age with a selection of pots and chopping implements, but inside a room devoted to Baekje treasures is the museum's pride and joy: a **bronze incense burner** that has become the town symbol. Elaborate animal figurines cover the outer shell of this 0.6m-high egg-shaped sculpture, which sits on a base of twisted dragons; it's considered one of the most beautiful Baekje articles ever discovered, displaying the dynasty's love of form, detail and restrained opulence.

Gungnamji

궁남지 • Daily 24hr • Free

A short walk south of General Gyebaek's statue is **Gungnamji**, a beautiful lotus pond with a pavilion at its centre, and surrounded by a circle of willow trees. Outside this weepy perimeter lie acres of lotus paddies, making this peaceful idyll feel as if it's in th middle of the countryside. There's a particularly good café (see page 283) just off the park area's north flank.

ARRIVAL AND INFORMATION BUYEO

By bus Buses arrive at a tiny station in the centre of town; from here most major sights – as well as the majority of motels and restaurants – are within walking distance, though it's easy to hunt down a taxi if necessary.

Destinations Daecheon (11 daily; 1hr); Daejeon (2–3 hourly; 1hr 30min); Gongju (1–2 hourly; 1hr); Seoul (Nambu terminal; 1–2 hourly; 3hr 30min).

Tourist information There's a tourist office next to the fortress entrance (daily 9am–6pm; ☎041 830 2523).

6

ACCOMMODATION

As long as you're not too fussy, **accommodation** is easy to find in Buyeo, and there's a higher-end resort just outside the city. Try to avoid the area around the bus terminal, which contains some rather insalubrious places to stay.

Baekje 백제호텔 108 Bukpo-ro ☎041 835 0870. Inconveniently located a short taxi ride from the bus terminal, this is the only official tourist accommodation near central Buyeo. Rooms are a little drab and motel-like; unless you want to sleep on mats on the floor, go for the "foreign" ones. There's also a small café-bar on site. __W88,000__

★ **Lotte Resort** 롯데 리조트 400 Baekjemun-ro ☎041 939 1000, ⓦlottebuyeoresort.com. Superbly designed resort hotel, whose pleasing, twin-horseshoe-shaped exterior is best described as "neo-Baekje". Although

service is occasionally patchy, the place is good value if you can knock something off the rack rates. The presence of good restaurants is welcome in such a far-flung location – it's located a W8000 taxi ride from central Buyeo, next to Baekje Cultural Land. __W270,000__

Motel VIP 모텔VIP 701 Dongnam-ri ☎041 832 3700. Near Boganso Rotary, this has the best rooms in central Buyeo, though this admittedly isn't saying much. The place is spotless though, with mood lighting in the rooms and piped music in the corridors. __W35,000__

EATING

267 Brunch Café 56 Seodong-ro ☎041 835 0267. A nice little addition to bucolic Buyeo, this airy café has a great location overlooking lotus ponds, plus decent coffee, lots of herbal teas and munchables including bacon-and-cheese omelette (W7500) and burgers (from W8500). Daily 9am–11pm.

Baekje-ui Jip 백제의집 252 Seongwang-ro ☎041 834 1212. On the main road just outside the Busosan entrance, this is the place to hunt down before or after a fortress visit. Here you can have a gigantic set meal of leaves, duck meat (or beef, though duck is a local speciality) and innumerable side dishes, for around W20,000 per person; solo diners may have to contend with the almost equally delectable *yeonipbap* (연잎밥; W10,000), a

surprisingly large set whose main component is rice and other goodies wrapped in a lotus leaf. Daily 9am–9pm.

★ **Minsokgwan** 민속관 64 Naruteo-ro ☎041 835 2445. Fascinating, traditionally styled restaurant with a courtyard full of old Korea paraphernalia, and tables and chairs inside fashioned from tree trunks. The cold buckwheat noodles (*naengmyeon*; 냉면) are good for cooling off in the summer and a snip at W7000; alternatively, try the home-made *kimchi*-tofu mix (두부김치; W10,000). The restaurant is on a road west of Busosan; keep an eye out for a Chinese-language sign with a pair of stone turtles straining their necks towards it. Daily 1–10pm.

Daecheon beach and around

대천 해수욕장

Long, wide and handsome, **Daecheon beach** is by far the most popular on Korea's western coast, attracting a predominantly young crowd. In the summer this 3km-long stretch of sand becomes a sea of people, having fun in the water by day, feasting on the delicious local **shellfish** (see page 285), then drinking and letting off fireworks until the early hours. In summer, visitors can rent banana boats, jet skis and large rubber tubes, or even a **quad bike** to ride up and down the prom; there's also a **zip-wire** ride here. The revelry reaches its crescendo each July with the **Boryeong mud festival**, a week-long event that seems to rope in, and sully, almost

6

THE BORYEONG MUD FESTIVAL AND OTHER ACTIVITIES

English teachers and American soldiers across the land circle the **Boryeong mud festival** (ⓦmudfestival.or.kr) in their diaries, but there's plenty going on by the beach for most of the year. For two July weekends, and the space in between them, the beach is a sea of mud-splattered foreigners and their Korean buddies. The stuff is everywhere, allowing participants to wrestle or slide around in it, throw it at their friends or smear it all over themselves, then take lots and lots of pictures – some will end up on TV, in newspapers or even on tourism posters. The focus of activities is a fenced-off area filled with inflatable slides, mud pools and the like (9.30am–12.30pm & 1.30–6pm; W10,000), though for many the event is simply a fine excuse to get smashed on the beach at night. This is all loads of fun, though it pays to book **transport** and **accommodation** well ahead – take trains rather than buses if at all possible, since the latter can get caught up in horrendous traffic jams. Secondly, if you're going with a group, figure out assembly points when you arrive – the mobile phone network gets strained during the festival, and it can prove almost impossible to meet your buddies.

As with any Korean beach worth its salt, there are a whole bunch of watery activities to enjoy, including speedboat trips (W15,000), banana-boat rides (W20,000) and Iron Man-style water-jet thingies (W50,000). You can also zoom across the beach on a 600m-long zip-wire (W18,000), or pedal across it on a monorail-like "sky-bike" (W22,000 for two people); the latter is a bit of a slow-going selfie-fest, with piped music for the enjoyment of those who just can't stand the sound of waves. Lastly, there are more karaoke places than you can count – just follow the noise (and some words of advice on the local way of doing things; see page 88).

every expat in the country (see page 284). In addition, it's a short ferry trip from the mainland bustle to the **West Sea islands**, a sleepy crew strung out beyond the horizon (see page 286).

Mud House

머드 하우스 • Jun–Aug daily 8am–6pm • W4000

You don't have to visit Daecheon during festival time to get nice and mucky – throughout the summer you can sample the brown stuff at the **Mud House**, the most distinctive building on the beachfront. The ticket gets you entry to an on-site **sauna**, at which you can bathe in a **mud pool** or even paint yourself with the stuff; all manner of mud-based cosmetics are on sale at reception, including mud shampoo, soap and body cream.

ARRIVAL AND INFORMATION   DAECHEON BEACH

Daecheon beach is just 15km from the town of **Boryeong** (보령), and the two places have been known to trade names on occasion – hence the "Boryeong" Mud Festival. Coming from elsewhere in Korea you'll arrive either at Boryeong train station (known as Daecheon) or Boryeong bus station (this time Boryeong), and will then need to take onward transport to the beach. The train and bus stations are visible from each other.

By train Daecheon station sits on a relatively quiet track, with trains every hour or so to Seoul's Yongsan station (2hr 40min), via Suwon and Cheonan. Most services are going to or from Iksan to the south (1hr); change here for high-speed services to Gwangju, Mokpo or Jeonju.

By bus The bus terminal has regular services to Buyeo (7 daily; 1hr); Daejeon (1–2 hourly; 1hr 40min); Gongju (1–2 hourly; 1hr 40min); and Seoul (1–2 hourly; 2hr).

To the beach Buses to the beach run from the train and

bus stations (W1400); the #100 goes to the port first (for the West Sea islands; see page 286), then down the beach from north to south, while the #101 goes the opposite way around the loop, so choose your number wisely (they leave alternately every 10min). Alternatively, the beach is a set W9000 by taxi from either station.

Tourist information There's a small booth near the mud centre; staff can reserve accommodation both in Daecheon and on the offshore islands.

ACCOMMODATION

Although there's very little at the top end of the scale, **motels** and **minbak** are everywhere, and even at the peak summer you can usually find a bed without too much difficulty; prices can go through the roof on summer weekends an holidays, though with time, patience and a few words with the ubiquitous *ajummas*, you should find a room for W30,000. Travellers and locals alike often save money by cramming as many people as possible into a room, or staying out all night on the beach with a few drinks. Lastly, there's a small **campground** behind the mud centre (W10,000 per tent, W2000 per shower).

Motel Coconuts 모텔 코코너츠 7 Haesuyokjang 2-gil ☎041 934 6595. Family-run motel whose rooms have been decorated with occasionally eye-searing wallpaper and bed linens; they're all en suite, with decent showers and cable TV. **W55,000**

Mudrin 리조트 머드린 28 Haesuyokjang 8-gil ☎041 934 1111, ⌂mudrin.com. The best of several higher-end options on the beachfront. The spick-and-

span rooms all boast a sea view, and there's a café and convenience store in the lobby. **W150,000**

Pine Motel 파인 모텔 9 Haesuyokjang 2-gil ☎041 931 7172. Easy to spot on account of its distinctive oriental roof, this motel's rooms are wood-panelled and quite pleasing; all have en-suite facilities. Handily, the place is now on a few international booking engines. **W40,000**

EATING

Daecheon's culinary scene is simple – fish, fish and more fish. The seafront is lined with **seafood restaurants** displaying their still-alive goods in outdoor tanks; among the myriad options are eel, blue crabs and sea cucumbers, but most are here for the **shellfish barbecues** (see page 285), which usually cost W40,000 for two diners. Since all of these restaurants serve the same thing and none have English-language menus, it would be unfair to recommend any particular establishment – just go for a popular place. A more rustic patch of restaurants can be found near **Daecheon harbour**; these are quite atmospheric, especially in the evenings when the ramshackle buildings, bare hanging bulbs and coursing sea water may make you feel as though you've been shunted back in time a couple of decades. If seafood's not your bag, try to hunt down one of the **bakeries** or pork cutlet places; instant noodles, snacks and cheap booze are also available from umpteen **convenience stores**.

Dinghowa 띵호와 2F 891 Daehae-ro ☎041 931 7172. A good option for pescaphobes, this Chinese restaurant serves simple staples such as black-bean-paste noodles (*jjajangmyeon*; W5000), fried rice (*bokkeumbap*; W7000) or fried dumplings (*gun-mandu*; W4000). Veggies may also find solace in their tofu dishes. Daily 11am–11pm.

★ **Susan Market** 수산 시장. Out by the harbour, Daecheon's fish market is one of the best in the country;

it also makes a good place to eat, since whatever you buy on the ground floor can be cooked and served upstairs for a small fee. The grilled eel here (장어구이) is nothing short of divine – it'll cost around W15,000 for a small eel serving two, plus another W10,000 to have it cooked. Daily 6am–7pm.

SHELLFISH BARBECUES

For the uninitiated, Korean seafood can be a little daunting: the prey is often both unfamiliar and alive; English-language menus are hard to find; and the vast majority of meals are for groups rather than single diners. However, it would be a huge pity to leave Daecheon without enjoying a **shellfish barbecue** (*jogae-gui*; 조개구이). The West Sea coast is famed for this bounty, and if you bear in mind a few tips the experience isn't too tricky at all.

First of all, choose a restaurant – any busy one will do. Secondly, set a price: it's usually W40,000 for two people, and another W15,000–20,000 for each additional person; single diners will eventually get lucky for W30,000 if they ask at enough places. The charcoal briquettes at your table will then be fired up, and you'll be presented with a huge round of shellfish, as well as free side dishes such as noodles, pancakes and cheesy corn. Pop the shells on the grill a bunch at a time; the closed ones are ready when they've opened up, while the already-open ones are good when they've been bubbling for a while. You'll also have been handed a tin-foil tray; squirt a bit of pepper paste in from the bottle, and add the "juice" from the various shells as they cook. This makes a broth for the giant **kijogae** (키조개), something like a giant mussel, and for many the tastiest shellfish of all; when cooked, the critter effectively becomes a sort of seafood steak, and has to be chopped up with the scissors you'll have on your table. Throw the pieces into the tin-foil broth, broil them up for a while, and enjoy – some of the tastiest food Korea has to offer.

West Sea islands

From Daecheon harbour, a string of tiny islands – many under the umbrella of the **Taean Haean National Park** (태안해안 국립 공원) – stretch beyond the horizon into what Koreans term the **West Sea**, a body of water known internationally as the Yellow Sea (see page 127). From their distant shores, the mainland is either a lazy murmur on the horizon or altogether out of sight, making this a perfect place to kick back and take it easy. **Beaches** and **seafood** constitute the main draws, but it's also a joy to sample an unhurried island lifestyle that remains unaffected by the changes that swept through the mainland on its freewheeling course to First World status. Fishing boats judder into the docks where the sailors gut and prepare their haul with startling efficiency; it's sometimes possible to buy fish directly from them. Restaurants on the islands are usually rickety, family-run affairs serving simple Korean staples.

There are two main **ferry circuits** heading out from Daecheon: the first is a loop taking in **Sapsido**, **Janggodo** and **Anmyeondo**; while the second hits **Hodo** and **Nokdo** before terminating at **Oeyeondo**, a full 53km out to sea. The ferries on the latter circuit are for foot passengers only, and the islands they visit are thus a fair bit quieter. Remember to bring enough money for your stay, as most of the isles lack **banks**; the majority have mini-markets, but these can be hard to find as they tend to double as family homes.

The Sapsido loop

Sapsido (삽시도; pronounced "sap-shi-doe") is the most popular island in the area. Its shores are dotted with craggy rock formations, while the island's interior is crisscrossed with networks of dirt tracks – it's possible to walk from one end to the other in under an hour. Depending on the tides, ferries will call at one of two ports: make sure that you know which one to go to when you're leaving the island.

Near here, little **Janggodo** (장고도) is home to some stupendous rock formations, it's popular with families and – thanks to some particularly good beaches – the trendier elements of the Korean beach set. Local buses wait at the northern terminal (there are two) to take passengers to the *minbak* area (it's a little far to walk).

Anmyeondo (안면도) is the largest island in the group, and the only one connected to the mainland by road; white-sand beaches fill the coves that dot its west coast, many of them only accessible by footpath from a small road that skirts the shore between **Anmyeon** (안면), the main settlement and transport hub, and **Yeongmok** (영목), a port village at the southern cape that receives ferries from Daecheon and other West Sea islands. Buses connect the two, running approximately once an hour.

The Oeyeondo route

One of the first stops on the Oeyeondo route, **Hodo** (호도) attracts beach-hunters without the fuss of similar places on the mainland. The island's best beach is a curl of white sand just a short walk from the ferry dock and is great for swimming. Around the terminal are plenty of *minbak* rooms – pretty much every dwelling in the village will accept visitors, though there are only around sixty on the whole island.

The smallest island hereabouts is **Nokdo** (녹도), which is home to some superb hill trails. Unlike on the other islands, the hillside town and its accommodation options are a fair walk from the ferry dock – everyone will be going the same way, so you should be able to hitch a lift without too much bother.

The ferries make their final stop at **Oeyeondo** (외연도), a weather-beaten family of thickly forested specks of land. Though the most remote of any of the islands surrounding Daecheon, Oeyeondo possesses the busiest and most built-up port area on the loop, with walking trails heading up to the island's twin peaks, as well as a tiny beach that's good for sunsets.

ARRIVAL AND DEPARTURE

By ferry Ferries connect the islands in two main circuits, though with so few sailings, you won't be able to see more than one or two islands in a day. There are usually three daily sailings from Daecheon (7.40am, noon & 3pm at the time of writing, though this changes frequently) to Sapsido, Janggodo and Anmyeondo. For the Oeyeondo route, there

WEST SEA ISLANDS

are two sailings daily from Daecheon (8am & 2pm; 40min to Hodo, 20min more to Nokdo and a further 30min to Oeyeondo). To get an idea of price, tickets cost W9900 to Sapsido, and W16,500 for the long haul to Oeyeondo.
By bus Anmyeondo is connected by bus to Seoul (15 daily; 3hr 30min), Daejeon (3 daily; 2hr), and almost nowhere else.

ACCOMMODATION AND EATING

All islands have *minbak* and pension **accommodation**, though don't expect anything too fancy – the rooms will be small and bare, and in the *minbak* you'll probably have to sleep on a blanket on the floor. Prices start at W25,000 per night, and increase in summer; when the weather's warm you may need to book ahead, which is easier said than done since almost nobody on the islands speaks English. Your best bet is to arrange things through the Daecheon beach tourist office (see page 284), or even one of their counterparts in Seoul (see page 97). Eating can be tricky – the islands all have **shops** and **restaurants**, though they tend to close early and no menus will be in English. Your accommodation may be able to whip up a meal, though on the larger islands it's quite common for restaurants to pick up customers for free. If you don't like seafood you may have to stick to instant noodles.

Gwangcheon Minbak 광천 민박 Hodo ☎ 010 3474 3385. One of the more reliable places to stay on the islands, with a friendly owner able to speak at least a little English; he also owns basically the only land vehicle on Hodo, and can often be persuaded to give rides across the mudflats when the tide is out. W30,000

Bamseom Pension 밤섬 펜션 Sapsido ☎ 010 5228 1131. Between two beaches (one nice and sandy) at the south end of Sapsido, this pension has large, bright upstairs rooms; the owners speak no English, but are also able to prepare meals for fair prices, or arrange for a pick-up from one of the few island restaurants. W50,000

Cheonan

천안

After years in the shadows, **CHEONAN** – an easy day-trip from the capital – is a city on the up: now connected to Seoul by subway and high-speed train, its population has boomed in recent years, and boasts a notable non-Korean contingent (most pertinently Chinese and Southeast Asians). The new **KTX line** has enabled commuters to work in Seoul while living in a cheaper, more manageable city, but despite the flashy new department stores and housing complexes, there's little here to detain travellers bar the superb **Arario Gallery** and the fascinating **Independence Hall of Korea**, which sits some way out of town.

Arario Gallery

아라리오 갤러리 • Daily 11am–7pm • W3000 • ⍵ arariogallery.com

The only sight of note in central Cheonan is the excellent **Arario Gallery** next to the bus terminal; it's the hub of a wide gallery and museum network, whose tentacles reach to Seoul, Jeju and even China. Outside the main entrance sits one of Damien Hirst's generic body-with-bits-exposed sculptures, alongside a tall tower of car axles that pokes fun at the city's ever-declining reputation as a mere transit hub; inside are two exhibition floors, both small but almost always brimming with high-quality modern art. The gallery has excellent connections to China, which means that it's often possible to catch glimpses of the burgeoning art scene across the West Sea.

Independence Hall of Korea

독립 기념관 • Tues–Sun: March–Oct 9.30am–6pm; Nov–Feb 9.30am–5pm • Free • ⍵ i815.or.kr • Bus #400 from train station or bus terminal (40min)

JAPANESE OCCUPATION

If you've done any sightseeing in Korea, you'll no doubt have come across information boards telling you when, or how often, certain buildings were burned down or destroyed by the Japanese. The two countries have been at loggerheads for centuries, but the 1910–45 **occupation period** caused most of the tension that can still be felt today. In this age of empire, Asian territory from Beijing to Borneo suffered systematic rape and torture at the hands of Japanese forces, but only Korea experienced a full-scale assault on its **national identity**. Koreans were forced to use Japanese names and money, books written in *hangeul* text were burnt and the Japanese language was taught in schools. These measures were merely the tip of the iceberg, and Japan's famed attention to detail meant that even the tall trees were chopped down: straight and strong, they were said to symbolize the Korean psyche, and they were replaced with willows which drifted with the wind in a manner more befitting the programme. The most contentious issue remains the use of over 100,000 **"comfort women"**, who were forced into slave-like prostitution to sate the sexual needs of Japanese soldiers; Koreans never discuss this, but women from other occupied countries suffered the same fate too.

The **atomic bombs** that brought about the end of the World War II also finished off the occupation of Korea, which slid rapidly into civil war. This post-occupation preoccupation kept both factions too busy to demand compensation or apologies from Japan – they were, in fact, never to arrive. While some countries have bent over backwards to highlight wartime misdeeds, Japan has been notoriously stubborn in this regard – its prime ministers have regularly paid respects at **Yasukuni**, a shrine to those who died serving the empire, but notably also to at least a dozen Class A war criminals, and school textbooks have increasingly glossed over the atrocities. This has led to repeated and continuing protests; surviving comfort women, having still not been compensated, hold weekly **demonstrations** outside the Japanese Embassy in Seoul. Korea, for its part, has failed to debate successfully the role of **local collaborators** during the resistance, or to acknowledge fully in its own schoolbooks and museums the foreign influences that ended both the Japanese occupation and the Korean War.

Set in a wooded area east of Cheonan, Korea's largest museum, the **Independence Hall of Korea**, is a concrete testament to the country's continued struggle for independence during its most troubled time, from 1910 to 1945, when it suffered the indignity of being **occupied by Japan**. Though this was a relatively short period, the effects were devastating (see above), and despite the Korean government's initial appeal for locals not to be "filled with bitterness or resentment", the popularity of the place and the size of its seven large exhibition halls – each of which would probably function quite well as individual museums – show that the wounds are still sore. Scarcely an opportunity is missed to insert a derogatory adjective against the Japanese people and policies of the time, but this combination of vitriol and history makes for an absorbing visit.

Each hall highlights different aspects of the occupation, with the most important displays labelled in English. Many locals head straight for those detailing **Japanese brutality** during the colonial period; "Torture done by Japan", a life-size display featuring some unfortunate mannequins, is one of the most popular exhibits.

ARRIVAL AND DEPARTURE   CHEONAN

By train Cheonan station is pretty central, a 20min walk or W3000 taxi ride from the centre. Slow trains from Seoul or Daejeon take an hour; high-speed services (30min from either) stop at Cheonan Asan station, three subway stops to the west – including transfers, it saves no time and costs more travelling this way.

By subway One branch of Seoul's subway line 1 heads to Cheonan train station, though it takes two hours to get here – a tedious ride.

By bus The city's two bus terminals sit almost side by side in the city centre: the express (고속) terminal is for Seoul alone (45min), while intercity (시외) services head to other destinations including Daecheon (1–2 hourly; 2hr 40min), Daejeon (every 30min; 1hr) and Gongju (3–4 hourly; 1hr 10min).

6

Songnisan National Park

석리산 국립 공원 • Daily 2hr before sunrise to sunset • W4000 (usually only levied at Beopjusa entrance) • ⓦ english.knps.or.kr

The myriad trails of **Songnisan National Park** are a joy to hike, its paths winding uphill alongside gentle streams to heady 1000m-high peaks – just what you'd expect from an area whose name translates as "mountains far from the ordinary world". This is justly one of the most popular parks in Korea, with most visitors here to gawp at fantastically photogenic **Beopjusa**, a temple featuring a visually arresting **33m-high bronze Buddha**. The park's popularity is also due, in no small part, to its highly central location – geographically speaking, the peak of Birobong can credibly claim to be the very centre of the country, since a drop of rain falling here – depending on what face it lands on – will end up flowing down the Nakdong River to Busan in the south, running through Gongju on its way to the west coast, or pouring north into the Han River and exiting the mainland through Seoul.

Located just down from Beopjusa, Songnisan's main accommodation area is provincial in feel and highly pleasant – stay the night if you can. The main road is lined with gingko trees, which glow a shimmering yellow in autumn months, though even at these times they're a mere prelude to the leafy pyrotechnics on offer in the park itself.

Beopjusa

법주사 • Daily 6am–6pm • ⓦ beopjusa.org

Inside the park, a short, shaded path leads to Songnisan's main draw – the glorious temple of **Beopjusa**. Entirely surrounded by pine and peaks, its name means – somewhat tautologically – "the temple where Buddhist teachings reside", and indeed it has been an active place of worship and religious study since it was built in 653. Standing with his back to the west (the direction of his death), the huge bronze **Buddha statue** stands atop an underground hall housing hundreds of figurines, including a rather splendid golden **goddess of compassion**.

Back outside and facing the statue is **Palsangjeon** (팔상전), an unconventional five-storey building that, despite a rather squat appearance fostered by the shallow lattice windows, is also the tallest wooden structure in Korea. As with all Korean temple halls bearing this name, it contains eight painted murals depicting various stages from the

HIKING SONGNISAN

Plenty of **hiking** opportunities lie beyond Beopjusa. The main target is the 1054m-high summit of **Munjangdae**, three hours away from Beopjusa; locals often make a wish after their third visit to this peak. From Munjangdae, the peak of **Birobong** (1008m) is a short walk away, or an easy ninety-minute ridge trail will bring you to **Cheonhwangbong**, the park's highest peak (1058m); a further two-hour walk west will bring you back down to the main park entrance, or you can continue east towards Sango-ri in Gyongsang province.

6

life of the Buddha; however, this is likely to be the oldest such building in the land. Nearby are two elaborately decorated **stone lanterns**; two lions hold up the torch segment on one (though the flames have long been extinguished), while the other is adorned with four carved devas and a statue of a bodhisattva. This deity incarnate once held an incense burner until he was consumed by fire, presumably reaching nirvana during his show of determination.

ARRIVAL AND DEPARTURE   SONGNISAN NATIONAL PARK

By bus There are direct bus connections to Songnisan from Cheongju (every 20min or so; 1hr 30min), as well as regular services from Daejeon (1hr 30min) and from the Dong-Seoul terminal in the capital. Buses stop just under 1km away from the park entrance itself, and their arrival is often delayed on summer and autumn weekends by the solid traffic running into the park.

ACCOMMODATION

There are plenty of simple places to stay in the village-like area between the bus terminal and Beopjusa, as well as plenty of restaurants and karaoke rooms. Beopjusa also runs **templestay** courses (W40,000), with English-language options available if you book ahead (see page 35).

★ **Birosanjang** 비로산장 Inside park ☎010 5456 4782; map p.290. Why don't all Korean national parks have something like this? This fascinating budget option lies inside the park itself, hanging over a trickling stream; chipmunks, frogs and colourful moths pop by for regular visits. On the down side, prices have gone up of late and they no longer serve food or alcohol (mercifully, there's a restaurant a little back down the path). Slightly overpriced it may be, but this could be the most atmospheric stay in all Korea. W50,000

Lake Hills 레익 힐즈 198 Sanae-ri ☎043 542 5281, ⓦ lakehills.co.kr; map p.290. Snuggled up to the park entrance, this is the most comfortable accommodation in the area. Prices pack a bit of a punch, but the rooms are just about worth it; note that "standard" ones are Korean-style sleep-on-the-floor affairs, though "deluxe" ones come with bed and cost no more. Away from weekends and the summer peak, you can probably chop the price in two. W150,000

Songnisan Pension 속리산 펜션 280-1 Sanae-ri ☎043 544 3844; map p.290. Best value of the motel clutch, with large, comfortable rooms, satellite TV and wi-fi. It's on a small alley parallel to the main road. W30,000

EATING

You know the drill by now – after a hike you're supposed to eat *pajeon* (a kind of savoury pancake), and sling it back with a pot of **makgeolli**; try to hunt down the local brand, a tasty number made with jujube (대추). Corn jelly (도토리묵; *dotorimuk*) and grilled bellflower root (더덕구이; *deodeok gui*) are the official **local specialities**, but you'll find all sorts of mountain cuisine on offer here; there are a few pancake places in the park itself.

Beopjusa Chatjip 법주사 찻집 Inside the park; map p.290. Located right next to the eponymous temple, this calm tearoom serves Korean infusions from around W6000 – try the jujube tea (대추차). Daily 10am–6pm.

★ **Songni Tosokeum Sikdang** 속리 토속음 식당 51 Sanae-ri ☎043 543 3917; map p.290. Mighty the place to eat on the main road. Their mainly veggie bellflower-root set meal (더덕정식; W15,000) comes with over twenty separate dishes and is absolutely huge, making good use of local mushrooms and herbs; there's usually a two-person minimum, but they'll feed single diners who ask nicely. Other choices include good savoury pancakes and various kinds of *bibimbap*, all from W8000. Daily 9am–9pm.

6

JIKJI: THE WORLD'S FIRST BOOK

To the west of Songnisan lies the city of **Cheongju** (청주), an uninteresting place with just one claim to fame: it witnessed the birth of **Jikji** (직지), the first-ever book produced with **movable metal type** rather than single-use page-blocks, and as such a direct ancestor of every newspaper, magazine or novel you've ever read. A guide to Seon Buddhism (better known as Zen in the West), *Jikji* was produced in 1377, thereby predating Germany's **Gutenberg Bible** by some 78 years. Initially two books were made, but one was destroyed in a fire. The remaining copy was taken to Paris as a form of compensation for the murder of French missionaries towards the end of the Joseon dynasty, and has now become Korea's equivalent of the Elgin Marbles – despite attempts at repatriation, it still lies in Paris at the Bibliothèque Nationale de France.

Danyang and around

단양

With its rarified and almost resort-like air, the sleepy town of **DANYANG** has become extremely popular of late, especially with families and young couples. However, it remains pleasantly relaxing, since there's little of the noise and clutter found in other urban areas; life dawdles by at a snail's pace, which is quite appropriate, really, since river snails are a local delicacy. These are dredged from **Chungju Lake**, a river-like expanse that curls a C-shape around the town centre. Green, pine-covered outcrops rise up from the lake, making for a thoroughly enchanting backdrop. The area's loftiest peaks converge at **Sobaeksan**, a pretty national park easily accessible from Danyang; on its cusp is **Guinsa**, one of the most distinctive temples in the whole of the land, and perhaps the highlight of the area.

Danuri Aquarium

다누리 아쿠아움 • Daily: July & Aug 9am–9pm; Sept–June 9am–6pm • W10,000

Danyang's newest sight is the large **Danuri Aquarium**, a slightly over-twee venue set in a building connected to the bus terminal. Over 16,000 fish call these tanks home; most are local varieties, though there are some interesting imports, such as the Amazon stingray.

Chungju Lake

충주호 • Ferry rides W12,000 or so (price and departure times vary with season)

Green-blue **Chungju Lake** is outstandingly beautiful, and impossible to miss if you're spending any time in the area. The lake is a man-made creation, having come into being after the building of a dam downstream in 1986. It swallowed what was once Danyang town centre, and many old buildings still lurk beneath the surface – few locals give these any mind today.

ONDAL, THE EYEBROW WARRIOR

Anyone spending any time in Danyang is sure to catch occasional glimpses of **Ondal** (온달), the town mascot – you'll see him, and his huge eyebrows, on everything from restaurant signs to toilet doors. According to local legend, he was the town fool until wooing a **local princess** (perhaps using those eyebrows) to one of the town's caves for an underground tryst; after their subsequent marriage, Ondal became a soldier of such skill that he eventually found himself promoted to general, fighting fierce battles at the **fortress** up the hill. The extremely Korean moral of the story seems to be that anything is possible with a good woman at your side.

A **lakeside promenade** runs for a couple of kilometres from the bus terminal to the *Edelweiss Hotel*, offering staggeringly beautiful views of the unspoiled mountain range; another one starts on the opposite side of the road from the bus terminal, running deep into the countryside. The effect is often ruined by music blaring from the speakers, put up to help Korean city-dwellers adjust to the scary countryside, but chances are that you'll find it quite romantic, especially at night.

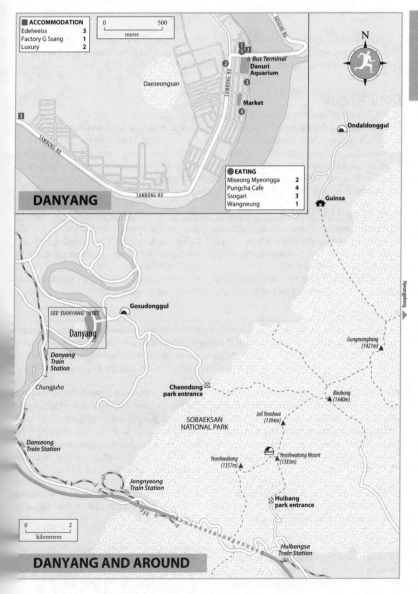

■ ACCOMMODATION
Edelweiss	3
Factory G Ssang	1
Luxury	2

0   500
metre

● EATING
Miseong Myeongga	2
Pungcha Cafe	4
Ssogari	3
Wangneung	1

DANYANG

Daeseongsan

Bus Terminal
Danuri Aquarium

Market

Ondaldonggul

Guinsa

Hyeongbong

Gosudonggul

SEE 'DANYANG' INSET

Danyang

Gungmangbong
(1421m)

Danyang Train Station

Chungjuho

Cheondong park entrance

Birobong
(1440m)

SOBAEKSAN NATIONAL PARK

Jeil Yeonhwa
(1394m)

Danseong Train Station

Yeonhwabong
(1357m)

Yeonhwabong Mount
(1383m)

Jongnyeong Train Station

Huibang park entrance

0   2
kilometres

Huibangsa Train Station

DANYANG AND AROUND

6

6

> **OUTDOOR ACTIVITIES IN DANYANG**
>
> There's one big reason why domestic tourism has blossomed in Danyang of late: **paragliding**. On any sunny weekend, you'll see dozens of tourists dropping to the ground like confetti from the Sobaeksan foothills. Several offices on the waterfront road will be able to get you (and your instructor) airborne for W80,000, including a transfer to the jumping point. The same companies offer **rafting trips** for W20,000 per person, and you can hire a two-person **all-terrain vehicle** for W40,000 per day.

A little further afield, it's possible to take a **ferry** ride for a view of the oddly shaped rocks and crags that pop out of the lake in and around Danyang; these depart from Janghoe downstream, accessible by bus (ask at the terminal) or taxi.

Gosudonggul

고수동굴 • Daily 9am–5pm • W11,000 • 20min walk from Danyang, across the bridge

Within walking distance of the centre is **Gosudonggul**; dating back millennia, this 1.7km-long grotto was discovered less than forty years ago. Underground, its honey-yellow stalagmites and stalactites ripple through the dim, damp tunnel, and are visible from metal walkways and staircases. Note, however, that the cave is a popular stopover with families out for a weekend drive through the countryside, and can become uncomfortably crowded: visit on a weekday, if possible.

ARRIVAL AND DEPARTURE
DANYANG

By train Danyang's station is inconveniently located a few kilometres west of the centre; it's a W7000 taxi ride into town, there are buses every 20–40min (W1400), or it's a 40min walk along the lakeside trail.

Destinations Andong (7 daily; 1hr 15min); Busan (Bujeon station; 2 daily; 5hr); Gyeongju (2 daily; 3hr 30min); Seoul (Cheongnyangni station; 7 daily; 2hr 15min).

By bus The bus terminal is more central than the train station, and can be found near the western end of the bridge crossing the lake.

Destinations Busan (1 daily; 5hr); Guinsa (13 daily; 40min); Seoul (2–3 hourly; 3hr).

ACCOMMODATION

As with most of provincial Korea, there's next to nothing at the higher end of the **accommodation** scale. A few smart new motels have opened up around the bus station, though surprisingly few make use of the phenomenal lake view. Note that on weekends it can be hard to find a room (at which times you can make use of sleeping rooms at two central 24-hour jjimjilbang spa facilities; see page 36); contrarily, on weekdays, you'll pay less than the prices stipulated here.

Edelweiss 단양 관광 호텔 31 Sanbong-ro ☎043 423 7070, ⓦdanyanghotel.com; map p.293. Away from the centre, and just across the river from the train station, this is an upmarket place with a sauna and the cushiest rooms in town. The prices are fair, though there's little of interest in the immediate area. **W115,000**

★**Factory G Ssang** 팩토리 지쌍 6-4 Byeolgok 11-gil ☎010 8668 0346; map p.293. The town's new default budget spot, and for several good reasons – prices are low (and include breakfast), rooms are decent and sport comfy beds, the owners are friendly English-speakers, and it's

bookable on several online engines. It's tucked into a small alley near the bridge, though you shouldn't be looking for long. Dorms **W20,000**, doubles **W50,000**

Luxury 호텔 럭셔리 125 Subyeon-ro ☎043 42¹ 9911; map p.293. Though this place calls itself a hote it's manifestly a love motel, as evidenced by the fre condoms in the rooms. However, as far as love motels g it's a pretty good one, with large flatscreen TVs, excelle showers and a great deal of attention paid to decoratio – take your pick from a dozen different room styles at th entrance. **W70,000**

EATING

For such a small place, Danyang has some great places to eat, with many of the dishes revolving in some way around t **garlic** for which the town is famed (see page 295). Note, however, that most **restaurants** in Danyang shut by 9p apart from some burger and pizza places on the main drag that stay open later, and convenience stores that are op around the clock. Also consider eating at the town market, which has many stalls serving garlic sundae, a kind of blood sausage (W8000–12,000 per portion).

Miseong Myeongga 미성명가 4 Byeolgok 4-gil ☎043 421 9295; map p.293. For a good sit-on-the-floor feed, head to this place, which specializes in *sutbul dakgalbi* (숯불 닭갈비; W8000), a special sort of chicken *galbi* cooked on a grill, rather than the regular pan. Pay an extra W1000 and you can try the super-spicy version. Daily 10am–8pm.

Pungcha Cafe 풍차 카페_61-1 Subyeon-ro ☎010 7138 9573; map p.293. The container café is just the treat for a Danyang morning – good coffee (most W4000) with strong wi-fi and river views from the roof. Daily 11am–9pm.

Ssogari 쏘가리 77 Sambong-do ☎043 421 8826; map p.293. River-facing restaurant that's the place to come for *olgaengi haejanguk* (see page 295); a bowl of the good stuff will set you back W8000. Daily 8am–7pm.

★**Wangneung** 왕릉 식당 13 Jungang 2-ro ☎043 423 9292; map p.293. In terms of presentation and taste, this restaurant has the best *maneul ddeok-galbi* (see page 295) in town – and, commendably, it's the only one prepared to serve single diners. These gut-busting meals will set you back W20,000 a head, and they're worth every won. Smaller staples include decent *naengmyeon* (W6000). Daily 10.30am–10pm.

Guinsa

구인사 • Daily 24hr • Free • Buses from Danyang (1–2 hourly from bus terminal or road outside; 40min), Seoul (hourly; 3hr) and a few others from elsewhere in Korea; note that most services dry up by 6pm

Shoehorned into a tranquil valley northeast of Danyang is **Guinsa**, one of Korea's more remarkable **temple** complexes. A great divider among Koreans, it's viewed by many as the most un-Korean temple, which is emphatically true – the colours and building styles are hard to find anywhere else in the country, and the usual elegant restraint of the traditional layouts has been replaced by a desire to show off. On the other hand, numbers alone bear witness to its importance – well over one thousand monks may reside here at any one time, and the kitchens can dish up food for twice that number on any given day.

Guinsa is the headquarters of the Buddhist **Cheontae sect**, once the most powerful in the country, and resuscitated in the 1940s (see page 296). Here, the usual black slate of Korean temple roofing has occasionally been eschewed for a glazed orange finish remini-scent of that in Beijing's Forbidden City, and some buildings show hints of Lhasa's Potala Palace, with their use of height and vertical lines. Buildings swarm up the valley and connect in unlikely ways, with alleys and bridges crisscrossing like the dragons depicted around the complex; you'll often wander up a path, and on looking back discover three or four routes that could have brought you to the same place. Despite being infested with an almost plague-like number of dragonflies in late summer, it's one of the most scenic temples in all Korea.

DANYANG TREATS

Danyang is famed for its **garlic**, which often fills the market in the town centre; there's even a festival related to the bulbs each July, which features a Miss Garlic contest. Don't miss the local dish, **maneul dolsotbap** (마늘 돌솥밥), in which four types of grain are served in a hot earthenware bowl speckled with chestnuts, dates, ginkgo nuts and a whole lot of garlic; it's often served as a huge side-dish with meals revolving around burger-like meat patties (*ddeok-galbi*; 떡갈비). Hunt around the market and you'll find a couple of places serving dumplings (*mandu*; 만두) with garlic mixed into the meat or veg filling, and many more selling garlicky blood sausage (*sundae*; 순대). Another town speciality is **olgaengi haejangguk** (올갱이 해장국), a warming vegetable soup filled with tiny **river snails** from the lake outside. Finally, there are a few good **makgeolli** brands to hunt down in the town's shops and restaurants, including Sobaeksan Geomeunkong (소백산 검은콩), a greyish, gloopy number made with black bean – probably the best such variety in the country.

6

THE CHEONTAE SECT

Cheontae (천태) is a Buddhist sect whose Korean followers number almost two million, making it one of the biggest in the country. As with other Korean sects, the school descended from China, where it was created in the sixth century and known as Tiantai (天台). On crossing the West Sea the sect's beliefs were polished into a local form deemed more logical, consistent and holistic than its Chinese predecessor; after wrestling with competitors during Unified Silla rule, the school became fully established in the eleventh century. Cheontae declined to near-extinction by the 1940s, but was given a second lease of life in 1945 by **Songwol Wongak**, a monk who put his overseas studies to good use by creating an altogether different temple – the Guinsa that you see today.

The temple

Entry to the main body of the complex is through the **Gate of Four Heavenly Kings**, from where you'll head up to the five-storey **law hall**; this is one of the largest such facilities in Korea, and like many other buildings on the complex is elaborate both in terms of painting and structural design. Inside you'll find a golden Shakyamuni Buddha and two attendants – tempting as it may be, you are not allowed to take photos in this building. Further along the maze of paths is a courtyard, sometimes barely visible under the masses of *kimchi* pots used for making dinner, which is cooked up in colossal kitchens and served in the huge **canteen**. Close by are several buildings which serve as **living quarters**; the one with the sheer vertical face is the newest and largest structure in the still-growing complex. Head up alongside this on a wonderful pine-covered path and you come to the **Great Teacher Hall**, the achingly gorgeous golden crown of the complex, and a gleaming shrine to its creator, whose statue stands proud at the centre of the hall. Continuing on the uphill path will bring you to his well-tended gravesite, while further on are the western slopes of **Sobaeksan National Park** (see page 296).

ACCOMMODATION AND EATING   GUINSA

Guinsa is one of the most interesting places in Korea to embark on a **templestay** programme (W40,000). Failing that, there are **minbak** at the foot of the complex (figure on W25,000), as well as plenty of **restaurants**. It's most enjoyable, however, to take a simple rice-and-spice lunch in the huge temple **canteen** (daily 11.30am–1.30pm) for a voluntary donation.

Sobaeksan National Park

소백산 국립 공원 • Daily from 2hr before sunrise to 2hr after sunset • Free • ⓦ english.knps.or.kr

Far quieter than most Korean parks on account of its location, **Sobaeksan National Park** is an unheralded delight. It is best visited at the end of spring (around May or June), when a carpet of royal **azalea blooms** paints much of the mountainside a riot of pink, but at any time of the year the views are impressive – the park is traversed by a relatively bare ridge heading in an admirably straight line from northeast to southwest, crossing numerous high peaks. A steep three-hour uphill path runs from the main entrance at Cheondong-ri to **Birobong**, the park's highest peak at 1440m. After reaching the ridge most head straight back down, but if you follow it along in either direction you will be rewarded with a succession of amazing views. Many opt to head northeast to Gungmangbong (1421m), an hour or so away, but only the hardcore continue all the way to Hyeongjebong. Southwest of Birobong are three peaks, confusingly, all named Yeonhwabong; on the central crest, taking advantage of the park's clean air and lofty elevation, is Korea's main **astronomical observatory**, though unfortunately it is closed to visitors. From here it's possible to exit the park to the south through the Huibang park entrance, the two-hour walk mopping up small waterfalls and a secluded temple on the way.

| ARRIVAL AND DEPARTURE | SOBAEKSAN NATIONAL PARK |

To Cheondong The Cheondong entrance is close to Danyang – just beyond Cheondonggul cave – and is best reached by taxi (W6000), though there are local buses every hour or so from the town's bus terminal. The park's other entrances aren't easily accessible by public transport.

To Huibang The Huibang entrance is a 2km walk from Huibangsa train station (희방사), just two stops away from Danyang; between the two, the track at one point dives into the mountain, and makes a 360-degree turn before coming out again much further up.

ACCOMMODATION

Most visitors to Sobaeksan stay in Danyang, though there's plenty of choice around the park entrance. **Minbak** rooms cluster by the Cheondong entrance; the price goes down and the quality up the further away you get from the entrance. Both park entrances have **camping** grounds (from W2000 per person).

6

Carpe Diem 카르페디엠 569 Darian-ro ☎043 421 2155. The best rooms in the area are in this chic pension, about 1km down the road from the Cheondong park entrance. It boasts a café and art gallery, rooms filled with modern art, plastic fruit strewn liberally about the place and an incongruous statue of Marilyn Monroe at the entrance. W80,000

Jeju Island

JUSANGJEOLLI

Jeju Island

The mass of islands draped along Korea's southern coast fades into the Pacific, before coming to an enigmatic conclusion in crater-pocked Jeju Island, known locally as Jejudo (제주도). This tectonic pimple in the South Sea is the country's number one holiday destination, particularly for Korean honeymooners, and it's easy to see why – the volcanic crags, innumerable beaches and colourful rural life draw comparisons with Hawaii and Bali, a fact not lost on the local tourist authorities. This very hype puts some foreign travellers off, but the island makes for a superb visit if taken on its own terms; indeed, those who travel into Jeju's more remote areas may come away with the impression that little has changed here for decades. In many ways it's as if regular Korea has been given a makeover – splashes of tropical green fringe fields topped off with palm trees and tangerine groves – and while Jeju's weather may be breezier and damper than the mainland, its winter is eaten into by lengthier springs and autumns, allowing oranges, pineapples and dragon fruit to grow.

Jeju City is the largest settlement, and whether you arrive by plane or ferry, this will be your entry point. You'll find the greatest choice of accommodation and restaurants here, and most visitors choose to hole up in the city for the duration of their stay, as the rest of the island is within day-trip territory. Although there are a few sights in the city itself, getting out of town is essential if you're to make the most of your trip.

The eastern half of Jeju is wonderfully unspoiled – think unhurried fishing villages, stone walls and lush green fields. On the east coast is **Seongsan**, a sumptuously rural hideaway crowned by **Ilchulbong**, a green caldera that translates as "Sunrise Peak"; ferries run from here to **Udo**, a tiny islet that somehow manages to be even more bucolic. Inland are the **Manjanggul lava tubes**, evidence of Jeju's turbulent creation and one of the longest such systems in the world, and **Sangumburi**, the largest and most accessible of Jeju's many craters.

All roads eventually lead to **Seogwipo** on the south coast; this relaxed, waterfall-flanked city is Jeju's second-largest settlement, and sits next to the five-star resort of **Jungmun**. Sights in Jeju's **west** are a little harder to access, but this makes a trip all the more worthwhile – the countryside you'll have to plough through is some of the best on the island, with the fields yellow with rapeseed in spring, and carpeted from summer to autumn with the pink-white-purple tricolour of cosmos flowers. Those with an interest in calligraphy may want to seek out the remote former home of Chusa, one of the country's most famed exponents of the art.

In the centre of the island is **Hallasan**, an extinct volcano and the country's highest point at 1950m, visible from much of the island, though often obscured by Jeju's fickle weather.

TEDDY BEAR MUSEUM

Highlights

❶ Walking the Jeju Olle Trail A delightful walking trail now circumnavigates more or less the entire island – if you've no time for the whole lot, at least try a section. See page 305

❷ Ilchulbong There's no better place in Korea to enjoy the sunrise than atop this distinctive mountain, looming over the cute town of Seongsan. See page 312

❸ Udo by bike There are few more enjoyable activities in all Korea than gunning around this tiny island's narrow lanes on a scooter. See page 314

❹ Seogwipo Flanked by waterfalls, Jeju's second-largest city is a relaxed base for tours of the sunny southern coast. See page 316

❺ Teddy Bear Museum The moon landings and the fall of the Berlin Wall are just some of the events to be given teddy treatment at this shrine to high kitsch. See page 319

❻ Yakcheonsa Turn up for the evening service at this remote temple for one of Jeju's most magical experiences. See page 320

❼ Hallasan Korea's highest point at 1950m, this mountain dominates the island and just begs to be climbed. See page 326

HIGHLIGHTS ARE MARKED ON THE MAP ON PAGE 302

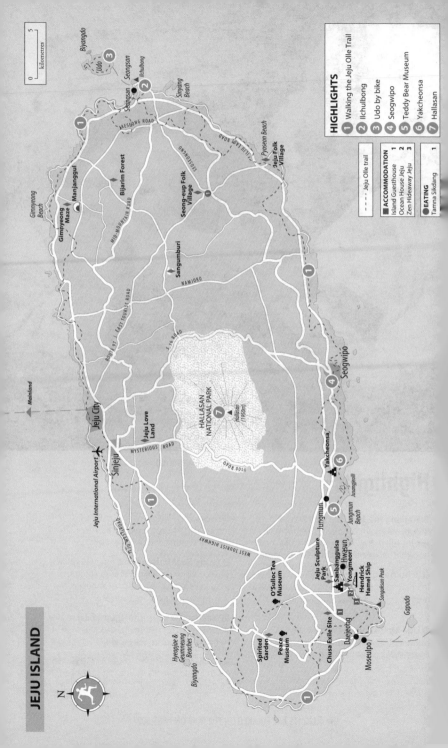

JEJU ISLAND

N

HIGHLIGHTS

1 Walking the Jeju Olle Trail
2 Ilchulbong
3 Udo by bike
4 Seogwipo
5 Teddy Bear Museum
6 Yakcheonsa
7 Hallasan

- - - Jeju Olle trail

■ ACCOMMODATION
Island Guesthouse 1
Ocean House Jeju 2
Zen Hideaway Jeju 3

● EATING
Tamna Sikdang 1

0 — 5 kilometres

Mainland

Jeju International Airport ✈

Jeju City

Sinjeju

MYSTERIOUS ROAD

Jeju Love Land

HALLASAN NATIONAL PARK

Hallasan (1950m) 7

1100 ROAD

S.16 ROAD

WEST TOURIST HIGHWAY

O'Sulloc Tea Museum

Spirited Garden
Peace Museum

Chusa Exile Site

Daejeong

Moseulpo

Hendrick Hamel Ship

Songaksan Peak

Gapado

Sanbangulsa
Yongmeori
Hwasun

Jeju Sculpture Park

Jungmun Beach
Jusangjeolli

Jungmun 5

Yakcheonsa 6

Seogwipo 4

1

Hyeopjae & Geumneung Beaches

Biyangdo

Gimnyeong Beach

Gimnyeong Maze
Manjanggul

Bijarim Forest

MID-MOUNTAIN ROAD

Sangumburi

NAMJORO

RUTE 97 / EAST TOURIST ROAD

Seong-eup Folk Village

JEJU EAST ROAD

Jeju Folk Village

Pyoseon Beach

Sinyang Beach

Seongsan
Ilchulbong 2

Seongsan

Udo 3
Biyangdo

JAESSEONG ROAD

1

1

JEJU'S UNIQUE CULTURE

Around the island, you'll see evidence of a rich local culture quite distinct from the mainland, most notably in the form of the **hareubang** – these cute, grandfatherly statues of volcanic rock were made for reasons as yet unexplained, and pop up all over the island (see page 307). Similarly ubiquitous are the **batdam**, walls of hand-stacked volcanic rock that separate the farmers' fields: like the drystone walls found across Britain, these were built without any bonding agents, the resulting gaps letting through the strong winds that often whip the island. Jeju's distinctive **thatch-roofed houses** are also abundant, and the island even has a breed of miniature horse; originally brought across during the Mongolian invasions, these are of particular interest to Koreans due to the near-total dearth of equine activity on the mainland, and their meat also turns up on some local menus. Also unique to Jeju are the *haenyeo*, **female divers** who plunge without breathing apparatus into often treacherous waters in search of shellfish (see page 314). Although once a hard-as-nails embodiment of the island's matriarchal culture, their dwindling numbers mean that this occupation is in danger of petering out.

7

Brief history

Jejudo burst into being around two million years ago in a series of volcanic eruptions, but prior to an annexation by the mainland Goryeo dynasty in 1105 its history is sketchy and unknown. While the mainland was being ruled by the famed Three Kingdoms of Silla, Baekje and Goguryeo, Jeju was governed by the mysterious **Tamna kingdom** (see page 304). The *Samguk Sagi* – Korea's main historical account of the Three Kingdoms period – states that Tamna in the fifth century became a tributary state to the Baekje kingdom on the mainland's southwest, then hurriedly switched allegiance before the rival Silla kingdom swallowed Baekje whole in 660. Silla itself was consumed in 918 by the Goryeo dynasty, which set about reining in the island province; Jeju gradually relinquished autonomy before a full takeover in 1105. The inevitable **Mongol** invasion came in the mid-thirteenth century, with the marauding Khaans controlling the island for almost a hundred years. The horses bred here to support Mongol attacks on Japan fostered a local tradition of horsemanship that continues to this day – Jeju is the only place in Korea with significant equine numbers – while the visitors also left an audible legacy in the Jejanese dialect.

Under the Joseon dynasty

In 1404, with Korea finally free of Mongol domination, Jeju was eventually brought under control by an embryonic **Joseon dynasty**. Its location made it the ideal place for Seoul to exile radicals. Two of the most famed of these were **King Gwanghaegun**, the victim of a coup in 1623, and **Chusa**, an esteemed calligrapher whose exile site can be found on the west of the island (see page 322). It was just after this time that the West got its first reports about Korea, from **Hendrick Hamel**, a crewman on a Dutch trading ship that crashed off the Jeju coast in 1653 (see page 323).

The Jeju Massacre

With Jeju continually held at arm's length by the central government, a long-standing feeling of resentment against the mainland was a major factor in the **Jeju Massacre** of 1948. The Japanese occupation having recently ended with Japan's surrender at the end of World War II, the Korean-American coalition sought now to tear out the country's Communist roots, which were strong on Jeju. Jejanese guerrilla forces, provoked by regular brutality, staged a simultaneous attack on the island's police stations. A retaliation was inevitable, and the rebels and government forces continued to trade blows years after the official end of the **Korean War** in 1953, by which time this largely ignored conflict had resulted in up to thirty thousand deaths, the vast majority on the rebel side.

THE TAMNA CREATION MYTH

Jeju's aloofness is no modern creation, for even during Korea's Three Kingdoms period, it conspired to be ruled by a fourth – the **Tamna kingdom**. With no historical record of Tamna's founding, it is left to Jeju myth to fill in the gaps: according to legend, the three founders of the country – Go, Bu and Yang – rose from the ground at a spot now marked by **Samseonghyeol** shrine in Jeju City (see page 306). On a hunting trip shortly after this curious birth, they found three maidens who had washed up on a nearby shore armed with grain and a few animals. The three fellows married the girls, and using the material and livestock set up agricultural communities, each man kicking off his own clan. Descendants of these three families conduct twice-yearly (in spring and autumn) ceremonies to worship their ancestors.

Recent times

Things have since calmed down significantly. Jeju returned to its roots as a rural backwater with little bar fishing and farming to sustain its population, but its popularity with mainland **tourists** grew and grew after Korea took off as an economic power, with the island becoming known for the *samda*, or three bounties: rock, wind and women. Recently, domestic tourist numbers have decreased slightly, with richer and more cosmopolitan Koreans increasingly choosing to spend their holidays abroad. However, Jeju still remains the country's top holiday spot, as well as a magnet for tourists from other Asian countries – the number of Chinese visitors, in particular, ballooned after visa restrictions to the island were lifted, but have recently decreased thanks to a diplomatic spat prompting Beijing to advise its citizens against travelling to Korea.

ARRIVAL AND GETTING AROUND   JEJU ISLAND

Jeju is accessible by plane from almost every other airport in the country, as well as by ferry from certain mainland ports (see page 308 for details about flights and sailings). Whichever way you arrive from the mainland, Jeju's special **visa rules** (it's open to Chinese and several other Asian nations who'd otherwise need a Korean visa) mean that it's necessary to bring along your **passport**.

By bus Most of the island is easily accessible by bus; all routes start in Jeju City (see page 309 for details), and most finish down south in Seogwipo.

By car or bike Jeju is one of the few places in Korea where renting a car or bicycle makes sense (see page 309). Outside Jeju City, roads are generally empty and the scenery is almost always stunning, particularly in the inland areas, where you'll find tiny communities, some

of which will never have seen a foreigner. Bicycle trips around the perimeter of the island are becoming ever more popular, with riders usually taking four days to complete the circuit – Seongsan, Seogwipo and Daecheong make logical overnight stops.

On foot It's now possible to make a circuit of Jeju on the island's excellent "Olle" trails (see page 305).

Jeju City

제주시

JEJU CITY (*jeju-shi*) is the provincial capital and home to more than half of the island's population. Markedly relaxed and low-rise for a Korean city, and loomed over by the extinct volcanic cone of Hallasan, it has a few sights of its own to explore, though palm trees, beaches, tectonic peaks and rocky crags are just a bus ride away, thus making it a convenient base for the vast majority of the island's visitors.

Jeju City was, according to local folklore, the place where the island's progenitors sprung out of the ground (see above); you can still see the holes at **Samseonghyeol**. While there are few concrete details of the city's history up until Joseon times, the traditional buildings of **Mokgwanaji**, a governmental office located near the present centre of the city, shows that it has long been a seat of regional power. Other interesting sights include **Jeju Hyanggyo**, a Confucian academy, and **Yongduam** ("Dragon Head

Rock"), a basalt formation rising from the often-fierce sea. Further east along the seafront, there's an appealing walk along the **promenade**; in bad weather the waves scud in to bash the rocks beneath the boardwalk, producing impressive jets of spray. There are also a couple of vaguely interesting **museums**, best reserved as a means of shelter on one of Jeju's many rainy days. Finally, south of the centre along the **Mysterious Road**, where objects appear to roll uphill, is the entertainingly racy **Love Land**.

Yongduam

용두암 • Daily 24hr • Free

Who'd have thought that basalt could be so romantic? The knobbly seaside formation of **Yongduam**, or "Dragon Head Rock", appears in the honeymoon albums of the many Korean couples who choose to celebrate their nuptials in Jeju, and is the defining symbol of the city. From the shore, and in a certain light, the crag does indeed resemble a dragon, though from the higher of two viewing platforms a similar formation to the right appears more deserving of the title. According to Jeju legend, these are the petrified remains of a regal servant who, after scouring Hallasan for magical mushrooms, was turned into a dragon by the offended mountain spirits. Strategically positioned lights illuminate the formation at night, and with fewer people around, this may be the best time to visit.

Jeju Hyanggyo

제주 향교 • Daily: March–Oct 8.30am–6pm; Nov–Feb 9am–5.30pm • Free

On the way back east from Yongduam towards the city centre, you may be tempted to take one of the gorgeous paths that crisscross into and over tiny, tree-filled Hancheon creek, eventually leading to **Jeju Hyanggyo**, a Confucian shrine and school built at the dawn of the Joseon dynasty in the late fourteenth century. Though not quite as attractive as other such facilities around the country, this academy is still active, and hosts age-old ancestral rite ceremonies in spring and autumn.

Mokgwanaji

목관아지 • Daily 9am–6pm • W1500

In the centre of the city are the elegant, traditional buildings of **Mokgwanaji**, a recently restored site that was Jeju's political and administrative centre during the Joseon dynasty; it's a relaxing place that makes for a satisfying meander. Honghwagak, to the back of the complex, was a military officials' office established in 1435 during the rule of King Sejong – the creator of *hangeul*, Korea's written text, and featured on the W10,000 note – and has since been rebuilt and repaired countless times. The place

---

THE JEJU OLLE TRAIL

One of the most pleasing recent additions to the Jeju tourism scene is the **Jeju Olle** trail (w jejuolle.org), a walking route that circumnavigates the entire island – 425km in total, along 25 marked sections. These take three to seven hours each, and if attempting one you're advised to get an early start – Jeju often clouds over in the afternoon, when there's also more chance of rain. It's also possible to book a trail **guide** to accompany you and provide useful information about the island (see website for details).

Most of the trail is walking only, though some routes do venture onto roads for stretches. One of the nicest sections is **#1**, which takes in beaches, fields and a couple of extinct volcanoes near Seongsan (see page 312). Another good route is **#8**, which hits the stunning temple of Yakcheonsa (see page 320), the Jusangjeolli basalt columns (see page 319) and Jungmun beach (see page 319), and a couple more mini-volcanoes.

also provides evidence that vice and nit-picking are far from new to Korean politics – several buildings once housed **concubines**, entertainment girls and "female government slaves", while the pond-side banquet site near the site entrance was repossessed due to "noisy frogs". Lastly, be sure to check out the two hareubang statues (see page 307) by the pavilion outside the entrance.

Arario Museum

아라리오 박물관 • Daily 10am–7pm • Exhibitions usually W6000–10,000

The Sanjicheon creek has been prettified of late, and strolling its banks is even more worthwhile now that there's actually something to see here – set in two converted motels, the double-wing **Arario Museum** is merely the latest offshoot of an art chain based in Cheonan (see page 288), and the exhibitions are usually very rewarding.

Samseonghyeol

삼성혈 • Daily 8am–6pm • W2500

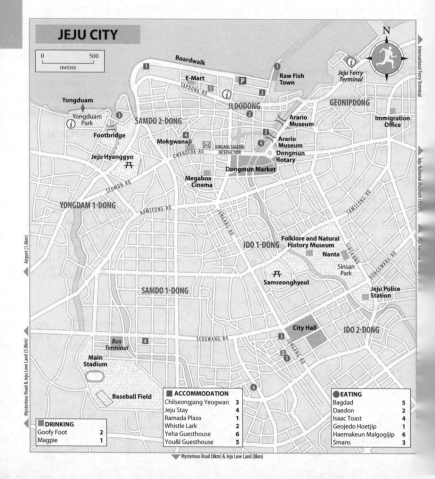

JEJU CITY

0 — 500 metres

Boardwalk
E-Mart
TAPDONG-RO
Raw Fish Town
Jeju Ferry Terminal
International Ferry Terminal
ILDODONG
GEONIPDONG
Yongduam
Yongduam Park
SAMDO 2-DONG
Arario Museum
Immigration Office
Footbridge
Mokgwanaji
Arario Museum
Jeju Hyanggyo
GWANDEOK-RO
JUNGANG SAGEORI INTERSECTION
Dongmun Rotary
Dongmun Market
Megabox Cinema
SEOMUN-RO
YONGDAM 1-DONG
NAMSEONG-RO
SAMSEONG-RO
JUNGANG-RO
IDO 1-DONG
Folklore and Natural History Museum
Nanta
Sinsan Park
SAMDO 1-DONG
Samseonghyeol
ILSAND-RO
DONGGWANG-RO
Jeju National Museum (900m)
Jeju Police Station
Airport (1.8km)
City Hall
IDO 2-DONG
SEOGWANG-RO
Bus Terminal
JUNGANG-RO
Main Stadium
Mysterious Road & Jeju Love Land (5.8km)
Baseball Field

■ **ACCOMMODATION**
Chilseongjang Yeogwan   3
Jeju Stay   4
Ramada Plaza   1
Whistle Lark   2
Yeha Guesthouse   6
You&I Guesthouse   5

● **EATING**
Bagdad   5
Daedon   2
Isaac Toast   4
Geojedo Hoetjip   1
Haemakeun Malgogijip   6
Smans   3

■ **DRINKING**
Goofy Foot   2
Magpie   1

▼ Mysterious Road (8km) & Jeju Love Land (8km)

GRANDFATHERS OF ROCK

What is it with Pacific islands and **statues**? The *moai* of Easter Island are the most famous, but similar relics have been found on Fiji, Tahiti, Hawaii and Okinawa, among other places. Jeju's own version is the *dolhareubang*, or "**stone grandfather**". Commonly abbreviated to **hareubang** (하르방), they can be found all over Korea – nowadays usually outside fish restaurants wishing to drum up custom. Bulgy-eyed and often cheery, they differ from their Polynesian counterparts by being quite expressive. Their hands rest on their tummies as if full of food; those with their left hands above their right are said to be military, as opposed to the more scholarly right-above-left brigade.

Like the *moai*, the origin and purpose of the statues remain shrouded in mystery, though it seems likely that they were placed at village entrances as a means of protection. Another theory, and one supported by their extremely **phallic appearance**, is that they served as sources of fertility – today, miniature versions are sold to women who are having trouble getting pregnant, as well as tourists wanting a souvenir of their trip to Jeju.

Today, only a few dozen **authentic** *hareubang* remain; the most accessible can be found in Jeju City, at the entrance to the Folklore and Natural History Museum, and outside Samseonghyeol.

7

Jeju's spiritual home, **Samseonghyeol**, is a shrine that attracts a fair number of Korean tourists year-round. Local legend has it that the island was originally populated by Go, Bu and Yang, three local demigods that rose from the ground here (see page 304). The glorified divots are visible in a small, grassy enclosure at the centre of the park, though it's hard to spend more than a few seconds looking at what are, in effect, little more than holes in the ground. The pleasant wooded walking trails that line the complex will occupy more of your time, and there are a few buildings to peek into as well as an authentic *hareubang* (grandfather statues; see page 307) outside the entrance.

Folklore and Natural History Museum

민속 자연사 박물관 • Daily 8.30am–6.30pm • W2000 • ⊕ museum.jeju.go.kr

Just east of Samseonghyeol, along Samseongno, you'll come to the **Folklore and Natural History Museum**. Local animals in stuffed and skeletal form populate the first rooms, before the diorama overload of the folklore exhibition, where the ceremonies, dwellings and practices of old-time Jeju are brought to plastic life. Unless you're planning to visit the folk villages out east (see page 315), there are few better ways to get a grip on the island's history.

Jeju National Museum

제주 국립 박물관 • Tues–Fri 10am–6pm, Sat & Sun 10am–7pm • Free • ⊕ jeju.museum.go.kr • Taxis around W4000 from city centre, and on numerous bus routes from Dongmun Rotary

As with all other "national" museums around the country, **Jeju National Museum**, 2km east of the centre, focuses almost exclusively on regional finds, but this particular institution – despite its size – has surprisingly little to see. Highlights include some early painted maps, a collection of celadon pottery dating from the twelfth century and a small but excellent display of calligraphy – be sure to take a look at the original **Sehando**, a letter-cum-painting created by Chusa, one of Korea's most revered calligraphers (see page 322). The upper floor is not open, so you'll have to make do with staring up at the sprawling stained-glass ceiling from the lobby.

Mysterious Road

도깨비도로 • Best accessed by taxi (around W12,000 from Jeju City), or just off #740 bus route • Daily 24hr • Free

THE WORLD'S BUSIEST FLIGHT ROUTE

Of the world's ten **busiest flight routes**, nine are domestic connections between major cities – Beijing to Shanghai, Sydney to Melbourne, Rio to Sao Paulo, and so on. However, trumping them all is the hour-long hop between **Gimpo** and **Jeju**, the course travelled by a whopping **178 flights** on an average day: at certain periods, there are four such departures allotted to a five-minute slot. Adding to the craziness, all other cities in the aforementioned top ten have populations of well over a million; Jeju Island as a whole has a mere 620,000, which just goes to show how popular a holiday destination it is with Koreans.

A few kilometres southwest of Jeju City, a short section of Route 99 – christened the **Mysterious Road** – has achieved national fame. Though no scheduled buses run to this notorious stretch of tarmac, there's always plenty of traffic: cars and tour buses, or indeed pencils, cans of beer or anything else capable of rolling down a hill, are said to roll upwards here. Needless to say, it's a visual illusion created by the angles of the road and the lay of the land. Some people think it looks convincing, while others wonder why people are staring with such wonder at objects rolling down a slight incline, but it makes for a surreal pit stop.

Jeju Love Land

제주 러브 랜드 · Daily 9am–midnight · W12,000 · ⓦ jejuloveland.com · Best accessed by taxi (around W12,000 from Jeju City), or just off #740 bus route

Right next door to the Mysterious Road, the tourists themselves constitute part of the attraction – **Jeju Love Land** is Korea's recent sexual revolution contextualized in a theme park. This odd collection of risqué sculpture, photography and art has been immensely popular with the Koreans, now free to have a good laugh at what, for so long, was high taboo. There are statues that you can be pictured kissing or otherwise engaging with, a gallery of sexual positions (in Korean text only, but the pictures need little explanation), several erotic water features, and what may be the most bizarre of Korea's many dioramas – a grunting plastic couple in a parked car. You may never be able to look at a *hareubang* in the same way, or see regal tombs as simple mounds of earth – maybe this park is the continuation of a long-running trend.

ARRIVAL AND DEPARTURE

JEJU CITY

By plane There are flights to Jeju from almost all mainland airports (bar Incheon, weirdly) – for as little as W20,000 one-way with a low-cost carrier, booked in advance, but more commonly around W90,000 – as well as a fair few cities across eastern Asia. This has long been the preferred form of arrival for locals, and the resultant closure of ferry routes means that planes are generally the way to go for foreign travellers too. The airport is a few kilometres west of the city centre, which is around W5000 by cab; in addition, six bus routes make the short run to the city centre, the most useful of which is #100 (W1200), which heads east every 15min or so to the bus terminal, then on to Dongmun Rotary in the city centre. Bus #600 runs at similar intervals to the top hotels in Jungmun and Seogwipo (both W5000), on the south of the island.

Destinations Busan (1–4 hourly; 55min); Cheongju (1–3 hourly; 1hr); Daegu (9 daily; 1hr); Gwangju (12 daily; 45min); Jinju (5 weekly; 50min); Mokpo (11 daily; 45min); Seoul Gimpo (up to 12 hourly; 1hr 10min); Ulsan (1 daily; 1hr); Wonju (daily; 1hr 10min); Yeosu (3 daily; 45min).

By ferry Schedules have long been in a state of flux, but at the time of writing there were daily ferries to Jeju City from Mokpo (1–3 daily; 4hr 30min–5hr 30min; from W32,000), Wando (2–3 daily; 1hr 40min–4hr; from W26,000) and Yeosu (6 weekly; 5hr; from W32,000), as well as an overnight ferry from Busan (3 weekly; 12hr; W43,000). Prices often drop a little on weekdays, and there's a W1500 terminal tax when departing Jeju. There are two terminals in town, each using the same large harbour; the Jeju Ferry Terminal is closer to the city centre (a short walk, or under W4000 by taxi), while the International Ferry Terminal is another 2km up the same road. With the terminals used by each company often shifting around, it's best to clarify with a tourist information office if departing Jeju in this manner.

By bus A number of bus routes spread out across the island from Jeju City (see page 309 for details).

GETTING AROUND

By bus Jeju City is small and relaxed enough to allow for some walking, but you may occasionally need to hop on a city bus (daily 6am–9pm; W1200).

By taxi Rides in the centre are unlikely to top W6000.

By bike Several outfits rent out bicycles in Jeju City, including Biketrip (☎064 744 5990, ⓦbiketrip.co.kr), within walking distance of the airport, and Yongduam Hiking (☎064 757 7777) in the town centre. You'll pay W7000–15,000 per day, depending upon the bike selected, and some places charge an extra W10,000 per day to keep your luggage. You may have to leave your passport behind as a security deposit.

By car A multitude of companies jostle for business at the city airport. Rates for car rental start at around W35,000 per day, and you'll need an international licence.

By motorbike Mr. Lee's Bike Shop (☎064 758 5296, ⓦjejubike.co.kr), near the bus station, has motorcycles and scooters to hire (W30,000–50,000 per day), and an English-speaking owner. Discounts available for multi-day hires.

INFORMATION

Tourist information There are two information desks just metres apart from each other at the airport. At least one will be open from 8am to 10pm (☎064 742 8866), but both can supply you with English-language maps and pamphlets and help with anything from renting a car to booking a room. Another booth at the ferry terminal offers less useful assistance (daily 10am–8pm; ☎064 758 7181). English-language help can also be accessed by phone on ☎064 1330.

Hiking equipment There are shops all over the city, especially in the shopping area around Jungang Sagori. Prices are higher than you might expect, but Treksta is a fairly safe choice.

Hospital The best place for foreigners is the Jeju University hospital (☎064 750 1234); call ☎119 in an emergency.

Post office Post offices across the island are open weekdays from 9am–5pm, with the central post office (☎064 758 8602), near Mokgwanaji, also open on Saturdays until 1pm.

ACCOMMODATION

Jeju's capital is firmly fixed on Korea's tourist itinerary; most visitors choose to base themselves here. However, many establishments were built when Korea's economy was going great guns in the 1980s, and are now beginning to show their age. All higher-end **hotels** slash their rates by up to fifty percent outside July and August, so be sure to ask about **discounts**. Often you'll be asked whether you'd like a "sea view" room facing north, or a "mountain view" facing Hallasan; the latter is usually a little cheaper. There are many cheap **motels** around the nightlife zone near City Hall, and in the rustic canalside area between Dongmun market and the ferry terminal; there are a few super-cheap *yeoinsuk* near Black Pork Street, but these generally don't take foreigners.

JEJU BUS ROUTES

Public buses scoot across much of the island, with the bulk of routes running from Jeju City's bus terminal. The #780 route is the fastest means of travelling between Jeju City and the southern resorts of Jungmun and Seogwipo.

#701 – East Coast (every 15–25min)
Jeju City–Gimnyeong–Seongsan–Pyoseon–Seogwipo

#702 – West Coast (every 15–25min)
Jeju City–Hallim–Sanbangsan (not all buses)–Jungmun–Seogwipo

#710 – Seongsan (every 50min–1hr 20min)
Jeju City–Sangumburi (not all buses)–Seongsan

#720 – Pyoseon (every 20–40min)
Jeju City–Sangumburi (not all buses)–Seong-eup Folk Village–Pyoseon (for Jeju Folk Village)

#730 – Seogwipo (every 20–40min)
Jeju City–Seogwipo

#740 – 1100 Highway (every 20–40min)
Jeju City–Yeongsil (Hallasan entrance)–Eorimok (Hallasan entrance)–Jungmun

#750 – Daejeong (every 20min)
Jeju City–Sanbangsan–Daejeong

#755 – Moseulpo (every 50min–1hr 20min)
Jeju City–O'Sulloc Tea Museum–Moseulpo

#780 – Express Road (every 15–20min)
Jeju City–Seongpanak (Hallasan entrance)–Jungmun–Seogwipo

Chilseongjang Yeogwan 칠성장 여관 43 Chilseongno-gil, ☎064 751 5701; map p.306. There are a few bare-bones *yeogwan* near the creek, and this is as low as you're going to want to go – grubby, yes, but budget travellers should find it just about acceptable. **W25,000**

★**Jeju Stay** 제주 스테이 호텔 22 Mugeunseong 7-gil ☎064 755 7945; map p.306. A fantastic choice in this price bracket – essentially a motel divested of the sleazy bits, its rooms have been smartened up to make them more than acceptable for mid-range travellers. Staff are informative, a simple breakfast is included in the rates and it's a short walk from the seafront promenade. **W40,000**

Ramada Plaza 라마다 프라자 66 Tapdong-ro ☎064 729 8100, ⓦramadajeju.co.kr; map p.306. A modern, cavernous hotel that's even bigger than it appears from outside. Vertigo-inducing interior views, plush interiors and some of Jeju's best food make it the hotel of choice for those who can afford it, though the atmosphere may be a little mall-like, especially when it hosts conventions. Breakfast included in rates, which usually get discounted down to W200,000, and sometimes even further. **W340,000**

★**Whistle Lark** 호텔 휘슬락 26 Seobudu 2-gil ☎064 795 7000, ⓦwhistlelark.co.kr; map p.306. Now this is a fine deal, at this price level. Not only is it right next to the seafront promenade, and just across the road from Raw Fish Town (see below), it has tidy rooms (some with balconies) and a sea-facing infinity pool, plus a café, restaurant and pub on the ground level. **W80,000**

Yeha Guesthouse 예하 게스트하우스 9 Samo-gil ☎064 756 5506, ⓦyehaguesthouse.com; map p.306. The Yeha team have opened at a new location, very close to City Hall and Jeju's best bars. As with the original, it's a friendly and immaculately clean place, and within walking distance of the bus terminal. Dorms **W19,000**, doubles **W60,000**

★**You&I Guesthouse** 예하유앤아이 게스트하우스 Gwanyang 8-gil ☎064 753 5648, ⓦuniguesthouse.com; map p.306. Handily located in the downtown area, this hostel boasts a gigantic kitchen area that's great for cooking. Staff are super-friendly, and local tangerines pop up in the free breakfasts. Dorms **W19,000**, twins **W40,000**

EATING

Jeju prides itself on its **seafood**, and much of the city's seafront is taken up by fish restaurants. These congregate in groups, most pertinently "Raw Fish Town", the large, ferry-like complex at the eastern end of the seafront promenade. A little inland from that, there's a street dedicated to – and newly named after – Jeju's speciality: "black pork", meat made from black-haired pigs, which is just a little tastier than usual. Lastly, there are some good places in the trendy **student** area west of City Hall.

Bagdad 바그다드 38 Seogwang-ro 32-gil ☎064 757 8182; map p.306. This Indian/Nepali restaurant has been doling out tasty curries for years now; they'll set you back W11,000–18,000, though with the decor and laidback air, you'll possibly be expecting French food to be plonked on your table instead. Daily 11am–3pm & 5.30–11pm.

★**Daedon** 대돈 29 Gwandeok-ro 15-gil ☎064 757 7400; map p.306. The restaurants on "Black Pork Street" basically all offer the same dishes at the same prices, but this one stands out on account of its being the only one willing to serve single portions (Koreans rarely eat alone, but some travellers do). It's W18,000 per portion of black piggy *moksal* (neck meat) or *ogyeopsal* (pork belly), with the former particularly tasty; they're served with a copious amount of excellent side-dishes. Lastly, customers have often found themselves walking out with free portraits – a nice surprise, if you're in luck. Daily 11.30am–11.30pm.

Isaac Toast 이작 토스트 1 Gwandeok-ro 15-gil; map p.306. In keeping with this cheapie chain's other branches across the country, this is a great little breakfast target for toast made the Korean way (ie mostly on a buttered-up hotplate). You'll rarely need to pay more than W3000, and they make cheap fruit juice too (though maybe ask them not to put in the usual insane amount of sugar syrup). Mon–Sat 10am–10pm, Sun noon–10pm.

Geojedo Hoetjip 거제도 횟집 22-1 Seobudu-gil ☎064 758 3737; map p.306. Watch Jeju's air traffic glide over the sea from the outside tables of this fish restaurant, located in the Raw Fish Town complex. Their huge mixed sashimi set meal (W40,000) are a good choice, though if you're looking for something smaller and cheaper, go for a *hoedeop-bap* (sashimi on rice with spicy sauce; W15,000). Daily 10am–midnight.

Haemakeun Malgogijip 해맑은 말고기집 48-1 Donam-ro ☎064 726 5073; map p.306. Jeju is famed for its horses, and inevitably they also crop up on the menus of a few dedicated restaurants here. This place looks simple but the food is fantastic – try your horsemeat barbecued (말고기 구이), or raw and served with slices of Korean pear (말육회); these dishes will set you back W25,000 each. The place is a bit hard to find, but it's only 10min on foot from the bus terminal. Daily 11am–7pm.

Smans 스만스 3-16 Donghandugi-gil ☎064 901 9899; map p.306. The best of the café options near Yongduam, with marvellous sea views from its roof deck Coffees are good (W3500 and up), but there are various other milky concoctions to choose from, plus freshly made churros (W2500, or W3500 with chocolate sauce). Dail 10.30am–1.30pm.

DRINKING

Most of the city's **drinking** takes place in the tightly crammed area west of City Hall. At the time of writing you could barely walk for five minutes without stumbling across a flavoured-beer and cheese-sticks bar – a fad on the decline on the mainland, but still going strong here.

★**Goofy Foot** 구피푸트 B1 11 Gwangyang 10-gil ☎010 2689 4173; map p.306. It's not really the "surf bar" it claims to be (bar the surfboard-shaped drinks menu), but fun times can be had nonetheless at this basement drinking hole. It has the usual roster of liquid and non-liquid enjoyment: pool table, dartboard, cheap beer (from W4000) and strong cocktails (W8000). A good place to pre-game and

rustle up new friends before heading on. Daily 6pm–3am.

Magpie 맥파이 맥주 3 Tapdong-ro 2-gil ☎070 4228 5300; map p.306. Seoul's craft beer scene has reached Jeju in the form of this *Magpie* branch, which constitutes some of the only decent nightlife near the seafront; everything's actually brewed on the island. Most beers cost around W6000. Daily 5pm–1am.

ENTERTAINMENT

Megabox Cinema In a large complex a short walk south of Mokgwanaji, this is the island's best place to catch a film; tickets cost W8000.

Nanta 난타 Ido 2-dong 837-20 ☎064 723 8878. The Jeju outpost of Seoul's wacky kitchen-based musical (see page 114) has been going strong since opening up here.

Tickets W50,000. Performances daily 5pm & 8pm.

Ramada Plaza Casino 66 Tapdong-ro ☎064 729 8100, ⓦramadajeju.co.kr. There are precious few casinos in Korea, but Jeju City has a few, including in this stylish hotel (see page 310), and also the Oriental across the road; Koreans themselves aren't allowed in.

The northeast coast

For one reason or another, most travellers making a circuit of Jeju do so in a clockwise direction. After escaping Jeju City's modest sprawl, rice paddies will suddenly be upon you, often bordered with the delightful stone walls for which the island is famed. **Gimnyeong** is the most pleasing of several **beaches** hereabouts, and makes a good place to stay the night; even if you don't, it's easy to mop up the area's other main sights – the lava tubes of **Manjanggul** and a neat little **maze** – on your way east to Seongsan.

Gimnyeong beach

김녕 해수역장 • On #701 bus route from Jeju City, Seongsan and Seogwipo
One of the island's most popular beaches on account of its exceptionally bright sand, **Gimnyeong beach** lies within easy swiping distance of Jeju City; it boasts the area's greatest concentration of restaurants and accommodation, and is accessible on the buses that run along the coastal road. There are three main swimming areas here, with the central one most conducive to swimming – best at low tide, since there are rocky outcrops at the top of the beach.

Manjanggul

만장굴 • Daily: April–Oct 9am–6pm; Nov–March 9am–5pm • W2000 • #700 bus from Jeju City or Seogwipo to Manjanggul stop, then 20min walk
Not too far in from the coast is **Manjanggul**, a long underground cave formed by pyroclastic flows – millions of years ago, underwater eruptions caused channels of surface lava to crust over or burrow into the soft ground, resulting in subterranean tunnels of flowing lava. Once the flow finally stopped, these so-called "**lava tubes**" remained. Stretching for at least 9km beneath the fields and forests south of the small port of Gimnyeong, Manjanggul is one of the longest such systems in the world, though only 1km or so is open to the public. This dingy and damp "tube" contains a number of hardened lava features, including balls, bridges and an 8m-high pillar at the end of the course – all in all, quite spectacular.

Seongsan

성산

You're unlikely to be disappointed by **SEONGSAN**, an endearing rural town with one very apparent tourist draw looming over it: **Ilchulbong**, or "Sunrise Peak", so named as it's the first place on the island to be lit up by the orange fires of dawn. The town can easily be visited as a day-trip from Jeju City, but many visitors choose to spend a night here, beating the sun out of bed to clamber up the graceful, green slope to the rim of Ilchulbong's crown-shaped caldera.

Besides the conquest of Ilchulbong, there's little to do in Seongsan bar strolling around the neighbouring fields and tucking into a fish supper, though the waters off the coast do offer some fantastic **diving** opportunities (see page 312). South of town is **Sinyang beach**, where the water depth and incessant wind make it a good place to windsurf; equipment is available to rent. Head the other way for the charming island of Udo (see page 313), which lies just offshore; this makes a better place to stay if you're not going to get up at dawn for the Ilchulbong sunrise.

Ilchulbong

일출봉 • Daily 1hr before sunrise to 8pm • W2000

From Seongsan town it's a twenty-minute or so walk to the summit of **Ilchulbong**, a delightfully verdant caldera. A steep set of steps leads up to the 182m-high **viewing platform** at the top, and although the island's fickle weather and morning mists usually conspire to block the actual emergence of the sun from the sea, it's a splendid spot nonetheless. Powerful bulbs from local squid boats dot the nearby waters; as the morning light takes over, the caldera below reveals itself as beautifully verdant, its far side plunging sheer into the sea – unfortunately, it's not possible to hike around the rim. If you turn to face west, Seongsan is visible below, and the topography of the surrounding area – hard to judge from ground level – reveals itself. Ilchulbong is an especially popular place for Koreans to ring in the New Year – a small **festival** celebrates the changing of the digits.

ARRIVAL AND DEPARTURE
SEONGSAN

By bus Seongsan lies on the #701 coastal bus route, which links Jeju City with Seogwipo (around 1hr 30min from either). From Jeju City, you'll save a little time by taking the more direct #710 (1hr). Leaving Seongsan by bus can be a little tricky, since some stops handle services to both Jeju City and Seogwipo, depending upon the route; always be sure to confirm where you're headed.

By ferry There are ferries to Udo (on the hour, 8am–4pm; 10min) from a small terminal a 15min walk from town – it's the terminus of the #710 bus route, but not on the #701.

ACTIVITIES

Diving Sungsan Scuba (☎ 064 782 6117), near *Haechon* restaurant, offers diving trips – these are at their most spectacular during May and June, when the summer rains are yet to hit and visibility is at its best. It'll set you back around W50,000 per small group for the boat out, and W40,000 for costume and equipment hire; they also run three-day PADI courses for W700,000.

ACCOMMODATION AND EATING

There's no higher-end accommodation in Seongsan, but *minbak* can be found in abundance – hang around for long enough and the *ajummas* will find you, and after a bit of haggling the price should drop to under W30,000. For food, there are loads of fish restaurants around, and plenty of cafés and snack stands clustered around the Ilchulbong ticket booth; there are also some 24-hour convenience stores.

Breeze Bay 브리즈베이 호텔 42 Seongsandeungyong ☎ 064 784 0000, ⑩ breezebayhotel.com. Finally, Seongsan has a place that might appeal to middle-range sorts. It's a good one too, though some rooms have Korean-style bedding, which isn't to every traveller's taste; take one of the "regular" ones with floor-to-ceiling windows (well, nearly) sportin ocean views. <u>W60,000</u>

Dosirak Guesthouse 도시락 게스트하우스 48 Seongsanjungang-ro ☎010 4095 2525. Seongsan's hostel has okayish (if slightly noisy) dorms and a few private rooms. It's all cheerfully decorated, though as with hostels all over Korea, quite overpriced. Dorms <u>W20,000</u>, doubles <u>W50,000</u>

★**Haechon** 해촌 22 Ilchul-ro ☎064 784 8001.

This restaurant is simply fantastic. Not only does it have optimum views of Ilchulbong rising up above the waters (grab a seat as close to the windows as you can), but the seafood here is quite superb. They have the regular *hoe-deop bap* (sashimi on rice; W10,000) and grilled mackerel (W13,000), but think about trying the local speciality, cutlassfish (*kalchi*), served on *bibimbap* – quite unusual, but very tasty (W12,000). Daily 8am–9pm.

Udo

우도

Visible from Ilchulbong is **UDO**, a rural speck of an island whose stacked-stone walls and rich grassy hills give it the air of a Scottish isle transported to warmer climes. Occasionally, the nomenclature of Korea's various peaks and stony bits reaches near-Dadaist extremes; "Cow Island" is one of the best examples, its contours apparently resembling the shape of resting cattle. This sparsely populated dollop of land is a wonderful place to hole up for a few days, and one of the best places to spot two of Jeju's big draws – the stone walls (밭담; *batdam*) that line the island's fields and narrow roads, and the **haenyeo**, female divers long famed for their endurance (see page 314). Bring enough money for your stay if possible – there's an ATM in the supermarket at the very centre of the island, but it's a bit of an uphill slog from the coast.

Sanho beach

산호 해수역장

Within walking distance of the main ferry terminal, westward-facing **Sanho beach** is the largest and most popular on the island, and boasts its greatest concentration of restaurants and accommodation (see page 314). Even if you're staying elsewhere on the island, be sure to come by for sunset if the weather's looking agreeable – these can be even more spectacular than the famed sunrises on Ilchulbong (a peak which is, in fact, the most conspicuous thing on the horizon).

Geommeolle beach

검멀레 해수역장

Geommeolle is a black-sand beach, located on the southeast coast of Udo. It's not exactly the best of places to work on your tan, but the rock formations backing it up are quite beautiful. Rising up over the beach, **Lighthouse Hill** protrudes from the very far south of the island, and can make quite a spectacular sight when viewed from certain angles around the coast. Scampering up the hill will give you the best possible vantage point for viewing Udo, which looks thrillingly rural from up here.

Biyangdo

비양도

If Udo is an island-off-an-island, then minute **Biyangdo** is an island-off-an-island-off-an-island. It's tethered to Udo by a bridge, and there are often just two people resident here: the owners of *Deungmeoeul* guesthouse (see page 314). Biyangdo used to be one of the main jump-off points for Jeju's famed diving women (see page 314), though a few of its sparse collection of buildings have now fallen into disrepair.

7

JEJU'S DIVING GRANNIES

It may be hard to believe in a place that once was, and in many ways still is, the most Confucian country on earth, but for a time areas of Jeju had **matriarchal** social systems. This is said to have begun in the nineteenth century as a form of tax evasion, when male divers found a loophole in the law that exempted them from tax if their wives did the work. So were born the **haenyeo** (해녀), literally "**sea women**"; while their husbands cared for the kids and did the shopping, the females often became the breadwinners, diving without breathing apparatus for minutes at a time in search of shellfish and sea urchins. With women traditionally seen as inferior, this curious emancipation offended the country's leaders, who sent delegates from Seoul in an attempt to ban the practice. It didn't help matters that the *haenyeo* performed their duties clad only in loose white cotton, and it was made illegal for men to lay eyes on them as they worked.

Today, the *haenyeo* are one of Jeju's most famous sights. Folk songs have been written about them, their statues dot the shores, and one can buy postcards, mugs and plates decorated with dripping sea sirens rising from the water. This romantic vision, however, is not entirely current; the old costumes have now given way to **black wetsuits**, and the *haenyeo* have grown older: even tougher than your average *ajumma*, many have continued to dive into their seventies. Modern life is depleting their numbers – there are easier ways to make money now, and few families are willing to encourage their daughters into what is still a dangerous profession. The figures peaked in the 1950s at around thirty thousand, but at the last count there were just a few dozen practising divers, the majority **aged over fifty**. Before long, the tradition may well become one of Jeju's hard-to-believe myths.

ARRIVAL AND GETTING AROUND UDO

By ferry Udo is reached on hourly ferries (daily 8am–4pm; 10min; W3500 each way, plus W1500 Udo entry fee on the outbound leg) from Seongsan port (see page 312). These dock at one of two terminals, so on arrival it may come in handy to note what time the ferries return; if you're staying the night, your accommodation will advise on which terminal to head to for the return leg.

By bicycle, scooter or buggy The best ways to get around the island are the bicycles (W5000/3hr), scooters (W22,000/2hr) and buggies (W30,000/2hr) available for rent outside both ferry terminals. Udo is so small that it's hard to get lost for too long, and most people simply fire around the island's near-empty lanes until it's time to return their vehicle. Don't worry if you're a bit late – this is Udo, after all.

On foot Udo has its own segment of the Jeju Olle trail (route 1-1; see page 305). The 11.3km circuit takes 4–5hr to complete.

ACCOMMODATION AND EATING

Minbak are readily available on Udo, though the rural ambience comes at a slightly higher price than you'd pay in Seongsan; prices are around W40,000 per night, and few people speak English. Udo has become somewhat trendy of late – the cue for lots of samey **cafés** to open up and charge huge mark-ups. **Seafood** is king here, but those in the mood for something else will find a couple of other eating options dotting the coastal road; there's also a **supermarket** (daily 8am–10pm) in the very centre of the island. Udo has its own brand of **makgeolli**, made with the peanuts for which the island is famed. It costs a fair bit more than regular brands (W5000, even in shops), since Udo has no machinery to get the oil out of the nuts – they're exported to Chungcheong on the mainland, turned into *makgeolli*, then brought back here.

★ **Deungmeoeul** 등머울 Biyangdo ☏ 064 784 3878. The chance to sleep on tiny Biyangdo is something special – even if it's a full house here, the island's entire population for the night won't exceed a dozen, making for a truly end-of-the-world feel. Rooms are a little bare, but the floor-to-ceiling windows afford views of naught bar sky, sea and grass – except at night, when the horizon becomes a pearl-like chain of squid boats. The friendly couple who run the *minbak* speak a little English, and will collect you from the ferry terminal if you give them a call. **W70,000**

Green Jeju Pension 그린 제주 펜션 Udo-myeon 2471 ☏ 064 782 7588. The best value of the several places lining Sanho beach – rates will drop considerably on weekdays and during the off season. Rooms are all en-suite with lovely, warm showers, and there's cooking apparatus if you fancy making your own meals. **W70,000**

Haewa Dal Geurigo Seom 해와 달 그리고 섬 Udo-myeon 78-5 ☏ 064 782 0940. Just off the Udo side of the bridge to Biyangdo is this seafood restaurant, which specializes in colossal, fist-sized sea snails called *sora* 소라; W20,000 per portion). They've gone all hipster o

7

late, with a mobile beer shack outside and some outdoor seating. Daily 10am–9pm.

★ **Hoeyanggwa Guksugun** 회양과 국수군 Udomyeon 2473 ☎ 064 782 0150. This place has been on TV a whole bunch of times, and certainly deserves the attention

– not least because it stays open the latest of any place on the Sanho stretch. Their speciality is flatfish sashimi on spicy, cold noodles (화국수; W10,000 per person) – once a very rare dish, but thanks to its popularity here it's now served all over the island. Daily 9am–9.30pm.

Route 97

With a volcanic crater to see and two folk villages to explore, rural **Route 97** – also known as the East Tourist Road – is a delightful way to cut through Jeju's interior. All three attractions covered here can be visited on a day-trip from Jeju City, or as part of a journey between the capital and Seogwipo on the south coast, though it pays to start reasonably early.

7

Sangumburi

산굼부리 • Daily 9am–7pm • W6000 • Bus #710 or #720 from Jeju City, though not all buses stop here – ask at the bus terminal

If you head south from Jeju City on Route 97 the first place worth a stop is **Sangumburi**, one of Jeju's many **volcanic craters** – possibly its most impressive, certainly its most accessible, though currently the only one you have to pay to visit. Hole lovers should note that this particular type is known as a Marr crater, as it was produced by an explosion in a generally flat area. One can only imagine how big an explosion it must have been: the crater, 2km in circumference and 132m deep, is larger than Hallasan's (see page 326). A short climb to the top affords sweeping views of some very unspoiled Jejanese terrain; peaks rise in all directions, with Hallasan 20km to the southwest, though not always visible. The two obvious temptations are to walk into or around the rim, but you must refrain from doing so in order to protect the crater's wildlife – deer and badgers are among the species that live in Sangumburi. Consequently there's not an awful lot to do here other than stroll and take pictures, though there's a small art gallery on site.

Seong-eup Folk Village

성읍 민속 마을 • Daily 24hr • Free • Bus #720 from Jeju City or Pyoseon

A twenty-minute bus ride southeast of Sangumburi lies dusty **Seong-eup Folk Village**, a functioning community living in traditional Jeju-style housing surrounded by an immaculate town wall. Within its confines, you're free to wander at will among the thatch-roofed houses; the residents, given financial assistance by the government, are used to curious visitors nosing around their yards. Here you'll see life carrying on as if nothing has changed in decades – farmers going about their business and children playing while crops sway in the breeze. Most visitors spend a couple of pleasant hours here, and if you're lucky you'll run into one of the few English-speaking villagers, who act as guides.

Jeju Folk Village

제주 민속 마을 • Daily: April–Sept 8.30am–6pm; Oct–March 8.30am–5pm; folk performances 11.20am, 1.30pm & 3.30pm • W10,000; audio guides W2000 • Bus #720 from Jeju City, or #701 from Seogwipo

Route 97 terminates near the coast at the **Jeju Folk Village**. This coastal clutch of traditional Jeju buildings may be artificial, but provides an excellent complement to the Seong-eup village to its north. Information boards explain the layout and structures of the buildings, and tell you what the townsfolk used to get up to before selling tea and baggy orange pants to tourists. The differences between dwellings on different parts of

7

JEJU TRADITIONS

Essentially a frozen piece of the past, Seong-eup Folk Village is a wonderful place to get a handle on Jeju's ancient **traditional practices**, but you'll see evidence of these age-old activities all over the island. Many locals still wear *galot* (갈옷), comfy Jejanese **costumes** of apricot-dyed cotton or hemp; these are available to buy in Seong-eup and Jeju Folk Village. Local homes are separated from each other with *batdam* (밭담), gorgeous **walls** of hand-stacked volcanic rock built with no adhesive whatsoever – ironically, this actually affords protection against Jeju's occasionally vicious winds, which whip straight through the gaps. The homes themselves are also traditional in nature, with **thatched roofs** and near-identical gates consisting of three wooden bars, poked through holes in two stone side columns. This is a quaint local **communication system** known as *jeongnang* (정낭), unique to Jeju and still used today – when all bars are up, the owner of the house is not home, one bar up means that they'll be back soon, and if all three are down, you're free to walk on in. Some houses still have a traditional open-air Jeju **toilet** in their yard; these were located above the pig enclosures so that the family hogs could transform human waste into their own, which could then be used as fertilizer. Needless to say, no locals now use these toilets – traditional, for sure, but some things are best left in the past.

the island are subtle but interesting – the island's southerners, for example, entwined ropes outside their door with red peppers if a boy had been born into their house. However, the buildings may all start to look a little samey without the help of an English-language **audio guide**, available from a hidden office behind the ticket booth. There are three daily **folk performances**, free with the price of your ticket.

EATING

ROUTE 97

Tamna Sikdang 탐라 식당 1627 Seongeum-ni ☎ 064 787 0007; map p.302. Just outside the Seong-eup Folk Village perimeter walls, this restaurant is renowned for its black pork (yet another Jeju speciality food). Tasty set meals of black pork and side dishes (*heukdwaeji jeongsik* 흑돼지 정식) go from W11,000 per head, while the restaurant also makes its own *makgeolli*. Daily 9am–7pm.

Seogwipo

서귀포

Sitting pretty on Jeju's fair southern coast, charming **SEOGWIPO** is Korea's sunny-side-up. Whereas days up north in Jeju City are curtailed when the sun drops beneath Hallasan's lofty horizon, there's no such impediment here; evidence of this extra light can be seen in a series of tangerine groves, famed across the land, which start just outside the city. Seowipo is the most pleasant place to base oneself on the island, and while there's plenty to do – gorgeous waterfalls flank the city, and water-based activities range from diving to submarine tours – the real attraction here is the chance to kick back and unwind.

Lee Joong Seop Gallery

이중섭 미술관 • Daily 10am–noon & 1pm–5pm • W1500

In the centre of the city is an interesting **gallery** devoted to the works of **Lee Joong-seop** (1916–56), who used to live in what are now the gallery's grounds. During the Korean War, he made a number of pictures on **silver paper** from cigarette boxes, which now take centre stage in a small but impressive collection of local modern art. Many of Lee's pieces echo the gradual breakdown of his private life, which culminated in his early demise. Just across the road from the gallery is *Geonchuk*, Seogwipo's most characterful café (see page 318).

Jeongbang waterfall

정방 폭포 • Daily 8am–6pm • W2000 • 10–15min walk from central Seogwipo

To the east of central Seogwipo is **Jeongbang**, a 23m-high cascade claimed to be the only one in Asia to fall directly into the ocean. Unique or not, once you've clambered down to ground level it's an impressive sight, especially when streams are swollen by the summer monsoon, at which time it's impossible to get close without being drenched by spray.

Cheonjiyeon waterfall

천지연 폭포 • Daily sunrise–10pm • W2000 • 10–15min walk from central Seogwipo

Seogwipo's western falls, **Cheonjiyeon**, are shorter but wider than Jeongbang, and sit at the end of a pleasant gorge that leads from the ticket office, a signposted downhill walk from the city centre. Many prefer to visit at night, when there are fewer visitors and the paths up to the gorge are bathed in dim light.

Saeseom

새섬 • Daily sunrise–10pm • Free

The small islet of **Saeseom** sits across a bridge that you'll see poking up south of Seogiwo – certainly at night, when it hosts a light show of sorts. The uninhabited island itself has nothing more than a pleasant walking trail – a simple pleasure, maybe, but fully worth the walk here.

ARRIVAL AND GETTING AROUND   SEOGWIPO

By bus Numerous bus routes connect Seogwipo to Jeju City (see page 309). All stop at Seogwipo's large bus station, inconveniently located several kilometres east of the city centre, near the World Cup Stadium. If coming from the east, for central Seogwipo you should get out at Jungmun Rotary stop, which is on all routes bar the #702;

if coming from the west, take a connecting bus on to that same stop, or hail a cab.

By motorbike Several places rent motorbikes (from around W30,000 per day); your accommodation will have pamphlets directing you to the nearest.

INFORMATION AND ACTIVITIES

Tourist information The main office (daily 9am–6pm; ☏ 064 732 1330) is at the entrance to the Cheonjiyeon falls (see page 317).

Submarine tours Near Cheonjiyeon is the launch point for a submarine tour (every 40min; W56,000, ⓦ submarine.co.kr); the subs dive down to 35m, allowing

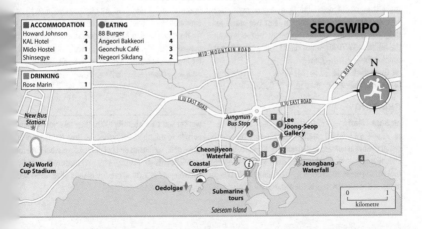

ACCOMMODATION		EATING	
Howard Johnson	2	88 Burger	1
KAL Hotel	4	Angeori Bakkeori	4
Mido Hostel	1	Geonchuk Café	3
Shinsegye	3	Negeori Sikdang	2

DRINKING	
Rose Marin	1

SEOGWIPO

MID-MOUNTAIN ROAD

5.16 ROAD

ILJU EAST ROAD

ILJU EAST ROAD

New Bus Station

Jeju World Cup Stadium

Jungmun Bus Stop

Lee Joong-Seop Gallery

Cheonjiyeon Waterfall

Coastal caves

Jeongbang Waterfall

Oedolgae

Submarine tours

Saeseom Island

0   1
kilometre

glimpses of colourful coral and marine life, including octopus, clownfish and the less familiar "stripey footballer". Boat trips around the coast and offshore islets are also available; check with the tourist office for details.

Diving and snorkelling The islands just south of Seogwipo are popular with divers. Big Blue 33, a German-run operation (☎064 733 1733), offers a range of courses starting at W110,000 per person. Failing that, head to *Mido Hostel* (see below), who rent snorkelling gear from W10,000.

ACCOMMODATION

Seogwipo has a range of accommodation to suit all budgets, though things often get booked out on summer weekends – if you're stuck, you can try your luck in the motel/pension area uphill from the Cheonjiyeon falls (see page 317). For a cheap and slightly bizarre place to stay, there's a **jjimjilbang** (W8000) in the World Cup Stadium to the west of the city.

★**Howard Johnson** 하워드존슨 호텔 436 Taepyeong-ro ☎070 8900 2202, ⓦwyndhamhotels. com; map p.317. A delightful addition to central Seogwipo, this is by far the city's best option at this price range. For these prices, you simply shouldn't be getting rooms so nice, but that's only half the story – all have balconies, though the best one is on the rooftop, where you can enjoy the hot-tub baths with superlative ocean views. **W75,000**

KAL Hotel KAL 호텔 242 Chilsimni-ro ☎064 733 2001, ⓦkalhotel.co.kr; map p.317. This is a very business-like tower that stands proudly over its surroundings. It's immaculate – though a little too clinical for some – and the grounds are beautiful. There's also a tennis court, a jogging track and various on-site restaurants and cafés.

Off-peak discounts can bring rooms down to under W90,000 – a bargain. **W170,000**

★**Mido Hostel** 미도 호스텔 13-1 Dongmundong-ro ☎064 762 7627, ⓦmidohostel.com; map p.317. The best and most professionally run of Seogwipo's many hostel options. The staff are full of local knowledge, while the outdoor common area occasionally doubles as an open cinema; in addition, rooms are clean and quiet, and many have small balconies. Dorms **W17,000**, doubles **W55,000**

Shinsegye 신세계 2-2 Jungang-ro ☎064 732 5800; map p.317. Officially a hotel, but in reality a less-seedy-than-average motel, this is a great cheapie – though this doesn't mean that you shouldn't try to haggle down further. Some rooms have internet-ready computer terminals, and others boast pleasant ocean views. **W50,000**

EATING

88 Burger 88 버거 63 Dongmun-ro ☎064 733 8488; map p.317. Great if you're looking for something non-Korean, selling a pleasing range of big-patty burgers for W8000 or thereabouts; try black-pig pork, a Jeju speciality. Tues–Sun 10am–3pm & 5.30–10pm.

★**Angeori Bakkeori** 안거리밖거리 6-1 Soldongsan-ro ☎064 763 2552; map p.317. This homely restaurant serves colossal set meals for W8000 – a small price to pay for a table near-covered with no fewer than fifteen delectable (and largely vegetarian) *banchan* side dishes. You'll need at least two orders for this meal; solo diners will have to content themselves with the *bibimbap* (W7000), which comes with a "mere" eight *banchan*. Daily 10am–9pm.

★**Geonchuk Café** 건축 카페 409-10 Taepyeong-ro ☎064 762 2597; map p.317. Opposite the Lee

Joong Seop Gallery you may make out a small treehouse – this almost certainly constitutes Jeju's most distinctive coffee spot. This rambling café has an almost bewildering selection of indoor and outdoor tables, as well as exhibitions of modern art, in its various nooks and crannies; the coffee and teas are good, too (from W4000), and the curious layout may tempt you to return for a beer in the evening. Daily 10am–10pm.

Negeori Sikdang 네거리 식당 Seogwidong 320-9 ☎064 762 5513; map p.317. Seogwipo now has a dedicated "food street", and this restaurant is a good pick for the many serving hairtail, a local speciality – have it braised (W25,000) or in soup (W15,000), with both meals feeding two, or try some mackerel (W8000). Daily 8am–3pm & 5–10pm.

DRINKING

★**Rose Marin** 로즈마린 13 Namseongjung-ro ☎064 762 2808; map p.317. Is this the most distinctive bar in Korea? Located down by the harbour near Cheonjiyeon waterfall, this is basically a shop with some cool seating areas attached to it – buy some super-cheap drinks and snacks cheap (a bottle of *makgeolli*, beer or *soju*

will set you back about W3000), then take your goodies outside to a harbour-facing seating area festooned with scuba gear, surfboards and goodness knows what. Give the pink-labelled *Jeju Makgeolli* a try – it's made with "friendly" bacteria, and is a cut above the island's other, oversweet brands. Daily noon–midnight.

Jungmun

중문

Korea's most exclusive resort curls along a beautiful beach west of Seogwipo, a place where expense-account tourists come from the mainland and abroad to play a few rounds of golf, shop for designer bags or relax in five-star pools in between business conventions. However, to write off **JUNGMUN** on account of this would be a mistake – the surrounding area has the island's greatest and most varied concentration of sights, accessible on any budget, and can even credibly claim to possess the most distinctive temple, gallery and museum of Korea's inexhaustible collection – all this shoehorned amid beaches, gardens and waterfalls. **Jungmun beach** itself is a real looker, though be warned – the waves rolling in from the Pacific can often be fierce, and this short stretch of sand claims at least one victim each year. Every August the beach is the starting point for the **Ironman Korea Triathlon**, when competitors thrash out a few kilometres in the ocean, followed by a 180km bike ride across the island and a 42km marathon for dessert.

7

Teddy Bear Museum

테디베어 박물관 • Daily 9am–7pm • ₩10,000

Although it may sound like the epitome of Jeju tack, the **Teddy Bear Museum** impresses even its most sceptical visitors. The main building is filled with floors of bears, but the diorama room is the museum highlight, with furry depictions of historical events – one for every decade of the twentieth century. As the scenes move backwards in time, you'll encounter teddies bashing down the Berlin Wall and fighting in World War II. Then following on from the battle, what appears to be a roller-skating teddy Hitler races into view, though he's soon revealed to be a teddy Charlie Chaplin. Other delights include a teddy Elvis, a "Teddycotta" Army, and a vision of what teddies may be up to in the year 2050, as well as a shop (no prizes for guessing what's on sale here) and garden.

Cheonjeyeon waterfall

천제연 • Daily 8am–6pm • ₩2500

A short walk east of the Teddy Bear Museum you can stretch your legs on the paths around **Cheonjeyeon**, a string of three small **waterfalls** (not to be confused with the similar-sounding Cheonjiyeon falls in Seogwipo). Note the seven white nymphs painted onto the vermilion humpback bridge – these fairies were said to bathe in the falls in the moonlight; a performance in their honour is put on by the falls every May. The uppermost fall gushes into a pool of almost unnatural sapphire, from where paths head through subtropical flora.

Jusangjeolli

주상절리 • Daily 8am–7pm • ₩2000 • A 2km walk from the resort, or a short taxi ride away (₩4000 or so)

East of Jungmun beach, waves smash against the hexagonal basalt columns of **Jusangjeolli**, which rise in angular

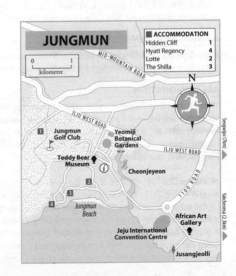

JUNGMUN

MID-MOUNTAIN ROAD

0 1
kilometre

N

ILJU WEST ROAD

■ **ACCOMMODATION**
Hidden Cliff   1
Hyatt Regency   4
Lotte   2
The Shilla   3

Seogwipo (7km)

Yakcheonsa (2.3km)

Jungmun Golf Club

Yeomiji Botanical Gardens

ILJU WEST ROAD

Teddy Bear Museum ⓘ

Cheonjeyeon

1100 ROAD

Jungmun Beach

African Art Gallery

Jeju International Convention Centre

Jusangjeolli

beauty from the sea in formations similar to the Giant's Causeway in Ireland. These strange creations were created when lava from one of Jeju's many volcanic explosions came in contact with sea water, and they can be viewed from a loop platform that runs along the coast.

African Art Gallery

아프리카 미술 박물관 • Daily 9am–7pm; musical performances Tues–Sun 11.30am, 2.30pm & 5.30pm • W8000 • A 2km walk from the resort, or a short taxi ride away (W4000 or so)

A stone's throw away from Jusangjeolli is the **African Art Gallery**, which was the brainchild of Mr Han, a traveller and interior designer who developed his collection into a museum. The collection was moved in 2004 from Seoul to a larger and more interesting building – a large faux-dirt structure peppered with logs on the outside, built to resemble the world's largest adobe building, the spectacular Grand Mosque in Djenné, Mali. Inside there's an interesting display of African photography on the ground floor, while the upper levels are mostly filled with sub-Saharan carved wood. Make sure your visit coincides with one of the entertaining **musical performances**; the groups are usually from Ghana, Nigeria and Senegal.

Yakcheonsa

약천사 • Daily 24hr • Free • Bus #645 from Seogwipo, but best accessed by rented scooter

A few kilometres east of Jungmun is the stunning temple of **Yakcheonsa**. It was built in the 1990s, and what it lacks in historical value it more than makes up for with its main building, a feast of intricate decoration despite its colossal size – the cavernous four-storey main hall is claimed to be the biggest in Asia, and is one of the most impressive in the country. The huge golden Buddha at the centre is best viewed from the encircling upper levels, which are themselves crowded with thousands of Buddhist figurines. Yet more (over five hundred, and all individually crafted) can be found in an exterior hall to the front of the complex; most are jovial (cheer up, #184) and many are individually interesting – take a look at no. 145's disturbing party trick, if you can find him. The best time to visit is 7pm on a summer evening, when worshipping locals **chant** under the interior glow with their backs to the sunset. Insect and bird calls add extra resonance to the bell rings that mark the beginning of the service, while squid boats out at sea shine like fallen stars on the horizon.

ARRIVAL AND DEPARTURE   JUNGMUN

By bus Limousine bus #600 (every 15min; 50min; W3900) runs directly from the airport to the hotels listed here. There are also no fewer than four routes here from Jeju City's bus terminal (see page 309 for details).

ACCOMMODATION

Standards are among the highest in the country at Jungmun. Accommodation caters almost exclusively to the well-heeled, especially in the resort area, where a slew of **hotels** have presidential suites with rack rates of W5,000,000. More affordable rooms are, of course, available, but travellers on low budgets are advised to stay in nearby Seogwipo. Given Jungmun's price levels, it's hardly surprising that most guests eat at their hotel, though there are a few **restaurants** at the top of the resort, near the Teddy Bear Museum.

★ **Hidden Cliff** 히든 클리프 호텔 550 Yeraehean-ro ☏ 064 752 7777, ⓦ hiddencliff.kr; map p.319. Located just outside the resort, this is something different to the beachside biggies – as you may infer from the name, it boasts a relatively secluded air, best imbibed while gazing over exotic-looking treetops from the infinity pool. Most of the rooms provide excellent views too, though you may well end up spending more time in the on-site spa. **W250,000**

Hyatt Regency 햐야트 리젠시 Jungmun Resor ☏ 064 733 1234, ⓦ jeju.regency.hyatt.com; ma p.319. This is the most relaxed of the three major hotel whose attention to detail is much as you'd expect of th chain; a leaf-filled atrium leads to ample, muted-ton rooms, and the on-site bars and restaurants are top-notch. A health club, spa and nine-hole putting green can also be found on site, and there's a walking trail down to the beach. **W340,000**

Lotte 롯데 호텔 Jungmun Resort ☎ 064 731 1000, ⓦ lottehotel.com; map p.319. The *Lotte* prides itself on being the "finest resort hotel in the world", but can be a little overblown for some. Aimed squarely at designer-handbag-toting guests from Japan and Hong Kong, the busy interior resembles a shopping mall, with the outside a theme park where every evening is celebrated with a

Vegas-style volcano show. Though the rooms are excellent, the outside bustle can often be hard to escape. **W450,000**

The Shilla 신라 Jungmun Resort ☎ 064 738 4466, ⓦ shilla.net/jeju; map p.319. Immaculately designed, the *Shilla* is the hotel of choice for Western tourists, on account of traditional designs woven into rooms and common areas alike. Soft music tinkles through the lobby and plush corridors, and it's a big place – though it may look low-rise from the outside, there are seven large floors and 429 soothing rooms. **W480,000**

Southwestern Jeju

Jeju's windswept **southwestern** corner boasts a collection of sights, three of them within walking distance of each other around the mountain of Sanbangsan: **Sanbanggulsa** is a temple hewn out of the peak itself, which looks down on **Yongmeori**, a jagged and highly photogenic coastline pounded mercilessly by waves; adjacent to this sits a replica of a Dutch vessel which came a cropper near these crags. In the distance lie the wind- and wave-punished islets of **Gapado** and **Marado**, the latter being Korea's southernmost point. Just north of Sanbangsan are a couple of arty attractions: fans for contemporary work may appreciate the large outdoor **sculpture park**, while traditionalists should head to the former exile site of **Chusa**, one of Korea's foremost calligraphers.

7

Sanbangsan

산방산 • Daily 8.30am–7pm • W1000, combined ticket with Yongmeori W2500 • Bus #750 from Jeju City, or #702 from Seogwipo

Jeju's far southwest is presided over by the mountain of **Sanbangsan**, which rises crown-like from the surrounding terrain. According to local folklore, this mountain once lay in what is now Hallasan's crater area, and was blasted to the edge of the island when the mountain erupted. Although the sharp cliffs that separate Sanbangsan's lower regions from its tree-flecked summit would make rock climbers go weak at the knees, the mountain has long been considered holy, and the highest you're allowed to go is the cave temple of **Sanbanggulsa** (산방굴사), about halfway up (there are, however, some challenging rock trails lower down). The holy grotto, created by a monk in Goryeo times, is bare but for a Buddha on its rear wall, while fresh, drinkable mountain water drips unceasingly from the ceiling near the entrance; slow as the flow is, try to catch the drops directly in one of the plastic cups provided, as the pool that they land in is hardly ever cleaned. After sweating up the hundreds of steps that lead here you'll have a superlative view of the ocean and the area's surrounding communities. This view is partially obscured by some ugly metal mesh at the top of the grotto opening, which provides important protection from falling rocks, a fact hammered home by several large indentations.

THE HWASUN ISSUE

The community settled just east of Sanbangsan is **Hwasun** (화순), situated at what would be an idyllic place were it not for the ugly power station that was built by the shore to supply much of Jeju's energy. As if this blight were not enough, the depth of the bay (and its convenient location, as far as possible from Pyongyang) recently attracted the **South Korean navy**, which opened up a large, purpose-built naval port in 2016 – this despite regular protests from Jeju locals. However, the site is also starting to attract cruise liners, with more than one million annual visitors set to land on Jeju in such a manner by 2020; after berthing alongside warships, they may well think twice about Jeju's designation as the "Island of World Peace".

Yongmeori

용머리 • Daily 8.30am–7pm • W2000, combined ticket with Sanbangsan W2500 • Bus #750 from Jeju City, or #702 from Seogwipo

The dramatic, wind-swept cliffs of **Yongmeori** stretch into the sea beneath Sanbangsan. A fissure-filled walkway curls around the rocks, but be warned that it may be closed if the waves are coming in with a lot of force: the seas in this unsheltered corner of Jeju are notoriously unpredictable, so don't venture too near the edge. The rock formations are stunning, their beauty somehow heightened by the strong winds that usually race in from the South Sea, and once around the outermost tip the contrast between the golden horizontal strata of the cliffside and the vertical grey crags of Sanbangsan becomes apparent. Keep an eye out for naturally made water paths that surge through the rock, where small fish peek out and dash between the crevices. *Ajummas* sometimes set up stalls along here to sell freshly caught fish.

Hendrick Hamel Ship

하멜 상선 전시관 • Daily 8.30am–6pm • Free • Bus #750 from Jeju City, or #702 from Seogwipo

From Sanbangsan's slopes you should be able to make out what appears to be a marooned ship just inland from the coast. This, the **Hendrick Hamel Ship**, is a replica of a Dutch trading ship that crashed off Jeju's shores in 1653, with important consequences for Korea and its relationship with the West (see page 323). An account of the ship and her crew's story is provided in an **exhibition** inside the vessel; some of this has, rather tenuously, been devoted to a more recent Dutch connection – South Korea's 2002 World Cup manager Guus Hiddink, immortalised in statue form outside the ship.

Jeju Sculpture Park

제주 조각 공원 • Daily 8am–7pm • W4500 • Bus #702 from Jeju City, Jungmun or Seogwipo

A few kilometres north of Sanbangsan – off Route 95 – is **Jeju Sculpture Park**, a large, open-air exhibition of contemporary sculpture from around the world. If you can imagine Copenhagen's Little Mermaid having a garden party with a bunch of oddly shaped friends, you're on the right track, but though metal sculptures are the predominant features around the park's grassy confines, there are several themed areas too, as well as a couple of indoor painting exhibitions.

Chusa's exile site

추사 적거리 • Daily 9am–6pm • W500 • Bus #702 from Jeju City, Jungmun or Seogwipo

The **exile site** of a calligrapher named **Chusa** sits a couple of kilometres west of Jeju Sculpture Park in the midst of some beautiful farmland. Kim Chun-hee, better known by his pen name, was exiled here in 1840 for his involvement in a political plot. Like a naughty boy sent to his room to consider his actions, he took to drawing on the walls, eventually honing his brushstrokes to such a degree that he is now revered as one of Korea's greatest artists and calligraphers. A letter-cum-painting named **Sehando** is his most famous piece, though the one on display is a replica, the original having been moved to Jeju National Museum (see page 307). The exhibition room is small with few actual articles, and there's no English-language information.

After you've seen the art you can wander around the nearby traditional buildings that Chusa once called home. While there's little here to detain any but ardent devotees of his work, the surrounding area – particularly that leading up to the distinctive mountain to the south – contains some achingly bucolic farming communities, a timeless land where elderly women sow grain, beasts plough the fields and mainland Korea feels a lifetime away.

A PEEK INSIDE THE "HERMIT KINGDOM"

In 1653 a **Dutch trading ship** bound for Nagasaki in Japan encountered a fierce typhoon south of the Korean peninsula and ran aground on the tiny island of **Gapado**. Just half of its crew of 64 survived the shipwreck, but despite their obvious status as victims rather than aggressors, they had entered the **"Hermit Kingdom"** and found themselves treated with scant respect – Joseon-era Korea was a highly isolationist land, whose policy (one rarely triggered) was to bar any foreigners who washed ashore from returning to their homeland. Forced into servitude, the survivors made repeated attempts to escape, but it was not until 1666 that a group of eight managed to flee to Japan from Yeosu, a port city in what is now Jeonnam province. Unfortunately, the survivors found Japan little more welcoming, but one year later a second escape took them back to the Netherlands. The accounts of survivor **Hendrick Hamel** became a bestseller in his homeland, and gave the West its first real portrayal of the Korean peninsula; English-language copies of *Hamel's Journal: A Description of the Kingdom of Korea 1653–1666* have been published, but are hard to track down.

Gapado and Marado

Ferries (4 daily to Gapado, W13,100 return; 5 daily to Marado, W17,000 return) from Moseulpo port, on the #755 bus route from Jeju City, and a 25min walk from the #702 buses linking Jeju City and Seogwipo

Off Jeju's southwestern shores lie the islets of **GAPADO** (가파도) and **MARADO** (마라도), home to tiny (and car-less) communities of just a few dozen people who somehow manage to eke out a living from land and sea. Low-lying **Gapado** was the unlikely conduit for the West's first contact with Korea, as it was where Hamel's ship ran aground (see page 323); it's now apparently carbon-free, as part of a wider experiment intended to encompass the whole of Jeju by 2030. **Marado** is smaller, loftier and more popular than its twin, attracting fans of geographical extremities who come to stand at Korea's southernmost speck of land. The place achieved national fame in a popular TV commercial in which a parachutist floated onto the island asking who had ordered the *jjajang-myeon*, a black-bean noodle dish; now an essential part of any Korean tourist's visit, the dish is served in all of the island's few restaurants. From the ferry, you may notice caves in the cliffs – these were military storage cavities made by the Japanese during their occupation of Korea, in anticipation of American attacks on strategically important Jeju. Even today, getting to these islands can be tough – ferries are often cancelled due to inclement weather or sea conditions, so check with local tourist authorities to see whether they're running.

ACCOMMODATION

SOUTHWESTERN JEJU

★ **Island Guesthouse** 아일랜드 게스트하우스 12-5 Boseongha-ro ☎070 7096 3899, ⓦislandguesthouse.kr; map p.302. It's possible to stay just a few hundred metres from Chusa's exile site (see page 322) at this surprisingly fresh hostel. It's almost literally in the middle of nowhere, which is what many Jeju travellers are looking for, but it'll be hard to find by yourself; staff will be willing to meet you at the nearest bus stop if you phone ahead. Breakfast included. Dorms <u>W25,000</u>, doubles <u>W60,000</u>

Ocean House Jeju 오션 하우스 제주 123 Sagye-ro ☎064 794 4541, ⓦoceanhouse.co.kr; map p.302. Nestling between Sanbangsan and the sea, and therefore easy to find, this wood cabin sports cooking facilities in every room; outside peak season, expect to lop around forty percent off the rack rates. <u>W100,000</u>

★ **Zen Hideaway Jeju** 젠하이더웨이 186-8 Sagyenam-ro ☎064 794 0133, ⓦzenhideawayjeju.com; map p.302. One of the more distinctive places to stay on the southern coast, located near the seafront just southwest of Sanbangsan. The industrial-chic exterior carries through into the rooms, which are a bit overpriced – ask about discounts. There's a great restaurant on site (daily 11am–9pm), selling an odd-but-tasty fusion of Italian, Thai and Korean cuisine, including pad Thai (W15,000) and pizzas topped with pesto (W19,000) or Jeju tangerines (W21,000). <u>W220,000</u>

The western interior

Jeju's **western interior** is strikingly beautiful, and covered with the purples, pinks and whites of cosmos bloom from summer to autumn – Jeju at its rural best. Those who've been drawn to the island by promises of empty roads, bucolic villages and unspoilt terrain should look no further – to many, this is quintessential Jeju. Its remoteness is very much part of the appeal, but it also makes it harder to reach its sights, and if you have no **transport** you may have to resort to the occasional spot of hitchhiking. Those who make it this far can hunt down a **tea plantation**, a **bonsai park** and the underground tunnels and rusty munitions of a **peace museum**.

O'Sulloc Tea Museum

오설록 차 재배단지 • Daily 9am–6pm • Free • On the #755 bus route between Jeju City and Moseulpo

Tour buses descend en masse to the open-plan **O'Sulloc Tea Museum**, which is a pleasant pit stop for groups touring the west of the island. A café in the **visitor centre** serves a stash of green-tea-related goods: try *nok-cha* tiramisu, cookies, ice cream – or even have a cup of tea – before visiting the viewing deck on the top level. The big building on view is the factory itself, one of two that the company uses to make the nation's favourite tea (though to keep costs down, much of it is now grown in China). The real attraction here is the opportunity to walk through the **tea fields**. If you've been to Boseong in Jeolla (see page 240) you'll know what to expect, though the fields here are flatter, and despite the plantation's popularity with Korean tourists, a short walk will find you alone among the leaves.

Spirited Garden

생각하는 정원 • Daily 8.30am–6pm • W10,000

Not so long ago the site on which the picturesque **Spirited Garden** bonsai garden now sits was wild, uncultivated land; nowadays, thanks primarily to the efforts of a lone botanist, this site claims to be the largest bonsai exhibition in the world. Though the English language uses the Japanese word, bonsai culture actually originated in China, where it was known as *penjing*, and hit Korea (known here as *bunjae*) before finally making it to Japan. There's lots of English information to read as you take a sweet-smelling walk around the gentle mounds of earth that make up the complex. A five-hundred-year-old juniper stands in tiny pride as the star of the show.

The Peace Museum

평화박물관 • Museum daily 8.30am–6pm • W3000 • Botanical garden daily 9am–5pm • W1000 • 10min walk from Cheongsu-ri bus stop on #900 route from Jeju City

Tucked away in countryside near the tea plantation is the **Peace Museum**, one of many such places in Korea. Like the others, it's entirely devoted to Japan's occupation of the Korean peninsula, and not so peaceful at all when groups of school kids are having nationalistic rhetoric barked at them through megaphones. If you're lucky enough to avoid these, you'll be rewarded with a modest but absorbing exhibition.

Deeming Jeju a strategically important hub between China, Korea and the Japanese mainland, Japanese forces established headquarters on the site of the museum during their occupation of Korea, and at one point planned to station up to seventy thousand soldiers on the island. Korean slaves were used to dig the 2km of **tunnels** that still snake underfoot, some of which are open to the public – cool, squat and dark, they're not for claustrophobes. There are relics from the occupation period on show in the main building (guns, grenades and the like), where staff will be pleased to show you

an English-language film. This contains interviews with survivors from the camp, and explains the site with a refreshing lack of vitriol, though as there are a few gory pictures, it's not really for kids.

Across the road is a **botanical garden**, which is a great place to reward yourself with a nice cup of herbal tea for getting this far.

Hallasan National Park

한라산 국립 공원

Arriving by ferry or plane on a clear day, you can see the whole of Jeju tapering slowly to **Hallasan**, a dormant volcano at the centre of the island, and Korea's highest point at 1950m. Blanketed with pink azalea in the spring, and snow in the winter, the centre of the island has long been a **national park**, with four well-trodden hikes heading to Hallasan's crater, a grassy bowl pocked with grey volcanic rocks, and home to a couple of small lakes. As long as the weather cooperates, a climb up Hallasan is one of the main goals for adventurous visitors from the mainland. The **four main routes**, starting from the north and heading clockwise, are Gwaneumsa, Seongpanak, Yeongsil and Eorimok.

Gwaneumsa route

Entrance open daily: May–Aug 5–10am; Sept–April 6–10am • 8.3km; 4hr up • Around W30,000 by taxi from Jeju City

The **Gwaneumsa route**, heading to the peak from the north, is the best if you'd like to tackle the peak without the crowds. This path is more challenging and **less accessible** than others – there are no public buses here, and though it's only an 11km taxi ride from Jeju City, you may have to pay almost double for the trip, as the driver will have

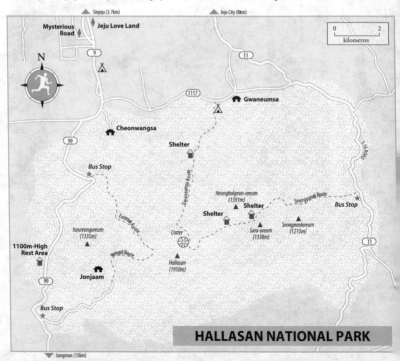

HALLASAN NATIONAL PARK

HALLASAN HIKING PRACTICALITIES

Jeju's porous volcanic rock means that Hallasan's climbing trails provide more grip than your average Korean national park, even in wet weather. Though the climb is not a terribly difficult walk, hikers should take certain **precautions** if attempting to reach the summit. In order to stop lots of feet stomping indelible lines into the mountain, trail sections – or even whole routes – are regularly **closed off**; your first point of call should be one of Jeju's many tourist offices, or telephone the tourist information line (❶064 1330) for up-to-date information. To make sure that everyone gets down in time, routes may close earlier than expected, sometimes even at 9am. This also reduces the chance of getting wet, which becomes increasingly likely towards evening as the air cools – bear in mind, though, that even a sunny morning may degenerate rapidly into thick fog and zero visibility at higher elevations; **bad weather** is the number one cause of most failed attempts to the summit. Even if you avoid the rain, strong winds can bite – bring at least a few layers of decent clothing. Also remember to bring enough **water** – Halla's rock absorbs most of the rainwater, so there are very few springs on the trails. With the longer walks some energy-giving **snacks** are a must; cooking and camping are prohibited, though the usual snack shops can be found at the trailheads.

7

next to no chance of picking someone up for the return leg. The most important advice is to get to the entrance early. Initially, it's easy going, but things soon get steeper. There are a lot of steps on this route, so many hikers opt to use it for their **downhill** run. The park's only **campsite** is near the start of the trail – book from one of Jeju's tourist offices.

Seongpanak route

Entrance open daily: May–Aug 5–10am; Sept–April 6–10am • 9.6km; 4–5hr up • On #780 bus route between Jeju City and Seogwipo

The popular **Seongpanak route** heads to the summit from the east. It's longer than the Gwaneumsa trail, but the gradient is gentle and makes for a much **easier climb** – it's possible to complete it in a moderately sturdy pair of trainers, as long as the weather agrees. The route is especially popular in the spring, when the path is surrounded by pink azaleas and other flowers.

Yeongsil route

Entrance open daily: March, April, Sept & Oct 6am–2pm; May–Aug 5am–3pm; Nov–Feb 6am–1pm • 5.8km; 2hr 30min up • Near #740 bus route between Jeju City and Jungmun

The **Yeongsil route** is the easiest and **shortest** path up the mountain, although at the time of writing the final burst to the **summit** was closed – this will no doubt change at some point, so ask at a tourist office for advice. The picturesque course starts off higher up the mountain than other routes, heading past some impressive rock scenery on the way to the top. There's currently no **public transport** to the park entrance, which is at least an hour's walk uphill from the "Yeongsil" bus stop – get hold of an up-to-date schedule at a tourist office or the Jeju City bus terminal. Alternatively, you could try flagging down a car heading up from the main road.

Eorimok route

Entrance open daily: March, April, Sept & Oct 6am–2pm; May–Aug 5am–3pm; Nov–Feb 6am–1pm • 6.8km; 3hr up • #740 bus between Jeju City and Jungmun

At the time of writing, the **Eorimok route** also terminated before the summit, coming to an end at the same point as the **Yeongsil** route. It's a **moderately difficult** trail, approaching the park from the northwest, and passing through lush forest at the beginning before heading into bamboo. Many Koreans believe this to be the most beautiful of the park's paths.

North Korea

MANSUDAE GRAND MONUMENT

PYEONGYANG SUBWAY

Basics

Getting there

First things first: yes, it is possible to enter North Korea (Democratic People's Republic of Korea, or DPRK), though at the time of writing US and Malay citizens were among those forbidden from doing so by their own governments. However, even those hailing from the "correct" nation can't just pop in on a whim, and those permitted entry will only be able to visit government-approved sights, and even then only in the company of a local guide. The process is often lengthy and never cheap, but it can be surprisingly simple: a travel agency usually does all the hard work with visas, permits and suchlike. The price of your tour will include pretty much everything: transport (most commonly a flight from Beijing to Pyongyang and a flight or overnight train back out, as well as all internal travel), accommodation, meals and entry fees.

The second question most ask about North Korea is whether one can enter from the South: the best answer here is a simple "no", though it's technically possible – if only for a minute or two, and even then only on the right days – on a tour to the Joint Security Area in the DMZ (see page 355). Though extremely enjoyable, these certainly don't offer a true taste of the DPRK – for this, you'll just have to head to Pyongyang.

From China

While several routes into North Korea exist, almost all Western travellers start their journey in **Beijing**. From here you can either take a flight or an overnight train; which one you use will depend on your tour operator (see page 331 for a few of these), and the cost will be factored into your tour price. Most tour groups fly into Pyongyang and take the train out, the latter leg giving a warts-and-all view of the North Korean countryside.

Flights into Pyongyang's Sunan International Airport have improved dramatically since Air Koryo – the DPRK's flag-carrier, and currently the only airline flying into the country – replaced their 1970s Soviet relics with a newer fleet of Russian Tupolevs and Ukrainian Antonovs in 2011. The EU lifted its travel ban for the most modern Koryo planes in 2010, though flights to Europe have yet to resume; at the time of writing, there were scheduled international flights to Pyongyang from Beijing (5 weekly; 2hr), Shanghai (2 weekly from spring to autumn; 2hr 20min) and Shenyang (2 weekly; 1hr 20min) in China, and to the Russian city of Vladivostok (2 weekly; 2hr).

Train journeys take around 24 hours from Beijing, though with the permission of your tour company you'll also be able to get on in Dandong, a Chinese city near the North Korean border; from here it's only a seven-hour trip to Pyongyang. Carriages are split into four-bed berths, with foreigners usually grouped together in the same carriage. There's also a restaurant car. Note that if you're crossing the border by train, you'll find that the toilets are often locked for hours: go before you reach Dandong on the way to North Korea, and before arriving at Sinuiju, a city just a few kilometres from the Chinese border, on the way out. At Sinuiju station, those able to escape the guards' attention may be able to take a quick look out over the main square of this little-visited city.

Customs inspections are usually thorough, so expect to be questioned (see page 332 for information on what not to bring); procedures are far faster at Pyongyang airport than at Sinuiju train station.

Tours and packages

A surprising number of travel operators offer **tours** into North Korea (see page 331 for a few of the best), most lasting for four to seven days. All visit the same core of Pyongyang-based sights, though some of the more expensive head to locations around the country. Group tours are cheapest – the size of the party can be anything from four to forty – but some also offer **individual packages**. These may sound appealing, but ironically you get more freedom on group trips – it's simply a lot harder for the two guides to keep tabs on twenty people than one or two, so those on group tours get far more leeway when walking around, leading to more picture-taking opportunities, the occasional chance to wander off by yourself for a few minutes and less official spiel. Many is the tale of woe from an individual traveller who has been marched around the same sights as group tourists, had no foreign company to bounce ideas, questions or frustrations off, and paid three times the price for the privilege.

To travel with the following operators, try to apply at least four weeks in advance; you may be asked for proof of employment.

TOUR OPERATORS

When going into somewhere as tricky as the DPRK, it's essential to use the services of a trustworthy company. As such, it's worth mentioning the British-run Young Pioneers group by way of warning – though angled towards the younger, cheaper end of the market, their tours have frequently run into bother, most pertinently during the tragic case of Otto Warmbier (see page 342). Rates here are based on sleeping two to a room (single-person supplements almost always available) and exclude the €50 visa fee (though this is always organized for you).

PLAN AHEAD, AVOID TROUBLE

Be careful when **packing your bags** for North Korea – with your trip likely to cost a pretty penny, it would be a shame to have to end it at **customs control**. Beware of taking anything that's very obviously American or South Korean – while K-pop on your music player is unlikely to be picked up, any clothing emblazoned with the stars and stripes surely will. Literature deemed to be of a subversive nature (including this guidebook) will also be confiscated.

The good news is that many restrictions on electronic devices have been lifted of late – almost all cameras and video recorders are fine, and tourists are now allowed to bring (and keep hold of) their **mobile phones**. You can even buy local SIM cards – a fun souvenir.

★ **Koryo Tours** Near Yashow Market, Sanlitun, Beijing, China ☎ 010 6416 7544, ⓦ koryogroup.com. This company takes more than half of the DPRK's foreign tourists, and its success is fully deserved – their tours are the best informed and most enjoyable ones available. The group has also made valiant efforts to open up as much of the country as possible to tourism, and to foster all-important cultural exchange with this reclusive nation. All tours head off from Beijing and range from two nights (€790) to three weeks (€4490); their budget tours are good value at €990 for four nights. Individual and themed tours are available, as are visits to cities and sights inaccessible to any other company.

KTG Room 1233, Yamao Building, Zhongshan Rd, Heping, Shenyang, China ☎ 010 6416 7544, ⓦ north-korea-travel.com. "Budget travel to North Korea" isn't really possible, but these guys try their best. They usually stick to five-day, four-night tours (€995), though destinations on these vary; you'll pay more if you want to fly in and/or out. Though based in Shenyang, all tours start and end in Beijing.

Regent Holidays Froomsgate House, Rupert St, Bristol, UK ☎ 020 7666 1244, ⓦ regent-holidays.co.uk. This agency has more than two decades of experience of sending travellers to North Korea and other far-out destinations. A standard tour gives five nights in the DPRK for £1500 or so (not including flights), while the seventeen-day whopper clocks in at around £3250.

Visas and entry requirements

Everyone needs a visa to enter North Korea, and though the process of obtaining one is lengthy, as long as you've got money and make your plans a couple of months in advance you should find it pretty easy to get in.

Journalists can find it hard, though it's not impossible – it's the travel agency's responsibility to vet applicants, so if you say that you're a circus performer and they believe you, you're in. Many try to avoid fraud by asking for signed confirmation from your employer.

Your **visa** is organized prior to arrival by the travel agency, and forms part of your tour price. Unless you make out your own visa application in a country that has diplomatic relations with the DPRK, it will come on a slip of paper (not as an insert in your passport) that you'll only possess for a short time on entry to North Korea. You won't receive a stamp, so your passport will show no evidence of your visit – probably a good thing. If you really want a stamp, try to pick up your visa at a DPRK embassy – ask your tour company for information on how best to do this.

Getting around

Once inside North Korea, you'll have precious little say in your day-to-day travels – all transport requirements will be arranged before you set foot inside the country, with the cost factored in as part of the tour price, and you'll be obliged to stick to the schedule.

Most travel is done by **tour bus** if you're in a group, and by **car** on independent tours, both within Pyongyang and for most trips to nearby destinations. Contrary to popular belief, the countryside around the highways hasn't been overhauled to present a false face to foreign tourists, and you'll see a great deal of poverty. The roads themselves are getting busier and busier – Pyongyang now has a few traffic lights to augment the semaphoring traffic ladies (see page 351), and even plays host to occasional traffic jams – quite an amazing change, considering the fact that roads across the land were near-empty as recently as 2008. There's also a **subway system** in Pyongyang, which figures on many tour schedules (see page 347), though the city's trams and buses are included on very few. **Internal flights** also exist, and those heading to Paekdusan or other more remote locations may find themselves taking one.

Accommodation, food and drink

As with transportation, all of your accommodation and dining requirements will

be taken care of and paid for prior to your arrival. While the country has occasional – and often severe – problems sourcing food, and leans heavily on the outside world for aid, try not to feel too guilty about eating here: the money you're paying is more than enough to cover what you eat, and at least part of it will be used to help feed the locals.

Most travellers spend every night of their tour in **Pyongyang**, where there are a few decent hotels (see page 351), but some tours include a night or two outside the capital; the two most common provincial bases are **Kaesong**, near the DMZ (see page 353), and **Myohyangsan**, home to a giant hall dedicated to gifts given (apparently) to the Kims from around the world.

The quality of your own **food** will vary according to financial, political and climatic conditions, but most visitors emerge well fed. If you have special dietary requirements you should make them clear to your tour company on application. Local **specialities** include *naengmyeon* (a buckwheat noodle dish similar to Japanese *soba*, but served in a cold, spicy soup) and barbecued duck.

There's more choice with local **drink**, as it's one of the only things that you'll have to pay for once inside the country; many travellers buy a few bottles of grog to take home (perhaps more for the bragging rights than the taste). Local hooches include some curious mushroom, ginseng and berry concoctions, as well as one apparently made from seal penis. **Soju** is tastier than it is in the South (see page 41) and available in most hotel bars, while the same can be said of some of the **beers** – Taedonggang is the most popular, but try to hunt down Ryongsong, which has a distinctive hoppy taste (partly thanks to a lack of preservatives, though this also means it'll spoil after a few days).

The media

While locals subsist on the "Rodong Shinmun" ("Workers' Daily"), North Korea also produces a surprising amount of English-language printed material, and is more than happy to offload it on foreign visitors. Of course, reportage by international media is usually a wee bit more grounded in fact, and there are a couple of DPRK specialist websites to choose from (see below).

In addition to the books written by Kim Jong Il – he was said to have authored well over a thousand, and many have been translated into various languages

for foreign consumption – there are a few interesting newspapers and periodicals, some of which may be dropped into your lap on the flight from Beijing.

Once you get to your hotel, you'll be able to tune into KCTV, the state television channel. For locals, this is off-air for much of the day, but foreign visitors get a full 24 hours of looped North Korean news and period drama. The latter is mainly made up of patriotic heroes refusing to capitulate to foreign forces, the themes a mix of Japanese occupation period, Korean War times and not much else. In addition, there's wkcna.co.jp, the official news website of the DPRK; the near-daily stories (some real, some not) of South Korean unrest against American military presence bring to mind the news reports about Eurasian and Eastasian activity in Orwell's Nineteen Eighty-Four.

Periodicals to look out for include Korea Pictorial, a colourful, glossy A3 monthly – with the word "Korea" on the front – that focuses more on photography than reportage, though some stories are rather absorbing. Korea Today is a smaller, far wordier version, with a songsheet reading of the "Song of General Kim Il Sung" on the inside cover. The articles are rather insipid, but good for the odd laugh-out-loud gem (do the laughing when you're back out of the country). The weekly newspaper, the Pyongyang Times, is not always easy to find inside the country, though its stories are fascinating ("School performs well"; "Factory increases shoe production"), and inevitably Kims-obsessed.

INTERNATIONAL WEBSITES

★ **NK News** ⓦ nknews.org. One of the best, and most up-to-date, sources of news pertaining to North Korea; they also include snippets from the official KNCA agency.

Yonhap News ⓦ english.yonhapnews.co.kr. A huge news agency in the South, Yonhap's website has a dedicated section for articles related to North Korea.

Festivals

North Korea was once famed for its utterly incredible Mass Games performances, but at the time of writing, this once-annual fixture had not been held since 2013. However, rumours suggested that they were due to return, either temporarily or permanently, so do check with tour agencies which head to North Korea.

However, special events are still held on important anniversaries – there's usually something going on to celebrate the birth of long-dead leader Kim Il-sung each April. That's also the month of the Pyongyang Marathon, which has been drawing in

GIFT GIVING

It's a good idea to bring **gifts**, not just for your guides and driver but for the locals who you're likely to run into along the way. Make sure that they're appropriate – nothing overtly capitalist, American or South Korean in origin. Western cigarettes go down well with local men and postcards from home with everyone, while balloons and small toys are always popular with children; try to ask a parent's permission before handing anything over.

ever-greater numbers of foreign entrants, eager to chalk off 26 miles (shorter courses also available) in this back-of-beyond nation.

Culture and etiquette

The first rule when travelling through North Korea is simple: do not disrespect the Kims. Disobeying could lead to dramatic consequences, but the sheer madness of the place makes acquiescence a hard line to toe – it's difficult not to pass comment on something that's likely to run contrary to your own upbringing. While the propaganda stuffed down your throat may be hard to stomach, it's unwise to react to it – asking questions or making accusations is not going to change the way that anybody thinks, much less the running of the country, and doing so can lead to trouble.

You'd be foolish to travel to North Korea with the intention of creating a stink, even after your visit: while a critical blog or travel article will not be of any danger to its author, the North Korean guides tarnished by association may get into a lot of trouble, and travel agencies have been known to lose their licences.

Good behaviour is required in private as well as public places – rumours abound of hotel rooms being bugged, and these cannot be wholly discounted. Even seemingly innocent activity is not above suspicion – there's one oft-quoted tale of a traveller who got into serious trouble after stubbing out his cigarette on a newspaper, inadvertently desecrating the holy face of Kim Jong Il.

However frightening all of this may seem, note that the vast majority of travellers encounter no problems whatsoever, and most have a fantastic time. Simply do as you're told, don't go running off, don't take pictures when you've been told not to and keep any frustrations bottled up until you're back in Beijing. The local guides are usually amiable folk; getting into their good books at the beginning of the tour by behaving yourself and asking permission to take pictures is likely to result in greater leeway as you make your way around. Neither should you fear the local North Korean people, who end up being the highlight of many a journey. Repeated contact with Western tour groups has convinced many Pyongyangers that foreigners are not to be feared – acting in a courteous manner will continue the trend.

Shopping

While staunchly anti-capitalist North Korea isn't exactly renowned for its shopping possibilities, there are a number of interesting things to buy, most of which are impossible to get anywhere else, and make fantastic souvenirs.

The race to stock up on as much North Korean material as possible often starts on the plane – wet-wipe packets, tissues, cutlery sleeves and even sick bags can be sold for a quick buck on the internet, though most people choose to hang on to these little mementos. You may also be handed propaganda-filled North Korean periodicals during your flight (see page 333). Once you're in North Korea, you'll find plenty to purchase in Pyongyang (see page 352).

Travel essentials

Communications

There are now more than two million **mobile phones** in the DPRK, all connected to the local Koryolink network. These cannot be used to make international calls, or to call any foreigner inside the DPRK. Foreign visitors can buy a local phone, or a local **SIM card** to put in their own; you won't be able to call any North Koreans, but can make and receive international calls (this is the best way to stay in touch with friends and family while on a trip), and the SIM cards themselves make good souvenirs. Those willing to pay more can even get a 3G SIM card, which gets you restricted Internet use – many social media and South Korean sites are blocked, though this issue can often be circumvented with the use of a VPN.

Bear in mind that whatever you say or read is likely to be monitored. This also applies to **post**, which will be read and understood, whatever the language; anything that seems cryptic or anti-establishment will most likely be thrown away.

Costs and money

All accommodation and transport will be included in your tour fee, as well as two or three meals per day, but for drinks, snacks and souvenirs you'll have to use hard currency, as there are no ATMs or banks accessible to foreigners. Most prices for tourist goods are quoted in **euros**, though American dollars and Chinese yuan are just as widely accepted.

The official currency of the DPRK is the **North Korean won**, but you're unlikely to have much contact with it as foreigners aren't allowed to use local money. There was a time when the won was pegged at 2.16 to the dollar, a fiscally ridiculous nod to Kim Jong Il's birthday on February 16, but this policy was abandoned in 2001. Note that it's illegal to export **North Korean currency** out of the country.

Electricity

In your hotel, you'll probably find sockets taking two pins (often both round and flat), at either 110V or 220V; you may need a converter as well as an adaptor. Power cuts are commonplace all over the land, though far less likely to strike the places you'll be visiting or staying at than places where locals live and work.

Insurance

It's wise to have **travel insurance** wherever you go, and North Korea is no exception. Most travel policies cover North Korea, but do check by making a quick call to your company.

Photography

In terms of pictures taken per traveller per minute, North Korea must be one of the most photographed nations on earth, a hugely ironic fact given that most of it is closed off, and even official sights are subject to **photographic restrictions**. This is a nation where even the mundane is incredible, and even on the shortest trips some visitors end up with thousands of images to sift through.

Some of the photographic **rules** are those that apply worldwide: don't take pictures of military installations or soldiers (unless you're in the DMZ, where it is almost expected), and ask permission if taking any photographs of people. Others are a little harder to guess, many of them surrounding **the Kims** – if you're taking a picture of a statue, mural or painting of the great men, try to get the whole body into your shot, as anything else may be viewed as disrespectful. (This can be quite a feat when snapping the huge bronze statues at Mansudae; see page 344.) It's also risky to photograph anything that might be taken as a **criticism of the country**. In practice, though, these rules are hard to police, and customs officials simply can't sift through each and every picture.

Tipping

Tipping is not a Korean custom, but will obviously be appreciated in a country as poor as this. A representative from most tour groups will usually pass the hat around on your final day, then split the pooled money between the various guides and drivers, who are not well paid despite their regular contact with foreigners – North Korean convention tends to reward work on the basis of danger, so guiding tourists is not high on the list. A tip of €10 per day for each guide and driver is about right; they're also happy to receive cigarettes and alcohol as gifts – even if they don't drink or smoke, these can be sold easily on the black market.

Travellers with disabilities

Travellers with **disabilities** can travel to North Korea, but there are next to no access facilities laid on for wheelchairs, and there are far easier countries to visit. It's interesting to note that disabled locals are highly revered in North Korea, a country where brave resistance is the theme of most songs, films and TV dramas; many women, indeed, consider it their duty to marry injured soldiers.

Travelling with children

It's quite possible to travel to North Korea with **children**, but there are two points to consider. First, the sight-packed days can be hard even on adults – you'll spend a lot of time in a tour bus or taxi, and yet more standing at sights while being bombarded with the greatness of the Kims. Second, there are precious few facilities for children, either in the hotels or around the country – bring everything that your child will need. That said, every housing block in Pyongyang has a small playground area; while tightly planned group tours are unlikely to squeeze this in, independent tours should be able to work a quick play into the schedule.

North Korea

A riddle, wrapped in a mystery, inside an enigma – a cliché it may be, but North Korea is far more deserving of Churchill's famous quip than Russia ever was. This is, quite simply, the world's least-understood nation, with reams of international reporters, scholars and diplomats devoting their whole careers towards making some kind of sense of the place. Espionage, famine and nuclear brinkmanship; perpetrator-in-chief of an international axis of evil; a rigidly controlled population under the shadowy rule of a president long deceased... you've heard it all before, but North Korea's dubious charms make it the Holy Grail for hard-bitten travellers. A trip to this tightly controlled Communist society is only possible as part of an expensive package, but a high proportion of those fortunate and intrepid enough to visit rank it as their most interesting travel experience.

North Korea is officially known as the **Democratic People's Republic of Korea**, or the DPRK for short. However, of the world's five remaining Communist countries, this remains the most committed to the system, and real democracy is thin on the ground. Comparisons with the police state in Orwell's *Nineteen Eighty-Four* are impossible to avoid: in addition to a regime that acts as a single source of information, residents of Pyongyang, and many other cities, do indeed wake up to government-sent messages and songs broadcast through speakers in their apartments, which can be turned down but never off – the fact that this is often the cue for callisthenic exercises further strengthens associations with the book. (Messages are also often relayed into many South Korean apartments, though these tend to be about garbage disposal and missing children, and the speakers can be turned off.) Other Big Brother similarities include verified claims that the country is crawling with informants, each seeking to further his or her own existence by denouncing friends, neighbours or even family for such crimes as letting their portrait of the Great Leader gather dust, singing unenthusiastically during a march, or simply being related to the wrong person. Also true is the rumour that locals have to wear a **pin-badge** portraying at least one of the deceased leaders – **Kim Il Sung**, the country's inaugurator and "Great Leader", and the "Dear Leader", his eldest son **Kim Jong Il**. Interestingly, Kim Il Sung remains the country's official president, despite having died in 1994. Both Kims, as well as present-day leader **Kim Jong Un**, are revered almost as gods, by a people with precious little choice in the matter.

For all this, North Korea exerts a **unique appeal** for those willing and able to visit. Whether you're looking out over Pyongyang's oddly barren cityscape or eating a bowl of rice in your hotel restaurant, the simple fact that you're in one of the world's most inaccessible countries will bring an epic feel to everything you do. It's also important to note the human aspect of the North Korean machine. Behind the Kims and their carefully managed stage curtain live real people leading real lives, under financial, nutritional, political and personal restrictions unimaginable in the West. Thousands

MUNSU WATER PARK

Highlights

❶ Kumsusan Memorial Palace of the Sun
Pay a visit to the two dead Kims, who lie in
state beyond a labyrinthine warren of corridors,
elevators and moving walkways. See page 344

❷ Ryugyong Hotel Rising 105 stories into the
Pyongyang sky, this half-finished mammoth is
off limits to tourists and impossible to miss; it
may eventually reopen as one of the world's
largest hotels. See page 345

❸ Pyongyang subway Most of the capital's
subway system is now accessible to foreigners;
you'll certainly get a kick out of the depth and
design of these palaces of the proletariat. See
page 347

❹ Munsu Water Park One of the capital's
most "normal-country" sights, and a unique
opportunity to mingle with North Koreans in
your swimming togs. See page 350

❺ Shopping It's somewhat ironic that anti-
capitalist North Korea makes such a great place in
which to purchase souvenirs – think local booze,
pins and stamps, or even some Socialist Realist
art at the Mansudae Art Studio. See page 352

❻ The DMZ Get a slightly different take on the
Korean crisis during a visit to the northern side of
the world's most fortified frontier. See page 355

HIGHLIGHTS ARE MARKED ON THE MAP ON PAGES 338 AND 343

upon thousands have found conditions so bad that they've risked imprisonment or even death to escape North Korea's state-imposed straitjacket. All the more surprising, then, that it's often the locals who provide the highlight of a visit to the DPRK – many, especially in Pyongyang, are extremely happy to see foreign visitors, and you're likely to meet at least a couple of people on your way around, whether it's sharing an outdoor *galbi* meal with a local family, chatting with the staff at your hotel, or saluting back to a marching gaggle of schoolchildren. This fascinating society functions in front of an equally absorbing backdrop of brutalist architecture, bronze statues, red stars and colossal murals, a scene just as distinctive for its lack of advertising or Western influence.

A visit to North Korea will confirm some of the things you've heard about the country, while destroying other preconceptions. One guarantee is that you'll leave with more questions than answers.

NORTH KOREA

N

C H I N A

Tuman River

Rajin

HAMGYEONGBUK-DO

Paekdusan

Chongjin

Hyesan

RYANGGANG-DO

CHAGANG-DO

▲ Chilbosan

Kanggye

Kilju

Amnok River

HAMGYEONGNAM-DO

Dandong
(China)

PYEONGANBUK-DO

Huichon

Tanchon

Sinuiju

Hamhung

Pakchon

MYOHYANGSAN
International
Friendship
Exhibition

PYONGANNAM-DO

EAST SEA
(SEA OF JAPAN)

Pyongyang Sunan
International Airport

Wonsan

PYONGYANG

Nampo

KANGWON-DO

Kosong

Sariwon

HWANG-
HAEBOK-DO

KUMGANGSAN

DMZ

HWANGHAENAM-DO

Sokcho

Haeju

Kaesong

6

Panmunjom

S O U T H
K O R E A

0   5
kilometres

WEST SEA
(YELLOW SEA)

SEOUL

HIGHLIGHTS
6 The DMZ

BUSTING MYTHS

A lot has been said and written about the current situation in North Korea, much of it true. These crazy truths, however, make it awfully easy to paint **rumours**, assumptions and hearsay as cast-iron fact. Political falsehoods have been detailed by excellent authors such as Cumings, Winchester and Oberdorfer, who take a more holistic view (see page 381 for some recommended reading), but a few of the more straightforward rumours can be easily debunked.

The first great untruth to put to bed is that North Koreans are somehow **evil**; whatever their leader's state of mind, remember that the large majority of the population have no choice whatsoever in the running of the country or even their own lives, much less than other populations that have found themselves under authoritarian rule. Another myth is that you'll be escorted around by a **gun-wielding soldier**; it's true that you'll have guides with you whenever you're outside the hotel, but they're generally very nice people and it's occasionally possible to slip away for a few minutes.

Sometimes even the myths are myths. The tale of Kim Jong Il hitting **eleven holes in one** on his first-ever round of golf is bandied about in the West as evidence of mindless indoctrination; the so-called rumour itself is actually unheard of in North Korea.

Brief history

The Democratic Republic of Korea was created in 1948 as a result of global shifts in power following the Japanese defeat in World War II and the **Korean War** that followed (see page 368). The Korean War, which ended in 1953, left much of the DPRK in tatters; led by **Kim Il Sung**, a young, ambitious resistance fighter from Japanese annexation days, the DPRK busied itself with efforts to haul its standard of life and productive capacity back to prewar levels. Kim himself purged his "democratic" party of any policies or people that he deemed a threat to his leadership, fostering a personality cult that lasts to this day. Before long, he was being referred to by his people as *Suryong*, meaning "Great Leader", and *Tongji*, a somewhat paradoxical term describing a higher class of comrade (in North Korea, some comrades are evidently more equal than others). He also did away with the elements of Marxist, Leninist or Maoist thought that did not appeal to him, preferring instead to follow "**Juche**", a Korean brand of Communism that focused on national self-sufficiency (see page 347). For a time, his policies were not without success – levels of education, healthcare, employment and production went up, and North Korea's development was second only to Japan's in East Asia. Its GDP-per-head rate actually remained above that of South Korea until the mid-1970s.

The **American threat** never went away, and North Koreans were constantly drilled to expect an attack at any time. The US Army had, in fact, reneged on a 1953 armistice agreement by reintroducing **nuclear weapons** into South Korea, and went against an international pact by threatening to use such arms against a country that did not possess any; North Korea duly got to work on a reactor of their own at Yongbyon.

There were regular skirmishes both around the **DMZ** and beyond, including an attack on the USS *Pueblo* in 1968 (see page 348), assassination attempts on Kim Il Sung and South Korean president Park Chung-hee around the same time, and the famed "Axe Murder Incident" that took place in the Joint Security Area in 1976 (see page 137). During the 1970s at least three tunnels were discovered heading under the DMZ (see page 139), which if they had been left undetected could have seen Korean People's Army (KPA) forces in Seoul within hours.

Decline to crisis

Then came the inevitable **decline** – Juche was simply not malleable enough as a concept to cope with external prodding or poor internal decision-making. Having developed into a pariah state without parallel, North Korea was forced to rely on the help of fellow Communist states the Soviet Union and China – the latter busy solving problems of its own under the leadership of Chairman Mao. The economy ground almost to a halt during the 1970s, while in the face of an American-South Korean threat that never diminished, military spending remained high. It was around this time that **Kim Jong Il** was being groomed as the next leader of the DPRK – the Communist world's first dynastic succession.

During the 1990s North Korea experienced alienation, famine, nuclear threats and the death of its beloved leader. The break-up of the **Soviet Union** in 1991 nullified North Korea's greatest source of funds, and a country officially extolling self-sufficiency increasingly found itself unable to feed its own people. Despite the **nuclear crisis** with the US (see page 341) the DPRK was making a few tentative moves towards peace with the South; indeed, it was just after examining accommodation facilities prepared for the first-ever North-South presidential summit that Kim Il Sung suffered a heart attack and died. This day in July 1994 was followed by a long period of intense public mourning – hundreds of thousands attended his funeral in Pyongyang, and millions more paid their respects around the country – after which came a terrible **famine**, a period known as the "Arduous March". Kim was elected "Eternal President", despite being dead; his son, Kim Jong Il, eventually assumed most of the duties that require the authorization of a living body, and was made Supreme Commander of the army.

The Sunshine Policy

The year 1998 brought great changes to North-South relations. **Kim Dae-jung** was elected president of South Korea, and immediately started his "**Sunshine Policy**" of reconciliation with the North, which aimed for integration without absorption (assimilation having been the main goal of both sides up until this point). With US president **Bill Clinton** echoing these desires in the White House, all three sides seemed to be pulling the same way for the first time since the Korean War. The two Kims held a historic Pyongyang summit in 2000, the same year in which Kim Dae-jung was awarded the Nobel Peace Prize. The southern premier revealed to the Western media that Kim Jong Il actually wanted the American army to remain in the South (to keep the peace on the peninsula, as well as for protection from powerful China and an ever more militarist Japan), as long as Washington accepted North Korea as a state and pursued reconciliation over confrontation. Clinton was in fact set for a summit of his own in Pyongyang, but the election of **George W. Bush** in 2000 put paid to that. Bush immediately undid much of the progress that had been made, and antagonized the DPRK, famously labelling it part of an "Axis of Evil" in 2002.

The **second nuclear crisis**, in 2002 (see page 341), brought about a surprise admission from the North: Kim Jong Il apologised to Japanese prime minister **Junichiro Koizumi** for a long-suspected series of **kidnappings** on the Japanese coast in the late 1970s and early 1980s, ostensibly as a rather convoluted way of teaching his secret service personnel Japanese. Though the number of abductions was probably higher, Kim admitted to thirteen people having been taken, of whom eight had died; one of the survivors had married **Charles Robert Jenkins**, an American defector from the post-Korean War period. The belief that more hostages were unaccounted for – and possibly still alive – made it impossible for Koizumi to continue his policy of engagement with the DPRK.

In 2002 **Roh Moo-hyun** was elected South Korean president, and adhered to the precepts of the Sunshine Policy. While the course under his tenure was far from smooth – the US and the DPRK continued to make things difficult for each other, South Korean youth turned massively **against reunification** and Roh himself suffered impeachment for an unrelated issue – there was still some movement, notably the symbolic reopening of train lines across the DMZ in 2007.

Return to crisis

In 2008, a South Korean tourist was **killed** after entering a high-security area on a visit to the Geumgang mountains. Seoul suspended these cross-border trips, choking off a much-needed source of income for Pyongyang, which eventually confiscated all South Korean-owned property in the area. Tensions rose, and in 2010 two catastrophic incidents brought inter-Korean relations to a postwar low (see page 372). First came the **sinking of the** *Cheonan*, a South Korean naval vessel, which was followed later in the year by the shelling of the West Sea island of **Yeonpyeongdo**, and retaliatory attacks by the South. Though North Korea continues to deny involvement in the sinking of the *Cheonan*, the attack may well have had something to do with the country's change of leadership – Kim Jong Il had been unwell for some time, and knew that elements of his military would be against yet another dynastic transfer of power to his son and intended successor, Kim Jong Un. Many analysts suggested that the younger Kim may have ordered the attack on the *Cheonan* as a way of proving to the military that, despite his youth, he possessed the necessary fortitude for leadership of the country.

The day duly arrived in December 2011, when Kim Jong Il passed away. According to the state media, the ice on Paekdusan's lake (see page 356) cracked so loudly that it "seemed to shake the heavens and the Earth", while the prevailing snowstorm paused in order to allow a glowing red sunset. Kim Jong Il was posthumously given the title of "**Generalissimo**" or "**Grand Marshal**", and you are likely to hear him referred to as such on your tours.

NUCLEAR BRINKMANSHIP

8

Say this about North Korea's leaders: they may be Stalinist fanatics, they may be terrorists, they may be building nuclear bombs, but they are not without subtlety. They have mastered the art of dangling Washington on a string. David Sanger, New York Times, March 20, 1994

Since the opening of a reactor at **Yongbyon** in 1987, North Korea has kept the outside world guessing as to its **nuclear capabilities**, playing a continued game of bluff and brinkmanship to achieve its aims of self-preservation and eventual reunification with the South. The folding of the Soviet Union in 1991 choked off much of the DPRK's energy supply; with few resources of their own, increasing importance was placed on nuclear energy, but the refusal to allow international inspectors in strengthened rumours that they were also using the facilities to create weapons-grade plutonium. **Hans Blix** and his crew at the International Atomic Energy Agency (IAEA) were finally permitted entry in 1992, but were refused access to two suspected waste disposal sites, which would have provided strong evidence about whether processed plutonium was being created or not. North Korea was unhappy with the sharing of information between American intelligence (the CIA) and the independent IAEA, but after threatening to withdraw from the **Nuclear Nonproliferation Treaty** (NPT) they agreed in 1994 to freeze their programme in exchange for fuel. This only happened after an election within the White House – Bill Clinton was more willing to compromise than his predecessor George Bush Senior.

The second part of the crisis erupted more suddenly. In 2002, after making veiled threats about a possible resumption of their nuclear programme, North Korea abruptly booted out IAEA inspectors. Regular six-party talks between China, Russia, Japan, the US and the two Koreas achieved little, but in 2006 North Korea conducted its **first nuclear test**, sending a missile into the Sea of Japan; having shown this card up its sleeve, talks continued with greater candour. In July 2007 Pyongyang finally announced that it was shutting down its Yongbyon reactor in exchange for aid, though it was only two years before they were cranking up the "permanently disabled" machinery once more, in response to UN criticism of a failed missile launch. More tests followed in 2012 and 2013, but things went into overdrive in 2016, which saw the first detonation of a nuclear warhead – **sanctions** on North Korea were tightened up (with even China, in a rare move, getting off the fence during UN Security Council votes), but these didn't stop ever larger tests going ahead in 2017. With Trump at the helm in the US and suggesting that pre-emptive strikes were a serious option, tensions went off the charts; as this book was going to print, the world was holding its breath for a first-ever meeting between the leaders of the US and DPRK.

Kim the Third

The third of North Korea's Holy Trinity, **Kim Jong Un**, ascended to power in April 2012. Little was known about Lil' Kim, bar the fact that he had spent part of his youth in Switzerland; only one verified picture of him existed, and even the year of his birth was a mystery, though it now seems that he was aged 30 when he attained leadership of the country. His relative youth, combined with his international upbringing, prompted hopes abroad that North Korea would finally crawl out of its hidey-hole. These were dashed as early as December 2013, when Kim's uncle **Jang Sung Taek** was executed, after a very public dismissal from his post as a chief of the Workers' Party. To compound the shock abroad, Jang had been seen as one of the more reform-minded elements of the North Korean elite. The country's international reputation took another huge blow, one compounded when Donald Trump was elected president of the US in late 2016 – Kim and Trump quickly began hurling insults and threats at each other (including Kim's reprise of the word "dotard", and Trump's suggestion that he had the "bigger" nuclear button), with a nervous world watching on as these two self-styled strongmen gave each other the long-distance eyeball treatment. Complicating the matter was the case of Otto Warmbier, a young American tourist to North Korea who in 2016 found himself imprisoned for fifteen years for alleged theft; he was released early but comatose, and died shortly after his return to the States, with both his family and the American government blaming North Korea for his illness. At the time of writing, the situation remained tense, especially in South Korea, where many long-term expats had, for the first time, started to draw up contingency plans for evacuation.

While the country's international reputation has gone through the wringer, much has changed domestically under Kim's leadership – incremental **improvements**, largely ignored by global media. Restrictions on business have been relaxed, and restaurants, bars and shops are now quite visible in Pyongyang and other cities; there are many more cars on the road now (including local brand Pyonghwa, many of whose models are based on those of Fiat); and agricultural reform has allowed farmers to keep a share of their produce for themselves. There's simply more bustle about the country now, and though these things are hard to measure, people do seem happier than they did a decade ago. Indeed, Chinese residents of Pyongyang have been heard to compare the pace of

---

2014: A DPRK ODDITY

The year 2014 was a bit of an odd one, even by North Korean standards. NBA legend **Dennis Rodman** set things rolling with his visit in January; after making a couple of visits to North Korea the previous year, he'd headed to Pyongyang again to enact some "sports diplomacy" with a cohort of basketball stars. The trip quickly descended into farce: Rodman was visibly inebriated during a shouty interview with CNN on January 7, and also while leading a "Happy Birthday, Mister President" sing-song at a basketball match the following day – the North Korean crowd clapped along diligently, despite being unfamiliar with the fact that it was Kim's birthday (until that point, something approaching a state secret). Following his return to the US, Rodman was investigated for violating state sanctions by donating luxury goods, including vodka (his own brand, as it turns out) and watches, to the Kims. The whole shebang was covered in an entertaining documentary: Dennis Rodman's *Big Bang in Pyongyang* (see page 380).

December saw the release of **The Interview**, a comedy in which Seth Rogen and James Franco play hapless journalists sent into North Korea with orders to assassinate Kim Jong-un. The North Korean government had, six months previously, threatened the US with "merciless retaliation" were they to permit the film's release. The computer systems at Sony Pictures were hacked, and sensitive company information leaked, by the "Guardians of Peace", a cyber-terrorist group suspected by the FBI of having strong ties to North Korea – whose government, of course, denied all involvement. Promises to attack the premiere, and any theatres showing the film, came to nought; all publicity being good publicity, *The Interview* raked in the cash, despite mixed reviews.

change to that of Beijing in the 1990s – except "they're changing even faster than we did". This may turn out to be a false dawn, but at least there are reasons to be optimistic about the future of this most reclusive of nations, and its long-suffering populace.

Pyongyang

평양

A strange concrete and marble experiment in socialist realism, the North Korean capital of **PYONGYANG** stands as a showcase of North Korean might, its grey high-rises and wide boulevards a faint echo of Le Corbusier's visions of utilitarian urban utopia – albeit one with Communist slogans screaming from the tallest buildings. Every street, rooftop, doorway and windowsill here has been designed in keeping with a single grand vision, meaning that this could, credibly, claim to be the most distinctive capital on earth – a maze of huge monuments and high-rises, studded with bronze statues and colourful murals in honour of its idolized leaders. On closer inspection, however, you'll notice that most buildings are dirty and crumbling, and the people under very apparent control.

Hard as it may be to believe, Pyongyang's near three million inhabitants live a relatively privileged existence. Life here is far better than in the countryside, though you'll still see signs of poverty: power cuts are commonplace, and each evening the city tumbles into a quiet darkness hard to fathom in a capital city.

Recent years have, however, seen some seismic shifts in the cityscape – and, perhaps, in the minds of its populace. Following Kim Jong Un's loosening of rules regarding private business, there is more and more visible commerce on the streets. **Restaurants** and **bars** have been present in number for decades, but now most of them actually have

8

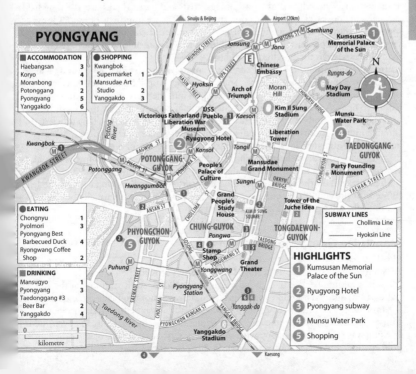

signboards to mark their presence, and indeed many have gone for flashy LED numbers – the lineaments of China's first baby steps towards capitalism are not hard to recognize.

You'll be taken by around a selection of officially sanctioned sights during your stay. These include **Kumsusan Memorial Palace of the Sun**, where the bodies of Kim and Kim lie in state, and **Mansudae**, site of their colossal statues; the distinctive granite **Juche Tower** overlooking the Taedong river; and the **Pyongyang metro**, one of the world's most intriguingly secretive subway systems. However, all sights aside, whether you're simply eating at a restaurant or relaxing in your hotel, Pyongyang always exudes a rather particular fascination.

Kumsusan Memorial Palace of the Sun

금수산 태양궁전 • No chewing gum, no smoking, no shorts, no sunglasses; all cameras, coats and bags to be left at reception

The huge **Kumsusan Memorial Palace of the Sun** is a North Korean cathedral, labyrinth and palace all rolled into one, and the single most important place in the country. It's here that the bodies of **Kim Il Sung** and **Kim Jong Il** lie in state, though only invitees, such as tour groups, are allowed to see them – you'll witness a lot of high-ranking military proudly wearing their medals and stripes. The official residence of Kim Il Sung until his death in 1994, it was transformed into his final resting place under the orders of his son, heir and future partner in rigor mortis, Kim Jong Il. While perceived disrespect to the leaders isn't advisable anywhere in the country, it will not be tolerated here – be on your best behaviour, dress smartly and keep any conversation hushed.

The tour

The walk around the palace and past the Kims is a long, slow experience, one that usually takes well over an hour. **Security** is understandably tight – you'll be searched at the entrance and relieved of your cameras, coats and bags. Then starts the long haul through corridor after marble corridor, some of which are hundreds of metres long; thankfully, moving walkways are in place, but stand on them, rather than walk – locals view this as an experience to be savoured for as long as possible, and you're likely to see many in tears, even the butchest of soldiers.

After accessing an upper floor by elevator, your proximity to **Kim Il Sung's body** will be heralded by a piped rendition of the "Song of General Kim Il Sung", composed after his death. Absolute silence is expected as visitors pass into the main room, which is bathed in a dim red light. A queue circles around the illuminated body – follow the North Korean lead and take a deep bow on each side. After paying your respects, you'll be ushered through more corridors. In one room are Kim Il Sung's many medals, prizes, doctorates and awards – note that a few of the universities on his dozens of diplomas have never existed – while in others there's a wall map of the world showing the countries that he visited, and the train carriage and car that he did some of his travelling in.

After this, you do the same again for objects pertaining to **Kim Jong Il** – and the fella himself. At the end of the tour, after collecting your things, you'll usually be allowed out onto the adjacent park for a much-needed stroll.

Mansudae Grand Monument

만수대 • No chewing gum, no smoking, no shorts, no sunglasses

At **Mansudae**, west of the river, huge **bronze statues** of Kim Il Sung and Kim Jong Il stand in triumph, backed by a mural of Mount Paekdu – spiritual home of the Korean nation (see page 361). Unlike the mausoleum, this was not originally a memorial – Kim Il Sung's statue was cast when he was still alive, a sixtieth birthday present to himself, paid for by the people and with monies donated by the Chinese government (Beijing was said to be unhappy with the unnecessary extravagance of the original gold coating, and it was soon removed). In 2012 the authorities added a statue of the recently deceased Kim Jong Il, and replaced Kim Il Sung's original stern-looking statue with a jollier one, so that the two chaps are both beaming with benevolent smiles.

So important are the statues that, despite their size (a full 20m) they're given a thorough scrub with disturbing regularity – not a single bird poo is ever seen on them, and if you ask your guide the reason why, they'll likely tell you that the birds respect them just as much as the people do. Indeed, said respect is also expected of foreigners: each individual, or every second or third person if it's a large tour party, will have to **lay flowers** at the divine metal feet (these will be purchased on the walk towards the monument, and you may be asked to chip in). Each group must also line up and perform a simultaneous bow – stay down for at least a few seconds. Note that taking any pictures that might be deemed "offensive", which includes those cutting part of the statue off, may result in your phone or camera being confiscated. Guides also usually ask people to smarten up a bit here, and to be on their best behaviour – no larking about.

Sloping up from the monument is **Moran Hill**, a small park crisscrossed with pleasant paths, and used by city-dwellers as a place to kick back and relax. While there's nothing specific to see, those who visit on a busy day will get a chance to see North Korean life at first hand – this is one of the best places in the country to make a few temporary friends. A simple smile, wave or greeting (in Korean, preferably) has seen travellers invited to scoff *bulgogi* at a picnic or dance along to traditional tunes with a clutch of chuckling grannies.

THE WORLD'S LARGEST SHELL

8

The Ministry of Truth – Minitrue, in Newspeak – was startlingly different from any other object in sight. It was an enormous pyramidal structure of glittering white concrete, soaring up, terrace after terrace, three hundred metres into the air... the Ministry of Truth contained, it was said, three thousand rooms above ground level, and corresponding ramifications below. George Orwell, Nineteen Eighty-Four

It's somewhat ironic that North Korea's most distinctive building seems to have had its design lifted from the pages of *Nineteen Eighty-Four*, a book banned across the country. In a Pyongyang skyline dominated by rectangular apartment blocks, the **Ryugyong Hotel** (류꽁 호텔) is the undisputed king of the hill – a bizarre triangular fusion of Dracula's castle and the Empire State Building. Despite the fact that it sticks out like a sore and rather weathered thumb, a whole generation of locals have viewed it as a taboo subject – this was something that couldn't be painted over with the regular whitewash of propaganda.

Construction of the pyramidal 105-floor structure started in 1987, a mammoth project intended to showcase North Korean might. The central peak was to be topped with several revolving restaurants, while the two lower cones may have held smaller versions of the same. For a time, rather amazingly, Pyongyang was one of only three cities in the world that could boast a hundred-storey-plus building, the others being New York and Chicago. Kim Il Sung had expected the *Ryugyong* to become one of the world's most admired hotels, its near-3000 rooms filled with awestruck tourists; however, no sooner had the concrete casing been completed than the foreign funding fell through (so much for the Juche Idea; see page 347), and the project was put on indefinite hold. It was left empty, a mere skeleton devoid of electricity, carpeting and windows.

Work only recommenced in earnest in 2008. By 2010, the crane that had maintained a lonely, sixteen-year vigil atop the structure had disappeared, and most of the naked exterior had finally been covered with tinted windows. At the time of writing everything was back on hold again, and tourists are still not allowed to enter its immediate area (though those who have the Victorious Fatherland Liberation War Square on their schedules will get quite near). In 2017, the wall surrounding the site came down, and the spring of 2018 saw a large LED display shining from the building's exterior – all being well, in years to come the world's largest shell will finally become one of its most distinctive places to stay.

The Arch of Triumph

개선문

The huge, white granite **Arch of Triumph**, at the bottom of Moran Hill, is on almost every tourist itinerary; you may even be taken here before checking in to your hotel. Modelled on the Arc de Triomphe in Paris, but deliberately built a little higher than its French counterpart, it's the largest such structure in the world. The arch was completed in 1982 to commemorate Korea's resistance to Japan, whose occupation ended in 1945. Despite the fact that it was actually Soviet forces that liberated the city, the on-site guide will tell you that **Kim Il Sung** did all the hard work. Just a minute's walk away, and easily visible from the arch, is a tremendous **mural** of the Great Leader receiving the adulation of his public, while set further back is the 50,000-seater **Kim Il Sung Stadium**. This is the venue for the start and finish of the Pyongyang marathon (see page 351).

Kim Il Sung Square

김일성 광장

South of Mansudae is **Kim Il Sung Square**, a huge paved area where the sense of space is usually heightened by a near-total dearth of people. First-time visitors may also get a sense of déjà vu – this is the square which features in all the stock North Korean footage of goose-stepping soldiers shown whenever the country is in the news (incidentally, this act is far from a daily event, and not even an annual one – it's only performed on important military anniversaries). State propaganda peers down into the square from all sides in the form of oversized pictures and slogans. The message on the party headquarters on the north side of the square reads "Long live the Democratic People's Republic of Choson!" Others say "With the Revolutionary Spirit of Paekdu Mountain!" and "Follow the Three Revolutionary Flags!" – the red flags in question read "history", "skill" and "culture", and the horse rearing away from them is Chollima, a winged horse of Korean legend. Visible to the east across the river is the soaring flame-like tip of the Juche Tower (see page 346).

Grand People's Study House

인민 대학 습당

At the west of the square is the **Grand People's Study House**, effectively an oversized library and one of the few buildings in the city to be built with anything approaching a traditional style – a little ironic, considering its status as a vault of rewritten history. This isn't on all tour itineraries, but anyone given the chance to enter will doubtless be impressed by the super-modern filing system.

Juche Tower

주체 사상탑

While the Mansudae Grand Monument was Kim Il Sung's sixtieth birthday gift to himself, the **Tower of the Juche Idea** – as it's officially referred to – is what he unwrapped when he turned 70 in 1982: a giant, 150m-high candle topped with a 20m red flame, rising up from its site on the banks of the Taedong river. Named after the North Korean take on Communist theory (see page 347) it's the tallest granite tower in the world, and one of the few points of light in Pyongyang's dim night sky. A kind of socialist version of Cheomseongdae in South Korea (see page 190), but without the astrological capabilities, it is made out of 25,550 granite slabs – one for each day of Kim's seventy years (leap years perhaps being deemed decadent and bourgeois in North Korea).

It's possible to take a **lift** to the torch level for stupendous views over Pyongyang. Alternatively, you could choose to stay behind, citing a fear of heights, for a guide-free walk around the area: your minder will have to go up with the group, leaving you alone to wander the riverside park. Given the slug-like speed of the lift, you may be on your own for a pleasantly long time. Take a look across the river, and to the right you'll see a sector of Pyongyang that some are now referring to as "**Mini Dubai**" (around Sungni subway station) – a slew of high-rise buildings, and rather attractive ones at that, which may well be a sneak peek into the architectural future of this city.

Mangyongdae Schoolchildren's Palace

만경대 학생 소년궁전

Behind their strained faces, you sense all the concentration that goes into playing the music, and especially into trying to keep up those Miss World smiles…It's all so cold and sad. I could cry.   Guy Delisle, Pyongyang

The **Mangyongdae Schoolchildren's Palace** showcases the impressive talents of some of the most gifted youths in the country – you'll be escorted from room to room, taking in displays of everything from volleyball and gymnastics to embroidery and song. For some visitors, this by-product of Kim Il Sung's contention that "children are the treasure of the nation" is a sweet and pleasant part of the tour, for others the atmosphere can be more than a little depressing – while there's no denying the abilities of the young performers, it's hard to ignore the level of intensity required in their training. At the end of the tour is an impressive but brutally regimental **performance** of song and dance in the large auditorium, showcasing North Korean expertise to foreign guests; many leave wondering what the country would be like if similar efforts were put into more practical educational pursuits.

Pyongyang subway

평양 지하철

Many visitors find it incredible that a country as poor as North Korea has something as decadent as a functioning **subway system**, one that even has two lines; in fact, there are likely to be several more for government-only use, though details are kept well under wraps. Several of the sixteen known stations are now open to foreign visitors.

The first thing you'll notice is the length of the escalator; Pyongyang has some of the world's **deepest** subway platforms, said to be reinforced and deep enough to

8

THE JUCHE IDEA

A local take on Marxist-Leninist theory, **Juche** is the official state ideology of the DPRK, and a system that informs the decision-making of each and every one of its inhabitants. Though Kim Il Sung claims the credit for its invention, the basic precepts were formed by *yangban* scholars in the early twentieth century, created as a means of asserting Korean identity during the Japanese occupation. The basic principle is one of **self-reliance** – both nation and individual are intended to be responsible for their own destinies. Kim Il Sung introduced Juche as the official ideology in the early 1970s, and the doctrines were put to paper in 1982 by his son Kim Jong Il in a book entitled *On the Juche Idea*. Foreign-language editions are available at hotels in Pyongyang, though the core principle of the treatise is as follows:

…man is a social being with independence, creativity and consciousness, which are his social attributes formed and developed in the course of social life and through the historic process of development; these essential qualities enable man to take a position and play a role as master of the world.

As one local puts it, "Juche is more centred around human benefit than material gain relative to the theories of Marx or Lenin. There's no time for asking why we don't have something, or excusing yourself because of this absence… if the state doesn't provide something, make it yourself." In spite of this apparent confidence, there are some pretty serious flaws and contradictions evident in the DPRK's pursuit of its own creed – the country preaches self-reliance but has long been heavily dependent on the international community for aid, and though Juche Man is said to be free to make his own decisions, **democracy** remains little more than a component part of the state's official title.

provide protection in the event of a military attack. Marble-floored, with sculpted columns and bathed in the dim glow of low-wattage chandelier lights, these platforms look surprisingly opulent, and are backed by large socialist realist mosaics. The trains themselves are a mix of Chinese rejects and relics of the Berlin U-Bahn, the latter evident in the occasional bit of ageing German graffiti (there's none at all in Korean); all feature the obligatory Kim pictures in each carriage.

The journey between stations doesn't last long, but will give you the chance to make a little contact with the locals. Photos of the subway or the boards that mark it from the outside – "*ji*" (지) in Korean text, short for *jihacheol* – go down particularly well with South Koreans, most of whom are totally unaware that such a facility exists in the North.

The Victorious Fatherland Liberation War Museum

조국 해방전 쟁승리 기념관 • No photography allowed inside

If you have any say in your schedule, make sure that it includes a visit to the **Victorious Fatherland Liberation War Museum**. Right from the huge, cheery mural at the entrance, you'll be subjected to the most fervent America-bashing that you're likely to hear in North Korea; the terms "aggressors", "imperialists" and "imperialist aggressors" are used avidly. You'll be escorted through rooms filled with photos and documents relating to atrocities said to have been inflicted on Korea by the Americans, many of which were apparently seized after the liberation of Seoul during the Korean War. The important bits on the documents are underlined, which helps to steer the eye away from some suspiciously shoddy English – however obvious the forgeries may be (and there are some), don't be tempted to point it out, and just treat it as part of the game.

Outside the museum you'll see pieces of war machinery – several bullet-ravaged planes, a torpedo ship and some captured guns and trucks. Of most interest is a **helicopter** shot down over North Korean territory; next to the vehicle's carcass is an extraordinary photograph of the pilot surrendering next to his dead friend. A statue of Kim Il Sung (looking, notably, for all the world like Kim Jong Un) greets you in the foyer; from here, you'll be led around three floors of exhibits. Perhaps most interesting is the **panorama room**, where the depiction of a battle in the Daejeon area – rendered on an apparently seamless 15m x 132m length of canvas – slowly revolves around a central platform. This latest incarnation of the museum dates back to 2013, and, in a sign of changing times, there are some computer terminals on which visitors can look at photos of the war. There are also three small coffee bars at which you can rest up if the rhetoric gets to you.

USS Pueblo

푸에블로 호납치 사건

A piece of history floating on the Potong river, the **USS Pueblo** would count as a Pyongyang must-see were it not for the fact that you'll probably have to see it anyway – it's actually part of the War Museum complex (see page 348). On January 23, 1968, this small American research ship was boarded and captured by KPA forces in the East Sea – whether it was in North Korean or international waters at the time depends on who you ask. The reasons for the attack, in which one crew member was killed, also vary from one side to the other – the North Koreans made accusations of espionage, the Americans contend that the Soviet Union wanted an on-board encryptor – as do accounts of what happened to the 83 captured crew during their enforced stay in the DPRK; the misty cloak of propaganda makes it hard to verify tales of torture, but they're equally difficult to reject. What's known for sure is that Pyongyang spent months waiting for an **apology** which the Americans deferred for months, and it was only on December 23 that the crew finally crossed to safety over Panmunjom's "Bridge of No Return" (see page 138).

Mangyongdae

만경대

A visit to **Mangyongdae** – the purported **birthplace** of Kim Il Sung on April 15, 1912 – is almost guaranteed to feature on your itinerary. Despite the lack of things to see, the park-like area is pretty in a dull sort of way, and kept as modest as possible, its wooden buildings surrounded by greenery and meandering paths providing a nod to Kim's peasant upbringing. You'll likely be offered spring water from the on-site well, which supposedly gets visitors "into the revolutionary spirit of things". The nearby funfair is marginally more interesting, and features a coconut shy where you can hurl projectiles at targets dressed up as American and Japanese soldiers.

Munsu Water Park

문수 물공원 • Entry usually €10 • Usually only open to foreigners on weekends and holidays

Pyongyang now has the **Munsu Water Park**, and to the surprise of many visitors, it's not dissimilar to such facilities in the West. The tallest of several slides allows you to drop like a stone from 26m, but the main draw here is the chance to mingle with "normal" North Koreans, without your guide in attendance – you'll basically be left to your own devices for an hour or more, and will likely be asked to feature in a fair few local selfies (don't leave your camera in your locker if you want some of your own!). The park doesn't yet feature on many tours, but ask your operator or guides in advance, and you may be allowed to swing by.

8

ARRIVAL AND DEPARTURE

Most visitors to Pyongyang are here to start a guided excursion, so whether you arrive by **plane** or **train** – your only two options – a bus or private car will be waiting. Given the tightness of the average itinerary, you're likely to visit at least one sight on the way to your hotel.

By plane The semi-decrepit Sunan International Airport (순안국제공항) received a thorough overhaul in 2015, and is now relatively pleasant. Customs inspections can be thorough, and they use their X-ray machines to find books; anything religious, pornographic or pertaining to South Korea will be confiscated, as will guidebooks such as this one. The 20min journey from the airport to central Pyongyang is a fascinating one for first-time visitors, displaying as it does an impoverishment that the authorities have made surprisingly little effort to conceal. **By train** Pyongyang station (평양역) is far more central than the airport. Before you leave, check out the pleasing 1920s-vintage architecture of the station.

GETTING AROUND

Getting around the city is usually as simple as waking up in time to catch your **tour bus** (those left behind will be stuck in the hotel until their group returns), but there are a few other ways in which to get around town – usually for locals only, though included on some tours.

By subway The city's subway system counts as a sight in its own right (see page 347), and forms part of most tours. The price will be included, but locals pay five won per ride – that's just a fraction of a cent.
By bus and tram Pyongyang's crammed public buses and trams feature on some tours. The buses are pretty photogenic, many of them Hungarian relics from the 1950s. Look out for the stars on their sides – each one represents 50,000 accident-free kilometres.
By taxi Pyongyang received its first-ever fleet of marked taxis in 2013; the largest firms are now KKG, a growing conglomerate, and Air Koryo, whose planes you probably flew in on. Rather interestingly, most cabs are adorned with the word "Taxi" in English as well as Korean – a rare sign of globalization in this Juche-oriented society, which tends to create new words of its own for new concepts. Ask your tour company if you'd like to take a cab, and also if you'd like one of the prepaid cards that some locals are using to pay for their trips (see page 353).

INFORMATION

Guides There's no such thing as a tourist information office in North Korea, but your guide will be on hand to answe

TRAFFIC LADIES

At many major intersections in Pyongyang, you'll spot women in uniform directing, or supervising, traffic from the roadsides. Chosen for their beauty by the powers that be, and evidently well schooled, these **traffic ladies** sport distinctive blue (sometimes white) jackets, hats and skirts, as well as regulation white socks. The traffic ladies are rather popular with some visitors, and one or two tour groups have persuaded their guides to stop by for a brief photo-shoot.

any questions. Most topics are fine, but asking anything that could be construed as disparaging of the regime could land you or your host in hot water. The guides are usually amiable sorts, and many of them are heaps of fun – especially if you can tempt them into the hotel bar after the day's touring is over. However, at some sights you'll be in the hands of specialists employed to bark out nationalistic vitriol (which, you'll notice, increases in force and volume when either of the Kims are mentioned).

Mass Games This incredible event has been off the event calendars (if such things exist in North Korea) since 2013, but at the time of writing rumours were suggesting a return – travel agencies listed here (see page 331) should be able to fill you in.

Pyongyang Marathon Starting and finishing at the whopping Kim Il Sung Stadium, this event takes place every April, and the guys at Koryo Tours (see page 331) lay on special tours for those wishing to take part in it.

ACCOMMODATION

There are fewer than a dozen hotels in Pyongyang designated for foreigners, and which one you end up at will be organized in advance by your tour operator. Most groups stay at Pyongyang's **top hotels**, the Koryo and Yanggakdo; there's little between them in terms of service and quality. Both provide a memorable experience and are tourist draws in their own right, which is a good thing, considering the amount of time you'll be spending there – in the evening, when your daily schedule is completed, there's not really anywhere else to go.

Haebangsan 해방산 호텔; map p.343. This is the cheapest hotel for foreigners, and a recent renovation has made it a perfectly acceptable place to stay – at least in warmer months, since 24-hour running water is not guaranteed. Another drawback is a near-total lack of atmosphere or on-site activities.

Koryo 고려 호텔; map p.343. The salmon-pink twin towers of this forty-storey hotel sit on a main thoroughfare, making for a decent appreciation of local life. Rooms are well kept and the on-site restaurants passable, while the ground-floor mini-market is stocked with foreign drinks, biscuits and other comestibles.

Moranbong 모란봉 호텔; map p.343. A boutique hotel in Pyongyang – whatever next? There are just twelve rooms here, and the fitness centre and pool exude an atmosphere rather contrary to the rest of the country. However, it's popular with diplomats, and as such a little hard to book.

Potonggang 포통강 호텔; map p.343. Just west of central Pyongyang, in a dull part of town, this is the only hotel to feed a couple of American TV channels into the

rooms. Despite the acceptable facilities, few Westerners end up staying here; if you do, you'll find it hard to miss the huge Kim mural in the lobby.

Pyongyang 평양 호텔; map p.343. The first official hotel in the country, this has benefitted enormously from recent renovations. Unlike the island-based Yanggakdo or the lofty Koryo, it's a low-level affair set right in the middle of things. If you're in a streetside room (highly recommended, if you have any say), look out of the window in the morning and you'll see locals heading to work; you may also hear fragments of quiet conversation drifting in from outside when you're falling asleep.

Yanggakdo 양각도 호텔; map p.343. This 47-storey hotel sits on an islet in the Taedong, and commands superb views of both the river and the city from its clean, spacious rooms. The isolated location means that you'll be able to wander around outside without provoking the ire of guides or guards, though to be honest there's precious little to do. The on-site restaurants are excellent, as are the bars (see page 352). Also on site are a bowling alley, a karaoke room and a tailor.

EATING

As with accommodation, all your dining requirements will be sorted out in advance. The best restaurants are closed to all but foreigners and the party elite, and you'll probably eat at a different one on each day of your stay. The North Korean authorities seem to think that foreigners will only enjoy their meal if they're rotating slowly – most "fancy" places, including both the Koryo and Yanggakdo hotels, have **revolving restaurants**. You usually have **breakfast** in your hotel, and on some days perhaps lunch or dinner too. Both the volume and the quality of food will depend on the prevailing food situation at the time of your visit – experienced diplomats suggest that it seems to improve when big groups or important folk are in town.

8

Chongnyu 청류; map p.343 A popular choice with tour operators, particularly in colder months, this long-established restaurant specializes in Korean hotpot. It's opposite the Romanian and Iranian embassies – the latter featuring Pyongyang's only mosque.

Pyolmori 별머리; map p.343 Those staying at the *Koryo* should ask to be taken to this nearby café-cum-bakery – in addition to tasty snacks, it serves good coffee.

Pyongyang Best Barbecued Duck 평양 제일 오리고기; map p.343 A popular tour stop, and only open when booked by an agency, this place serves duck and little else.

Ryongwang Coffee Shop; map p.343 Located on Kim Il Sung Square (see page 346), this offers some of the best coffee in the city – and, by extension, the whole country.

DRINKING

Drinking can be one of Pyongyang's most unexpected delights – while you won't exactly be painting the town red, many travellers stagger to bed from the **hotel bar** every single night of their stay (and then have to get up at 7am to catch the tour bus). There are also a handful of **local bars** – a couple of classier joints and some proletarian places – now licensed to allow foreign visitors; ask the guides to take you to one, since the chance to mingle with the locals is truly memorable.

Mansugyo 만수교; map p.343 Pester your guide in advance of a visit to the War Museum, and you may get to drop by this locals' bar. They serve all seven strains of Taedonggang beer at super-low prices (around $0.50), plus there's a pleasing outdoor section. Amiable staff – and, usually, customers – round out the picture.

Pyongyang 평양 호텔; map p.343 Hunt down the fourth-floor bar if you're staying here – it's usually the most fun option of the several dotted around the establishment. Unfortunately its most regular customer, a Scottish lawyer who lived at this hotel for years, is no longer around (better call Seoul).

Taedonggang #3 Beer Bar 태동강 재삼 맥주점;

map p.343 About 100m east of the Juche Tower, this impressive-looking bar is popular with Pyongyang's emerging middle-class, and has up to seven beers on tap (all made by the eponymous brewery; avoid the number five) from $2 each, plus cocktails, snacks and full meals.

Yanggakdo 양각도 호텔; map p.343 This landmark hotel boasts two of the most interesting bars in town. One revolves slowly at the top of the tower, and makes a great place for a nightcap with a view of Pyongyang's galaxy of faint lights. The ground-floor bar brews its own beer ($3.50 or so, making this the most expensive bar in the land), which can be quite delicious after a hard day slogging around sights.

SHOPPING

While staunchly anti-capitalist North Korea isn't exactly renowned for its **shopping** possibilities, "regular" commerce has become much more common in recent years – those able to read Korean may even spy the odd sale, discount or two-for-one sign here and there, things that would have been next to nonexistent not all that long ago. Tourists have to stick to a limited number of government-approved shops, but there are a number of interesting things to buy in Pyongyang, most of which are impossible to get anywhere else – many make fantastic souvenirs.

Food and drink Your hotel is likely to have a shop at which you can buy North Korean booze – beer and *soju* are common purchases, though the bold can try some of the harder spirits, made with all sorts, from mushroom to seal penis. A few tours feature the fantastic new Kwangbok supermarket, in which purchases can only be made in North Korean money (there's a market-rate exchange booth at the front); the local honey's a sweet treat, while South Korean friends will get a kick out of the *naengmyeon* noodles – spelled "*raengmyeon*" (랭면) in the North, these are clearly definable as contraband, though there's nothing to stop you sending or taking them into the South. The same goes for booze, though South Korean customs only tend to allow incoming travellers to carry one bottle of alcohol.

Kim-lit Imagine if your local bookstore only sold works from writers with the same surname – that's pretty much what it's like in the DPRK. Shops in hotels and various other

places around Pyongyang sell books from the pen of Kim, Kim and Kim, the trio of leaders holding forth on all sorts of subjects from cinema to social policy.

Kim suits The *Yanggakdo* (see page 351) has a tailor on the third floor, and it's often possible to make a special visit even if you're not staying at this hotel – and you'll find ideal fodder for Hallowe'en parties. A variety of jackets and trousers are available, though most popular are the buttoned-up-to-the-collar "Kim suits", as popularized by Kim Jong Il; it's also possible to nab a green, military-style jacket with gold buttons.

Local money It's technically illegal for foreigners to use (and therefore, by extension, export) North Korean money though there are certainly ways in which to get your hand on some. Those visiting in warmer months may spot women selling ice cream from tiny booths, most often tasty stick-bar called an *Eskimo* – if you pay slightly over the odds in foreign currency you'll get some local change

The same goes at the snack kiosks you'll see streetside all over the city. In all cases, hard Chinese currency certainly goes down well.

Pre-paid cards These have become rather popular of late in North Korea (with the Narae Card being the original and most widely used), and can be used for all sorts from paying at grocery stores to taking local taxis. You may not actually ever get to use one, but ask your guide and they should be able to get you one for a few dollars during your trip. The cards make fantastic souvenirs, and attempting to pay for something with one south of the border will provoke a fair bit of head-scratching, then wide-eyed astonishment as the poor cashier finally realizes where the card comes from.

Socialist realist stamps and badges A visit to the stamp shop comes as part of many tours, and their socialist realist designs are really quite striking – a good purchase, even if you're not a philatelist. Your hotel's shop is also likely to stock a series of similarly cool badges.

Socialist realist art Some tourists end up spending hundreds of dollars on Socialist realist art, often coming back for more – prospective owners (or dealers, since there's money to be made) should ask to swing by the Mansudae Art Studio, though a shop down south in Panmunjom (see page 354) has cheaper, slightly lower-quality fare for sale too.

Other sights in the DPRK

Most of the country is closed off to foreign visitors, but even the shortest tour itinerary is likely to contain at least one sight outside Pyongyang. The most common trip is to **Panmunjom** in the DMZ, via **Kaesong**, the closest city to the border, but there are other popular excursions to **Paekdusan**, the mythical birthplace of the Korean nation and its highest peak, and the wonderful "Diamond Mountains" of **Kumgangsan** near the South Korean border.

8

Kaesong

개성

Other than Pyongyang, **KAESONG** is usually the only North Korean city that foreign travellers get to see. From the capital, it's an easy ninety-minute trip south along the traffic-free **Reunification Highway**; the road actually continues all the way to Seoul, just 80km away, though it's blocked by the DMZ a few kilometres south of Kaesong. Kaesong's proximity to the border means that the surrounding area is crawling with soldiers, and it's hardly surprising that Kaesong's long-suffering citizens often come across as a little edgy.

SPECIAL EXCURSIONS

This section details a few of the most common DPRK sights outside Pyongyang. All regularly feature on tour itineraries, but new areas are opened up from time to time – largely thanks to Koryo Tours (see page 331), who take a hugely proactive stance in these regards. Here are a few lesser-visited places to look out for when choosing a tour:

Haeju (해주) A great side trip for history buffs: the city is home to a huge pavilion erected in 1500, while the surrounding area is home to a Goryeo-dynasty mountain fortress and a Joseon-era Confucian academy. It's possible to stay the night here.

Hamhung (함흥) This major east-coast city only opened to tourism in 2010 – your presence will cause quite a stir. It's visually interesting, with lots of buildings designed by East German architects, while attractions include factory tours and trips to local farms.

Nampo (남포) A major city just 45 minutes west of Pyongyang by bus. Sights are low-key, but interesting in their own way – most visitors get shown around the 8km-long West Sea Barrage, the steelworks and a couple of factories. Ask for a trip to the hot-springs resort.

Wonsan (원산) A large port city – visitors usually get shown around the docks, though more interesting is the chance to swim in the sea at Songdowon beach, just down the coast. On the way to or from Pyongyang (a 4hr drive) you may be able to stop at the gorgeous Ulim waterfalls – ask permission for a dip, if it's warm.

The palpable tension, Kaesong – romanized as "Gaeseong" in the South – is actually a place of considerable history: this was once the capital of the **Goryeo dynasty** (see page 364), which ruled over the peninsula from 936 to 1392, though thanks to wholesale destruction in the Korean War, you'll see precious little evidence of this today. One exception is **Sonjuk Bridge**, which was built in the early thirteenth century; it was here that an eponymous Goryeo loyalist was assassinated as his dynasty fell.

Kim statues

Guaranteed to catch the eye in Kaesong are two huge **statues** of **Kim Il Sung** and **Kim Jong Il**. One of the most prominent such statue-pairings in the country (and there are many), and even visible from the Reunification Highway on the way to Panmunjom, they're illuminated at night come what may owing to a generator, which enables them to surf the crest of any power shortages that afflict the rest of the city.

The tomb of Wang Kon
왕건 왕릉

There are a few officially sanctioned sights in Kaesong's surrounding countryside. West of the city on the road to Pyongyang is the tomb of **Wang Kon**, the first leader of Goryeo and the man responsible for moving the dynasty's capital to Kaesong, his home town. In the South, he's more commonly known as King Taejo, and his decorated grass-mound tomb is similar to those that can be found in Seoul (see page 91).

The tomb of Wang Jon
왕전 왕릉

West of Wang Kon is another tomb, this one belonging to **Wang Jon**. Also known as King Kongmin, he ruled (1351–74) during Mongol domination of the continent; in keeping with the traditions of the time, he married a Mongol princess and was buried alongside her – the tiger statues surrounding the tomb represent the Goryeo dynasty, while the sheep are a nod to the Mongol influence. North of Wang Kon's tomb is **Pakyon**, a forest waterfall whose surroundings include a fortress gate and a beautiful temple.

ACCOMMODATION AND EATING   **KAESONG**

Groups heading to or from Panmunjom often have a **lunch stop** in Kaesong, which was famed for its cuisine prior to the division of Korea – there are plenty of restaurants south of the border named after the city. It's also possible to **stay** in Kaesong, which is provided as an interesting add-on to many tours.

Kaesong Folk Hotel A parade of traditional rooms running off a courtyard, set in a complex dotted with swaying trees and bisected by a peaceful stream. Rooms are basic, and sometimes fall victim to power outages, but it's a unique experience with an entirely different vibe from the big hotels in Pyongyang.

★ **Tongil** The option favoured by most tour leaders, the "Unification" restaurant lays on a superb spread, apportioned into little golden bowls – perhaps the best food you're likely to encounter in the whole country.

Panmunjom
판문점

The village of **PANMUNJOM** sits bang in the middle of the **Demilitarized Zone** that separates North and South Korea (see page 135 for more information on how it can be reached from the South, where it's romanized as Panmunjeom, but pronounced the same). You'll see much the same from the North, but with the propaganda reversed – all of a sudden it was the US Army that started the Korean War and Kim Il Sung who won it. Interestingly, many visitors note that the cant is just as strong on the American side (and not always much more balanced).

Into the DMZ

The route to Panmunjom follows the Reunification Highway from Kaesong. Your first stop will be at the **KPA guardpost**, which sits just outside the northern barrier of the DMZ; the southern flank is just 4km away, though it feels much further. After being given a short presentation of the site by a local soldier, it's time for the ride into the DMZ itself – note the huge slabs of concrete at the sides of the road, ready to be dropped to block the way of any invading tanks (this same system is in place on the other side). A short way into the DMZ is the **Armistice Hall**, which was cobbled together at incredible speed by North Korean soldiers to provide a suitable venue for the signing of the Korean Armistice Agreement, a document which brought about a ceasefire to the Korean War on July 27, 1953. Tucked away in a corner is what is said to be a weapon from the famed "Axe Murder Incident", an incident for which North Korea claims little responsibility (see page 137).

The Joint Security Area

From the Armistice Hall you are taken to the **Joint Security Area** (see page 137), where Panmun Hall looks across the border at a South Korean building of similar size. From here, you're led into one of the three halls that straddle the official line of control, and are permitted to take a few heavily guarded steps into South Korean territory. The whole experience is bizarre, but fascinating, and it's an oddly tranquil place, despite its status as one of the world's most dangerous border points.

Kumgangsan

금강산

Before partition, the **Kumgangsan** mountain range – which sits just north of the DMZ on Korea's east coast – was widely considered to be the most beautiful on the peninsula. The DPRK's relative inaccessibility has ensured that this remains the case. Spectacular crags and spires of rock tower over a skirt of pine-clad foothills, its pristine lakes and waterfalls adding to a richly forested beauty rivalled only by Seoraksan just across the border (see page 156). There are said to be more than twelve thousand pinnacles, though the principal peak is Birobong, which rises to 1638m above sea level.

Kumgangsan can be visited as part of a North Korean tour, and was indeed once visitable on **a trip from South Korea** (where the name is romanized as "Geumgangsan", but pronounced the same) – until a South Korean tourist was killed in 2008 and the tours put on indefinite hold.

Myohyangsan

묘향산

Many North Korean tours include a visit to **Myohyangsan**, a pristine area of hills, lakes and waterfalls around 150km north of Pyongyang. Though it's about as close as the DPRK comes to a mountain resort, the main reason to come here isn't to walk the delightful hiking trails, but to visit the **International Friendship Exhibition** – a colossal display showing the array of presents given to the Kims by overseas well-wishers. After the exhibition you're likely to be taken to see **Pohyonsa**, an eleventh-century temple just a short walk away, and **Ryongmun** or **Paengryong**, two stalactite-filled limestone caves which burrow for a number of kilometres under the surrounding mountains.

The International Friendship Exhibition

국제 친선 전람관

The halls of the **International Friendship Exhibition** burrow deep into a mountainside – insurance against any nuclear attacks that come the DPRK's way. Inside the exhibition hall, gifts numbering 200,000 and rising have been arranged in order of country of origin, the evident intention being to convince visitors that the Kims command immense respect all over the world – of course, this is not the place to air any painful truths.

The first rooms you come to are those dedicated to **Kim Il Sung**. For a time, gifts were pouring in from all over the Communist world, including a limousine from Stalin and an armoured train carriage from Chairman Mao. There are also a number of medals, tea sets, pots, cutlery and military arms, as well as more incongruous offerings such as fishing rods and a refrigerator. The **Kim Jong Il** rooms are less stacked with goodies, and instead feature heavily corporate treats and electronic gadgets. Perhaps most interesting is the **basketball** donated by former American Secretary of State Madeleine Albright, signed by Michael Jordan, of whom Kim was apparently a big fan. And, of course, there are now rooms dedicated to **Kim Jong Un**, including a few gifts (some sanctionable) left behind by one Dennis Rodman.

ACCOMMODATION   MYOHYANGSAN

Chongchon 청천 Basic three-storey place with a bar and regular power cuts – good enough for one night, however, and a tour including this instead of the *Hyangsan* will be far cheaper.

Hyangsan 향산 Pyramidal hotel that's currently the best in the land, with an on-site health complex and stupendous pool, as well as the obligatory top-floor revolving restaurant.

Paekdusan

백두산

The highest peak on the Korean peninsula at 2744m, the extinct volcano of **Paekdusan** straddles the border between North Korea and China, and is the source of the Tuman and Amnok rivers (Tumen and Yalu in Mandarin) that separate the countries. Within its caldera is a vibrant blue **crater lake** surrounded by a ring of jagged peaks; it's a beguiling place steeped in myth and legend. This was said to be the landing point for

---

NORTH KOREA FROM THE OUTSIDE

If budgetary constraints or possession of the wrong kind of passport make a trip to North Korea impossible, there are a number of ways to peer into the country from outside.

FROM SOUTH KOREA

The two Koreas share a 250km-long border, and though the area around the Demilitarized Zone that separates them is largely off limits, there are a number of vantage points from which you can look across. **DMZ tours from Seoul** are highly popular (see page 138); itineraries vary, but can include views of the North from an observatory, a trip inside tunnels dug by North Koreans in preparation for an attack on Seoul, as well as the chance to step onto **DPRK territory** in the Joint Security Area. Note that there's another observatory just north of **Sokcho** on the east coast (see page 151).

FROM CHINA

The large city of **Dandong** is right on the North Korean border, with only the Yalu river ("Amnok" in Korean) separating it from Sinuiju on the other side. The two cities offer a rather incredible contrast, with the tall, neon-seared skyscrapers on the Chinese side overlooking poor, low-rise Sinuiju across the water. On Dandong's riverside promenade you'll be able to buy North Korean banknotes and pin-badges, or take a boat trip to within a single metre of the North Korean shore; you can get just as close from **Tiger Mountain**, 25km east of the city and the easternmost section of China's Great Wall.

With the mountain and its crater lake straddling the border, it's also possible to visit **Paekdusan** (see page 356) from the Chinese side, a trip highly popular with South Koreans. The best form of access is Chiangbaishan airport, served by flights from most of China's largest cities.

Dangun, the divine creator of Korea, after his journey from heaven in 2333 BC (see page 361). More recently, it was also the apparent birthplace of **Kim Jong Il**, an event said to have been accompanied by flying white horses, rainbows and the emergence of a new star in the sky – records seem to suggest that he was in fact born in Soviet Siberia, but who needs history when the myth is so expressive?

The main attraction for foreign visitors, however, is simple – extreme natural beauty. Paekdusan's ring of mountains is cloaked with lush forest, which is home to bears, wolves, boar and deer. As long as the weather holds – and at this height, it often doesn't – you may be able to hike up to the very top of the Korean peninsula. A cable car also whisks guests down to the lakeside, where you may be tempted to have a swim in warmer months – not a problem on the Chinese side, but since these waters are "sacred" to Koreans, anything more than sticking your feet in is usually frowned upon.

With Paekdusan being a place of such importance, every person in the country is expected to make the pilgrimage at some point; the journey is usually paid for in full by the government. Foreign tourists wishing to visit must take a **chartered flight** from Pyongyang, and then a car the rest of the way, though due to weather conditions the journey is usually only possible during warmer months. It's also possible to visit from the Chinese side, as thousands of South Koreans do each year (see page 356).

8

INDEPENDENCE HALL OF KOREA

Contexts

History

With its two-millennium-long chain of unbroken regal rule interspersed by regular conflict, the Korean peninsula offers plenty for history buffs to get their teeth into. The country's early beginnings are shrouded in mystery, though events have been well documented since before the birth of Christ, a period when Korea's famed Three Kingdoms were springing into existence. Replacing Gojoseon – the first known Korean kingdom – these were Silla, Goguryeo and Baekje, three states that jostled for peninsular power for centuries, seeing off other nascent fiefdoms while dealing with the Chinese and Japanese states of the time. Even today, tangible evidence of all three kingdoms can still be seen. It was Silla that eventually prevailed, emerging victorious from a series of battles to bring the peninsula under unified control. Infighting and poor governance led to its demise, the slack taken up by the Goryeo dynasty, which lasted for almost five hundred years before folding and being replaced by Joseon rule. This was to last even longer, but was snuffed out by the Japanese at a time of global turmoil, bringing to an end Korea's succession of well over one hundred kings. World War II ended Japanese annexation, after which Korea was split in two in the face of the looming Cold War. There then followed the brutal Korean War, and in 1953 the Communist north and the capitalist south went their separate ways, each writing their own historical versions of the time – and in the case of North Korea, skewing historical events even prior to partition. The war was never technically brought to an end, and its resolution – either peaceable, or by force – will add the next chapter to Korea's long history.

The beginnings

Remains of *Homo erectus* show that the Korean peninsula may have been home to hominids for more than half a million years. The first evidence of habitation can be found in several clusters of Neanderthal sites dating from the Middle Paleolithic period (roughly 100,000–40,000 BC). The assortment of hand axes, scrapers and other tools made of stone and bone hauled from the complexes suggest a **hunter-gatherer** existence. **Neolithic** sites (8000–3000 BC) are far more numerous than those from the Paleolithic era, and in these were found thousands of remnants from the peninsula's transition from the Stone to the Bronze Age. In addition to the use of metal tools, from 7000 BC **pottery** was being produced with distinctive comb-toothed patterns

2333 BC	7th century BC	c.109 BC
Founding of Gojoseon, Korea's first known kingdom, by semi-mythical bear-child Dangun	First mentions of Gojoseon in Chinese records	Demise of Gojoseon at hands of Chinese Han dynasty

KOREA'S MAJOR HISTORICAL ERAS	
Gojoseon	c.2333 BC to c.109 BC
Three Kingdoms	c.57 BC to 668 AD
Silla	c.57 BC to 668 AD
Goguryeo	c.37 BC to 668 AD
Baekje	c.18 BC to 660 AD
Unified Silla	668–935
Goryeo	918–1392
Joseon	1392–1910
Japanese colonial period	1910–45
Republic of Korea (South)	1945–present day
Democratic People's Republic of Korea (North)	1945–present day

(*jeulmun*) similar to those found in Mongolia and Manchuria. Fired earth also came to play a part in death rituals, a fact made evident by small, shell-like "jars" into which the broken bodies were placed together with personal belongings; these were then lowered into a pit and covered with earth. An even more distinctive style of burial was to develop, with some tombs covered with large stone slabs known as **dolmen** ("*goindol*" in Korean). Korea is home to over thirty thousand burial mounds. Three of the most important sites – Gochang and Hwasun in the Jeolla provinces, and Ganghwado, west of Incheon – are UNESCO World Heritage Sites.

Gojoseon

The peninsula's first kingdom was known as Joseon, though today it is usually referred to as **Gojoseon** (고조선; "Old Joseon") in an effort to distinguish it from the later Joseon period (1392–1910). Its origins are obscure to say the least; most experts agree that it got going in 2333 BC under the leadership of **Dangun**, who has since become the subject of one of Korea's most cherished myths (see page 361). Joseon initially functioned as a loose federation of fiefdoms covering not only parts of the Korean peninsula, but large swathes of Manchuria too. By 500 BC it had become a single, highly organized dominion, even drawing praise from Confucius and other Chinese sages. Accounts of the fall of Joseon are also rather vague, but large parts of its Manchurian population were squeezed onto the Korean peninsula during the Chinese **Warring States Period** (470–221 BC), and it seems likely to have fallen victim to a nascent Han dynasty in 109 BC. Joseon's historical name lives on: North Korea continues to refer to its land as such (and South Korea as Namjoseon, or "South Joseon"), while many South Korean tourist brochures use "The Land of Morning Calm" – a literal translation of the term – as a national motto.

The Three Kingdoms period

By 109 BC, after the fall of Gojoseon, power on the peninsula was decentralized to half-a-dozen fiefdoms, the most powerful of which – **Silla**, **Goguryeo** and **Baekje** – went on to become known as the Three Kingdoms. Though exact details regarding their beginnings

57 BC	**c.37 BC**	**18 BC**
Founding of Silla dynasty, first of Korea's "Three Kingdoms", by King Hyeokgeose, who supposedly hatched from an egg laid by a horse	Founding of Goguryeo dynasty by Jumong, another king hatched from an egg	Founding of Baekje dynasty by King Onjo

are just as sketchy as those surrounding Gojoseon – two of the inaugurators are said to have hatched from eggs – this period saw the first definitive drawing of borders in Korean history, although it must be noted that none of them became fully fledged kingdoms for a couple of centuries, each existing initially as a loose confederation of fiefdoms. Several of those jostling for power after Gojoseon's demise are not included under the Three Kingdoms banner; most notably, these include the states of **Gaya**, which was absorbed by Silla, and **Buyeo**, parts of which were incorporated by Goguryeo and Baekje. The kingdom of **Tamna**, isolated on Jeju Island, also came under Baekje control.

Territorial borders shifted continuously as all three kingdoms jostled for power, and a number of fortresses went up across the land, many of which can still be seen today. Outside forces were occasionally roped in to help; interestingly, Baekje was closely aligned with Japan for much of its time, while Silla sided with the Chinese Tang dynasty, despite their positions on the "wrong" sides of the peninsula. Because of these close ties with China and Japan, Korea acted as a conduit for a number of customs imported from the continent: Chinese characters came to be used with the Korean language and the import and gradual flourishing of **Buddhism** saw temples popping up all over the peninsula. However, it was **Confucianism**, another Chinese import, that provided the social building blocks, with a number of educational academies supplying the *yangban* scholars at the head of the aristocracy. Great advances were made in the arts, particularly with regard to jewellery and pottery; wonderful relics of the time have been discovered in their thousands from the grassy hill-tombs of dead kings and other formerly sacred sites. After **centuries of warring** that saw the kingdoms continually changing allegiance to each other and to Chinese and Japanese dynasties, matters finally came to a head in the mid-seventh century. In 660, supplemented by Tang forces from China, Silla **triumphed in battle** against Baekje, whose people leapt to their death from a cliff in the city of Buyeo. Muyeol died just a year later, but within a decade his son King Munmu defeated Goguryeo, setting the scene for a first-ever **unified rule** on the peninsula.

THE LEGEND OF DANGUN

The Korean peninsula has played host to some of the world's longest-running monarchies, and such regal durability has made for comprehensive records. However, much of what's known about the years preceding the Three Kingdoms period remains obscure, and Korea has resorted to mythology to fill in the gaps of its creation – primarily the legend of **Dangun**.

The story begins with **Hwanin**, the "Lord of Heaven", whose son **Hwanung** desired to live as a mortal being on Earth. Hwanin set his son down on Mount Paekdu (located in present-day North Korea) together with an army of three thousand disciples. Hwanung and his tribe took charge of the locals, and fostered celestial ideals of law, art and social structure. Two of his pets – a bear and a tiger – prayed to Hwanung that they be made human, just as he had been; they were each given twenty cloves of garlic and a bundle of mugwort, and told to survive on nothing else for a hundred days, before being sent to a cave. The tiger failed the challenge, but the bear prevailed, and on being made human soon bore Hwanung's child, Dangun, who went on to found **Joseon** in 2333 BC.

In 1993 North Korean officials announced that they had found Dangun's tomb in a location close to Pyongyang; unfortunately, they've been unwilling to share this evidence with the rest of the world.

372	**660**	**668**
Buddhism introduced to Korea; it slowly starts to replace shamanism	Silla defeats Baekje	Silla defeats Goguryeo, unifies rule on peninsula by 676

Goguryeo

The kingdom of **Goguryeo** (고구려) covered the whole of present-day North Korea, a large chunk of Chinese Manchuria and much of what is now Gangwon-do in the South, making it by far the largest of the Three Kingdoms by territory. Because of its location, the majority of Goguryeo's relics are a little harder to come by today than those from the Baekje or Silla kingdoms, and the history even more vague; most guesses place the inauguration of the first Goguryeo king, Dongmyeong, at 37 BC. At this point Goguryeo was still paying tax and tribute to China, but when the **Han dynasty** started to weaken in the third century, Goguryeo advanced and occupied swathes of territory; they eventually came to rule over an area (much of which is now in the Chinese region of Dongbei) almost three times the size of the present-day Korean peninsula. Baekje and Silla forces mounted sporadic attacks from the south, and the Chinese Tang invaded from the north, squeezing Goguryeo towards the Tuman and Anmok rivers that mark North Korea's present boundary. The Tang also provided pressure from the south by allying with the Silla dynasty, and when this **Tang-Silla coalition** defeated Baekje in 660, the fall of Goguryeo was inevitable; it was finally snuffed out in 668.

Baekje

The **Baekje** (백제) dynasty, which controlled the southwest, was created as the result of great movements of people on the western side of the Korean peninsula. **Buyeo**, a smaller state not considered one of the Three Kingdoms, was pushed southward by the nascent kingdom of Goguryeo, and some elements decided to coalesce around a new leader – **Onjo**, the son of Dongmyeong, the first king of Goguryeo. Jealous of his brother's inheritance of that kingdom, Onjo proclaimed his own dynasty in 18 BC. Baekje is notable for its production of fine jewellery, which exhibited more restraint than that found in the other kingdoms, a fact often attributed to the dynasty's relatively early adoption of Buddhism as a state religion. Evidence of Baekje's close relationship with the **Japanese kingdom of Wa** can still be seen today – the lacquered boxes, folding screens, immaculate earthenware and intricate jewellery of Japan are said to derive from the influence of Baekje artisans. Unfortunately for Baekje, the Wa did not provide such protection as the Chinese Tang dynasty gave Silla, and much of its later history was spent conceding territory to Goguryeo. The capital shifted south from a location near present-day Seoul to Ungjin (now known as Gongju), then south again to Sabi (now Buyeo); after one final battle, fought in 660 against a Tang-Silla coalition, Baekje's small remaining population chose death over dishonour, and committed suicide from Sabi's riverside fortress.

Silla

Although it held the smallest territory of the Three Kingdoms, in the southeast, and was for centuries the most peaceable, it was the **Silla** (신라) dynasty that defeated Baekje and Goguryeo to rule over the whole peninsula. Unlike its competitors, it only had one dynastic capital – Gyeongju – and many of the riches accumulated in almost a millennium of power (including over two hundred years as the capital of the whole peninsula) can still be seen today.

Silla's first king – Hyeokgeose – was crowned in 57 BC, but it was not until the sixth century AD that things got interesting. At this time, Silla accepted Buddhism as its state religion (the last of the Three Kingdoms to do so), and created a Confucian "bone

774	918	935
Completion of Bulguksa, still one of Korea's most revered temples	Inauguration of Goryeo dynasty by Wang Geon, later known as King Taejo	Official transfer of power from Silla to Goryeo

rank" system in which people's lives were governed largely by heredity: Buddhism was used to sate spiritual needs, and Confucianism as a regulator of society. Following threats from the Japanese kingdom of Wa, they also began a rapid build-up of military strength; under the rule of King Jinheung (540–76) they absorbed the neighbouring **Gaya** confederacy, and started to nibble away at the other neighbouring kingdoms. Initially they sided with Baekje to attack Goguryeo, a dynasty already weakened by internal strife and pressure from the Chinese Tang to the north; a century later, Silla turned the tables on Baekje by allying with the **Tang**, then used the same alliance to finish off Goguryeo to the north and bring the Korean peninsula under unified rule.

Unified Silla

Following the quickfire defeats of its two competitor kingdoms in the 660s, the **Silla dynasty** gave rise to the Korean peninsula's first-ever unification, keeping Gyeongju as the seat of power. This was, however, no easy matter: small pockets of Baekje and Goguryeo resistance lingered on, and a new (perhaps necessarily) nationalistic fervour developed by the king meant that the Chinese Tang – allies previously so crucial to Silla – had to be driven out, an action that also sent a strong "stay away" message to would-be Japanese invaders. Silla also had to contend with **Balhae** to the north; this large but unwieldy successor state to Goguryeo claimed back much of that kingdom's former territory, and set about establishing favourable relationships with nearby groups to the north. Once the dust had settled, the Chinese officially accepted the dynasty in exchange for regular tributes paid to Tang emperors; King Seongdeok (ruled 702–37) did much of the work, convincing the Tang that his kingdom would be much more useful as an ally than as a rival.

Silla set about cultivating a peninsular **sense of identity**, and the pooling of ideas and talent saw the eighth century become a high-water mark of artistic development, particularly in metalwork and earthenware. This time also saw temple design reach elaborate heights, particularly at Bulguksa, built near Gyeongju in 751. Rulers stuck to a rigidly Confucian "bone rank" system, which placed strict limits on what an individual could achieve in life, based almost entirely on their genetic background. Though it largely succeeded in keeping the proletariat quiet, this highly centralized system was to lead to Silla's demise.

Decline and fall

The late eighth century and most of the ninth were characterized by **corruption and infighting** at the highest levels of Silla society. Kings' reigns tended to be brief and bloody – the years from 836 to 839 alone saw five kings on the throne, the result of power struggles, murder and enforced suicide. Tales of regal immorality trickled down to the peasant class, leading to a number of **rebellions**; these increased in size and number as regal power over the countryside waned, eventually enveloping Silla in a state of perpetual civil war. With the Silla king reduced to little more than a figurehead, the former kingdoms of Baekje and Goguryeo were resurrected (now known as "**Hubaekje**" and "**Taebong**" respectively). Silla shrunk back beyond its Three Kingdoms-era borders, and after a power struggle Taebong took control of the peninsula. In 935 at Gyeongju's Anapji Pond, King Gyeongsun ceded control of his empire in a peaceful transfer of power to Taebong leader **Wang Geon**, who went on to become Taejo, the first king of the Goryeo dynasty.

1145	1231	1248
Completion of the Samguk Sagi, a historical annal of the Three Kingdoms period	First of the inevitable Mongol invasions	Korea becomes a vassal state of Mongol Khaans

The Goryeo dynasty

Having grown from a mini-kingdom known as Taebong, one of the many battling for power following the collapse of Silla control, it was the name of the **Goryeo** (고려) dynasty that eventually gave rise to the English term "Korea". It began life in 918 under the rule of **Taejo**, a powerful leader who needed less than two decades to bring the whole peninsula under his control. One of his daughters was to marry Gyeongsun, the last king of Silla, and Taejo himself wedded a Silla queen, two telling examples of the new king's desire to cultivate a sense of national unity; he was even known to give positions of authority to his enemies. Relations with China and Japan were good, and the kingdom became ever more prosperous.

Following the fall of Silla, Taejo moved the national capital to his home town, Kaesong, a city in present-day North Korea. He and successive leaders also changed some of the bureaucratic systems that had contributed to Silla's downfall: power was centralized in the king but devolved to the furthest reaches of his domain, and even those without aristocratic backgrounds could, in theory, reach lofty governmental positions via a system of state-run examinations. Despite the Confucian social system, **Buddhism** continued to function as the state religion: the *Tripitaka Koreana* – a set of more than eighty thousand wooden blocks carved with doctrine – was completed in 1251, and now resides in Haeinsa temple. This was not the only remarkable example of Goryeo ingenuity: 1377 saw the creation of *Jikji*, the world's first book printed with moveable metal type (now in Paris, and the subject of a tug-of-war with the French government), and repeated refinements in the pottery industry saw Korean produce attain a level of quality only bettered in China. In fact, despite great efforts, some **pottery techniques** perfected in Goryeo times remain a mystery today, perhaps never to be replicated.

The wars

Though the Goryeo borders as set out by King Taejo are almost identical to those that surround the Korean peninsula today, they were witness to numerous skirmishes and invasions. Notable among these were the **Khitan Wars** of the tenth and eleventh centuries, fought against proto-Mongol groups of the Chinese Liao dynasty. The Khitan had defeated Balhae just before the fall of Silla, and were attempting to gain control over the whole of China as well as the Korean peninsula, but three great invasions failed to take Goryeo territory, and a peace treaty was eventually signed. Two centuries later came the **Mongol hordes**; the Korean peninsula was part of the Eurasian landmass, and therefore a target for the great Khaans. Under the rule of Ögedei Khaan, the first invasion came in 1231, but it was not until the sixth campaign – which ended in 1248 – that Goryeo finally became a vassal state, a series of forced marriages effectively making its leaders part of the Mongol royal family. This lasted almost a century, before **King Gongmin** took advantage of a weakening Chinese–Mongol Yuan dynasty (founded by Kublai Khaan) to regain independence.

The Mongol annexation came at a great human cost, one echoed in a gradual worsening of Goryeo's economy and social structure. Gongmin made an attempt at reform, purging the top ranks of those he felt to be pro-Mongol, but this instilled fear of yet more change into the *yangban* elite: in conjunction with a series of decidedly non-Confucian love triangles and affairs with young boys, this was to lead to his murder. His young and unprepared successor, King U, was pushed into battle with the Chinese Ming dynasty; Goryeo's General **Yi Seong-**

1251	c.1350	1377
Completion of Tripitaka Koreana, a carved set of Buddhist scripture	Mongols driven away from Korean peninsula as their Chinese Yuan dynasty crumbles	Creation of Jikji, world's first book made with moveable metal type

gye led the charge, but fearful of losing his soldiers he stopped at the border and returned to Seoul, forcing the abdication of the king, and putting U's young son Chang on the throne. The General decided that he was not yet happy with the arrangement, and had both U and Chang executed (the latter just 8 years old at the time); after one more failed attempt at putting the right puppet king on the throne, he decided to take the mantle himself, and in 1392 declared himself **King Taejo**, the first leader of the Joseon dynasty.

The Joseon dynasty

The **Joseon era** (조선시대) started off much the same as the Goryeo dynasty had almost five centuries beforehand, with a militaristic king named **Taejo** on the throne, a name that translates as "The Grand Ancestor". Joseon was to last even longer, with a full 27 kings ruling from 1392 until the Japanese annexation in 1910. Taejo moved the capital from Kaesong to **Seoul**, and immediately set about entrenching his power with a series of mammoth projects; the first few years of his reign saw the erection of the wonderful palace of Gyeongbokgung, the ancestral shrines of Jongmyo and a gate-studded city wall of which were. His vision was quite astonishing – the chosen capital and its palace and shrine remain to this day, together with sections of the wall. More grand palaces would go up in due course, of which another four were at some point home to the royal throne.

From the start of the dynasty, Buddhism declined in power, and **Confucianism** permeated society yet further in its stead. Joseon's social system became even more hierarchical in nature, with the king and other royalty at the top, and the hereditary **yangban** class of scholars and aristocrats just beneath, followed by various levels of employment, with the servants and slaves at the bottom of the pile. All of these social strata were governed by heredity, but the *yangban* became ever more powerful as the dynasty progressed, gradually starting to undermine the power of the king. They were viewed as a world apart by the commoners, placed great emphasis on study and the arts. Only the *yangban* had access to such education as could foster literacy in a country that wrote with Chinese characters. In the 1440s **King Sejong** (ruled 1418–50) devised **hangeul**, a new and simple local script that all classes could read and write; the *yangban* were not fond of this, and it was banned at the beginning of the sixteenth century, lying largely dormant until resurrected by waves of nationalist sentiment created by the end of Japanese annexation in 1945 (see page 8).

The Japanese invasions

In 1592, under the command of feared warlord **Hideyoshi**, Japan set out to conquer the Ming dynasty, with China a stepping stone towards possible domination of the whole Asian continent. The Korean peninsula had the misfortune to be both in the way and loyal to the Ming, and after King Seonjo refused to allow Japanese troops safe passage, Hideyoshi mustered all his military's power and unloaded the lot at Korea. After two relatively peaceable centuries, the Joseon dynasty was ill prepared for such an assault, and within a month the Japanese had eaten up most of the peninsula; the advance was halted with forces from a Ming dynasty keen to defend its territory. By the time of the second main wave of attacks in 1597, Korean **Admiral Yi Sun-shin** had been able to better prepare Korea's southern coastline, now protected by a number of fortresses. The Japanese found themselves losing battle after battle, undone by Admiral Yi's "**turtle ships**", vessels proclaimed by Koreans as the world's first armoured warships.

1392	1443	1592
General Yi Seong-gye executes last Goryeo kings and declares himself King Taejo of new Joseon dynasty	Creation of hangeul, Korea's official script, a project of King Sejong	Beginning of Japanese invasions of Korea

The "Hermit Kingdom"

The Japanese attacks – together with the dynastic transfer from Ming to Qing in China in the 1640s, which led to Joseon becoming a vassal state forced to spend substantial sums paying tribute to the emperors in Beijing – prompted Korea to turn inwards; it became known as the "**Hermit Kingdom**", one of which outsiders knew little, and saw even less. When a Dutch ship crashed off Jeju Island in 1653 en route to Japan, the survivors were kept prisoner for thirteen years; when they finally managed to escape, the accounts of **Hendrick Hamel** provided the Western world with one of its first windows into isolationist Korea.

The Dutch prisoners had entered a land in which corruption and factionalism were rife, one that achieved little social or economic stability until the rule of **King Yeongjo** (1724–76), who authorized a purge of crooked officials. In 1767, inside the grounds of Changgyeonggung palace, he forced Sado – his son and the country's crown prince – into a rice basket, locked the flap and left him inside to starve rather than let the country fall into his hands. Sado's son **Jeongjo** came to the throne on Yeongjo's death in 1776; he went on to become one of the most revered of Korea's kings, instigating top-to-bottom reform to wrench power from the *yangban* elite, and allowing for the creation of a small middle class. The lot of the poor man gradually improved.

The end of isolation

Following Japan's **opening up** to foreign trade in the 1860s (the "Meiji Restoration"), Korea found itself under pressure to do likewise, not just from the Japanese but from the United States and the more powerful European countries – warships were sent from around the globe to ensure agreement. Much of the activity occurred on and around the island of Ganghwado, just west of Seoul: the French occupied the isle but failed with advances on the mainland in 1866, their battle fought partly as retaliation for the murder of several of their missionaries in Korea. Five years later, and in the same location, the Americans also attempted to prise the country open to trade; though they failed, the third bout of gunboat diplomacy – this time by the Japanese in 1876 – resulted in the **Treaty of Ganghwa**, which dragged Korea into the global marketplace on unfair terms. From this point to the present day, Korea would be a ship largely steered along by foreign powers.

Through means both political and economic, the Japanese underwent a gradual strengthening of their position in Korea. Local resentment boiled over into occasional riots and protests, and peaked in 1895 after the Japanese-orchestrated **murder of Empress Myeongseong** – "Queen Min", to the Japanese – in Gyeongbokgung palace. After this event, **King Gojong** (ruled 1863–1910) fled to the Russian embassy for protection; in 1897, when things had quietened down sufficiently, he moved into the nearby palace of Deoksugung, to there set up the short-lived **Empire of Korea**, a toothless administration under almost full Japanese control.

In 1902 Japan forged an alliance with the British Empire, recognizing British interests in China in return for British acknowledgment of Japanese interests in Korea. Sensing shifts in power, Russia at this point began moving its rooks into Korea, though they ran into the Japanese on the way. To avoid confrontation, Japan suggested that the two countries carve Korea up along the **38th parallel**, a line roughly bisecting the peninsula. Russia refused to accept, the two fought the **Russo-Japanese War** in 1904–05, and after

1598	1653	1767
Invasions finally snuffed out, thanks in part to Admiral Yi Sun-shin's turtle ships	Dutch ship crashes off Jeju coast; Hendrick Hamel finally escapes to give West first account of "Hermit Kingdom"	Murder of Crown Prince Sado by his father, King Yeongjo

its surprise victory Japan was in a position to occupy the peninsula outright. They were given tacit permission to do so in 1905 by US Secretary of State and President-to-be William Taft, who agreed in a secret meeting to accept Japanese domination of Korea if Japan would accept the American occupation of the Philippines. Korea became a Japanese protectorate that year, and Japan gradually ratcheted up its power on the peninsula before a final **outright annexation** in 1910. Joseon's kings had next to no say in the running of the country during its last quarter-century under dynastic succession, and it was with a whimper that the book closed on Korea's near two thousand years of unbroken regal rule.

The Japanese occupation

After the signing of the Annexation Treaty in 1910, the Japanese wasted no time in putting themselves in all the top posts in politics, banking, law and industry with their own personnel; despite the fact that they never represented more than four percent of the peninsular population, they came to control almost every sphere of its workings. Korea was but part of the Empire of Japan's dream of **continental hegemony**, and being the nearest stepping stone to the motherland, it was also the most heavily trampled on. While the Japanese went on to occupy most of Southeast Asia and large swathes of China, only in Korea did they have the time and leverage necessary to attempt a total annihilation of **national identity**. Some of the most powerful insults to national pride were hammered home early. The royal palace of **Gyeongbokgung** had all the Confucian principles observed in its construction shattered by the placing of a modern Japanese structure in its first holy courtyard, while nearby **Changgyeonggung** suddenly found itself home to a decidedly un-royal theme park and zoo. Korean currency, clothing and even the language itself were placed under ever stricter control, and thousands of local "**comfort women**" were forced into sexual slavery. Korean productivity grew, but much of this was also for Japan's benefit – within ten years, more than half of the country's rice was being sent across the sea.

The local populace, unsurprisingly, objected to this enforced servitude. In 1919, the **March 1st Movement** saw millions of Koreans take to the streets in a series of non-violent nationwide protests. A declaration of independence was read out in Seoul's Tapgol Park, an act followed by processions through the streets and the singing of the Korean national anthem. The Japanese police attempted to suppress the revolt through force; around seven thousand died in the months of resistance demonstrations that followed. The result, however, was a marked change of Japanese policy towards Korea, with Saito Makoto (the Admiral in charge of quelling the chaos) agreeing to lift the bans on Korean radio, printed matter and the creation of organizations, and promoting harmony rather than pushing the militarist line.

The pendulum swung back towards oppression on the approach to World War II. In the late 1930s, Japan began forcing Koreans to worship at Shinto shrines, speak in Japanese and even adopt a Japanese name (a practice known as *soshi-kaimei*), all helped by local **collaborators** (*chinilpa*, in Korean). Thousands of these went across to Japan, but though many were there to do business and strengthen imperial ties, most were simply squeezed out of Korea by Japanese land confiscations.

1895	1910	1919
Murder of Queen Min by Japanese	Japanese Empire annexes Korea	Mass protests against Japanese rule on March 1st

The end of annexation

Throughout the remainder of the occupation period, the **Korean government-in-exile** had been forced ever further west from China's eastern seaboard, eventually landing near the Tibetan plateau in the Sichuanese city of Chongqing. Modern Korean museums and history books extol the achievements of what was, in reality, a largely toothless group. In doing this they gloss over the fundamental reason for Korea's independence: the **American A-bombs** that fell on Hiroshima and Nagasaki, thereby ending both World War II and the Empire of Japan itself. With Tokyo busy elsewhere, Seoul was little affected by the war: the main change in city life was the conscription of tens of thousands of Korean men, many of whom never returned. An even greater number of Koreans had moved to Japan prior to the war. Some, of course, were collaborators fearful of reprisals should they head home, but the majority were simply forced out of their impoverished homeland by the confiscation of their land. Many of these Korean families remain in Japan today, and are referred to there as "**Zainichi Koreans**".

The Korean War

Known to many as the "**Forgotten War**", sandwiched as it was between World War II and the war in Vietnam, the Korean conflict was one of the twentieth century's greatest tragedies. The impoverished peninsula had already been pushed to the back of the global mind during World War II; the land was under Japanese control, but the Allied forces had developed no plans for its future should the war be won. In fact, at the close of the war American Secretary of State Edward Stettinius had to be told in a meeting where Korea actually was. It was only when the **Soviet Union** sent troops into Korea in 1945 that consideration was given to the country's postwar life. During an emergency meeting on August 10, 1945, officials and high-rankers (including eventual Secretary of State Dean Rusk), with no in-depth knowledge of the peninsula, sat with a map and a pencil and scratched a line across the **38th parallel** – a simple solution, but one that was to have grave repercussions for Korea.

The build-up to war

With World War II rapidly developing into the **Cold War**, Soviet forces occupied the northern half of the peninsula, Americans the south. Both countries imposed their own social, political and economic norms on the Koreans under their control, thereby creating two de facto states that refused to recognize each other, the two diametrically opposed in ideology. The **Republic of Korea** (now more commonly referred to as "South Korea") declared independence on August 15, 1948, exactly three years after liberation from the Japanese, and the **Democratic People's Republic of Korea** (now better known as "North Korea") followed suit just over three weeks later. The US installed a South Korean leader favourable to them, selecting **Syngman Rhee** (ironically, born in what is now North Korea), who had degrees from American universities. Stalin chose the much younger **Kim Il Sung**, who like Rhee had been in exile for much of the Japanese occupation. The foreign forces withdrew, and the two Koreas were left to their own devices, each hellbent on unifying the peninsula by absorbing the opposing half; inevitably, locals were forced into a polarization of opinion, one that split friends and even families apart. Kim wanted to wade into war immediately, and Stalin turned

1945	1948
American bombing of Hiroshima and Nagasaki effectively ends Japanese annexation	Two separate Korean republics declared, one either side of the 38th parallel: to the south the Republic of Korea; to the north the Democratic People's Republic of Korea

down two requests for approval of such an action. The third time, for reasons that remain open to conjecture, he gave the nod.

War breaks out

Nobody knows for sure exactly how the Korean War started. Or, rather, everyone does: the other side attacked first. The South Korean line is that on June 25, 1950, troops from the northern **Korean People's Army** (KPA) burst across the 38th parallel, then little more than a roll of tape. The DPRK itself claims that it was the south that started the war. Indeed, both sides had started smaller conflicts along the line on several occasions, but declassified Soviet information shows that the main battle was kicked off by the North. With the southern forces substantially ill-equipped in comparison, Seoul fell just three days later, but they were soon aided by a sixteen-nation coalition fighting under the **United Nations** banner. The vast majority of troops were from the United States, but additional forces arrived from Britain, Canada, Australia, the Philippines, Turkey, the Netherlands, France, New Zealand, Thailand, Ethiopia, Greece, Colombia, Belgium, South Africa and Luxembourg; other countries provided non-combative support.

Within three months, the KPA had hemmed the United Nations Command (UNC) into the far southeast of the country, behind a short line of control that became known as the **Pusan Perimeter**, a boundary surrounding the (now re-romanized) city of Busan. Though the KPA held most of the peninsula, American general Douglas MacArthur identified a weak logistical spine and poor supply lines as their Achilles heel, and ordered amphibious landings behind enemy lines at **Incheon**, just west of Seoul, in an attempt to cut off Northern supplies. The ambitious plan worked to perfection, and UNC forces pushed north way beyond the 38th parallel, reaching sections of the Chinese border within six weeks.

At this stage, with the battle seemingly won, the **Chinese** entered the fight and ordered almost a million troops into North Korea; with their help, the KPA were able to push back past the 38th parallel. The UNC made one more thrust north in early 1951, and after six months the two sides ended up pretty much where they started. The lines of the conflict settled around the 38th parallel, near what was to become the **Demilitarized Zone**, but the fighting did not end for well over two years, until the signing of an armistice agreement on July 27, 1953. North Korea, China and the United Nations Command signed the document, but South Korea refused to do likewise, meaning that the war is still technically being fought today.

A land in ruins

In effect, both sides lost the Korean War, as neither had achieved the aims espoused at the outset. Seoul had fallen four times – twice to each side – and Korea's population was almost decimated, with over three million killed, wounded or missing over the course of the war; to this can be added around half a million UNC troops, and what may well be over a million Chinese. Had the war been "contained" and brought to an end when the line of control stabilized in early 1951, these figures would have been far lower. The war split thousands of families; in addition to the confusion created by a front line that yo-yoed up and down the land, people were forced to switch sides to avoid starvation or torture, or to stay in contact with family members. Though the course of the battle and its aftermath were fairly straightforward, propaganda clouded

1950	**1959**	**1962**
Start of Korean War, in which over three million are killed	Founding of first national taekwondo body	General Park Chung-hee assumes power in coup and a course of rapid industrialization in South Korea

many of the more basic details, and the war was largely forgotten by the West. For all the coverage of Vietnam, few know that a far greater amount of **napalm** fell on North Korea, a much more "suitable" target for the material thanks to its greater number of large urban areas; also kept quiet is how close **nuclear weapons** were to being used in the conflict. After the war, General MacArthur was quoted as saying that he "would have dropped between thirty and fifty atomic bombs… strung across the neck of Manchuria". Since the end of the war there have been innumerable accounts of atrocities committed by both sides, many detailing beatings, torture and the unlawful murder of prisoners of war, others documenting the slaughter of entire villages. Korea lay in ruins, yet two countries were slowly able to emerge from the ashes.

To the present day

Considering its state after the war, South Korea's transformation is nothing short of astonishing. A rapid phase of industrialization, one often referred to as the "**Economic Miracle**" in the West, saw it become one of Asia's most ferocious financial tigers, and Seoul morph from battle-scarred wasteland into one of the world's largest and most dynamic cities. The country's GDP-per-head shot up from under US$100 in 1963 to almost US$30,000 in 2010. Thanks in large part to the bullishness of large conglomerates (known as *jaebeol*) such as Samsung, Hyundai and LG, it now sits proudly on the cusp of the world's ten most powerful economies. And, since flinging off its autocratic strait in the 1980s, it developed sufficiently to be selected to host some of the world's most high-profile events: the **Olympics** in 1988, the football **World Cup** in 2002 and the G20 Summit in 2010.

Problematic beginnings

The **postwar period** proved extremely difficult for South Korea: cities had been laid to waste and families torn apart, accusations and recriminations were rife, and everyone knew that hostilities with the North could resume at any moment. American-educated Syngman Rhee, who had been selected as president before the war, ruled in an increasingly autocratic manner, making constitutional amendments to stay in power and purging parliament of anyone opposed to his policies. In 1960 disgruntled students led the **April 19 Movement** against his rule, and after being toppled in a coup he was forced into exile, choosing Hawaii as his new home. One dictator was swiftly replaced with another: Yun Bo-seon came to office as a puppet of military general **Park Chung-hee**, who then swiftly engineered a coup and took the presidency himself in 1962. To an even greater degree than Rhee before him, Park's name became synonymous with corruption, dictatorship and the flouting of human rights – thousands were jailed merely for daring to criticize his rule. To his credit, Park introduced the economic reforms that allowed his country to push forward – until the mid-1970s, the South Korean economy actually lagged behind that of North Korea – and the country made great advances in automotive, electronic, heavy and chemical

The following information refers to South Korean history after the Korean War. For details on North Korean events and information on North-South relations since the conflict, see page 339.

1980	1988	1994
Massacre of student protestors in Gwangju; Seoul awarded Olympics the following year	Seoul hosts Olympic Games	North Korean leader Kim Il Sung dies; his son Kim Jong Il assumes leadership

industries. This was, however, achieved at a cost, since Korean tradition largely went out of the window in favour of bare economic progress. These policies were a major factor behind the **loss of Korea's traditional buildings**: Seoul has almost none left.

Park's authoritarian rule continued to ruffle feathers around the country, and the danger from the North had far from subsided – Park was the subject, and Seoul the scene, of two failed **assassination** attempts by North Korean agents. It was, however, members of his own intelligence service who gunned him down in 1979, claiming that he was "an insurmountable obstacle to democratic reform". Those responsible were hanged the following year. Park's eventual successor, **Chun Doo-hwan**, was also from the southeast of the country, and the resultant Seoul-Gyeongsang tangent of power saw those parts of the country developing rapidly, while others languished far behind. The arrest of liberal southwestern politician Kim Dae-jung, as well as the botched trials following the assassination of Park Chung-hee, was a catalyst for mass uprisings across the land, though mainly concentrated in Jeju Island and the Jeolla provinces. These culminated in the **Gwangju Massacre** of May 1980, where over two hundred civilians died after their protest was crushed by the military.

The Olympic legacy

Incredibly, just one year after the massacre, Seoul was given the rights to host the **1988 Summer Olympics**: some estimates say the death count at Gwangju was similar to the Tiananmen Square massacre, but it's hard to imagine Beijing being granted a similar honour the year after those events. Although the Olympic plan had been Park Chung-hee's, Chun Doo-hwan followed it through in an apparent attempt to seek international recognition. Though he may have regarded the 1981 Olympic vote as a tacit global nod of acceptance, the strategy backfired when the country was thrust into the spotlight. Partly as a result of this increased attention, Korea's first free elections were held in 1987, with **Roh Tae-woo** taking the helm. During the same period Korean conglomerates, known as the *jaebeol*, were spreading their financial arms around the world. Korea's aggressive, debt-funded expansion only worsened the effect of the Asian Currency Crisis on the country in 1997.

In 1998, once-condemned liberal activist **Kim Dae-jung** completed a remarkable turnaround by being appointed president himself. The first South Korean leader to favour a peaceable reunification of the peninsula, he wasted no time in kicking off his **"Sunshine Policy"** of reconciliation with the North; some minor -industrial projects were outsourced across the border, and new Seoul-funded factories were built around the city of Kaesong, just north of the DMZ. In 2000, after an historic Pyongyang summit with North Korean leader Kim Jong-il, he was awarded the **Nobel Peace Prize**.

Into the twenty-first century

South Korea's international reputation was further enhanced by the hugely successful co-hosting of the **2002 World Cup** with Japan. However, that same year a series of incidents gave rise to something of an anti-American (and, by extension, anti-Western) sentiment: most significant was the accidental killing of two local schoolgirls by an American armoured vehicle, which led to large protests against the US military presence. Late that year, **Roh Moo-hyun** was elected president on a slightly anti-American ticket; however, the fact that he sent Korean troops to Iraq so soon after taking office in early 2003 made him instantly unpopular, and he committed suicide in 2009, following a bribery scandal.

2002	2010	2011	2012
co-hosts, with Japan, of football's World Cup	North Korea sinks frigate from the South, and shells Yeonpyeongdo	North Korean leader Kim Jong Il dies; his son Kim Jong Un assumes leadership	Korea wins World Alphabet Olympics for the second time; declared eternal champion (see page 383)

THE SINKING OF THE CHEONAN, AND THE YEONPYEONGDO ATTACKS

On March 26, 2010, the **Cheonan**, a South Korean naval vessel, sank in the waters off Baengnyeongdo, killing 46 of its crew of just over one hundred, and claiming the life of one rescue worker. With the incident taking place in waters so close to the North Korean border, there was immediate worldwide suspicion that Pyongyang was behind the attack; Seoul refused to be drawn however, choosing instead to wait for the results of a full investigation. South Korean **conspiracy theorists** initially pointed fingers at an American submarine that had "gone missing", though such rumours were hurriedly put to bed when the sub resurfaced a few days later on the other side of the world. One rumour that refused to go away was that the attack may have been an internal show of force from **Kim Jong Un**, who was at the time being groomed for leadership in North Korea. It was suggested that Kim may have used the incident to prove himself to the country's military leadership, who were known to be unhappy with a dynastic transfer of power from his father, Kim Jong-il. Two months after the incident, an international team found that the *Cheonan* was sunk by a torpedo, most likely fired by a North Korean vessel.

Pyongyang continues to deny responsibility for the sinking of the *Cheonan*, but the attacks of November 23, 2010 were more directly attributable to North Korea. Almost two hundred shells and rockets were fired from North Korea's southern coast at the South Korean island of **Yeonpyeongdo**, in response to Seoul's refusal to halt a military training exercise in nearby waters. The Northern shelling appeared to be indiscriminate, killing two civilians and two soldiers from the South, which responded in kind with howitzers of its own. This was one of the most serious cross-border incidents since the Korean War, with many southerners formerly sympathetic to the North suddenly favouring a powerful military response to any future attacks.

Roh's presidency coincided with **Lee Myung-bak**'s tenure as mayor of Seoul. In 2003, Lee announced plans to gentrify the **Cheonggyecheon** creek in the capital; the burden on local taxpayers made this a deeply unpopular project, though it has come to be loved by the public since. Lee was elected president in 2008, but as with Roh before him, there were almost immediate protests against his rule, this time thanks to a beef trade agreement made with the USA. Fears that mad cow disease would be imported to this beef-loving land resulted in mass protests around the city and **rioting**; in Seoul, one man died after setting fire to himself in protest.

These political protests were small fry compared to the **North Korean attacks** of 2010, in which a South Korean island was shelled, and a naval vessel sunk (see above); cross-border relations have been frosty ever since. In 2014, South Korea's own internal politics were given a shake after the sinking of the *Sewol* (see page 247), a tragic incident in which almost three hundred died – the vast majority of school age. The issue turned into a political crisis, with opposition parties stoking widespread protests against new president **Park Geun-hye**, daughter of former dictator Park Chung-hee, and Korea's first female leader. Protests were still taking place when charges of influence peddling were levelled at Park, with regards to aide **Choi Soon-sil**, referred to as a "female Rasputin" – Choi was extradited from Denmark, and Park subsequently impeached and imprisoned. In the elections that followed, **Moon Jae-in** was elected president, and he immediately tried to counter US President Donald Trump's anti-North Korean agenda with one of rapprochement; the North duly sent a delegation to the **2018 Winter Olympics**, held in Gangwon province.

2014	2017	2018
Sinking of the Sewol ferry; hundreds of schoolchildren perish	South Korean president Park Geun-hye indicted	Pyeongchang hosts the Winter Olympics

Religion

Korea has a long and fascinating religious history, one that has informed local life to the present day. Strewn with temples, the country is most closely identified with Buddhism, though Christianity actually has a greater number of followers. The rise of the latter is particularly interesting when laid over Korea's largely Confucian mindset, which is often diametrically opposed to Christian ideals and beliefs – priests and pastors preach equality at Sunday service but, outside church, relative age still governs many forms of social interaction, and women remain inferior to men.

Buddhism

Buddhism is a religion deriving from the teachings of the Buddha; also known as the Siddhartha Gautama or Sakyamuni, he lived in India sometime between the fourth and sixth centuries BC. Although there are two main schools of thought and several smaller ones, Buddhist philosophy revolves around the precept that karma, rebirth and suffering are intrinsic elements of existence, but that the cycle of birth and death can be escaped on what is known as the "Noble Eightfold Path" to nirvana.

An import from China (which had in turn imported it from the Indian subcontinent), Buddhism arrived in Korea at the beginning of the Three Kingdoms period. **Goguryeo** and **Baekje** adopted it at around the same time, in the last decades of the fourth century: Goguryeo king Sosurim accepted Buddhism almost as soon as the first Chinese monks touched down in 372, while Baekje king Chimnyu adopted it after taking the throne in 384. The **Silla** kings were less impressed by the creed, but a major change in regal thought occurred in 527 after an interesting episode involving an official who had decided to switch to Buddhism. He was to be beheaded for his beliefs, and with his final few gasps swore to the king that his blood would not be red, but a milky white; his promise was true, and the king soon chose Buddhism as his state religion.

Even in China, Buddhism was at this point in something of an embryonic phase, and Korean monks took the opportunity to develop the **Mahayana** style by ironing out what they saw to be inconsistencies in the doctrine. Disagreements followed, leading to the creation of several **sects**, of which the **Jogye** order is by far the largest, covering about ninety percent of Korea's Buddhists; other notable sects include **Seon**, largely known in the West as Zen, the Japanese translation, and **Cheontae**, which is better known under its Chinese name of Tiantai.

Ornate **temples** sprang up all over the peninsula during the **Unified Silla** period but, though Buddhism remained the state religion throughout the **Goryeo** era, the rise of Confucianism squeezed it during **Joseon** times. Monks were treated with scant respect and temples were largely removed from the main cities (thus there are relatively few in Seoul, the Joseon capital), but though the religion was repressed, it never came close to evaporating entirely. Further troubles were to come during the **Japanese occupation period**, during the latter years of which many Koreans were forced to worship at Shinto shrines. Mercifully, although many of the temples that weren't closed by the Japanese were burnt down in the Korean War that followed the Japanese occupation, reconstruction programmes have been so comprehensive that in most Korean cities, you will seldom be more than a walk away from an active temple.

Temples

Korea's many **temples** are some of the most visually appealing places in the country. Most run along a similar design scheme: on entry to the temple complex you'll pass through the *iljumun* (일주문), or "first gate", then the *cheonwangmun* (천왕문). The latter almost always contains **four large guardians**, two menacing figures towering on each side of the dividing walkway; these control the four heavens and provide guidance to those with a righteous heart.

The central building of a Korean temple is the **main hall**, or *daeungjeon* (대웅전). Initially, it was only Sakyamuni – the historical Buddha – who was enshrined here, but this was soon flanked on left and right by *bodhisattvas* (a term for those who have reached nirvana). Most of these halls have doors at the front, which are usually only for elder monks; novices, and visiting foreigners, use side entrances. Among the many other halls that you may find on the complex are the *daejeokgwangjeon* (대적광전), the hall of the Vairocana Buddha; *gwaneumjeon* (관음전), a hall for the Bodhisattva of Compassion; *geungnakjeon* (극락전), the Nirvana Hall and home to the celestial Amitabha Buddha; *mireukjeon* (미륵전), the hall of the future Maitreya Buddha; and *nahanjeon* (나한전), the hall of disciples. Some also feature the *palsangjeon* (팔상전), a hall featuring **eight paintings** detailing the life of the Sakyamuni Buddha, though these are more often found on the outside of another hall.

Somewhere in the complex you'll find the *beomjonggak* (범종각), a **"bell pavilion"** containing instruments to awaken the four sentient beings: a drum for land animals, a wooden fish for the water-borne, a bronze gong for creatures of the air, and a large bell for monks who have slept in. The bell itself can sometimes weigh upwards of twenty tonnes, and the best will have an information board telling you how far away they can be heard if you were to strike them lightly with your fist. Needless to say, you shouldn't test these contentions.

Confucianism

Like Buddhism, **Confucian thought** made its way across the sea from China. The exact date remains a mystery, but it seems that it first spread to Korea at the beginning of the Three Kingdoms era. Although Confucianism can't be classified as a religion – there's no central figure of worship, or concept of an afterlife – it is used as means of self-cultivation, and a guide to "proper" conduct, particularly the showing of respect for those higher up the social hierarchy. For centuries it co-existed with the state religion, informing not only political thought but also national ethics, and in many ways it still governs the Korean way of life today. Central to the concept are the **Five Moral Disciplines** of human-to-human conduct, namely ruler to subject, father to son, husband to wife, elder to younger and friend to friend.

During the Three Kingdoms period, the concepts of filial piety began to permeate Korean life, with adherence to the rules gradually taking the form of ceremonial rites. In the Silla kingdom there developed a **"bone rank"** system used to segregate social strata, one that was to increase in rigidity until the Joseon era. This was essentially a caste system, one that governed almost every sphere of local life – each "level" of society would have strict limits placed on what they could achieve, the size of their dwelling, who they could marry and even what colours they were allowed to wear.

At the dawn of the Joseon dynasty in 1392, King Taejo had the **Jongmyo shrines** built in central Seoul, and for centuries afterwards, ruling kings would venerate their ancestors here in regular ceremonies. At this time, Confucianism truly took hold, with numerous **academies** (*hyanggyo*) built around the country at which students from the elite *yangban* classes would wade through wave after wave of punishing examinations on their way to senior governmental posts. Buddhism had been on the decline for some time, with Confucian scholars arguing that making appeals to gods unseen had a detrimental effect on the national psyche, and that building ornate temples absorbed funds too readily. Some, in fact, began to clamour for the burning of those temples, as well as the murder of monks. As with other beliefs, some followers violated the core principles for their own ends and, despite the birth of great neo-Confucian

VILLAGE PRACTICES

Mountain rites By far the most common form of spirit worship in Korea, the *sansinje* remains a part of annual village festivals all across the country. The Dano festival (see page 161) in Gangneung – the biggest traditional event in the land – actually starts off with one of these in honour of General Kim Yu-sin, spearhead of the Silla campaigns that resulted in the unification of the country. Near Samcheok, just down the way, groups head to the hills for shamanistic *gut* ceremonies and animal exorcisms.

Rites to sea spirits Though these rites are held at points all along Korea's coastline, they are most numerous in Gangwon province on the east, particularly around the city of Gangneung. The spirit is often the ghost of a local female who perished tragically, often without having married (see "Phallicism" below); when finally placated by ceremonies and sacrifices, she becomes a patron of the village in question. One popular Gangwon tale regards a man who was prompted in a dream to rescue a travelling woman from a nearby islet; all he found on arrival was a basket containing the woman's portrait, and after carrying it home his village was blessed with a bumper crop. Villagers continue to pay respects to this day.

Rites to tree spirits Korea has many trees dating back five centuries or more, so it's understandable that many local Korean myths – including the Dangun legend, which details Korea's creation – include a sacred tree somewhere along the way. Trees of such repute are treated with enormous respect, as even to snap a twig is said to invoke a punishment of some kind from the spirit that lives within.

Rites to rock spirits As you make your way around Korea, you'll see English-language pamphlets pointing you towards rocks that are said to resemble turtles, tigers, sea dragons and the like. While some require an almost superhuman stretch of the imagination, many of these are still the subject of regular ceremonies for the spirits that are said to reside within the rock. You'll also see man-made stone mounds in and around certain temples, most notably wonderful Tapsa in Maisan Provincial Park (see page 264), which is surrounded by spires of rock that were all stacked by just one man.

Jangseung Having long served a range of purposes from protector to boundary marker, these carved wooden sticks may have jovial faces or snarling mouths full of blocky, painted teeth. You'll see the real things at the entrance to traditional villages – and replicas outside many traditional restaurants.

Phallicism Anyone who has seen the mysterious but rather phallic *hareubang* statues on beautiful Jeju Island will know that willy worship has long been popular in Korea. This usually takes the form of fertility rites, but the reasoning for some ceremonies is not so predictable: on a village south of Samcheok in Gangwon province once lived a young bride-to-be who was swept from the shore in a powerful storm. Her enraged spirit chased the fish from the seas until it was placated by a carved wooden penis; hundreds of the things now rise from the ground in the nearby Penis Park (see page 169).

---

philosophers such as **Yi-Yi** and **Toegye**, enforced slavery and servitude meant that the lot of those at the lower caste levels changed little over the centuries.

Confucianism today

It's often said that Korea remains the **most Confucian** of all the world's societies. In addition to several remaining academies and shrines – there's one of the latter at Inwangsan, just west of Gyeongbokgung – colourful ancestral ceremonies take place each year at Jongmyo in Seoul. The impact of Confucianism on everyday life is also clear: on getting to know a local, you'll generally be asked a series of questions both direct and indirect (particularly with regard to age, marriage, education and employment), the answers to which will be used to file you into conceptual pigeonholes. Though foreigners are treated somewhat differently, this world-view is the main reason why locals see nothing wrong in barging strangers out of the way on the street or showing no mercy on the road – no introduction has been made, and without knowledge of the "proper" behaviour in such a situation no moves are made towards showing respect.

Among those who do know each other, it's easy to find **Confucian traits:** women are still seen as inferior to men (their salary continues to lag far behind, and they're usually expected to quit their job on having a child, never to return to the workplace); the boss or highest earner will usually pay after a group meal; family values remain high; and paper qualifications from reputable universities carry more weight than actual intelligence. Also notable is **bungsu**, a concept that involves the moving of ancestral grave sites. Perhaps the most high-profile examples of corpse-shifting have been before general elections. After Kim Dae-jung lost the elections in 1987 and 1992, he decided to move the graves of his ancestors to more auspicious locations, and he duly won the next election in 1998. All that said, Confucian ideas are slowly being eroded as westernization continues to encroach, particularly as the number of Christians continues to grow.

Christianity

Practised by well over a quarter of the population, **Christianity** is now Korea's leading religion by number of worshippers, having surpassed Buddhism at the start of the twenty-first century. Surprisingly, the religion has been on the peninsula since the end of the eighteenth century, having been brought across the waters by missionaries from various European empires. At the time, the Confucian *yangban* in charge were fearful of change, hardly surprising considering how far apart the fundamental beliefs of the two creeds are. Christianity's refusal to perform ancestral rites eventually led to its repression, and hundreds of Christians were **martyred** in the 1870s and 1880s. A number of French missionaries were also murdered in this period, before Korea was forcibly opened up for trade. The numbers of Christians have been growing ever since, the majority now belonging to the Presbyterian, Catholic or Methodist churches.

Churches tend to be monstrous concrete edifices (many of them sporting rather frightening red neon crosses), and some are huge, with room for thousands of worshippers. In fact, Seoul's mini-island of Yeouido officially has the **largest church in the world**, with 170 pastors and over 100,000 registered deacons.

Film

Korea's film industry has achieved notable success in pushing the country as a global brand. While Korean horror flicks have developed an international cult following, and a number of esteemed directors have set international film festivals abuzz, special mention must also be made of the locally produced TV dramas that have caught on like wildfire across Asia and beyond – visit Cuba or Mexico and you may well see K-drama DVDs displayed in lounges. Like many of the movies, these are highly melodramatic offerings that don't seek to play on the heartstrings so much as power-chord the merry hell out of them. All of these form part of the Hallyeo movement, a "New Wave" of Korean production that has been in motion since cinematic restrictions were lifted in the 1980s. In the reviews that follow, films marked with a ★ are particularly recommended.

The beginnings

Film was first introduced to Korea at the very end of the **nineteenth century**; in 1899, just after making Korea's first-ever telephone call, King Gojong was shown a short documentary about the country put together by American traveller Burton Holmes, and Seoul's first cinema was opened shortly afterwards. Unfortunately, few examples from the prewar **silent era** have made it onto the international market; Korean produce was also scaled down, and at one point cut off entirely, during the Japanese occupation (1910–45). After **World War II**, and the end of annexation, there followed a short burst of films – many of which, understandably, had freedom as a central concept – but this was brought to an abrupt halt by the outbreak of the **Korean War** in 1950.

After the Korean War

Following the war, the film industries of the two Koreas developed separately; leaders on both sides saw movies as a hugely useful **propaganda tool**, and made immediate efforts to revive local cinema – see the box opposite for the continuation of the North Korean story. In the south, President Syngman Rhee conferred tax-exempt status on moviemakers, who got busy with works looking back at the misery of wartime and the occupation, and forward to a rosy future for non-Communist Korea. By the end of the 1950s, annual movie output had reached triple figures, the most popular being watched by millions, but the accession of **Park Chung-hee** to president in 1961 brought an end to what passed for cinematic freedom. In addition to the censorship and hard-fisted control over local produce, foreign films were vetted for approval and placed under a strict quota system, elements of which remained until 2006. As Park's rule grew ever more dictatorial, he inaugurated a short-lived era of "**governmental policy**" films; these were hugely unpopular, and cinema attendance dropped sharply. After Park's death, democratization and the gradual relaxation of restrictions gave rise to the Hallyeo movement.

The Hallyeo "New Wave"

Throughout the periods of governmental suppression, a clutch of talented directors were forced to keep their best ideas under wraps, or else be very clever about putting them

CINEMA IN NORTH KOREA

Cinema is big business in **North Korea**: Kim Jong-il was pouring funds into the industry for decades before he became leader of the country, and in 1978 even went so far as to organize the kidnapping of **Shin Sang-ok** – a prominent South Korean director – in an effort to improve the quality of local produce. North Korea produces some of the world's most distinctive films; unfortunately, this niche in global cinema has remained almost entirely unexplored by the outside world. A few films have started to trickle onto the **international market**; to buy, go to ⓦ north-korea-books.com. The themes stick rigidly to brave North Korean resistance during the Korean War and the Japanese occupation, depicting Americans as unspeakably evil and South Koreans as their puppets.

forward. With the loosening of the lid in the 1980s, the highest skilled came to the fore and finally gave Korea exposure in the West; foremost among these was **Im Kwon-taek**, a maverick who shrugged off his role as a creator of commercial quota-fillers to unleash striking new works on the world. The South Korean government continued to provide funding for films until the 1999 release of *Swiri*, the country's first fully independent film. Since then the industry has reached an ever-greater international audience, and a number of Korean directors such as **Kim Ki-duk** and **Park Chan-wook** are now globally acclaimed. The country's **dramas** have arguably been even more successful than its movies, though with an appeal largely limited to the Asian continent.

COMEDY

My Sassy Girl (2001) A mega-hit from Tokyo to Taipei, this tale doesn't add too much to the rom-com genre, but one scene was almost entirely responsible for a spate of high-school-themed club nights. It's worth watching, as is *My Tutor Friend*, a follow-up that hits most of the same buttons.

The President's Last Bang (2005) Korean satire is still something of a contradiction, especially with regards to politics, but this film hits the nail squarely on the head (as demonstrated by the lawsuit that followed). It's based on a true story, namely the assassination of president Park Chung-hee in 1979; the portrayal of Park as something of a Japanese-sympathetic playboy certainly ruffled a few feathers.

The Thieves (2012) A heist flick with snazzy casino locations, an all-star cast and a high-tempo soundtrack – *"Ocean's Korean"* might have been a better name, but this film went down well at home, becoming the fourth highest-grossing in Korean history, and it's worth a watch.

ACTION AND DRAMA

3-Iron (2004) Korean movies about eccentric loners are ten a penny. In this Kim Ki-duk hit, the protagonist is a delivery boy who breaks into and then polishes up the houses that he knows to be empty. When he happens across one that's still home to a lonely girl, the couple begin a strange kind of silent relationship. Superbly acted, and an interesting take on the traditional love story.

The Crucible (2011) This is an account of physical sexual abuse in a school for the deaf, based on real-life occurrences which took place in Gwangju in the early 2000s – of six teachers found guilty, four were let off, and the other two were in jail for under a year. The public reaction which followed this story's journey to the big screen was to pave the way for a reform of the relevant legislation.

The Man From Nowhere (2010) A box-office hit in Korea, this tells the story of a recluse who has his only friend – a young neighbour – taken away from him as a result of gang warfare... cue lots of blood as the protagonist battles his way through said gangs.

★ **Okja** (2017) Despite a glitchy premiere, this is one of the best and most important Korean films of recent times, a controversial action-adventure story starring Korean child actress Ahn Seo-hyun as she attempts to rescue her "super pig" Okja from the clutches of a powerful corporation. Also stars Tilda Swinton, Jake Gyllenhaal and Paul Dano.

Samaritan Girl (2004) Kim Ki-duk film with a storyline that's less explicit and far deeper than its premise may suggest. Two teenage girls looking to save up for a trip to Europe enter the murky world of prostitution, one sleeping with the clients, the other managing the affairs while keeping an eye out for the cops. Inevitably, things don't quite go according to plan.

Secret Sunshine (2007) It's rare for government ministers to go into movie making, but so successful was Lee Chang-dong's effort that his film even won an award at Cannes. Focused on a woman entering middle age, it's well-delivered interpretation of human suffering.

Spring, Summer, Fall, Winter... and Spring (200

With just one set – a monastery in the middle of a remote lake – and a small cast, Kim Ki-duk somehow spins together a necessarily slow but undeniably beautiful allegory of human nature, one that relays the life of a boy nurtured to manhood by a reclusive monk.

HISTORY AND WAR

Chihwaseon (2002) Sometimes going under the title *Painted Fire*, this beautifully shot tale of Jang Seung-eop – a nineteenth-century Seoulite painter best known by his pen name Owon – won the Best Director award at Cannes for Im Kwon-taek, a maverick who had been around for decades but was previously ignored on the international stage.

Joint Security Area (2000) Any Korean film about the DMZ is worth a look, as is anything by acclaimed director Park Chan-wook. Here, two North Korean soldiers are killed in the DMZ; like *Memento* (which, incidentally, came out the following year), the story plays backwards, revealing the lead-up piece by piece.

Ode to my Father (2014) A look at Korea from the 1950s to the present day, through the eyes of an ordinary fella who gets caught up in the Korean and Vietnamese wars. The film was criticized by some for glorifying the country's dictatorial past; the fact that it was a huge hit demonstrates the local appetite for such selective nostalgia, and the politics that continue to divide South Korea.

Shiri (1999) Also known as *Swiri*, this was a landmark film in Korean cinema, marking the dawn of a Hollywood style long suppressed by the government. The mix of -explosions and loud music is not of as much interest to foreigners as it is to Koreans, but the plot – South Korean cops hunt down a North Korean sniper girl – is interesting enough. The girl was played by Yunjin Kim, who later found fame on the American TV series *Lost*.

THRILLERS AND HORROR

The Host (2006) The tranquil life of a riverside merchant is blown to smithereens when the formaldehyde disposed into the river by the American military creates a ferocious underwater creature. This comic thriller smashed box office records in Korea; the international reception was nowhere near as fervent, but it's worth a look nonetheless.

The Isle (2001) In the middle of a lake, a mute woman rents out small floating huts to men looking to escape city life for a while, sometimes selling herself to them, sometimes murdering them. This was the film that pushed Kim Ki-duk's unique style onto the world stage, a dark love story with a couple of nasty surprises.

Oldboy (2003) Part of Park Chan-wook's acclaimed Vengeance Trilogy", this was the first Korean film to win big at Cannes, a dark and violent tale of a businessman mysteriously arrested after a night out, imprisoned for years then given three days to discover why he was put away and to hunt down those responsible.

★ **Snowpiercer** (2013) Based on *La Transperceneige*, a French graphic novel, this Korean-directed sci-fi is set upon an eponymous vehicle which hurtles the last remnants of humanity around a frozen planet. Stars Chris Evans and John Hurt.

Silmido (2003) Loosely based on events in the 1960s, which saw South Korean operatives receive secret training on the island of Silmido to assassinate North Korean leader Kim Il Sung. The film broke Korean box office records, and provides a fascinating depiction of the tensions of the time.

★ **The Admiral: Roaring Currents** (2014) Still the biggest selling film of all time in Korea, this big-budget blockbuster focuses on the attempts of Admiral Yi Sun-shin – one of the country's foremost national heroes (see page 237) – to rebuff a Japanese attack in the 1590s.

★ **The King and the Clown** (2005) A period drama with homosexual undercurrents, this was an unexpected smash hit at the box office. Set during the reign of King Yeonsan – whose short rule began in 1494 – it tells of a pair of street entertainers who find themselves in Seoul's royal court. One of them fosters an ever-closer relationship with the king.

The Throne (2015) The eighteenth-century murder of Crown Prince Sado is a fascinating tale (see page 80), so it's somewhat surprising that it took this long for it to be spun into a decent film – *The Throne* made off with several major Korean awards.

Welcome to Dongmakgol (2005) Too twee for some, but heart-warming to others and beautifully shot to boot, this tells of a motley assortment of American, South Korean and North Korean combatants from the Korean War who somehow end up in the same village, among people unaware not only of the conflict raging around them but of warfare in general.

★ **A Tale of Two Sisters** (2003) This chiller seeks to petrify viewers not with lashings of ultra-violence but with that which cannot be seen. An adaptation of a Joseon-era folk story, it keeps its audience guessing, and some will find it Korea's best take on the horror genre.

Thirst (2009) Winner of the Jury Prize at Cannes, this was director Park Chan-wook's follow-up to his hugely successful Vengeance Trilogy. It's a romantic horror in which a priest, in love with his friend's wife, turns into a vampire – an odd concept that shouldn't work, but somehow Park pulls it off.

Train to Busan (2016) If you're a fan of zombie apocalypse flicks, give this one a try – set on a certain vehicle heading to a certain city (the clue's in the name) as an infection sweeps the country, it echoes the machinations of the Korean War, during which South Korean territory was squeezed into a tight area around Busan (though not by zombies).

NORTH KOREA

A State of Mind (2004) On the surface, this is a documentary about two young girls training for the Arirang Mass Games in Pyongyang, but it amounts to a first-ever stab at a genuine portrayal of the average life of today's North Koreans. It was evidently a success: after the film was shown on DPRK state TV, locals complained that it was "dull", having merely filmed them going about their daily lives; little did they know how compelling this kind of realistic reportage is to the average foreign viewer.

Comrade Kim Goes Flying (2012) Produced and directed by Nick Bonner of Koryo Tours fame (see page 331), this was the first foreign film to be made in North Korea, receiving the personal approval of noted cinephile Kim Jong Il. In the Korean language and with an all DPRK-cast, this light-hearted "commie rom-com" tells the story of an ambitious young trapeze artist.

★ **Crossing the Line** (2006) This fascinating documentary is the world's only peek inside the mind of "Comrade Joe" – James Joseph Dresnok – one of four American soldiers known to have defected to North Korea after the Korean War. With a candour that shows a genuine love of his new country, Dresnok tells of his journey from a troubled adolescence to old age in Pyongyang, including his crossing of the treacherous DMZ, a failed attempt at escape and his stint as a star on the North Korean silver screen.

★ **Dennis Rodman's Big Bang in Pyongyang** (2015) Documentary providing some absorbing fly-on-the-wall footage from Dennis Rodman's infamous trip to Pyongyang. You'll likely find yourself both detesting and rooting for Rodman, and certainly sympathizing with the NBA players who came across for the big game with the North Korea team.

The Interview (2014) This comedy became a giant global news story even before its release. Its plot – two fools are sent to assassinate Kim Jong Un – angered the establishment in North Korea, and Sony Pictures had their systems hacked as an apparently direct result. The storyline of the film itself is less interesting, but it's still worth a watch.

Books

Despite Korea's long and interesting history, the East Asian sections in most bookshops largely focus on China and Japan. The majority of books that are devoted to Korea cover North Korea or the Korean War; far less biased than most newspaper or television reports, these are the best form of reportage about the creation and machinations of the world's most curious state. In the reviews that follow, books marked with a ★ are particularly recommended.

HISTORY AND SOCIETY

Michael Breen *The New Koreans: the Story of a Nation.* A 2017 follow up to Breen's esteemed *The Koreans*, this is an excellent, sideways look at the Korean psyche, at a time of profound social and cultural change. As with the initial tome, his accounts are relayed with warmth and a pleasing depth of knowledge.

Bruce Cumings *Korea's Place in the Sun: A Modern History.* The Korean peninsula went through myriad changes in the twentieth century, and this weighty tome analyses the effects of such disquiet on its population, showing that the South's seemingly smooth trajectory towards democracy and capitalism masked a great injury of the national psyche.

Euny Hong *The Birth of Korean Cool.* A good rundown of Korea's attempts to conquer Asia, and then the world at large, with its pop culture; as well as the more obvious effects on drama and music, it looks at how this impacted upon Korea's place at the global business table.

Keith Pratt *Everlasting Flower: A History of Korea.* This thoroughly readable book provides a chronicle of Korean goings-on from the very first kingdoms to the modern day, its text broken up with interesting illustrated features on the arts and customs prevalent at the time.

★ **Simon Winchester** *Korea: A Walk Through the Land of Miracles.* This highly entertaining book details Winchester's walk from southern Jeju to the North Korean border. Written in the 1980s, it's now an extremely dated snapshot of Korean society, but this is actually a plus point: it is amazing to witness, even at second hand, how much has changed in such a short time.

NORTH KOREA AND THE KOREAN WAR

★ **Bruce Cumings** *North Korea: Another Country.* The US-North Korean dispute is far more complex than Western media would have you imagine, and this book provides a revealing – if slightly hard to digest – glance at the flipside. Cumings' meticulous research is without parallel, and the accounts of American atrocities and cover-ups both in the "Forgotten War" and during the nuclear crisis offer plenty of food for thought.

Guy Delisle *Pyongyang.* A comic strip describing his time as a cartoonist in Pyongyang, Delisle's well-observed and frequently hilarious book is a North Korean rarity – one that tells it like it is, and doesn't seek to make political or ideological statements. His illustrations are eerily accurate.

★ **Barbara Demick** *Nothing to Envy.* An admirably well-researched look at modern-day life in North Korea, based on the experiences of six residents of Chongjin, a major city in the northeast of the country. Gulags, the Kim cult, famine and poverty all get a mention, juxtaposed with the views of a seemingly unwavering believer in the regime.

Max Hastings *The Korean War.* A conflict is not quite a war until it has been given the treatment by acclaimed historian Max Hastings. With this book, he has provided more than his usual mix of fascinating, balanced and well-researched material; the account of the stand of the

Gloucesters on the Imjin is particularly absorbing.

Kang Chol-Hwan *The Aquariums of Pyongyang.* Having fled his homeland after spending time in a North Korean gulag, Kang's harrowing accounts of squalor, starvation and brutality represent one of the only windows into the world's most fenced-off social systems. He's not a natural author, however, and the confused sermonizing at the end rather dilutes the book's appeal.

Hyeonseo Lee *The Girl with Seven Names.* There has been a recent glut of books by North Korean defectors, and sadly a desire for ever-juicier stories means that many of them contain a fair dose of BS. This is one of the better-written and more believable ones, penned by a girl who attempted to flee North Korea with her family.

Bradley K. Martin *Under the Loving Care of the Fatherly Leader.* Almost 900 pages long – 200 of which are references – this isn't one to carry around in your backpack, but for an in-depth look at the first two Kims and the perpetration of their personality cult, it's hard to beat.

★ **Don Oberdorfer** *The Two Koreas: A Contemporary History.* Lengthy, but engaging and surprisingly easy to read, this book traces the various events in postwar Korea, as well as examining how they were affected by the actions and policies of China, Russia, Japan and the US. You'd be hard-pressed to find a book about North Korea more neutral in tone.

★ **Daniel Tudor & James Pearson** *North Korea Confidential.* The publishers of this book, and the newspapers who its authors worked for, got into hot water with Pyongyang, for daring to tell the truth about how capitalism has become an unofficial but integral part of present-day North Korea.

FICTION

Cho Se-hui *The Dwarf.* Even miracles have a downside: Seoul's economy underwent a truly remarkable transformation in the 1970s, but at what cost to its people and culture? This weighty, tersely delivered novel uncovers the spiritual decline of Seoul's nouveau riche, via twelve interconnected stories; *A Dwarf Launches a Little Bell* is particularly recommended, and has been reprinted hundreds of times in Korea.

★ **Adam Johnson** *The Orphan Master's Son.* Winner of the 2013 Pulitzer Prize for fiction, this tells the story of an orphan who struggles through life in North Korea, and ends up employed as a kidnapper of Japanese citizens.

★ **Han Kang** *The Vegetarian.* Written in 2007 but only translated to English in 2015 (winning the prestigious Man Booker prize the following year), this is the visceral tale of an ordinary married couple, for whom family life begins to implode upon the wife's decision to become vegetarian.

Kim Young Ha *Your Republic is Calling You* and *I Have the Right to Destroy Myself.* Two books from a man whose international reputation is growing by the year, his popularity and his existentialist tendencies marking him out as a potential Korean Murakami. The first book revolves around a North Korean spy torn between his homeland and the South, while the second, set in Seoul, is the dark tale of a refined thinker with suicidal tendencies.

Kyung-sook Shin *Please Look After Mom* The story of a family's search for an elderly lady who goes missing in Seoul subway station, and their subsequent self-discoveries, this has been given the Oprah seal of approval, and also turned into a stage play and musical.

★ **Yi Munyeol** *Our Twisted Hero.* This tale of psychological warfare at a Korean elementary school has a deceptively twee plotline, managing to explore the use and misuse of power while providing metaphorical parallels to Korean politics of the 1970s.

RECIPE BOOKS

Debra Samuels and **Taekyung Chung** *The Korean Table.* One hundred easy-to-follow recipes "from barbecue to *bibimbap*", accompanied by droolworthy photos, this will have you getting your kitchen stinky and covered with chilli paste in no time at all.

Marja Vongerichten and **Jean Georges Vongerichten** *The Kimchi Chronicles: Korean Cooking for an American Kitchen.* A very useful cookbook that takes account of the fact that its readers may not have access to a full Korean kitchen's-worth of utensils.

A–Z of contemporary Korea

A: Alphabet Olympics
Seoul hosted the Summer Games in 1988, and Pyeongchang the Winter version in 2018. However, there's one festival at which Korea has been declared the eternal champion: the **Alphabet Olympics**. The first event was held in 2009, with Korea's *hangeul* beating off fifteen other national and international scripts. Lee Yang-ha, the (Korean) president of the World Alphabet Olympic Committee, explained with joy that while "the 26 letters of English can only express 300 or more sounds, the 24 Korean characters can theoretically express more than 11,000" – all rather odd, since the Korean script is very limited when transliterating words from other languages. The second event was held in 2012; with *hangeul* again the victor, the heads of the World Alphabet Academy (again all Korean, and with a manifesto to propagate *hangeul* and Christianity throughout the world) decided to make Korea the champion forever, because "scripts do not change as fast as language". Meanwhile, English teachers across Korea struggle to help local students pronounce the letters Z or V, distinguish between L and R, or end syllables with most consonantal sounds.

B: Burberry man
What's generally known as a "flasher" in English is referred to as a **Burberry man** in Korea. These gents – dressed in a three-quarter-length jacket and little else – hang around universities in order to expose themselves to female students, most commonly when large crowds are gathered in the front enclosures. They're surprisingly common – most Korean girls will have seen at least one, and many schools see a Burberry man show up regularly. Korea's love of conformity means that even these sex pests have a uniform of sorts: while the Burberry label is not essential, most of their jackets are brown, and for some reason knee-length grey socks seem almost mandatory.

C: City branding
Cities and countries around the world have long attempted to rope in extra visitors with clever slogans, and in the early 2000s Korea took this idea and ran with it. Local consultants raked in the cash with a slew of **city branding**, which often verged on the comical. Some of the more "interesting" examples include "Aha! Suncheon", "Oh, Yeosu!", "Happy Citizen, Proud Jeongeup", "It's Daejeon", "Just Sangju", "Yes! Uiwang", "Hi-touch Gongju" (an odd name for an ancient capital) and "Pyeongtaek Super". Then along came Psy, who did more for Korean branding with one silly dance than any city slogan ever achieved.

D: Dotjari
Open the boot of a Korean's car, or peek into the storage space in their apartment, and you'll likely find a **dotjari**. These woven mats were, in the days before air conditioning, used for outdoor sleeping (often in conjunction with a "bamboo wife", a hollow pillow made from bamboo), but their modern equivalent – generally fashioned from plastic and tin foil – can transform any flat space into a picnic spot at the drop of a hat.

E: Eyelid surgery
In a country where appearance is not quite everything but pretty damn close, beauty is big business. The large and thriving plastic surgery industry sees women – and more than a few men – get all sorts from nose jobs to a nip and tuck, but the most popular alteration by far is **eyelid surgery**. This involves the creation of a crease in the upper eyelid, the results being apparently more beautiful to Koreans, but distinctly non-oriental.

F: "Fan death"

"**Fan death**" is a truly curious phenomenon – whereas around the world people fall asleep with a fan or the air conditioning left on, only in Korea does such folly regularly seem to result in fatalities. The reasons given include air currents starving the victim of air, reduced room temperatures inducing hypothermia, or even fan blades actually cutting the oxygen molecules in two. This is enough to convince most Koreans that the humble electric fan is an instrument to be feared – even broadsheet newspapers run fan-death stories, and the Korean government has issued warnings against using fans at night. Such beliefs are of much amusement to Korea's expat population (unless they find themselves sharing a room with a Korean in the summer).

G: Grandmother techno

While modern K-pop has swept across continental Asia, there's another strain of music that you're likely to come across on your way around Korea: "*bongjak*" songs – best described as a kind of **grandmother techno** – are fast-paced ballads, set to odd synthesized rhythms and crooned out in a semi-compulsory warble. Some of the best places to get a handle on *bongjak* are Korea's national parks: older locals are fond of drinking and listening to music both during and after their hikes, which makes it all the more likely that you'll get to see the accompanying dance (something like bouncing on a toilet seat while handling a steering wheel).

H: Homosexuality

Homosexuality has long been a bit of a taboo in Korea, but in line with the development of other countries, a couple of high-profile comings out have made such matters more acceptable to the wider populace. There was the case of **Hong Seok-cheon**, an actor who lost pretty much everything after coming out in 2000. After taking a risk by opening up an LGBT+ venue in Itaewon, he went on to own around a dozen bars and restaurants in the area, and appears on television pretty much every day. **LGBT+** issues, more broadly, are also slowly becoming more acceptable topics of conversation. **Harisu** was assigned male at birth, but flew in the face of a conservative society to become the first transgender celebrity in the country; she was also one of the first in the queue to change gender when it became legal to do so.

I: Internet deaths

Koreans are famed for their use of computers, most notably the amount of time they spend playing online games. In fact, there is a growing backlash among the non-Korean gaming community: such is the domination of the country's gamers that they are accused of taking over international gaming sites and tournaments. They even hit the international headlines with occasional **internet deaths**: stories of gamers making mammoth stints (one was measured at 92 hours) at PC bars have become less common since the government ordered tighter controls, but there's still the occasional death behind closed doors.

J: Jaebeol

Korean business is dominated by a troupe of gigantic business conglomerates known as **jaebeol**. A few of these organizations have achieved fame around the world, though perhaps bar Samsung, most foreigners probably wouldn't know that the company is Korean even if the name is familiar to them. Some of the largest and most renowned *jaebeol* include LG, Hyundai, SK, Lotte, Daewoo and Kumho Asiana. Most are still family-controlled, leading to enormous riches for those at the helm; their power was a driving force behind Korea's "Economic Miracle". Times have changed; after the Asian Financial Crisis and the resultant reforms, many chose (or were forced) to break up into smaller units.

K: K-pop

For all its success in international business and mobile telephony, it's Korea's pop music – usually referred to as **K-pop** – which has best marketed the country as a brand. While the term is broad, it usually refers to saccharine boy- and girl-band pap, which since the turn of the century has seen accompanying music videos become ever more raunchy.

L: Louis Vuitton

Though the numbers are gradually starting to decline, patterned brown handbags from French designer **Louis Vuitton** have long been standard issue on female Korean arms. However, high prices – and increased expertise of counterfeiting in China – oblige many to invest in a fake bag instead. Watch what happens if it starts to rain.

M: Military service

South Korea still has compulsory **military service** for its young men. This was once 36 months, but is now around 24 months and likely to decrease further. Conscientious objectors will be jailed, but there are ways around the rule – many students manage to tie their service into university courses such as logistics and electronic engineering. Military service is also mandatory for men in North Korea, and women are actively encouraged to enrol as volunteers.

N: Nocheonnyeo

A **nocheonnyeo** is an "over-the-hill spinster", a woman who has gone past the perceived outer boundary of marriageable age; thirty has long been the feared number, though the Korean age-counting system (whereby children are born aged 1 and become 2 on the date of the next Lunar New Year) makes this 28 or 29 in international terms. While it remains harder for a woman to marry after achieving *nocheonnyeo* status, societal shifts (notably an increase in divorce rates, and the slow decline of the resign-from-your-job-after-marriage path for females) mean that it's by no means impossible.

O: Oktapbang

Korea is the world's second most densely populated country of any substantial size, and as such there's understandable pressure for living space. From the 1980s on, many landlords increased the rents that they could accrue from low-rise buildings by making a tiny extra room on the roof; known as **oktapbang** ("home-top room"), these minuscule abodes are generally inhabited by students.

P: Private tutoring

With Korea's mix of generous salaries and relatively poor level of proficiency in foreign languages, there's a large and growing market for English teachers. Most of these go – at least initially – to teach children at after-school **private tutoring** institutes known as *hagwon*. These are not just for English lessons – the huge pressures inherent in Korea's educational system prompt an extremely high proportion of parents to push their kids into extra-curricular classes from ages as young as 5. In addition to language classes and "regular" school, the little mites may have violin lessons, computer training, art classes, dance groups and piano recitals crammed into their weekly schedule.

Q: Questionable English

Anyone spending time in Korea will see T-shirts splashed with **questionable English** all over the place – "Skinny Bitch" got to be popular with young girls, though "Hey Guy! Lay Me" was a mercifully short-lived fad. The mirth is not restricted to T-shirt slogans: Maeil Milk is available at every convenience store, there's an energy drink called Coolpis, a bakery chain called Gout and children's clothing shops called Hunt Kids and Baby Hunt. There are also spelling mistakes galore: "crab" is spelt with a "p" on a surprising number of the country's menus, and a certain hamburger chain is often spelled "Bugger King" on English-language maps.

R: Red Devils

Having casually pinched their nickname from England's Manchester United, the South Korean national football team is often referred to as the "**Red Devils**", as are their main supporters' group. A noisy but friendly bunch, the latter were one of the highlights of the 2002 World Cup, an event half-hosted in Korea; most fans wore a T-shirt emblazoned with "Be The Reds!", perhaps the best-known example of "Konglish" (a hybrid of Korean and English which makes little sense in either language). The inventors of the logo initially neglected to copyright it, and it was eventually superseded by the official slogan of the supporters' club, the more grammatically correct "Reds Go Together".

S: StarCraft

Korea was one of the first countries in which online gaming became truly huge, with **StarCraft** a particularly popular game – at one point, sales in Korea accounted for sixty percent of the global total, while 24-hour television channels were dedicated to it, and a number of deaths were attributed to playing the game for far too long. Indeed, it could be said that the Korean addiction to StarCraft helped to facilitate the rise of eSports around the world; the country successfully lobbied to have them included at the Asian Games, and they'll make their debut as a medal event at the 2022 edition in Hangzhou.

T: Table gifts

A first birthday party is a pretty special event wherever you are in the world, but Korea has added its own distinctive twist to proceedings – **table gifts**. At some point in the occasion, the baby will be seated on or dangled over a table laid out with money, rice, thread and a pencil, and pushed to make a selection that, it is said, will influence their future path. Money speaks for itself, but the selection of rice is said to lead to a comfortable life, thread to a long one, and a pencil to a scholarly career. Of course, this is not enough to satisfy many modern parents, who throw contemporary choices such as golf balls, footballs, DVDs or microphones onto the table too, often giving their young one precious little choice in the selection.

U: Unconstitutional law

Koreans were, until recently, banned from marrying anyone of the same clan. This may have sounded like an extremely severe rule in a country with so few family names (around one-quarter of Koreans are named Kim, another fifteen percent Lee, and almost ten percent Park), but the ruling only in fact covered those who had both the same name and the same ancestral clan; some of these subdivisions, however, were over a million-strong in number. Same-clan marriages were termed incestuous, even if the pair were a dozen generations apart, but this law was found **unconstitutional** by the Korean court in 1997, and thousands have since taken advantage of this ruling.

V: VANK

The Voluntary Agency Network of Korea, also known as **VANK**, is an online club with over 120,000 members. Their remit is to promote Korea overseas, though the primary focus generally seems to be getting one over on arch-enemy Japan – any international organization that dares to use "Takeshima or Sea of Japan" on a map, rather than Dokdo or the East Sea, will likely be bombarded with emails by these cyber-nationalists.

W: Work meals

Work meals, known as *hoe-sik*, are the bane of many a Korean office worker's life. In the West, many employees would doubtless appreciate being treated to a big meal by their boss (not to mention the free booze); however, there's understandable resentment when it becomes a weekly occurrence that one can't back out of. It's common for bosses to announce the *hoe-sik* at the last minute, forcing the cancellation of any plans not involving the work team.

X: Xenophobia

Koreans tend to make foreigners feel very welcome, but this friendliness conceals a rampant **xenophobia**. Korea remains one of the most homogenous societies on Earth, and traces of the "Hermit Kingdom" remain, mainly thanks to history lessons that paint the motherland in virginal white while detailing every single injustice inflicted on her; most of the official ire is reserved for the Japanese, but anti-Americanism is also rife. Korea is simply seen as a world apart, and foreigners will always be viewed as such, even if they were born in Korea and speak the language fluently. This explains the surprise that many Koreans will show to Westerners able to use chopsticks – no matter how close you live to a Chinatown, it's simply not in your DNA. However, the benefits of being white in Korea usually outweigh the negatives; the same cannot always be said for those of African, South Asian or Southeast Asian descent.

Y: Yoo Jae-suk

It's quite possible that no person has ever clocked up more television hours than Korean chat show personality **Yoo Jae-suk**. Nicknamed "The Grasshopper" on account of his distinctive appearance, Yoo started life as one of Korea's many young, lower-level stand-up comedians, but soon made the transition from stage to small screen, and married a local beauty queen. His chat shows, often set in *jjimjilbang* (see page 36) and incorporating a distinct reality-TV element, are on television almost every single day of the year, and rope in washed-up A-listers like moths to a flame.

Z: Zainichi Koreans

After the Chinese, **Zainichi Koreans** form Japan's largest ethnic minority group. Unlike "regular" ethnic Koreans, who made the journey across the sea in dynastic times or recent decades, they're the descendants of those who went to Japan during the country's occupation of Korea (1910–45). Many originated from the North, and maintain close ties with the DPRK – a whopping 217 "Chongryon" schools across Japan (plus one university) teach a pro-North Korean syllabus, and their students often go to Pyongyang on field trips.

Korean

The sole official tongue of both North and South Korea, the Korean language is used by almost eighty million people, making it one of the world's twenty most-spoken tongues. It's a highly tricky language to pick up – much to the chagrin of linguists, it remains stubbornly "unclassified" on the global language tree, its very origins something of a mystery. Some lump it in with the Altaic group (itself rather vague), which would put it on the same branch as Turkish and Mongolian, though many view it as a language isolate. Korean is therefore in the same boat as Japanese, its closest linguistic brother; both share a subject-object-verb syntax and similar grammar, though well over half of the Korean words themselves actually originate from China. Korea also used Chinese text for centuries, even after creating its own characters (known as hangeul; 한글) in the 1440s, but now almost exclusively uses the local system for everyday functions.

Native speakers of European languages will encounter some pretty significant **grammatical differences** when attempting to get a handle on the Korean tongue. Korean **nouns** remain unaffected whether they refer to singular or plural objects, very little use is made of **articles**, and **verbs** do not change case according to who or what they're referring to – *gayo* can mean "I go", "he/she/it goes" or "we/they go", the meaning made clear by the context. Verbs do, however, alter depending on which **level of politeness** the speaker desires to use, and the relationship between speaker and listener; the conversation will sound quite different depending on whether it's between a child and a mother, a boss and an employee, or even good friends of slightly different age. In general, it's pretty safe to stick to verbs with the polite **-yo** ending; the verb forms given here are in a formal style which should suffice for most travellers. Unfortunately, there are few good **books** from which to learn Korean; those from the *Teach Yourself* and *Colloquial* series fall short of the two companies' usually high standards, but are about as good as you'll find. There are plenty of dictionary and language-learning apps, though none of them have really nailed it yet.

Korean characters

Though it consists of a highly distinctive scrawl of circles and Tetris shapes, many foreigners find Korean text surprisingly **easy to learn**. Koreans tend to assume that foreigners don't have the inclination or mental capability to decipher *hangeul*, so your efforts will not go unappreciated. Koreans are immensely proud of *hangeul*, which they see as the world's most logical written system (see page 389). While this is no great exaggeration, the efficiency also has a downside – user-friendly it may well be, but in reality *hangeul* is a very narrow system that cannot cope with sounds not found in the Korean language, a fact that partially explains the Korean people's occasionally curious pronunciation of foreign words.

Pronunciation

Pronouncing Korean words is a tough task – some sounds simply do not have English-language equivalents. You'll see from the *hangeul* box (see page 389) that there's only one character for "l" and "r", with its actual sound some way in between the two – try

HANGEUL

Korean characters are grouped into **syllabic boxes** of more or less equal size, and generally arranged left to right – if you see a line of text made up of eighteen of these character-chunks, it will have eighteen syllables when spoken. The way in which the **characters** fall into the boxes is rather unique and takes a bit of figuring out – some have two characters in the top half and one at the bottom (the top two are read left to right, followed by the bottom one, so 한 makes *han*), while others have two or three characters arranged vertically (these are read downwards, so 국 makes *guk*). Thus put together, we have 한국 – *hanguk*, meaning "Korea". The basic building blocks are listed in the box below, though note that some of these symbols **change sounds** depending on whether they're at the beginning or end of a syllable or word (syllable-ending sounds are bracketed in the boxed text), and that "ng" is used as an initial null consonant for syllables that start with a vowel.

ㄱ	g (k)
ㄴ	n
ㄷ	d (t)
ㄹ	r/l
ㅁ	m
ㅂ	b (p)
ㅅ	s (t)
ㅈ	j (t)
ㅊ	ch (t)
ㅋ	k
ㅌ	t
ㅍ	p
ㅎ	h
ㅇ	ng
ㅏ	a
ㅑ	ya
ㅓ	eo
ㅕ	yeo
ㅗ	o
ㅛ	yo
ㅜ	u
ㅠ	yu
ㅡ	eu
ㅣ	i
ㅔ	e
ㅐ	ae
ㅖ	ye
ㅒ	yae
ㅟ	wi
ㅞ	we
ㅙ	wae
ㅘ	wa
ㅚ	oe
ㅢ	ui
ㅝ	wo

saying both phonemes at the same time. The letters "k", "d", "b" and "j" are often written "k", "t", "p" and "ch", and are pronounced approximately halfway towards those Roman equivalents; unfortunately, the second set also have their place in the official system, and are usually referred to as **aspirated consonants**, accompanied as they are by a puff of air. Consonants are fairly easy to master – note that some are doubled up, and spoken more forcefully – but pronunciation guides to some of the tricky **vowels** and **diphthongs** are as follows (British English readings offer the closest equivalents):

TRANSLITERATION TROUBLES

Rendering the Korean language in Roman text is, simply, a battle that can never be won – a classic problem of square pegs and round holes. Numerous systems have been employed down the years, perhaps best exemplified in the Korean family name now usually romanized as "Lee": this has also been written as Rhee, Li, Ri, Lih, Rhi, Ree, Yi, Rii and more besides. Under the current system it would be "I", but the actual pronunciation is simply "ee" – it's amazing how much trouble a simple vowel can cause (especially when almost a fifth of the country has this name).

A Korean's age, schooling, family and even lifestyle influence the way that they'll romanize a given word, but official standards have long been in place. The **Yale** and **McCune–Reischauer** systems became widely accepted in the 1940s, and the latter is still much in evidence today; under its rules, aspirated consonants are marked with apostrophes, and certain vowels with breves. One problem – other than looking ugly – was that these punctuation markings are often neglected, even in language study books; though it remains the official system in North Korea, the South formulated its own system of **Revised Romanization** in the year 2000. While this is far from perfect, it's the official standard, and has been used throughout this book; exceptions include names of the many hotels, restaurants, universities and individuals who cling to the old ways. One other issue is the Korean syllable *shi*; this is now romanized as *si*, a rather ridiculous change since it takes Koreans years of language classes before they can pronounce the syllable without palatalizing it – "six" and "sister" will be pronounced "shix" and "shister". We've written it as *shi* in the language listings to help you achieve the correct pronunciation, but obeyed the official system in the rest of the book – Sinchon is pronounced "Shinchon", and so on.

Koreans themselves find it hard to render **foreign words** in *hangeul* as there are many sounds that don't fit into the system – the difficulties with "l" and "r" sharing the same character being an obvious example – but even when parallels exist they are sometimes distorted. The letter "a" is usually written as an "e" or "ae" in an unsuccessful effort to Americanize the pronunciation – "hat", for example, will be pronounced "het" by the majority of the population.

a as in "car"	**ae** as in "air"
ya as in "yap"	**ye** as in "yet"
eo as in "hot"	**yae** as in "yeah"
yeo as in "yob"	**wi** as in "window"
o pronounced "ore"	**we** as in "wedding"
yo pronounced as the British "your"	**wae** as the beginning of "where"
u as in "Jew"	**wa** as in "wag"
yu pronounced "you"	**oe** as in the beginning of "way"
eu no English equivalent; widen your mouth and try an "euggh" sound of disgust	**ui** no English equivalent; add an "ee" sound to *eu* above
i as in "pea"	**wo** as in "wad"
e as in "bed"	

USEFUL WORDS AND PHRASES

BASICS

Yes *ye/ne* 예/네
No *aniyo* 아니요
Please (asking for something) ...*juseyo* ...주세요
Excuse me *shillye hamnida* 실례 합니다
I'm sorry *mian hamnida* 미안 합니다
Thank you *gamsa hamnida* 감사 합니다
You're welcome *gwaenchan-ayo* 괜찮아요
What? *muot?* 무엇?
When? *eonje?* 언제?
Where? *eodi?* 어디?

Who? *nugu?* 누구?
How? *eotteokke?* 어떻께?
How much? *eolma-eyo?* 얼마에요?
How many? *myeokke-eyo?* 몇 개에요?
I want... ...*hago-shipeoyo* ...하고 싶어요
Please help me *dowa-juseyo* 도와주세요

COMMUNICATING

I can't speak Korean *jeo-neun hangugeo-reul mot haeyo* 저는 한국어를 못 해요

I can't read Korean *jeo-neun hangugeo-reul mok ilgeoyo* 저는 한국어를 못 읽어요

Do you speak English? *yeongeo halsu-isseoyo?* 영어 할수 있어요?

Is there someone who can speak English? *yeongeo-reul haljul a-neun bun isseoyo?* 영어를 할줄 아는 분 있어요?

Can you please speak slowly? *jom cheoncheonhi mal haejuseyo?* 좀 천천히 말 해주세요?

Please say that again *dashi han-beon mal haejuseyo* 다시 한번말 해주세요

I understand/I see *alasseoyo* 알았어요

I (really) don't understand *(jal) mollayo* (잘) 몰라요

What does this mean? *i-geot museun ddeushi-eyo?* 이것 무슨 뜻이에요?

How do you say (x) in Korean? *(x) eul/reul hanguk-eoro eotteokke mal hayo?* (x) 을/를 한국어로 어떻게 말하요

Please write in English *yeongeo-ro jegeo jushillaeyo* 영어로 적어 주실래요

Please wait (a moment) *(jamggan) gidariseyo* (잠깐) 기다리세요

Just a minute *jamggan manyo* 잠깐 만요

MEETINGS AND GREETINGS

Hello; Good morning/ afternoon/evening *annyeong haseyo* 안녕 하세요

Hello (polite) *annyeong hashimnikka* 안녕 하십니까

How are you? *jal jinaesseoyo?* 잘 지냈어요?

I'm fine *jal jinaesseoyo/jo-ayo* 잘 지냈어요 / 좋아요

Nice to meet you *bangapseumnida* 반갑습니다

Goodbye (when staying) *annyeong-hi gaseyo* 안녕히 가세요

Goodbye (when leaving) *annyeong-hi gyeseyo* 안녕히 계세요

What's your name? *ireum-i eotteokke doeshimnikka?* 이름이 어떻게 되십니까?

My name is… *ireum-i … imnida* 이름이… 입니다.

Where are you from? *eodi-eso wasseoyo?* 어디에 왔어요?

I'm from… *…eso wasseoyo* 에서 왔어요

Korea *han-guk* 한국

Britain *yeong-guk* 영국

Ireland *aillaendeu* 아일랜드

America *mi-guk* 미국

Australia *oseuteureillia/hoju* 오스트레일리아 / 호주

Canada *kae-nada* 캐나다

New Zealand *nyu jillaendeu* 뉴질랜드

South Africa *nam apeurika* 남 아프리카

How old are you? *myeot-sal ieyo?* 몇 살이에요?

I am (age) *(age)-sal ieyo* (age)-살 이에요

Do you like…? *…o-a hayo?* …좋아 해요?

I like… *jo-a hayo* 좋아 해요

I don't like… *an jo-a hayo* 안 좋아해요

Do you have (free) time? *shigan-i isseoyo?* 시간이 있어요?

NUMBERS

Rather confusingly, the Korean language has two separate number systems operating in parallel – a **native Korean** system, and a **Sino–Korean** system of Chinese origin – and you'll have to learn according to the situation which one to use. To tell the time, you'll actually need both – amazingly, minutes and hours run on different systems. The native Korean system only goes up to 99, and has been placed on the right-hand side of the readings. Dates and months use the Sino–Korean system alone, with *il* (sun) used as a suffix for days, and *wol* (moon) for months: June 7 is simply *yuk-wol chil-il.*

Zero *yeong/gong* 영/공

One *il/hana* 일/하나

Two *i* (pronounced "ee")/*dul* 이/둘

Three *sam/set* 삼/셋

Four *sa/net* 사/넷

Five *o/daseot* 오/다섯

Six *yuk/yeoseot* 육/여섯

Seven *chil/ilgop* 칠/일곱

Eight *pal/yeodeol* 팔/여덟

Nine *gu/ahop* 구/아홉

Ten *ship/yeol* 십/열

Eleven *shib-il/ yeol-hana* 십일/ 열하나

Twelve *shib-i/yeol-dul* 십이/열둘

Twenty *i-shib/seumul* 이십/스물

Thirty *sam-ship/ seoreun* 삼십/ 서른

One hundred *baek* 백

Two hundred *i-baek* 이백

Thousand *cheon* 천

Ten thousand *man* 만

One hundred thousand *shim-man* 십만

One million *baeng-man* 백만

One hundred million *eok* 억

TIME AND DATES

Now *jigeum* 지금

Today *o-neul* 오늘

Morning *achim* 아침

Afternoon *ohu* 오후

Evening *jeonyok* 저녁

Night *bam* 밤

Tomorrow *nae-il* 내일

Yesterday *eoje* 어제

Week *ju* 주

Month *wol/dal* 월/달

Year *nyeon* 년

Monday *wolyo-il* 월요일

Tuesday *hwayo-il* 화요일

Wednesday *suyo-il* 수요일

Thursday *mogyo-il* 목요일

Friday *geumyo-il* 금요일
Saturday *toyo-il* 토요일
Sunday *ilyo-il* 일요일
What time is it? *myo-shi-eyo?* 몇시에요?
It's 10 o'clock *yeol-shi-eyo* 열시에요
10.20 *yeol-shi i-ship-bun* 열 시 이십분
10.30 *yeol-shi sam-ship-bun* 열시 삼십분
10.50 *yeol-shi o-ship-bun* 열 시 오십분

TRANSPORT AND TRAVEL

Aeroplane *bihaenggi* 비행기
Airport *gonghang* 공항
Bus *beoseu* 버스
Express bus (terminal) *gosok beoseu (teominal)* 익스프레스 (터미널)
Intercity bus (terminal) *shi-oe beoseu (teominal)* 시외 버스(터미널)
City bus *shinae beoseu* 시내 버스
Airport bus *gonghang beoseu* 공항 버스
City bus stop *jeong-nyu-jang* 정류장
Train *gicha* 기차
Train station *yeok* 역
Subway *jihacheol* 지하철
Ferry *yeogaek-seon* 여객선
Ferry terminal *yeogaek teominal* 여객 터미널
Left-luggage office *jimbogwanso* 짐보관
Ticket office *maepyoso* 매표서
Ticket *pyo* 표
Platform *seunggangjang* 승강장
Bicycle *jajeon-geo* 자전거
Taxi *taek-shi* 택시

DIRECTIONS AND GENERAL PLACES

Where is (x)? *-i/ga eodi-eyo?* -이/가 어디에요?
Straight ahead *jikjin* 직진
Left *oen-jjok (pronounced "wen-chok")* 왼쪽
Right *oreun-jjok* 오른쪽
Behind *dwi-e* 뒤에
In front of *ap-e* 앞에
North *buk* 북
South *nam* 남
East *dong* 동
West *seo* 서
Map *maep/jido* 맵/지도
Entrance *ip-gu* 입구
Exit *chul-gu* 출구
Art gallery *misulgwan* 미술관
Bank *eunhaeng* 은행
Beach *haebyeon* 해변
Department store *baekhwajeom* 백화점
Embassy *daesagwan* 대사관
Hot-spring spa *oncheon* 온천
Museum *bangmulgwan* 박물관
Park *gongwon* 공원

Sea *haean/bada* 해안/바다
Temple *Jeol/sachal* 절/사찰
Toilet *hwajang-shil* -화장실
Tourist office *gwan-gwang annaeso* 관광 안내소

ACCOMMODATION

Hotel *hotel* 호텔
Motel *motel* 모텔
Guesthouse *yeogwan* 여관
Budget guesthouse *yeoinsuk* 여인숙
Rented room *minbak* 민박
Youth hostel *yuseu hoseutel* 유스 호스텔
Korean-style room *ondol-bang* 온돌방
Western-style room *chimdae-bang* 침대방
Single room *shinggeul chimdae* 싱글 침대
Double room *deobeul chimdae* 더블 침대
Twin room *chimdae dugae* 침대 두개
En-suite room *yokshil-ddallin bang* 욕실 딸린방
Shower *syaweo* 샤워
Bath *yokjo* 욕조
Key *ki* 키
Passport *yeogwon* 여권
Do you have any vacancies? *bang isseoyo?* 방 있어요?
I have a reservation *yeyak haesseoyo* 예약 했어요
I don't have a reservation *yeyak anhaesseoyo* 예약 안했어요
How much is the room? *bang-i eolma-eyo?* 방이 얼마에요?
Does that include breakfast? *achim-shiksa poham-dwae isseoyo?* 아침식사 포함돼 있어요?
One/two/ three nights *haruppam/ i-bak/ sam-bak* 하룻밤/이박/삼박
One week *il-ju-il* 일주일
May I see the room? *bang jom bolsu- isseoyo?* 방 좀 볼수 있어요?

SHOPPING, MONEY AND BANKS

Bank *eunhaeng* 은행
Foreign exchange *woe-hwan* 외환
Won *won* 원
Pounds *pa-un-deu* 파운드
Dollars *dalleo* 달러
Cash *don* 돈
Travellers' cheque *yeohaengja supyo* 여행자 수표
How much is it? *eolma-eyo?* 얼마에요?
It's too expensive *neomu bissayo* 너무 비싸요
Please make it a little cheaper *jom kkakka-juseyo* 좀 깎아주세요
Do you accept credit cards? *keurediteu kadeu gyesan dwaeyo?* 크레디트 카드 계산 돼요?

POST AND TELEPHONES

Post office *uche-guk* 우체국

Envelope *bongtu* 봉투
Letter *pyeonji* 편지
Postcard *yeopseo* 엽서
Stamp *u-pyo* 우표
Airmail *hanggong u-pyeon* 항공 우편
Surface mail *seonbak u-pyeon* 선박 우편
Telephone *jeon-hwa* 전화
Fax *paekseu* 팩스
Telephone card *jeonhwa kadeu* 전화카드
Internet café *PC-bang* 방
I would like to call... *...hante jeonhwa hago- shipeeoyo* 좀바꿔 주세요
May I speak to... *...jom baggwo juseyo* 저는 아파요
Hello? *yeoboseyo?* 여보세요?

HEALTH

Hospital *byeongwon* 병원
Pharmacy *yak-guk* 약국
Medicine *yak* 약

Doctor *uisa* 의사
Dentist *chigwa-uisa* 치과의사
Diarrhoea *seolsa* 설사
Nausea *meseukkeo-um* 메스꺼움
Fever *yeol* 열
Food poisoning *shikjungdok* 식중독
Antibiotics *hangsaengje* 항생제
Antiseptic *sodok-yak* 독약
Condom *kondom* 콘돔
Penicillin *penishillin* 페니실린
Tampons *tampon* 탐폰
I'm ill *jeo-neun apayo* 저는 아파요
I have a cold *gamgi geoll-yeosseoyo* 감기 걸렸어요
I'm allergic to... *...allereugi-ga isseoyo* ...알레르 기가 있어요
It hurts here *yeogi-ga apayo* 여기가 아파요
Please call a doctor *uisa-reul bulleo juseyo* 의사를 불러 주세요

FOOD AND DRINK

PLACES

Restaurant *sikdang* 식당
Korean barbecue restaurant *galbi-jip* 갈비집
Seafood restaurant *hoet-jip* 횟집
Western-style restaurant *reseutorang* 레스토랑
Chinese restaurant *jungguk-jip* 중국집
Japanese restaurant *ilshik-jip* 일식집
Burger bar *paeseuteu-pudeu-jeom* 패스트푸드점
Convenience store *pyeonui-jeom* 편의점
Market *shijang* 시장
Café *kape* 카페
Bar *ba/suljip* 바/술집
Club *naiteu-keulleob* 나이트클럽
Expat bar *woeguk-in ba* (pronounced 외국인 바 "*way-guk-in ba*")
Makgeolli bar *makgeolli-jip* 막걸리집
Soju tent *pojangmacha* 포장마차
Where's (a) ... ? *...eodi isseoyo?* ...어디 있어요?

ORDERING

Waiter/Waitress (lit. "Here!") *yeogiyo!* 여기요!
How much is that? *eolma-eyo?* 얼마에요?
I would like... *...hago shipeeoyo* ...하고 싶어요
May I have the bill? *gyesanseo juseyo?* 계산해 주세요
I'm a vegetarian *jeo-neun chaeshikju uija-eyo* 저는 채식주의자에요
Can I have this without meat? *gogi bbaego haejushilsu isseoyo?* 고기 빼고 해주실수 있 어요?
I can't eat spicy food *maeun-geot mot meogeoyo* 매운 것 못 먹어요
Delicious! *mashisseoyo!* 맛있어요!
Chopsticks *jeot-garak* 젓가락
Fork *po-keu* 포크

Knife *nai-peu/kal* 나이프/칼
Spoon *sut-garak* 숟가락
Menu *menyu* 메뉴

STAPLE INGREDIENTS

Beef *so-gogi* 쇠고기
Chicken *dak-gogi* 닭고기
Duck meat *oti-gogi* 오리고기
(Raw) fish *saengsun (hoe)/* 생선(회)
Ham *haem* 햄
Kimchi *kimchi* 김치
Meat *gogi* 고기
Noodles *myeon* 면
Pork *dwaeji-gogi* 돼지고기
Red-pepper paste *gochu-jang* 고추장
Rice *bap* 밥
Rice cake *ddeok* 떡
Seaweed laver *gim* 김
Shrimp *sae-u* 새우
Squid *ojing-eo* 오징어
Tuna *chamchi* 참치
Vegetables *yachae* 야채

RICE DISHES

Bibimbap *bibimbap* 비빔밥
Fried rice (usually with egg and vegetables) *bokkeumbap* 볶음밥
Marinaded beef on rice *bulgogi (deop-bap)* 소고기 (덮밥)
Rice rolls *gimbap* 김밥

MEAT DISHES

Barbecued ribs *galbi* 갈비

Boiled beef rolls *syabu-syabu* 샤부샤부
Dog-meat soup *boshintang/yeongyangtang* 보신탕/
영양탕
Marinaded beef *bulgogi* 소고기
Pork belly slices *samgyeopsal* 삼겹살
Spicy squid on rice *ojingeo deop-bap* 오징어 덮밥
Steamed ribs *galbi-jjim* 갈비찜

STEWS AND SOUPS

Beef and noodle soup *seolleong-tang* 설렁탕
Beef rib soup *galbi-tang* 갈비탕
Cold buckwheat noodle soup *naengmyeon* 냉면
Dumpling soup *mandu-guk* 만두국
Kimchi broth *kimchi jjigae* 김치 찌개
Ginseng-stuffed chicken soup *samgye-tang* 삼계탕
Noodles with vegetables and meat *makguksu* 막국수
Soybean broth (miso) *doenjang jjigae* 된장 찌개
Spicy fish soup *maeun-tang* 매운탕
Spicy noodle soup *ramyeon* 라면
Spicy tofu soup *sundubu* 순두부
Tuna broth *chamchi jjigae* 참치 찌개

SNACKS AND KOREAN FAST FOOD

Battered flash-fried snacks (tempura) *twigim* 튀김
Breaded pork cutlet *donkkaseu* 돈까스
Dumplings *mandu* 만두
Fried dumplings *gun-mandu* 군만두
Rice wrapped in omelette *omeuraiseu* 오므라이스
Rice cake in red-pepper paste *ddeokbokki* 떡볶이
Savoury pancake with vegetables *pajeon* 파전
Steamed dumplings *jjin-mandu* 찐만두
Stuffed sausage *sundae* 순대

SEAFOOD

Broiled fish *saengseon-gu-i* 생선구이
Fried baby octopus *nakji bokkeum* 낙지 볶음
Raw fish platter *modeum-hoe* 모듬회
Sliced raw fish *saengseon-hoe* 생선회

WESTERN FOOD

Bread *bbang* 빵
Cereal *shiri-eol* 시리얼
Cheese *chi-jeu* 치즈
Chocolate *chokollit* 초콜릿
Eggs *gyeran* 계란

Fruit *gwa-il* 과일
Pizza *pija* 피자
Spaghetti *seupageti* 스파게티
Steak *seuteikeu* 스테이크

TEA

Black tea (lit. "red tea") *hong-cha* 홍차
Chrysanthemum tea *gukhwa-cha* 국화차
Cinnamon tea *gyepi-cha* 계피차
Citron tea *yuja-cha* 유자차
"Five flavours" tea *omija-cha* 오미자차
Ginger tea *saenggang-cha* 생강차
Ginseng tea *insam-cha* 인삼차
Green tea *nok-cha* 녹차
Honey ginseng tea *gyulsam-cha* 귤삼차
"Job's Tears" tea *yulmu-cha* 율무차
Jujube tea *daechu-cha* 대추차
Medicinal herb tea *yak-cha* 약차
Plum tea *maeshil-cha* 매실차
Wild herb tea *ma-cha* 마차

ALCOHOLIC DRINKS

Baekseju *baekseju* 백세주
Beer *maekju* 맥주
Blackberry wine *bokbunja* 복분자
Bottled beer *byeong maekju* 병 맥주
Cocktail *kakteil* 칵테일
Dongdongju *dongdongju* 동동주
Draught beer *saeng maekju* 생맥주
Ginseng wine *insamju* 인삼주
Makgeolli *makgeolli* 막걸리
Plum brandy *maeshilju* 매실주
Soju *soju* 소주
Wine *wain* 와인
Whisky *wiseuki* 위스키

OTHER DRINKS

Coffee *keopi* 커피
Orange juice *orenji jyuseu* 오렌지 쥬스
Fruit juice *gwa-il jyuseu* 과일 쥬스
Milk *uyu* 우유
Mineral water *saengsu* 생수
Water *mul* 물

GLOSSARY

ajeossi an older or married man.

ajumma an older or married woman.

-am hermitage.

anju bar snacks.

-bang room.

-bawi boulder or large rock.

-bong mountain peak. The highest peak in a park is often referred to as *ilchulbong* ("Number One Peak").

buk- north.

buncheong a Korean style of pottery that became popular in Joseon times. The end product is often bluish-green in colour.

celadon a Korean style of pottery (also common in China and Japan), used since the Three Kingdoms period but largely overtaken by *buncheong* in Joseon times. The end product is often pale green in colour, with a cracked glaze.

cha tea.

-cheon stream or river of less than 100km in length.

Chuseok Korean Thanksgiving.

dae- big, large, great.

Dangun mythical founder of Korea.

DMZ the Demilitarized Zone that separates North and South Korea.

-do island.

-do province.

-dong city neighbourhood; part of a *–gu*.

dong- east.

dongdongju a milky rice wine much favoured by Korean students; very similar to *makgeolli*.

DPRK Democratic People's Republic of Korea.

-eup town.

-ga section of a major street.

-gang river of over 100km in length.

-gil street.

gisaeng Female entertainers popular in dynastic times.

-gu district of a city, subdivided into *–dong* neighbourhoods.

-gul cave.

-gun county.

-gung palace.

gwageo civil service examinations in the Joseon era.

Gyopo Koreans, or people of Korean descent, living overseas.

hae sea. Korea's East, West and South seas are referred to as *Donghae*, *Seohae* and *Namhae* respectively, though the international nomenclature of the first two (more readily referred to as the "Sea of Japan" and the "Yellow Sea" abroad) is a touchy subject with Koreans.

hagwon private academy for after-school study. Many expats in Korea are working at an English academy (*yeongeo hagwon*).

hallyu the "Korean New Wave" of pop culture, most specifically cinematic produce.

hanbok traditional Korean clothing.

-hang harbour.

hangeul the Korean alphabet.

hanja Chinese characters, which are still sometimes used in Korea.

hanji traditional handmade paper.

hanok a style of traditional, tile-roofed wooden housing.

-ho lake; also used for those artificially created after the construction of a dam.

hof a Korean-style bar.

insam ginseng.

jaebeol major Korean corporation.

-jeon temple hall.

jjimjilbang Korean spa-cum-sauna facilities, often used by families, youth groups and the occasional budget traveller (see page 36).

KNTO Korea National Tourism Organization.

KTX the fastest class of Korean train.

makgeolli a milky rice wine much favoured by Korean students; very similar to *dongdongju*.

minbak rented rooms in a private house or building, most commonly found near beaches and national park entrances.

mudang practitioner of shamanism; usually female.

mugunghwa Korea's third-highest level of train, one below a *saemaeul*. Named after Korea's national flower, a variety of hibiscus, also known as the "Rose of Sharon", which flowers punctually each July.

-mun city or fortress gate.

-myo Confucian shrine.

nam- south.

-ni village; sometimes pronounced – *ri*.

-no large street; sometimes pronounced – *ro*.

nocheonnyeo an "over-the-hill" female – Korean women have long been expected to marry by the age of thirty, though this is slowly changing.

noraebang a "singing room" often the venue of choice for the end of a night out.

oncheon hot-spring bath or spa.

ondol traditional underfloor system of heating, made by wood fires underneath traditional buildings, but replaced with gas-fired systems in Korean apartments and modern houses.

pansori Korean opera derived from shamanistic songs, sung by female vocalists to minimalist musical accompaniment.

-pokpo waterfalls.

pyeong Korean unit of measurement equivalent to approximately 3.3 square metres; still commonly used to measure the floors pace of housing or offices.

Red Devils a nickname for the South Korean national football team, or their noisy supporters.

-ri village; sometimes pronounced – *ni*.

-ro large street; sometimes pronounced – *no*.

ROK Republic of Korea.

-sa temple.

Saemaeul Korea's second-highest level of train, one faster than a *mugunghwa* but slower than a KTX. Also the name of the "New Community Movement" inaugurated by Korean president Park Chung-hee in the 1970s.

-san mountain; often used to describe an entire range.

sanseong mountain fortress.

seo- west.

Seon Korean Buddhist sect proximate to Zen in Japan.

seonsaengnim title for a teacher, which goes before the family name, or (mistakenly) after the given name in the case of most expat teachers in Korea. Hence, a teacher named Martin will usually be referred to as "Martin *seonsaengnim*".

seowon Confucian academy, most prevalent in Joseon times.

-si city, subdivided into *-gu* districts.

soju clear alcoholic drink (around 25 percent alcohol by volume) which is often compared to vodka, and usually cheaper than water at convenience stores up and down the land.

ssireum a Korean wrestling style inevitably compared to sumo, but far closer in form to Mongolian or Greco-Roman styles.

STO Seoul Tourism Organization.

taekwondo Korean martial art, now practised around the world.

tap pagoda.

tongil unification, a highly important concept on the divided Korean peninsula.

trot a very distinctive style of Korean music much favoured by older generations.

woeguk-in foreigner; pronounced "way-goog-in". *Woeguk-saram* is also used.

yangban the scholarly "upper class" in Joseon-era Korea.

yeogwan Korean form of accommodation, similar to a motel but privately run and almost always older.

yeoinsuk Korean form of accommodation, similar to a *yeogwan* but with communal toilets and showers.

Small print and index

A ROUGH GUIDE TO ROUGH GUIDES

Published in 1982, the first Rough Guide – to Greece – was a student scheme that became a publishing phenomenon. Mark Ellingham, a recent graduate in English from Bristol University, had been travelling in Greece the previous summer and couldn't find the right guidebook. With a small group of friends he wrote his own guide, combining a contemporary, journalistic style with a thoroughly practical approach to travellers' needs.

The immediate success of the book spawned a series that rapidly covered dozens of destinations. And, in addition to impecunious backpackers, Rough Guides soon acquired a much broader readership that relished the guides' wit and inquisitiveness as much as their enthusiastic, critical approach and value-for-money ethos. These days, Rough Guides include recommendations from budget to luxury and cover more than 120 destinations around the globe, from Amsterdam to Zanzibar, all regularly updated by our team of roaming writers.

Browse all our latest guides, read inspirational features and book your trip at **roughguides.com**.

Rough Guide credits

Editor: Georgia Stephens
Cartography: Carte, Katie Bennett
Managing editor: Rachel Lawrence
Picture editor: Michelle Bhatia

Cover photo research: Phoebe Lowndes
Senior DTP coordinator: Dan May
Head of DTP and Pre-Press: Rebeka Davies

Publishing information

This fourth edition published in 2018 by
Rough Guides Ltd

Distribution
UK, Ireland and Europe
Apa Publications (UK) Ltd; sales@roughguides.com
United States and Canada
Ingram Publisher Services; ips@ingramcontent.com
Australia and New Zealand
Woodslane; info@woodslane.com.au
Southeast Asia
Apa Publications (SN) Pte; sales@roughguides.com
Worldwide
Apa Publications (UK) Ltd; sales@roughguides.com
Special Sales, Content Licensing and CoPublishing
Rough Guides can be purchased in bulk quantities
at discounted prices. We can create special editions,
personalised jackets and corporate imprints tailored to
your needs. sales@roughguides.com.

roughguides.com
Printed in China by CTPS
All rights reserved
© 2018 Apa Digital (CH) AG license edition © Apa
Publications Ltd UK.
All rights reserved. No part of this publication may be
reproduced, stored in or introduced into a retrieval system,
or transmitted in any form, or by any means (electronic,
mechanical, photocopying, recording or otherwise) without
the prior written permission of the copyright owner.
A catalogue record for this book is available from the
British Library
The publishers and authors have done their best to
ensure the accuracy and currency of all the information
in **The Rough Guide to Korea**, however, they can accept
no responsibility for any loss, injury, or inconvenience
sustained by any traveller as a result of information or
advice contained in the guide.

Help us update

We've gone to a lot of effort to ensure that the fourth
edition of **The Rough Guide to Korea** is accurate and up-
to-date. However, things change – places get "discovered",
opening hours are notoriously fickle, restaurants and
rooms raise prices or lower standards. If you feel we've got
it wrong or left something out, we'd like to know, and if
you can remember the address, the price, the hours, the
phone number, so much the better.

Please send your comments with the subject line
"Rough Guide Korea Update" to mail@uk.roughguides.
com. We'll credit all contributions and send a copy of the
next edition (or any other Rough Guide if you prefer) for
the very best emails.

Readers' updates

Thanks to all the readers who have taken the time to write in with comments and suggestions (and apologies if we've
inadvertently omitted or misspelt anyone's name):

Jonghyeon Choe, Ms. M. MacPolin, Meriel, Jane Park, Klaus Schröer, Dana Weiser, Fran Wormald

Acknowledgements

Norbert Paxton: Norbert would like to thank his usual
Seoul peeps for their company during his latest research
trip, including Jason Strother, David Carruth and Matt
Crawford, as well as Mike Spavor for his entertaining
cameo appearances. He would also like to thank Nuri Kim
and Minjeong Lee from the Gangwon tourism board, Kim
Rye Han from the Gwangju city government, Matt Baldwin
for the meal and company in Daejeon, Ting for the floor
space and parties in Suwon and Maria Azafran for the
barbecue back in Seoul.

ABOUT THE AUTHOR

Norbert Paxton first visited Korea in early 2002, and has been
travelling the world almost non-stop since then. In that time he has
written or contributed to over thirty Rough Guides, but all of his roads
seem to lead back to Seoul, and you'll often find him somewhere
around the Cheonggyecheon – or, occasionally, swimming in it.

Photo credits
(Key: T-top; C-centre; B-bottom; L-left; R-right)

Index

Main references are in **bold** type

Map symbols

The symbols below are used on maps throughout the book

	International boundary		Post office		Monument
	Regional boundary		Hospital		Campsite
	Demilitarized zone	E	Embassy		Palace
	Motorway		Spring/spa		Border checkpoint
	Main road		Museum		Mountain refuge/lodge
	Minor road		National park		Cave
	Pedestrian road		Mountain peak		Picnic
	Path		Mountain range		Skiing
	Wall		Waterfall		Golf course
	Ferry		Crater		Observatory
	Railway		Lighthouse		Building
	Cable car		Gate		Church (town maps)
	Point of interest		Memorial/statue		Stadium
(i)	Information office		Shrine		Beach
(M)	Subway station		Buddhist temple		Park
	Airport		Hindu temple		Marshland
★	Transport stop		Pagoda		

Listings key

- ■ Accommodation
- ● Eating
- ■ Drinking/nightlife
- ● Shopping